AMERICAN
INTERNATIONAL
PICTURES

GARLAND REFERENCE LIBRARY
OF THE HUMANITIES
(VOL. 492)

AMERICAN INTERNATIONAL PICTURES
A Filmography

Robert L. Ottoson

GARLAND PUBLISHING, INC. • NEW YORK & LONDON
1985

Library of Congress Cataloging in Publication Data

Ottoson, Robert, 1947–
  American International Pictures.

  (Garland reference library of the humanities ;
vol. 492)
  Includes index.
    1. Moving-pictures—United States—Catalogs.
2. American International Pictures (Firm)   I. Title.
II. Series: Garland reference library of the humanities ;
v. 492.
PN1998.078   1985   791.43′0973   83-49335
ISBN 0-8240-8976-6 (alk. paper)

Cover design by Larry Walczak

Printed on acid-free, 250-year-life paper
Manufactured in the United States of America

To Chris and Mary

CONTENTS

Preface   ix

Introduction   xi

Selected Bibliography   xv

Filmography

The Fifties   3

The Sixties   55

The Seventies   184

Title Index   336

Name Index   346

PREFACE

The author has attempted to make this AIP filmography as complete as possible. Much of the filmography has been limited to movies that have been included in U.S. copyright entries as being AIP films. Excluded have been the features bought by AIP and sold directly to television, e.g., the numerous grade-Z Mexican horror films. Also excluded are the films distributed under the two AIP subsidiaries, Hallmark Releasing and Trans American Films, and a group of features bought from the defunct Commonwealth United years after they were produced. If there are any gaps in this filmography, they are with some of the foreign films AIP bought for distribution in the 70s, for which material is practically nonexistent. Finally the small number of films that AIP coproduced with its new partners, Filmways, have been excluded, since AIP by this time had been absorbed by Filmways.

For reference to AIP products I have consulted such works as *Variety*, *The New York Times Film Reviews*, *Monthly Film Bulletin*, *Filmfacts*, *Screen World*, *Reference Guide to Fantastic Films*, *Horror and Science Fiction Films*, Vols. I and II, *The American Film Institute Catalog of Motion Pictures: Feature Films 1961–1970*, and material supplied from the Academy of Motion Picture Arts and Sciences Library. If the reader spots any omissions in this filmography, after considering the above limitations, then this author would like to hear about them.

The author wishes to thank the staff at the Iowa State University Library in Ames and the University of Iowa Library in Iowa City for their assistance. The photos are all from Eddie Brandt's Saturday Matinee in North Hollywood, California. Funds for the photos were provided by the Iowa State University Library Faculty Research Fund. Special thanks go to Lynette Reed for her expert typing of the final manuscript.

INTRODUCTION

"I suppose time can dignify anything."—Samuel Z. Arkoff, President of American International Pictures, after the Museum of Modern Art in New York City announced a 25th-anniversary retrospective tribute to AIP in 1979.

With MOMA's recognition AIP became somewhat respectable among *cinéastes,* although that audience should not hold its collective breath for an institution like MOMA to unveil a tribute to the gore films of Herschell Gordon Lewis. Respectable in its old age or not, AIP is most fondly remembered not for its big-budget flops of the mid- and late 1970s, but for its floridly titled horror and teenage exploitation films of the 50s and its mindlessly benign beach films and violent biker films of the 60s. The story of the rise and fall of AIP closely follows the ebb and flow of the American film industry from 1955 to 1980.

In 1954 a young lawyer, Samuel Z. Arkoff, representing a client in a title copyright infringement, walked into the office of Jack Broder, head of Realart Pictures, and met James H. Nicholson, a sales manager for Realart. Nicholson was impressed with Arkoff's business deal with Broder, and soon after both men combined about $3,000 and started their own distribution company—American Releasing Corporation. After distributing other producers' low-budget films for almost two years, they changed the name of the company to American International Pictures and began to produce and distribute their own films.

Arkoff and Nicholson could not have started AIP at a worse time. After a postwar Hollywood boom the motion picture industry went into a slump. In the late 40s the studios finally lost a protracted antitrust battle whereby they had to divest themselves of their vertically integrated monopoly. They were no longer allowed to exhibit the product that they produced and distributed. At the same time television began to enter the living rooms of millions of American homes. By 1953–54 the big studios were scrambling for a dwindling audience with such enticements as 3-D and Technicolor Cinemascope epics. With fewer and fewer "B" movies being made, Arkoff and Nicholson took a plunge into the marketplace with a series of low-budget black-and-white double bills. Rarely costing more than $100,000 (which would not even pay for the catering bills for location filming nowadays), these films, shot in about two weeks, never lost money.

AIP's early films were created in an interesting fashion. Nicholson would conjure up a title, e.g., *The Beast with a 1,000,000 Eyes,* and develop an advertising plan around it. After this was done, the screenplay would be written and the film quickly produced. Among independents AIP was one of the first to offer saturation bookings. Such films as *Dragstrip Girl* and *I Was a Teenage Frankenstein* would be teamed up with thematically related features and play in four or five dozen theatres in an urban location split almost equally among drive-ins and indoor theatres. Since these exploitation films supposedly did not have any redeeming characteristics, they were shown for only a week or two but would always garner a profitable economic return. Arkoff and Nicholson catered to the same audience that larger companies, which produce such films as *Valley Girl* and *Friday the 13th,* do now—primarily the high school and college-aged youths who are looking for some cheap thrills with their dates on a Friday or Saturday night.

AIP continued to do well with these double bills until around 1959, when other companies, such as Allied Artists, began to copy its format. Soon after AIP began importing and distributing foreign films, such as the Goliath movies, and British sleaze "shockers," like *Circus of Horrors* and *Horrors of the Black Museum.* While continuing to import and produce their own films, Arkoff and Nicholson in the early 60s began a cycle of films based on the stories of Edgar Allan Poe. Most of them were directed by Roger Corman, who had been making films for AIP since its inception. For the most part these films were quite well made and were responsible for the 60s being the most financially stable period for AIP.

Beginning in 1963 the beach-party-type films solidified AIP's reputation as being the supreme producer of youth exploitation films. Unlike other youth-oriented films, these particular ones always eliminated the young peoples' parents. This surf-and-sand crowd seemed to exist in a sort of nether world where they never went home. As the 60s wore on and blacks in Alabama were being blown up and attacked with dogs and fire hoses, and Lyndon Johnson escalated the war in Vietnam, the tenor of AIP productions changed. Young people were now shown as not existing in a hermetically sealed world where all they had to worry about was a bad sunburn or a sand crab bite (or worse). AIP films became more contentious—engaged, if you will. Such films as *The Wild Angels* ushered in a whole group of biker films, which often starred such terminal "nut" cases as Bruce Dern and Adam Roarke portraying violence-crazed cyclists. Not wanting to avoid the subject of the so-called "drug culture" AIP produced one of the seminal drug films of the period—*The Trip*. As the 60s closed, AIP had two of its largest grossers in 1968 with *Wild in the Streets* and *3 in the Attic*.

The 70s would see a slow but continuous decline in the fortunes of the company. Nicholson left in 1972 to produce films independently and died six months later. AIP's audience now seemed to have changed a bit. While its main audience had been white teenagers, the 70s saw the demographics change, as the company built up a slightly older audience (the teenagers of the 50s and 60s had grown up along with AIP) of blue-collar working-class whites and urban blacks. Blacks in particular constituted a sizable new audience, and AIP responded with a whole slew of what is often referred to as blaxploitation action films starring such people as Jim Brown, Pam Grier, and Fred Williamson. In the early and mid-70s AIP mixed up its film fare with the abovementioned blaxploitation crime and horror films, foreign films picked up for American distribution, and violence-filled horror films. Soon AIP found itself in direct competition with the major studios, which, ironically, were making AIP-type exploitation films, such as *American Graffiti*, *Jaws*, and *The Exorcist*, but with much larger budgets. From the mid-70s on AIP's production and advertising costs were well above the inflationary spiral. The company had to keep up with the other companies and their substantial budgets because the sales to television (which for many years had been a very profitable area for AIP) necessitated a product as expensive and desirable as the majors.

The handwriting was on the wall. In the first nine months of 1977 AIP had a 14-percent jump in domestic film rentals yet showed lower profits than in the previous year. By 1978 first-half profits were down 76 percent from 1977, and in 1979 the company recorded its first losing year in history. AIP's attempt at competing with the major studios proved disastrous, as it lost money on such big-budget "turkeys" as *Force 10 from Navarone* and *Meteor*. In October 1978 AIP and Filmways announced a merger agreement. This was supposed to have been a mutually beneficial pact, whereby AIP would have access to some of Filmways' production capital, while Filmways would have access to AIP's well-developed distribution system. The merger became an on-off-on-again situation. After calling off merger talks in December 1978, the two parties finally signed an agreement in March 1979. Arkoff, by now AIP's president and chief stockholder, became an independent producer inside the Filmways organization. Arkoff, the maverick, quickly became dissatisfied with the constraints put upon him in being just a cog in a large corporation. In December 1979 he resigned as AIP president just after he had reported to Filmways that he had discovered that AIP's television production assets had been overstated by $5,000,000.

However, this is not the end of AIP. Samuel Z. Arkoff is now an independent producer and has started a new AIP—Arkoff International Pictures. Its first release in 1982 was Larry Cohen's tongue-in-cheek *Q*. This old AIP fan hopes that this signals only a beginning.

SELECTED BIBLIOGRAPHY

Aside from the movie trade papers, such as *Variety* and *Box Office*, relatively little has been written about AIP. The following bibliography is only an introduction to the reader. Such sources as the *Film Literature Index* and the *International Index to Film Periodicals* contain additional article citations for AIP productions and personnel.

BOOKS

McCarthy, Todd, and Charles Flynn, eds. *Kings of the Bs: Working Within the Hollywood System*. New York: Dutton, 1975.

McGee, Mark T. *Fast and Furious: A History of American International Pictures*. Jefferson, N.C.: McFarland, 1984

McGee, Mark T., and R.J. Robertson. *The J.D. Films: Juvenile Delinquency in the Movies*. Jefferson, N.C.: McFarland, 1982.

Meyers, Richard S. *For One Week Only: The World of Exploitation Films*. Piscataway, N.J.: New Century, 1983.

Naha, Ed. *The Films of Roger Corman: Brilliance on a Budget*. New York: Arco, 1982.

Warren, Bill. *Keep Watching the Skies!: American Science Fiction Movies of the 1950s*. Jefferson, N.C.: McFarland, 1982.

Weldon, Michael, with Charles Beesley, Bob Martin, and Akira Fitton. *The Psychotronic Encyclopedia of Film*. New York: Ballantine, 1983.

Willemen, Paul, David Pirie, David Will, and Lynda Myles. *Roger Corman: The Millennic Vision*. Edinburgh: Edinburgh Film Festival, 1970.

ARTICLES

Ansen, David, and Martin Kasindorf. "The Incredible Horror Mogul." *Newsweek,* June 18, 1979, pp. 56–57.

Bean, Robin. "Muscles and Mayhem." *Films and Filming,* June 1964, pp. 14–18.

Bean, Robin, and David Austen. "U.S.A. Confidential." *Films and Filming,* November 1968, pp. 16–31.

Byron, Arthur. "The Last Tycoon." *Village Voice,* April 16, 1979, p. 39.

Diehl, Digby. "Roger Corman." *Show,* May 1970, pp. 26–30 + .

Dyer, Peter John. "Z Films." *Sight and Sound,* Autumn 1964, pp. 179–181.

Ginnane, A.I. "The Man in the Black Car; Samuel Z. Arkoff." *Cinema Papers,* January 1977, pp. 215–17 + .

Goldman, Charles. "An Interview with Roger Corman." *Film Comment,* Fall 1971, pp. 49–54.

Harmetz, Aljean. "The Dime Store Way to Make Movies—and Money." *The New York Times Magazine,* August 4, 1974, pp. 12–13 + .

—————. "Museum Celebrates Drive-In Movies." *The New York Times,* July 27, 1979, Sec. C., p. 1.

Joyce, Paul. "Roger Corman Starts the Long Ride Home." *Film,* Autumn 1965, pp. 28–32.

Koszarski, Richard. "The Films of Roger Corman." *Film Comment,* Fall 1971, pp. 42–48.

Lazarus, P.N. "Motion Pictures Today Is an Obstacle Course." *Film Bulletin,* January 1976, p.5 + .

Sauvage, P. "The Whole Business Stinks from the Top." *Action,* January–February 1978, pp. 49–51.

American International Pictures

The Fast and the Furious

THE FIFTIES

THE FAST AND THE FURIOUS. 1954. 65 minutes. *Directors:*
Edwards Sampson and John Ireland. *Screenplay:* Jerome
Odlum and Jean Howell; from a story by Roger Corman.
Cinematography: Floyd Crosby. *Cast:* John Ireland (Frank
Webster); Dorothy Malone (Connie Adair); Bruce Carlisle
(Faber); Marshall Bradford (Race Official); Jean Howell
(Sally); Larry Thor (Police Sergeant); Robin Morse (Gas
Station Attendant); Bruno Ve Sota (Truck Driver); Iris
Adrian (Waitress).

It is appropriate that the first AIP release (under the
banner of the American Releasing Corporation) should star and
be co-directed by that quintessential "B" actor--John Ireland.
Here he plays a truck driver falsely imprisoned on a murder
charge. He escapes and commandeers a sports car owned by race
driver Dorothy Malone. She has entered a race, which, she
finds, does not allow female contestants. Ireland drives her
car in the race, which will take him to Mexico and freedom.
A heroic act by Ireland during the race proves to Malone that
he is not a murderer. Realizing that Malone loves him,
Ireland goes back to give himself up and clear his name. In
the final race sequence Ireland drove the race car himself,
as does producer Roger Corman with one of the other cars.
    This accent on speed and racing set a pattern that could
be seen in the AIP hot-rod films of the 50s and the motorcycle-
gang films of the 60s and early 70s.

APACHE WOMAN. 1955. 82 minutes. Color. *Director:* Roger
Corman. *Screenplay:* Lou Rusoff. *Cinematography:* Floyd
Crosby. *Cast:* Lloyd Bridges (Rex Moffet); Joan Taylor
(Anne Libeau); Lance Fuller (Armand); Morgan Jones (Macy);
Paul Birch (Sheriff); Jonathan Haze (Tom Chandler); Paul
Dubov (Ben); Lou Place (Carrom Bentley); Gene Marlowe
(White Star); Dick Miller (Tall Tree); Chester Conklin
(Mooney); Jean Howell (Mrs. Chandler).

A government agent (Bridges) is sent to check on a series
of robberies and murders that have been supposedly committed
by reservation Apaches. He meets a local half-breed (Taylor),

whom he falls for. It turns out that the guilty party is
Taylor's brother (Fuller), the leader of a group of bandits,
who pose as Indians to cover up their crimes. Taylor learns
about her brother and goes to warn Bridges before he can be
caught in a trap set for him by Fuller. The men have a fist
fight in which Fuller falls to his death.

Roger Corman made an attempt here to deal with racial
prejudice--a subject hardly touched upon in AIP films. About
six years later he made a much bolder film on prejudice entitled *The Intruder*, which failed miserably at the box office.

THE BEAST WITH A 1,000,000 EYES. 1955. 78 minutes. *Director:*
    David Kramarsky. *Screenplay:* Tom Filer. *Cinematography:*
    Everett Baker. *Cast:* Paul Birch (Allan Kelly); Lorna
    Thayer (Carol Kelly); Donna Cole (Sandy Kelly); Dick
    Sargent (Larry); Leonard Tarver (Carl, the mute); Chester
    Conklin (Old Man Webber).

A family living in the California desert find themselves
being menaced by an evil force emanating from an alien creature in its spaceship out in the desert. The alien seeks to
take over the Earth by projecting its mind on all living
things, as birds attack humans and gentle household pets,
such as dogs, suddenly turn vicious. It is only the power of
the family's love that finally wards off the alien.

One of the strange aspects of this first feature by David
Kramarsky is the mute farm handyman (Tarver). In his behavior
he provides much more of an unsettling presence than the alien
out in the desert. The ad campaign for the film featured a
rendering of a million-eyed monster. When the exhibitors saw
the finished product sans the million eyes, they were aghast.
As an eight-year-old this author recalls a similar feeling of
disappointment of not seeing a horrendous monster, but instead
a vicious dog and an out-of-control cow. This film was one
of the early examples when Nicholson and Arkoff thought up a
title and ad campaign before the film was actually shot.

FIVE GUNS WEST. 1955. 78 minutes. Color. *Director:* Roger
    Corman. *Screenplay:* R. Wright Campbell. *Cinematography:*
    Floyd Crosby. *Cast:* John Lund (Govern Sturges); Dorothy
    Malone (Shalee); Touch (Mike) Connors (Hale Clinton);
    Bob Campbell (John Candy); Jonathan Haze (Billy Candy);
    Paul Birch (J.C. Haggard); James Stone (Uncle Mime);
    Jack Ingraham (Stephen Jethro); Larr Thor (Confederate

Captain).

Five Guns West was Roger Corman's directing debut. Made
in only about nine days, this was a reasonably ambitious western with some good action and color photography.

Five Civil War prisoners (Lund, Connors, Birch, Haze, and
Campbell) are pardoned and put into the Confederate Army for
a dangerous mission out West. They must capture an army de-
serter (Ingraham), along with a gold shipment in his possession aboard a stagecoach. They stop the stage at an isolated
depot, where they fight off Yankee troops in a skirmish. It
turns out that Lund is a Confederate officer, whose job it is
to bring Ingraham back to Confederate authorities. There is
no gold on the stage, so the four other prisoners storm the
depot where Lund has his prisoner. They plan to have Ingraham
take them to the hidden gold. With the help of the depot's
custodian (Stone) and his niece (Malone), Lund is able to fight
the four off and return Ingraham to prison.

OPERATION MALAYA. 1955. 65 minutes. *Director:* David
  MacDonald. *Screenplay:* John Croydon and David MacDonald.
  Cinematography: Geoffrey Faithful and Arthur Graham.
  Narrators: John Humphrey, Winford Vaughn Thomas, John
  Slater, and Chips Rafferty.

This is a filmed account of Communist-inspired guerilla
activities in Malaya from the British government viewpoint.
It combines some staged sequences, as well as newsreel footage,
to show how British officials are aiding the local authorities
in combating native insurgents. The film portrays the guerrillas as fighting against workers at tin mines and rubber
plantations, when in fact it was mainly the British and their
colonial rule that they wanted to do away with. The narrators,
representing four distinct personality types, throw out all
sorts of data about the situation in Malaya--more information
than most people would care to hear. One wonders who this
type of film was made for. American audiences, even during
the height of the Cold War, were not all that interested in
paying money to see the British attempt to hold on to a piece
of their colonial empire. *Operation Malaya* seems to have been
a film made for audiences in Great Britain.

OUTLAW TREASURE. 1955. 65 minutes. *Director:* Oliver Drake.
  Screenplay: John Carpenter. *Cinematography:* Clark Ramsey.

Cast: John Forbes (Dan Parker); Adele Jergens (Rita); with Glenn Langan, Michael Whalen, Frank Carpenter, Hal Baylor.

Outlaw Treasure is utterly negligible, even by the paltry standards of early AIP westerns. It reminds one of those westerns churned out by Monogram and PRC in the 40s, which had a bunch of cowboys shooting guns and riding aimlessly around the familiar terrain of the Southern California hills.

To give this film some semblance of interest the filmmakers have tossed into the plot the James brothers (Frank and Jessie) in a story concerning stolen government gold shipments during the post Civil War Period. The government hires a man (Forbes) to investigate the series of gold-shipment robberies, and after 65 minutes of fast guns and chases on horseback Forbes not only captures the desperados but gets the girl (Jergens) as well. For those of us who harbor an appreciation of Adele Jergens, it should be noted that she appears in only about five or six minutes of the film.

THE DAY THE WORLD ENDED. 1956. 81 minutes. *Director:* Roger
    Corman. *Screenplay:* Lou Rusoff; based on a story by
    Rusoff. *Cinematography:* Jock Feindel. *Cast:* Richard
    Denning (Rick); Lori Nelson (Louise); Adele Jergens
    (Ruby); Touch (Mike) Connors (Tony); Paul Birch
    (Maddison); Raymond Hatton (Pete); Paul Dubov (Radek);
    Jonathan Haze (Contaminated Man); Paul Blaisdell (Mutant).

The time--the mid-1970s. A nuclear war has caused an almost total destruction of the world. Seven people survive, presumably the only survivors. A former sea captain and his daughter, a gangster and his girlfriend, a geologist and a burned radiation victim, and an old prospector find shelter in a farmhouse in a secluded valley. After being threatened by a three-eyed mutant and fighting among themselves for food and water, the only two survivors (Denning and Nelson) venture out into the world as a postnuclear Adam and Eve.

The flamboyantly madeup mutant, who has been able to survive nuclear destruction in a grotesque form, ironically collapses and dies when it is subjected to one of the most vivifying forces of nature--rainwater. During the 50s AIP paired many of its films on a prepared double bill. In the case of *The Day the World Ended* it appeared with the ludicrous *The Phantom from 10,000 Leagues.*

Female Jungle

FEMALE JUNGLE. 1956. 70 minutes. *Director:* Bruno Ve Sota.
    Screenplay: Burt Kaiser and Bruno Ve Sota. *Cinematog-
    raphy:* Elwood Bredell. *Cast:* Lawrence Tierney (Sergeant
    Stevens); John Carradine (Claude Almstead); Jayne
    Mansfield (Candy Price); Burt Kaiser (Alec Voe); Kathleen
    Crowley (Peggy Voe); James Kodl (Joe); Rex Thorsen (Ser-
    geant Duane); Jack Hill (Captain Kroger); Bruce Carlisle
    (Chuck); Connie Cezon (Connie); Robert Davis (George);
    Gordon Urquhart (Larry Jackson); Alan Frost (Dr.
    Urquhart); Bill Layne (Heckler); Bruno Ve Sota (Frank);
    Jean Lewis (Monica Madison).

    Female Jungle is imbued with a Mickey Spillane-like mood.
Police detective Lawrence Tierney has to redeem himself by
finding the murderer of a blonde movie star. It seems that
he was off-duty and drunk in the vicinity of the murder when
it took place. Like Mike Hammer, he spends much of the film
going through back alleys and women's bedrooms to look for the
killer.
    This film contains some unusually baroque camerawork and
a variety of acting styles. We have the theatricality of John
Carradine (as a gossip columnist!), the hardboiled demeanor
of Tierney, Mansfield's breathless allure, and the repulsive
oiliness of Burt Kaiser as the murderer. *Female Jungle* is usually shown on television in an abbreviated 56 minute version.

GIRLS IN PRISON. 1956. 86 minutes. *Director:* Edward L. Cahn.
    Screenplay: Lou Rusoff. *Cinematography:* Frederick E.
    West. *Cast:* Richard Denning (Reverend Fulton); Joan
    Taylor (Anne Carson); Adele Jergens (Jenny); Helen Gilbert
    (Melanee); Lance Fuller (Paul Anderson); Jane Darwell
    (Matron Jamieson); Raymond Hatton (Pop Carson); Phyllis
    Coates (Dorothy); Diana Darrin (Meg); Mae Marsh (Grandma);
    Laurie Mitchell (Phyllis); Diane Richards (Night Club
    Singer); Luana Walters (Female Guard); Riza Royce (Female
    Guard).

    Beginning with the excellent *Caged*, made in 1950, the 50s
saw an unusual number of films about women in prison. Most
of these films were mediocre at best, and *Girls in Prison* is
no exception.
    Joan Taylor believes she has been falsely imprisoned,
and the prison chaplain (Denning) believes her. One of
Taylor's cellmates (Jurgens) thinks that she hid money from
a bank robbery. She organizes a prison break and takes Taylor
along to retrieve the money. The women escape when an

earthquake destroys the prison. In the ensuing action Jergens
is shot by Taylor's accomplice (Fuller) in the bank robbery,
and Taylor goes back to prison to wait for an early parole.
   The girl-fights in *Girls in Prison* are rather poorly
staged. However, the film does have Phyllis Coates, the first
Lois Lane in television's *Superman*, playing a psychotic inmate.

GUNSLINGER. 1956. 77 minutes. Color. *Director:* Roger
   Corman. *Screenplay:* Charles B. Griffith and Mark Hanna.
   Cinematography: Fred West. *Cast:* John Ireland (Cane
   Miro); Beverly Garland (Rose Hood); Allison Hayes (Erica
   Page); Martin Kingsley (Gideon Polk); Jonathan Haze (Jake
   Hays); Chris Alcaide (Joshua Tate); Richard Miller (Jimmy
   Tonto); Bruno Ve Sota (Zebelon Tabb); Margaret Campbell
   (Felicity Polk); William Schallert (Scott Hood); Aaron
   Saxon (Nate Signo); Chris Miller (Tessie-Belle).

   Of all the westerns distributed by AIP in its early years,
Gunslinger might very well be the most interesting. It gives
an unconventional twist to the traditional western, with its
feminist point of view.
   Beverly Garland portrays a female marshal in a lawless
town who took over for her slain husband. John Ireland is a
hired gun brought into town by the local saloon proprietress
(Hayes), who is attempting to buy up the town because a railroad is coming through. Her plans go awry when Ireland and
Garland fall in love. In a final shootout Ireland kills Hayes,
but Garland guns him down. Garland does not let her emotions
get in the way because she has agreed to uphold the law.
   Both Garland and Hayes come across very strong in *Gunslinger*. Beverly Garland brought a conviction to just about
every role she portrayed, and Allison Hayes, along with Marie
Windsor, was one of the great "floozies" of the "B" films of
the 50s.

HOT ROD GIRL. 1956. 79 minutes. *Director:* Leslie Martinson.
   Screenplay: John McGreevey. *Cinematography:* Sam Leavitt.
   Cast: Lori Nelson (Lisa); John Smith (Jeff); Chuck Connors
   (Ben); Frank J. Gorshin (Flat-Top); Roxanne Arlen (L.P.);
   Mark Andrews (Bronc); Carolyn Kearney (Judy); Ed Reider
   (Two Tanks); Del Erickson (Steve); Fred Essler (Yo-Yo);
   Russ Thorsen (Logan); Charles Keane (Pat); Dabbs Greer
   (Henry).

Hot Rod Girl is just about the first of AIP's teenage
exploitation films. Here Chuck Connors is a cop who is waging
a one-man war on teenage hot rodders. In order to stop viola-
tors he promotes the idea of an organized dragstrip that the
young drivers can use. One of the young drivers (Smith) with-
draws his support when his brother is killed in a street race.
Stepping into this power vacuum is a troublemaker (Andrews),
who attempts to take over the leadership of the hot-rod group,
but everything is resolved after a fatal road race.

This is not at all a bad film of its kind, but indicative
of the type of comments made by contemporary reviews was this
insight: "The film presents an alarming picture of American
youth (who are depicted as naive, ingenuous and moronic) ..."
(*Monthly Film Bulletin*, September 1956, p. 117). I can think
of no greater compliment.

IT CONQUERED THE WORLD. 1956. 71 minutes. *Director:* Roger
    Corman. *Screenplay:* Credit is given to Lou Rusoff, but
    the film was actually written by Charles B. Griffith.
    Cinematography: Frederick E. West. *Cast:* Peter Graves
    (Dr. Paul Nelson); Lee Van Cleef (Dr. Tom Anderson);
    Beverly Garland (Claire Anderson); Sally Fraser (Joan
    Nelson); Russ Bender (General Pattick); Jonathan Haze
    (Private Manuel Ortiz); Dick Miller (Sergeant Neil);
    Charles B. Griffith (Pete Shelton); Karen Kadler (Ellen
    Peters); Paul Blaisdell (Visitor from Venus).

It Conquered the World is one of Roger Corman's better
early efforts. It contains some witty and vivid dialogue and
is graced by fine performances by Peter Graves and Beverly
Garland.

A scientist (Van Cleef) establishes radio contact with
Venus and discovers that the Venusians are going to send an
invasion party to Earth. Thinking that the aliens will improve
the state of affairs on Earth, Van Cleef helps to guide them
on his ham radio set. Once here, a Venusian monster sends out
his army of bats, who bite their victims on the neck, thereby
turning them into the type of emotionless zombies found in
Invasion of the Body Snatchers. Van Cleef's naiveté about the
alien's motives do not set well with his fellow scientist
(Graves), especially after Graves had to dispatch his wife
with a gun after she turned into a zombie. When Van Cleef's
wife (Garland) is killed by the monster, he kills it by putting a blowtorch to its eyes, but he dies in the process.

The alien monster is one of the most ridiculous looking
monsters on record--part inverted cone, part cucumber with
crablike arms, and a mouth like a chainsaw.

THE OKLAHOMA WOMAN. 1956. 71 minutes. *Director:* Roger
   Corman. *Screenplay:* Lou Rusoff. *Cinematography:* Fred
   West. *Cast:* Richard Denning (Steve Ward); Peggie Castle
   (Marie "Oklahoma" Saunders); Cathy Downs (Susan Grant);
   Tudor Owen (Ed Grant); Martin Kingsley (Sheriff Bill
   Peters); Touch (Mike) Connors (Tom Blake); with Dick
   Miller, Bruno Ve Sota, Jonathan Haze.

   The essentially conservative nature of the western genre
does not lend itself to the ludicrous energy that we find in
some of AIP's science-fiction and teenage films. *The Oklahoma
Woman* is a standard western, which revolves around a black-
hearted woman played by Peggie Castle. She excelled in these
roles in the 50s, in such gritty *films noirs* as *I, the Jury*
and *99 River Street*.
   A former gunfighter (Denning) returns to his hometown
from a stretch in prison. He finds himself in the middle of
a power struggle between the "law-abiding" citizens, such as
Ed Grant (Owen) and his daughter (Downs), and the town's power
structure. This structure is partly embodied by Denning's old
"flame" (Castle, our eponymous villainess) and her hired
pistolero (Connors). Connors murders Owen and implicates
Denning in the crime. Before Denning can be hanged by the
townsfolk, Downs forces a confession out of Castle, and he is
cleared.
   The highlights of this film are the saloon fight between
Castle and Downs, when she forces the confession from her, and
Connors's portrayal of the psychotic gunslinger. Connors reminds one of Raymond Burr, in that both men were more interesting as "heavies" in their early films than they were when
they later appeared successfully on television as the upholders
of law and order.

THE PHANTOM FROM 10,000 LEAGUES. 1956. 80 minutes. *Director:*
   Dan Milner. *Screenplay:* Lou Rusoff; based on a story by
   Dorys Lukather. *Cinematography:* Bryden Baker. *Cast:*
   Kent Taylor (Ted Baxter); Cathy Downs (Lois King); Michael
   Whalen (Professor King); Helene Stanton (Wanda); Philip
   Pine (George Thomas); Rodney Bell (Bill Grant); Pierce
   Lyden (Andy); Vivi Janiss (Ethel Hall); Michael Garth
   (Sheriff).

   This is another of the monster-affected-by-radiation
films that were quite common to the science-fiction genre of
the 50s. Here, a mutant lives off the California coast guard-
ing an underwater atomic light (actually a deposit of uranium
ore). When a number of fishermen and swimmers are killed by

the mutant, the Defense Department, in the person of Kent
Taylor, decides to investigate. There is also a subplot concerning foreign agents that is never really developed. It
turns out that the mutant is a result of an errant experiment
by a professor of oceanography (Whalen), who ends up destroying
the creature, the deposit of uranium ore, and himself.
If there is a saving grace to *The Phantom from 10,000
Leagues* it is the fine underwater photography. But this is
balanced by a terrible musical score and a phantom that is
talked about more than seen.

THE SHE CREATURE. 1956. 76 minutes. *Director:* Edward L.
Cahn. *Screenplay:* Lou Rusoff; based on a story by Rusoff.
Cinematography: Frederick E. West. *Cast:* Chester Morris
(Carlo Lombardi); Marla English (Andrea); Tom Conway
(Timothy Chappel); Cathy Downs (Dorothy); Lance Fuller
(Ted Erickson); Ron Randell (Lieutenant James); Frieda
Inescort (Mrs. Chappel); Frank Jenks (Police Sergeant);
El Brendel (Olaf); Paul Dubov (Johnny); Bill Hudson (Bob);
Flo Bert (Marta); Jeanne Evans (Mrs. Brown); Kenneth
MacDonald (Professor Anderson); Paul Blaisdell (Creature).

The She Creature is a film that is played with the utmost
sincerity, headed by that always dependable "B" actor Chester
Morris. It combines a mixture of Svengali and the Bridey
Murphy theme.
Morris is a sideshow hypnotist who is able to call upon
a prehistoric monster (a cross between *The Creature from the
Black Lagoon* and *The Hideous Sun Demon*) from the past existence
of his assistant (English). When English becomes romantically
interested in a psychic researcher (Fuller), Morris attempts
to resurrect the monster to kill Fuller. But English's sub-
conscious rejects this notion as the monster turns on Morris
and kills him. Prior to this the monster has eliminated much
of the cast. At the end the she creature shuffles back into
the sea.

THE AMAZING COLOSSAL MAN. 1957. 81 minutes. *Director:* Bert
I. Gordon. *Screenplay:* Mark Hanna and Bert I. Gordon.
Cinematography: Joe Biroc. *Cast:* Glenn Langan (Lieutenant-
Colonel Glenn Manning); Cathy Downs (Carol Forrest);
William Hudson (Dr. Paul Lindstrom); James Seay (Colonel
Hallock); Larry Thor (Dr. Eric Coulter); Russ Bender
(Richard Kingman); Lynn Osborn (Sergeant Taylor); Diana

Darrin (Typist); William Hughes (Control Officer); Jack Kosslyn (Lieutenant in Briefing Room); Jean Moorhead (Girl in Bath); Jimmy Cross (Sergeant at Reception Desk); Hank Patterson (Henry); Frank Jenks (Delivery Man); Harry Raybould (Army Guard at Gate); Scott Peters (Sergeant Lee Carter); Myron Cook (Captain Thomas); Michael Harris (Police Lieutenant Keller); Bill Cassaday (Lieutenant Peterson); Dick Nelson (Sergeant Hanson); Edmund Cobb (Dr. McDermott); Judd Holdren (Robert Allen); Paul Hahn (Attendant); June Jocelyn (Nurse); Stanley Lachman (Lieutenant Kline).

An army officer (Langan) is exposed to plutonium from an atomic test. Badly burned, he is taken to a local hospital, where his skin quickly heals and he starts to grow rapidly. Because of his size (having grown to 70 feet), he is chained and put into a large tent. When an attempt is made to inject him with a hypodermic needle the size of a guided missile, he escapes. Langan has now become more than slightly unhinged, as he wanders about wondering where he is going to find the nearest men's big-and-tall store. Before we know it, he is rampaging through downtown Las Vegas, where his scorched-earth policy of urban renewal is not looked at too kindly. He finally topples from Boulder Dam, supposedly to his death, but for the climax see *War of the Colossal Beast*.

Beginning with *King Dinosaur* in 1955, Bert I. Gordon has directed an inordinate number of science-fiction films that are concerned with the super-tall or the very small. In this film he does make you sympathize with Langan's plight, but what one remembers from *The Amazing Colossal Man* are the atrocious matte shots.

BLOOD OF DRACULA. 1957. 68 minutes. *Director:* Herbert L. Strock. *Screenplay:* Ralph Thornton; based on a story by Thornton. *Cinematography:* Monroe Askins. *Cast:* Sandra Harrison (Nancy Perkins); Louise Lewis (Miss Branding); Gail Ganley (Myra); Jerry Blaine (Tab); Heather Ames (Nola); Malcolm Atterbury (Lieutenant Dunlap); Mary Adams (Mrs. Thorndyke); Thomas B. Henry (Mr. Perkins); Don Devlin (Eddie); Jeanne Dean (Mrs. Perkins); Richard Devon (Sergeant Stewart); Paul Maxwell (Mike); Carlyle Mitchell (Stanley Mather); Shirley De Lancey (Terry); Michael Hall (Glenn).

This film follows much the same plot of the successful *I Was a Teenage Werewolf*. All that was changed was the gender

of the main character, and here she was made a vampire instead
of a werewolf.

An emotionally upset young woman (Harrison) is put into
a girl's school by her father (Henry), who has just remarried
shortly after his wife's death. A chemistry teacher (Lewis),
sensing Harrison's vulnerability, uses her as a guinea pig in
a series of experiments she is undertaking with an ancient and
mysterious Carpathian amulet. Those who are in the know realize that the Rumanian Carpathians are the home of the vampire.
Under a spell Harrison turns into a vampire and begins killing
off her classmates. When Lewis refuses to release Harrison
from her condition, she strangles Lewis and is herself eventually impaled.

Despite the plot description, *Blood of Dracula* is a cut
or two above many of AIP's films from this period, especially
in the believability that Sandra Harrison brings to the character of Nancy Perkins. In *I Was a Teenage Frankenstein* the
screenplay credit is given to Ralph Thornton, a pseudonym for
Herman Cohen and Aben Kandel. We can assume that this is the
case here as well.

CAT GIRL. 1957. 67 minutes. *Director:* Alfred Shaughnessy.
Screenplay: Lou Rusoff. *Cinematography:* Peter Hennessy.
Cast: Barbara Shelley (Leonora); Robert Ayres (Dr. Mar-
lowe); Kay Callard (Dorothy); Paddy Webster (Cathy);
Ernest Milton (Edmund); Lilly Kahn (Anna); Jack May
(Richard); John Lee (Allan); Martin Body (Cafferty); John
Watson (Roberts); Selma Vas Dias (Nurse); John Baker (Male
Nurse); Frank Atkinson (Guard); Geoffrey Tyrrell (Care-
taker).

Along with *Rock Around the World* this was one of the first
films that AIP produced or distributed that came out of Great
Britain. Aside from the fact that *Cat Girl* is just plain flat,
much of the dialogue is difficult to comprehend. *Cat Girl* is
a poor man's *Cat People*.

Barbara Shelley believes that she has inherited a family
curse that will cause her to turn into a blood-lusting leopard.
When a leopard terrorizes the community, Shelley believes she
is responsible, while her psychiatrist (Ayres) thinks she is
suffering from an emotional disorder. Since she is in love
with Ayres, she devises a plan to kill his wife (Callard). In
the end, of course, what Ayres believes to be Shelley's obsession turns out to be something much more. Barbara Shelley
would later go on to appear in many more British horror films.

Dragstrip Girl

DRAGSTRIP GIRL. 1957. 69 minutes. *Director:* Edward L. Cahn.
  Screenplay: Lou Rusoff. *Cinematography:* Frederick E.
  West. *Cast:* Fay Spain (Louise Blake); Steve Terrell
  (Jim Donaldson); John Ashley (Fred Armstrong); Frank
  Gorshin (Tommy Burns); Russ Bender (Lieutenant Bradley);
  Tommy Ivo (Rick Camden); Gracia Narsico (Mama); Tito
  Vuolo (Papa); with Dorothy Bruce, Don Shelton, Carla
  Merey, Leon Tyler, George Dockstader, Bill Welsh, Edmund
  Cobb, Woody Lee, Judy Bambert.

Hot rods and a love triangle dominate *Dragstrip Girl*.
This film comes about as close as any AIP teen exploitation
film to exhibiting any sort of class conflict.
  Poor, but honest, Jim Donaldson (Terrell) is at odds with
rich and spoiled Fred Armstrong (Ashley) for the affections
of Fay Spain. Ever since they were kids, Terrell has had the
upper hand on Ashley. Both young men enter a car race that
offers a scholarship prize, which Terrell could use for his
schooling. Not needing the prize, Ashley is determined to win
just to spite his rival. Before the big race Ashley steals
Terrell's hot rod and kills a pedestrian. Terrell is arrested
for the crime on the day of the race, and Spain takes his place
and wins the race for him. She then gives the authorities
evidence implicating Ashley in the hit and run.

FLESH AND THE SPUR. 1957. 78 minutes. Color. *Director:*
  Edward L. Cahn. *Screenplay:* Charles B. Griffith and Mark
  Hanna. *Cinematography:* Frederick E. West. *Cast:* John
  Agar (Luke/Matthew Random); Marla English (Willow); Touch
  (Mike) Connors (Stacey Dark); Raymond Hatton (Windy);
  Maria Monay (Lola); Joyce Meadows (Rena); Kenne Duncan
  (Tanner); Frank Lackteen (Indian Chief); Mel Gaines
  (Blackie); Michael Harris (Deputy Marshal); Eddie Kafafian
  (Bud); Richard Alexander (Bartender); Kermit Maynard,
  Bud Osborne, Buddy Roosevelt (Outlaws).

I am afraid that *Flesh and the Spur* is nowhere near as
suggestive or kinky as the title would indicate. Like *Rancho
Notorious*, this is a western tale of hate, murder, and revenge,
as John Agar sets out to find the man who murdered his twin
brother. Joining him is a gunman (Connors), who is seeking a
member of the outlaw gang that the killer might be with. In
the end Agar discovers that Connors is the man who murdered
his brother, and the two of them fight to the death.
  Along the way to this denouement there appear a number
of old Hollywood faces: Raymond Hatton, who was a regular in

Hollywood since the days of D.W. Griffith; Kenne Duncan, who often portrayed gangsters or outlaws; Frank Lackteen, known for playing exotic foreigners; and Kermit Maynard, brother of cowboy star Ken Maynard and a western actor in his own right. The title *Flesh and the Spur* is never really explained in the film, unless it refers to a fight between two men using spurs, and a young girl being burned at the stake.

I WAS A TEENAGE FRANKENSTEIN. 1957. 72 minutes. Part Color. *Director:* Herbert L. Strock. *Screenplay:* Kenneth Langtry (pseudonym for Aben Kandel). *Cinematography:* Lothrop Worth. *Cast:* Whit Bissell (Professor Frankenstein); Phyllis Coates (Margaret); Robert Burton (Dr. Karlton); Gary Conway (Teenage Monster); George Lynn (Sergeant Burns); John Cliff (Sergeant McAfee); Marshall Bradford (Dr. Randolph); Claudia Bryar (Arlene's Mother); Angela Blake (Beautiful Girl); Russ Whiteman (Dr. Elwood); Charles Seel (The Jeweler); Paul Keast (Man at Crash); Gretchen Thomas (Woman in Corridor); Joy Stoner (Arlene); Larry Carr (Young Man); Pat Miller (Police Officer).

Following closely on the heels of the success of *I Was a Teenage Werewolf*, this film contains none of the teenager-as-misfit theme that appears in the former film. Whit Bissell appears here as the evil doctor who is interested in body transplants. He and his assistant (Burton) gather up parts of bodies from auto crashes and plane wrecks and put together a muscular young teenager (Conway) with a hideous face. It remains this way until Conway and Bissell go to a local lovers' lane and bring back a handsome replacement head inside a birdcage. The monster eventually rebels in the laboratory and feeds Bissell to the alligator he keeps to dispose of excess body parts. When the police arrive, the monster backs into an electronic panel and is electrocuted.

I Was a Teenage Frankenstein is primarily remembered for the witty screenplay, especially some of the lines given to Whit Bissell (which he plays straight). Also, the last minute or so of this film, as Conway is being electrocuted and Bissell being eaten by the alligator, is in color.

I WAS A TEENAGE WEREWOLF. 1957. 76 minutes. *Director:* Gene Fowler, Jr. *Screenplay:* Ralph Thornton (pseudonym for Herman Cohen and Aben Kandel). *Cinematography:* Joseph La Shelle. *Cast:* Michael Landon (Tony Rivers); Yvonne

Lime (Arlene); Whit Bissell (Dr. Alfred Brandon); Tony
Marshall (Jimmy); Dawn Richard (Theresa); Barney Phillips
(Detective Donovan); Ken Miller (Vic); Cindy Robbins
(Pearl); Michael Rougas (Frank); Robert Griffin (Police
Chief Baker); Joseph Mell (Dr. Hugo Wagner); Malcolm
Atterbury (Charles); Eddie Marr (Doyle); Vladimir Sokoloff
(Pepi); Louise Lewis (Miss Ferguson); John Launer (Bill);
Guy Williams (Chris Stanley); Donna Crehan (Mary).

I Was a Teenage Werewolf is simply one of the best teenage
exploitation films of the 50s. Both Michael Landon and Whit
Bissell give an authority to their roles that is not often
found in these types of films.
The film explores the theme of the teenager as the "other"
--a misfit, an outsider, not a Jerry Lewis spastic schlep.
Landon is a young man (not unlike James Dean in *Rebel Without
a Cause*) who has a problem controlling his temper. A friendly
policeman (Phillips) and Landon's girlfriend (Lime) convince
him to seek psychiatric help. The psychiatrist (Bissell)
figures that Landon would be a fitting subject for a series
of experiments in regression. Lo and behold, Landon soon re-
verts to a werewolf state and kills a couple of his classmates.
After he has also dispatched Bissell and his assistant, the
police arrive and he is himself shot and killed.
The sincerity of the film's presentation does not negate
the one glaring incongruity in the plot. It is never explained
just where on the evolutionary scale man was a werewolf. Nonetheless, *I Was a Teenage Werewolf* grossed more than ten times
its cost.

INVASION OF THE SAUCER MEN. 1957. 69 minutes. *Director:*
Edward L. Cahn. *Screenplay:* Robert J. Gurney, Jr., and
Al Martin; based on the story "The Cosmic Frame," by
Paul W. Fairman. *Cinematography:* Frederick E. West.
Cast: Steve Terrell (Johnny); Gloria Castillo (Joan);
Frank Gorshin (Joe); Raymond Hatton (Larkin); Lyn Osborn
(Art); Russ Bender (Doctor); Douglas Henderson (Lieutenant
Wilkins); Sam Buffington (Colonel); Jason Johnson (Detec-
tive); Don Shelton (Mr. Hayden); Scott Peters (Soldier);
Jan Englund (Waitress); Kelly Thordsen (Sergeant Bruce);
Bob Einer (Soda Jerk); Patti Lawler (Irene); Calvin Booth
(Paul); Ed Nelson (Boy); Jim Bridges (Boy); Roy Darmour
(Sergeant Gordon); Audrey Conti (Girl); Joan Dupuis
(Girl); Jimmy Pickford (Boy in Soda Shop); Buddy Mason
(Policeman); Orv Mohler (Boy in Soda Shop).

This could be described as a typical AIP film from this period--ridiculous but fun. *Invasion of the Saucer Men* is a satire on the little-green-men-from-Mars films, such as *Invaders from Mars*.

These extraterrestrials arrive in a town called Hicksville, where they encounter all sorts of hostility from local teenagers, the military, a farmer, and even a brahma bull. They are destroyed when the teenagers get together and turn the headlights of their hot rods on the creatures, thereby rendering them into puffs of smoke.

The aliens have a startling appearance, with their large vein-covered heads, bulging lizardlike eyes, and oversized hands with an eyeball on top. Their strange method of killing consists of using needles that pop out of their fingers, which contain alcohol. An injection of this given to an already-drunk Frank Gorshin proves lethal. This film was remade in 1965 as *The Eye Creatures* for an AIP television release.

MOTORCYCLE GANG. 1957. 78 minutes. *Director:* Edward L. Cahn. *Screenplay:* Lou Rusoff. *Cinematography:* Frederick E. West. *Cast:* Anne Neyland (Terry); Steve Terrell (Randy); John Ashley (Nick); Carl Switzer (Speed); Raymond Hatton (Uncle Ed); Russ Bender (Joe); Jean Moorhead (Marilyn); Scott Peters (Hank); Eddie Kafafian (Jack); Shirley Falls (Darlene); Aki Aleong (Cyrus Wong); Wayne Taylor (Phil); Hal Bogart (Walt); Phyllis Cole (Mary); Suzanne Sydney (Birdie); Edmund Cobb (Bill); Paul Blaisdell (Don); Zon Murray (Hal); Felice Richmond (Hal's Wife).

Motorcycle Gang is not much more than a remake of *Dragstrip Girl*, with both Steve Terrell and John Ashley respectively playing the hero and villain. Ashley has just returned from a jail term for a hit-and-run accident. He taunts Terrell, who is on probation for the same accident, into an illegal motorcycle race. Being a member of a police-supervised motorcycle club, Terrell declines because he wants to win a trophy in a legally sponsored race. Between the two of them steps Anne Neyland, who teases both young men to test their masculinity in a "chicken run." Terrell's participation in this race disqualifies him from the big race, but he is eventually reinstated. Just in time, as a matter of fact, because in the middle of the race he learns that Ashley and his gang are terrorizing the citizens of a small town a la *The Wild One*. Terrell and his boys ride into the town and quickly restore things to the status quo.

One of the characters to look for in this film is Carl
Switzer, better known as "Alfalfa" of the *Our Gang* comedies
of the 30s and 40s. This was one of the last films he made
before he died.

THE NAKED PARADISE. 1957. 68 minutes. Color. *Director:*
    Roger Corman. *Screenplay:* Charles B. Griffith and Mark
    Hanna. *Cinematography:* Floyd Crosby. *Cast:* Richard
    Denning (Duke Bradley); Beverly Garland (Max McKenzie);
    Lisa Montell (Keena); Leslie Bradley (Zac Cotton); Richard
    (Dick) Miller (Mitch); Jonathan Haze (Stony Gratoni);
    with Carol Lindsay.

This Roger Corman produced and directed film was shot in
Hawaii in tandem with *The She Gods of Shark Reef*. About the
only things *The Naked Paradise* has going for it are the exotic
locations, the good camerawork, and the title.
    Richard Denning is a captain of a yacht that is chartered
by a gang who have just robbed a plantation of its payroll.
Beverly Garland is the "secretary" to the leader of the gang
(Bradley). When Denning and Garland discover a mutual attraction for one another, they decide to leave Bradley and his
henchmen (Miller and Haze), but a hurricane alters their plans.
This leads to a violent climax in which the gang is routinely
dispatched, and the two of them are able to be together.
    Also known as *Thunder Over Hawaii*, this film flopped when
it first appeared. However, when it was later released as an
AIP Encore Hit it turned a tidy profit.

REFORM SCHOOL GIRL. 1957. 71 minutes. *Director:* Edward
    Bernds. *Screenplay:* Edward Bernds. *Cinematography:*
    Floyd Crosby. *Cast:* Gloria Castillo (Donna Price); Ross
    Ford (David Lindsay); Edward Byrnes (Vince); Ralph Reed
    (Jackie); Jan Englund (Ruth); Yvette Vickers (Roxy);
    Helen Wallace (Mrs. Trimble); Donna Jo Gribble (Cathy);
    Luana Anders (Josie); Diana Darrin (Mona); Nesdon Booth
    (Deetz); Wayne Taylor (Gary); Sharon Lee (Blonde); Jack
    Kruschen (Mr. Horvath); Linda Rivera (Elena); Elaine
    Sinclair (Midge); Dorothy Crehan (Matron); Claire Carleton
    (Mrs. Horvath); Lillian Powell (Mrs. Patton); Sally
    Kellerman (A Girl).

Director Edward Bernds visited a couple of girls' refor-
matories before he scripted *Reform School Girl*. The result

is a typically fast-paced, lurid, AIP youth exploitation film.

The film begins with Gloria Castillo almost being raped by her uncle (Kruschen). Right after this she takes a ride with a young car thief (Edd "Kookie" Byrnes). He runs down a pedestrian in a hit-and-run accident, and Castillo is sent to a girls' reform school because she refused to "squeal" on him. Byrnes convinces the other girls in the reformatory that Castillo is a "squealer," so they do such things as put a snake in her bed and pour hot coffee on her. Castillo retaliates by starting a fight with a pair of scissors. She is eventually cleared of complicity in the hit-and-run when Byrnes is captured attempting to enter the institution to kill her.

Despite the amount of violence in the film, much of it is not well staged. But the film did employ a number of young Hollywood starlets (including Sally Kellerman), and in the words of *Variety* it contains "mucho leg display" (August 28, 1957, p. 6).

ROCK ALL NIGHT. 1957. 62 minutes. *Director:* Roger Corman. *Screenplay:* Charles B. Griffith; based on a story by David P. Harmon. *Cinematography:* Floyd Crosby. *Cast:* Dick Miller (Shorty); Abby Dalton (Julie); The Platters (Themselves); The Blockbusters (Themselves); Robin Morse (Al); Richard Cutting (Steve); Bruno Ve Sota (Charlie); Chris Alcaide (Angie); Mel Welles (Sir Bop); Barboura Morris (Syl); Clegg Hoyt (Marty); Russell Johnson (Jigger); Jonathan Haze (Joey); Richard Carlan (Jerry); Jack De Witt (Philippe); Bert Nelson (Bartender); Beech Dickerson (The Kid); Ed Nelson (Pete).

Shot in about six days, all the action in this Roger Corman "cheapie" takes place in a neighborhood bar called Al's Place. The habitues of this bar are sitting around one evening when a man rushes in off the street to say that he witnessed a murder. When he "fingers" two of the bar patrons (Johnson and Haze) as the murderers, they shoot him and hold the rest of the bar hostage. It takes one of the bar's regulars, Shorty (Miller), who is known for his verbose excesses and shortage of gray matter, to subdue the two thugs. He does this not with his fists, but with his sarcastic remarks.

Along with *A Bucket of Blood*, this is one of Dick Miller's best roles in that he carries off many of the wisecracks in the script very well. Those who are going to see this film just for The Platters had better not miss the first ten minutes, since this is the only time they appear in the film.

ROCK AROUND THE WORLD. 1957. 71 minutes. *Director:* Gerald
Bryant. *Screenplay:* Norman Hudis. *Cinematography:*
Peter Hennessey. *Cast:* Tommy Steele (Himself); Patrick
Westwood (Brushes); Hilda Fenemore (Mrs. Steele); Charles
Lamb (Mr. Steele); Peter Lewiston (John Kennedy); John
Boxer (Paul Lincoln); Mark Daly (Junkshop Man); Lisa
Daniely (Hospital Nurse); Byran Coleman (Hospital Doctor);
Cyril Chamberlain (Chief Steward); Bernard Hunter (Busker-
Guitarist); Alan Weighell (1st Steelman-Bass); Dennis
Price (2nd Steelman-Pianist); Leo Pollini (3rd Steelman-
Drummer); Alan Stuart (4th Steelman-Saxophonist); Tom
Littlewood (Judo Instructor); with Calypso Bands--Chris
O'Brien's Caribbeans and Tommy Eytle's Calypso Band;
Teenage Party Artists--Humphrey Lyttelton's Band, Chas.
McDevitt Skiffle Group; with Nancy Whiskey, Hunter
Hancock.

This film, made to exhibit British rocker Tommy Steele
to the American public, includes added American footage of an
introduction by Los Angeles disc jockey Hunter Hancock. The
plot is negligible even by the standards of rock-and-roll
films, but it does include about 12 numbers by Steele, whose
singing voice betrays none of his Bermondsey Cockney background.

Much of *Rock Around the World* consists of stock footage
shot at a London concert, and thus gives us a good look at
some of the early pre-Beatles rock and roll from Great Britain.
Especially noteworthy is the rendition of "Freight Train" done
by Nancy Whiskey and the Chas McDevitt Skiffle Group.

RUNAWAY DAUGHTERS. 1957. 90 minutes. *Director:* Edward L.
Cahn. *Screenplay:* Lou Rusoff; based on a story by
Rusoff. *Cinematography:* Frederick E. West. *Cast:* Marla
English (Audrey Barton); Anna Sten (Ruth Barton); John
Litel (George Barton); Lance Fuller (Tony Forrest); Adele
Jergens (Dixie); Mary Ellen Kaye (Mary Rubeck); Gloria
Castillo (Angela Forrest); Jay Adler (Rubek); Steven
Terrell (Bob Harris); Nicky Blair (Joe); Frank J. Gorshin
(Tommy); Maureen Cassidy (Maureen); Reed Howes (Henry);
Anne O'Neal (Miss Petrie); Edmund Cobb (Detective).

Runaway teenagers today are even a larger problem than
when *Runaway Daughters* was made, but the causes for leaving
never vary to any great extent. At 90 minutes this was one
of AIP's longer features, even though it had only a nine day
shooting schedule and a budget of under $100,000.

Three young girls leave home to go to Los Angeles. Marla
English comes from a wealthy family that gives her everything
but love. Gloria Castillo is neglected by her mother, who is
always traveling, and Mary Ellen Kaye has a domineering father.
When they get to Los Angeles, they find nothing but trouble.

A humorous story is told about veteran actress Anna Sten,
who plays English's mother, and who once was under contract
to Sam Goldwyn. On her first day on the AIP set she brought
champagne and caviar sandwiches, only to be told that she
would be sharing a dressing room with brassy Adele Jergens
(Mark Thomas McGee and R.J. Robertson, *The J.D. Films: Juvenile
Delinquency in the Movies*. Jefferson, N.C.: McFarland, 1982,
p. 65). This is tantamount to George Sanders sharing a dressing room with Dick Miller.

SHAKE, RATTLE AND ROCK. 1957. 74 minutes. *Director:* Edward
    L. Cahn. *Screenplay:* Lou Rusoff; based on a story by
    Rusoff. *Cinematography:* Frederick E. West. *Cast:* Fats
    Domino (Himself); Joe Turner (Himself); Lisa Gaye (June);
    Touch (Mike) Connors (Garry); Sterling Holloway (Axe);
    Raymond Hatton (Horace); Douglas Dumbrille (Eustace);
    Margaret Dumont (Georgianna); Tommy Charles (Himself);
    Annita Ray (Herself); Paul Dubov (Bugsy); Eddie Kafafian
    (Nick); Clarence Kolb (Judge); Percy Helton (Hiram);
    Choker Campbell (Himself); Charles Evans (Bentley); Frank
    Jenks (Director); Pierre Watkin (Armstrong); Joe Devlin
    (Police Captain); Jimmy Pickford (Eddie); Nancy Kilgas
    (Nancy); Giovanna Fiorino (Helen); Leon Tyler (Aloysius);
    Patricia Gregory (Pat).

Shake, Rattle and Rock has one of the most improbable
casts you could ever want to find. It also contains only a
modicum of music when you compare it with *Rock Around the
World*.
    Connors is a television personality (much like Dick
Clark), who is attempting to help disadvantaged young people
by setting up a recreation center where they can listen and
dance to rock and roll. The conflict comes when a small group
of "upright" citizens (led by Dumbrille) claim that rock and
roll is a pernicious influence among the young and leads to
delinquency. A television program is setup so that both sides
can present their arguments and let the public act as jury.
The citizen's group show a film comparing rock with "primitive"
aboriginal dances. Then Connors shows a film displaying the
Black Bottom and the Charleston and explains that they were
the rock and roll of their day. This helps convince the older

Shake, Rattle and Rock

group that they have nothing to fear from rock and roll.

An interesting sidelight to this film is that some of the slang dialogue delivered by Sterling Holloway was subtitled. The plot for *Shake, Rattle and Rock* was very similar to Columbia's *Don't Knock the Rock*, which highlighted Bill Haley and the Comets and the great Little Richard.

SORORITY GIRL. 1957. 61 minutes. *Director:* Roger Corman. *Screenplay:* Ed Waters and Leo Lieberman. *Cinematography:* Monroe P. Askins. *Cast:* Susan Cabot (Sabra Tanner); Dick Miller (Mort); Barboura (Morris) O'Neill (Rita Joyce); June Kenney (Tina); Barbara Crane (Ellie Marshall); Fay Baker (Mrs. Tanner); Jeane Wood (Mrs. Fessenden), with Margaret Campbell.

Loosely based on Calder Willingham's *End as a Man* (filmed in 1957 as *The Strange One*), *Sorority Girl* is one of the most downbeat of AIP's teenage exploitation films. Susan Cabot is a maladjusted young rich girl who cannot adjust to living in a sorority, but she must graduate from college to achieve her inheritance. She takes out all her neuroses on her sorority sisters. She blackmails one of the more popular girls (O'Neill) to keep her under her domination. When Cabot's allowance is stopped, she blackmails a pregnant student (Kenney), which misfires with almost tragic results. The film ends with Cabot alone on a beach, as her peers refuse to have anything to do with her.

The Susan Cabot character is considerably whitewashed compared with her depraved counterpart, Ben Gazarra, in *The Strange One*. Corman claims that the film was meant "to deal with the social structure of a university as a microcosm of the social structure in society.... The movie's best scenes were the comedy relief" (Ed Naha, *The Films of Roger Corman: Brilliance on a Budget*. New York: Arco, 1982, p. 19).

THE UNDEAD. 1957. 71 minutes. *Director:* Roger Corman. *Screenplay:* Charles B. Griffith and Mark Hanna. *Cinematography:* William Sickner. *Cast:* Pamela Duncan (Helene/Diana); Richard Garland (Pendragon); Allison Hayes (Livia); Val DuFour (Quintus); Mel Welles (Smolkin); Dorothy Neuman (Meg Maud); Billy Barty (The Imp); Bruno Ve Sota (Scroop); Aaron Saxon (Gobbo); Richard Devon (Satan).

A psychotherapist experimenting with time (Garland) picks up a prostitute (Duncan) and through hypnosis sends her back 1,000 years to the Middle Ages. It turns out that Duncan was executed as a witch. She attempts to save herself from death, even if it means her present self would have never been born. Garland aids her in her journey back into time, and both find themselves allied against a sexy witch (Hayes) and even Satan (Devon). They both learn the dangers of trying to alter history, as Duncan finally lets herself be beheaded as a witch. When she awakens from her trance, she finds that Garland has become trapped in the past.

The Undead was another of Roger Corman's ten-day wonders, supposedly filmed in a reconverted supermarket. *Variety* summed up the results: "A retrogression theme and bosomy dames are used in this minor league horror subject as ballyhoo pegs for quickie playdates" (February 27, 1957, p. 6).

THE VIKING WOMEN AND THE SEA SERPENT. 1957. 63 minutes.
    Director: Roger Corman. *Screenplay:* Louis Goldman; based on a story by Irving Block. *Cinematography:* Monroe P. Askins. *Cast:* Abby Dalton (Desir); Susan Cabot (Enger); Brad Jackson (Vedric); June Kenney (Asnild); Richard Devon (Stark); Betsy Jones-Moreland (Thyra); Jonathan Haze (Ottar); Jay Sayer (Senja); Gary Conway (Jarl); with Lynn Bernay, Sally Todd, Mike Forrest, Wilda Taylor.

A group of Viking women take a boat and go out to look for their missing menfolk. Their boat is destroyed in the area where a sea serpent lives. The four survivors are washed ashore and captured by a primitive tribe called the Grimaults. The women are made slaves by the tribe and find that their men are also being used as slaves. They all finally make their escape, and in the process the Grimaults run afoul of the sea serpent.

The Viking Women and the Sea Serpent stands right up there with *A Bucket of Blood* and *The Little Shop of Horrors* as one of the most perversely enjoyable of Roger Corman's films. Filmed in what looks like the canyons above Hollywood, the actors here all show a type of enthusiasm that is more appropriate for Hollywood Boulevard than ninth-century Scandinavia. The Grimaults, a so-called warrior race, sprang from what only could have been a defective gene pool. When this film appears on television, keep an eye out for the "campy" portrayal of a Grimault sissy.

VOODOO WOMAN. 1957. 77 minutes. *Director:* Edward L. Cahn.
Screenplay: Russell Bender and V.I. Voss. *Cinematography:*
Frederick E. West. *Cast:* Marla English (Marilyn
Blanchard); Tom Conway (Dr. Roland Gerard); Touch (Mike)
Connors (Ted Bronson); Lance Fuller (Rick Brady); Mary
Ellen Kaye (Susan Gerard); Paul Dubov (Marcel Chateau);
Martin Wilkins (Chaka); Norman Willis (Harry West); Otis
Greene (Bobo); Emmett E. Smith (Gandor); Paul Blaisdell
(Monster); Giselle D'Arc (Singer); Jean Davis (Native
Girl).

  Voodoo Woman could easily make a list of one of the worst
films ever made. It stars Tom Conway, who at one time was a
creditable actor. Here he shows the ravages of his lengthy
bout with alcohol, as this film certainly represents the nadir
of his career.
  Conway is a mad doctor, who for some reason is living in
a voodoo village. He is working on a formula for a mental
slave who will be the start of a new superrace and seeks out
only beautiful women for these experiments. Women who are
pure of heart will not do, so Conway offers to pay ruthless
jungle adventuress Marilyn Blanchard (English) if she will
participate in his experiment. She turns into a monster and
kills a number of the local natives, and Conway as well. When
English returns to her natural form, she accidentally falls
into a crater, but the last shot of the film shows her crawling
back out, now transformed again into a monster.
  Voodoo Woman has been called "an inept jumble of jungle
melodrama, voodoo, evil science, and greed" (Bill Warren, *Keep
Watching the Skies! American Science Fiction Movies of the
Fifties: Volume 1, 1950-1957.* Jefferson, N.C.: McFarland,
1982, p. 401). It contains as its lone highlight a song, performed by Giselle D'Arc, entitled "Black Voodoo."

THE ASTOUNDING SHE-MONSTER. 1958. 59 minutes. *Director:*
Ronnie Ashcroft. *Screenplay:* Frank Hall. *Cinematography:*
William C. Thompson. *Cast:* Robert Clarke (Dick Cutler);
Kenne Duncan (Nat Burdell); Marilyn Harvey (Margaret
Chaffee); Jeanne Tatum (Esther Malone); Shirley Kilpatrick
(Monster); Ewing Brown (Brad Conley).

  The Astounding She-Monster is right up there with *Lost
Women*, *Robot Monster*, and *Plan 9 from Outer Space* as one of
the most disreputable science-fiction films of the 50s, which,
of course, means of all time.

As in *The Day the World Ended*, a motley group of people--
three kidnappers, their victim, and a geologist--find themselves in a remote wilderness cabin. Here they are confronted
with an alien female dressed to the nines in one of Tina
Turner's old dresses--a shimmering, radioactive quasi-leotard.
When she is first sighted moving about the forest, she appears
to look more like an overgrown lightning bug. By the end of
the film the three kidnappers and the alien female have been
killed, with the geologist (Clarke) and the kidnap victim
(Harvey) the only ones left alive. At this point we realize
that the she-monster was actually not a menace, but a messenger
of peace from another planet.

ATTACK OF THE PUPPET PEOPLE. 1958. 78 minutes. *Director:*
    Bert I. Gordon. *Screenplay:* George Worthing Yates; based
    on a story by Bert I. Gordon. *Cinematography:* Ernest
    Laszlo. *Cast:* John Agar (Bob Westley); John Hoyt (Mr.
    Franz); June Kenney (Sally Reynolds); Michael Mark (Emil);
    Jack Kosslyn (Sergeant Patterson); Marlene Willis
    (Laurie); Ken Miller (Stan); Laurie Mitchell (Georgia);
    Scott Peters (Mac); Susan Gordon (Agnes); June Jocelyn
    (Brownie Leader); Jean Moorhead (Janet); Hank Patterson
    (Doorman); Hal Bogart (Mailman); Troy Patterson (Elevator
    Operator); Bill Giorgio (Janitor); George Diestel (Switch-
    board Operator); Jaime Forster (Ernie); Mark Lowell
    (Salesman).

    Most of Bert I. Gordon's science-fiction films from *The
Amazing Colossal Man* to *Empire of the Ants* deal with giants
of one sort or another. In this respect *Attack of the Puppet
People* is an anomaly in his oeuvre, as this was certainly made
to capitalize on the success of *The Incredible Shrinking Man*.
    A dollmaker and one-time puppeteer (Hoyt) invents a ma-
chine that reduces humans to about six inches tall. He does
not have any nefarious reason for doing this, for he does it
only to relieve his loneliness. The main conflict in the film
revolves around two people (Agar and Kenney) whom Hoyt has
miniaturized and their efforts to escape and regain their
height. Hoyt destroys his creations and himself before the
police can capture him, but both Agar and Kenney are successful
in changing back to normal size.
    This film contains neither the inventiveness of *The Devil
Doll* nor the pathos of *The Incredible Shrinking Man*. The most
preposterous part of *Attack of the Puppet People* comes when
one of the puppet people sings "Living Doll" in an echo
chamber.

THE BRAIN EATERS. 1958. 60 minutes. *Director:* Bruno Ve Sota.
Screenplay: Gordon Urquhart. *Cinematography:* Larry
Raimond. *Cast:* Ed Nelson (Dr. Kettering); Alan Frost
(Glenn); Jack Hill (Senator Powers); Joanna Lee (Alice);
Jody Fair (Elaine); David Hughes (Dr. Wyler); Robert Ball
(Dan Walker); Greigh Phillips (Sheriff); Orville Sherman
(Cameron); Leonard Nimoy (Protector); Doug Banks (Doctor);
Henry Randolph (Telegrapher).

This low-budget effort was produced by actor Ed Nelson,
who up until this time had only appeared in bit parts. *The
Brain Eaters* takes as its premise an idea borrowed from *It
Conquered the World.*
   A scientist (Nelson) and a U.S. Senator (Hill) investigate
occurrences of murder and mayhem. It seems that parasites who
come from deep within the earth are attaching themselves to
people's necks and controlling their brain functions. If they
are removed, the affected person will lapse into a short period
of insanity and die. When all ordinary means of eliminating
the creatures fail, an electric cable is put over the craft
where they live. The ensuing explosion shrinks up and destroys
the parasites.
   This film was made early in the careers of three actors
who later became better known. Ed Nelson would go on to star
as Dr. Rossi in the television version of *Peyton Place*, Leonard
Nimoy would gain popularity as Mr. Spock in *Star Trek*, and
Jack Hill went on to become a director of horror films.

THE BONNIE PARKER STORY. 1958. 79 minutes. *Director:* William
Witney. *Screenplay:* Stanley Shpetner. *Cinematography:*
Jack Marta. *Cast:* Dorothy Provine (Bonnie Parker); Jack
Hogan (Guy Darrow); Richard Bakalyan (Duke Jefferson);
Joseph Turkel (Chuck Darrow); William Stevens (Paul);
Ken Lynch (Restaurant Manager); Douglas Kennedy (Tom
Steel); Patti Huston (Chuck's Girl); Joel Colin (Bobby);
Jeff Morris (Marv); Jim Beck (Alvin); Stanley Livingston
(Little Boy); Carolyn Hughes (Girl); John Halloran (Ranger
Chief); Madeline Foy (Ranger's Secretary); Sid Lassick
(Scoutmaster); Howard Wright (Old Man); Karl Davis
(Texan); Raymond Guth (Louisiana Sheriff); Vince Williams
(Narrator); Frank Evans (Announcer).

Dorothy Provine is perhaps best remembered as a light-
hearted nightclub entertainer in the old television series
The Roaring Twenties. In this film she portrays Depression
criminal Bonnie Parker in a much tougher and unsentimental

style than did Faye Dunaway in *Bonnie and Clyde*.

Provine is a waitress in a greasy spoon when she marries Duke Jefferson (Bakalyan), totally unaware he is a bank robber. When he is captured and sent to prison for life, she begins her life of crime along with two brothers (Hogan and Turkel). Provine proves tougher than the men, smoking big cigars and handling a tommy gun with the ease of eyeliner. After Turkel's death she becomes the leader of the gang, only to be killed in an ambush by Texas Rangers.

Unlike Arthur Penn's *Bonnie and Clyde*, *The Bonnie Parker Story* makes no attempt either to glamorize or to preach to the audience. The film shows the drab and grim environment of the Depression in the Southwest, and gives only a casual nod to the environmental factors that lead to Bonnie's life of crime. Her crime spree is shown with relish, aided by the manic, edgy style of Ronald Stein's musical score.

THE COOL AND THE CRAZY. 1958. 78 minutes. *Director:* William Witney. *Screenplay:* Richard C. Sarafian. *Cinematography:* Harry Birch. *Cast:* Scott Marlowe (Bennie Saul); Gigi Perreau (Amy); Dick Bakalyan (Jackie Barzan); Dick Jones (Stu Summerville); Shelby Storck (Lieutenant Sloan); Marvin J. Rosen (Eddie); Caroline von Mayrhauser (Mrs. Ryan); Robert Hadden (Cookie); Kenneth Plumb (Marty); Anthony Pawley (Mr. Saul); James Newman (Sergeant Meyers); Joe Adelman (Police Sergeant); Jackie Storck (Amy's mother); Leonard Belove (Amy's Father); Jim Bysol (Blue Note Proprietor); John Hannahan (Drunk).

Of all the AIP films of the 50s none has come as close to achieving the level of a cult film as has *The Cool and the Crazy*. The reason for this, most likely, is the subject of marijuana and drug addiction, which usually was not treated to much scrutiny in the AIP films of the period.

Bennie Saul (Marlowe), just out of reform school, quickly organizes a gang at school. Through his local pusher (Rosen) Marlowe is able to lead the other boys into the world of drugs. One of the boys (Bakalyan) refuses the temptation thanks to the influence of his girlfriend (Perreau). Soon Marlowe and the others are committing violent acts while they are "high." The moral to the story comes about when Marlowe, in a drugged state, misinterprets some traffic lights and drives his car over a cliff.

Apparently no one involved in this film believed that marijuana led to harder drugs, but the inclusion of drugs made for a nice twist from the other AIP youth films. When *The Cool*

and the Crazy was being filmed in Kansas City, two of the actors were supposedly arrested by the police because they looked
too much like delinquents.   Incidentally, Scott Marlowe has
gone from Bennie Saul the drug addict to television directing.

DRAGSTRIP RIOT. 1958. 68 minutes. *Director:* David Bradley.
   Screenplay: George Hodgins; based on a story by O. Dale
   Ireland and Hodgins; additional story and dialogue by
   V.J. Rheims. *Cinematography:* Gil Warrenton. *Cast:* Yvonne
   Lime (Janet Pearson); Gary Clarke (Rick Martin); Fay Wray
   (Mrs. Martin); Bob Turnbull (Bart Thorsen); Connie Stevens
   (Marge); Gabe Delutri (Silva); Marcus Dyrector (Cliff);
   Ted Wedderspoon (Gramps); Barry Truex (Gordie); Marilyn
   Carroll (Rae); Marla Ryan (Helen); Steve Ihnat (Dutch);
   Tony Butula (Joe); Carolyn Mitchell (Betty); Joan Chandler
   (Lisa); Marc Thompson (Gary); Allan Carter (Mike).

By the time *Dragstrip Riot* came out, the hot-rod youth
film had built up a regular series of predictable conventions.
This is much like *Motorcycle Gang*, but instead of a "bad" boy
just returning from jail we have the hero (Clarke) returning
from six months in a reformatory for beating up a boy in a
fight.   Clarke and his upper-middle-class friends all drive
shiny sportscars and are naturally at odds with the local bikers.   A young tough (Turnbull) makes a play for Clarke's girl
(Lime).   Both boys have a race on a railroad track, Turnbull
loses and joins the motorcycle gang.   One of the gang members
is killed in an attempt to run Clarke and Lime off the road.
Clarke, because of his past, is naturally suspected of being
responsible for the youth's death.   By now the resolution has
become well established.
   The plot of *Dragstrip Riot* and some similar films revolves
around a tension between upper-class and working class youngsters.   In this respect they become an American version of the
British battle between the Mods and the Rockers in the 50s and
early 60s.

HELL SQUAD. 1958. 64 minutes. *Director:* Burt Topper.
   Screenplay: Burt Topper; based on a story by Topper.
   Cinematography: Erik Daarstad and John Morrill. *Cast:*
   Wally Campo (Russo); Brandon Carroll (German Officer);
   Fred Gavlin (Clemens); Greg Stuart (Nelson); Cecil Addis
   (Lippy); Leon Schrier (Roth); Don Chambers (American Cap-
   tain); with Larry Shuttleworth, Jerry Bob Weston, Gordon

Edwards, Jack Sowards, Jim Hamilton, Ben Bigelow, Jon
Hearne, Jack N. Kramer, Dick Walsh, Curtis Lozer, Bob
Williams.

During World War II a small American patrol is lost in
the Tunisian desert after having blown up a German oil depot.
All of the members of the patrol perish, except for one soldier, Russo (Campo), who is wounded and trapped in a German
minefield. The only other person in the vicinity is a German
officer (Carroll) starving for water and delirious. He also
has a map of the mine placements. The two men play a cat-and-
mouse game. Just as it appears that the German has the upper
hand, Campo is rescued by the arrival of reinforcements.

HIGH SCHOOL HELLCATS. 1958. 69 minutes. *Director:* Edward
Bernds. *Screenplay:* Mark and Jan Lowell. *Cinematography:*
Gil Warrenton. *Cast:* Yvonne Lime (Joyce); Bret Halsey
(Mike); Jana Lund (Connie); Suzanne Sydney (Dolly);
Heather Ames (Meg); Nancy Kilgas (Laurie); Rhoda Williams
(Miss Davis); Don Shelton (Martin); Viola Harris (Mrs.
Martin); Robert Anderson (Lieutenant Manner); Martin
Braddock (Rip); Arthur Marshall (Mr. Anderson).

High School Hellcats was one of the first films of this
period that dealt with female delinquent gangs. Yvonne Lime
is a new student in a high school that has a girls' gang called
the Hellcats. It is run by the sadistic Connie (Lund) and her
dim-witted second in command, Dolly (Sydney). Since Lime does
not receive enough "strokes" at home from her parents, she decides to join the Hellcats so that she will have a feeling of
belonging. One night the gang breaks into a deserted house
to throw a party. Sydney desires to become leader of the Hellcats, so she pushes Lund down a flight of stairs to her death.
She believes that Lime witnessed this, so she maneuvers to
meet Lime in the deserted movie theatre that the gang uses as
a clubhouse. In her attempt on Lime's life Sydney falls off
the theater balcony to her death. Now Lime can console herself
with her cipher boyfriend (Halsey).
    High School Hellcats has some great teenage tough-girl
names--Connie, Dolly, Meg, etc. The buxom Suzanne Sydney,
who convincingly portrays the demented Dolly, is sort of a
teenage equivalent of Allison Hayes. This would turn out to
be her biggest role, as she ended up relegated to bit parts
and some "cheesecake" pinups.

HOT ROD GANG. 1958. 71 minutes. *Director:* Lew Landers.
Screenplay: Lou Rusoff; based on a story by Rusoff. *Cine-
matography:* Floyd Crosby. *Cast:* John Ashley (John Aber-
nathy III); Jody Fair (Lois Cavendish); Gene Vincent
(Himself); Steve Drexel (Mark); Henry McCann (Dave):
Maureen Arthur (Marley); Gloria Grant (Tammy); Dorothy
Neuman (Anastasia Abernathy); Helen Spring (Abigail Aber-
nathy); Lester Dorr (Dryden Philpot); Doodles Weaver
(Wesley Cavendish); Russ Bender (Bill); Claire Dubray
(Agatha); Dub Taylor (Al Berrywhiff); Scott Peters
(Jack); Robert Whiteside (Jimmy); Simmy Bow (Johnny Red
Eye); Earl McDaniel (Himself); Kay Wheeler (Specialty
Dancer).

By all accounts *Hot Rod Gang* really scrapes the bottom of
the barrel of youth exploitation films. It contains a mixture
of both hot rods and rock and roll, but the two never mesh.
John Ashley portrays a young heir who lives with his two
maiden aunts and must lead a life of rectitude in order to
inherit his grandfather's fortune. But on the side he has
organized a hot-rod gang and a rock-and-roll group. He disguises himself with a fake beard and calls himself "Big Daddy,"
so he can play with Gene Vincent's rock group. With the money
he earns singing he and his gang can build a custom-made hot
rod to enter in a national meet. Some of the more impatient
gang members decide to get some money for the hot rod illegal-
ly, and Ashley is implicated in the crime. But he is cleared
and eventually converts his aunts and stuffy family lawyer to
the merits of rock and roll.
Gene Vincent and his Red Caps perform about four numbers,
including "Dance in the Streets" (not to be confused with
"Dancin' in the Streets" by Martha and the Vandellas). The
film could have been called "I was a Swingin' Teenage Jekyll
and Hyde Driving My 409," but whatever the title the "general
level is decidedly moronic" (*Monthly Film Bulletin*, February
1959, p. 19).

HOW TO MAKE A MONSTER. 1958. 75 minutes. Part Color. *Director:* Herbert ·L. Strock. *Screenplay:* Kenneth Langtry
(pseudonym for Aben Kandel) and Herman Cohen. *Cinematography:* Maury Gertzman (also spelled Gertsman). *Cast:*
Robert H. Harris (Pete Drummond); Paul Brinegar (Rivero);
Gary Conway (Tony Mantell); Gary Clarke (Larry Drake);
Malcolm Atterbury (Richards); Dennis Cross (Monahan);

with Walter Reed, Morris Ankrum, Heather Ames, John
Ashley.

Despite its title *How to Make a Monster* is more of a mur-
dur mystery than a monster film. It is full of in-house gim-
micks and references to AIP and the making of monster films.
   A group of East Coast business executives take over a
Hollywood motion picture studio. They decide to offer musicals
to the public and abandon the string of horror films that the
studio was known for. The studio makeup man (Harris) is fired,
but he is not going to let his horrific artistic creations go
to waste. He concocts a new makeup that contains a drug in it
that induces hypnosis to whoever puts it on. Harris applies
the makeup to two young actors (Conway and Clarke), and they
take on the personalities and appearance of the teenage Frankenstein and teenage wolfman respectively. Under this guise
they kill the new studio executives. Harris even makes himself
up as a caveman to go out and commit murders. He decides to
kill the two young men, so he can have their heads in his personal collection of makeup art. A fire breaks out in a room
filled full of Harris's grotesque masks, and he and all his
creations perish.
   The final scene in the film is in color, just as in *I Was
a Teenage Frankenstein* and *War of the Colossal Beast*. The
illusion of the teenage monster is broken here, as we witness
the behind-the-scenes work of how the monsters were made up.
How to Make a Monster was AIP's last teenage-monster film.

JET ATTACK. 1958. 68 minutes. *Director:* Edward L. Cahn.
   Screenplay: Orville H. Hampton; based on a story by Mark
   Hanna. *Cinematography:* Frederick E. West. *Cast:* John
   Agar (Tom Arnett); Audrey Totter (Tanya); Gregory Walcott
   (Bill); James Dobson (Sandy); Leonard Strong (Major Wan);
   Nicky Blair (Chick); Victor Sen Yung (Chon); Joe Hamilton
   (Olmstead); Guy Prescott (Major Garver); George Cisar
   (Colonel Catlett); Stella Lynn (Muju); Robert Carricart
   (Colonel Kuban); Weaver Levy (Orderly); Paul Power
   (Phillips); Hal Bogart (AP Sergeant); Madeline Foy (WAAC
   Corporal); Bob Gilbreath (Signalman).

Jet Attack has the rather questionable distinction of being one of the first of the AIP war films of the late 50s.
One is not quite sure for whom these low-budget films were
made. Teenagers formed the bulk of the AIP audience at this
time, among whom war themes were not all that popular.
   During the Korean War an American flight crew (Agar,

Walcott, and Blair) go behind North Korean lines to find if a
scientist (Hamilton) is alive. They are aided by a Russian
nurse (Totter), as they transport Hamilton out of enemy hands.
Totter is killed in the process, but Agar escapes with Hamilton
aboard a captured North Korean airplane.

MACHINE GUN KELLY. 1958. 84 minutes. *Director:* Roger Corman.
   Screenplay: R. Wright Campbell. *Cinematography:* Floyd
   Crosby. *Cast:* Charles Bronson (George R. "Machine Gun"
   Kelly); Susan Cabot (Flo); Morey Amsterdam (Fandango);
   Jack Lambert (Howard); Wally Campo (Maize); Bob Griffin
   (Vito); Barboura Morris (Lynn); Richard Devon (Apple);
   Ted Thorp (Teddy); Mitzi McCall (Harriet); Frank De Kova
   (Harry); Shirley Falls (Martha); Connie Gilchrist (Ma);
   Mike Fox (Clinton); Larry Thor (Drummond); George
   Archambeault (Frank); Jay Sayer (Philip Ashton).

   Having been successful in the horror and teenage exploitation genre, AIP decided to try its hand with gangster films.
In *Machine Gun Kelly* the company came up with one of its best
efforts, a film that gave Roger Corman some international recognition. It contains some high-pitched action and is peopled
with such underworld pug ugly types as Charles Bronson, Jack
Lambert, and Frank De Kova.
   The story follows the exploits of 30s bank robber/kidnap-
per George "Machine Gun" Kelly (Bronson). Kelly is a man with
an enormous inferiority complex, who started with "nickel and
dime" robberies and graduated to big-time kidnapping. Along
the way Bronson has a difficult time keeping his moll (Cabot)
and his gang members in line. It turns out that one of the
disgruntled underlings (Amsterdam) is the one who "squeals"
on Bronson. When he is cornered, Bronson surrenders to the
police. Unlike other famous Depression-era criminals, such
as Bonnie and Clyde or Dillinger, Kelly lived to 1954.
   Machine Gun Kelly, like *The Bonnie Parker Story*, is enhanced with a musical score that integrates well with the rest
of the film. Corman also gives some of the minor actors an
extra dimension in their characterizations.

NAKED AFRICA. 1958. 71 minutes. Color. *Director:* Ray
   Phoenix. *Cinematography:* Ray Phoenix. *Narrator:* Quentin
   Reynolds.

   This early AIP documentary was paired with the feature

White Huntress. It was made at a time when ethnocentrism was
still a strong factor in documentary travel films. In *Naked
Africa* some of the advertising lines contained such questionable statements as: "See the Shocking Dance of the Virgins,"
"Primitive Passions Unleashed!," and "Africa--Land of Beauty--
Land of Promise--Land of Darkness."
     Shown are the Xhosa tribe of southeast Africa and some
of their ancient rituals; the city of Durban, South Africa;
and a community outside of Durban, where the Indian immigrant
population lives. Also seen is a Christian sect of natives
performing a mass wedding ceremony. The film concludes with
some footage of African wildlife.

NIGHT OF THE BLOOD BEAST. 1958. 65 minutes. *Director:*
     Bernard L. Kowalski. *Screenplay:* Martin Varno; based on
     a story by Varno. *Cinematography:* John Nicholaus, Jr.
     Cast: Michael Emmet (Major John Corcoran); Angela Greene
     (Dr. Julie Benson); John Baer (Steve Dunlap); Ed Nelson
     (Dave Randall); Tyler McVey (Dr. Alex Wyman); Georgianna
     Carter (Donna Bixby); Ross Sturlin (The Creature).

     Also known as *The Creature from Galaxy 27*, this film has
an interesting premise: a man impregnated with alien embryos.
Astronaut Major John Corcoran (Emmet) returns from a flight
in a damaged space capsule. While outside the Earth's atmosphere he has been impregnated with microscopic embryos from
an alien whose planet was destroyed by a nuclear blast.
Emmet's body becomes the conduit by which the creature may
gain entrance to Earth. The alien plans to bring a superior
intelligence to Earth to save the planet from destruction.
When Emmet learns of its mission, he sacrifices his own life,
and the creature dies along with him (thanks to the use of
some Molotov cocktails). Before it dies, the alien makes it
clear that more of its kind will follow.
     The parasite that invades John Hurt's body in *Alien* has
its forerunner in *Night of the Blood Beast*. The poster art
was even gorier than the film, showing a severed head dripping
with blood. This low-budget effort is best exemplified in the
outfit of the alien, which resembles something that dropped
out of a garbage bag under a kitchen sink and gestated for
five years.

THE SCREAMING SKULL. 1958. 68 minutes. *Director:* Alex Nicol.
     Screenplay: John Kneubuhl. *Cinematography:* Floyd Crosby.

Cast: John Hudson (Eric); Peggy Webber (Jenni); Toni
Johnson (Mrs. Snow); Russ Conway (Reverend Snow); Alex
Nicol (Mickey).

The Screaming Skull is a mixture of *Gaslight* and *Rebecca*.
It has a husband attempting to drive his wife insane and a
custodian who idolizes the former mistress of the mansion.

A husband (Hudson) takes his new wife (Webber) to live
in his palatial home. The house was left to Hudson by his
first wife, who died under mysterious circumstances. Webber,
who had been hospitalized for a nervous breakdown, now starts
to question her sanity when strange events (such as mobile
skulls) occur in the house. We are made to suspect that the
gardener (Nicol), who idolized Hudson's first wife, is responsible for the unusual occurrences. But in fact it is Hudson
who is trying to drive his wife insane, to get his hands on
her money. When his plan is uncovered, he is pursued by several ghostly skulls. One of them attaches itself to his neck,
and he falls in a pond and drowns.

What starts out as a gothic mystery ends with a supernatural event. Alex Nicol acts as a red herring, but he provides
enough of a minatory presence to remind us of the Leonard
Tarver character in *The Beast with a 1,000,000 Eyes*.

SHE GODS OF SHARK REEF. 1958. 63 minutes. Color. *Director:*
Roger Corman. *Screenplay:* Robert Hill and Victor Stoloff.
Cinematography: Floyd Crosby. *Cast:* Don Durant (Lee);
Bill Cord (Chris); Lisa Montell (Mahia); Jeanne Gerson
(Dua); Carol Lindsay (Hula Dancer).

She Gods of Shark Reef was held up for release for about
a year and a half, which is understandable. When it did appear, it came out on an improbable double bill with *Night of
the Blood Beast*.

A killer (Durant) convinces his brother (Cord) to help
him escape. Shipwrecked on a reef, they are rescued by a native girl (Montell). She takes them to an island inhabited
solely by young female pearl divers. Cord and Montell fall
in love, but the island matriarch (Gerson) orders Montell to
be sacrificed to appease the shark god. However, Cord rescues
her, and they go away together. When Durant attempts to escape
with the islands' pearls, he is devoured by sharks.

This is just about as insubstantial a film as Roger
Corman's other film made in Hawaii, *The Naked Paradise*. It
could be argued that aside from exceptions, such as King
Vidor's *Bird of Paradise* and Murnau's *Tabu*, the South Seas

milieu does not lend itself to very interesting film material. *She Gods of Shark Reef* is nothing more than an old 40s South Sea adventure like *South of Pago Pago* or *Aloma of the South Seas*.

THE SPIDER. 1958. 72 minutes. *Director:* Bert I. Gordon. *Screenplay:* Laszlo Gorog and George Worthing Yates; based on a story by Bert I. Gordon. *Cinematography:* Jack Marta. *Cast:* Ed Kemmer (Kingman); June Kenney (Carol Flynn); Gene Persson (Mike Simpson); Gene Roth (Sheriff Cagle); Hal Torey (Mr. Simpson); June Jocelyn (Mrs. Flynn); Mickey Finn (Mr. Haskel); Sally Fraser (Helen Kingman); Troy Patterson (Joe); Skip Young (Sam); Howard Wright (Jake); Bill Giorgio (Sheriff Sanders); Hank Patterson (Hugo); Jack Kosslyn (Mr. Fraser).

Bert I. Gordon is back again here with another giant-mutant movie, filmed around the Carlsbad Caverns. However, unlike *The Amazing Colossal Man*, the special effects in *The Spider*, with the use of a split screen and traveling matte photography, are creditable.
  Two teenagers (Kenney and Persson) come upon a giant spider in a cave. It is sprayed with insecticide and transported to the high school auditorium. When it revives, it escapes and terrorizes the town. Since this is an isolated community, the military does not become involved. The responsibility falls upon the local police department and upon high school students and their parents. The spider finally returns to the cave. The entrance to the cave is dynamited by a teacher (Kemmer) and the sheriff (Roth), but teenagers Kenney and Persson are accidentally trapped inside. Working against time, Kemmer finally electrocutes the monster.

SUICIDE BATTALION. 1958. 79 minutes. *Director:* Edward L. Cahn. *Screenplay:* Lou Rusoff. *Cinematography:* Floyd Crosby. *Cast:* Michael Connors (Major Matt McCormick); John Ashley (Tommy Novello); Jewell Lain (Elizabeth Ann Mason); Russ Bender (Harry Donovan); Bing Russell (Lieutenant Chet Hall); Scott Peters (Wally Skilzowski); Walter Maslow (Marty Green); John McNamara (Colonel Craig); Clifford Kawada (Colonel Hiosho); Bob Tetrick (Bill); Marjorie Stapp (Beverly); Jan Englund (Annette); Isabel Cooley (Julie); Hilo Hattie (Mama Lily); Sammy Tong (Papa Lily); Gordon Barnes (Peter Hendry); Art Gilmore (Captain Hendry); Jackie Joseph (Cho Cho).

Another AIP war film. This time it takes place during
World War II in the Philippines. Six soldiers (Connors,
Ashley, Bender, Peters, Russell, and Maslow) form a volunteer
group. They are ordered to go behind enemy lines to destroy
important papers that have been left behind at an abandoned
American military headquarters. Along the way the men run into
a female news photographer (Lain) and bar girls (Stapp,
Englund, and Cooley). Only two of the volunteers survive the
mission. Both Connors and Lain fall in love and make their
escape. Some of the battle scenes in *Suicide Battalion* are
staged, while others resort to stock footage.

TANK BATTALION. 1958. 80 minutes. *Director:* Sherman A. Rose.
Screenplay: Richard Bernstein and George W. Waters; based
on a story by Waters. *Cinematography:* Frederick Gately.
Cast: Don Kelly (Brad); Marjorie Hellen (Alice); Edward G.
Robinson, Jr. (Corbett); Frank Gorshin (Skids); Regina
Gleason (Norma); Barbara Luna (Nikko); Bob Padget
(Collins); Mark Sheeler (Captain Caswell); Baynes Barrow
(Bulk); Tetsu Komai (Egg Charlie); John Trigonis (Lieu-
tenant); Don Devlin (1st Soldier); Warren Crosby (2nd
Soldier); Troy Patterson (Soldier).

This Korean War film was on a double bill with *Hell Squad*.
A four-man tank crew (Kelly, Robinson, Gorshin, and Padget)
fight for their lives behind enemy lines. The climactic scene
occurs when their tank is damaged and is under enemy fire.
Many of the battle scenes in *Tank Battalion* are interspersed
with love scenes.
The only thing that stands out about this film is a late-
night picnic on which three members of the tank crew take their
girlfriends. It ends up being broken up by snipers. Incidentally the musical score contains a number of variations on
Debussy.

TEENAGE CAVEMAN. 1958. 65 minutes. *Director:* Roger Corman.
Screenplay: R. Wright Campbell. *Cinematography:* Floyd
Crosby. *Cast:* Robert Vaughn (The Boy); Darrah Marshall
(The Maiden); Leslie Bradley (Symbol Maker); Frank De Kova
(The Villain); Joseph Hamilton, Marshall Bradford, Robert
Shayne, Beech Dickerson, June Jocelyn, Charles P.
Thompson, Jonathan Haze (Members of the Tribe).

This film was originally going to be titled *Prehistoric
World*, but the title *Teenage Caveman* appealed nicely to the

teenage drive-in trade. Actually this is not as bad a film
as the title would indicate.

A teenage boy (Vaughn) of independent mind attempts to
venture out from the environment of his tribe. The tribe has
something called The Law, which requires that no members of
the tribe leave their rocky and barren terrain for the verdant
land across the river. Any tribal member who does so will be
killed, and so will any outsider who dares to set foot on the
tribe's land. Vaughn defies The Law and goes across the river.
There he runs into the "monster" the tribe is terrified of.
It turns out that this "monster" is actually a survivor of an
atomic war. What the audience has assumed was a story set in
prehistory is actually a story set in a postnuclear age.

Appearing a number of years before *The Man From
U.N.C.L.E.*, Robert Vaughn here seems to be taking his role
seriously. The film's plea against nuclear war was not force-
fully presented because of an impecunious budget.

TERROR FROM THE YEAR 5000. 1958. 66 minutes. *Director:*
Robert J. Gurney, Jr. *Screenplay:* Robert J. Gurney, Jr.;
based on a story by Gurney. *Cinematography:* Arthur
Florman. *Cast:* Ward Costello (Robert Hedges); Joyce
Holden (Claire Erling); John Stratton (Victor); Frederic
Downs (Professor Erling); Fred Herrick (Angelo); Beatrice
Furdeaux (Miss Blake); Jack Diamond (1st Lab Technician);
Fred Taylor (2nd Lab Technician); Salome Jens (Woman from
A.D. 5000).

Robert J. Gurney, Jr., is virtually a one-man gang with
this film, having produced, directed, and written the screenplay and original story of *Terror from the Year 5000*. Taking
place somewhere in the Southern swampland, this film could be
described as a "guilty pleasure," a film that one enjoys, even
though it grates against all our critical faculties.

An assistant (Stratton) to a professor (Downs) is conducting experiments with a time machine. He has already produced a highly radioactive statuette from the future. Next a
hideously disfigured woman (Jens) from the year A.D. 5000 appears out of the machine and attempts to take Stratton into
the future with her. There his preatomic genes would be used
to begin a new race of noncontaminated people. But the machine
develops a defect, and both of them are electrocuted.

What one remembers from this film is the time machine,
which looks like the booth from *The $64,000 Question*, and
Jens's outfit, a black body stocking with sequins. Her dis-
figurement consists of what seems like a few moles, and a set

of teeth in need of orthodontic work. At least Jens showed
the relatively good sense to pick Stratton to be the progenitor
of a new race. After all she could have chosen the local
handyman (Herrick), who lived in a squalid shack lined with
pinups.

WAR OF THE COLOSSAL BEAST. 1958. 68 minutes. Part Color.
    Director: Bert I. Gordon. *Screenplay:* George Worthing
    Yates; based on a story by Bert I. Gordon. *Cinematog-*
    raphy: Jack Marta. *Cast:* Sally Fraser (Joyce Manning);
    Dean Parkin (Colonel Glen Manning); Roger Pace (Major
    Baird); Russ Bender (Dr. Carmichael); Charles Stewart
    (Captain Harris); George Becwar (Swanson); Robert
    Hernandez (Miguel); Rico Alaniz (Sergeant Luis Murillo);
    George Alexander (Army Officer); George Navarro (Mexican
    Doctor); John McNamara (Neurologist); Bob Garnet
    (Correspondent-Pentagon); Howard Wright (Medical Corps
    Officer); Roy Gordon (Major); George Milan (General
    Nelson); Warren Frost (Switchboard Operator); Bill Giorgio
    (Bus Driver); Loretta Nicholson (Joan); June Jocelyn
    (Mother); Jack Kosslyn (Newscaster).

    This is the third and final part of Bert I. Gordon's Cy-
clops trilogy (the others being *The Amazing Colossal Man* and
The Cyclops). *War of the Colossal Beast* is the weakest of
the three. Confusion reigns in this film, as there are different actors portraying roles from *The Amazing Colossal Man*,
as well as some of the same actors from that film playing different roles here.
    We begin where *The Amazing Colossal Man* ended, as Colonel
Glen Manning (Parkin), a mutated giant, falls off Boulder Dam.
He survives the fall, but he is horribly mutilated in the
process. He is captured, but no one knows what to do with him.
He is taken to Los Angeles, where he will be transported to
an uninhabited Pacific island. Before the authorities can
send him away, he escapes and terrorizes Los Angeles. He holds
a busload of teenagers hostage, but his sister (Fraser) convinces him to let them go. No longer able to endure his existence, Parkin deliberately walks into high-tension wires and
is electrocuted. The death scene was filmed in color.

WHITE HUNTRESS. 1958. 75 minutes. Color. *Director:* George
    Breakston. *Screenplay:* Dermot Quinn. *Cinematography:*
    John Lawrence. *Cast:* Robert Urquhart (Jim Dobson);

War of the Colossal Beast

Susan Stephen (Ruth Meetcham); John Bentley (Paul Dobson);
Howarth Wood (Meetcham); Alan Tarlton (Seth); Morea
Soutter (Mrs. Church); Tom Lithgow (Peter Johnson);
Maureen Connell (Elizabeth Johnson); Kip Kamoi (Kip).

White Huntress was made in Kenya in 1954 and was sold to
AIP as part of a package with *Naked Africa*. Set in 1890, this
film resembles nothing more than a western story transposed
to Africa.

Two white-hunter brothers (Urquhart and Bentley) join up
with a group of white settlers in British East Africa on their
way to locate a valuable amount of ivory. The unscrupulous
Bentley diverts the settlers away from the ivory and into hostile native country. The settlers convince the natives that
they have come to live in peace. But Bentley, who believes
he has found gold on the land, convinces the natives to attack
and dispossess the new immigrants. When they do so, and find
that Bentley has tricked them, they kill him. Urquhart now
becomes the settlers' protector.

The British title of this film is *Golden Ivory*, which
seems more appropriate than *White Huntress*. The eponymous
heroine (Stephen) is not given much to do except run away from
pythons and natives.

ATTACK OF THE GIANT LEECHES. 1959. 61 minutes. *Director:*
Bernard L. Kowalski. *Screenplay:* Leo Gordon. *Cinematog-
raphy:* John Nicholaus, Jr. *Cast:* Ken Clark (Steve
Benton); Yvette Vickers (Liz Walker); Bruno Ve Sota (Sher-
iff Walker); Jan Shepard (Nan Greyson); Michael Emmet
(Cal Moulton); with Tyler McVey, Gene Roth, Jody Fair.

Several inhabitants of a community in the Florida swamps
disappear, including local nympho (Vickers) and her lover
(Emmet). The game warden (Clark) believes that some type of
monster is in the swamp. He detonates an explosive charge in
the swamp and several desanguinated bodies rise to the surface.
Clark changes into frogman gear and dives into a part of the
swamp where he is attacked by a giant leech. He manages to
work his way free and finds Vickers still alive in the underwater cave where the leeches hide. He rescues her from the
monsters and sets off another dynamite charge. But unbeknownst
to Clark one of the leeches has escaped.

Aside from the fact that *Attack of the Giant Leeches* contains some of the most repulsive specimens in the animal kingdom, what makes the film watchable is Bruno Ve Sota. Ve Sota
appeared in bit parts in a number of AIP films through the

mid- and late 50s and even directed a few of them. Here he
plays a tub of lard masquerading as a "good old boy" backwoods
sheriff. He spends much of his time wondering why his wife,
Yvette Vickers, is disgusted with him, as he wanders around
looking for his "Liz, honey."

A BUCKET OF BLOOD. 1959. 66 minutes. *Director:* Roger Corman.
    Screenplay: Charles B. Griffith. *Cinematography:* Jack
    Marquette. *Cast:* Dick Miller (Walter Paisley); Barboura
    Morris (Carla); Anthony Carbone (Leonard); Julian Burton
    (Max Brock); Ed Nelson (Art Lacroix); John Brinkley
    (Will); John Shaner (Oscar); Judy Bambert (Alice); Myrtle
    Domerel (Mrs. Surchart); Burt Convy (Lou Raby); Jhean
    Burton (Naolia).

    Roger Corman's *A Bucket of Blood* and his *The Little Shop
of Horrors* constitute two of the most bizarre black comedies
ever to come out of Hollywood. Shot in only five days, *A
Bucket of Blood* contains a performance by Dick Miller of "sustained poignancy as the half-wit hero" (*Monthly Film Bulletin*,
January 1960, p. 6).
    Miller is a busboy and resident schlemiel in a beatnik
coffeehouse. Listening to the obscurantist verse of beat poet
Max Brock (Burton), Miller yearns for attention as a beat artist. He returns to his rooming house with a lump of clay and
decides to become a sculptor. He is not able to get the clay
to do anything, so he angrily throws his sculpture knife into
the wall and accidentally kills a cat that had gone in there
to hide. He covers the cat with clay and brings it in to the
coffeehouse, where everybody becomes impressed with the new
artist-in-residence. Success goes to Miller's head, and for
his next project he goes after bigger game—people. The owner
of the coffeehouse (Carbone) decides to have a display show-
casing Miller's creations. During the show one of the clay
figures begins to melt, revealing a body underneath. With the
police on his trail Miller returns to his rooming house, covers
himself with clay, and hangs himself.
    The Little Shop of Horrors has probably become more of a
cult film than *A Bucket of Blood*, but from this writer's point
of view the latter is a funnier film. Charles B. Griffith's
script has some trenchant observations about the beat subcul-
ture and its artistic pretensions. Also Dick Miller's portrayal has more subtlety to it than Jonathan Haze's in *Little
Shop*, where he acts as a Jerry Lewis clone.

A Bucket of Blood

DADDY-O. 1959. 74 minutes. *Director:* Lou Place. *Screenplay:*
    David Messinger. *Cinematography:* Perry Finnerman. *Cast:*
    Dick Contino (Phil Sandifer); Sandra Giles (Jana Ryan);
    Bruno Ve Sota (Sidney Chillas); Gloria Victor (Marcia);
    Ron McNeil (Duke); Jack McClure (Bruce Green); Sonia
    Torgeson (Peg); Kelly Gordon (Ken); Joseph Donte (Frank
    Wooster); Bob Banas (Sonny Di Marco); Hank Mann (Barney);
    Joseph Martin (Kerm).

    Even by AIP standards circa 1959, *Daddy-O* is a minor ef-
fort. It stars Dick Contino, who was known more for his accor-
dion playing than his acting.
    A truck driver and amateur sportscar racer (Contino) is
forced off the road by a playgirl (Giles) in her sportscar.
They meet later at a club where the multitalented Contino
sings, when he is not racing or repairing cars. She challenges
him to a race, but they are stopped by the police, who want to
question Contino about the death of a friend (Banas). When
Contino is cleared, he goes to look for Banas's killer. He
learns that a nightclub owner (Ve Sota) had Banas killed when
he refused to smuggle illegal goods into the country for him.
All this time Contino has been working undercover for the police, as he offers to drive for Ve Sota. In the end he rounds
up Ve Sota and his gang and decides to give up his racing and
stick to singing.

DIARY OF A HIGH SCHOOL BRIDE. 1959. 72 minutes. *Director:*
    Burt Topper. *Screenplay:* Burt Topper and Mark and Jan
    Lowell. *Cinematography:* Gil Warrenton. *Cast:* Anita Sands
    (Judy Lewis); Ronald Foster (Steve Redding); Chris
    Robinson (Chuck); Wendy Wilde (Gina); Louise Arthur (Mrs.
    Lewis); Barney Biro (Mr. Lewis); Richard Gering (Richie);
    Peggy Miller (Patty); Elvira Corona (Dancer); Clark Alan
    (Guitarist); Joan Connors (Madge); Al Laurie (Tony);
    Glenn Hughes (Beatnik); Dodie Rake (Beatnik); Lili Rosson
    (Lydia); Luree Nicholson (Verna); Loretta Nicholson
    (Jerry); Laura Nicholson (Edie); John Hurt, John Garrett,
    Don Hix (Policemen); Larry Shuttleworth (Truck Driver);
    Gloria Victor (Wife of Truck Driver).

    Seventeen-year-old Judy Lewis (Sands) has just married a
24-year-old law student (Foster) against her parents' objec-
tion. The parents attempt to alienate the couple by giving
them gifts that the prideful Foster refuses to accept. Sands's
old boyfriend (Robinson) also intervenes. This creates an
argument between the young couple, and Sands returns home to

her parents.   Now Robinson makes his move, as he lures Sands
to his father's empty film studio, where he plans to rape her.
But he is accidentally killed on one of the catwalks when he
touches a high-voltage wire.   Sands and Foster are now happily
reunited.

Diary of a High School Bride is an AIP exploitation film
with a capital "E."   It contains a note of false piety in the
opening titles, stating how this film is addressing itself to
the urgent social problem of high school marriages.   It then
proceeds for the next 70 minutes to do everything it can to
exploit this theme.   The teenage films of this period were at
their best when they went in for cheap thrills and were socially unredeeming.   For the most part the intended audience
knew exactly what these movies were up to and did not pay attention to any introductory statement of concern.

GHOST OF DRAGSTRIP HOLLOW.   1959.   65 minutes.   *Director:*
   William Hole, Jr.   *Screenplay:* Lou Rusoff.   *Cinematog-
   raphy:* Gil Warrenton.   *Cast:* Jody Fair (Lois); Martin
   Braddock (Stan); Russ Bender (Tom); Leon Tyler (Bonzo);
   Elaine Dupont (Rhodo); Henry McCann (Dave); Sanita Pelkey
   (Amelia); Dorothy Neuman (Anastasia); Kirby Smith
   (Wesley); Jean Tatum (Alice); Jack Ging (Tony); Nancy
   Anderson (Nita); Beverly Scott (Hazel); Bill St. John
   (Ed); Judy Howard (Sandra); Tom Ivo (Allen); Paul
   Blaisdell (Monster); George Dockstader (Motor Cop);
   Marvin Almars (Leon); Rosemary Johnston (Lois's Double);
   Marilyn Moe (Nita's Double).

Ghost of Dragstrip Hollow illustrates the creative paucity
that was developing among AIP's teenage exploitation films by
1959.   This particular film is a sort of AIP mulligan stew of
hot rods, monsters, ghosts, rock and roll, and a parrot.

The story hangs by a thread.   A hot-rod club loses its
headquarters and moves into a haunted house.   The only thing
that haunts the house is a former actor in monster films.   In
the end the club inaugurates its new headquarters with a spook
party.

Much of the film is an extended commercial plug for AIP's
record division, since the songs performed are on its label.
Intended as a comedy, *Ghost of Dragstrip Hollow* includes a
talking car, as well as Paul Blaisdell dressed up in the creature costume he created for *The She Creature*.   The AIP teen
cycle would not hit its stride again until the Beach Party
films of the early and mid-60s.

GOLIATH AND THE BARBARIANS. 1959. 85 minutes. Color. *Direc-*
    tor: Carlo Campogalliani. *Screenplay:* Carlo Campogalli-
    ani, Gino Mangini, Nino Stresa, and Giuseppe Taffarel;
    based on a story by Mangini and Emmimo Salvi. *Cinematog-*
    raphy: Adalberto Albertini. *Cast:* Steve Reeves
    (Emiliano); Chelo Alonso (Londo); Bruce Cabot (Alboyna);
    Giulia Rubini (Sabina); Livio Lorenzon (Igor); Luciano
    Marin (Svevo); Arturo Dominici (Delfo); Furio Meniconi
    (Marco); Fabrizio Capucci (Bruno); Andrea Checchi
    (Agnese); Gino Scotti (Count Daniele); with Fosco
    Giacchetti, Carla Calo, Ugo Sasso, and Gabriele Tinti.

    Along with *Sign of the Gladiator*, this was one of the
first of the Italian historical films distributed by AIP. The
color and the wide screen cannot disguise the low-budget mentality of *Goliath and the Barbarians*.
    Italy, A.D. 568--the Longobards, led by their ruler
(Cabot), enter Verona with rape and pillage on their minds.
Local strong boy Emiliano (Reeves), better known as Goliath,
dons a cat-man costume and leads the peasants in a guerrilla
revolt against the invaders. He also falls for one of the
daughters (Alonso) of the barbarians. After numerous battles
the Longobards are expelled by Reeves and his citizen army.
    This film is no more or less silly than the others of its
ilk. Scenes are mismatched so we are able to tell that they
were shot on different days, and Chelo Alonso cavorts in a
sixth-century bikini. But then that is not so unusual, since
one of the prime motives for these films is a kind of pectoral
exploitation of both the musclebound hero and his leading lady.

THE HEADLESS GHOST. 1959. 63 minutes. *Director:* Peter Graham
    Scott. *Screenplay:* Kenneth Langtry (pseudonym for Aben
    Kandel) and Herman Cohen. *Cinematography:* John Wiles.
    Cast: Richard Lyon (Bill); Liliane Sottane (Ingrid); David
    Rose (Ronnie); Clive Revill (The Fourth Earl); Jack Allen
    (Earl of Ambrose); Alexander Archdale (Randolph); Carl
    Bernard (Sergeant Grayson); with Josephine Blake, John
    Stacy, Donald Bissett, Mary M. Barclay, Patrick Connor,
    Trevor Barnett.

    Three foreign students (Lyon, Sottane, and Rose) are on
a holiday in England. They visit Ambrose Castle, which, according to the present Earl of Ambrose (Allen), is haunted.
To satisfy their curiosity, the three students stay overnight
in the castle. Before they know it, the Fourth Earl of Ambrose
(Revill), a friendly ghost, appears. He requests their help

in restoring peace to the ghosts in the castle. To do so they must help another dead ancestor find his head, which, of course, they do.

The fine British actor Clive Revill has some good scenes portraying the ghostly Fourth Earl, but that cannot be said for the rest of the cast. *The Headless Ghost* is neither humorous or scary. The ending left room for a sequel, but, mercifully, none was made.

HORRORS OF THE BLACK MUSEUM. 1959. 94 minutes. Color. *Director:* Arthur Crabtree. *Screenplay:* Aben Kandel and Herman Cohen. *Cinematography:* Desmond Dickinson. *Cast:* Michael Gough (Edmond Bancroft); June Cunningham (Joan Berkley); Graham Curnow (Rick); Shirley Ann Field (Angela); Geoffrey Keen (Superintendent Graham); Gerald Anderson (Dr. Ballan); John Warwick (Inspector Lodge); Beatrice Varley (Aggie); Austin Trevor (Commissioner Wayne); Malou Pantera (Peggy); Howard Greene (Tom Rivers); Dorinda Stevens (Gail); Stuart Saunders (Fun Fair Barker); Hilda Barry (Woman in Hall); Nora Gordon (Woman in Hall).

When the middle-brow critics of *The New York Times* excoriate a horror film, you can be assured that horror buffs will love it. *Horrors of the Black Museum* is such a film, for it is a precursor of the gore films of the 70s and 80s. Given a lavish New York opening and an expensive ad campaign, this polished production was the first AIP film in both color and cinemascope.

Edmond Bancroft (Gough), a psychopathic writer of crime fiction, has a "black museum" in his house, a sort of chamber of horrors. He drugs his young assistant (Curnow), so the young man will commit gruesome murders that provide Gough with new material for his crime books. After a series of murders, which include a guillotining, impalement with ice tongs, and dissolving a body in a bath of acid, Gough asks Curnow to kill his girlfriend (Cunningham). Curnow resists and ends up stabbing Gough to death.

The beginning of *Horrors of the Black Museum* contains the most horrifying murder and acts as a foreshadowing of events. A young woman receives a package in the mail. She opens it and it turns out to be a pair of binoculars. She points them out the window and focuses the lenses, and as she does, two spikes come out of the viewing end. They go right through her eyes and penetrate her brain. Originally this film came out with a 13-minute prologue in which hypnotist Emile Franchel performs, but, alas, this is not included in most television prints.

Horrors of the Black Museum

OPERATION DAMES. 1959. 74 minutes. *Director:* Louis Clyde
  Stoumen. *Screenplay:* Ed Lakso; based on a story by
  Stanley Kallis. *Cinematography:* Edward R. Martin. *Cast:*
  Eve Meyer (Lorry Evering); Chuck Henderson (Sergeant
  Valido); Don Devlin (Tony); Ed Craig (Hal); Cindy Girard
  (Roberta); Barbara Skyler (Marsha); Chuck Van Haren
  (Billy); Andrew Munro (Dinny); Byron Morrow (Benny);
  Alice Allyn (Marge); Ed Lakso (George).

The director of this film, Louis Clyde Stoumen, is primarily known as a documentary filmmaker--*The Naked Eye*, *Black
Fox*, etc. This foray into feature work did not prove entirely
successful, as *Operation Dames* alternates between unintentional
humor and grim battle scenes.
  Some USO entertainers become stranded behind enemy lines
during the Korean War. Caught with them is a group of American
infantrymen. The main part of the film deals with how they
all make their way to safety after a long march.
  The star of the film is Eve Meyer, who at the time was
married to softcore director Russ Meyer. If the intent of
Stoumen's film was to spotlight the late Ms. Meyer in risqué
poses, then it failed almost completely.

PARATROOP COMMAND. 1959. 77 minutes. *Director:* William
  Witney. *Screenplay:* Stanley Shpetner. *Cinematography:*
  Gil Warrenton. *Cast:* Richard Bakalyan (Charlie); Ken
  Lynch (Lieutenant); Jack Hogan (Ace); Jimmy Murphy (Ser-
  geant); Jeffrey Morris (Pigpen); Jim Beck (Cowboy);
  Carolyn Hughes (Gina); Patricia Huston (Amy).

Paratroop Command has the dubious distinction of being
the best of the tepid AIP war films of the late 50s. It is
sort of a low-budget *Walk in the Sun*, in which Richard Bakalyan
gives one of his most restrained performances. Shpetner's
script also includes believable and sympathetic characters.
  An American paratrooper (Bakalyan) in North Africa during
World War II accidentally kills one of his fellow paratroopers.
Bakalyan had been a shiftless nobody in civilian life and now
becomes an outcast among the other paratroopers. Further tension is created as the troops hopscotch from North Africa to
Sicily, and finally to Italy. The other soldiers had planned
to kill Bakalyan when they had the chance, but before they can
he sacrifices his life while reporting vital information back
to headquarters.

ROAD RACERS. 1959. 78 minutes. *Director:* Arthur Swerdloff.
   Screenplay: Ed Lakso and Stanley Kallis; based on a story
   by Kallis. *Cinematography:* Carl Guthrie. *Cast:* Joel
   Lawrence (Rob); Marian Collier (Liz); Skip Ward (Greg);
   Sally Fraser (Joanie); Alan Dinehart, Jr. (Kit); Irene
   Windust (Alice); John Shay (Harry); Michael Gibson (Bar-
   tender); Richard G. Pharo (Wilkins) Sumner Williams (Me-
   chanic); Haile Chace (McKenzie); Gloria Marshall (Sally).

   Most of the AIP road-racing films dealt with teenagers
and hot rods. *Road Racers* was an attempt to put car racing
on a professional level, with the results proving much more
conventional than the hot-rod films.
   A young professional racer (Lawrence) is banned from racing in the United States after causing the death of another
driver. He goes to Europe for two years and becomes a racing
star. He eventually comes back to the U.S. and is allowed to
drive once again. He finds that his girlfriend (Collier) is
now being courted by another driver (Ward). Lawrence enters
a race that Ward is in hoping to run him off the road. He has
the opportunity, but he backs off and his car crashes. He
walks away, unhurt, but is now resolved to quit racing.

SIGN OF THE GLADIATOR. 1959. 84 minutes. Color. *Director:*
   Vittorio Musy Glori. *Screenplay:* Antonio Thellung,
   Francesco De Feo, Sergio Leone, Giuseppe Mangione, and
   Guido Brignone. *Cinematography:* Luciano Trasatti. *Cast:*
   Anita Ekberg (Zenobia); George Marchal (Marcus Valerius);
   Folco Lulli (Semanzio); Chelo Alonso (Erika); Jacques
   Sernas (Julian); Lorella De Luca (Bathsheba); Alberto
   Farnese (Marcel); Mimo Palmara (Lator); Alfredo Varelli
   (Ito); Sergio Sauro (Tullius); Paul Muller (Head Priest);
   Gino Cervi (Emperor Aurelian).

   This heavily edited French, German, and Italian co-
production reduces history to the level of a comic-book story,
with bad color to boot. As *Variety* said, "*Sign of the Gladiator* is a crudely-made spectacle. The deepest thing about it
is Anita Ekberg's cleavage" (October 28, 1959, p. 6).
   It is A.D. 217, and the state of Palymra (Syria) under
its queen (Ekberg) has broken away from its alliance with Rome.
A Roman general (Marchal) is taken prisoner and pretends to
hate Roman rule, so he can gain Ekberg's confidence. He is
actually a spy, as the Romans defeat Palymra in a battle, and
Ekberg is taken prisoner. But Marchal has fallen in love with
her and is able to convince the Roman Senate to spare her life.

Sign of the Gladiator is really not much worse than most
other dubbed historical epics. It just does not have the in-
genuity to include something like the half-man-half tree that
is found in *The Loves of Hercules*.

SUBMARINE SEAHAWK. 1959. 83 minutes. *Director:* Spencer
    Bennet. *Screenplay:* Lou Rusoff and Owen Harris. *Cinema-
    tography:* Gil Warrenton. *Cast:* John Bentley (Paul
    Turner); Brett Halsey (David Shore); Wayne Heffley (Dean
    Stoker); Steve Mitchell (Andy Flowers); Henry McCann
    (Ellis); Frank Gerstle (Captain Boardman); Paul Maxwell
    (Bill Hallohan); Jan Brooks (Ellen); Mabel Rae (Maisie).

As in *Paratroop Command*, the main character in this World
War II film, set in the South Pacific, must prove himself worthy of his compatriots' respect. Paul Turner (Bentley) is an
unsociable submarine officer who takes over command of the
sub *Seahawk* from a popular commander. His crew becomes rest-
less when Bentley seems more concerned with reconnaissance
activities against the Japanese fleet than engaging it more
directly. In the end his methodical plan of operation pays
off, as the sub destroys a Japanese carrier.
    Like many war films, *Submarine Seahawk* is weakest when
it leaves the battle sequences and attempts to develop various
human relationships. It also includes quite a bit of stock
footage, but the miniature work is good.

TANK COMMANDOS. 1959. 79 minutes. *Director:* Burt Topper.
    Screenplay: Burt Topper. *Cinematography:* John Nicholaus,
    Jr. *Cast:* Robert Barron (Lieutenant Blaine); Maggie
    Lawrence (Jean); Wally Campo (Lazzotti); Donato Farretta
    (Diano); Leo V. Netranga (Shorty); Jack Sowards (Todd);
    Anthony Rich (Sands); Larry Hudson (Captain Paxton); Maria
    Monay (Italian Girl); Carmen D'Antonio (Tessie); David
    Addis (Clifften); Russ Prescott (Taylor); Freddy Roberto
    (Italian Prisoner); Jerry Lear (Bartender); Fred Gavlin
    (German Prisoner); Joan Connors (Streetwalker); Larry
    Shuttleworth (GI Sergeant); Lee Redman (GI); Norberto
    Kermer (Nazi Sergeant).

Placed on a double bill with *Operation Dames*, *Tank Commandos* was one of the last of the AIP war films made in the
1958-59 period. It contains a good deal of action footage
but is saddled with quite a few clichés.

An American demolition squad in Italy during World War II is ordered to destroy an underwater bridge that is giving the Germans a route for their tanks and equipment. The only person knowing the location of the bridge is a young Italian war orphan (Farretta). He leads the squad through the cellars of a Nazi-occupied city. They eventually destroy the bridge, but the boy and all of the squad, except for two, are killed.

THE SIXTIES

THE AMAZING TRANSPARENT MAN. 1960. 60 minutes. *Director:*
Edgar G. Ulmer. *Screenplay:* Jack Lewis. *Cinematography:*
Meredith M. Nicholson. *Cast:* Marguerite Chapman (Laura);
Douglas Kennedy (Joey Faust); James Griffith (Krenner);
Ivan Triesault (Dr. Ulof); Red Morgan (Julian); Carmel
Daniel (Maria); Edward Erwin (Drake); Jonathan Ledford
(Smith); Norman Smith (Security Guard); Patrick Cranshaw
(Security Guard); Kevin Kelly (Woman); Dennis Adams (State
Policeman); Stacy Morgan (State Policeman).

Edgar G. Ulmer was a director who was known throughout
his long career as someone who could do wonders on a small budget. But doing anything imaginative with *The Amazing Transparent Man* proved beyond his capabilities.
    The girlfriend (Chapman) of a spy helps a criminal
(Kennedy) break out of prison. She takes him to a ranch owned
by her lover (Griffith). While there, Kennedy is made invisible by a scientist (Triesault), whom Griffith holds prisoner.
He plans to build an invisible army and orders Kennedy to obtain the proper radioactive materials. Instead Kennedy robs
a bank, but he suddenly turns visible during the holdup. He
escapes with Chapman, with whom he has fallen in love.
Triesault tells Kennedy that he is radioactive and will soon
die. As his last act Kennedy kills Griffith and sets
Triesault free. He then destroys the ranch with an explosion.
    This attempt to mix genres by combining the science-
fiction and the gangster film never works. The actors appear
uncommitted and the production values are penurious. Compared
with this, its companion feature, *Beyond the Time Barrier*,
looks like *2001: A Space Odyssey*.

THE ANGRY RED PLANET. 1960. 83 minutes. Color. *Director:*
Ib Melchior. *Screenplay:* Ib Melchior and Sidney Pink;
based on a story by Pink. *Cinematography:* Stanley Cortez.
Cast: Gerald Mohr (Tom O'Banion); Nora Hayden (Dr. Iris
Ryan); Les Tremayne (Professor Theodore Gettell); Jack
Kruschen (Sergeant Sam Jacobs); Paul Hahn (General George
Treegar); J. Edward McKinley (Professor Weiner); Tom
Daly (Dr. Gordon); Edward Innes (General Prescott).

The Angry Red Planet is standard interplanetary fare. A
spaceship leaves Earth for Mars with four people on board
(Mohr, Hayden, Tremayne, and Kruschen). When they land on
Mars, they find a very unfriendly planet. They are attacked
by alien organisms, such as carnivorous plants, a giant amoeba,
and a monster that is a combination bat/rat/spider/crab. Of
the four people on the expedition only two return safely.

If this film is known for anything it is for a technique
called Cinemagic. This was a photographic process that produced the quality of a negative. Filmed in pink-colored tones,
the shadings become reversed--light things look dark and dark
things light. One wonders whether this effect was used by the
makers of the film solely to obscure the cardboard cutouts
masquerading as the Martian landscape.

BEYOND THE TIME BARRIER. 1960. 75 minutes. *Director:* Edgar
     G. Ulmer. *Screenplay:* Arthur G. Pierce; based on a story
     by Pierce. *Cinematography:* Meredith M. Nicholson. *Cast:*
     Robert Clarke (Major William Allison); Darlene Tompkins
     (Trirene); Arianne Arden (Markova); Vladimir Sokoloff
     (The Supreme); Stephen Bekassy (Karl Kruse); John van
     Dreelen (Dr. Bourman); Red Morgan (The Captain); Ken Knox
     (Colonel Martin); Don Flournoy (Mutant); Tom Ravick (Mu-
     tant); Neil Fletcher (Air Force Chief-of-Staff); Jack
     Herman (Dr. Richman); William Shapard (General York);
     James Altgens (Secretary Patterson); John Loughney (Gen-
     eral Lamont); Russell Marker (Colonel Curtis).

This Edgar Ulmer film was made simultaneously with *The
Amazing Transparent Man*. Both were shot in a period of less
than two weeks, and it shows.

A space explorer (Clarke) crosses the fifth dimension and
winds up in the year 2024. He discovers a postnuclear underground society that is threatened by aboveground mutants. A
nuclear plague has wiped out much of the world, with most of
the subterranean people being sterile, except for the daughter
(Tompkins) of the group's benevolent despot (Sokoloff). After
unsuccessful attempts to leave Clarke comes upon something
called "reverse relativity paradox," which helps take him back
to 1960. The film ends with Clark intending to tell the world
what is in store if it tampers with nuclear weapons.

An attempt was made to make this film look like more than
it is. Ernst Fegte's geometric Neo-Cubist set designs look
more tacky than futuristic. The electronic music by Darrell
Calker is appropriately avant-garde. Use is also made of the
triangular wipes featured in old-time serials.

Beyond the Time Barrier

CIRCUS OF HORRORS.   1960.   88 minutes.   Color.   *Director:*
   Sidney Hayers.   *Screenplay:* George Baxt.   *Cinematography:*
   Douglas Slocombe.   *Cast:* Anton Diffring (Dr. Schuller);
   Erika Remberg (Elissa); Yvonne Monlaur (Nicole); Donald
   Pleasence (Vanet); Jane Hylton (Angela); Kenneth Griffith
   (Martin); Conrad Phillips (Inspector Arthur Ames); Jack
   Gwillim (Superintendent Andrews); Vanda Hudson (Magda);
   Yvonne Romain (Melina); Colette Wilde (Evelyn Morley);
   William Mervyn (Dr. Morley); John Merivale (Edward
   Finsbury); Carla Challoner (Nicole as a Child); Peter
   Swanwick (Inspector Knopf); Walter Gotell (Von Gruber);
   Chris Christian (Ringmaster); Sasha Coco (Luis); Jack
   Carson (Chief Eagle Eye); Glyn Houston (Barker); Malcolm
   Watson (Elderly Man); Kenneth Warren (1st Roustabout);
   Fred Haggerty (2nd Roustabout).

   Along with *Horrors of the Black Museum*, and the extraordinary *Peeping Tom*, this film is one in a trilogy of what David
Pirie calls "Sadian films" (David Pirie, *A Heritage of Horror:
The English Gothic Cinema 1946-1972*.   London: Gordon Fraser,
1973, p. 99).   *Circus of Horrors* delights in the audience's
voyeuristic interest in the violent, sensational, and grotesque
elements of life.   It also contains a strong streak of misogyny
in it.
   A disreputable plastic surgeon (Diffring) leaves England
for France after he has botched an operation on a once-
beautiful woman (Wilde).   He takes over the operation of a
small circus as a front for his experiments.   He restructures
the faces of beautiful women who have been badly disfigured.
Most of them have criminal backgrounds, so Diffring is able
to blackmail them into performing for the circus.   Whenever
any of the women attempts to leave him, he sees to it that
they will have a convenient "accident" under the Big Top.
While the circus is in England, the police become suspicious
about these numerous "accidents."   Before they can apprehend
Diffring, the woman whose face he ruined years before runs him
down in her car.
   Circus of Horrors is a wonderful mixture of *Grand Guignol*
and kink, especially the scene in which Diffring caresses and
embraces one of his lovers wrapped in bandages after an operation.   The song in the film, "Look for a Star," was a hit record in 1960 and acts here as an antithetical element to the
sordid story.

GOLIATH AND THE DRAGON.   1960.   90 minutes.   Color.   *Director:*
   Vittorio Cottafavi.   *Screenplay:* Marco Piccolo and

Circus of Horrors

Archibald Zounds, Jr. *Cinematography:* Marco Montuori.
Cast: Mark Forest (Goliath); Broderick Crawford (King
Eurystheus); Leonora Ruffo (Dejanira); Philippe Hersent
(Illus); Sandro Maretti (Ismene); Federica Ranchi (Thea);
Gaby André (Alcinor); with Gian Carlo Sbragia, Ugo Sasso,
Carla Calo, Franco Loffredi, Pietro Pastore, Spartaco
Nale, Nino Milano, Renato Terra, Fedele Gentile.

By the early 1960s the American market was glutted with
films recounting the adventurous exploits of mythological heroes. *Goliath and the Dragon*, a French-Italian co-production
was no different, except it had a new hero--"Man Mountain"
Mark Forest.
     Forest is the King of Thebes, Emilius, better known as
Goliath. The convoluted story concerns rival monarchs (Forest
and Crawford), and Forest's son (Maretti) and Crawford's daughter (Ranchi), who are in love. Before the film is finished,
Forest has had to go through a series of heroic tests arranged
for him by Crawford. Among the struggles he must endure are
a bull elephant; Cerebus, the three-headed dog; a large bear;
a pit of vipers; and your standard everyday smoke-belching
dragon.
     Forest performs his acting duties in about as cardboard
a fashion as some of the scenery. Crawford just goes through
the motions. The director, Vittorio Cottafavi, has gained
some critical recognition from European critics. Here he dem-
onstrates a rather creative use of screen space and some ener-
getic traveling shots.

HOUSE OF USHER. 1960. 79 minutes. Color. *Director:* Roger
     Corman. *Screenplay:* Richard Matheson; based on the story
     "The Fall of the House of Usher," by Edgar Allan Poe.
     Cinematography: Floyd Crosby. *Cast:* Vincent Price
     (Roderick Usher); Mark Damon (Philip Winthrop); Myrna
     Fahey (Madeline Usher); Harry Ellerbe (Bristol); Bill
     Borzage, Mike Jordon, Nadajan, Ruth Oklander, George Paul,
     David Andar, Eleanor Le Faber, Geraldine Paulette, Phil
     Sylvestre, John Zimeas (Ghosts).

This was AIP's first excursion into Poe's world of de-
spair, death, and obsession. *House of Usher* romanticizes the
Poe story somewhat but makes up for this failing with an im-
pressive (by AIP standards) *mise en scene*.
     Philip Winthrop (Damon) has come to the mansion of the
Usher family to claim his fiancée, Madeline Usher (Fahey).
He is met by her older brother, Roderick (Price), who tells

Damon that his sister cannot marry anyone. Price and Fahey
are the last two descendants of a family that has a history
of madness and murder. He intends to kill both himself and
his sister rather than propagate the malignant family line.
Price tells Damon that Fahey has died of a heart attack, but
when Damon learns that she is subject to cataleptic fits, he
realizes that Price has buried her alive in the family crypt.
Fahey escapes from her coffin and is now stark raving mad.
Like most Ushers, when threatened with death she gains super-
human strength. Fahey kills Price, as the house catches fire.
Damon staggers out of the burning house and manages to escape.

Vincent Price's anemic-looking Roderick Usher might very
well be his best performance in an AIP film. As for Damon and
Fahey, you could have put them in a pair of Levis and tight
sweaters, and they would have thought it was just another of
AIP's teenage monster movies.

THE JAILBREAKERS. 1960. 63 minutes. *Director:* Alexander
    Grasshoff. *Screenplay:* Alexander Grasshoff. *Cinematog-
    raphy:* W. Merle Connell. *Cast:* Robert Hutton (Tom); Mary
    Castle (June); Michael O'Connell (Lake); Gabe Delutri
    (Joe); Anton Van Stralen (Stearn); Toby Hill (Karen);
    Carlos Chavez (Bushman).

Three criminals (O'Connell, Delutri, and Van Stralen) escape from prison intending to recover $400,000 hidden after a
bank robbery. They meet up with O'Connell's stepson (Hutton),
whom they plan to use in finding the stolen money. Unaware
of the scheme, Hutton takes his wife (Castle) along, and both
are taken prisoner by the three men. The five of them go to
a desert ghost town where the money is supposedly hidden.
There they meet the fourth member of the gang (Chavez), who
is the only one who knows where to find the stolen loot. His
three confederates force Chavez to disclose the hiding place
and then kill him. When the three convicts start arguing among
themselves, Hutton and Castle take the opportunity to free
themselves.

JOURNEY TO THE LOST CITY. 1960. 95 minutes. Color. *Direc-
    tor:* Fritz Lang. *Screenplay:* Fritz Lang and Werner Jörg
    Lüddecke; based on a novel by Thea von Harbou and a script
    by von Harbou and Lang. *Cinematography:* Richard Angst.
    Cast: Debra Paget (Seetha); Paul Hubschmid (Harald
    Berger); Walter Reyer (Chandra); Claus Holm (Dr. Walter

Rhode); Sabine Bethmann (Irene); Valery Inkijinoff (Yama);
René Deltgen (Prince Ramigani); Jochen Brockmann (Padhu);
Jochen Blume (Asagara); Luciana Paluzzi (Bahrani); Guido
Celano (General Dagh); Angela Portulari (Peasant);
Richard Lauffen (Bhowana); Helmut Hildebrand (Ramigani's
Servant); Panos Papadopoulos (Messenger); and Victor
Francen.

Made in 1958, this was Fritz Lang's first film for a German company since the pre-Hitler era. *Journey to the Lost
City* had a big budget and opulent sets and is a remake of a
1919 film directed by Joe May in Germany.
  Filmed in the state of Rajasthan in India, this film recalls "a lost tradition of chivalry, love forbidden or obses-
sive, the Mystery of the East and its grisly excitement ..."
(*Monthly Film Bulletin*, May 1962, p. 64). A Western architect
(Hubschmid) comes to the so-called "lost city" of Eshnapur on
a construction project for Prince Chandra (Reyer). Eshnapur
seems mainly populated by maneating tigers, dancing girls, and
lepers. While here Hubschmid falls in love with a dancing
girl (Paget). He also becomes involved in palace intrigue,
as Ramigani (Holm) is attempting to take over the throne from
his brother, Prince Chandra.
  This was actually two different films that originally
ran for over 200 minutes. Dubbed and cut more than in half
it is a totally different film from the original. Debra Paget
actually wears different dresses in the same scene. Needless
to say, Fritz Lang had the good sense to disown this severely
truncated version.

WHY MUST I DIE? 1960. 86 minutes. *Director:* Roy Del Ruth.
  Screenplay: George W. Waters and Richard Bernstein. *Cine-
matography:* Ernest Haller. *Cast:* Terry Moore (Lois King);
  Debra Paget (Dottie Manson); Bert Freed (Adler); Juli
  Reding (Mitzi); Lionel Ames (Eddie); Richard LePore
  (Sinclair); Selette Cole (Peggy Taylor); Dorothy Lovett
  (Mrs. Benson); Phil Harvey (Kenny Randall); Fred Sherman
  (Red King); Robert Shayne (Charlie Munro); Damian O'Flynn
  (Denison); Holly Harris (Mrs. Bradley); Mark Sheeler
  (Jim); Jhean Burton (Trixie); Abbagail Shelton (Dawn).

Lois King (Moore) leaves her criminal father (Sherman)
to strike out on her own. She is able to obtain a job as a
singer in a nightclub called The Cockatoo, and falls in love
with the owner (Harvey). One of her father's partners (Ames)
and his girlfriend (Paget) force Moore to help them rob the

nightclub. In the process Paget murders Harvey. But on cir-
cumstantial evidence Moore is accused of the murder and is
sentenced to be executed in the electric chair. Paget, who is
now on death row for the murder of a blind news vendor, runs
through the corridors of the jail desperately confessing to
the murder of Harvey. However, her confession comes moments
after innocent Terry Moore has been executed.

Clearly made as an anti-capital-punishment film, *Why Must
I Die?* is a lurid ripoff of *I Want to Live!* Hoping perhaps
to win an Oscar as Susan Hayward had in the latter film, Terry
Moore here gives an overwrought performance. In answer to her
plea of "Why must I die," perhaps the answer is "Because you
can't act."

ALAKAZAM THE GREAT. 1961. 84 minutes. Color. *Director:*
Lee Kresel (U.S. version). Teiji Yabushita, Osamu Tezuka,
and Daisaku Shirakawa (Japanese version). *Screenplay:*
Lou Rusoff and Lee Kresel (English-language version).
Osamu Tezuka and Keinosuke Uekusa (Japanese version).
Cinematography (Animation): Seigo and Harusato Otsuka,
Komei Ishikawa, and Kenji Sugiyama. *Cast:* Frankie Avalon
(Alakazam); Dodie Stevens (De De); Jonathan Winters (Sir
Quigley Broken Bottom); Arnold Stang (Lulipopo); Sterling
Holloway (Narrator).

This was the first, and one of the few, animated films
distributed by AIP. It was made by the Toei Company of Japan
in 1960. AIP bought the copyright, and reedited the film,
and dubbed an English-language version. There is some good
imaginative animation from the Toei animators, even if it is
imitative of Disney.

Alakazam the Great is a children's fantasy about a shy
monkey who is chosen by the other monkeys as leader of all
the Earth's animals. He becomes arrogant in his new position
and is punished by a king and imprisoned in a cave. He is released from the cave only if he agrees to perform nothing but
good deeds. He now becomes a humble monkey and returns to
his peers.

ASSIGNMENT--OUTER SPACE. 1961. 79 minutes. Color. *Director:*
Anthony Daisies (Pseudonym for Antonio Margheriti).
Screenplay: Vassily Petrov. *Cinematography:* Marcello
Masciocchi. *Cast:* Rick von Nutter (Ray Peterson);
Gabriella Farinon (Lucy); Dave Montresor (George);

Archie Savage (Al); Alan Dijon (The Commander); with
Frank (Franco) Fantasia, Aldo Pini, Joe Pollini, David
Maran, José Néstor, Anita Todesco, Jack Wallace (English-
Version Narrator).

This originally opened in Europe in 1960 under the title
Space Men. As they did with so many other foreign films in
the 60s, AIP picked up the American distribution and retitled
the movie *Assignment--Outer Space*.

A spaceship, *Alpha II*, is on an uncontrolled deadly course
to Earth. The pilot has died, and the ship's own automatic
pilot, an electronic brain, is now in control. In order to
stop certain death and destruction when it lands, a reporter
(von Nutter), a commander of a space station (Dijon), and his
assistant (Farinon), attempt to stop *Alpha II* before it can
reach the Earth. Tension arises when both men find themselves
attracted to Farinon. In the end von Nutter is able to sever
the link to the electronic brain on *Alpha II* and the Earth is
saved.

BEWARE OF CHILDREN. 1961. 87 minutes. *Director:* Gerald
    Thomas. *Screenplay:* Norman Hudis and Robin Estridge;
    based on the novel by Verily Anderson. *Cinematography:*
    Alan Hume. *Cast:* Leslie Phillips (David Robinson);
    Geraldine McEwan (Catherine Robinson); Julia Lockwood
    (Vanilla); Noel Purcell (Tandy); Irene Handl (Mrs.
    Spicer); Joan Hickson (Cook); June Jago (Matron); Cyril
    Raymond (Colonel Matthews); Esma Cannon (District Nurse);
    Alan Gifford (Edgar Treadgold); Sydney Tafler (Mr. Rock-
    bottom); Brian Oulton (Vicar); Eric Pohlmann (King);
    Brian Rawlinson (Will); Michael Sarne (Henri); Joy Shelton
    (Mrs. Rockbottom); Patricia Jessel (Queen); Earl Cameron
    (Colored Father); Pearl Prescod (Colored Mother); Peter
    Howell (Angus' Father); Marian Mather (Helen Treadgold);
    Peggy Simpson (Angus' Mother); Nöel Hood (Vicar's Wife);
    Cyril Chamberlain (Cafe Owner), and the Children--
    Christopher Witty (Richard Robinson); Martin Stephens
    (Angus); Francesca Annis (Priscilla); Haydn Evans
    (Lionel); Michael Gowdy (Dandy Big); Jeanette Bradbury
    (Dandy Little); Keith Lacey (Hassan); Mark Mileham
    (Suleiman); Louise Redman (Margaret); Millicent Kerr
    (Eileen).

Made by the director of many of the Carry On films, *Beware
of Children* (British title--*No Kidding*) is a hodgepodge of
unruly slapstick and a sappy sort of sentimentality. It

touches upon some of the historic class differences among the British but never really develops that theme.

A young couple (Phillips and McEwan) inherit an old country home and decide to turn it into a resort for the neglected children of rich parents. Trouble arises when the children turn out to be a bunch of unmanageable spoiled brats. Compounding the couple's problems are an alcoholic cook (Hickson) and a local councilwoman (Handl), who would like to have the home used for underprivileged children. The rich children refuse to leave until their parents give them more attention. Handl then realizes that Phillips and McEwan's resort is actually helping these emotionally starved children and decides not to bother them any further about giving up the home.

BLACK SUNDAY. 1961. 84 minutes. *Director:* Mario Bava. *Screenplay:* Ennio De Concini, Mario Serandrei, Mario Bava, and Marcello Coscia; based on the story "The Vij," by Nikolai Gogol. *Cinematography:* Ubaldo Terzano and Mario Bava. *Cast:* Barbara Steele (Princess Asa/Princess Katia); John Richardson (Dr. Andrej Gorobek); Ivo Garrani (Prine Vajda); Andrea Checchi (Dr. Choma Kruvajan); Arturo Dominici (Javutich); Enrico Olivieri (Constantino); Antonio Pierfederici (Priest); Clara Bindi (Innkeeper); Germana Dominici (Her Daughter); Mario Passante (Nikita); Tino Bianchi (Ivan); with Renato Terra.

Black Sunday stars British actress Barbara Steele, probably the only woman ever to become a star in the horror genre. She appeared in a slew of horror films, mainly during the 60s in Italy, and has over the years developed a legion of fans.

Moldavia in 1830. A physician (Checchi) accidentally awakens Asa, a witch (Steele) who has been dead for 200 years. She and her servant (Dominici) were put to death by her brother. Now, along with the resurrected Dominici, she plans to kill her brother's three remaining descendants. Steele first kills Checchi, turns him into a vampire, and commands him to kill one of the descendants (Garrani). A young doctor (Richardson) investigates the disappearance of his colleague, Checchi. He meets Katia, the last of the three relatives to be killed. Asa fights Richardson for the soul of Katia, by attempting to enter her body. But Richardson prevails when he gives Asa to a priest (Pierfederici), who kills the witch/vampire.

This film is one of the best ever made in the horror genre. Mario Bava has the camera zooming and moving around the dark corners of a castle and the nearby countryside. The

Black Sunday

art direction by Bava and Giorgio Giovannini is also exemplary
in its atmospheric details. *Black Sunday* is a film to be sa-
vored on a large screen in a darkened theatre and not on a
small television set.

FIVE MINUTES TO LIVE. 1961. 74 minutes. *Director:* Bill Karn.
 Screenplay: Cay Forester; based on a story by Palmer
 Thompson; adapted by Robert L. Joseph. *Cinematography:*
 Carl Guthrie. *Cast:* Johnny Cash (Johnny Cabot); Donald
 Woods (Ken Wilson); Cay Forester (Nancy Wilson); Pamela
 Mason (Ellen); Midge Ware (Doris); Victor Tayback (Fred
 Dorella); Ronny Howard (Bobbie Wilson); Merle Travis
 (Max); Howard Wright (Pop); Norma Varden (Priscilla).

This feature starring country and western singer Johnny
Cash was purchased for rerelease by AIP in 1966 under the title
Door-to-Door Maniac. In keeping with that exploitation title,
new footage was added, including a rape sequence.
 A fugitive (Cash) has settled in a small town. A crook
(Tayback) approaches Cash with a plan for a bank holdup. Cash
breaks into the home of a bank president (Woods) and holds his
wife (Forester) for a $70,000 ransom. Meanwhile Tayback goes
to the bank and demands the ransom money from Woods. He almost
refuses the demand, since he is planning to leave his wife
anyway, but he finally capitulates. Tayback is captured by a
bank guard. Woods then leads the police back to his house,
where Cash is killed by the police. Woods is now reunited
with his wife.

FLIGHT OF THE LOST BALLOON. 1961. 91 minutes. Color. *Direc-
 tor:* Nathan Juran. *Screenplay:* Nathan Juran. *Cinematog-
 raphy:* Jacques Marquette. *Cast:* Mala Powers (Ellen);
 Marshall Thompson (Dr. Joseph Faraday); James Lanphier
 (The Hindu); Douglas Kennedy (Sir Hubert); Robert Gillette
 (Sir Adam); Felippe Birriel (Golan); A.J. Valentine
 (Giles); Blanquita Romero (The Malkia); Jackie Donoro
 (Native Dancer).

When *Flight of the Lost Balloon* came out theatres handed
out to customers a "motion-sickness pill." Apparently this
was to take the spectators' minds off the fact that what they
were seeing were not people actually in the air in a balloon,
but instead positioned in front of a rear-projection screen.
 A noted British explorer (Kennedy) is being held prisoner

in a fort near the Nile by a ruthless Hindu (Lanphier), until
he discloses the whereabouts of Cleopatra's lost treasure.
Lanphier goes to London and maneuvers the Geographic Society
to launch an expedition to find Kennedy. Included in the expedition is Kennedy's fiancée (Powers), whom Lanphier plans to
torture so Kennedy will talk. Explorer Dr. Joseph Faraday
(Thompson) convinces the Society to make the expedition in a
balloon. The party has several dangerous episodes with cannibals, gorillas, and a group of condors that attack the balloon.
Powers and Thompson finally reach the fortress. Lanphier has
Powers tortured on the rack, but Kennedy still refuses to tell
where the treasure is hidden. Thompson comes to their rescue.
The greedy Kennedy is killed attempting to load the treasure
on the balloon, and Powers and Thompson go away together.

GUNS OF THE BLACK WITCH. 1961. 81 minutes. Color. *Director:*
    Domenico Paolella (Italian version). Lee Kresel (U.S.
    version). *Screenplay:* Luciano Martino and Ugo Guerra.
    Cinematography: Carlo Bellero. *Cast:* Don Megowan (Jean);
    Silvana Pampanini (Delores); Emma Danieli (Elisa); Livio
    Lorenzon (Guzman); Germano Longo (Michel); Loris Grizzi
    (The Governor); Philippe Hersent (Jean's Stepfather);
    Anna Alberti (Elisa's Maid); with Corrado Annicelli,
    Franco Lamonte, Giovanni Baghino, Nando Angelini, Cesare
    Lancia, Tullio Altamura, Pasquale De Filippo, Dora Corra,
    Francesco De Leone.

    In the 17th-century Caribbean a buccaneer colony is mas-
sacred by soldiers of the Spanish Governor's aide (Lorenzon).
Two young boys, Jean and Michel, escape and are found and
raised by pirates. Twelve years later both of them (Megowan
and Longo) are pirate captains of the *Black Witch*. They plan
to overthrow the local government, which was responsible for
the massacre 12 years before. In a raid Megowan is wounded.
The captured Longo unwittingly betrays Megowan and the pirates,
through the influence of a woman (Pampanini) who had been re-
buffed by Megowan. Megowan is aided by the daughter (Danieli)
of the Spanish Governor (Gizzi). In a battle at the end Longo,
Lorenzon, and Pampanini are killed.
    Guns of the Black Witch has a standard revenge theme that
could have easily been transposed to two other favorite genres
of Italian filmmakers, the western and the costume epic.

THE HAND. 1961. 61 minutes. *Director:* Henry Cass. *Screenplay:* Ray Cooney and Tony Hilton. *Cinematography:* James Harvey. *Cast:* Derek Bond (Captain Roberts/Roger Crawshaw); Reed De Rouen (Private Michael Brodie); Bryan Coleman (Corporal Adams); Walter Randall (Japanese Commander); Tony Hilton (Sergeant Foster); Harold Scott (Charlie Taplow); Ray Cooney (Detective Sergeant Pollitt); Gwenda Ewen (Nurse Johns); Michael Moore (Dr. Metcalfe); Ronald Leigh-Hunt (Inspector Munyard); Ronald Wilson (Doctor); Garard Green (Dr. Simon Crawshaw); Jean Dallas (Nurse Geiber); David Blake Kelly (Marshall); Reginald Hearne (Noel Brodie); Madeleine Burgess (Mrs. Brodie); Frances Bennett (Mother); Susan Reid (Little Girl); Pat Hicks (Mrs. Adams); John Norman (Peter Adams).

In Burma during World War II three British soldiers (Bond, De Rouen, and Coleman) are captured by the Japanese. De Rouen and Coleman have their right hands severed because they refuse to divulge intelligence information, but Bond gives in and has his hand saved.

In modern-day London the police are investigating the murder of an alcoholic who had recently had his hand amputated. The trail eventually leads to the deranged Derek Bond. He kills the surgeon who amputated the alcoholic's hand and also murders De Rouen, who had been harassing Bond all these years. With the police pursuing him, Bond runs across some train tracks, falls, and has a speeding train sever his hand.

The Hand is about as insubstantial a film as those 60-minute British-made films based on Edgar Wallace stories. It would only be of interest to those who have an amputation fetish.

HOUSE OF FRIGHT. 1961. 89 minutes. Color. *Director:* Terence Fisher. *Screenplay:* Wolf Mankowitz; based on the story "The Strange Case of Dr. Jekyll and Mr. Hyde," by Robert Louis Stevenson. *Cinematography:* Jack Asher. *Cast:* Paul Massie (Dr. Henry Jekyll/Mr. Edward Hyde); Dawn Addams (Kitty Jekyll); Christopher Lee (Paul Allen); David Kossoff (Ernest Litauer); Francis De Wolff (Inspector); Norma Marla (Maria); Joy Webster and Magda Miller (Sphinx Girls); William Kendall (Clubman); Helen Goss (Nannie); Pauline Shepherd (Girl in the Gin Shop); Percy Cartwright (Coroner); Joe Robinson (Corinthian); Arthur Lovegrove (Cabby).

This Hammer film reworking of the Jekyll and Hyde story
has a slight twist. Dr. Jekyll is a rather moody, bearded
figure, while Mr. Hyde is a cleanshaven urbane man-about-town.
Dr. Henry Jekyll (Massie) is conducting drug experiments
attempting to separate the good and evil in man's nature. He
injects himself with the experimental drug and is transformed
into Mr. Hyde. He goes out to a nightclub, where he finds
his wife (Addams) and her paramour (Lee). Massie tries to
control his evil nature, but is unable to, as he plots Lee's
death. After Lee has been killed by a python, Massie, in the
guise of Hyde, sexually assaults his wife. The hysterical
Addams ends up killing herself. Massie is now totally subsumed
by the Mr. Hyde personality, and he kills two more people.
He attempts to pass off one of the deaths as actually being
that of Dr. Jekyll. However, during the coroner's inquest,
the Dr. Jekyll side of Massie's personality reemerges and the
truth comes out.

JOURNEY TO THE SEVENTH PLANET. 1961. 80 minutes. Color.
    Director: Sidney Pink. *Screenplay:* Ib Melchior and Sidney
    Pink. *Cinematography:* Age Wiltrup. *Cast:* John Agar
    (Don); Greta Thyssen (Greta); Ann Smyrner (Ingrid); Mimi
    Heinrich (Ursula); Carl Ottosen (Eric); Ove Sprogoe
    (Barry); Louis Miehe-Renard (Svend); Peter Monch (Karl);
    Annie Birgit Garde (Ellen); Ulla Moritz (Lise); Bente
    Juhl (Colleen).

    In the year A.D. 2001 a five-man United Nations space ex-
pedition lands on Uranus to explore the possibility of life.
They encounter an unseen evil power that is able to conjure
up all of the spacemen's unconscious fears and desires. Not
only do they experience giant rats and spiders, but they also
run across women they have known from the past. The men realize that the only way to escape their past thoughts is to find
and kill the being that is responsible. They finally track
it down in a sub-zero cave and kill it with liquid nitrogen.
    Journey to the Seventh Planet is a dubbed U.S./Danish co-
production. It has an intriguing premise but flounders in
its execution. The monsters are rubbery-looking, and the all-
powerful being is nothing more than a giant eye.

KONGA. 1961. 90 minutes. Color. *Director:* John Lemont.
    Screenplay: Aben Kandel and Herman Cohen. *Cinematography:*
    Desmond Dickinson. *Cast:* Michael Gough (Dr. Charles

Decker); Margo Johns (Margaret); Jess Conrad (Bob Kenton);
Claire Gordon (Sandra Banks); Austin Trevor (Dean Foster);
Jack Watson (Superintendent Brown); George Pastell (Pro-
fessor Tagore); Vanda Godsell (Bob's Mother); Stanley
Morgan (Inspector Lawson); Grace Arnold (Miss Barnesdell);
Leonard Sachs (Bob's Father); Nicholas Bennett (Daniel);
Kim Tracy (Mary); Rupert Osborne (Eric); Waveney Lee
(Janet); John Welsh (Commissioner Garland); Sam Sylvano
(Konga, as a Chimp).

The preproduction title of this film was *I Was a Teenage
Gorilla*. Even with the title *Konga* it is little more than an
amalgam of the Frankenstein monster and King Kong.
  A scientist (Gough) returns from a year in the African
jungle. While there Gough discovered a link in the evolutionary cycle between plant and animal. He injects his pet chimpanzee Konga with a growth serum taken from a carnivorous
plant, and it grows to the size of a gorilla. Gough hypnotizes
the gorilla to kill off his scientific and romantic rivals.
His assistant (Johns), who is jealous of his attraction to a
young student (Gordon), gives the gorilla`a serum overdose.
This causes it to grow to an immense size. Konga picks Gough
up in his hand and goes out into the streets of London. The
military bombards the animal with artillery fire; it throws
Gough to the crowd just before it dies.

LOST BATTALION. 1961. 83 minutes. *Director:* Eddie Romero.
  Screenplay: Eddie Romero and César Amigo. *Cinematography:*
  Felipe Sacdalan. *Cast:* Leopoldo Salcedo (Ramón, Guerrilla
  Leader); Diane Jergens (Kathy); Johnny Monteiro (Bruno,
  Bandit Leader); Joe Dennis (Landis); Jennings Sturgeon
  (Hughes); Joe Sison (Pepe); Bruce Baxter (Jimmy); Renato
  Robles (2nd Guerrilla); Rosi Acosta (Pepe's Wife); Arsenio
  Alonso (3rd Guerrilla).

This was one of the first AIP films made by Filipino director Eddie Romero. In the 1970s he would make other films
in the Philippines for AIP, e.g., *Savage Sisters*.
  In the Philippines during World War II a band of Filipino
guerrillas are convoying a group of stranded Americans to a
rendezvous with a submarine on the coast. During their trek
through the jungle one of the Americans (Jergens) falls in
love with the guerrilla leader (Salcedo). The group is set
upon by local bandits and Jergens is kidnapped. She is rescued
by Salcedo, and they in turn are rescued by a band of pygmies.
The bandits reappear, and Salcedo and the bandit leader

(Monteiro) have a fight. Both men are killed, while the Americans make it to the coast and are picked up by the submarine.

MASTER OF THE WORLD. 1961. 104 minutes. Color. *Director:*
    William Witney. *Screenplay:* Richard Matheson; based on
    the novels *Master of the World*, and *Robur, The Conquerer*,
    by Jules Verne. *Cinematography:* Gil Warrenton. *Cast:*
    Vincent Price (Robur); Charles Bronson (Strock); Henry
    Hull (Prudent); Mary Webster (Dorothy); David Frankham
    (Philip); Richard Harrison (Alistair); Vito Scotti
    (Topage); Wally Campo (Turner); Steve Masino (Weaver);
    Ken Terrell (Shanks); Peter Besbas (Wilson).

    In the middle of the 19th century a government agent
(Bronson) and three others (Hull, Webster, and Frankham) sail
a balloon over a crater in Pennsylvania. They are investigating a series of eruptions that have emanated from the crater. Their balloon is shot down by a rocket, and they are
taken prisoner aboard a flying ship, *The Albatross*, by its
inventor, Robur (Price). It is Price's mission to destroy
all materials of war throughout the world. When this is accomplished, he will become master of a peaceful world. The four
prisoners go around the world with Price and his crew, as the
ship bombs naval vessels and armies in Egypt and other countries. In order to stop Price's "kill for peace" scheme,
Bronson sets an explosive charge aboard the ship, as he and
the other three escape. When the explosion occurs, Price and
his crew decide to go down with *The Albatross* instead of jumping ship.
    Master of the World is a departure for Vincent Price from
many of the horror roles he portrayed for AIP in the 60s, but
he fits in nicely here as a demented idealist. Charles
Bronson, who possesses a 20th-century urban physiognomy, looks
more than a bit out of place as a Department of the Interior
representative circa 1848.

OPERATION CAMEL. 1961. 74 minutes. *Director:* Sven Methling,
    Jr. *Screenplay:* Bob Ramsing. *Cinematography:* Age
    Wiltrup, Ole Lytken, Ib Lonvang, and Per Staehr. *Cast:*
    Nora Hayden (The Dancer); with Paul Hagen, Ebbe Langberg,
    Preben Kaas, Carl Miehe-Renard, Klaus Pagh, Svend
    Johansen, Ole Dixon, Tor Stokke, Lisbet Kurt, Mogens
    Brandt, Vera Stricker, Annie Birgit Garde, Raggah Jussef,
    Maria Velasco, Majour Poulsen, Addison Mayers.

This comedy trifle originally came out in Denmark in color as part of the "Soldaterkammerater" series. A group of Danish soldiers undergo training in Denmark and then are sent to Gaza in the Middle East, as part of a United Nations peacekeeping force. One of the soldiers finds that his girlfriend (Hayden) is a dancer in a local nightclub. She wants to leave, but the club owner will not return her passport to her. The soldier boyfriend goes to the club with some of his army chums to get the passport back. This results in a finale that turns into a slapstick free-for-all.

THE PHANTOM PLANET. 1961. 82 minutes. *Director:* William Marshall. *Screenplay:* Fred Gebhardt. *Cinematography:* Elwood J. Nicholson. *Cast:* Dean Fredericks (Captain Frank Chapman); Coleen Gray (Liara); Anthony Dexter (Herron); Dolores Faith (Zetha); Francis X. Bushman (Sesom); Richard Weber (Lieutenant Makonnen); Al Jarvis (Judge Eden); Dick Haynes (Colonel Lansfield); Earl McDaniel (Pilot Leonard); Michael Marshall (Lieutenant White); John Herrin (Captain Beecher); Mel Curtis (Lieutenant Cutler); Jimmy Weldon (Navigator Webb); Akemi Tani (Communications Officer); Lori Lyons (Radar Officer); Richard Kiel (Solarite); with Susan Cembrowska, Marissa Mathes, Gloria Moreland, Judy Erickson, Marya Carter, Allyson Ames, Marion Thompson, Warrene Ott.

An American astronaut (Fredericks) is sent to investigate the disappearance of a spacecraft near the vicinity of a "phantom planet" called Rehton. He lands on the planet and finds that the atmosphere has reduced him to the same small size as the inhabitants of the planet. This diminutive race is ruled by Sesom (Bushman), who possesses the secret of gravity control (which he controls by a wave of his hand). Fredericks grows fond of the people and helps them defend themselves against their ancient enemy, the Solarites. He regains his normal size as soon as he puts on his spacesuit. Fredericks leaves for Earth realizing that no one will believe the adventures he has encountered.

Unless one is a hardcore science-fiction addict, the only reason to see *The Phantom Planet* is to view one of the last film appearances of Francis X. Bushman. Also in the cast, as one of the Solarite enemies, is Richard Kiel, better known as "Jaws" in the James Bond films.

THE PIT AND THE PENDULUM. 1961. 85 minutes. Color. *Director:* Roger Corman. *Screenplay:* Richard Matheson; based on the story by Edgar Allan Poe. *Cinematography:* Floyd Crosby. *Cast:* Vincent Price (Nicholas Medina); John Kerr (Francis Barnard); Barbara Steele (Elizabeth Barnard Medina); Luana Anders (Catherine Medina); Anthony Carbone (Dr. Charles Leon); Patrick Westwood (Maximillian); Lynn Bernay (Maria); Larry Turner (Nicholas as a Child); Mary Menzies (Isabella); Charles Victor (Bartolome).

In the 16th century a young Englishman (Kerr) comes to Spain after he has learned of his sister's death. He reaches the ancestral castle of the Medina family, into which his sister (Steele) had married. Kerr finds that no one wants to talk about his sister's death. Gradually he learns, through his brother-in-law (Price), how Steele became upset with the decaying environment of the Medina castle. She supposedly died of fright in the castle's torture chamber, which at one time had been used by Price's father, an executioner for the Inquisition. Price is obsessed with the thought of his wife having been buried alive, as his mother was. One night he finds that his wife is actually alive and is plotting with the family doctor (Carbone) to drive him insane. Price goes off the deep end and assumes his late father's personality. He locks Steele in an iron maiden and in his madness mistakes Kerr for Carbone. He ties Kerr to a table underneath a giant pendulum, with a razor-sharp blade. However, before he can be cut in half, Kerr is rescued, and Price falls to his death in a pit.

The Pit and the Pendulum is even more thematically bizarre and visually opulent than its predecessor, *House of Usher*. The final shot in the film provides quite a shock. Kerr is being led out of the dungeon torture chamber by Price's sister (Anders) and the butler (Westwood). The camera swish pans to a closeup of Steele, still locked in the iron maiden, and still alive.

PORTRAIT OF A SINNER. 1961. 96 minutes. *Director:* Robert Siodmak. *Screenplay:* Audrey Erskine Lindop and Dudley Leslie; based on the novel *The Rough and the Smooth*, by Robin Maugham. *Cinematography:* Otto Heller. *Cast:* Nadja Tiller (Ila Hansen); Tony Britton (Mike Thompson); William Bendix (Reg Barker); Natasha Parry (Margaret Goreham); Norman Wooland (David Fraser); Donald Wolfit (Lord Drewell); Tony Wright (Jack); Adrienne Corri (Jane Buller); Joyce Carey (Mrs. Thompson); John Welsh (Dr.

Thompson); Martin Miller (Piggy); Michael Ward (Head-
waiter); Edward Chapman (Willy Catch); Norman Pierce
(Barman); Beatrice Varley (Hotel Manageress); Myles Eason
(Bobby Montagu-Jones); Cyril Smith (Taxi Driver); Geoffrey
Bayldon (Ransom).

A young archaeologist (Britton) dumps his fiancée (Parry)
when he meets the enigmatic Ila Hansen (Tiller). Britton becomes angry when he finds that Tiller is living with her boss
(Bendix), but he is told that the living situation is only a
business arrangement. A man (Wright) from her past, who is in
a desperate situation, asks to borrow some money from her.
Tiller asks both Britton and Bendix for the money, but neigher
can help her. Angrily, she admits to both men that Wright is
the only one who could ever sexually satisfy her. Bendix cannot bear to live without her and commits suicide. The other
two men both leave her, and when Tiller realizes this, she
goes out and picks up the first man she meets.
    The director of *Portrait of a Sinner*, Robert Siodmak, is
best remembered for a series of excellent *films noirs* he directed in the 40s. This British-made film opened in England
in 1959 under the suggestive title *The Rough and the Smooth*.
It is imbued with some *film noir* touches: its photography; the
central character, a *film noir* "black widow"; and a general
tone of misogyny.

TWIST ALL NIGHT. 1961. 76 minutes. Color Prologue. *Direc-
    tor:* William J. Hole, Jr. *Screenplay:* Berni Gould.
    Cinematography: Gene Polito. *Cast:* Louis Prima (Louis
    Evans); June Wilkinson (Jenny Watson); Sam Butera and the
    Witnesses (Themselves); Gertrude Michael (Letitia
    Clunker); David Whorf (Riffy); Hal Torey (The Mayor);
    Ty Perry (Mr. Arturo); Fred Sherman (Julius); Dick Winslow
    (Du Bois); Gil Fry (Policeman).

Twist All Night was obviously made to capitalize on the
dance craze of the early 60s--The Twist. It originally contained a ten-minute prologue in color called "Twist Craze,"
but this has been cut out of most television prints.
    Musician Louis Evans (Prima) and his cohorts, Sam Butera
and the Witnesses, cannot pay the rent on their nightclub.
The teenagers who frequent the place just occupy the tables
and do not spend any money. The young people are being paid
by an art-gallery owner (Perry) who lives in the same building
and wants to force the musicians out. Prima confronts Perry,
assaults him, and lands in jail. It later turns out that Perry

Twist All Night

is an art thief and is arrested. Prima now throws a successful
block party, and the club becomes a big success.

This hopeless comedy has much of the action taking place
within 20 feet of the bandstand. Louis Prima and Sam Butera
and the Witnesses were in their time the quintessential Las
Vegas lounge act--a heady mixture of brilliantine, mohair, and
garlic. Here they perform such "classics" as "Oh, Mama Twist,"
"Better Twist Now, Baby," and "Tag That Twistin Dollie." *Twist
All Night* faithfully exploits The Twist but misses the opportunity to do the same with the statuesque June Wilkinson.

THE BRAIN THAT WOULDN'T DIE. 1962. 71 minutes. *Director:*
    Joseph Green. *Screenplay:* Joseph Green; based on a story
    by Rex Carlton and Green. *Cinematography:* Stephen Hajnal.
    Cast: Virginia Leith (Jan Compton); Herb Evers (Dr. Bill
    Cortner); Adele Lamont (Doris Powell); Bruce Brighton
    (Dr. Cortner); Doris Brent (Nurse); Leslie Daniel (Kurt);
    Bonnie Shari (Stripper); Paula Maurice (B-Girl); Lola
    Mason (Donna Williams); Audrey Devereau (Jeannie); Bruce
    Kerr (Announcer); Eddie Carmel (Monster).

The Brain That Wouldn't Die ranks right up there as one
of the sleaziest films ever made. After watching it, you want
to take a nice hot shower.

A young doctor (Evers) robs graves to receive parts for
his organ transplants. He and his fiancée (Leith) are in an
auto accident, and she is decapitated. He rushes her head
back to his laboratory, where with the aid of various drugs
he is able to keep it alive. Evers goes out at night looking
for a body for Leith's head, even though Leith has begged him
to let her die. His search takes him to low-life bars where
he finds plenty of perfect bodies in the form of prostitutes
and bar girls. He finally settles on a photographer's model
(Lamont), with a disfigured face, but a perfect body. Meanwhile Leith has communicated her thoughts to a disgusting-
looking monster (Carmel), which Evers keeps locked up in a
room in his lab. Before he can perform the body transplant,
the monster escapes and kills Evers and his assistant (Daniel);
The lab catches fire, as Lamont escapes and Leith's agony ends.

BURN, WITCH, BURN. 1962. 90 minutes. *Director:* Sidney
    Hayers. *Screenplay:* Charles Beaumont, Richard Matheson,
    and George Baxt; based on the novel, *Conjure Wife*, by
    Fritz Leiber. *Cinematography:* Reginald Wyer. *Cast:*

The Brain That Wouldn't Die

Janet Blair (Tansy Taylor); Peter Wyngarde (Norman
Taylor); Margaret Johnson (Flora Carr); Anthony Nicholls
(Harvey Sawtelle); Colin Gordon (Professor Lindsay Carr);
Kathleen Byron (Evelyn Sawtelle); Reginald Beckwith
(Harold Gunnison); Jessica Dunning (Hilda Gunnison);
Norman Bird (Doctor); Judith Stott (Margaret Abbott);
Bill Mitchell (Fred Jennings); George Roubicek (Cleaner's
Man); Frank Singuineau (Truck Driver); Gary Woolf (His
Mate).

This film about black magic and the occult is a worthy
effort in the genre. In some respects *Burn, Witch, Burn* is a
companion piece to Jacques Tourneur's *Curse of the Demon*, another British-made film on the same subject.
Tansy Taylor (Blair) practices witchcraft to further her
husband's (Wyngarde) academic career. He discovers her black-
magic paraphernalia and destroys it. A streak of bad luck now
follows Wyngarde, such as being accused of rape and having an
auto accident. Blair disappears, and Wyngarde finds her in a
graveyard. When she is taken home, she starts to exhibit violent behavior. It turns out that the wife (Johnson) of one
of Wyngarde's academic rivals (Gordon) has hypnotized Blair
into following her orders. Wyngarde is attacked by a piece
of masonry come to life, shaped like an eagle. Later a piece
of the masonry supporting the eagle collapses, falls on top
of Johnson, and kills her.

INVASION OF THE STAR CREATURES. 1962. 75 minutes. *Director:*
Bruno Ve Sota. *Screenplay:* Jonathan Haze; based on the
story "Monsters from Nicholson Mesa," by Haze. *Cinema-
tography:* Basil Bradbury. *Cast:* Robert Ball (Philbrick);
Frankie Ray (Penn); Gloria Victor (Dr. Tanga); Dolores
Reed (Professor Puna); Mark Ferris (Colonel Rank); with
Slick Slavin, Mark Thompson, Sid Kane, Mike Del Piano,
Lenore Bond, Anton Van Stralen, James Almanzar, Allen
Dailey, Joseph Martin.

Two young soldiers (Ball and Ray) become lost from their
platoon and happen to follow some odd-looking plantlike creatures into a cave. Inside the cave are two beautiful women
scientists (Victor and Reed), who have come from another planet
to conquer Earth. Bell and Ray seduce the two aliens with
kisses and transform them from would-be conquerers to obedient
women.
This inept science-fiction comedy certainly contains some
reactionary sexual elements. Directed by Bruno Ve Sota and

written by Jonathan Haze, two actors who appeared regularly
in AIP films, *Invasion of the Star Creatures* has about the most
pathetic-looking outer-space creatures one could find. Their
outfits consist of "leg stockings, potato sacks, flappy pitch-
fork hair, and ping-pong ball eyes" (Harry and Michael Medved,
The Golden Turkey Awards. New York: Perigee, 1980, p. 135).

MARCO POLO. 1962. 95 minutes. Color. *Director:* Hugo
    Fregonese and Piero Pierotti. *Screenplay:* Piero Pierotti,
    Oreste Biancoli, Duccio Tessari, Antoinette Pellevant,
    Ennio De Concini, and Eliana De Sabata; based on a story
    by Pierotti and Biancoli. *Cinematography:* Riccardo
    Pallottini. *Cast:* Rory Calhoun (Marco Polo); Yoko Tani
    (Princess Amuroy); Robert Hundar (Mongka); Camillo Pilotto
    (Great Khan); Pierre Cressoy (Cuday); Michael Chow (Ciu-
    Lin); Thien-Huong (Tai-Au); with Poing Ping.

One would have thought that we had seen the last of the
Americanized Marco Polos with Gary Cooper in 1938 in *The Adventures of Marco Polo*. But veteran "B" Western actor Rory
Calhoun continues the questionable tradition in *Marco Polo*.
    Marco Polo, a Venetian, is in route to China in the 13th
century when he saves the life of a young man (Chow). He also
rescues the daughter (Tani) of the Great Khan (Pilotto) from
bandits. Calhoun becomes involved with the internal feuding
between the forces of the Khan and those of the tyrant Mongka
(Hundar). He meets an old man, who is the inventor of gunpowder. With this new weapon Calhoun builds a cannon, which
helps defeat Hundar and his troops. Now that Peking has been
saved, Calhoun is asked by Tani to marry her, but he declines
so he can continue his travels.

PANIC IN THE YEAR ZERO. 1962. 92 minutes. *Director:* Ray
    Milland. *Screenplay:* Jay Simms and John Morton; based
    on a story by Simms. *Cinematography:* Gil Warrenton.
    Cast: Ray Milland (Harry Baldwin); Jean Hagen (Ann Bald-
    win); Frankie Avalon (Rick Baldwin); Mary Mitchell (Karen
    Baldwin); Joan Freeman (Marilyn Hayes); Richard Garland
    (Mr. Johnson); Richard Bakalyan (Carl); Rex Holman
    (Mickey); Neil Nephew (Andy); Willis Bouchey (Dr. Strong);
    O.Z. Whitehead (Hogan); Byron Morrow (Haenel); Shary
    Marshall (Mrs. Johnson); Russ Bender (Harkness); Hugh
    Sanders (Becker); with Andrea Lane, Scott Peters, Bud
    Slater, Kelton Crawford.

Panic in the Year Zero is a film that will gladden the
hearts of the bomb-shelter crowd. Its attitude toward the nuclear devestation of Los Angeles is about as urgent as if it
had been a smog alert.

Harry Baldwin (Milland) and his family leave Los Angeles
on a fishing trip. A couple of hours after they leave they
hear an explosion and later learn that Los Angeles has been
leveled by a nuclear attack. Realizing that looters will be
out in force, they continue to their vacation rendezvous, only
stopping to buy food and ammunition. The Baldwins take shelter
in a cave. Later they are menaced by three young toughs, two
of whom rape Milland's daughter (Mitchell). They are promptly
blown away by Milland and his son (Avalon). The two of them
find a young woman (Freeman) who had been held prisoner by the
hooligans and they take her back to the cave. A radio report
now tells them that Los Angeles is safe, and they all return
to help rebuild the city.

It is inconceivable that a film such as this could be
made nowadays, although there are those who still attempt to
convince us that it is possible to survive a nuclear holocaust.

THE PREMATURE BURIAL. 1962. 81 minutes. Color. *Director:*
    Roger Corman. *Screenplay:* Charles Beaumont and Ray
    Russell; based on the story by Edgar Allan Poe. *Cinema-
    tography:* Floyd Crosby. *Cast:* Ray Milland (Guy Carrell);
    Hazel Court (Emily Gault); Richard Ney (Miles Archer);
    Heather Angel (Kate Carrell); Alan Napier (Dr. Gideon
    Gault); John Dierkes (Sweeney); Richard Miller (Mole);
    Brendan Dillon (Minister); with Clive L. Halliday.

The Poe story from which this film was taken was more of
a treatise on the "disadvantages" of being buried alive.
Screenwriters Beaumont and Russell adapted the material and
concocted a story with many of the same obsessions found in
The Pit and the Pendulum and *House of Usher*.

Guy Carrell (Milland), a rather old medical student in
19th-century London, fears that he has his father's catalepsy
and will be buried alive during a seizure. He even hesitates
to marry Emily Gault (Court) and retreats to his family estate.
When his sister (Angel) convinces him to marry, Milland builds
a tomb with numerous escape devices. A friend (Ney) gets
Milland to open his father's crypt to prove to him that his
father was dead when he was buried. When they find that the
"dead" man struggled to get out, Milland has a seizure and is
pronounced dead. Two grave robbers steal his coffin, but
Milland awakes and kills them both. Now totally mad, he takes

his wife and buries her alive. When Ney confronts Milland
with his crimes, the two of them struggle, and Milland is shot
dead by Angel. She put him out of his misery, since she discovered that his wife was using Milland's morbid obsession to
inherit his money.

PRISONER OF THE IRON MASK. 1962. 80 minutes. Color. *Direc-*
     tor: Francesco De Feo (Italian version). Lee Kresel (U.S.
     version). *Screenplay:* Silvio Amadio, Ruggero Jacobbi,
     and Francesco De Feo; based on the novel *The Man in the*
     Iron Mask, by Alexandre Dumas. *Cinematography:* Raffaele
     Masciocchi. *Cast:* Michel Lemoine (Marco); Wandisa Guida
     (Christina); with Andrea Bosic, Jany Clair, Giovanni
     Materassi, Pietro Albano, Tiziana Casetti, Alan Evans,
     Mimmo Poli, Francesco De Leone, Nando Tamberlani, Marco
     Tulli, Joe Camel, Silvio Bagolini, Erminio Spalla, Emma
     Baron, Andrea Fantasia, Piero Pastore.

     Prisoner of the Iron Mask is loosely based on the Dumas
novel, which was put to film with much more fidelity in 1939
as *The Man in the Iron Mask.*
     In 18th-century Italy a duke is being slowly poisoned by
one of his unscrupulous advisers, Count Astolfo. Marco
(Lemoine), the duke's son, who has proof of the adviser's per-
fidy, is captured by Astolfo's men. He is put in an iron mask,
but not before he has hidden the evidence against Astolfo. A
friend of Lemoine's rescues him. Just before his sister is
forced to marry Astolfo, Lemoine has a duel with him and is
victorious. Astolfo is now put in the iron mask and is sent
to the battlefield where he must do battle with the French.

REPTILICUS. 1962. 81 minutes. Color. *Director:* Sidney Pink.
     Screenplay: Sidney Pink and Ib Melchior. *Cinematography:*
     Aage Wiltrup. *Cast:* Carl Ottosen (Mark Grayson); Ann
     Smyrner (Lise Martens); Mimi Heinrich (Karen Martens);
     Asbjorn Andersen (Professor Martens); Marla Behrens
     (Connie Miller); Bent Mejding (Svend Viltofft); Poul
     Wildaker (Dr. Dalby); Dirk Passer (Dirk Mikkelsen); Ole
     Wisborg (Captain Brandt); with Bodil Miller, Mogens
     Brandt, Kjeld Petersen, Alex Suhr, Alfred Wilken, Bent
     Vejlby, Knud Hallest, Benny Juhlin, Martin Stander, Borge
     Moller Grimstrup, Hardy Jensen, Poul Thomsen, Svend
     Johansen, Jorgen Blaksted, Birthe Wilke, Claus Toksvig.

From the team that brought us *Journey to the Seventh Planet* comes *Reptilicus*, another conventional sci-fi/horror film with an added twist. In the former film the monster was able to bring to life people's unconscious thoughts and desires. In *Reptilicus* we have a monster with the power of spontaneous regeneration.

While drilling in Lapland, Danish engineers unearth the frozen tail of a prehistoric monster. It is sent to a professor (Andersen) in Copenhagen to study. At room temperature the tail thaws and begins to grow new living tissue. An American military man (Ottosen) is sent to maintain security around the growing creature. By now the monster has generated itself into a huge reptile, which can walk, swim, or fly--a real triple threat. It escapes into the forest, where conventional military weapons have no effect on its impenetrable scaly body. It proceeds to stomp out a good portion of Copenhagen, until a rocket with a lethal poison is fired at it. It now appears to be dead. However, one of the creature's feet, which had been severed by a depth charge in the ocean, now begins to regenerate.

SAMSON AND THE SEVEN MIRACLES OF THE WORLD. 1962. 80 minutes. Color. *Director:* Riccardo Freda. *Screenplay:* Oreste Biancoli. *Cinematography:* Riccardo Pallottini. *Cast:* Gordon Scott (Samson); Yoko Tani (Princess Lei-Ling); Gabriele Antonini (Cho); Leonardo Severini (Garak); Valery Inkijinoff (High Priest); Hélène Chanel (Liutai); Dante Di Paolo (Bayan); with Chu-La-Chit, Luong-Ham-Chau, Franco Ressel, Antonio Cianci, Ely Yeh, Giacomo Tchang.

What Samson is doing in China is never made clear; perhaps he was clearing a path for Marco Polo. Anyway, the plot of this film is remarkably similar in many respects to AIP's *Marco Polo*. Both films were made by the same production company in Europe and use the same screenwriter.

Samson (Scott) rescues a Chinese prince and princess after their father has been murdered by a Tartar leader. Scott takes the heirs to a monastery. The Tartars attack and the young prince is killed. The Chinese revolt against the Tartar invasion when Scott rings the "Gong of Freedom" (the Chinese equivalent of the Liberty Bell). The musclebound Scott, not being too fast on his feet, is knocked down and out by the swinging gong. The tartars capture him and bury him in an underground tomb. When he frees himself, Scott starts an earthquake, which is instrumental in defeating the Tartar ogre and his army. The princess is now free to assume the throne.

TALES OF TERROR. 1962. 90 minutes. Color. *Director:* Roger
    Corman. *Screenplay:* Richard Matheson; based on the sto-
    ries "Morella," "The Black Cat," "The Cask of Amontil-
    lado," and "The Facts in the Case of M. Valdemar," by
    Edgar Allan Poe. *Cinematography:* Floyd Crosby. *Cast for*
    "Morella": Vincent Price (Locke); Maggie Pierce (Lenora);
    Leona Gage (Morella); Edmund Cobb (Driver). *Cast for*
    "The Black Cat": Vincent Price (Fortunato); Peter Lorre
    (Montresor Herringbone); Joyce Jameson (Annabel Herring-
    bone); Lennie Weinrib (Policeman); Wally Campo (Bar-
    tender); Alan De Witt (Chairman); John Hackett (Police-
    man). *Cast for "The Facts in the Case of M. Valdemar":*
    Vincent Price (Ernest Valdemar); Basil Rathbone (Mr.
    Carmichael); Debra Paget (Helene Valdemar); David
    Frankham (Dr. Elliot James); Scotty Brown (Servant).

This horror anthology of four of Poe's short stories combined into three is for the most part quite successful. Humor
was used here along with horror to much greater effect than
the later Poe film *The Raven.*
    "Morella" is pure Poe. A man (Price) has lived alone
for 26 years in a decaying mansion, after his wife (Gage) had
died in childbirth. His terminally ill daughter (Pierce)
comes to visit him after being away at boarding school for
many years. Price keeps Gage's mummified body in the bedroom.
During the night Gage's spirit enters the body of the sleeping
Pierce. Now it is Pierce who is the mummified body, and Gage
is 26 years younger and beautiful again. She confronts Price
and announces that she has come back to avenge her death. She
strangles him, as the house goes up in flames consuming them
all.
    "The Black Cat" concerns the revenge brought on by a jeal-
ous husband. Peter Lorre is a drunken lout, who neglects his
beautiful wife (Jameson). He participates in a boisterous
wine-tasting contest with connoisseur Vincent Price. Price
takes the drunken Lorre home and finds himself immediately
attracted to Jameson. They fall in love, and Lorre extracts
his revenge by walling them up in the cellar. When the police
check Price's disappearance, they venture into the cellar.
There they hear the cries of Jameson's cat, which Lorre had
hated. The animal was accidentally entombed with the lovers,
and now it has gained revenge on Lorre for the abuse it suffered at his hands.
    The final story concerns the subject of mesmerism, which
interested Poe. A dying man (Price) has hired a mesmerist
(Rathbone) to put him in a trance just before he dies, in order
to see how long death can be forestalled. Price's body dies,
but his mind lives on. Against the wishes of Price's wife

(Paget), Rathbone keeps him in this state for scientific purposes. In fact he refuses to release Price unless Paget marries him. When he makes advances toward her, Price rises out
of bed. Walking toward Rathbone in his advanced state of pu-
trefaction, Price grasps Rathbone by the throat, and Rathbone
dies of fright.

WARRIORS 5. 1962. 84 minutes. *Director:* Leopoldo Savona.
  Screenplay: Gino De Santis, Ugo Pirro, and Leopoldo
  Savona; based on a story by Lino Del Fra. *Cinematography:*
  Claudio Racca. *Cast:* Jack Palance (Jack); Giovanna Ralli
  (Italia); Serge Reggiani (Libero); Folco Lulli (Marzi);
  Venantino Venantini (Alberto); Franco Balducci (Conti);
  Miha Baloh (Sansone); Vera Murco (Matalda); Vida Levstik
  (Ida); Ajsa Mesic (Luisa); Valeria Sila (Old Woman);
  Isabella Chiurco (Carla); Guido Bertone (Carlo); Bruno
  Scipioni (Angelino).

The only thing that differentiates *Warriors 5* from *Tank
Commandos* is that it was filmed in Italy and not in the United
States. In Italy during World War II an American paratrooper
(Palance) is dropped into German-occupied territory to commit
acts of sabotage. He is captured but manages to escape with
four Italian prisoners. They go their separate ways, but
Palance runs into the four once again and asks them to aid
him in blowing up a bridge vital to the Germans. They are
successful in their mission, but the four Italians are killed.
Now only Palance and a prostitute (Ralli), who had met up with
the group, are left to fight the Germans.

WHITE SLAVE SHIP. 1962. 92 minutes. Color. *Director:* Silvio
  Amadio. *Screenplay:* Sandro Continenza, Marcello Coscia,
  and Ruggero Jacobbi. *Cinematography:* Aldo Giordani.
  Cast: Pier Angeli (Polly); Edmund Purdom (Dr. Bradley);
  Armand Mestral (Calico Jack); Ivan Desny (Captain Cooper);
  Michèle Girardon (Anna); with Franca Parisi Strahl, Mirko
  Ellis, Maria Pia Luzi, Paolo Petrini, Ruth von Hagen,
  Ivy Holsen, Renato Speziali, Franco Capucci, Germana
  Francioli, Fiorella Ferrero, Letitia Bollante, Charles
  Borromel.

In 1675 a young woman (Angeli) is taken out of a British
prison along with other women to be sold into slavery in the
Colonies. They are put on a ship, the *Albatross*, which has a

hidden shipment of male convicts aboard. The women, obviously
not desiring to be slaves, free the convicts. A political
prisoner (Purdom) and a brigand (Mestral) now assume control
of the ship. Mestral and his thugs go out of control and kill
most of the crew. When the vessel runs into trouble during a
storm, Purdom helps restore the ship's captain (Desny) to control. Realizing that mutiny is punishable by death, Mestral
and his men imprison all on board. With rations running low,
the mutineers plan to throw the women prisoners overboard. But
Angeli and the other women help to free Desny and Purdom. They
now battle the mutineers and defeat them. Because of their
aid in suppressing a mutiny, both Purdom and Angeli are once
again given their freedom.

BATTLE BEYOND THE SUN. 1963. 75 minutes. Color. *Director:*
   Thomas Colchart. *Screenplay:* Nicholas Colbert and Edwin
   Palmer. *Cinematography:* Nikolay Kulchitskiy. *Cast:* Edd
   Perry (Kornev); Arla Powell (Korneva); Andy Stewart
   (Gordiyenko); Gene Tonner (Verst); Barry Chertok (Somov);
   Lawrence Loben (Sashko); Kirk Barton (Klark); Linda
   Barrett (Olga); with Bruce Hunter, Frederick Farley,
   Thomas Littleton, Mary Kannon.

   This film originally appeared in the Soviet Union in 1959
under the title *Nebo Zovyot*. Roger Corman, with the help of
Francis Ford Coppola, adapted the American-release version,
which included additional footage. The directors', screenwriters' and actors' names are pseudonyms.
   In the future Earth has been divided into two great na-
tions--The North Hemis and the South Hemis. Spaceships from
both states land on a platform at a space station. They end
up on a race to Mars. One of the ships is drawn toward the
sun, forcing the other ship to rescue its rivals and take them
on board. Now low on fuel, the lone ship must land on Astar,
which is in Mars' orbit. All aboard now appear to be perma-
nently stranded, but another spaceship lands on Astar with
enough fuel to make it back to Earth. The pilot of this ship
dies from his arduous journey. The crews of the North and
South Hemis spacecraft decide to unite in their efforts in
space travel in honor of the dead pilot.
   A substantial amount of *Battle Beyond the Sun* was changed
by Coppola, who spent six months translating the Russian into
English. One thing is clear, however, and that is that the
Soviet notions of comradeship and martydom are still very much
in evidence.

BEACH PARTY. 1963, 101 minutes. Color. *Director:* William
   Asher. *Screenplay:* Lou Rusoff. *Cinematography:* Kay
   Norton. *Cast:* Bob Cummings (Professor Sutwell); Dorothy
   Malone (Marianne); Frankie Avalon (Frankie); Annette
   Funicello (Dolores); Harvey Lembeck (Eric Von Zipper);
   Jody McCrea (Deadhead); Morey Amsterdam (Cappy); John
   Ashley (Ken); Eva Six (Eva); Dick Dale and the Del Tones
   (Themselves); David Landfield (Ed); Dolores Wells (Sue);
   Valora Noland (Rhonda); Bobby Payne (Tom); Duane Ament
   (Big Boy); Andy Romano, John Macchia, Jerry Brutsche,
   Bob Harvey (Motorcycle Rats); Linda Rogers, Alberta
   Nelson (Motorcycle Mice); Candy Johnson (Perpetual Motion
   Dancer); Roger Bacon (Tour Guide); Yvette Vickers, Sharon
   Garrett (Yogi Girls); Mickey Dora, John Fain, Pam Colbert,
   Donna Russell, Mike Nader, Ed Garner, Laura Lynn, Susan
   Yardley, Brian Wilson (Surfers); Lorie Summers, Meredith
   MacRae, Luree Nicholson, Paulette Rapp, Marlo Baers (Beach
   Girls); John Beach, Bill Slosky, Brent Battin, Roger
   Christian, Gary Usher, Bill Parker (Beach Boys); Vincent
   Price (Big Daddy).

   This is it--the film that started the trend of having
American teenagers believe they were ersatz Californians.
Beach Party and its successors always had a mixture of veterans
and aspiring young actors and actresses in basically similar
plots, with only minimal variations.
   In this inaugural beach picture Bob Cummings portrays an
anthropology professor who is studying the sex habits of teenagers. He naturally picks Frankie and Annette and their group
of surfers and surf bunnies to study. What he does not realize
is that their squeaky-clean variations on boy/girl relations
is similar to the goings on at an Osmond Family concert.
Funicello gets to know Cummings after he has rescued her from
the pea-brained motorcyclist Eric Von Zipper (Lembeck), and
soon Avalon becomes jealous. When the teenagers find out that
Cummings has been studying them like guinea pigs, they become
angry. The ending has everyone reconciled, as the surfers
have a large pie fight with Lembeck and his gang.
   Beach Party and its sequels were quite popular for two
or three years. By the time the mid-60s rolled around, young
people were becoming more concerned about such issues as Vietnam. Youth films from around 1966 onward generally became
much more confrontational and less frivolous.

CALIFORNIA. 1963. 86 minutes. *Director:* Hamil Petroff.
   Screenplay: James West. *Cinematography:* Edward

Fitzgerald. *Cast:* Jock Mahony (Don Michael O'Casey);
Faith Domergue (Carlotta Torres); Michael Pate (Don
Francisco Hernandez); Susan Seaforth (Marianna De La
Rosa); Rudolpho Hoyos (Padre Soler); Penny Santone (Dona
Ana Sofia Hicenta); Jimmy Murphy (Jacinto); Nestor Paiva
(General Micheltorena); Roberto Contreras (Lieutenant
Sanchez); Felix Locher (Don Pablo Hernandez); Charles
Horvath (Manuel).

California stars Jock Mahony, who gained a small degree
of popularity in the 50s by appearing as the star in such television shows as *The Range Rider* and *Yancy Derringer*.
    In California in 1841 the people are restless under Mexi-
can rule and seek to gain statehood. Don Francisco (Pate), a
Mexican collaborator, poisons his father (Locher), who is a
resistance leader. Pate's half-brother (Mahony) now takes up
the fight for independence. Mahony receives aid from Pate's
mistress (Domergue). Pate trys to force her to seduce a Mexican general (Paiva), but she refuses and kills herself. Eventually the Mexicans are defeated, as Pate is killed by one of
his own men. Mahony is now free to marry Pate's fiancée
(Seaforth) and take over ownership of his father's land.

THE COMEDY OF TERRORS. 1963. 88 minutes. Color. *Director:*
    Jacques Tourneur. *Screenplay:* Richard Matheson. *Cine-*
    matography: Floyd Crosby. *Cast:* Vincent Price (Waldo
    Trumbull); Peter Lorre (Felix Gillie); Boris Karloff
    (Amos Hinchley); Basil Rathbone (John F. Black); Joe E.
    Brown (Cemetary Keeper); Joyce Jameson (Amaryllis
    Trumbull); Beverly Hills (Mrs. Phipps); Paul Barselow
    (Riggs); Linda Rogers (Phipps' Maid); Luree Nicholson
    (Black's Servant); Buddy Mason (Mr. Phipps); "Rhubarb"
    the Cat (Cleopatra); with Alan De Witt, Doug Williams.

    The unfortunate aspect of AIP's horror films of the 60s
was their lapse into comedy. One of the episodes in *Tales of*
Terror was amusing, but continuing with *The Raven* and culminating with *The Comedy of Terrors*, the comedic elements are
just too "hammy". The veterans in this cast look to be enjoy-
ing themselves immensely, but with its broad humor and bosomy
women the film resembles nothing more than a burlesque skit.
    A drunken and lazy undertaker (Price) has taken over his
father-in-law's (Karloff) funeral business. Price works only
when money is needed; with the aid of his assistant (Lorre)
he goes out to "drum up" business by killing people. He kills
a wealthy man (Mason), but his wife (Hills) leaves town without

paying for the funeral. On the verge of losing his lease, Price decides to kill his landlord (Rathbone). Rathbone, a victim of catalepsy, refuses to stay dead. He comes back to Price's mortuary for revenge, and Price finally does him in. Meanwhile Lorre and Price's wife (Jameson) have fallen in love. When the police enter the premises, Price pretends to be unconscious, so as not to be blamed for Rathbone's death. Karloff takes this opportunity to administer to Price some poisoned medicine meant for Karloff. Now Jameson and Lorre go away together.

THE CRAWLING HAND. 1963. 89 minutes. *Director:* Herbert L. Strock. *Screenplay:* Herbert L. Strock and William Idelson; based on a story by Robert Young and Joseph Cranston. *Cinematography:* Willard Van Der Veer. *Cast:* Peter Breck (Steve Curan); Kent Taylor (Doc Weitzberg); Rod Lauren (Paul Lawrence); Sirry Steffen (Marta Farnstrom); Alan Hale, Jr. (Sheriff); Arline Judge (Mrs. Hotchkiss); with Richard Arlen, Ross Elliott, Allison Hayes, Ed Wermer, Tris Coffin, Syd Saylor, G. Stanley Jones, Ashley Cowan, Jock Putnam, Beverly Lunsford, Andy Andrews.

The disembodied-hand-type horror film is almost a subgenre that appears every now and then. In the 40s it was *The Beast with Five Fingers*, and more recently it was *The Hand*. Neither of these films was very good, which puts them in league with *The Crawling Hand*.
An astronaut in space has been taken over by an alien form. He pleads with the scientists over the radio to destroy him and his spacecraft. The only part of the astronaut that makes it back through reentry intact is his hand. It is found on a beach by a young medical student (Lauren). He takes it home, where the hand comes to life and kills his landlady. The hand now begins to exert a strange control over Lauren, giving him the impulse to kill. He finally attempts to combat the hand's influence upon him. In a grisly ending he throws the hand to a pack of hungry cats, who finish it off as if it were a can of Purina cat chow (meow, meow, meow).

DEMENTIA 13. 1963. 81 minutes. *Director:* Francis Coppola. *Screenplay:* Francis Coppola. *Cinematography:* Charles Hannawalt. *Cast:* William Campbell (Richard Haloran); Luana Anders (Louise Haloran); Bart Patton (Billy

Haloran); Mary Mitchell (Kane); Patrick Magee (Justin
Caleb); Eithne Dunne (Lady Haloran); Peter Read (John
Haloran); Karl Schanzer (Simon); Ron Perry (Arthur);
Derry O'Donovan (Lillian); Barbara Dowling (Kathleen).

Roger Corman was so satisfied with the work that Francis
Coppola did on *Battle Beyond the Sun* that he provided the financial backing for *Dementia 13*. Filmed in Ireland, this tale
contains all the trappings of the gothic horror story, as well
as some very effective photography.
    During an argument with his wife (Anders) over his moth-
er's will, John Haloran (Read) dies of a heart attack. Anders
believes she will be out of the old woman's (Dunne) will if
she discovers her son is dead. She decides to conceal Read's
death and claims he has gone on a trip. Her plan is to drive
Dunne insane by convincing her that she can communicate with
her granddaughter, who died eight years before. Anders is
savagely axed to death before she has an opportunity to carry
out her plan, and Dunne is murdered shortly thereafter. A wax
statue of the long-dead child is found, as is the murderer--
her brother (Patton). He is homicidal and was responsible for
the death of his sister, which supposedly had been a drowning
accident.

ERIK THE CONQUEROR. 1963. 90 minutes. Color. *Director:*
    Mario Bava. *Screenplay:* Oreste Biancoli, Mario Bava, and
    Piero Pierotti. *Cinematography:* Ubaldo Terzano and Mario
    Bava. *Cast:* Cameron Mitchell (Iron); Giorgio Ardisson
    (Erik, Duke of Helfort); Andrea Checci (Gunnar); Françoise
    Christophe (Queen Alice); Ellen Kessler (Daja); Alice
    Kessler (Rama); Folco Lulli (Aello); Franco Giacobini
    (Rustichello); Joe Robinson (Iron's Rival) Raffaele
    Baldassarre (Blak); Enzo Doria (Bennet); Franco Ressel
    (King Lotar); Livia Contardi (Hadda); with Jean-Jacques
    Delbo.

Also known as *Fury of the Vikings*, this film by Mario
Bava is a far cry from the gothic horror films for which he
is known. *Erik the Conqueror* is one of the few Italian sword
epics that takes place in Northern Europe.
    In the tenth century the English defeat the Vikings, and
the English queen (Christophe) adopts a Viking child, who
grows up to be Erik, Duke of Helfort (Ardisson). Meanwhile
his brother (Mitchell) has become chief of the Vikings. During
another war with the Vikings the queen is betrayed by one of
her power-hungry advisers (Checci), who takes over the throne.

Ardisson returns home to overthrow Checci, who is now being
guarded by the Vikings. Mitchell is killed by Checci, in
hopes of blaming Ardisson. However, the Vikings decide to
unite behind Ardisson and Checci is overthrown.

FREE, WHITE AND 21. 1963. 102 minutes. *Director:* Larry
    Buchanan. *Screenplay:* Larry Buchanan, Hal Dwain, and
    Cliff Pope. *Cinematography:* Ralph K. Johnson. *Cast:*
    Frederick O'Neal (Ernie Jones); Annalena Lund (Greta Mae
    Hansen); George Edgley (Judge); George Russell (Defense
    Attorney Tyler); John Hicks (Prosecuting Attorney Atkins);
    Hugh Crenshaw (Assistant Prosecuting Attorney); Miles
    Middough, James Altgens, Bill McGee, Jonathan Ledford,
    Ted Mitchell, Jack Dunlop (Witnesses).

Free, White and 21 exploits the racial tension existing
in the South of the early 60s by focusing on a case of attempted rape. It was directed by Larry Buchanan, who directed
a number of AIP's cut-rate films, which were distributed solely
to television.
    A black businessman (O'Neal) in Texas is on trial for the
attempted rape of a young Scandinavian woman (Lund), who came
to Texas as a Freedom Rider. Both parties describe the events.
The prosecution claims that Lund sought refuge in a hotel owned
by O'Neal. She had to leave the local YMCA because of her
association with blacks. O'Neal is supposed to have raped her
after offering her a job. His defense attorney (Russell) says
that Lund, as an adult, was fully aware of her relationship
with O'Neal. The judge (Edgley) makes the audience the jury,
and the jury finds for the defendant. In essence the film
has concluded that Lund is free, white, and 21.

GOLIATH AND THE SINS OF BABYLON. 1963. 80 minutes. Color.
    Director: Michele Lupo. *Screenplay:* Roberto Gianviti,
    Francesco Scardamaglia, and Lionello De Felice. *Cinema-
    tography:* Guglielmo Mancori and Mario Sbrenna. *Cast:*
    Mark Forest (Goliath); Eleanora Bianchi (Regia/Chelmia);
    José Greci (Xandros); Giuliano Gemma (Alceo); John Chevron
    (Evandro); Erno Crisa (Pergaso); Piero Lulli (Meneos);
    Arnaldo Fabrizio (Morakeb); with Mimmo Palmara, Livio
    Lorenzon, Jacques Herlin, Paul Müller.

A ruler (Crisa) of the city of Cafaus is victorious over
the neighboring city of Nefer and orders the vanquished to

provide him with 24 virgins. Goliath (Forest) frees one of
the virgins, and then joins with a group of men from the conquered city to rescue the remaining virgins. Forest takes
part in a chariot race, replacing Xandros (Greci), one of the
men from Nefer who had been injured by Crisa's men. Forest
is victorious and is ordered arrested, but he escapes and
joins the men from Nefer. Together they revolt and capture
Crisa's palace and depose him. Greci now becomes the new ruler, while Forest returns to his peaceful life in the country.

   Forest's role in this film is somewhat like the samurais
in *Seven Samurai* or Toshiro Mifune in *Yojimbo*. He intervenes
on the side of the underdog and then goes his own way--a sort
of "lone gun" concept.

THE HAUNTED PALACE. 1963. 85 minutes. Color. *Director:*
   Roger Corman. *Screenplay:* Charles Beaumont; based on the
   poem by Edgar Allan Poe and the story "The Case of Charles
   Dexter Ward," by H.P. Lovecraft. *Cinematography:* Floyd
   Crosby. *Cast:* Vincent Price (Charles Dexter Ward/Joseph
   Curwen); Debra Paget (Ann Ward); Lon Chaney, Jr. (Simon
   Orne); Frank Maxwell (Dr. Marinus Willet); Leo Gordon
   (Edgar Weeden); Elisha Cook (Peter Smith); John Dierkes
   (Jacob West); Milton Parsons (Jabez Hutchinson); Cathy
   Merchant (Hester Tillinghast); Guy Wilkerson (Leach);
   Harry Ellerbe (Minister); I. Stanford Jolley (Boat Cap-
   tain); Darlene Lucht (Young Woman Victim); Barbara Morris
   (Mrs. Weeden); Bruno Ve Sota (Bartender).

   While *The Haunted Palace* is supposed to take place in
New England, it has the feeling of a European village. Perhaps
it is those villagers running through claustrophobic studio-
created woods carrying torches, as they do in the old horror
films, that gives the film this European feeling.

   In about 1875 Charles Dexter Ward (Price) and his wife
(Paget) come to the New England village of Arkham to reopen
his family's palace, which he has inherited. Over a hundred
years before Price's ancestor Joseph Curwen had been burned
to death by the villagers for being a sorcerer. Before he
died, he put a curse on the town and the descendants of his
killers. Price and Paget find that the town has a high propor-
tion of mutated offspring as a result of Curwen's curse. Soon
Price begins to manifest his ancestor's behavior as Curwen's
spirit takes possession of him. He plans to sacrifice Paget
in the dungeon of the palace. The villagers attack the palace
again as they had a century before and set fire to the house
(why they did not burn the house down before is never

explained). In the process a portrait of Curwen is burned.
This frees Price from the spirit of Curwen, and he and Paget
are able to excape the burning house. The final closeup of
the film shows Price, who now possesses Curwen's physical coun-
tenance.

THE MIND BENDERS. 1963. 99 minutes. *Director:* Basil Deardon.
Screenplay: James Kennaway. *Cinematography:* Denys Coop.
Cast: Dirk Bogarde (Dr. Henry Longman); Mary Ure (Oonagh
Longman); John Clements (Major Hall); Michael Bryant (Dr.
Tate); Wendy Craig (Annabelle); Harold Goldblatt (Profes-
sor Sharpey); Geoffrey Keen (Calder); Terry Palmer
(Norman); Norman Bird (Aubrey); Roger Delgado (Dr. Jean
Bonvoulois); Edward Fox (Stewart); Terence Alexander
(Coach); Georgina Moon (Persephone); Teresa Van Hoorn
(Penny); Timothy Beaton (Paul); Christopher Ellis (Peers);
Edward Palmer (Porter); Elizabeth Counsell (Girl Student
on Station); Anthony Singleton (Student on Station);
Pauline Winter (Mother); Philip Ray (Father); Rene Setan
(1st Indian Student); Ashik Devello (2nd Indian Student);
Robin Hawdon (Student in Oxford); Terence Edmond (1st
Student at Party); Ian Dewar (Crowd Ringleader).

Unlike many of the films that AIP distributed, *The Mind
Benders* is a quality production with a fine cast, headed by
Dirk Bogarde. Aside from Ken Russell's *Altered States*, very
few films have dealt with the subject of experiments in sen-
sory deprivation.
A professor (Goldblatt) has committed suicide after becoming involved in sensory-deprivation experiments for a British space agency. A security officer on the project (Clements)
claims that Goldblatt was a traitor. An Oxford scientist and
friend of Goldblatt's (Bogarde) refuses to believe such a
charge. Thinking that his friend was brainwashed and in a
vulnerable state when he died, Bogarde agrees to undergo the
experiments to prove his point. He is immersed in a tank of
warm water and ends up in a state of emotional collapse.
Clements and an associate (Bryant) attempt to brainwash Bogarde
by subverting his love for his wife (Ure). The experiment
looks to be a failure, but suddenly Bogarde begins to act in
ways that cause a strain in his marriage. Concerned about his
behavior, Clements tries to reverse the damage done in the
brainwashing session. Bogarde comes back to his senses only
when the pregnant Ure falls and induces labor.

NIGHT TIDE. 1963. 84 minutes. *Director:* Curtis Harrington.
Screenplay: Curtis Harrington. *Cinematography:* Vilis
Lapenieks. *Cast:* Dennis Hopper (Johnny Drake); Linda
Lawson (Mora); Gavin Muir (Captain Murdock); Luana Anders
(Ellen Sands); Marjorie Eaton (Madame Romanovitch);
Cameron (Woman in Black); H.E. West (Lieutenant Hender-
son); Tom Dillon (Merry-Go-Round Owner); with Ben Roseman.

This strange oneiric film is rather an anomaly for AIP.
Night Tide was completed a few years before AIP picked up the
distribution rights. In 1961 it was screened at both the Venice and Spoleto Film Festivals. Even if it is not a totally
successful film, it is at least a very personal film, by Curtis
Harrington.

A lonely sailor on leave (Hopper) meets a young woman
(Lawson) who works as a "mermaid" at a Santa Monica boardwalk
concession. He is warned by the concession owner (Muir) and
another boardwalk worker (Anders) to stay away from Lawson because a couple of men had died after being seen with her. Un-
deterred, Hopper follows a woman (Cameron) dressed in black
to Muir's house. Muir tells him a fanciful story about how
Lawson is descended from the Sea People, who, under the spell
of the full moon, are compelled to kill people. When Hopper
and Lawson go skindiving, she disappears. He next sees her
body on display at Muir's concession stall. Muir eventually
admits that he cast a spell on Lawson making her believe she
was a mermaid, so she would not leave him.

Night Tide has some unusual fantasy elements. It also
mixes up the theme of *She Creature* and the werewolf legend,
since Lawson supposedly killed lonely men during a full moon.

OPERATION BIKINI. 1963. 84 minutes. Color Sequences. *Direc-
tor:* Anthony Carras. *Screenplay:* John Tomerlin. *Cinema-
tography:* Gil Warrenton. *Cast:* Tab Hunter (Lieutenant
Morgan Hayes); Frankie Avalon (Seaman Joseph Malzone);
Scott Brady (Captain Emmett Carey); Jim Backus (Bosun's
Mate Ed Fennelly); Gary Crosby (Seaman Floyd Givens);
Michael Dante (Lieutenant William Fourtney); Jody McCrea
(Seaman William Sherman); Eva Six (Reiko); Aki Aleong
(Seaman Ronald Davayao); David Landfield (Lieutenant
Cale); Richard Bakalyan (Seaman Hiller); Joe Finnegan
(Seaman Morris); Vernon Scott (Seaman Fowler); Raymond
Guth (Seaman Rich); Tony Scott (CPO Perez); Steve Mitchell
(Seaman Nolan); Mickey McDermott (Seaman Fairley); Wayne
Winton (Seaman Patterson); Duane Ament (Seaman Kingsley);
Jody Daniels (Seaman Jones); Marc Cavell (Paul); Raynum K.

Night Tide

Tsukamoto (Kawai); Lan Nam Tuttle (Mika); Alicia Li (3rd
Native Girl); Nancy Dusina (Dream Girl Back Home); Judy
Lewis (Dream Siren).

With a title like *Operation Bikini* and a cast that includes Frankie Avalon and Jody McCrea, one would think that
this might be another beach picture. It actually came out
months before *Beach Party* and in many ways is similar to the
AIP war films of the late 50s.
In the South Pacific during World War II an underwater
demolition team headed by Tab Hunter is taken aboard a submarine piloted by Scott Brady. The demolition team's mission
is to destroy a sunken American sub with valuable equipment
aboard, before the Japanese can get to it. Brady's submarine
lands near Bikini Island. With the help of the local native
guerrillas they are able to find the exact location of the
sub. Hunter becomes romantically involved with one of the female guerrillas (Six), but she is killed by the Japanese.
Hunter's team is successful in blowing up the American sub and
escape safely.

THE RAVEN. 1963. 86 minutes. Color. *Director:* Roger Corman.
Screenplay: Richard Matheson; based on the poem by Edgar
Allan Poe. *Cinematography:* Floyd Crosby. *Cast:* Vincent
Price (Dr. Erasmus Craven); Peter Lorre (Dr. Adolphus
Bedlo); Boris Karloff (Dr. Scarabus); Hazel Court (Lenore
Craven); Jack Nicholson (Rexford Bedlo); Connie Wallace
(Maid Servant); William Baskin (Grimes); Aaron Saxon
(Gort); Jim Jr. (The Raven).

As a respite from the morbid Poe stories he was filming
for AIP, Roger Corman directed this comedy, which is very
loosely based on Poe's "The Raven." Mainly because of the
amusing characterizations from the veteran cast, the film becomes a baroque rendering of Poe turned topsy-turvy.
Price is a 16th-century magician who retires after the
apparent death of his wife (Court). He is visited one night
by a talking raven, who really is a Dr. Bedlo (Lorre). He
has been turned into a bird by a sorcerer (Karloff), but Price,
through his own magic, changes Lorre back into human form.
Acting as one of Karloff's minions, he tells Price that his
wife is alive and is at Karloff's castle living as his mistress. Karloff's plan is to lure Price to his castle, where
he can learn his magical secrets and become the most powerful
magician in the world. At the castle Karloff turns Lorre back
into a raven. By now Price has become Karloff's prisoner,

but Lorre/Raven helps Price to escape. Now the magicians are
pitted in a duel of their powers as they fire lightning bolts
at one another. They bring the castle to ruins, as Price
emerges victorious. He now takes the raven home with him and
obviously is in no hurry to change it back into human form.

SAMSON AND THE SLAVE QUEEN. 1963. 86 minutes. Color. *Director:* Umberto Lenzi. *Screenplay:* Guido Malatesta and
   Umberto Lenzi. *Cinematography:* Augusto Tiezzi. *Cast:*
   Pierre Brice (Zorro/Ramón); Alan Steel (Samson); Moira
   Orfei (Malva); Maria Grazia Spina (Isabella); Andrea
   Aureli (Rabek); Massimo Serato (Garcia); with Aldo Bufi
   Landi, Andrea Scotti, Loris Gizzi, Rosy De Leo, Nazzareno
   Zamperla, Gaetano Scala, Attilio Dottesio.

   This strong boy Samson really got around. You could find
him in 13th-century China, or Russia, and, in *Samson and the
Slave Queen*, 15th-century Spain. The title is misleading since
nowhere in the film is there a slave queen.
   King Philip II has died, and the throne is contested between his two nieces, the evil Malva (Orfei) and the good
Isabella (Spina). Inside a treasure chest is hidden the name
of the King's successor. Orfei hires Samson (Steel) to bring
the chest to her because she is sure that the King's will would
name Spina. Meanwhile Spina has hired the masked swordsman
Zorro (Brice) to bring the chest to her, after being advised
by a poet (Brice), with whom she is in love. Both Steel and
Brice go through a number of strength tests to gain possession
of the royal treasure chest. Steel prevails, but he realizes
that Spina should really be the new queen. He and Brice now
team up to fight Orfei's guards. When Spina becomes queen,
she realizes that Zorro and her poet lover are the same man.

SUMMER HOLIDAY. 1963. 100 minutes. Color. *Director:* Peter
   Yates. *Screenplay:* Peter Myers and Ronald Cass. *Cine-
matography:* John Wilcox. *Cast:* Cliff Richard (Don); Lauri
   Peters (Barbara); Melvyn Hayes (Cyril); Una Stubbs
   (Sandy); Teddy Green (Steve); Pamela Hart (Angie); Jeremy
   Bulloch (Edwin); Jacqueline Daryl (Mimsie); Madge Ryan
   (Stella); Lionel Murton (Jerry); Christine Lawson (Annie);
   Ron Moody (Orlando); David Kossoff (Magistrate); Wendy
   Barry (Shepherdess/Dancer); Nicholas Phipps (Wrightmore);
   The Shadows (Themselves); with Lindsay Dolan, Richard
   Farley, Terry Gilbert, Ian Kaye, Vincent Logan, John

MacDonald, Paddy McIntyre, Leon Pomerantz, Ben Stevenson,
Anne Briley, Leander Fedden, Sarah Hardenberg, Derina
House, Eithne Milne, Sheila O'Neill, Joan Palethorpe
(Dancers).

Summer Holiday is of note solely because it was the directorial debut of Peter Yates (*Breaking Away*, *Bullitt*, *The Deep*,
etc.).   This particular film is sort of a British equivalent
of the beach-party films--lots of music and good clean fun.
     Four young London auto mechanics (Richard, Hayes, Green,
and Bulloch) want to start a European travel bus service.   They
obtain a double-decker bus, adjust it into a living facility,
and go to France.   Near Paris they get into a minor auto accident with a car carrying three young female singers (Stubbs,
Hart, and Daryl) on their way to Greece.   They join the young
men as they travel across Europe.   Along the way they meet a
runaway American singer (Peters).   Peter's mother (Ryan) and
her press agent (Murton) attempt to use the group of youngsters
for publicity purposes.   So as they go across Europe they are
involved in a number of newspaper headlines.   When they finally
reach Athens, they have become minor celebrities.   Richard and
Peters become engaged, and the boys are given enough buses by
a bus company to start their own business.

THE TERROR.   1963.   81 minutes.   Color.   *Director:* Roger
     Corman.   *Screenplay:* Leo Gordon and Jack Hill.   *Cinema-
     tography:* John Nicholaus.   *Cast:* Boris Karloff (Baron von
     Leppe); Jack Nicholson (Lieutenant André Duvalier); Sandra
     Knight (Helene); Richard Miller (Stefan); Dorothy Neuman
     (Old Woman); Jonathan Haze (Gustaf).

The Terror was supposedly filmed in just a matter of days
using the sets left over from *The Raven*.   Roger Corman had
future directors Francis Coppola and Monte Hellman aid him in
this effort, which has all the earmarks of a home movie.   Cast
with AIP regulars, the film has an air of improvisation that
revolves around a negligible plot.
     An officer in Napoleon's army (Nicholson, recognizable
even with a full head of hair) finds himself in a state of ex-
haustion somewhere on the Baltic coast.   He collapses and is
revived by a beautiful woman (Knight), who promptly walks into
the sea.   After passing out again, Nicholson finds himself in
the hut of an old woman (Neuman) and her jibbering fool of a
servant (Haze).   Haze tells him that Knight can be found at
the castle of Baron von Leppe (Karloff).   It turns out that
Knight is Karloff's long-dead wife.   Karloff orders Nicholson

to leave the castle, but he comes back on the advice of the now dying Haze. Karloff's servant (Miller) tells him that Karloff is Neuman's son, who has been impersonating the baron, after having killed him. He finds Knight again and takes her away with him. To end the psychedelic experience that this movie provides, Knight now turns into a decomposing corpse before Nicholson's eyes.

X--THE MAN WITH THE X-RAY EYES. 1963. 80 minutes. Color. *Director:* Roger Corman. *Screenplay:* Robert Dillon and Ray Russell; based on a story by Russell. *Cinematography:* Floyd Crosby. *Cast:* Ray Milland (Dr. James Xavier); Diana Van Der Vlis (Dr. Diane Fairfax); Harold J. Stone (Dr. Sam Brandt); John Hoyt (Dr. William Benson); Don Rickles (Crane); John Dierkes (Preacher); Lorie Summers (Party Dancer); Vicki Lee (Young Girl Patient); Kathryn Hart (Mrs. Mart); Carol Irey (Woman Patient).

The alcoholic troubles that plagued Ray Milland in *The Lost Weekend* are nothing compared with what he goes through in this film. Actually *X--The Man with the X-Ray Eyes* is one of the best films that Roger Corman directed for AIP.

Dr. Xavier (Milland) is told that funds for his experiments in eyesight will be cut unless he comes up with some quick results. He decides to use himself as a guinea pig by putting drops of his experimental fluid in his eyes. Soon he finds that he can see through paper and living tissue. Milland is dismissed from the hospital because of a medical disagreement. By now his eyes have become so sensitive to sunlight that he wears protective lead glasses in a vain attempt to ward off his continuous headaches. Milland accidentally kills another doctor, so he flees and joins a carnival, where he performs a mentalist act. Needing money in order to continue the experiments in the hopes of finding an antidote, he becomes a gambler in Las Vegas. By now he is nearly mad, because he is able to see beyond the stars and into the outer reaches of the universe. He comes upon a revival meeting, where under the preacher's (Dierkes) command, he gouges his eyes out.

THE YOUNG RACERS. 1963. 82 minutes. Color. *Director:* Roger Corman. *Screenplay:* R. Wright Campbell. *Cinematography:* Floyd Crosby. *Cast:* Mark Damon (Stephen Children); William Campbell (Joe Machin); Luana Anders (Henny); Robert Campbell (Robert Machin); Patrick Magee (Sir

William Dragonet); Bruce McLaren (Lotus Team Manager);
Milo Quesada (Italian Driver); Anthony Marsh (Announcer);
Marie Versini (Sesia Machin); Beatrice Altariba (Monique);
Margaret Robsahn (Lea); Christina Gregg (Daphne).

Filmed on the European Grand Prix circuit, *The Young Racers* has a number of similarities to *Road Racers*, the most ob-
vious being the main character, who changes from a contemptible
person to someone who possesses some noble traits.

Joe Machin (William Campbell) is a thoughtless and reck-
less Grand Prix race driver, who manages to become involved
in a number of adulterous affairs. A former racer turned
writer (Damon) witnesses Campbell putting the make on his girlfriend (Altariba). Damon decides to write a book that will
be a hatchet job on Campbell. Unaware of Damon's intentions,
Campbell invites him to tag along on the Grand Prix circuit.
When they return to England, Campbell learns of Damon's planned
book and intends to get even. They both participate in a race
at Aintree. Damon's car begins to spin, but Campbell decides
at the last minute not to injure Damon, as his car crashes
and he is injured. At the hospital Damon learns from Campbell's brother (Campbell) that his arrogance is just a coverup
for a sensitive personality. To wrap up this "buddy" movie
neatly, the two now become the best of friends.

ATRAGON. 1964. 90 minutes. Color. *Director:* Inoshiro Honda.
Screenplay: Shinichi Sekizawa. *Cinematography:* Hajime
Koizumi. *Cast:* Tadao Takashima (Commercial Photographer);
Yoko Fujiyama (Captain Shinguji's Daughter); Yu Fujiki
(Captain Shinguji); with Kenji Sawara, Akemi Kita,
Tetsuko Kobayashi, Akihiko Hirata, Hiroshi Koizumi, Jun
Tazaki, Ken Uehara.

Atrogan is a cut above most other Japanese science-
fiction films in that it is actually watchable. How can anyone
not fall for a plot that combines a sort of Japanese Atlantis
and a group of Japanese soldiers left over from World War II?

The ancient kingdom of Mu sank beneath the Pacific Ocean
when an earthquake hit the continent. The civilization, which
has all the trappings of ancient Egypt instead of Japan, has
been able to survive for 2,000 years by harnessing energy from
the Earth's core. With this power the people of the Mu empire
plan to conquer and enslave the world. The only hope for Earth
is a land/sea ship known as *Atragon*. It was designed by a
Japanese commander (Fujiki) who had deserted during World War
II. Living on a remote island with other Japanese soldiers,

Fujiki refuses to use *Atragon*. Only when his daughter
(Fujiyama) is kidnapped by the Mu people does he agree to use
Atragon to defend the world. Needless to say, his invention
destroys the entire Mu empire, including a giant sea creature.

BIKINI BEACH. 1964. 100 minutes. Color. *Director:* William
    Asher. *Screenplay:* William Asher, Leo Townsend, Robert
    Dillon. *Cinematography:* Floyd Crosby. *Cast:* Frankie
    Avalon (Frankie/The Potato Bug); Annette Funicello (Dee
    Dee); Keenan Wynn (Huntingdon Honeywagon); Martha Hyer
    (Vivien Clements); Harvey Lembeck (Eric Von Zipper); Don
    Rickles (Big Drag); John Ashley (Johnny); Jody McCrea
    (Deadhead); Candy Johnson (Candy); Danielle Aubry (Lady
    Bug); Meredith MacRae (Animal); Dolores Wells (Sniffles);
    Paul Smith, James Westerfield (Police Officers); Donna
    Loren (Donna); Little Stevie Wonder (Himself); The Pyra-
    mids (Themselves); The Exciters Band (Themselves); Janos
    Prohaska (Clyde, the Chimpanzee); Timothy Carey (South
    Dakota Slim); Val Warren (The Teenage Werewolf Monster);
    Boris Karloff (Art Dealer); with Renie Riano.

This second in the series of beach-party films combines
the usual surfing along with some drag racing. *Bikini Beach*
came out just about the time when The Beatles were becoming
popular. Frankie Avalon does an impression of a British rock
star, which might very well be the most embarrassing piece of
"business" in the entire beach-party series.
    A representative (Wynn) of the local Moral Majority is
attempting to get the gang off the beach, so he can build a
retirement community. When he tells the young people that
they have sunk to the animal level, you feel like getting on
your feet and cheering. Other problems arise for Frankie
Avalon when his girlfriend (Funicello) begins flirting with a
rock star called The Potato Bug. Meanwhile a motorcycle gang
headed by Eric Von Zipper (Lembeck) decide to join Wynn's campaign against the surfers, because of their intrinsic dislike
for one another. Through the influence of a teacher (Hyer)
Wynn changes his opinion of the young people. In the end, as
in *Beach Party*, the surfers and the cyclists have a comical (?)
battle royal, in which the cyclists are defeated.
    With some very close inspection you can usually find some
thing of interest in these beach-party films. What is remembered from *Bikini Beach* is Frankie's hairdo--he had an anchor-
man's hairdo before anchormen did--and Annette's hairdo, which
looks like it was constructed by the Bechtel Corporation.
Little Stevie Wonder appears toward the end of the film doing
an impression of Eddie Murphy.

Bikini Beach

BLACK SABBATH. 1964. 99 minutes. Color. *Director:* Mario
    Bava. *Screenplay:* Alberto Bevilacqua, Mario Bava, and
    Ugo Guerra; based on the stories "The Drop of Water," by
    Anton Chekov; "The Telephone," by F.G. Snyder; and "The
    Wurdalak," by Leo Tolstoy. *Cinematography:* Ubaldo
    Terzano. *Cast for "The Drop of Water":* Jacqueline
    Pierreux (Helen Corey); Milly Monti (Miss Perkins' Maid).
    Cast for "The Telephone": Michèle Mercier (Rosy); Lidia
    Alfonsi (Mary); with Gustavo De Nardo. *Cast for "The
    Wurdalak":* Boris Karloff (Gorca); Susy Andersen (Sdenka);
    Mark Damon (Vladimir D'Urfé); Glauco Onorato (Giorgio);
    Rika Dialina (Giorgio's Wife); Massimo Righi (Pietro).
    Master of Ceremonies: Boris Karloff.

In "The Drop of Water" a nurse (Pierreux) comes to the
home of a sick clairvoyant only to find that the woman has already died. She steals the woman's diamond ring off her finger. That same night at home Pierreux finds herself scared
by the sound of dripping water. The ghost of the clairvoyant
appears and orders Pierreux to strangle herself. The next
day her body is found with a bruise on the finger, as if a
ring had forceably been taken off.
    "The Telephone" concerns a prostitute (Mercier) who is
receiving menacing phone calls from a man she had cheated and
who is supposedly dead. She asks a friend (Alfonsi) to stay
with her. The telephone caller enters their house and kills
Alfonsi by mistake. Mercier then stabs him, but the telephone
rings again with his warning to her.
    "The Wurdalak" is a vampire who yearns for the blood of
loved ones. A young traveler (Damon) spends the night with a
family whose father (Karloff) is a wurdalak. He begins killing
his relatives, but Damon and Karloff's daughter (Andersen),
who have fallen in love, escape and hide in a convent. Karloff
tracks them down and turns Andersen into a fellow wurdalak.
Damon is unaware of her condition and kisses her. She in turn
kills him, and he also becomes a wurdalak.

COMMANDO. 1964. 98 minutes. *Director:* Frank Wisbar. *Screen-
    play:* Giuseppe Mangione, Mino Guerrini, William Demby,
    Milton Krims, Frank Wisbar, and Eric Bercovici; based on
    a story by Arturo Tofanelli. *Cinematography:* Cecilio
    Paniagua. *Cast:* Stewart Granger (Captain Le Blanc);
    Dorian Gray (Nora); Maurizio Arena (Dolce Vita); Ivo
    Garrani (Colonel Dionne); Fausto Tozzi (Brascia); Riccardo
    Garrone (Paolo); Carlos Cesarvilla (Ben Bled); Peter
    Casten (Barbarossa); Hans von Borsody (Fritz); Rafael

Luis Calvo (Kappa-Kappa); Dietmar Schönherr (Petit
Prince); Leo Anchóriz (Garcia); with Alfredo Mayo,
Guillermo Carmona, Pablito Alonso, Jaime de Pedro,
Francisco Cornet.

Commando, a film about the Algerian war, is written by a
virtual committee, which reflects the international nature of
this Belgian/Italian/Spanish/West German co-production. Those
interested in the Algerian war from a different perspective
should see *The Battle of Algiers*.
Captain Le Blanc of the Foreign Legion (Granger) is ordered to capture an Algerian resistance leader (Cesarvilla).
He and his legionnaires capture him but in the process they
become stranded in guerrilla territory. Most of Granger's
men realize that the cause they are fighting for (a continuation of French rule in Algeria) is lost. After some bitter
fighting Granger and his surviving men take Casarvilla to the
authorities. It turns out that, because of a change in the
political situation, Casarvilla is now considered an important
figure in bringing about a peace treaty. The embittered and
disillusioned Granger considers murdering Casarvilla, but he
changes his mind.

THE DAY THE EARTH FROZE. 1964. 67 minutes. Color. *Director:*
Aleksandr Ptushko (Russian-Finnish version). Gregg
Sebelious (U.S. version). *Screenplay:* Viktor Vitkovich
and Grigoriy Yagdfeld; based on the Finnish oral-poetry
cycle "Kalevala," compiled by Elias Lönnrot. *Cinematog-
raphy:* G. Tsekaviy and V. Yakushev. *Cast* (U.S. version):
Nina Anderson (Anniky); Jon Powers (Lemminkainen); Ingrid
Elhardt (Loukhy the Witch); Peter Sorenson (Ilmarinen);
Marvin Miller (Narrator).

The title of this film makes it sound like a science fiction film, when in fact *The Day the Earth Froze* is based on a
Finnish folk fantasy. This is a Russian/Finnish co-production
that originally came out in 1959 under the title *Sampo*, in a
version about 30 minutes longer than the American release
version.
This fanciful tale deals with the struggle for possession
of the "sampo," a mill that not only produces grain, but gold
as well. Only a young blacksmith (Sorenson) from Kalevala
has the magic power to forge the sampo. A wicked witch
(Elhardt) wants the sampo for herself, so she kidnaps Sorenson's sister (Anderson). He and her lover (Powers) attempt
to rescue her. They are successful, but they destroy the sampo

before Elhardt can possess it. The revengeful witch now seizes
the sun, which causes the land to be covered with ice. Her
army and the Kalevalans do battle, and in the end the witch
is turned to stone. The sun comes back out and everyone else
celebrates.

DIARY OF A BACHELOR. 1964. 89 minutes. *Director:* Sandy
    Howard. *Screenplay:* Ken Barnett. *Cinematography:* Julian
    Townsend. *Cast:* William Traylor (Skip O'Hara); Dagne
    Crane (Joanne); Joe Silver (Charlie Barrett); Denise Lor
    (Jane Woods); Susan Dean (Barbara); Eleni Kiamos (Angie
    Pisano); Jan Crockett (Jennifer Watters); Arlene Golonka
    (Louise); Joan Holloway (Nancy Feather); Mickey Deems
    (Barney Washburn); Dom De Luise (Marvin Rollins); Jackie
    Kannon (Bob Haney); Leora Thatcher (Mother O'Hara);
    Bradley Bolke (Bugsy); Jim Alexander (Harley Peterson);
    Joey Faye (Bartender); Beatrice Pons (Thelma); Joy
    Claussen (Susan); Chris Noel (Carol); Saliha Tekneci
    (Belly Dancer); Bonnie Jones (Wanda Smith); Joanne
    MacCormack (Cynthia Brooks); Ellen Nevdal (Victoria
    Ampolski); Paula Stewart (Carlotta Jones); with Greta
    Randall, Carolyn Lasater, Darlene Enlow, Nai Bonet, Len
    Hammer, Larry Navarro.

This hapless comedy filmed in New York City incorporates
the Playboy lifestyle in a tale about promiscuity. It attempts
to use levity in a story whose moral is "What's sauce for the
goose is sauce for the gander."
    A bachelor (Traylor) decides to give up the single life
and marry one of his numerous girlfriends (Crane). Alone in
his apartment, Crane finds Traylor's "little black book" and
realizes that he has been seeing many other women while courting her. She then encounters another woman (Holloway) making
herself at home in his apartment. Crane leaves him, and
Traylor eventually marries Holloway. After a year's time he
has become domesticated, but Holloway, an airline stewardess,
is still seeing her other boyfriends in her travels.

EVIL EYE. 1964. 92 minutes. *Director:* Mario Bava. *Screen-*
    play: Ennio De Concini, Eliana De Sabata, Franco Prosperi,
    Enzio Corbucci, Mino Guerrini, and Mario Bava. *Cinema-*
    tography: Mario Bava. *Cast:* Leticia Roman (Nora
    Dralston); John Saxon (Dr. Marcello Bassi); Valentina
    Cortese (Laura Terrani); Dante Di Paolo (Landini); Robert

Buchanan (Dr. Alessi); Gianni Di Benedetto (Professor
Terrani); with Jim Dolen, Virginia Doro, Chana Coubert,
Peggy Nathan, Marta Melecco, Lucia Modugno, Franco Morigi,
John Stacy, Milo Quesada, Tiberio Murgia, Titti Tomaino,
Pini Lido, Dafydd Havard.

Mario Bava, who had previously made some successful horror
films, e.g., *Black Sunday*, decided on a change of pace in *Evil
Eye*. This is not a bad mystery melodrama, with some nice plot
twists.
　　A secretary (Roman) from the United States is visiting
her sick aunt in Rome. On the way to get a doctor for her
Roman is attacked and becomes unconscious. As she is awakening, she witnesses what appears to be a man killing a woman.
After a stay in the hospital she returns with a doctor (Saxon)
to the house of her now-deceased aunt. The house is now inhabited by a friend (Cortese) of her aunt and her doctor husband (Di Benedetto). Unsolved murders have occurred in the
near vicinity, and Roman believes Di Benedetto may be the murderer, since she has found newspaper headlines about the murders in his possession. She later finds him seriously stabbed.
Cortese is the killer; she had forced Di Benedetto to dispose
of the bodies. Before Cortese can kill Roman, the dying Di
Benedetto kills his wife.

GODZILLA VS. THE THING. 1964. 90 minutes. Color. *Director:*
　　Inoshiro Honda. *Screenplay:* Shinichi Sekizawa. *Cinema-
　　tography:* Hajime Koizumi. *Cast:* Akira Takarada (Ichiro
　　Sakai); Yuriko Hoshi (Junko Nakanishi); Hiroshi Koizumi
　　(Professor Miura); Yu Fujiki (Jiro Nakamura); Emi and
　　Umi Ito (The Guardians); Yoshifumi Tajima (Kumayama);
　　Kenji Sahara (Banzo Torahata); Jun Tazaki (Newspaper Edi-
　　tor); Ikio Sawamura (Priest); Kenzo Tadake (Mayor); Susume
　　Fujita (Public Relations Officer); Yutaka Sada (Old Man);
　　Yoshio Kosugi (Old Man in the Village); Yutaka Nakayama,
　　Hiroshi Iwamoto, Koji Uno (Fishermen); Yasuhisa Tsutsumi
　　(Longshoreman); Ren Yamamoto (Sailor); Haruo Nakajima
　　(Godzilla).

This is another in a series of monster and science-fiction
films from the prolific director Inoshiro Honda. As always,
Godzilla vs. the Thing should be viewed for its special effects
(such as they are) instead of for any of the acting. This is
especially true here, as we are subjected to those two unbear-
ably saccharine twins left over from *Mothra*.
　　The story concerns the battle between Mothra and Godzilla.

A gigantic egg has appeared on Japan's shore. Two diminutive twin girls (The Itos) come on the wings of Mothra from a radio-active island to take the egg away. Greedy local businessmen intend to use the egg as a tourist attraction (an example of Japanese postwar economic revival). Godzilla appears and be-gins to stomp out Tokyo. Mothra is used to combat it, but Godzilla dispatches the giant moth with no problem. The large egg hatches, and two large caterpillars emerge, who wrap a cocoon around Godzilla. Unable to move freely, the monster topples from a cliff to its death.

GOLIATH AND THE VAMPIRES. 1964. 91 minutes. Color. *Direc-tor:* Giacomo Gentilomo and Sergio Corbucci. *Screenplay:* Sergio Corbucci and Duccio Tessari. *Cinematography:* Alvaro Mancori. *Cast:* Gordon Scott (Goliath); Gianna Maria Canale (Astra); Leonora Ruffo (Julia); Annabella Incontrera (Magda); Rocco Vitolazzi (Ciro); Jacques Sernas (Buono); Mario Feliciani (Omar); Van Aikens (Amahil); Guido Celano (Kobrak); with Edy Vessel, Emma Baron, Renato Terra.

This is one of the few attempts to mix a horror film with a strongman costume epic. It stars Gordon Scott, who also portrayed Tarzan in films.
Goliath finds that everyone in his village has been killed, except for the young women. A group of bandits have taken the women to become slaves. Aided by a chemist (Sernas), Scott finds the women and frees them. Sernas learns that the bandit leader is actually a vampire, who turns men into willing robots. While searching for his fiancée (Ruffo), Scott is im-prisoned by an Amazon compatriot (Canale) of the vampire. He is freed with the help of Sernas. Meanwhile Sernas has learned a way to bring the robots back to their normal state. The vampire assumes Scott's identity and plans to kill Sernas and Ruffo. Scott comes to their rescue, slays the vampire, and returns home with Ruffo.

THE LAST MAN ON EARTH. 1964. 86 minutes. *Director:* Sidney Salkow (U.S. version); Ubaldo Ragona (Italian version). *Screenplay:* Logan Swanson and William Leicester; based on the novel *I Am Legend*, by Richard Matheson. *Cinema-tography:* Franco Delli Colli. *Cast:* Vincent Price (Robert Morgan); Franca Bettoja (Ruth); Emma Danieli (Virginia); Giacomo Rossi Stuart (Ben Cortman); with

Umberto Rau, Christi Courtland, Antonio Corevi, Ettore Ribotta.

Richard Matheson, who wrote a number of the screenplays for the AIP Poe cycle, is in his own right a famous writer of horror and science fiction. *The Last Man on Earth*, an Italian and American co-production, takes as its subject the novel Matheson wrote back in 1954. It is basically a science fiction story, but the intrusion of vampirism brings the horror element into play.

A mysterious plague has struck the Earth, with the survivors having turned into vampires. A scientist (Price) is immune to the plague because of a fever he had once contracted. Price clears away dead bodies during the day, and seeks out the vampires so he may kill them with a stake through the heart. During the night he fends off the vampires with the usual accouterments, e.g., garlic and mirrors. He meets a woman (Bettoja), who, while a vampire, is a member of a group that possesses a serum that makes them temporarily immune. Price administers a transfusion to her with his own blood to make her normal. However, the other members of her group refuse to heed Price's offer of salvation through him, and they kill him.

THE MASQUE OF THE RED DEATH. 1964. 90 minutes. Color. *Director:* Roger Corman. *Screenplay:* Charles Beaumont and R. Wright Campbell; based on the stories "The Masque of the Red Death" and "Hop-Frog," by Edgar Allan Poe. *Cinematography:* Nicolas Roeg. *Cast:* Vincent Price (Prince Prospero); Hazel Court (Juliana); Jane Asher (Francesca); David Weston (Gino); Patrick Magee (Alfredo); Nigel Green (Ludovico); Skip Martin (Hop Toad); John Westbrook (Man in Red-Death); Gaye Brown (Senora Escobar); Julian Burton (Senor Veronese); Doreen Dawn (Anna-Marie); Paul Whitsun-Jones (Scarlatti); Jean Lodge (Scarlatti's Wife); Verina Greenlaw (Esmeralda); Brian Hewlett (Lampredi); Harvey Hall (Clistor); Robert Brown (Guard); with David Davies, Sarah Brackett.

The Masque of the Red Death is often considered to be Roger Corman's best film. With its bold use of color and its stylized sets (borrowed from *Becket*), this British made film is certainly the best looking of the AIP Poe films.

In medieval Italy a nobleman and follower of Satan (Price) orders a plague-ridden village burned to the ground. He takes a woman (Asher) and two men (Weston and Green) from the village

as prisoners for questioning his authority. At his castle,
which is the scene of a number of debauched parties, Price decides to instruct Asher in the ways of the Prince of Darkness.
His mistress (Court) becomes jealous of the attention he is
giving Asher, so she helps her and the two men escape from the
castle. Price intercedes and spoils their escape attempt.
He has Weston and Green perform a test of will with a poisoned
knife as part of the entertainment at his masked ball. Green
dies and Weston is banished from the castle. In the forest
Weston meets a red-hooded figure, Death (Westbrook), who tells
him to go back to the castle to rescue Asher. Death arrives
at the party, and Price believes it is Satan dressed for the
party in costume. Westbrook contaminates all the revelers
with the Red Death, as Weston and Asher are allowed to escape.

MUSCLE BEACH PARTY. 1964. 94 minutes. Color. *Director:*
    William Asher. *Screenplay:* Robert Dillon; based on a
    story by Dillon and William Asher. *Cinematography:* Harold
    Wellman. *Cast:* Frankie Avalon (Frankie); Annette
    Funicello (Dee Dee); Luciana Paluzzi (Julie); John Ashley
    (Johnny); Don Rickles (Jack Fanny); Peter Turgeon (Theo-
    dore); Jody McCrea (Deadhead); Dick Dale (Dick); Candy
    Johnson (Candy); Little Stevie Wonder (Himself); Morey
    Amsterdam (Cappy); Buddy Hackett (S.Z. Matts); Peter
    Lupus, Jr. (Flex Martin); Dolores Wells (Sniffles); Donna
    Loren (Donna); Valora Noland (Animal); Alberta Nelson
    (Lisa); Amedee Chabot (Floe); Larry Scott (Biff); Bob
    Seven (Rock); Steve Merjanian (Tug); Don Haggerty (Riff);
    Chester Yorton (Sulk); Gene Shuey (Mash); Gordon Cohn
    (Clod); Luree Holmes, Laura Nicholson, Lorie Summers,
    Darlene Lucht (Beach Girls); Duane Ament, Gary Usher,
    Roger Christian, Guy Hemric (Beach Boys); Mary Hughes,
    Kathy Kessler, Salli Sachse, Linda Opie, Linda Benson,
    Patricia Rane (Surfer Girls); Butch Van Artsdalen, Mike
    Diffenderfer, Bill Graham, Charles Hasley, Larry Shaw,
    Duane King, Mike Nader, Ed Garner, John Fain, Mickey Dora
    (Surfer Boys); Peter Lorre (Mr. Strangdour); with The
    Del Tones.

    Muscle Beach Party contains a reversal of sex roles, of
sorts. Here it is the male who becomes a sex object, something
to be prized and coveted. As usual the musical interludes
are a joke (as they even were in 1964).
    The group of surfers headed by Avalon and Funicello become
upset when some musclemen from Jack Fanny's (Rickles) gym take
over part of the beach for exercising. Meanwhile, a wealthy

Italian contessa (Paluzzi) living on her yacht offshore has
her eye on one of the musclemen (Lupus). She checks him out
as if he were a slab of meat and is determined to have him as
another one of her kept men. Paluzzi, however, quickly tires
of all that brawn and becomes attracted to Avalon. She promises to make him a recording star, which appeals to him. His
friends reject him for "selling out," and not wanting to spend
the next 40 years in the sun, sand, and surf. Avalon learns
of Paluzzi's other temporary affairs from her business manager
(Hackett), so he leaves her and goes back to Funicello. The
finale contains an all out brawl between the surfers and the
body builders.

NAVAJO RUN. 1964. 63 minutes. *Director:* Johnny Seven.
   Screenplay: Jo Heims. *Cinematography:* Gregory Sandor.
   Cast: Johnny Seven (Mathew Whitehawk); Warren Kemmerling
   (Luke Grog); Virginia Vincent (Sarah Grog); Ron Soble
   (Jesse Grog).

   This western drama contains elements very similar to those
found in such films as *The Naked Prey* and *The Most Dangerous
Game.*
   A young Navajo half-breed (Seven) is bitten by a snake
and seeks out aid at a ranch run by a husband and wife
(Kemmerling and Vincent). Vincent discourages Seven from staying, but her husband tells her to nurse him back to health.
Seven becomes friends with Kemmerling's mute brother (Soble)
and later learns that Kemmerling's friendship is only a ruse.
He invites Seven to go hunting with him. Kemmerling then
leaves him in the wilderness without any food and begins to
hunt him down like an animal. He apparently has killed a number of other Indians this way. Seven is finally trapped by
Kemmerling, but he captures a rattlesnake and uses it to kill
him.

PAJAMA PARTY. 1964. 85 minutes. Color. *Director:* Don Weis.
   Screenplay: Louis M. Heyward. *Cinematography:* Floyd
   Crosby. *Cast:* Tommy Kirk (Go-Go); Annette Funicello
   (Connie); Elsa Lanchester (Aunt Wendy); Harvey Lembeck
   (Eric Von Zipper); Jesse White (J. Sinister Hulk); Jody
   McCrea (Big Lunk); Ben Lessy (Fleegle); Donna Loren
   (Vikki); Susan Hart (Jilda); Bobbi Shaw (Helga); Cheryl
   Sweeten (Francine); Luree Holmes (Perfume Girl); Candy
   Johnson (Candy); Buster Keaton (Chief Rotten Eagle);
   Dorothy Lamour (Head Saleslady); Andy Romano, Linda

Rogers, Alan Fife, Alberta Nelson, Jerry Brutsche, Bob
Harvey (The Rat Pack); Renie Riano (Maid); Joi Holmes
(Topless Bathing Suit Model); Kerry Kolmar (Little Boy);
Joan Neel, Patricia O'Reilly, Marion Kildany, Linda Opie,
Mary Hughes, Patti Chandler, Laura Nicholson, Linda
Benson, Carey Foster, Stacey Maxwell, Teri Hope, Margo
Mehling, Diane Bond, Keva Page, Toni Basil, Kay Sutton,
Connie Ducharme, Joyce Nizzari, Leslie Wenner (The Pajama
Girls); Ray Atkinson, Frank Alesia, Ned Wynn, Ronnie
Rondell, Howard Curtis, John Fain, Mike Nader, Rick
Newton, Guy Hemric, Ed Garner, Frank Montiforte, Ronnie
David, Gus Trikonis, Bob Pane, Roger Bacon, Ronnie Dayton,
(The Pajama Boys); The Nooney Rickett Four (Themselves).

Pajama Party might very well be the worst of the beach-
party-type films. It is unbearable enough to watch Buster
Keaton in these farces, but this picture even includes Dorothy
Lamour. There are also about seven musical numbers in the
film, and the guest artists are the mercifully forgotten Nooney
Rickett Four.
   A Martian emissary (Kirk) is sent to Earth to prepare
for an invasion. He lands on the property of an eccentric
woman (Lanchester). He meets her numbskull nephew (McCrea)
and his girlfriend (Funicello), to whom he is attracted. Trouble arises from two crooks (White and Lessy) who plan to steal
Lanchester's money and from the head of a motorcycle gang
(Lembeck), who is also attracted to Funicello. Lanchester
gives a pajama party for the teenagers, which is intruded upon
by White and Lessy. Kirk, with his Martian powers, effectively
deals with the crooks, as well as with Lembeck and his gang.
He now decides to stay on Earth and is able to convince his
fellow Martians not to attack.

PYRO. 1964. 99 minutes. Color. *Director:* Julio Coll.
   Screenplay: Luis de los Arcos and Sidney W. Pink; based
   on a story by Pink. *Cinematography:* Manuel Berenguer.
   Cast: Barry Sullivan (Vance Pierson); Martha Hyer (Laura
   Blanco); Sherry Moreland (Verna Pierson); Soleded Miranda
   (Liz Frade); Luis Prendes (Police Inspector); Fernando
   Hilbeck (Julio); Carlos Cesarvilla (Frade); Marisenka
   (Isabella Blanco); with Hugo Pimentel, Francisco Moran.

Filmed in Spain, *Pyro* stars Barry Sullivan, one of the
finest of "B" actors, who gives a fine performance here. In-
explicably, *Pyro* was paired on a double bill with *Goliath and
the Vampires*.

An engineer (Sullivan) moves to Spain to supervise the construction of a generator. He and his family move into a house owned by pyromaniac Martha Hyer. Sullivan becomes involved in an affair with her, which he breaks off. The revengeful Hyer sets fire to his house, killing his wife and daughter. Sullivan, who has been badly disfigured in the fire, escapes from the hospital and plans vengeance on Hyer and her family. He constructs a lifelike mask for his face and travels with a carnival while he looks for her. He sets a fire that kills some of Hyer's relatives. Then he finally comes upon her and burns her to death as well. Sullivan kidnaps Hyer's daughter and takes her back to the carnival, where he plans to throw her off a ferris wheel. Instead he spares the child and jumps to his death.

SOME PEOPLE. 1964. 93 minutes. Color. *Director:* Clive
    Donner. *Screenplay:* John Eldridge. *Cinematography:* John
    Wilcox. *Cast:* Kenneth More (Mr. Smith); Ray Brooks
    (Johnnie); Annika Wills (Anne); David Andrews (Bill);
    Angela Douglas (Terry); David Hemmings (Bert); Timothy
    Nightingale (Tim); Frankie Dymon, Jr. (Jimmy); Harry H.
    Corbett (Johnnie's Father); Fanny Carby (Johnnie's Moth-
    er); Michael Gwynn (Vicar); Cyril Luckham (Magistrate);
    Fred Ferris (Clerk of the Court); Richard David (Harper);
    Dean Webb (Mike).

Filmed in 1962, *Some People* is not much more than a fla-
grant piece of propaganda for the Duke of Edinburgh's Award
Scheme for young people. Even the profits from the film went
to the project. Its simpleminded and superficial attitude
toward teenagers was fully in keeping with the teen image AIP
was marketing in the early and mid 60s.
    In Bristol three young working-class youths (Brooks,
Andrews, and Hemmings) lose their driving licenses after a
motorcycle accident. When they are thrown out of a local teen
center, they go into a church and play rock on the church organ. The choirmaster (More), who is also the local head of
the Award Scheme, is impressed with their musical abilities,
and offers to let them practice in the church. Brooks soon
begins to date More's daughter (Wills). Meanwhile Andrews,
who does not trust More's altruism, leads a gang assault on
the church social hall. Brooks now feels that he will be ostracized from his new friends because of the activities of
Andrews. More finally persuades him to return to the church
so he may guide himself on the straight and narrow path of
life.

THE T.A.M.I. SHOW. 1964. 113 minutes. *Director:* Steve
   Binder. *Cinematography:* Jim Kilgore. *Featuring:* The
   Beach Boys, Chuck Berry, Marvin Gaye, Lesley Gore, The
   Rolling Stones, The Barbarians, James Brown and the
   Flames, Gerry and the Pacemakers, Jan and Dean, The Su-
   premes, Billy J. Kramer and the Dakotas, Smokey Robinson
   and the Miracles.

   The T.A.M.I. Show is one of the first, and best, of the
rock revue films. It was filmed at the Santa Monica Civic
Auditorium on October 29, 1964. This Teenage Awards Music
International Show is a must-see for anyone interested in 60s
rock and roll. Let's face it, any musical show that can incorporate Lesley Gore and James Brown on the same stage is of
more than casual interest.
   Included here are artists representing some of the then-
current trends in rock: the Southern California sound of Jan
and Dean and The Beach Boys; the Motown sound of Marvin Gaye,
The Supremes, and Smokey Robinson; and the British "invasion,"
with The Rolling Stones and Gerry and the Pacemakers. Some of
the songs performed are "Time Is on My Side" (The Rolling
Stones); "Johnny B. Goode" (Chuck Berry); "I Get Around" (The
Beach Boys); "Hitchhike" (Marvin Gaye); "It's My Party" (Lesley
Gore); and "Baby Love" (The Supremes).

THE TIME TRAVELERS. 1964. 83 minutes. Color. *Director:* Ib
   Melchior. *Screenplay:* Ib Melchior and David L. Hewitt.
   Cinematography: William (Vilmos) Zsigmond. *Cast:* Preston
   Foster (Dr. Eric von Steiner); Philip Carey (Steve
   Connors); Merry Anders (Carol White); John Hoyt (Varno);
   Dennis Patrick (Councilman Willard); Joan Woodbury
   (Gadra); Dolores Wells (Reena); Steve Franken (Danny
   McKee); Gloria Leslie (Councilwoman); Peter Strudwick
   (Deviant); Margaret Selden, Forrest J. Ackerman (Tech-
   nicians).

   A group of university scientists (Foster, Carey, and
Anders) are in the process of constructing a time portal
through which they may view the past and the future. A laboratory accident causes them to be transported to the year 2071.
They land on a desolate area of Earth after a nuclear war has
devastated almost everything. The group is chased into a cave
by genetic mutants, who had once been human beings. In the
cave they come across a race of androids (half-human/half-
robot). The androids have spent many years constructing a
spaceship that will take them to a new planet. The scientists

meanwhile attempt to fix their damaged time portal so they
may return to the past. They succeed, but they must take some
of the androids with them when their spaceship is destroyed
by the mutants. Inside the time portal the group ends up going
too far back in time. Carey's readjustment to the portal sets
them too far in the future. They now all find themselves
trapped in an endless time warp.

    The Time Travelers is marred by its obvious comparison to
the superior *The Time Machine* and by some bad acting. For one
of the actors, Philip Carey, the high point of his career came
in his starring in the Granny Goose potato chips television
commercial on the West Coast.

TORPEDO BAY. 1964. 95 minutes. *Directors:* Charles Frend and
    Bruno Vailati. *Screenplay:* Charles Frend, Pino Belli,
    Alberto Ca' Zorzi, Augusto Frassineti, and Bruno Vailati.
    Cinematography: Gabor Pogany. *Cast:* James Mason (Captain
    Blayne); Lilli Palmer (Lygia da Silva); Gabriele Ferzetti
    (Leonardi); Geoffrey Keen (Officer Hodges); Alberto Lupo
    (Magri); Renato De Carmine (Ghedini); Valeria Fabrizi
    (Susanne); Daniele Vargas (Brauzzi); Andrew Keir
    (O'Brien); Andrea Checchi (Micheluzzi); with Gabriele
    Tinti, Jeremy Burnham, Davide Montemuri, Gaia Germani,
    Mimmo Poli, Paul Müller, Luigi Visconti, Aldo Pini.

    Torpedo Bay is not unusual because it is a war film that
stresses brotherhood among men, even when they are at war
against one another. What it does show is something that American audiences do not see much of, namely a heroic Italian
military effort. In most non-Italian films, the Italian military was often portrayed as an ally that no one wanted on their
side.

    During World War II a damaged Italian submarine attempts
to cross the Straits of Gibralter. A British ship, commanded
by James Mason, waits to destroy the sub. Both ships find
themselves in the vicinity of Tangiers, in international waters, and must go into port. The British still have orders to
destroy the sub if it leaves port. While in Tangiers Mason
and the Italian commander (Ferzetti), and their men, learn a
newfound respect for one another. Eventually the time comes
when the Italians must leave port. Both sides, with great
hesitation, face off against one another, and the Italians are
victorious.

UNDER AGE. 1964. 90 minutes. *Director:* Larry Buchanan.
Screenplay: Larry Buchanan and Harold Hoffman. *Cinematography:* Henry Kokojan. *Cast:* Anne MacAdams (Ruby
Jenkins); Judy Adler (Linda Jenkins); Roland Royter
(George Gomez); George Russell (Defense Attorney Tyler);
John Hicks (Prosecuting Attorney Adkins); George Edgley
(The Judge); Tommie Russell (Mrs. Sybel Riley); Regina
Cassidy (Dr. Vivian Scott); Joseph Patrick Cranshaw (W.J.
Earnhardt, Justice of the Peace); Raymond Bradford (Wilbur
Neal); Jonathan Ledford (Barney Jenkins); Howard Ware
(Bailiff); Joretta Cherry (Court Reporter); Robert Alcott
(Assistant District Attorney); William Peck (News Photographer); Barnett Shaw (News Reporter).

Filmed in Dallas, *Under Age* is a companion piece to director Larry Buchanan's *Free, White and 21*. Again it uses sexual
permissiveness of the social, or illegal, sort as its central
theme.
A mother (MacAdams) is standing trial for the rape of her
14-year-old daughter (Adler). MacAdams had sanctioned Adler's
sexual relations with a 16-year-old boy (Royter) by giving
her a contraceptive and allowing them to use one of her bedrooms for sex. Adler attempts to break off with Royter, but
MacAdams claims that they are married according to God's law.
Adler runs away to her aunt (Tommie Russell), and what started
as a family argument ends up as a court case. MacAdams is on
trial for encouraging Adler and Royter to engage in an unlawful act. After a parade of witnesses the jury goes into deliberation as the film ends.

THE UNEARTHLY STRANGER. 1964. 68 minutes. *Director:* John
    Krish. *Screenplay:* Rex Carlton. *Cinematography:* Reginald
    Wyer. *Cast:* John Neville (Dr. Mark Davidson); Gabriella
    Licudi (Julie Davidson); Philip Stone (Professor John
    Lancaster); Patrick Newell (Major Clarke); Jean Marsh
    (Miss Ballard); Warren Mitchell (Dr. Munro).

A British scientist (Mitchell), who has been working on
experiments that would allow men to move through outer space
by teleportation, is found dead. Apparently scientists in
other countries, working on the same experiments, have died
the same way. Another scientist (Neville) replaces Mitchell
on the project. The security officer of the project (Newell)

learns that Neville's wife (Licudi) is an alien who cannot
blink her eyes and has no pulse. She has been sent from her
planet to kill Neville but could not because she loves him.
Licudi is killed by her fellow aliens since she failed in her
mission. Neville's life is threatened by another alien at
the research center (Marsh), posing as a secretary. At the
end both Neville and another scientist (Stone), find themselves
surrounded by a group of the alien women.

   The Unearthly Stranger is sort of a science-fiction love
story. The meeting and marrying of Neville and Licudi is
sketched out as a love story. When he learns that she sleeps
with her eyes open, the film moves into the science-fiction
realm. Actually Licudi, the impassive alien, shows more emotion than the pod people in *Invasion of the Body Snatchers*.

VOYAGE TO THE END OF THE UNIVERSE. 1964. 81 minutes. *Direc-
    tor:* Jack Pollack (Jindřich Polák). *Screenplay:* Jack
    Pollack and Pavel Juráček. *Cinematography:* Jan Kalis.
    Cast: Dennis Stephans (Expedition Commander Vladimir
    Abajev); Francis Smolen (Astronomer Anthony Hopkins);
    Dana Meredith (Nina Kirova); Irene Kova (Brigit); Rodney
    Lucas (MacDonald); Otto Lack (Michael); Myron March
    (Marcel Bernard); Joseph Adams (Zdenek Lorenc); Rudolph
    Dial (Ervin Herold); John Rose (Doctor); Martin Tapin
    (Peter Kubes); Jerry Tullis (Erik Svensson); John Mares
    (Milek Wertbowsky); Marcella Martin (Stefa); Svatava
    Hubeňáková (MacDonald's Wife); with Renza Nova, Jan
    Morris, Joe Irwin, Ludek Munzar, Emilie Vasayova.

   This oddity, a Czech science-fiction film, was originally
released under the title *Ikarie XB1*. The actors' names have
all been anglicized from the Czech.

   In the 25th century a spaceship called *Icarus* is transporting its crew to distant planets. In their travels the
crew come upon an abandoned space vehicle that contains unex-
ploded bombs. Members of the crew are killed investigating
the craft, and the rest continue their travels until they come
upon a dark star. The star's radiation causes the crew to go
into a period of sleep. They next encounter a nebula (rarefied
gas or dust in interstellar space), which is originating from
a planet. The nubula is protecting them from the dark star's
radiation. Thinking that this planet contains intelligent
and friendly life, the crew prepares to land on this unexplored
territory. It turns out to be Earth.

BEACH BLANKET BINGO. 1965. 98 minutes. Color. *Director:*
William Asher. *Screenplay:* William Asher and Leo
Townsend. *Cinematography:* Floyd Crosby. *Cast:* Frankie
Avalon (Frankie); Annette Funicello (Dee Dee); Deborah
Walley (Bonnie Graham); Harvey Lembeck (Eric Von Zipper);
John Ashley (Steve Gordon); Jody McCrea (Bonehead); Donna
Loren (Donna); Marta Kristen (Lorelei); Linda Evans (Sugar
Kane); Timothy Carey (South Dakota Slim); Donna Michelle
(Animal); Mike Nader (Butch); Patti Chandler (Patti);
The Hondells (Themselves); Don Rickles (Big Drop); Paul
Lynde (Bullets); Buster Keaton (Himself); Earl Wilson
(Himself); Bobbi Shaw (Bobbi); Andy Romano, Alan Fife,
Jerry Brutsche, John Macchia, Bob Harvey, Alberta Nelson,
Myrna Ross (Rat Pack).

Perhaps realizing that Avalon and Funicello could not
carry the picture alone, the producers of *Beach Blanket Bingo*
included Don Rickles, Paul Lynde, and Buster Keaton in the
cast. Also in the cast, and one of the film's saving graces,
is that bizarre character Timothy Carey. He looks to be im-
provising a good deal and in essence is directing himself.
Avalon and Funicello and the rest of the beach crowd witness a parachute jump, which is used as a publicity stunt for
a young singer (Evans). Being an impressionable group, they
all start to take skydiving lessons at Don Rickles's skydiving
school. Before you know it, both Avalon and Funicello begin
flirting with the two skydiving instructors (Walley and
Ashley). Complicating matters is Harvey Lembeck and his gang
of cyclists, who kidnap Evans. The surfers lead a rescue
party, which results in a large melee.
This was the fourth of the beach films, and, like polyes-
ter, prolonged exposure to these films can be hazardous to
one's health. The musical numbers reached a sustained level
of inanity with Harvey Lembeck and his gang's rendering of
"Follow Your Leader."

CONQUERED CITY. 1965. 91 minutes. *Director:* Joseph Anthony.
Screenplay: Guy Elmes, Eric Bercovici, and Marc Brandel;
based on the novel *The Captive City*, by John Appleby.
Cinematography: Leonida Barboni. *Cast:* David Niven (Major
Peter Whitfield); Lea Massari (Lelia); Ben Gazzara (Cap-
tain George Stubbs); Daniela Rocca (Doushka); Martin
Balsam (Feinberg); Michael Craig (Captain Elliot); Clelia
Matania (Miss Climedes); Giulio Bosetti (Narriman); Percy

Herbert (Sergeant Reed); Ivo Garrani (Mavroti); Odoardo
Spadaro (Janny Mendoris); Roberto Risso (Corporal Love-
day); Venantino Venantini (General Ferolou); Carlo
Hintermann (Sergeant); Adelmo Di Fraia (Andrea); Massimo
Righi (Pollit); Francesco Tensi (General Bennet); Renato
Moretti ("The Saint"); with Lamberto Antinori.

Conquered City tells the standard story about a small
group of people holed up somewhere under siege. This theme,
often filmed in the western genre, is here situated in Greece
during the German retreat of 1945.
    The Hotel Zeus is the headquarters for a polyglot group
of people--British and American military, Greek loyalists,
refugees, etc. Outside the hotel rival political groups are
fighting for control of Greece. A British officer (Niven),
with the aid of an American officer (Gazzara), defends the
hotel against attacks from Greek rebels. Apparently the hotel
is the hiding place for a large amount of weapons wanted by
the rebels. It is learned that the hotel has a traitor in
its midst. When Gazzara disappears, Niven suspects that he
has joined the rebels. The traitor turns out to be another
officer (Craig). He and Niven have a battle in the hotel's
basement, where the munitions are stored. An explosion destroys the weapons and Craig is killed. Niven manages to escape the hotel with the other survivors.

DIE, MONSTER, DIE! 1965. 80 minutes. Color. *Director:*
    Daniel Haller. *Screenplay:* Jerry Sohl; based on the story
    "The Colour Out of Space," by H.P. Lovecraft. *Cinematog-
    raphy:* Paul Beeson. *Cast:* Boris Karloff (Nahum Witley);
    Nick Adams (Stephen Reinhardt); Freda Jackson (Letitia
    Witley); Suzan Farmer (Susan Whitley); Terence De Marney
    (Merwyn); Patrick Magee (Dr. Henderson); Paul Farrell
    (Jason); George Moon (Cab Driver); Gretchen Franklin (Miss
    Bailey); Sydney Bromley (Pierce); Billy Milton (Henry);
    Leslie Dwyer (Potter). (Sources differ on the roles of
    the cabdriver and Miss Bailey. Some say the roles are
    performed by Harold Goodwin and Sheila Raynor.)

Die, Monster, Die! is taken from a story by the 20th-
century Poe, H.P. Lovecraft. Since both of his parents had
died after bouts with mental illness, Lovecraft, living a good
deal of his life in seclusion, became morbidly preoccupied
with the problems of heredity. His oeuvre almost equals that
of Poe's in its obsessional consistency.
    A young American scientist (Adams) comes to a small

English village to visit his fiancée (Farmer) and her parents
(Karloff and Jackson). He receives a hostile reception from
the villagers and Karloff. Jackson, who is an invalid and
wears a veil, asks Adams to take her daughter away from the
house. After some strange occurrences take place, Adams and
Farmer visit the family greenhouse, where they discover mutated
plants. The cellar of the greenhouse contains a large radioactive meteorite, which Karloff has used to create the plant
mutations. The same radiation has disfigured his wife. A
fire begins in the family home, as Karloff and Jackson perish,
but Adams and Farmer escape.

DR. GOLDFOOT AND THE BIKINI MACHINE. 1965. 90 minutes.
    Color. *Director:* Norman Taurog. *Screenplay:* Elwood
    Ullman and Robert Kaufman; based on a story by James
    Hartford. *Cinematography:* Sam Leavitt. *Cast:* Vincent
    Price (Dr. Goldfoot); Frankie Avalon (Craig Gamble);
    Dwayne Hickman (Todd Armstrong); Susan Hart (Diane); Jack
    Mullaney (Igor); Fred Clark (D.J. Pevney); Alberta Nelson
    (Reject No. 12); Milton Frome (Motorcycle Cop); Hal Riddle
    (News Vendor); Kaye Elhardt (Girl in Nightclub); William
    Baskin (Guard); Vince Barnett (Janitor); Joe Ploski
    (Cook); Sam and the Ape Men (Themselves); Diane De Marco
    (Herself); Patti Chandler, Salli Sachse, Sue Hamilton,
    Marianne Gaba, Issa Arnal, Pamela Rodgers, Sally Frei,
    Jan Watson, Mary Hughes, Luree Holmes, Laura Nicholson,
    China Lee, Deanna Lund, Leslie Summers, Kay Michaels,
    Arlene Charles (Robots); Annette Funicello, Deborah
    Walley, Harvey Lembeck, and Aron Kincaid (Guest Stars,
    Cameos); with David Shayer, Bob Harris, Ronnie Rondell,
    Carey Loftin, Louis Elias, Troy Milton, Mari Ann Leslie,
    Ronnie Dayton, Paul Stader, Harvey Parry, Jerry Summers,
    Fred Stromsoe.

    This film takes many of the young people from the beach-
party films and combines them with AIP's resident master of
horror, Vincent Price. Price has rarely looked more foolish.
    With the aid of a computer controlled laboratory, Dr.
Goldfoot (Price) has managed to develop attractive bikini-
wearing robots. Their purpose is to go out and seduce wealthy
men, so Price may obtain their fortunes. One of the robots
(Hart) wins over a rich playboy (Hickman). A secret government agent (Avalon), who is in love with Hart, intervenes and
attempts to rescue Hickman from Price's plot. Both Avalon
and Hickman are imprisoned in Price's torture chamber. They
manage to escape, with Price in hot pursuit.

Some of the ridiculous goings-on here are somewhat alleviated by the location work filmed in San Francisco. The beginning of the film even includes a trip down some of that city's hills, à la *Bullitt*. The scene in Price's torture chamber, with its iron maidens and swinging pendulums, is a clear spoof on the Corman/Poe films.

GO GO MANIA. 1965. 70 minutes. Color. *Director:* Frederic
     Goode. *Screenplay:* Roger Dunton. *Cinematography:*
     Geoffrey Unsworth. *Cast:* The Beatles, The Animals, Matt
     Munro, The Nashville Teens, Susan Maughan, The Rockin'
     Berries, The Honeycomb, Herman's Hermits, The Four Pen-
     nies, Peter and Gordon, The Fourmost, Sounds Incorporated,
     Billy Davis, Spencer Davis Group, Billy J. Kramer and
     the Dakotas, Tommy Quickly and the Remo Four.

This musical was filmed in various studio settings, and each act is introduced by London disc jockey Jimmy Saville. The opening and closing numbers are performed by The Beatles, filmed from a live concert. Among the numerous performers appearing in the film are some that never really made it big in the United States, e.g., The Fourmost, Susan Maughan, and Tommy Quickly and the Remo Four. With the inclusion of these less-well-known performers, *Go Go Mania* is somewhat similar to AIP's 1957 film *Rock Around the World*.

HOW TO STUFF A WILD BIKINI. 1965. 93 minutes. Color. *Direc-*
     tor: William Asher. *Screenplay:* William Asher and Leo
     Townsend. *Cinematography:* Floyd Crosby. *Cast:* Annette
     Funicello (Dee Dee); Dwayne Hickman (Ricky); Brian Donlevy
     (B.D.); Harvey Lembeck (Eric Von Zipper); Beverly Adams
     (Cassandra); Jody McCrea (Bonehead); John Ashley (Johnny);
     Marianne Gaba (Animal); Len Lesser (North Dakota Pete);
     Irene Tsu (Native Girl); Arthur Julian (Doctor Melamed);
     Bobbi Shaw (Khola Koku); Frankie Avalon (Frankie); Buster
     Keaton (Bwana); The Kingsmen (Themselves); Alberta Nelson
     (Puss); Andy Romano (J.D.); John Macchia, Jerry Brutsche,
     Bob Harvey, Myrna Ross, Alan Fife (Rat Pack); Alan
     Frohlich, Tom Quine, Hollis Morrison, Guy Hemric, George
     Boyce, Charles Reed (Ad Men); Patti Chandler (Patti);
     Mike Nader (Mike); Luree Holmes, Jo Collins, Mary Hughes,
     Stephanie Nader, Jeannine White, Janice Levinson (Beach
     Girls); Ed Garner, John Fain, Mickey Dora, Brian Wilson,
     Bruce Baker, Ned Wynn, Kerry Berry, Dick Jones, Ray

Atkinson, Ronnie Dayton (Beach Boys); Salli Sachse, Linda
Bent (Bookends); Marianne Gordon (Chickie); Sheila
Stephenson (Secretary); Rosemary Williams (English Girl);
Sue Williams (Peanuts); Tonia Van Deter (Italian Girl);
Uta Stone (German Girl); Toni Harper (Barberette); Michele
Barton (Manicurist); Victoria Carroll (Shoe Shine Girl);
and Mickey Rooney (Peachy Keane).

The highlight of *How to Stuff a Wild Bikini* is the opening credits, which are done with clay animation. One has to
question any film that uses television's Dobie Gillis, Dwayne
Hickman, as a playboy. Once again, as in *Beach Blanket Bingo*,
we are subjected to Harvey Lembeck and his gang's rendition
of "Follow Your Leader."
    Frankie Avalon has left the beach crowd, and is in the
Naval Reserves in the South Pacific. He asks a native witch
doctor (Keaton) for help in keeping Funicello away from other
men while he is gone. For some reason Keaton sends a pelican
(which makes sounds like a chimpanzee) to guard her. It is
not too long before a beachfront swinger (Hickman) makes a
move on Funicello. Keaton sends a girl (Adams) to distract
Hickman. Next thing we know an ad man (Rooney) is on the beach
looking for the "Girl Next Door" for a promotional campaign.
Somehow Harvey Lembeck and his motorcycle gang have become
mixed up in this mélange. By the end of the film Hickman is
courting Adams, Avalon has returned to Funicello, and Lembeck
has traded in his leather jacket for a grey flannel suit.

OPERATION SNAFU. 1965. 97 minutes. *Director:* Cyril Frankel.
Screenplay: Harold Buchman; based on the novel *Stop at a
Winner*, by Ronald Frederick Delderfield. *Cinematography:*
Edward Scaife. *Cast:* Alfred Lynch (Horace Pope); Sean
Connery (Pedlar Pascoe); Cecil Parker (Group Captain
Bascombe); Stanley Holloway (Mr. Cooksley); Alan King
(Technical Sergeant Buzzer); Eric Barker (Doctor); Wilfrid
Hyde-White (Trowbridge); Kathleen Harrison (Mrs. Cooks-
ley); Eleanor Summerfield (Flora McNaughton); Terence
Longdon (Air Gunner); Victor Maddern (1st Airman); Harry
Locke (Huxtable); John Le Mesurier (Hixon); Viola Keats
(Sister); Peter Sinclair (Mr. Pope); Edna Morris (Lil);
Thomas Heathcote (Sergeant); Brian Weske (Corporal); Jack
Lambert (Police Constable); Cyril Smith (Ticket Collec-
tor); Simon Lack (Flight Lieutenant Baldwin); Graham Stark
(Sergeant Ellis); Jean Aubrey (WAAF Corporal); Ann Beach
(Iris); Mirian Karlin (WAAF Sergeant); Bil Owen (Corporal
Gittens); Barbara Windsor (Mavis); Ian Whittaker

(Lancing); Harold Goodwin (Corporal Reeves); Kenneth J.
Warren (Dusty); Beatrix Lehmann (Lady Edith); Gary
Cockrell (U.S. Snowdrop); Lance Percival (MacTaggart);
Monty Landis (Conductor); with Jack Smethurst, Patsy
Rowlands, Priscilla Morgan, Richard Hart, Stuart Saunders,
Toni Palmer, Norman Coburn, Michael Sarne.

Filmed in 1961, this routine service comedy is of interest
for only one reason--Sean Connery. Appearing just prior to
his success as James Bond, Connery here portrays a brawny soldier.
Instead of serving a jail sentence, a con artist (Lynch)
enters the RAF during World War II. He meets a gypsy (Connery), and the two of them spend much of their time making
profits. They begin by selling transfer passes to other soldiers, and continue on to a variety of other money-making
schemes. They run afoul of an American military man (King),
who has Lynch and Connery transferred to the front lines in
France. Connery, who had been up to this time Lynch's lackey,
now assumes control of the situation. Both men distinguish
themselves in battle and end up as war heroes.

PLANET OF THE VAMPIRES. 1965. 86 minutes. Color. *Director:*
Mario Bava. *Screenplay:* Alberto Bevilacqua, Callisto
Cosulich, Mario Bava, Antonio Roman, and Raphael J.
Salvia; based on the story "One Night of 21 Hours," by
Renato Pestriniero. English-Language-Version Screenplay:
Ib Melchior and Louis M. Heyward. Story for the English-
Language Version: Ib Melchior. *Cinematography:* Antonio
Rinaldi. *Cast:* Barry Sullivan (Captain Mark Markary);
Norma Bengell (Sanya); Angel Aranda (Wess); Evi Marandi
(Tiona); Fernando Villena (Karan); Stelio Candelli (Mud);
Massimo Righi (Nordeg); Mario Morales (Eldon); Franco
Andrei (Garr); Ivan Rassimov (Kell/Derry); Rico Boido
(Keir/Key); Alberto Cevenini (Wan/Toby).

As one can expect from a Mario Bava film, *Planet of the
Vampires* contains a stylistic richness with its colorful and
imaginative atmosphere constructed on a small budget. Unfortunately, aside from *Black Sunday*, most of Bava's films have
nothing more than a surface splash to them. In this respect
Bava was a precursor of the imaginative Dario Argento.
Two spaceships are carrying a team of explorers and scientists on an expedition to the mist-covered planet of Aura.
One of the ships, the *Galliot*, disappears. The *Argos* lands
on Aura and the crew members begin to attack one another. The

Galliot is found with the ravaged bodies of its crew. The captain of the *Argos* (Sullivan) learns from a scientist (Villena) that the planet is inhabited by disembodied beings. The crew of the *Argos* are slowly killed off one at a time by the resurrected crew of the *Galliot*. Their bodies have been taken over by beings from Aura, who seek to leave the planet for another world. Sullivan and two assistants (Bengell and Aranda) manage to escape, but Aranda realizes that his cohorts have been possessed by the Aurans. He is killed attempting to foil their escape from Aura. Now Sullivan and Bengell manage to escape to a nearby planet--Earth.

SAMURAI PIRATE. 1965. 95 minutes. Color. *Director:* Senkichi Taniguchi. *Screenplay:* Takeshi Kimura and Shinichi Sekizawa. *Cinematography:* Takao Saito. *Cast:* Toshiro Mifune (Sukezaemon/"Luzon"); with Makoto Sato, Jun Funato, Ichiro Arishima, Mie Hama, Kumi Mizuno, Akiko Wakabayashi, Mitsuko Kusabue, Tadao Nakamaru, Jun Tazaki, Takashi Shimura.

Also known as *The Lost World of Sinbad*, this film stars one of the most popular Japanese actors, Toshiro Mifune. Famous for his samurai roles, Mifune here portrays an oddity--a Japanese pirate. *Samurai Pirate* is a fantasy that includes, among other things, Mifune flying on top of a large kite and a witch who changes into a flying insect.

In 16th-century Japan a wealthy man (Mifune) is accused of piracy and sentenced to death. He escapes and sets sail determined to regain his fortune through piracy. He abandons his ship when he is attacked by other pirates and swims safely to a nearby island. Here he meets an old wizard who tells him about the evil warlord who rules the island. It turns out that the warlord is also the leader of the pirates who had attacked Mifune. Mifune becomes involved in a scheme to overthrow the tyrant and restore the imprisoned king. He finally kills the villain in a sword fight and leaves to search for other adventures.

SERGEANT DEADHEAD. 1965. 90 minutes. Color. *Director:* Norman Taurog. *Screenplay:* Louis M. Heyward. *Cinematography:* Floyd Crosby. *Cast:* Frankie Avalon (Sergeant O.K. Deadhead/Sgt. Donovan); Deborah Walley (Colonel Lucy Turner); Cesar Romero (Admiral Stoneham); Fred Clark (General Rufus Fogg); Gale Gordon (Captain Weiskopf);

Harvey Lembeck (Private McEvoy); John Ashley (Private
Filroy); Buster Keaton (Private Blinken); Reginald
Gardiner (Lieutenant Commander Talbott); Eve Arden (Lieu-
tenant Kinsey); Pat Buttram (The President); Donna Loren
(Susan); Romo Vincent (Tuba Player); Tod Windsor (Sergeant
Keeler); Norman Grabowski, Mike Nader (Air Police); Edward
Faulkner (Radioman); Bobbi Shaw (Gilda); Patti Chandler
(Patti); Salli Sachse (Sue Ellen); Luree Holmes (Luree);
Sue Hamilton (Ivy); Jo Collins (Gail); Bob Harvey (Bell-
hop); Jerry Brutsche (Newsman); Andy Romano, John Macchia
(Marine MPs) Sallie Dornan (Secretary); Mary Hughes,
Astrid De Brea, Jean Ingram, Peggy Ward, Stephanie Nader,
Lyzanne Ladue, Janice Levinson, Alberta Nelson (WAFS).

Sergeant Deadhead uses a number of the old gang from the
beach pictures interspersed with a group of aging actors to
create a comedy that is sort of a poor man's *The Nutty Professor.* Frankie Avalon proves here that he does not fit into
the Jerry Lewis mold.

An inept Air Force sergeant (Avalon) is sent to the guardhouse after accidentally exploding a rocket during a military
review. He escapes from jail and hides in a test rocket.
Avalon and the chimpanzee inside the ship are launched into
space. When the rocket lands, Avalon is made a hero by the
military in order to quiet any controversy about a military
mistake. The space ride has changed Avalon from being mild-
mannered to aggressive. He is imprisoned again before he can
expose the military's blunder to the public. A wedding was
to have taken place between Avalon and Deborah Walley, but the
military finds Avalon's double in Sergeant Donovan and intend
to replace him during the marriage ceremony. Once more Avalon
escapes from the guardhouse and has a rendezvous with Walley
at their honeymoon hotel, where he changes back to his old
personality.

SKI PARTY. 1965. 90 minutes. Color. *Director:* Alan Rifkin.
Screenplay: Robert Kaufman. *Cinematography:* Arthur E.
Arling. *Cast:* Frankie Avalon (Todd Armstrong); Dwayne
Hickman (Craig Gamble); Deborah Walley (Linda Hughes);
Yvonne Craig (Barbara Norris); Robert Q. Lewis (Donald
Pevney); Bobbi Shaw (Nita); Aron Kincaid (Freddie Carter);
Steve Rogers (Gene); Mike Nader (Bobby); Jo Collins (Jo);
Mickey Dora (Mickey); John Boyer, Ronnie Dayton (Ski
Boys); Bill Sampson (Arthur); Patti Chandler (Janet);
Salli Sachse (Indian); Sigi Engl (Ski Instructor); Mikki
Jamison, Mary Hughes, Luree Holmes (Ski Girls); The

Hondells, James Brown and the Flames, and Lesley Gore
(Themselves); Dick Miller (Cab Driver); Annette Funicello
(College Professor).

Ski Party just proves that the Beach Party films are more
of a state of mind (lessness), and not necessarily a geographic
locale. This film begins with Annette Funicello in a cameo,
portraying a college professor giving a lecture on "Love Without Sex." For the next 90 minutes Frankie Avalon and Dwayne
Hickman do all they can to disprove the premise of her lecture.
   Two college boys (Avalon and Hickman) are jealous of all
the attention the girls lavish on a fellow classmate (Kincaid).
All of the gang decide to take a ski vacation. At the resort
Avalon and Hickman dress like girls and flirt with Kincaid in
an attempt to find out why girls find him so attractive. The
joke is on Hickman, as Kincaid begins to flirt with him. Meanwhile Avalon is spending his time coming on to an abundant
Swedish snow bunny (Shaw). When the group returns to Los Angeles, the boys' joke is found out, but all the girls forgive
them.
   This film could also have been called "Hormones Run Amok,"
as there must be something about the close confines of a ski
resort that causes this generally wholesome group to act this
way. James Brown and the Flames, decked out in ski sweaters,
perform "I Feel Good." Put in this setting, Brown and his
group remind one of Raymond Chandler's quote about a character
in *Farewell My Lovely*: "as inconspicuous as a tarantula on a
slice of angel food."

SWINGER'S PARADISE. 1965. 83 minutes. Color. *Director:*
   Sidney J. Furie. *Screenplay:* Peter Meyers and Ronald
   Cass. *Cinematography:* Ken Higgins. *Cast:* Cliff Richard
   (Johnnie); Walter Slezak (Lloyd Davis); Susan Hampshire
   (Jenny); Hank B. Marvin, Bruce Welch, Brian Bennett, and
   John Rostill (Mood Musicians); Melvyn Hayes (Jerry);
   Richard O'Sullivan (Edward); Una Stubbs (Barbara); Joseph
   Cuby (Miguel); Derek Bond (Douglas Leslie); Gerald Harper
   (Senior Sheik/Scotsman/Harold).

   With about a half-hour cut from its original length,
Swinger's Paradise is an innocuous beach-party clone. Like
those films, this musical comedy casts veteran actors along
with the young talent. In this case it is Walter Slezak and
Derek Bond.
   Cliff Richard and his musician friends are put off a lux-
ury liner after one of their electric guitars blows out the

the lights on the ship. Their raft lands them in the Canary
Islands. A film is being made there, and Richard takes a job
as a stuntman for another actor (Bond). He and his friends
decide they can make a better film than the director (Slezak).
Secretly they film added scenes and incorporate it into the
existing footage. Slezak attempts to sabotage their project,
but both versions are completed. Slezak combines both films,
and it turns out to be a success. Richard now becomes a famous
director, and asks the leading lady (Hampshire) to marry him.

TABOOS OF THE WORLD. 1965. 97 minutes. Color. *Director:*
     Romolo Marcellini. *Screenplay:* Romolo Marcellini and Ugo
     Guerra; story by Marcellini, Virgilio Lilli, Ettore Della
     Giovanna, and L. De Marchi. *Cinematography:* Rino
     Filippini. *Narrator:* Vincent Price.

     Taboos of the World is an imitation of another Italian
film, *Mondo Cane.* During the 60s a whole series of these Mondo
films (Bizzaro, Balordo, Pazzo, etc.) exploited the voyeuristic geeklike mentality of certain segments of the audience.
Purporting to be a survey of the strange customs and taboos
of the world, this ethnocentric film, filmed mainly in Asia,
contains an appropriately tongue-in-cheek narration by Vincent
Price.
     Among the oddities depicted here are a mass for lepers;
a funeral in the Ganges; atom bomb victims; addicts selling
their children to support their habit; Scandinavians blood
drinkers; tattooed women; and a Japanese sect who cut off their
little fingers as part of an initiation ceremony.

TOKYO OLYMPIAD. 1965. 93 minutes. Color. *Director:* Kon
     Ichikawa. *Screenplay:* Natto Wada, Yoshio Shirasaka,
     Shuntaro Tanikawa, and Kon Ichikawa. *Cinematography:*
     Juichi Nagano, Kinji Nakamura, and Tadashi Tanaka. Super-
     vised by Shigeo Hayashida and Kazuo Miyagawa.

     Noted Japanese director Kon Ichikawa used 164 cameramen
to make *Tokyo Olympiad,* one of the best films ever made about
the Olympic Games. Ichikawa brings to the film a sense of the
wonder and curiosity of an amateur spectator, instead of presenting a paean to physical prowess. The cameramen "have ob-
tained close, long and medium shots that lay bare the competi-
tive dash, the human endeavor and the beauty as well as the
underside of sweat, suffering and hurt" (*Variety*, May 26, 1965,

p. 15). Of special note is the beautifully edited sequence showing the women's volleyball final between Russia and Japan. Unfortunately most copies of *Tokyo Olympiad* have been cut down to 93 minutes from their original length of 132 minutes.

THE TOMB OF LIGEIA. 1965. 81 minutes. Color. *Director:* Roger Corman. *Screenplay:* Robert Towne; based on the story "Ligeia," by Edgar Allan Poe. *Cinematography:* Arthur Grant. *Cast:* Vincent Price (Verden Fell); Elizabeth Shepherd (Lady Ligeia/Lady Rowena); John Westbrook (Christopher Gough); Oliver Johnston (Kenrick); Derek Francis (Lord Trevanion); Richard Vernon (Dr. Vivian); Ronald Adam (Parson); Frank Thornton (Peperel); Denis Gilmore (Livery Boy); with Penelope Lee.

The Tomb of Ligeia was the last of the Poe adaptations directed by Roger Corman. Filmed on location in England, this is unlike the other Poe films. Instead of the claustrophobic world of the studio, there are actually scenes here filmed in sunlight.
     A wealthy man (Price) is grief-stricken over the death of his wife, Ligeia (Shepherd). She had such a capacity for life that Price actually believes she will return from the dead. Months later he marries another young woman (Shepherd). Their honeymoon goes well, and Price seems to be over his obsession for his dead wife. When the two of them return to live at his Gothic abbey, Price begins to leave Shepherd alone at night. At a party he mesmerizes her, and she begins to speak in Ligeia's voice. Soon after Shepherd begins to have a series of dreams about the dead woman and a black cat. An admirer of Shepherd's (Westbrook) decides to open Ligeia's grave and finds a wax dummy. On the brink of an emotional collapse, Shepherd one night finds herself in a passageway to a large tomb. Here she finds Price and the well-preserved body of Ligeia. It seems that the strong-willed Ligeia hypnotized Price to staying with her every night. In his madness Price attempts to strangle Shepherd, as a fire is started. Westbrook rescues her, and Price, the corpse of Ligeia, and the black cat perish in the burning tomb.

WAR GODS OF THE DEEP. 1965. 85 minutes. Color. *Director:* Jacques Tourneur. *Screenplay:* Charles Bennett and Louis M. Heyward; additional dialogue by David Whitaker; based on the poem "The Doomed City" and the story "A Descent

into the Maelstrom," by Edgar Allan Poe. *Cinematography:*
Stephen Dade and John Lamb. *Cast:* Vincent Price (The
Captain, Sir Hugh Tregathion); Tab Hunter (Ben Harris);
David Tomlinson (Harold Tiffin-Jones); Susan Hart (Jill
Tregellis); John Le Mesurier (Reverend Jonathan Ives);
Henry Oscar (Mumford); Derek Newark (Dan); Roy Patrick
(Simon); Tony Selby (George); Michael Heyland (Bill);
Steven Brooke (Ted); William Hurndell (Tom); Jim Spearman
(Jack); Dennis Blake (Harry); Arthur Hewlett, Walter
Sparrow, John Barrett (Fishermen); Barbara Bruce, Hilda
Campbell Russell (Women Guests); Bart Allison, George
Richards (Men Guests); and Herbert (Himself, a Rooster).

Veteran director Jacques Tourneur keeps the action moving
in *War Gods of the Deep*. By doing so he makes one forget about
the improbable story and the tacky sets.
A body washes ashore on the Cornwall coast. It is discovered by an American (Hunter), who proceeds to tell his
discovery to a young woman (Hart) and her artist friend
(Tomlinson). That night Hart disappears from the hotel she
owns, leaving behind only a trail of seaweed. Hunter and
Tomlinson follow her trail, which leads them down a passage-
way to an undersea city called Lyonesse. Here they find a
band of smugglers who have lived there for about a hundred
years. They are ruled by The Captain (Price), who has kidnapped Hart because she resembles his dead wife. The eruption
of a volcano threatens Lyonesse, and everybody escapes while
avoiding the quakes and the undersea creatures known as the
gillmen. All of the smugglers die in the escape attempt, except Price. When Price, Hart, Hunter, and the few others surface to sunlight, Price, now exposed to the air, quickly ages
and dies.

THE WAR OF THE ZOMBIES. 1965. 85 minutes. Color. *Director:*
Giuseppe Vari. *Screenplay:* Piero Pierotti and Marcello
Sartarelli; based on an idea by Ferruccio De Martino and
Massimo De Rita. *Cinematography:* Gabor Pogany. *Cast:*
John Drew Barrymore (Aderbal); Susy Andersen (Tullia);
Ettore Manni (Gaius); Ida Galli (Rhama); Mino Doro
(Lutetius); Philippe Hersent (Azer); Ivano Staccioli
(Sirion); with Matilda Calnan, Antonio Corevi, Giulio
Maculani, Livia Contardi, and Rosy Zichel.

The War of the Zombies stands on the verge of being a
cult movie. It contains plenty of action, mayhem, and overacting. This is especially true in the case of John Drew

War of the Zombies

Barrymore, who, taking some tips from his father, has a field
day in his role of a Roman Empire era cult leader.
    A Roman centurion (Manni) is sent to learn the whereabouts
of some treasure being sent to Rome. He finds that a self-
styled high priest (Barrymore) has the treasure. He is using
it as a lure to convince a local official (Doro) to aid him
in a revolt against Roman rule. Barrymore has Doro's wife
(Andersen) and her slave (Galli) under his influence. Manni
falls in love with Galli, and is quickly captured by Barrymore.
He escapes and learns that Barrymore has resurrected dead soldiers into an army of invincible zombies, ready to take over
the world. Manni foils Barrymore's plans by destroying the
eye of the cyclopean gold statue he idolizes, thereby depriving
him of his power.

BANG, BANG, YOU'RE DEAD! 1966. 92 minutes. Color. *Director:*
    Don Sharp. *Screenplay:* Peter Yeldham; based on a story
    by Peter Welbeck. *Cinematography:* Michael Reed. *Cast:*
    Tony Randall (Andrew Jessel); Senta Berger (Kyra Stanovy);
    Terry-Thomas (El Caid); Herbert Lom (Narim Casimir);
    Wilfrid Hyde-White (Arthur Fairbrother); Grégoire Aslan
    (Achmed); John Le Mesurier (George Lillywhite); Klaus
    Kinski (Jonquil); Margaret Lee (Samia Voss); Emile
    Stemmler (Hotel Clerk); Helen Sanguineti (Madame Bouseny);
    Sanchez Francisco (Martinez); William Sanguineti (Police
    Chief); Hassan Essakali (Motorcycle Policeman); Keith
    Peacock (Philippe); Burt Kwouk (Export Manager).

    This lighthearted espionage film made in Marrakesh would
be almost totally dismissed if it were not for the inclusion
of Klaus Kinski in the cast. After spending years appearing
in nondescript international co-productions, Kinski more recently has become associated with director Werner Herzog, acting as sort of his alter ego.
    A spy (Lom) in Marrakesh is waiting for an unidentified
agent to give him $2,000,000 in exchange for information that
would change an important vote at the United Nations. Among
the people Lom has his eye on are a CIA agent (Berger) posing
as a journalist. An American architect (Randall) unwittingly
becomes involved with her when Lom and his associates try to
"frame" her for murder. Both Randall and Berger lead the spies
on a merry chase into the hills outside Marrakesh. Berger is
captured by Lom, but Randall and a group of desert nomads rescue her. Lom is thwarted as the unidentified agent (Hyde-
White) is exposed.
    The plot for this film contains traces of Hitchcock's

The 39 Steps and *North by Northwest*, especially in the case of an innocent man becoming involved with spies. In this instance the usually weak-hearted Tony Randall proves that real men *do* eat quiche.

THE BIG T.N.T. SHOW. 1966. 93 minutes. Color. *Director:* Larry Peerce. *Screenplay:* Robert Boatman. *Featuring:* Roger Miller, Joan Baez, Ray Charles and His Orchestra, Donovan, Petula Clark, The Byrds, The Lovin' Spoonful, Ike and Tina Turner, The Modern Folk Quartet, The Ronettes, Bo Diddley, and David McCallum.

Attempting to repeat the success of *The T.A.M.I. Show*, this live concert, recorded at The Moulin Rouge in Hollywood on November 29, 1965, incorporates a wide variety of popular musical tastes. Each act is introduced by David McCallum, who at the time had a substantial female teenage following as one of the co-stars of *The Man from U.N.C.L.E.*
The film never quite captures the excitement of its predecessor. To be able to listen to Ike and Tina Turner, Bo Diddley, Ray Charles, The Ronettes, and The Byrds, we have to endure such acts as The Modern Folk Quartet, Donovan, and The Lovin' Spoonful. Some of the "blasts from the past" performed here are "Georgia on My Mind," and "What'd I Say," (Ray Charles); "It's Gonna Work Out Fine," (Ike and Tina Turner); "Be My Baby" (The Ronettes); and "Mr. Tambourine Man" and "Turn, Turn, Turn" (The Byrds).

BLOOD BATH. 1966. 80 minutes. *Directors:* Jack Hill and Stephanie Rothman. *Screenplay:* Jack Hill and Stephanie Rothman. *Cinematography:* Alfred Taylor. *Cast:* William Campbell (Antonio Sordi); Marissa Mathes (Daisy Allen); Linda (Lori) Saunders (Dorian/Melissa); Sandra Knight (Donna Allen); with Karl Schanzer, Jeff Elliot, Sid Haig, Jonathan Haze, David Ackles, Thomas Karnes, Frank Church, David Miller, and Jeff Nichols.

Blood Bath was co-directed by Stephanie Rothman, one of the few women directors who have worked in exploitation films. This was her first directorial credit. Since then she has gone on to direct such films as *The Student Nurses*, *The Velvet Vampire*, and *Terminal Island*.
A Venetian artist (Campbell) turns into a vampire at night. He either kills his victims or brings them back to

Blood Bath

his studio, where he drops them in a vat of boiling wax. He
uses the resultant statues as an inspiration for his paintings.
During the day Campbell has a romance of sorts with a young
woman (Saunders), who just happens to resemble a mistress of
one of his ancestors. He believes that he is the reincarnation of his ancestor, who had been executed in the 15th century
for sorcery. After several other killings Campbell confronts
Saunders in his belltower studio. In his demented state he
believes her to be the mistress who betrayed his ancestor.
Before Campbell can kill her, however, the bodies of his former
victims come to life and force him to fall into the vat of
boiling wax.

THE DIRTY GAME. 1966. 91 minutes. *Directors:* Terence Young,
    Christian-Jaque, Carlo Lizzani, and Werner Klingler.
    Screenplay: Jacques Laborie, Jacques Remy, Ennio De
    Concini, Christian-Jaque, and Philippe Bouvard. *English
    Language Screenplay by:* Jo Eisinger. *Cinematography:*
    Richard Angst, Pierre Petit, and Enrico Menczer. *Cast:*
    Henry Fonda (Kourlov); Robert Ryan (General Bruce);
    Vittorio Gassman (Perego, aka Ferrari); Annie Girardot
    (Nanette, aka Monique); Bourvil (Laland); Robert Hossein
    (Dupont); Peter Van Eyck (Berlin CIA Head); Maria Grazia
    Buccella (Natalia); Mario Adorf (Callagan); Jacques Sernas
    (Glazov); with Georges Marchal, Wolfgang Lukschy, Louis
    Arbessier, Jacky Blanchot, Gabriel Gobin, Helmut Wildt,
    Violette Marceau, Gabriella Giorgelli, Nino Crisman,
    Oreste Palella, Renato Terra.

A top cast is wasted in this international co-production.
This type of ethnic filmmaking always resulted in films that
did not contain any national characteristics but instead presented a homogenized internationalism.
    An American intelligence officer (Ryan) on his way to
meet his Russian counterpart recollects three stories of espionage. The first deals with how an Italian double agent
(Gassman) persuaded an Italian scientist to aid the West before the Russians could kidnap him. The second episode recalls
how a French oceanographic expert (Bourvil) helped in locating
a Russian base, which intended to attack American submarines
on maneuvers. The third story concerns an American spy (Fonda)
who has just escaped the Russians after 17 years in prison.
His hiding place is found by a traitorous CIA chief (Van Eyck).
Fonda is murdered but is able to leave a clue implicating Van
Eyck as a double agent.

DR. GOLDFOOT AND THE GIRL BOMBS. 1966. 85 minutes. Color.
   Director: Mario Bava. *Screenplay:* Louis M. Heyward,
   Robert Kaufman, Franco Castellano, and Pipolo; based on
   a story by James Hartford. *Cinematography:* Antonio
   Rinaldi. *Cast:* Vincent Price (Dr. Goldfoot); Fabian (Bill
   Dexter); Franco Franchi (Franco); Ciccio Ingrassia
   (Ciccio); Laura Antonelli (Rosanna); Moana Tahi (Gold-
   foot's Assistant); with Francesco Mulè.

   This was made as a sequel to the previous year's *Dr.*
Goldfoot and the Bikini Machine. Directed by top horror filmmaker Mario Bava, this film has nothing going for it but the
inclusion of Laura Antonelli, who has since gone on to international stardom.
   Dr. Goldfoot (Price) is in league with China in precipitating a war between the United States and Russia, by bombing
Moscow with a stolen American plane. Price must first eliminate a number of NATO generals, so he can pose as the final
survivor. He devises a bomb to put into the navels of his
robot girls, which will go off when they seduce the generals.
After a number of murders a secret agent (Fabian) is summoned
to investigate. For some reason he hires the services of two
cloddish doormen (Franchi and Ingrassia), who yearn to be secret agents. Needless to say the three stop Price during his
bombing mission by operating a hot-air balloon. All four bail
out, but Fabian is the only one to escape from Russia. Franco
and Ingrassia end up in a Russian gulag, where, much to their
surprise, Price has become the camp commander.

FIREBALL 500. 1966. 92 minutes. Color. *Director:* William
   Asher. *Screenplay:* William Asher and Leo Townsend. *Cine-*
   matography: Floyd Crosby. *Cast:* Frankie Avalon ("Fire-
   ball" Dave Owens); Annette Funicello (Jane Harris); Fabian
   (Sonny Leander Fox); Chill Wills (Big Jaw Harris); Harvey
   Lembeck (Charlie Bigg); Julie Parrish (Martha Brian);
   Douglas Henderson (Hastings); Baynes Barron (Bronson);
   Sandy Reed (Race Announcer); Mike Nader (Joey); Ed Garner
   (Herman); Vin Scully (Prolog Announcer); Sue Hamilton
   (Farmer's Daughter); Renie Riano (Herman's Wife); Len
   Lesser (Man in Garage); Billy Beck (Jobber); Tex Armstrong
   (Herman's Friend); Mary Hughes, Patti Chandler, Karla
   Conway, Hedy Scott, Salli Sachse, Jo Collins, Maria
   McBane, Linda Bent (Leander's Fans); with The Don Randi
   Trio Plus One, The Carole Lombard Singers.

By 1966 even the people who made the beach-party-type
films realized that the concept behind those films should be
changed. *Fireball 500* is an action melodrama, but it is broken up occasionally by the lightweight songs we heard in the
prior films.

In this picture two young men from South Philadelphia
(Avalon and Fabian) are turned into Southern race-car drivers.
Both are rivals on the same Southern stock-car-racing circuit.
Avalon is duped into transporting illegal moonshine whiskey.
Federal agents threaten him with prison if he will not help
them capture the moonshiners. Fabian, even though he does
not like Avalon, decides to help him after a mutual friend
(Nader) has been killed delivering the illegal liquor. They
set a trap and catch the man (Lembeck) responsible for the
illegal operations. Next comes the big race, which Avalon
ends up winning, while Fabian quits racing after being burned
in an accident.

FRANKENSTEIN CONQUERS THE WORLD. 1966. 87 minutes. Color.
Director: Inoshiro Honda. *Screenplay:* Kaoru Mabuchi;
from a synopsis by Jerry Sohl and a story by Reuben
Bercovitch. *Cinematography:* Hajime Koizumi. *Cast:* Nick
Adams (Dr. James Bowen); Tadao Takashima (Scientist); Kumi
Mizuno (Woman Doctor); with Yoshio Tsuchiya, Takashi
Shimura, Kenchiro Kawaji, Seuko Togami.

This film stars Nick Adams, who had gained some popularity
in the early 60s in the television show *The Rebel*. It was
films like *Frankenstein Conquers the World* that put Adams's
career on the skids. A couple of years after making this picture Adams was found dead from an overdose of a drug used to
treat nervous disorders and alcoholism.

Toward the end of World War II the Germans transport a
box out of one of their laboratories and send it to Japan.
The box contains the beating heart of the Frankenstein monster.
When the atomic bomb levels Hiroshima, the heart is one of the
few things to survive and flourish. Fifteen years later, an
American doctor (Adams) and his Japanese colleague (Mizuno)
come upon a primitive boy living off animal carcasses. They
bring him to their hospital, where they discover that he is
the Frankenstein monster, having developed from that beating
heart fifteen years before. His radiation-racked body causes
him to grow bigger and uglier. The confines of the hospital
cannot hold him any longer, and he escapes to a forest near

Mt. Fuji. Here he comes in contact with a prehistoric beast,
which has surfaced after an earthquake. The two of them have
what seems to be an interminable battle. The Frankenstein
monster finally kills the beast, but he also perishes during
a new earthquake.

THE GHOST IN THE INVISIBLE BIKINI. 1966. 82 minutes. Color.
   Director: Don Weis. *Screenplay:* Louis M. Heyward and
   Elwood Ullman; based on a story by Heyward. *Cinematog-
   raphy:* Stanley Cortez. *Cast:* Tommy Kirk (Chuck Phillips);
   Deborah Walley (Lili Morton); Aron Kincaid (Bobby); Quinn
   O'Hara (Sinistra); Jesse White (J. Sinister Hulk); Harvey
   Lembeck (Eric Von Zipper); Nancy Sinatra (Vicki); Claudia
   Martin (Lulu); Francis X. Bushman (Malcolm); Benny Rubin
   (Chicken Feather); Bobbi Shaw (Princess Yolanda); George
   Barrows (Monstro); Luree Holmes (Shirl); Piccola Pupa
   (Piccola); Alberta Nelson (Alberta); Andy Romano (J.D.);
   Basil Rathbone (Reginald Ripper); Patsy Kelly (Myrtle
   Forbush); Boris Karloff (Hiram Stokely); Susan Hart
   (Cecily, the Ghost); Bobby Fuller Four (Themselves); Ed
   Garner, Mary Hughes, Patti Chandler, Frank Alesia, Salli
   Sachse, Sue Hamilton (Boys and Girls); Myrna Ross, Jerry
   Brutsche, Bob Harvey, John Macchia, Alan Fife (Rat Pack);
   Elena and Herb Andreas (The Statues).

Another permutation of the beach-party films. Instead
of dealing with racing cars (*Fireball 500*) or mad doctors
(Dr. Goldfoot), this film concerns itself with ghosts and
haunted houses. Veteran actors like Francis X. Bushman, Boris
Karloff, and Basil Rathbone are on hand just to prove how badly
they needed the money.
A recently deceased man (Karloff) is visited, while in
his coffin, by the ghost of his old flame (Hart). Hart tells
him that he will go to heaven and will regain his youth if he
performs one last good deed: that being to keep Karloff's shy-
ster lawyer (Rathbone) from conniving Karloff's nephew (Kirk)
out of his rightful inheritance. Just as the will is to be
read in Karloff's mansion, another relative (Kincaid) comes
to stay for the weekend with all his swinging young friends.
Also on hand, for some reason, are Harvey Lembeck and his fu-
gitives from *The Wild One*. Amidst all the confusion, Rathbone
makes an attempt on Kirk's life in the mansion's dungeon.
Karloff and Hart intervene, and Kirk receives the inheritance.
Karloff is now taken to heaven, where he regresses to a three-
year-old state.

THE GIRL GETTERS. 1966. 93 minutes. *Director:* Michael
Winner. *Screenplay:* Peter Draper. *Cinematography:*
Nicolas Roeg. *Cast:* Oliver Reed (Tinker); Jane Merrow
(Nicola); Barbara Ferris (Suzy); Julia Foster (Lorna);
Harry Andrews (Larsey); Ann Lynn (Ella); Guy Doleman
(Philip); Andrew Ray (Willy); John Porter Davidson (Grib);
Clive Colin Bowler (Sneakers); Iain Gregory (Sammy);
David Hemmings (David); John Alderton (Nidge); Jeremy
Burnham (Ivor); Mark Burns (Michael); Derek Nimmo (James);
Pauline Munro (Sylvie); Derek Newark (Alfred); Stephanie
Beaumont (Marianne); Talitha Pol (Helga); Dora Reisser
(Ingrid); Susan Burnet (Jasmin); Victor Winding (Stan
Atty); Jennifer Tafler (Sonia); Ross Parker (Fred); with
Gwendolwn Watts.

The Girl Getters attempts to capture some of the mod
spirit of England in the mid-60s. Two men associated with
this production have gone on to become well known: Michael
Winner, the director of the vile but profitable *Death Wish*
and *Death Wish II*; and Nicolas Roeg, one of the few cinematog-
raphers actually to become an accomplished director.
   A savvy photographer (Reed) at an English seaside resort
has developed a way to meet women. He takes their pictures,
gets their addresses, and then takes his pick. He meets a
London fashion model (Merrow), who is at the resort visiting
her father for the summer. Reed develops what to all accounts
is an unrequited love for her and realizes that their differences in lifestyles would probably come between them. When
the summer ends, Merrow leaves for a modeling job in Rome.
Reed would like to go with her, but he does not have the confidence to compete outside his provincial setting. In the
end he realizes that, for Merrow, their affair was only tran-
sitory, and she has beat him at his own game.

THE GREAT SPY CHASE. 1966. 84 minutes. *Director:* Georges
Lautner. *Screenplay:* Michel Audiard and Albert Simonin.
Cinematography: Maurice Fellows. *Cast:* Lino Ventura
(Lagneau); Bernard Blier (Cafarelli); Francis Blanche
(Vassilieff); Mireille Darc (Amaranthe); Charles Millot
(Muller); André Weber (Rossini); Jess Hahn (O'Brien);
Jacques Balutin (Le Douanier); Robert Dalban (Le Camion-
neur); Michèle Marceau (Rosalinde); with Noël Roquevert.

The success of the James Bond films produced a raft of
imitations. This spy comedy is only one of a large group of

spy films that came out of Western Europe at this time.
A scientist has just died, and four agents attempt to
persuade the man's widow (Darc) to part with her husband's
secret papers. All the rivals go to her country home in the
hopes of convincing her. Also along is a large contingent of
agents from China intent on obtaining the information. The
four agents decide to stop fighting among themselves and eliminate the Chinese. The French agent (Ventura) makes an over-
ture of marriage to Darc, even though he is already married.
The two of them go to Lisbon, where the secret plans are being
kept in a bank. They are followed by the other spies, but
Darc is won over by Ventura. They set out for Paris, with
Ventura wondering about his future as a bigamist.

KING AND COUNTRY. 1966. 86 minutes. *Director:* Joseph Losey.
   Screenplay: Evan Jones; based on the play *Hamp*, by John
   Wilson, and the novel *Return to the Wood*, by James Lans-
   dale Hodson. *Cinematography:* Denys Coop. *Cast:* Dirk
   Bogarde (Captain Hargreaves); Tom Courtenay (Private
   Arthur Hamp); Leo McKern (Captain O'Sullivan); Barry
   Foster (Lieutenant Webb); James Villiers (Captain Midg-
   ley); Peter Copley (Colonel); Barry Justice (Lieutenant
   Prescott); Vivian Matalon (Padre); Jeremy Spenser (Pri-
   vate Sparrow); James Hunter (Private Sykes); David Cook
   (Private Wilson); Larry Taylor (Sergeant-Major); Jonah
   Seymour (Corporal Hamilton, MP); Keith Buckley (Corporal
   of the Guard); Richard Arthure (Guard); Derek Partridge
   (Captain at Court Martial); Brian Tipping (Lieutenant at
   Court Martial); Raymond Brody, Dan Cornwall, Terry Palmer
   (Soldiers in Hamp's Platoon).

   Originally appearing in 1964, *King and Country* is clearly
an antiwar picture carrying the same type of emotional punch
as *Paths of Glory* and *Breaker Morant*. It is interesting to
note that all three films deal with military (in)justice, during wars earlier than World War II, wars in which the moral
lines were perhaps not as clearly marked.
   During World War I a young soldier (Courtenay) is arrested
for desertion after having spent three years in frontline action. The captain (Bogarde) ordered to represent Courtenay
at his courtmartial is at first hesitant to believe his story.
Bogarde slowly comes to sympathize with him as he learns about
what Courtenay has been through--an unhappy childhood, the
death of his comrades, and the unfaithfulness of his wife.
He provides for Courtenay a fervent defense, claiming that
under the circumstances he was not responsible for what he was

doing. But the court, realizing that it must maintain disci-
pline at all costs, orders Courtenay to be executed. When
the shots of the firing squad fail to kill him, Bogarde mercifully puts a bullet in his head.

THE MAN FROM COCODY. 1966. 84 minutes. Color. *Director:*
    Christian-Jaque. *Screenplay:* Jean Ferry, Jacques
    Emmanuel, and Christian-Jaque; based on a story by Claude
    Rank. *Cinematography:* Pierre Petit. *Cast:* Jean Marais
    (Jean-Luc Herve de la Tommeraye); Liselotte Pulver (Baby);
    Philippe Clay (Renaud Lefranc); Nancy Holloway (Nancy);
    Maria Grazia Buccella (Angelina); Jacques Morel (Rouf-
    fignac); Robert Dalban (Pepe).

Filmed in the Ivory Coast, *The Man from Cocody* is an adventure melodrama in the vein of *That Man from Rio*. A secret
society called the Sons of the Panthers slays a lepidopterist.
A French attaché (Marais) investigates the death along with
another lepidopterist (Pulver). They are blocked in their
quest by members of the secret society. The two of them come
across an abandoned airplane with jewels on board. Pulver,
who is really the head of a gang of jewel thieves, desires
the booty. She is kidnapped by the Sons of the Panthers but
is rescued by Marais. After the two of them have gone through
other adventures, it is learned that Marais's boss at the
French Embassy (Morel) is the leader of the Sons of the Panthers. With Marais's urging Pulver turns over a new leaf and
asks her gang of thieves to help the police.

NASHVILLE REBEL. 1966. 91 minutes. Color. *Director:* Jay
    Sheridan. *Screenplay:* Ira Kerns and Jay Sheridan; based
    on a story by Click Weston. *Cinematography:* John
    Elsenbach. *Cast:* Waylon Jennings (Arlin Grove); Gordon
    Oas-Heim (Wesley Lang); Mary Frann (Molly Morgan); Cece
    Whitney (Margo Powell); with Tex Ritter, Henny Youngman,
    Sonny James, The Wilburn Brothers, Faron Young, Loretta
    Lynn, Porter Wagoner, Cousin Jody, Archie Campbell (Them-
    selves).

This was one of the earliest attempts AIP made in the
country-and-western field. At the time *Nashville Rebel* was
made Waylon Jennings was not well known nationally. Now, of
course, he has become one of the biggest names in country-and-
western music. The film revolves around a good many musical

numbers, and the story sounds very much like the lyrics to a C&W song.

A young man (Jennings) just out of the Army is robbed and beaten by a group of punks. He wakes up in the back of a country store/gas station. Jennings soon falls in love and marries a young woman (Frann), who is the niece of the store owner. He sings at a local music contest and is discovered by an unscrupulous agent (Oas-Heim). Jennings becomes tired of the agent's tactics, and attempts to break his contract. Oas-Heim decides to come between Jennings and his wife by having him meet another woman (Whitney) and obtaining for him a singing engagement in Chicago. His singing style is ridiculed by the big-city audience, and he soon begins to drink heavily. Frann asks Tex Ritter to help her husband by letting him sing at the Grand Ole Opry (Nashville's answer to La Scala). Jennings learns that Frann is pregnant and is sick in the hospital. After singing a song for her on the Opry stage, he rushes to her bedside to find that they now have a child.

QUEEN OF BLOOD. 1966. 81 minutes. Color. *Director:* Curtis
    Harrington. *Screenplay:* Curtis Harrington. *Cinematog-*
    raphy: Vilis Lapenieks. *Cast:* John Saxon (Allan); Basil
    Rathbone (Dr. Farraday); Judi Meredith (Laura); Dennis
    Hopper (Paul); Florence Marly ("Queen of Blood"); with
    Robert Boon, Don Eitner, Virgil Frye, J. Robert Porter,
    Teri Lee, Forrest J. Ackerman.

This measly production incorporated footage from *Battle Beyond the Sun*, plus additional material written and directed by Curtis Harrington. On television it is often shown under the title *Planet of Blood*.

In 1990 an alien spaceship crashes on Mars and issues a distress signal to Earth. A team of U.S. astronauts are sent to the ship's rescue. One of the crew (Saxon) comes upon the craft on one of the Martian moons. The sole survivor of the alien ship is a green-complexioned woman (Marly), who is taken by the crew back to Earth. It turns out that Marly is a vampire, and she soon begins dispatching various members of the crew. In a struggle with one of the crew members (Meredith) Marly is scratched and slowly bleeds to death. The hemophiliac alien has left some eggs behind, which one scientist (Rathbone) plans to study on Earth.

SANDS OF BEERSHEBA. 1966. 90 minutes. *Director:* Alexander
Ramati. *Screenplay:* Alexander Ramati; based on his novel
Rebel Against the Light. *Cinematography:* Wolfgang
Suschitzky. *Cast:* Diane Baker (Susan); David Opatoshu
(Daoud); Tom Bell (Dan); Paul Stassino (Salim); Didi
Ramati (Naima); Theodore Marcuse (Nuri); Wolfe Barzell
(Ayub); with Oded Kotler, and Avraham Ben-Yosef.

Filmed on location in Israel, *Sands of Beersheba* is a
modern version of the biblical story of David and Absalom.
Alexander Ramati's "locales are authentically ancient, stark
and simple. His drama is equally stark and simple" (A.H.
Weiler, *The New York Times Film Reviews*, vol. 5/1959-1968.
New York: Arno, 1969, p. 3610).

A young American woman (Baker) is visiting the site in
Israel where her fiancé died in the 1948 Palestinian war. She
falls in love with one of her fiancé's best friends (Bell),
who is a gun runner for the Israelis. Bell is set upon by a
group of Arab terrorists and takes refuge in an Arab village.
He is protected by the village elder (Opatoshu), whose son
(Stassino) happens to be the leader of the group who attacked
Bell. Stassino sets siege to his father's house in an attempt
to gain possession of Bell's ammunition truck. During a battle Stassino is killed and the wounded Bell has Baker come to
his aid.

SECRET AGENT FIREBALL. 1966. 89 minutes. Color. *Director:*
Martin Donan (Mario Donen). *Screenplay:* Julian Barry
(Sergio Martino). *Cinematogrpahy:* Richard Thierry
(Riccardo Pallottini). *Cast:* Richard Harrison (Robert
Fleming); Dominique Boschero (Liz); Wandisa Guida (Elena);
Alcide Borik (Taxi Driver); Jim Clay and Alan Collins
(Russian Agents); with Audrey Fisher, Franklyn Fred,
Clément Harari, Caroll Brown, Jean Ozenne, Freddy Unger.
(Jim Clay, Alan Collins, and Caroll Brown are pseudonyms
for Aldo Cecconi, Luciano Pigozzi, and Bruno Carotenuto.)

Often on the late show you can view, through droopy eyes,
spy films like *Secret Agent Fireball*. Usually made by West
German, Italian, or French companies, these dubbed films present travelogues of cities in Europe and the Middle East, with
plots that are, at best, vestigial.

Two scientists escape from the Soviet Union with important microfilm. Both are murdered in separate incidents in Europe. A CIA agent (Harrison) goes to Beirut, where a wealthy Lebanese supposedly has the microfilm, but he is murdered before Harrison can make contact with him. Harrison and the man's niece (Boschero) are captured by Soviet agents. Boschero tells them that the microfilm is buried with her uncle. His coffin is opened, and a double agent, posing as a Russian, but working for another country, steals the microfilm and kidnaps Boschero. Harrison gives chase in a helicopter. He locates the speedboat they are in and sets fire to it. Boschero is rescued, and it is discovered that the microfilm contains information on nuclear weaponry.

SPY IN YOUR EYE. 1966. 88 minutes. Color. *Director:* Vittorio Sala. *Screenplay:* Romano Ferrara, Adriano Baracco, and Adriano Bolzoni; based on a story by Lucio Marcuzzo. *Cinematography:* Fausto Luccoli. *Cast:* Brett Halsey (Bert Morris); Pier Angeli (Paula Krauss); Dana Andrews (Colonel Lancaster); Gaston Moschin (Boris); with Tania Beryl, Alessandro Sperli, Mario Valdemarin, Tino Bianchi, Aldo De Francesco, Renato Baldini, Marco Guglielmi, Luciana Angiolillo, George Wang, Luciano Pigozzi, Massimo Righi, Franco Baltimor, Giulio Mecale, Aghul Rain Bozan.

By the mid 60s the James Bond-style ripoffs were being made with great frequency. *Spy in Your Eye* is not much different from the rest, except that it contains the somewhat novel idea of a tiny camera being implanted in someone's eye.
In Berlin both Russian and American intelligence are attempting to obtain a secret formula from a recently deceased scientist. Supposedly the scientist's daughter (Angeli) knows something about the formula's whereabouts. She is kidnapped by Russian agents, and an American secret agent (Halsey) is ordered to rescue her. What the Americans are not aware of is that the Russians know all of their intelligence plans. The head of U.S. intelligence (Andrews) has had, unknown to him, a microscopic camera implanted in his eye by the Russians during an operation to implant an artificial eye. The Russians are able to monitor everything that Andrews does. However, the "spying eye" is uncovered, and American intelligence feeds false information to the Russians through it. The chaos that this causes allows Halsey to abduct Angeli from the Russians. It is now learned that the secret formula had been tattooed on Angeli--under her hair.

TARZAN AND THE VALLEY OF GOLD. 1966. 100 minutes. Color.
Director: Robert Day. *Screenplay:* Clair Huffaker; based
on characters created by Edgar Rice Burroughs. *Cinema-
tography:* Irving Lippman. *Cast:* Mike Henry (Tarzan);
Nancy Kovack (Sophia); David Opatoshu (Vinaro); Manuel
Padilla, Jr. (Ramel); Don Megowan (Mr. Train); Enrique
Lucero (Perez); Eduardo Noriega (Talmadge); John Kelly
(Voss); Francisco Riquerio (Manco); Frank Brandstetter
(Ruiz); Carlos Rivas (Romulo); Jorge Beirute (Rodriguez);
Oswald Olvera (Antonio).

Originally the character of Tarzan swung from the trees
in Africa. By the 60s Tarzan became quite the world traveler,
being found in Brazil, Thailand, India, and, in this film,
Mexico.
A young boy (Padilla) is kidnapped by a man (Opatoshu)
who believes that Padilla can lead him to a lost Aztec city
of gold. Tarzan (Henry) is sent by the authorities to help
find the lost city and thwart Opatoshu. Aided by a jaguar, a
lion, and his trusting chimpanzee, Henry locates Padilla and
also rescues Opatoshu's ex-mistress (Kovack). He then locates
the cave that leads into the lost city and meets the elderly
chief (Riquerio) of the city. Henry persuades him that violent measures must be taken to save the city from Opatoshu
and his band of mercenaries. Opatoshu commands an invasion
force that uses armored tanks. Riquerio leads him to a chamber where a shower of gold dust traps and suffocates Opatoshu
to death. Henry battles with Opatoshu's minions and defeats
them. He and Kovack now leave Riqueiro's city with everything
intact.

TRUNK TO CAIRO. 1966. 80 minutes. Color. *Director:* Menahem
Golan. *Screenplay:* Marc Behm and Alexander Ramati. *Cin-
ematography:* Itzhak Herbst. *Cast:* Audie Murphy (Mike
Herrick); George Sanders (Professor Schlieben); Marianne
Koch (Helga Schlieben); Hans von Borsody (Hans Klugg);
Joseph Yadin (Captain Gabar); Gila Almagor (Yasmin);
Elana Eden (Hadassa); Eytan Priver (Jamil); Zalman
(Ephraim); Bomba Zur (Ali); Tikva Mor (Christina); Zeev
Berlinski (Benz); Eliezer Young (Dr. Heider); Shlomo
Vichinsky (Jacob); Yoel Noyman (Egyptian Colonel); Cesar
Suberi (Old Mullah); Shlomo Paz (Joe); Mona Silberstein
(Hostess); Anna Shell (Belly Dancer); Suzanna Ratoni
(Fraulein Bruckner); Menashe Glazier (Mahmud); Karin
(Young German Girl).

This Israeli espionage film apparently was a fiasco, since it was well over a year before it made it into American theatres. The film is terribly miscast. There is a hero who sounds like a cowboy, and it also includes George Sanders, who looks bored with the entire affair. Director Menahem Golan has proven himself to be an exemplary hack over the years. All one has to do is look at the movie trade papers to see what kinds of questionable films he is now producing.

An agent (Murphy), working for Israel, is sent to Cairo to contact a scientist (Sanders), who is working on a nuclear rocket. Sanders's lab is guarded by the Egyptian army but Murphy is able to enter the premises and destroy the rocket blueprints. An Islamic group desires the completed rocket, but Murphy outwits them and escapes Egypt, along with Sanders's daughter (Koch), in a submarine. The Egyptians recapture him, but through a trick involving a trunk headed for Cairo, he escapes once again. Now Murphy is free to return Koch to her father.

WHAT'S UP TIGER LILY? 1966. 80 minutes. Color. *Director:*
    Senkichi Taniguchi (original version). *Screenplay for*
    English-Language Version: Woody Allen, Frank Buxton, Len
    Maxwell, Louise Lasser, Mickey Rose, Bryna Wilson, and
    Julie Bennett. *Screenplay for Japanese-Language Version:*
    Kazuo Yamada. *Cinematography:* Kazuo Yamada. *Cast:*
    Tatsuya Mihashi (Phil Moscowitz); Mie Hama (Terri Yaki);
    Akiko Wakabayashi (Suki Yaki); Tadao Nakamaru (Shepherd
    Wong); Susumu Kurobe (Wing Fat); Woody Allen (Narrator/
    Host); Frank Buxton, Len Maxwell, Louise Lasser, Mickey
    Rose, Julie Bennett, Bryna Wilson (Voices); The Lovin'
    Spoonful (Themselves); China Lee (Herself); with Kumi
    Mizuno.

This Japanese made spy film was sold to a couple of American investors and given over to Woody Allen for reediting and dubbing. *What's Up Tiger Lily?* (original title: *Kagi No Kagi*) was Woody Allen's first opportunity to exercise creative control over a film. The deliberate non sequiturs in the dialogue and the incongruous names of the characters are fresh and amusing for about the first 20 minutes or so. Then the novelty wears thin in this trumped-up story about the attempted theft of an egg-salad recipe. It is bad enough that the film becomes bogged down, but why must we be subjected to the totally unnecessary musical interludes by The Lovin' Spoonful? *What's Up Tiger Lily?* remains a film that appeals to the *Saturday Night Live* mentality. It would be a couple of years before Woody Allen fans could see his true comic talent on display.

THE WILD ANGELS. 1966. 90 minutes. Color. *Director:* Roger Corman. *Screenplay:* Charles Griffith. *Cinematography:* Richard Moore. *Cast:* Peter Fonda (Heavenly Blues); Nancy Sinatra (Mike); Bruce Dern (Loser); Lou Procopio (Joint); Coby Denton (Bull Puckey); Marc Cavell (Frankenstein); Buck Taylor (Dear John); Norman Alden (Medic); Michael J. Pollard (Pigmy); Diane Ladd (Gaysh); Joan Shawlee (Mama Monahan); Gayle Hunnicutt (Suzie); Art Baker (Thomas); Frank Maxwell (Preacher); Frank Gerstle (Hospital Policeman); Kim Hamilton (Nurse); with members of the Hell's Angels of Venice, California, and Peter Bogdanovich.

The Wild Angels is one of the most influential and controversial films produced by AIP. It was the film that began the series of motorcycle films so prevalent in the mid- and late 60s. It was an entry at the Venice Film Festival, much to the outrage of the middle-brow establishment film critics.

A group of Hell's Angels headed by Peter Fonda help one of their members (Dern) get his cycle back, by precipitating a fight with a rival gang. The police come and they shoot Dern as he is trying to escape. Members of the gang decide to, as they say, "rescue him," from the hospital. In doing so they get their "kicks" by raping a nurse (Hamilton). Not having any doctors among the gang, Dern dies because of a lack of proper medical care, and his body is sent back home. During a drunken binge the Angels decide to give Dern a proper Nazi-bedecked send-off. They tie up the minister, rape his widow, and have an orgy. Before they can bury him, the Angels are attacked by the outraged local citizens, and a violent melee erupts. When the police arrive, the gang get on their cycles and split. The pensive Fonda stays to mourn over Dern's grave.

BORN LOSERS. 1967. 112 minutes. Color. *Director:* T.C. Frank (Tom Laughlin). *Screenplay:* E. James Lloyd (Tom Laughlin). *Cinematography:* Gregory Sandor. *Cast:* Tom Laughlin (Billy Jack); Elizabeth James (Vicky Barrington); Jane Russell (Mrs. Shorn); Jeremy Slate (Danny Carmody); William Wellman, Jr. (Child); Robert Tessier (Cue Ball); Jeff Cooper (Gangrene); Edwin Cook (Crabs); Tex (Himself); Paul Prokop (Speechless); Julie Cahn (Lu Ann Crawford); Susan Foster (Linda Prang); Janice Miller (Jodell Shorn); Stuart Lancaster (Sheriff); Jack Starrett (Deputy); Paul Bruce (District Attorney); Robert Cleaves (Mr. Crawford); Ann Bellamy (Mrs. Prang); Gordon Hoban (Jerry Carmody).

I suppose one has to admire someone like Tom Laughlin,
who has had some success in producing and directing his own
films outside of the Hollywood establishment. However, his
Billy Jack character happens to be part sanctimonious bore
and part hero/avenger. In *Born Losers* he is flexing his muscles, getting ready for his role in the immensely successful
Billy Jack.
     A small California town is being terrorized by an outlaw
motorcycle gang headed by Jeremy Slate. A young half-breed
Indian (Laughlin) is arrested after helping one of the townsfolk fight off an attack by the gang. Slate's group next stage
an orgy, in which a number of the young women of the town are
gang-raped. Law-enforcement authorities are powerless to arrest anyone, because the people of the town have been threatened if anyone testifies against the gang. Laughlin decides
to show his mettle, so he gets on his motorcycle and heads
for the gang's mountain retreat. He murders Slate and rounds
up the rest of the gang, just as the police arrive. He leaves
the scene on his cycle, and one of the trigger-happy cops
shoots him by accident. Seriously wounded, he heads into the
mountains, but a young woman (James) leads a police rescue
squad to help him.

THE COBRA. 1967. 93 minutes. Color. *Director:* Mario Sequi.
     Screenplay: Gumersindo Mollo; based on a story by Adriano
     Bolzoni. *Cinematography:* Enrique Toran and Claudio Racca.
     Cast: Dana Andrews (Chief Kelly); Peter Martell (Mike
     Rand); Anita Ekberg (Lou); Elisa Montés (Corianne); Jesus
     Puente (Stiarkos); Peter Dane (Hullinger); Luciana
     Vincenzi (Ulla); George Histman (Crane); Omar Zoulfikar
     (Sadek); Giovanni Petrucci (King); Chang'e (Li Fang);
     Eshane Sadek (Gamel); with Lidia Biondi.

The Cobra is enlivened by lavish sets and some exotic
locations in the Middle East. This tale of international drug
smuggling takes a decidedly right-wing slant. At one point
Dana Andrews (doing an Efrem Zimbalist, Jr., impression) refers to some heroin as "a time bomb from Peking to destroy
the moral fiber of our nation" (*Variety*, April 10, 1968,
p. 22).
     The head (Andrews) of the U.S. Secret Service is in Istan-
bul to hire a former agent (Martell). He wants Martell to
find the identity of The Cobra, the leader of an international
ring of drug smugglers. Martell discovers that the drugs are
sent out of China and then transported across the Middle East
through oil pipelines. The Cobra turns out to be a wealthy

Greek ship owner (Puente). With the aid of one of Puente's
former associates (Ekberg) Martell is able to locate the drug
shipment. In a gun battle Ekberg is killed, and Martell confronts Puente. In a *Death Wish*-like twist, Martell coldblood-
edly murders Puente, because he thinks the courts of law would
let him go free.

DEVIL'S ANGELS. 1967. 84 minutes. Color. *Director:* Daniel
   Haller. *Screenplay:* Charles Griffith. *Cinematography:*
   Richard Moore. *Cast:* John Cassavetes (Cody); Beverly
   Adams (Lynn); Mimsy Farmer (Marianne); Maurice McEndree
   (Joel-the-Mole); Marc Cavell (Billy the Kid); Salli Sache
   (Louise); Nai Bonet (Tonya); Buck Taylor (Gage); Marianne
   Kanter (Rena); Leo Gordon (Sheriff Henderson); Buck
   Kartalian (Funky); John Craig (Robot); Kip Whitman (Roy);
   George Sims (Leroy); Mitzi Hoag (Karen); Russ Bender
   (Royce); Wally Campo (Grog); Richard Anders (Bruno); Paul
   Myer (Mayor); Lee Wainer (Cane); Roy Thiel and Ronnie
   Dayton (Deputies); Henry Kendrick (Store Owner).

   There seemed to be an attempt being made by AIP in *Devil's
Angels* to soften, somewhat, the nihilism displayed in *The Wild
Angels*. John Cassavetes plays the long-of-tooth (as many actual members of these outlaw cycle gangs are) leader of a gang
of cyclists, who shows enough of a conscience at the end of
the film to be on the verge of tears.
   When two members of The Skulls motorcycle gang become
involved in a fatal accident, their leader (Cassavetes) decides to move the gang to a hideout for outlaw cyclists. On
their way they stop in a small town. Some members attempt to
seduce a local girl (Farmer). The sheriff (Gordon) arrests
Cassavetes, thinking that Farmer had been raped. When the
truth comes out, he is allowed to leave with his gang as long
as they do not come back. Another gang enters the town and
embarks on an orgy of mayhem. Cassavetes realizes that he
will never find a safe place to hide for his gang, so he dis-
associates himself from the rest and rides off alone.

THE GLORY STOMPERS. 1967. 85 minutes. Color. *Director:*
   Anthony M. Lanza. *Screenplay:* James Gordon White and
   John Lawrence. *Cinematography:* Mario Tosi. *Cast:* Dennis
   Hopper (Chino); Jody McCrea (Darryl); Chris Noel (Chris);
   Jock Mahoney (Smiley); Saundra Gayle (Jo Ann); Jim Reader
   (Paul); Robert Tessier (Magoo); Astrid Warner (Doreen);

Gary Wood (Pony); Lindsay Crosby (Monk); Casey Kasem (Mouth); with Al Quick, Paul Prokop, Tony Acone, Ed Cook.

The title, *The Glory Stompers*, not only refers to the name of a motorcycle gang, but is also a colloquialism for the big heavy boots that the bikers wear. This film was co-produced by radio disc jockey Casey Kasem, and Mike Curb, a Pat Boone-type young Republican clone, who later became Lieutenant Governor of California.

Dennis Hopper and his outlaw gang of cyclists, The Black Souls, capture the leader (McCrea) of a rival group, The Glory Stompers, and his girlfriend (Noel). Noel is molested by a gang member (Tessier), as the rest do all they can to stomp McCrea into the ground. An ex-Glory Stomper (Mahoney) comes upon the injured McCrea, who has been left for dead. The two of them band together to rescue Noel. She has been kidnapped by the gang, who plan to sell her as a prostitute in Mexico. There is a bloody pitched battle in which Tessier and Hopper are killed. McCrea rescues Noel and they go off together.

HOUSE OF A THOUSAND DOLLS. 1967. 78 minutes. Color. *Director:* Jeremy Summers. *Screenplay:* (English-language version); Peter Welbeck (pseudonym for Harry Alan Towers). Carmen M. Roman (foreign version). *Cinematography:* Manuel Merino. *Cast:* Vincent Price (Felix Manderville); Martha Hyer (Rebecca); George Nader (Stephen Armstrong); Ann Smyrner (Marie Armstrong); Wolfgang Kieling (Inspector Emil); Sancho Gracia (Fernando); Maria Rohm (Diane); Luis Rivera (Paul); José Jaspe (Ahmed); Juan Olaguibel (Salim); Herbert Fux (Abdu); Yelena Samarina (Madame Viera); Diane Bond (Liza); Andrea Lascelles, Jill Echols, Kitty Swan, Ursula Janis, Loli Munoz, Karin Skarreso, Monique Aimé, Lara Lenti, Caroline Coon, Marisol, Sandra Petrelli, Françoise Fontages (The Dolls); with Milo Quesada, Fernando Cebrian, Irene G. Caba.

This British-German-Spanish co-production "could well serve as an object lesson in the kind of disaster that this type of international venture can produce" (*Monthly Film Bulletin*, May 1968, p. 78). *House of a Thousand Dolls* seems to have been a vehicle made solely to show a bevy of European starlets in various stages of undress.

A businessman (Nader) and his wife (Smyrner) are on a vacation in Tangiers. They meet a young man (Gracia), who believes that his fiancée (Rohm) is a prisoner in a local house of prostitution. The whorehouse, known as the House of a

Thousand Dolls, is operated by two illusionists (Price and Hyer), who use their magic act as a cover for kidnapping attractive young women into a life of slavery. Gracia is ordered killed by the brothel's madame (Samarina). Nader is hoodwinked by Price and led on a false trail, as Price and Hyer kidnap Smyrner. A rift occurs between the two of them. The finale has the women of the house, The Dolls, doing battle with Price and his henchman. Price falls to his death, while Hyer is arrested.

THE MILLION EYES OF SU-MURU. 1967. 95 minutes. Color. *Director:* Lindsay Shonteff. *Screenplay:* Kevin Kavanagh; based on a story by Peter Welbeck (pseudonym for Harry Alan Towers) and on characters created by Sax Rohmer. *Cinematography:* John Kotze. *Cast:* Frankie Avalon (Tommy Carter); George Nader (Nick West); Shirley Eaton (Su-Muru); Wilfrid Hyde-White (Colonel Baisbrook); Klaus Kinski (President Boong); Patti Chandler (Louise); Salli Sachse (Mikki); Ursula Rank (Erna); Christa Nell (Zoe); Maria Rohm (Helga); Paul Chang (Inspector Koo); Essie Huang (Kitty); Jon Fong (Colonel Medika); Denise Davreux, Mary Cheng, Jill Hamilton, Lisa Gray, Christine Lok, Margaret Cheung, Louise Lee (The Su-Muru Guard).

The Million Eyes of Su-Muru is played as a satire, since any film in which Frankie Avalon portrays a secret agent would have to be satirical. The relationship between the title character (Shirley Eaton, the Golden Girl from *Goldfinger*) and her female underlings carries more than a trace of lesbianism.

An officer in British Intelligence (Hyde-White) convinces two Americans (Nader and Avalon) to aid in the investigation of a murder of an official in the fictitious Asian country of Sinonesia. They learn that an organization of women plotting to enslave the world are behind the murder. Their next plan is to kill the President (Kinski) of Sinonesia. Nader is captured by the agents of Su-Muru and forced to infiltrate Kinski's security system. An attempt is made on Kinski's life, but his double is killed instead. Nader is now taken back to Su-Muru's torture dungeon, but Avalon rescues him just before Su-Muru's island fortress is blown up by a large explosion. There is left the intimation that Su-Muru escaped the blast, and that the film would lead to a sequel.

PSYCHO-CIRCUS. 1967. 65 minutes. *Director:* John Moxey.
Screenplay: Peter Welbeck (pseudonym for Harry Alan
Towers). *Cinematography:* Ernest Steward. *Cast:* Christo-
pher Lee (Gregor); Leo Genn (Inspector Elliott); Anthony
Newlands (Barberini); Heinz Drache (Carl); Eddi Arent
(Eddie); Klaus Kinski (Manfred); Margaret Lee (Gina);
Suzy Kendall (Natasha); Cecil Parker (Sir John); Victor
Maddern (Mason); Maurice Kaufmann (Mario); Lawrence James
(Manley); Tom Bowman (Jackson); Skip Martin (Mr. Big);
Fred Powell (Red); Gordon Petrie (Negro); Henry Longhurst
(Hotel Porter); Dennis Blakely (Armored Van Guard); George
Fisher (4th Man); Peter Brace and Roy Scammel (Speedboat
Men); Geoff Silk and Keith Peacock (Security Men).

Also known as *Circus of Fear*, this film was cut for U.S.
release by 18 minutes. *Psycho-Circus* contains a confused plot,
in which many of the main characters are involved in murder,
revenge, and blackmail.
   The police investigate a circus ground after some stolen
money from an armored car robbery has turned up there. An
inspector (Genn) finds that members of the troupe have a number of motives, after one of the robbery suspects and a circus
performer are found murdered. Eventually it is learned that
the lion tamer (C. Lee) found the stolen money. Before he
can escape with it, he is murdered by a mysterious disguised
figure. Genn does not believe that Lee was responsible for
the other two murders, so he arranges for a stunt that will
trap the real killer. After all the red herrings have been
eliminated, it turns out that the circus bookkeeper (Arent),
a frustrated circus performer, is the guilty one.

RIOT ON SUNSET STRIP. 1967. 85 minutes. Color. *Director:*
Arthur Dreifuss. *Screenplay:* Orville H. Hampton. *Cine-
matography:* Paul C. Vogel. *Cast:* Aldo Ray (Lieutenant
Walt Lorimer); Mimsy Farmer (Andy); Michael Evans (Ser-
geant Tweedy); Laurie Mock (Liz-Ann); Tim Rooney (Grady);
Gene Kirkwood (Flip); Hortense Petra (Marge); Anna Mizrahi
(Helen Tweedy); Schuyler Hayden (Herby); with Dick
Winslow, Bill Baldwin, Sr., Tony Benson, Jim LeFebvre,
Al Ferrara, Pat Renella, The Standells, Forrest Lewis,
George E. Carey, The Enemies, Deborah Travis, John Hart,
The Longhairs, The Chocolate Watch Band.

Riot on Sunset Strip was based on the actual teenage riots that took place on Sunset Boulevard in Hollywood in 1966.
Using some stock footage of the riots, AIP wasted no time in

RIGHTS, NOT FIGHTS

Riot on Sunset Strip

grafting a story line onto it. The music in the film is provided by such terminally insipid groups as The Chocolate Watch
Band and The Standells, among others.
    Aldo Ray is a police detective in Hollywood, where young
people have started to hang out on the street in droves. His
daughter (Farmer), who lives with his drunken wife, becomes
involved with a group who hang out on the Sunset Strip. Farmer
meets the spoiled son (Hayden) of a movie star. The two of
them and their friends trespass upon an unoccupied house, and
have a drug party. The noise of the party brings in the police, including Ray. He finds Farmer in a drugged state, and
she must be hospitalized. He exacts his revenge on Hayden and
his friends by giving them a severe beating.

SEXY MAGICO. 1967. 89 minutes. Color. *Directors:* Mino Loy
    and Luigi Scattini. *Screenplay:* Uncredited. *Cinematog-
    raphy:* Benito Frattari and Floriano Trenker. *Cast:* Black
    Eva, Nana Pilou, Leila Sohl, Rosetta Esperanza, Barbara
    Won, Jessica Rubicon, Belinda, Monty Landis, Marlene,
    Fernando Rego.

    It is surprising that *Sexy Magico* is under the AIP label
and not its subsidiary, Trans-American. Under the latter
title AIP usually distributed films that it was leery of distributing under its own banner. Made back in 1963, this film
is similar to other films of the early and mid-60s, e.g., *Europe in the Raw*, *Hollywood's World of Flesh*, and *Mondo Topless*.
Before hardcore films came into being with any frequency, these
types of films acted as a tame substitute. In *Sexy Magico* we
are shown the sexual rites of various tribal communities
throughout the world. They are all performed through dances
and acts by performers in various nightclubs. Among the exotic and "magical" acts depicted are those that originate at
such places as the Sombrero Club in Nairobi and the Crazy Horse
Saloon in Paris.

THOSE FANTASTIC FLYING FOOLS. 1967. 95 minutes. Color. *Di-
    rector:* Don Sharp. *Screenplay:* Dave Freeman; based on a
    story by Peter Welbeck (pseudonym for Harry Alan Towers).
    Cinematography: Reg Wyer. *Cast:* Burl Ives (Phineas T.
    Barnum); Troy Donahue (Gaylord Sullivan); Gert Frobe (Pro-
    fessor von Bulow); Hermione Gingold (Angelica); Lionel
    Jeffries (Sir Charles Dillworthy); Dalia Lavi (Madelaine);
    Dennis Price (Duke of Barset); Stratford Johns (Warrant

Officer); Graham Stark (Grundle); Terry-Thomas (Captain
Sir Henry Washington-Smythe); Jimmy Clitheroe (General
Tom Thumb); Joachim Teege (Bulgeroff); Joan Sterndale-
Bennett (The Queen); Renate von Holt (Anna); Edward De
Souza (Henri); Judy Cornwell (Electra); Derek Francis
(Puddleby); Allan Cuthbertson (Scotland Yard Man); with
Klaus Kinski.

Those Fantastic Flying Fools is supposedly taken from
some of the writing of Jules Verne. It is a science-fiction
comedy that is part *Around the World in Eighty Days* and part
Those Magnificent Men in Their Flying Machines.
    Phineas T. Barnum (Ives) and his star attraction, Tom
Thumb (Clitheroe), find themselves in Victorian England. They
meet a professor (Frobe), who has built a rocket that he claims
will go to the moon. Ives senses that money can be made from
a rocket-to-the-moon scheme. Soon upon the scene comes a number of spies trying to obtain the design of the space craft,
as well as a young American (Donahue), who has a plan for a
round-trip moon flight. The rest of this farcical plot involves kidnapping, sabotage, and chicanery. Eventually a Russian spy (Teege), and two other villains (Jeffries and Terry-
Thomas) sneak aboard the ship and are sent on a one way flight.
When they land on a desolate planet they find, much to their
amazement, that the inhabitants are all singing in Russian.

THUNDER ALLEY. 1967. 90 minutes. Color. *Director:* Richard
    Rush. *Screenplay:* Sy Salkowitz. *Cinematography:* Monroe
    Askins. *Cast:* Annette Funicello (Francie Madsen); Fabian
    (Tommy Callahan); Diane McBain (Annie Blaine); Warren
    Berlinger (Eddie Sands); Jan Murray (Pete Madsen); Stanley
    Adams (Mal Lunsford); Maureen Arthur (Babe); Michael T.
    Mikler (Harry Wise); Michael Bell (Leroy); Kip King (Dom);
    Sandy Reed (Announcer); with Sammy Shore, Baynes Barron,
    Michael Dugan, The Band Without a Name.

Thunder Alley is sort of a continuation of *Fireball 500*,
except without Frankie Avalon. The blandness of the two main
leads, Annette Funicello and Fabian, is somewhat made up for
by the sauciness of Maureen Arthur and Diane McBain, and the
cynicism of Jan Murray.
    A young stock car racer (Fabian) is suspended after he
blacks out during a race and kills another driver. The only
job he can find is with Jan Murray's auto-daredevil show.
Fabian is part of a team along with Murray's daughter
(Funicello) and her boyfriend (Berlinger) in staging hair-

raising crashes. Under Fabian's tutelage Berlinger enters a
race and wins. Arrogant with the thrill of victory, Berlinger
goes on to steal Fabian's speed-crazy girlfriend (McBain).
Despite both young men's dislike for one another, they end up
as teammates in a race. During the race Fabian suddenly discovers, after all these years, the reasons for his blackouts.
He goes on to win the race after Berlinger has crashed his
car, and is now united with Funicello.

THE TRIP. 1967. 85 minutes. Color. *Director:* Roger Corman.
    Screenplay: Jack Nicholson. *Cinematography:* Arch R.
    Dalzell. *Cast:* Peter Fonda (Paul Groves); Susan Strasberg
    (Sally Groves); Bruce Dern (John); Dennis Hopper (Max);
    Salli Sachse (Glenn); Katherine Walsh (Lulu); Barboura
    Morris (Flo); Caren Bernsen (Alexandra); Dick Miller
    (Cash); Luana Anders (Waitress); Tom Signorelli (Al);
    Mitzi Hoag (Wife); Judy Lang (Nadine); Barbara Renson
    (Helena); Susan Walters and Frankie Smith (Go-Go Girls);
    with Peter Bogdanovich.

The Trip is one of the more significant cinematic artifacts of the 60s. It has been rumored that director Roger
Corman embarked on an LSD trip before making the film.
    A director of television commercials (Fonda) is going
through a life crisis, with doubts about his job and an immi-
nent breakup with his wife (Strasberg). On the verge of becoming a basket case, Fonda asks a friend (Dern), a local guru,
to be his guide on an LSD trip. He takes Fonda to a psychedelic nightclub and later to a party at a pusher's (Hopper)
home. The two then go to Dern's house, where Fonda has his
first hit of acid. His trip begins serenely, with tranquil
thoughts and day-glo colors. Fonda's perceptions then start
to change, as he experiences scenes of medieval rites involving people he had met earlier in the evening. He soon visual-
izes his own funeral, and runs from Dern's pad. He is found
by Hopper, who takes Fonda to the home of a girl (Sachse) he
had met at Hopper's party. The two of them have sex, and in
the morning Fonda feels as if he has experienced a rebirth.
But Sachse tells him, "It's easy now. Wait until tomorrow."

WAR ITALIAN STYLE. 1967. 74 minutes. Color. *Director:* Luigi
    Scattini. *Screenplay:* Franco Castellano and Pipolo; based
    on an idea by Fulvio Lucisano. *Cinematography:* Fausto
    Zuccoli. *Cast:* Buster Keaton (General Von Kassler);

Franco Franchi (Frank); Ciccio Ingrassia (Joe); Martha
Hyer (Lieutenant Inge Schultze); Fred Clark (General
Zacharias); with Franco Ressel, Tommaso Alvieri, Barbara
Loy, Alessandro Sperli, Alfredo Adami, Ennio Antonelli.

This pathetic World War II comedy was severely edited
from almost 100 minutes down to its present length. It is
not exactly the most fitting memorial to one of the screen's
greatest comics--Buster Keaton. This was the last film he
made, and he is teamed up here with the Italian equivalent of
Abbott and Costello--Franco and Ciccio.

Two American soldiers in North Africa (Franchi and
Ingrassia) come upon the headquarters of a famous but incompetent Nazi general (Keaton). They are captured and sent back
out again with some false battle plans. What the Germans do
not know is that the two soldiers accidentally were given the
real plans. This leads to an important Allied victory. In
Italy Franchi and Ingrassia run into Keaton again and persuade
the bumbling officer to destroy his own gun placements. Keaton
is ordered to be executed, but the two GIs like the old man,
so they disguise him and help him to escape.

ANGELS FROM HELL. 1968. 86 minutes. Color. *Director:* Bruce
    Kessler. *Screenplay:* Jerome Wish. *Cinematography:* Herman
    Knox. *Cast:* Tom Stern (Mike); Arlene Martel (Ginger);
    Ted Markland (Smiley); Stephen Oliver (Speed); Paul
    Bertoya (Nutty Norman); James Murphy (Tiny Tim); Jack
    Starrett (Captain Bingham); Jay York (George); Pepper
    Martin (Dennis); Bob Harris (Baney); Saundra Gayle
    (Clair); Susan Walters (Millie); Luana Talltree (Angry
    Annie); Susan Holloway (Jennifer); Judith Garwood
    (Louise); Susanne Sidney (Buff); Steve Rodgers (Dude).

Another of your standard AIP biker movies, with your usual
Cro Magnon cretins on wheels. A Vietnam veteran (Stern) separates from his wife and resumes his old life as a cyclist.
He and a friend (Markland) start a new outlaw motorcycle gang.
Stern's Vietnam experience is put to good use as he combats
other gangs to become their undisputed leader. When the police try to curb his new found power, Stern decides to orga-
nize all the cycle gangs in the state as his own private army.
During one of his gang's orgies a young woman is killed. The
gang member responsible is murdered by the police, so Stern
calls for an all-out war against the cops. He is eventually
trapped in his hideout and dies in the ensuing shootout. *Angels from Hell* is an early, and prime, example of the notion
of bringing the Vietnam War home.

THE BRUTE AND THE BEAST. 1968. 88 minutes. Color. *Directors:* Lucio Fulci and Terry Vantell. *Screenplay:* Fernando Di Leo. *Cinematography:* Riccardo Pallottini. *Cast:* Franco Nero (Tom); George Hilton (Jeff); Nino Castelnuovo (Jason); Lyn Shayne (Brady); John MacDouglas (Mr. Scott); Rina Franchetti (Mercedes); with Aysanoa Runachagua, Tchang Yu, Tom Felleghi, Franco Morici.

The Brute and the Beast is one of the few Italian spaghetti westerns distributed by AIP. It contains the western themes used a number of times before: the outcast son, the strong-willed father, and the fight for land inheritence.

A young gold prospector (Nero) receives an unsigned note to return to his hometown, which he had left as a young boy. Neither his half-brother (Hilton) or the family retainer (Franchetti) knows who wrote the letter. Nero finds that the town is controlled by an old tyrant (MacDouglas) and his trigger-happy son (Castelnuovo). They have taken over Nero's family ranch. When Nero questions their right to the land, he is badly beaten by Castelnuovo's bully boys. It is eventually learned that MacDouglas sent Nero the letter, and that he is his father. Castelnuovo has been the prime villain all along. The two men have a gunfight and Nero kills him. He now reclaims the land that is rightfully his.

THE CONQUEROR WORM. 1968. 87 minutes. Color. *Director:* Michael Reeves. *Screenplay:* Michael Reeves and Tom Baker; additional scenes by Louis M. Heyward; based on the novel *Witchfinder General*, by Ronald Bassett. *Cinematography:* John Coquillon. *Cast:* Vincent Price (Matthew Hopkins); Ian Ogilvy (Richard Marshall); Rupert Davies (John Lowes); Hilary Dwyer (Sara); Robert Russell (John Stearne); Patrick Wymark (Oliver Cromwell); Wilfred Brambell (Master Loach); Nicky Henson (Trooper Swallow); Tony Selby (Salter); Bernard Kay (Fisherman); Godfrey James (Webb); Michael Beint (Captain Gordon); John Trenaman (Trooper Harcourt); Bill Maxwell (Trooper Gifford); Morris Jar (Paul); Maggie Kimberley (Elizabeth Clark); Peter Haigh (Lavenham Magistrate); John Kidd (Magistrate); Hira Talfrey (Hanged Woman); Ann Tirard (Old Woman); Peter Thomas (Farrier); Edward Palmer (Shepherd); David Webb (Jailer); Paul Dawkins (Farmer); Lee Peters (Infantry Sergeant); David Lyell (Foot Soldier); Alf Joint (Sentry); Martin Terry (Hoxne Innkeeper); Jack Lynn (Brandeston Innkeeper); Beaufoy Milton (Priest); Dennis Thorne and Michael Segal (Villagers); Toby Lennon (Old Man); Gillian

The Conqueror Worm

6803-26

Aldham (Young Woman in Cell); Paul Ferris (Young Husband);
Margaret Nolan, Sally Douglas, Donna Reading, Tasma
Brereton, Sandy Seager (Wenches at the Inn); with Philip
Waddilove, Derek Ware, Susi Field.

The director of *The Conqueror Worm*, Michael Reeves, was
a promising young director in the horror genre. Only about a
year after this film was made he died of a drug overdose.
England in 1645 is in the midst of chaos and civil war.
A cynical opportunist (Price) and his brutal henchman (Russell)
take advantage of people's fears and pose as witch finders.
For a fee they will torture local inhabitants into making them
confess to being witches, and then execute them. A local
priest (Davies) is accused by Price, and in order to save her
uncle's life a young woman (Dwyer) lets Price seduce her. Her
soldier fiancé (Ogilvy) vows revenge on Price and Russell.
He follows the two men throughout the countryside until he
finally confronts them in the village of Lavenham. Price captures both Dwyer and Ogilvy and plans to torture Dwyer until
Ogilvy will admit he is guilty of witchcraft. Two of Ogilvy's
fellow soldiers arrive to rescue him. Ogilvy mutilates
Russell, and just before he can finish carving Price up with
an ax, one of the soldiers shoots Price dead.
    There is a great contrast here between the lush beauty
of the English countryside and the superstition and barbarity
of some of its inhabitants. Some of the more violent scenes
are often cut for television.

THE DESPERATE ONES. 1968. 104 minutes. Color. *Director:*
    Alexander Ramati. *Screenplay:* Alexander Ramati; based
    on his book *Beyond the Mountains. Cinematography:*
    Christian Matras. *Cast:* Maximilian Schell (Marek); Raf
    Vallone (Victor); Irene Papas (Ajmi); Theodore Bikel
    (Kisielev); Maria Perschy (Marusia); Fernando Rey (Ibram);
    George Voskovec (Doctor); Alberto de Mendoza (Hamlat);
    Antonio Vico (Ulag Beg); Vincente Sangiovanni (Shura);
    Robert Palmer (Ukrainian NKVD); Danny Stone (NKVD Guard);
    Mariela Chatlak (Aka); Carmen Carbonell (Ulag Beg's Wife);
    with Fernando Hilbeck, Andres Monreal, Maruchi Fresno,
    Mark Malicz, Max Staten, Alexander Ramati, Ricardo
    Palacios, Cris Huerta, Antonio Dugue, Luis Castro, Luis
    Tejada.

    There is not much that even a formidable cast can do with
this international production. *The Desperate Ones* is terribly
miscast with actors from Switzerland, Italy, Greece, and Spain
here portraying Poles and Uzbeks.

Two Polish brothers (Schell and Vallone) have escaped
from a Siberian gulag. They travel to Uzbekistan, where a
smuggler (de Mendoza) will lead them out of the Soviet Union.
The two rent a room with a local couple (Rey and Papas) while
they wait for the proper moment to escape. Meanwhile the local head of the NKVD (Bikel) is keeping an eye on them. On
the day they are to leave, Vallone becomes ill, and Rey goes
to fetch medicine from a nearby town. While he is gone,
Schell, who has already fallen in love with Papas, makes love
to her. Her shame makes her attempt suicide, but Schell stops
her. Rey returns with the medicine and all of them plan to
escape together over the mountains. During their escape attempt Schell sacrifices his life for the others so they may
go free.

THE GLASS SPHINX. 1968. 91 minutes. Color. *Director:* Luigi
   Scattini. *Screenplay:* Rafael Sánchez Campoy, Jaime Camas
   Gil, and José Antonio Cascales; based on a story by
   Adalberto Albertini and Campoy; English dialogue by Louis
   M. Heyward and Adriano Bolzoni. *Cinematography:* Felix
   Mirón Martínez. *Cast:* Robert Taylor (Professor Karl
   Nichols); Anita Ekberg (Paulette); Gianna Serra (Jenny);
   Jack Stuart (Ray); Angel Del Pozo (Alex); José Truchado
   (Theo); Remó De Angelis (Mirko); Emad Hamdy (Fouad); with
   Ahmed Kamis and Lidia Biondi.

This is a run-of-the-mill melodrama filmed in Egypt and
starring an aged Robert Taylor. He portrays an archaeologist
who is looking for the tomb of the Glass Sphinx, which supposedly possesses the elixir of eternal life. His niece
(Serra) has some important documents stolen from her, and one
of his assistants is murdered. Two of Taylor's other assistants (Ekberg and Del Pozo) are plotting against Taylor and
plan to kill him as soon as the sphinx is uncovered. Ekberg
and Del Pozo make off with the treasure, but they are captured
by desert bandits. They are found by Taylor and an insurance
agent (Stuart) assigned to protect Taylor's life. Del Pozo
attempts to trade his freedom with the bandits in exchange for
Ekberg (quite a lopsided trade-off in favor of the bandits),
and in an ensuing struggle Ekberg is killed. With the aid of
the Cairo police Stuart manages to track down Del Pozo.

HELGA. 1968. 87 minutes. Color. *Director:* Erich F. Bender
   (German version). Terry Van Tell (English-language version). *Screenplay:* Erich F. Bender. *Cinematography:*

Fritz Baader and Klaus Werner. *Cast:* Ruth Gassmann
(Helga); Eberhard Mondry (Helga's Husband); with Asgard
Hummel and Ilse Zielstorff.

Made under the guidance of the West German Ministry of
Health, *Helga* is a dramatized documentary about sex education.
It is sincere but stilted. A big hit in Europe, this film
follows a young woman through the months of her pregnancy.
It depicts her doing various exercises to prepare for the birth
and shows her and her husband receiving information from medical personnel about sexuality. *Helga* contains micro photography that shows the development of the embryo and the fetus.

HIGH, WILD AND FREE. 1968. 105 minutes. Color. *Director:*
    Gordon Eastman. *Cinematography:* Gordon Eastman, Wes
    Marks, Lee Holen, Glen McLean, and John Payne. *Narrator:*
    Gordon Eastman.

High, Wild and Free is an anomaly for AIP to have distributed. This nature travelogue, shot in 16mm, is somewhat
similar to the types of films Sunn Classics began distributing
in great quantity during the early 70s. We witness Gordon
Eastman and his two sons as they traverse the rugged wilds of
British Columbia. It shows them fishing and trapping beaver,
as well as viewing the activities of grizzly bears, caribou,
elk, and the stone sheep. Eastman is a longtime nature filmmaker, who often toured and lectured with his films.

KILLERS THREE. 1968. 88 minutes. Color. *Director:* Bruce
    Kessler. *Screenplay:* Michael Fisher; based on a story
    by Fisher and Dick Clark. *Cinematography:* J. Burgi
    Contner. *Cast:* Robert Walker, Jr. (Johnny Ward); Diane
    Varsi (Carol Ward); Dick Clark (Roger); Norman Alden
    (Guthrie); Maureen Arthur (Elvira Sweeney); Tony York
    (J.J. Ward); Merle Haggard (Charlie); Bonnie Owens
    (Singer); John Cardos (Bates); Beach Dickerson (Scotty);
    Jerry Petty (R.C.); Clint Stringer (Sheriff Brown); Fairy
    Sykes (Mrs. Harmon); William Alspaugh (Lester Meed);
    Douglas Barger (Felix); The Strangers (Singing Group).

Dick Clark of *American Bandstand* fame can take either the
credit or the blame for this film, since he not only acts in
it, but produced and co-wrote it also. *Killers Three* turns
out to be a pallid reworking of *Bonnie and Clyde*, which had

come out the previous year. Merle Haggard has a small role
in the film and takes the time to sing a few songs.
   In 1947 a young war veteran (Walker) comes back to his
wife (Varsi) and son (York) in the hills of North Carolina.
Needing money to get to California, Walker and a friend (Clark)
decide to rob a bootlegger. During the robbery Walker kills
a federal agent. During their getaway both men gun down several more people. Varsi's policeman brother (Haggard) runs
into them and gives them ten minutes to leave town. Clark
walks in on the conversation and, not knowing what Haggard
wants, shoots him dead. The trio are eventually trapped inside a sawmill. Clark is killed, and Walker and Varsi drive
their car through a hail of police bullets. Walker realizes
that he will never make it to California, so he drives back
home, but he finds that Varsi has died of gunshot wounds on
the way.

MARYJANE. 1968. 104 minutes. Color. *Director:* Maury Dexter.
   Screenplay: Richard Gautier and Peter L. Marshall; based
   on a story by Maury Dexter. *Cinematography:* Richard
   Moore. *Cast:* Fabian (Phil Blake); Diane McBain (Ellie
   Holden); Kevin Couglin (Jordan Bates); Michael Margotta
   (Jerry Blackburn); Patty McCormick (Susan Hoffman); Russ
   Bender (Harry Braxton); Booth Colman (Maynard Parlow);
   Baynes Barron (Police Chief Otis Mosley); Henry Hunter
   (Mayor Arthur Ford); Phil Vandervort (Herbie Mueller);
   Ivan Bonar (Roger Campbell); Robert Lipton (Dick Marsh);
   Byron Morrow (Judge); Ward Ramsey (Mr. Blackburn); Tom
   Nolan (Frenchy); Bruce Mars (Toby); Steve Cory (Chuck
   Poe); Harold Ayer (Minister); Linda Cooper (Linda);
   Ronnie Dayton (George); Terry Garr (Terri); Jo Ann Harris
   (Jo Ann); Hilarie Thompson (Hilarie); David Meo (Ben);
   Wayne Heffley (Ice Cream Company Manager); Dodie Warren
   (Angela); Carl Gottlieb (Larry Kane); Peter Madsen
   (Kirby); Garry Marshall (Service Station Attendant); Joe
   E. Ross (Mr. Reardon); Floyd Mutrux (Ollie); Helen
   Steusloff (Waitress); Perry Cook (Ship Owner); Linda Sue
   Risk (Little Girl).

   Maryjane is an antimarijuana film in the vein of those
antidrug films of the 30s. Those who believe the theme of
this film are gullible enough to be convinced by Fabian's
portrayal of a high school teacher.
   In a small town the local citizens are up in arms over
the increasing use of marijuana in the local high school. A
high school teacher (Fabian) befriends a young man (Margotta),

who is the black sheep of the marijuana crowd. He allows
Margotta to use his car, which he takes to a pot party. The
police break up the party, and the leader (Coughlin) of the
pot crowd stashes some marijuana inside Fabian's car. The
cops find it and arrest Fabian for possession. He is bailed
out by another teacher (McBain). Meanwhile Margotta has agreed
to deliver some fake pot to a group of young hoods. Fabian
borrows McBain's car to stop Margotta before he can be beaten
up. He now learns that it has been McBain all along who has
been supplying the teenagers with marijuana. He rescues
Margotta and leaves Coughlin to be beaten up by the hoodlums.

THE MINI-SKIRT MOB. 1968. 82 minutes. Color. *Director:*
     Maury Dexter. *Screenplay:* James Gordon White. *Cinema-*
     tography: Arch R. Dalzell. *Cast:* Jeremy Slate (Lon);
     Diane McBain (Shayne); Sherry Jackson (Connie Logan);
     Patty McCormick (Edie); Ross Hagen (Jeff Logan); Harry
     Dean Stanton (Spook); Ronnie Rondell (L.G.).

     This is one of the more sadistic AIP cycle films. It
stars Diane McBain, here playing a miniskirted sadist bent on
revenge--quite a departure from her usual roles as a decorative
cupcake. Also in the cast is that unusual character actor
Harry Dean Stanton, who often portrays characters whose elevator does not quite go to the top. In its theme of a family
being terrorized in the desert *The Mini-Skirt Mob* is reminiscent of the quite later, and even more violent, *The Hills Have*
Eyes.
     Two newlyweds (Jackson and Hagen) are harassed by Hagen's
former girlfriend (McBain) and her gang of cyclists. The couple are in a honeymoon trailer in the desert when they are
attacked by the group. In a chase one of the cyclists goes
over a cliff. McBain's sister (McCormick) believes that the
violence has gone too far, so she decides to help the young
couple escape. She is caught in the trailer when the gang
deluge it with Molotov cocktails and is burned to death. In
a frenzy McBain and a crony (Slate) blame Hagen and Jackson
for McCormick's death. During the ensuing events Slate crashes
his cycle and is killed. McBain is caught on the edge of a
cliff, and Jackson hesitantly goes to her rescue. At the last
moment she loosens up her grip on McBain and lets her topple
to her death.

PSYCH—OUT. 1968. 88 minutes. Color. *Director:* Richard Rush.
Screenplay: E. Hunter Willett and Betty Ulius; based on
a story by Willett. *Cinematography:* Lazlo Kovacs. *Cast:*
Susan Strasberg (Jennie Davis); Dean Stockwell (Dave);
Jack Nicholson (Stoney); Bruce Dern (Steve Davis); Adam
Roarke (Ben); Max Julien (Elwood); Henry Jaglom (Warren);
Linda Gaye Scott (Lynn); I.J. Jefferson (Pandora); Tommy
Flanders (Wesley); Ken Scott (Preacher); Garry Marshall
(Plainclothesman); Geoffrey Stevens (Greg); Susan Bushman
(Little Girl); John Cardos (Thug); Madgal Dean (Mother);
William Gerrity (Little Boy); Robert Kelljan (Arthur);
Gary Kent (Thug Leader); Beatriz Monteil (Landlady);
David Morick (Stuntman); Barbara London (Sadie); with
The Strawberry Alarm Clock and The Seeds.

Psych-Out is one of the better films made by AIP during
the 60s. Not only does it contain a good cast, but it is directed with an unusual amount of flair by Richard Rush, who
later would direct *The Stunt Man.*
A young deaf runaway (Strasberg) ventures to the Haight-
Ashbury in San Francisco to look for her brother (Dern). She
runs into three laid-back musicians (Nicholson, Roarke, and
Julien), who help her look for Dern. It turns out that Dern
is also wanted by some local toughs. Strasberg and Dern meet
in a nightclub, but his pursuers appear and he runs away.
Distraught, Strasberg is taken by a friend of Nicholson's
(Stockwell) to a pad, where he attempts to seduce her by giving her STP. She escapes into the night in a heavily drugged
state and finds that Dern has barricaded himself in a burning
house. Nicholson finally tracks Strasberg to the Golden Gate
Bridge and rescues her.
Bruce Dern steals the film with his appropriately frenzied
style. With that crazed look in his eyes he portrayed a number of psychos in the 60s. The drug scenes here make use of
the psychedelic touch that was seen for one of the first times
in *The Trip.*

THE ROAD HUSTLERS. 1968. 95 minutes. Color. *Director:*
Larry E. Jackson. *Screenplay:* Robert Barron. *Cinema-
tography:* Gerhard Maser. *Cast:* Jim Davis (Noah Reedy);
Scott Brady (Earl Veasey); Bruce Yarnell (Matt Reedy);
Robert Dix (Mark Reedy); Victoria Carroll (Nadine); Andy

Devine (Sheriff Estep); Sue Raney (Helen); Christian
Anderson (Luke Reedy); Ted Lehmann (Hagar); John Cardos
(Chandler); Bill McKinney (Hays); Bill MacDowell (Basset);
Jack Lester (Eskie); Sid Lawrence (Deke); Monica Davis
(Martha Lu); Derek Hughes (Ted); Marshall Lockhart
(Nelly); Jim Quick (Imhoff); Jack Morey (Harrison).

Shot in North and South Carolina, *The Road Hustlers* is
much like the films made by that cornpone C.B. DeMille--Earl
Owensby. Though not as good as *Thunder Road*, it provides
enough action for those small group of films about moonshiners.
A local moonshining family (Davis and his sons Yarnell,
Dix, and Anderson) are being threatened by the local sheriff
(Devine), federal officials, and a local gangster (Brady).
Brady sends one of his hoods (Lawrence) out in an unsuccessful
attempt to kill Dix. Davis then decides to have a fight to
the finish with Brady and his gang. He rigs up electronic
devices to his own stills, and traps Brady's gang in a speedboat chase culminating in an ambush. They then raid Brady's
headquarters, where Davis manages to trick the federal authorities into arresting Brady and his men. Davis and his sons
are now free to work again making their moonshine.

THE SAVAGE SEVEN. 1968. 97 minutes. Color. *Director:*
Richard Rush. *Screenplay:* Michael Fisher; based on a
story by Rosalind Ross. *Cinematography:* Laszlo Kovacs.
Cast: Robert Walker, Jr. (Johnnie Little Hawk); Larry
Bishop (Joint); Adam Roarke (Kisum); Joanna Frank (Marie
Little Hawk); John Garwood (Stud); Max Julien (Grey Wolf);
Richard Anders (Bull); Duane Eddy (Eddie); Chuck Bail
(Taggert); Mel Berger (Fillmore); Billy Rush (Seely);
John Cardos (Running Buck); Susannah Darrow (Nancy);
Beach Dickerson (Fat Jack); Alan Gibbs (Stunt Man); Fabian
Gregory (Tommy); Gary Kent (Lansford); Gary Littlejohn
(Dogface); Penny Marshall (Tina); Walter Robles (Walt);
with Eddie Donno.

With bikers replacing cowboys, *The Savage Seven* is like
a modern-day western. The combination of violence and fast
action here makes one wonder whether George Miller, the director of *Mad Max* and the superb *The Road Warrior*, saw such
films as this while growing up.
A group of Indians living in a California desert town
are exploited by local businessmen and harassed by a group of
bikers. The leader (Roarke) of the cyclists is attracted to
one of the Indian girls (Frank). He helps out Frank's brother

(Walker) in a dispute with a local merchant (Berger), and the Indians and cyclists join together to ransack Berger's store. Frank is manhandled by Roarke, which causes the end of the short-lived alliance between the two groups. One of Roarke's gang members is killed, supposedly for raping an Indian woman. Roarke calls for an all-out conflict against the Indians. It is now learned that Berger killed the gang member, but this information is brought to light too late, as both groups decimate one another in a pitched battle.

3 IN THE ATTIC. 1968. 91 minutes. Color. *Director:* Richard Wilson. *Screenplay:* Stephen H. Yafa; based on his novel *Paxton Quigley's Had the Course. Cinematography:* J. Burgi Contner. *Cast:* Christopher Jones (Paxton Quigley); Yvette Mimieux (Tobey Clinton); Judy Pace (Eulice); Maggie Thrett (Jan); Nan Martin (Dean Nazarin); Reva Rose (Selma); John Beck (Jake); Richard Derr (Mr. Clinton); Eve McVeagh (Mrs. Clinton); Honey Alden (Flo); Tom Ahearne (Wilfred).

3 in the Attic turned out to be a big hit for AIP. Part of the reason was due to the inclusion of Christopher Jones, who had successfully appeared earlier in the year in AIP's *Wild in the Streets.* The other reason for the film's success is that it deals with the ultimate male fantasy, which is usually found in the films of Russ Meyer.

A local college stud (Jones) is always telling other male students about his numerous sexual conquests. He meets a young student (Mimieux), with whom he actually falls in love, as he spends the entire summer with her. When classes begin again, he begins juggling his time between Mimieux and two other coeds (Pace and Thrett). When all three discover how they are being used, they plan their revenge. They lock Jones up in an attic and make constant love to him daily, until his libido is destroyed. After initial enjoyment, Jones begs for them to release him and decides to go on a hunger strike. The women finally release him in such a weakened state that he must be hospitalized. While there, Jones realizes that Mimieux is really in love with him. The chastened former Lothario asks, and receives, her forgiveness.

THE WILD EYE. 1968. 91 minutes. Color. *Director:* Paolo Cavara. *Screenplay:* Paolo Cavara and Tonio Guerra, with collaboration by Alberto Moravia, based on a story by Cavara, Fabio Carpi, and Ugo Pirro. *Cinematography:*

Raffaele Masciocchi or Marcello Masciocchi (sources con-
flict on the credit). *Cast:* Philippe Leroy (Paolo);
Delia Boccardo (Barbara Bates); Gabriele Tinti (Valen-
tino); Luciana Angelillo (Mrs. Davis); Gianni Bongioanni
(The Hunter); Tullio Marini (Ruggero); Giorgio Gargiullo
(Rossi); Lars Bloch (John Bates).

This film takes a swipe at the voyeuristic tendencies of
the *Mondo Cane* type of filmmaker. Of course, while *The Wild
Eye* is casting aspersions on these practices it is also exploiting them for our own titillation.
  A documentary filmmaker (Leroy) searches around the world
for the more outlandish forms of human behavior. In the Sahara
he meets a woman (Boccardo), whom he follows to Bombay with
her husband (Block). Attracted to her, he makes her his leading lady. Together they wander throughout Asia, as Leroy films
various aspects of the human condition. Boccardo criticizes
him for his cynical exploitation of human misery, but she decides to follow him to Vietnam anyway. While filming the war,
Leroy is beaten up by the Vietcong. He learns of a bar that
is going to be blown up and sets up a hidden camera without
telling the people inside what is about to happen. The explosion kills Boccardo, and the grief-stricken Leroy asks his
cameraman (Tinti) to record his moment of sorrow.

WILD IN THE STREETS. 1968. 97 minutes. Color. *Director:*
    Barry Shear. *Screenplay:* Robert Thom; based on his story
    "The Day It All Happened, Baby." *Cinematography:* Richard
    Moore. *Cast:* Shelley Winters (Mrs. Flatow); Christopher
    Jones (Max Frost); Diane Varsi (Sally LeRoy); Ed Begley
    (Senator Allbright); Hal Holbrook (John Fergus); Millie
    Perkins (Mary Fergus); Richard Pryor (Stanley X); Bert
    Freed (Max Jacob Flatow, Sr.); Kevin Couglin (Billy Cage);
    Larry Bishop (Abraham); May Ishihara (Fuji Ellie); Michael
    Margotta (Jimmy Fergus); Don Wyndham (Joseph Fergus);
    Kellie Flanagan (Young Mary Fergus); Salli Sachse (Hippie
    Mother); Paul Frees (Narrator); with Walter Winchell,
    Melvin Belli, Kenneth Banghart, Louis Lomax, Dick Clark,
    Jack Latham, Pamela Mason, Allan J. Moll, Army Archerd,
    Gene Shacove.

This generation-gap satire is one of AIP's landmark films
of the 60s, along with *The Wild Angels* and *The Trip*. Produced
for about $1,000,000 (a large amount for AIP), *Wild in the
Streets* collects many of the societal concerns of the late
60s and wraps them all up in one tidy package.

A young rock star (Jones), who lives lavishly with his "space cadet" of a girlfriend (Varsi) and a host of flunkies, agrees to perform at a rally for a liberal politician (Holbrook). Jones (whose motto is "I don't want to live to be thirty, man.") calls for the voting age to be lowered to 14. The subsequent demonstrations by youth succeed in changing the voting age. Intoxicated with his newfound power, Jones next gets Varsi elected to Congress. The politicians are all drugged with LSD and pass a bill eliminating any age requirement for prospective politicians. Jones runs for President and is elected. One of his first acts is to put everyone over 35 in camps where they will be constantly supplied with LSD. Just as Jones achieves maximum control, an incident occurs that makes us suspect that the under-ten-year-olds will be the next ones in power.

THE WILD RACERS. 1968. 79 minutes. Color. *Director:* Daniel Haller. *Screenplay:* Max House. *Cinematography:* Nestor Almendros and Daniel Lacambre. *Cast:* Fabian (Jo-Jo Quillico); Mimsy Farmer (Katherine); Alan Haufrect (Charlie); Judy Cornwell (British Girl); David Landers (Manager); Warwick Sims (Jo-Jo's Partner); with Talia Coppola, Ursule Pauly, Dick Miller, Ron Gans, Fabienne Arel, Patricia Culbert, Mary Jo Kennedy, Kurt Boon.

At 79 minutes this is not only one of the shortest AIP films of the 60s, but it also might reach the nadir of AIP's films about racing. It is filled full of stock footage from other films, with a plot that barely hangs by a thread. It is difficult to believe that such talented people as Francis Coppola (2nd unit director), Nestor Almendros (cinematography), and Verna Fields (editing) had a hand in this production.
Fabian portrays an obnoxious, womanizing race driver who lives life in the fast lane. He spends much of his time dumping one woman for another, as he continues to win a number of races. A woman (Farmer) enters his life, and he begins to feel very close to her. She wants to get married, but Fabian is afraid of how it will alter his career, so he drops Farmer for someone else. The rest of the film is padded with racing footage.

THE YOUNG ANIMALS. 1968. 100 minutes. *Director:* Maury Dexter. *Screenplay:* James Gordon White. *Cinematography:* Kenneth Peach. *Cast:* Tom Nardini (Tony); Patty McCormick

(Janet); David Macklin (Bruce); Joanna Frank (Raquel);
Zooey Hall (Paco); Sammy Vaughn (Emmet); Michael Wood
(Jerry); Keith Taylor (Din-Din); Adolph Martinez (Johnny);
Alberto Isaac (Ramon); Russ Bender (Mr. Simms); Arthur
Peterson (Mr. Wilson); The American Revolution (Them-
selves).

Also known as *Born Wild*, this film made in Tucson, Arizona, will never win any awards for promoting interracial
harmony and understanding. While it does contain an inflam-
matory element, it never caused the type of disturbance during
its premiere that *The Warriors* did.

A young Chicano (Nardini) has just moved into a border
town where there is a great deal of anti-Mexican prejudice.
Nardini becomes the leader of a group of Chicano students at
the local high school, who are attempting to get the moss-
backed principal (Peterson) to give them a fair shake in school
affairs. A young liberal student (McCormick) becomes friends
with Nardini, much to the ire of her racist boyfriend
(Macklin). Macklin and his punk friends rape a young Mexican
girl (Frank) and beat up her boyfriend (Hall). Tension increases when Hall avenges himself on a member of Macklin's
gang. While the more enlightened students, headed by Nardini
and McCormick, are having a meeting, Hall and Frank are run
off the road and killed by Macklin and his friends. He next
goes after Nardini and McCormick by chasing them with a wreck-
ing machine in a junkyard, but they manage to escape. The
film ends with a united student body asking the principal to
hear their grievances.

THE YOUNG, THE EVIL AND THE SAVAGE. 1968. 82 minutes. Color.
   Director: Anthony Dawson (Antonio Margheriti). *Screen-
   play:* Anthony Dawson and Frank Bottar (Franco Bottari);
   based on a story by John Simonelli (Giovanni Simonelli).
   Cinematography: Frank Zuccoli (Fausto Zuccoli). *Cast:*
   Michael Rennie (Inspector Duran); Mark Damon (Richard);
   Eleonora Brown (Lucille); Sally Smith (Jill); Pat Valturri
   (Denise); Ludmilla Lvova (Miss Clay); Alan Collins/Luciano
   Pigozzi (Laforet); Gianni Di Benedetto (DeBrazzi); Franco
   DeRosa (Detective Gabon); Vivian Stapleton (Miss Tran-
   field); Esther Masing (Miss Martin); Valentino Macchi
   (Policeman); Aldo De Carellis (Professor); Sylvia
   Dionisio, Kathleen Parker, Paolo Natale, Malisa Longo
   (Girls); with Umberto Papiri and John Hawkwood.

Red herrings and hints of lesbianism abound in this film
about murders at an exclusive girl's school. While it uses
the same environment as Dario Argento's *Suspiria*, it is nowhere near as stylish.

A naked body of a young girl is found at a fashionable
college for girls. Soon afterward another student is murdered
while roaming around in the school's basement. The body is
found by another student (Brown), but it disappears while she
is summoning help. Two police detectives (Rennie and DeRosa)
arrive on the scene to investigate. One suspect on their list
is murdered, as now it becomes clear that Brown is the killer's
intended victim. This is proven when the killer makes an attempt on the life of a young girl (Valturri), thinking that
she is Brown. It is finally established that the killer is
one of Brown's relatives, who planned to kill her for her inheritance. Having masqueraded as a female teacher all this
time, the killer is finally trapped and captured by the detectives.

ANGEL, ANGEL, DOWN WE GO. 1969. 93 minutes. Color. *Direc-
     tor:* Robert Thom. *Screenplay:* Robert Thom. *Cinematog-
     raphy:* John F. Warren. *Cast:* Jennifer Jones (Astrid
     Steele); Jordan Christopher (Bogart); Roddy McDowall
     (Santoro); Holly Near (Tara Nicole Steele); Lou Rawls
     (Joe); Charles Aidman (Willy Steele); Davey Davison (Anna
     Livia); Marty Brill (Maitre'd); Hiroko Watanabe (Mas-
     seuse); with Carol Costello, Danielle Aubry, Sandrine
     Gobet, Joan Calhoun, Rudy Battaglia, George Ostos, Ron
     Allen, Romo Vincent.

For sheer excess, this overdone and kinky film can be
looked at as a late-60s equivalent of some of those great melodramas Douglas Sirk directed in the 50s.

A heavy, insecure teenager (Near) returns to her rich
family after being away at a European boarding school. Near's
family is the antithesis of the family in *Leave It to Beaver*--
her father (Aidman) is gay, and her mother (Jones) is a former
star of "party" films and a voracious social climber. They
plan a party for their daughter, but Near leaves the festivi-
ties and ends up meeting one of the musicians (Christopher)
hired for the affair. He makes love to her and wants to marry
her. Christopher soon starts getting it on with Jones and invites her to go skydiving with him and his band. When she
jumps from the plane her parachute does not open, and she falls

to her death. Near then finds her father murdered. She learns
that Christopher had been having an affair with both of her
parents simultaneously. Unable to fathom the disorder and confusion of what has transpired, she becomes insane.

CHASTITY. 1969. 85 minutes. Color. *Director:* Alessio De
    Paola. *Screenplay:* Sonny Bono. *Cinematography:* Ben
    Coleman. *Cast:* Cher (Chastity); Barbara London (Diana
    Midnight); Stephen Whittaker (Eddie); Tom Nolan (Tommy);
    Danny Zapien (Cab Driver); Elmer Valentine (1st Truck
    Driver); Burke Rhind (Salesman); Richard Armstrong (Hus-
    band); Joe Light (Master of Ceremonies); Dolly Hunt
    (Church Lady); Jason Clarke (2nd Truck Driver); and
    Autumn.

    Cher gives a performance of the utmost sangfroid in *Chas-
tity*. She reminds one of the French actress Stephane Audran,
both in her facial structure and impassive stare. Fortunately
Sonny Bono does not appear in the film, but he did write and
produce it. Anyone who has ever seen him pontificate on television talk shows knows that Sonny will never be compared in
his insights to Einstein, or even Mickey Rooney.
    A young woman (Cher) is hitchhiking on her own through-
out the Southwest. Living up to her name of Chastity, she refuses the propositions of the men who pick her up. A student
(Whittaker) gives her a lift but respects her feelings of
wanting to be left alone. Cher runs away from him anyway,
steals a car, and heads for Mexico. A cab driver (Zapien)
leads her to a whorehouse run by an American (London). She
spends a night at London's house and finds that she is a lesbian. After a night with London, she hits the road again.
Cher now recalls moments from her past, which include incestuous relationships. As soon as she snaps out of this recol-
lection she goes to the highway, and gets a ride from another
truck driver. For this very screwed-up young woman, the cycle
now starts again.

THE CYCLE SAVAGES. 1969. 82 minutes. Color. *Director:* Bill
    Brame. *Screenplay:* Bill Brame. *Cinematography:* Frank
    Ruttencutter. *Cast:* Bruce Dern (Keeg); Melody Patterson
    (Lea); Chris Robinson (Romko); Maray Ayres (Sandy); Karen
    Ciral (Janie); Mick Mehas (Bob); Jack Konzal (Bartender);
    Walter Robles (Tom); Daniel Ghaffouri (Marvin); Anna
    Sugano (Motorcycle Girl); Gary Littlejohn (Motorcycle
    Boy); Ron Godwin (Walter); Lee Chandler (Doug); Marjorie

Dayne (Motorcycle Girl); Randee Lee (One of the Girls);
Jerry Taylor (Storekeeper); Denise Gilbert (Little Girl);
Peter Fain and Steve Brodie (Police Detectives); Virginia
Hawkins (Woman); Tom Daly (Docky); Casey Kasem (Keeg's
Brother); Scott Brady (Vice Squad Detective); with Joe
McManus and Linda Banks.

Bruce Dern has commented about some of the overzealous
roles he portrayed in the AIP films of the 60s. In *The Cycle
Savages* he is at his most outlandishly psychotic. If given
the opportunity, he would not have hesitated to torch a child-
care center.
An artist (Robinson) has followed around a motorcycle
gang in order to make sketches of them. The gang leader (Dern)
attacks Robinson and later has his members injure Robinson's
hands. Dern is fearful that the sketches could be used to
identify him and his gang, who are involved in the prostitution racket in Las Vegas. One of the female gang members
(Patterson) takes a liking to Robinson, and they make love.
Meanwhile Dern and his merry band have been busy kidnapping a
high school girl (Ciral), giving her LSD, and gang-raping her.
Robinson is captured by the gang and they smash his hands in
a vice. Another girl (Ayres), who has been mistreated by the
gang, picks up a gun and shoots Dern. The cops now arrive at
the gang's headquarters and arrest them all.

THE DAY THE HOT LINE GOT HOT. 1969. 100 minutes. Color.
  Director: Etienne Périer. *Screenplay:* Paul Jarrico;
  based on a story by Guerdon Trueblood and Dominique Fabre.
  Cinematography: Manuel Berenguer. *Cast:* Charles Boyer
  (Vastov); Robert Taylor (Anderson); George Chakiris (Eric
  Ericson); Marie Dubois (Natasha); with Marta Grau, Irene
  D'Astrea, Josefina Tapias, Gérard Tichy, Gustavo Re,
  Oscar Pellicer, Frank Oliveras.

This is a French and Spanish co-produced espionage comedy. A computer operator in Sweden (Chakiris) asks his company to transfer him to Spain. He buys a large trunk for his
move in a store where three old women (Grau, D'Astrea, and
Tapias) are buying a similar trunk. The three of them work
for an international spy who plans to create a world crisis.
The three blackmail a woman (Dubois) who works at the international hot-line center to send caustic messages to both the
Americans and the Russians, so as to start a diplomatic incident. They put Dubois in their trunk, but on the flight to
Spain their trunk and Chakiris's are exchanged. When he finds

Dubois in his trunk, he calls the police, but the two of them
are quickly kidnapped by the old women. They manage to free
themselves, but the three women, with the help of Chinese ac-
robats, are able to escape from the police. Zzzzzzzzzzzz.

DE SADE. 1969. 113 minutes. Color. *Director:* Cy Endfield;
uncredited additional direction by Roger Corman and
Gordon Hessler. *Screenplay:* Richard Matheson and Peter
Berg; based on the correspondence of the Marquis de Sade
and *Vie du Marquis de Sade*, by Gilbert Lely. *Cinematog-
raphy:* Heinz Pehlke and Richard Angst. *Cast:* Keir Dullea
(Marquis de Sade); Senta Berger (Anne de Montreuil);
Lilli Palmer (Madame de Montreuil); John Huston (Abbé de
Sade); Anna Massey (Renée de Montreuil); Uta Levka (Rose
Keller); Herbert Weissbach (Monsieur de Montreuil);
Christiane Laura Krüger (de Sade's Mistress); Sonja
Ziemann (Le Beauvoisin); Max Kiebach (de Sade as a Boy);
Barbara Stanyk (Colette); Maria Caleita (Marie); Heinz
Spitzner (Inspector Marais); Friedrich Schönfelder (de
Sade's Father); Susanne von Almassy (de Sade's Mother);
with Tilly Lauenstein, Ortrud Gross, Susanne Hsiao, Rolf
Eden, Eva-Marie Gebel.

According to *Variety*, *De Sade* would "bridge the genera-
tion gap. It will attract both the turned-on hip and the dirty
old men" (October 1, 1969, p. 17).
De Sade (Dullea) escapes from a lunatic asylum and returns to the dilapidated mansion where he grew up. His uncle
(Huston), who lives there, makes Dullea recollect happenings
from the past. An extended flashback shows Dullea indulging
his sexual proclivities in a number of orgies, filmed in slow
motion and tinted pink. He is sent to prison for his debauch-
eries, and while there he begins to write antigovernment
tracts. When he gets out of prison, he marries a wealthy woman
(Massey), while he pursues his sister-in-law (Berger). Before
he can elope with her, however, she dies of the plague.
This X-rated feature turned out to be a very large flop
for AIP, despite the sexual nature of its content. *De Sade*
never really shows any hint of the society in which De Sade
existed. It is a hermetically sealed world, cut off from the
revolution that is transpiring all around it. The real De Sade
was a twisted genius (and a real world-beater), but here he
is shown as someone who only seemed to care for a plump der-
riére.

DESTROY ALL MONSTERS. 1969. 88 minutes. Color. *Director:*
Inoshiro Honda. *Screenplay:* Kaoru Mabuchi and Inoshiro
Honda. *Cinematography:* Taiichi Kankura. *Cast:* Akira
Kubo (Captain Katsuo Yamabe); Jun Tazaki (Dr. Yoshido);
Yoshio Tsuchiya (Dr. Otani); Kyoko Ai (Queen of the
Kilaaks); Yukiko Kobayashi (Kyoko); Kenji Sawara (Nishi-
Kawa); Andrew Hughes (Dr. Stevenson); with Nadao Kirino,
Susumu Kurobe, Hisaya Ito, Yoshifumi Tajima, Naoya
Kusakawa, Ikio Sawamura, Wataru Omura, Kazuo Suzuki,
Yutaka Sada.

Toho Studios made this film as a celebration: it was its
20th monster film. *Destroy All Monsters* is fun of sorts, in
a mindless way.
In the year 1999 all of the monsters that have terrorized
the world have been captured and put on a Japanese island
called Ogasawara (better known as Monsterland), both for security reasons and for scientific investigation. A mechanical
disturbance in the security system frees the monsters from
their island prison. Godzilla, Mothra, Rodan, and Manda go
out and destroy the great cities of the world. It turns out
that a group of aliens from the planet Kilaak have unleashed
the monsters in preparation for their takeover of Earth. Captain Yamabe of Moon Rocket SY-3 and his men infiltrate the
Kilaaks' underwater base and terminate them (with extreme prejudice). But the aliens have already brought forth Ghidrah,
the three-headed dragon, as a weapon, and it fights the four
other monsters. When Ghidrah is defeated, the other monsters
return to Monsterland.

THE DEVIL'S 8. 1969. 97 minutes. Color. *Director:* Burt
Topper. *Screenplay:* James Gordon White, William Huyck,
and John Milius; based on a story by Larry Gordon. *Cin-
ematography:* Richard C. Glouner. *Cast:* Christopher George
(Ray Faulkner); Ralph Meeker (Burl); Fabian (Sonny); Tom
Nardini (Billy Joe); Leslie Parrish (Cissy); Ross Hagen
(Frank Davis); Larry Bishop (Chandler); Cliff Osmond
(Bubba); Robert DoQui (Henry Reed); Ron Rifkin (Stewart
Martin); Baynes Barron (Bureau Chief); Joseph Turkel
(Sam); Lada Edmund, Jr. (Inez); Marjorie Dayne (Hallie).

The Devil's 8 is nothing more than an imitation of *The
Dirty Dozen.* Supposedly taking place in one of the Southern
states, the film was actually shot in California, near Camp
Pinecrest.

A federal law-enforcement officer (George) manufactures
the escape of a group of chain-gang prisoners. He promises
them paroles if they will help him eliminate a moonshine syndicate operated by Ralph Meeker. Once the men have been
trained in the nuances of throwing Molotov cocktails and high
speed driving, they go after their prey. With his operation
curtailed, Meeker is forced to cut George and the rest of the
group in on his business. Meeker arranges for George and
another man (Rifkin) to be caught by some cops on the "take."
Meanwhile another one of the convicts (Fabian) has located
Meeker's illegal stills. With the aid of the rest of the group
and their explosives they stage a raid and Meeker is captured.

FEARLESS FRANK. 1969. 78 minutes. Color. *Director:* Philip
    Kaufman. *Screenplay:* Philip Kaufman. *Cinematography:*
    Bill Butler. *Cast:* Jon Voight (Frank/False Frank);
    Monique Van Vooren (Plethora); Joan Darling (Lois); Severn
    Darden (The Good Doctor/Claude); Anthony Holland (Alfred);
    Lou Gilbert (The Boss); Ben Carruthers (The Cat); David
    Steinberg (The Rat); David Fisher (Screwnose); Nelson
    Algren (Needles); Ken Nordine (The Stranger).

    This low-budget fantasy-satire was shot on location in
Chicago and premiered at the Cannes Film Festival in 1967.
Both its director, Philip Kaufman, and its star, Jon Voight,
were unknowns when the film was made. Kaufman has gone on to
direct such films as *The White Dawn* and the remake of *Invasion
of the Body Snatchers*.
    A country bumpkin (Voight) comes to the big city to seek
fame and fortune. A group of gangsters kill him, but he is
revived by a doctor (Darden), who transfers him into a Super-
man-type character. The gangsters get Darden's evil brother
to construct a shopworn replica of Voight. Eventually both
of the creations undergo a change as they reverse roles. The
creation of the bad doctor turns against his maker and stops
the destruction of the city.

GOD FORGIVES, I DON'T. 1969. 101 minutes. Color. *Director:*
    Giuseppe Colizzi. *Screenplay:* Giuseppe Colizzi and
    Gumersindo Mollo. *Cinematography:* Alfio Contini. *Cast:*
    Terence Hill (Cat); Frank Wolff (Bill San Antonio); Bud
    Spencer (Earp Hargitay); Gina Rovere (Rose); José Manuel
    Martín (Bud); with Tito Garcia, Paco Sanz, Giovanna Lenzi,
    José Canalejas, Bruno Arie, Remo Capitani, Juan Olaguibel,

Rufino Inglés, Roberto Alessandri, Luis Bar Boo, Arturo Fuento, Giancarlo Bastianoni.

Aside from its wonderful title, this spaghetti western uses Spanish locations, which look very much like the American West. Terence Hill starred in numerous Italian westerns in the 60s and 70s and gained a certain degree of popularity in Europe. An attempt to become a star in the United States has never materialized for Hill (his real name is Mario Girotti). A gunfighter (Hill) is out to find the money from a train robbed by Bill San Antonio (Wolff). After they have a rigged card game, Hill unknowingly shoots Wolff with a gun filled with blanks. He is convinced he has killed him and continues on his way to the stolen money. An insurance agent (Spencer) joins up with him to search for the loot. When they find it, they are captured by Wolff and his gang. After escaping and being recaptured, Hill and Spencer have a showdown with Wolff. An explosive charge kills Wolff, and Hill and Spencer are now left to divide the money freely.

HELL'S ANGELS 69. 1969. 97 minutes. *Director:* Lee Madden. *Screenplay:* Don Tait; based on a story by Tom Stern and Jeremy Slate. *Cinematography:* Paul Loman. *Cast:* Tom Stern (Chuck); Jeremy Slate (Wes); Conny Van Dyke (Betsy); Steve Sandor (Apache); G.D. Spradlin (Detective); Sonny Barger (Sonny); Terry the Tramp (Terry); with Bobby Hall, Ray Renard, Michael Michaelian, Bud Elkins, Joe Hooker, Bob Harins, Ric Henry, Danielle Corn, Jerry Randall, Ed Mulder, The Oakland Hell's Angels.

It is interesting sometimes how art can imitate life, even on the level of an AIP cycle film. In the late 60s the Oakland Hell's Angels did a job for the cops when they beat up antiwar protesters at the Oakland Army Induction Center. In this film many of the same Angels from the Oakland chapter are given the opportunity to again do what law enforcement officers are paid to do.

Two bored half-brothers (Stern and Slate) decide to rob Caesar's Palace in Las Vegas just for kicks. They pose as a couple of East Coast bikers to win the respect of the Hell's Angels. They intend to use the unsuspecting gang as a decoy in their robbery scheme. They then rob the casino, as the police are busy coping with the antics of the Angels. One of the gang's women (Van Dyke) wants part of the money as well as Slate's attentions. The three escape into the desert. The police inform the Angels that they have been duped, so the gang goes out after the trio. Stern is killed trying to escape the gang when his motorcycle crashes. Slate and Van Dyck have their water and gasoline taken from them by the Angels and are left to die in the desert.

HELL'S BELLES. 1969. 98 minutes. Color. *Director:* Maury
    Dexter. *Screenplay:* James Gordon White and Robert
    McMullen. *Cinematography:* Kenneth Peach. *Cast:* Jeremy
    Slate (Dan); Adam Roarke (Tampa); Jocelyn Lane (Cathy);
    Angelique Pettyjohn (Cherry); Michael Walker (Tony);
    Astrid Warner (Piper); William Lucking (Gippo); Eddie
    Hice (Red Beard); Dick Bullock (Meatball); Jerry Randall
    (Crazy John); Jerry Brutsche (Rabbit); Kristin Van Buren
    (Zelda); Elaine Everett (Big Sal); Fred Krone (Burr);
    Ronnie Dayton (Barney); Henry Kendrick (Gas Station Attendant); Frank Kennedy (Store Owner); James Owens (Leo);
    Larry H. Lane (Charlie); Jackie Hummer (Girlfriend); Bill
    Thompson (L.G.); Michael Jones (Sonny).

Hell's Belles is a combination of a western quest like
The Searchers and De Sica's *The Bicycle Thief* on motorcycle.
Jeremy Slate has his expensive new cycle stolen. He traces
it to a ruffian (Roarke), who is in the Arizona hills with
his motorcycle gang. Slate is waylaid by the gang and is left
one of the girls (Lane) from the gang as compensation for the
cycle. She tells him that the group is on their way to Mexico.
While tracking them down they enter a town that has been terrorized by Roarke and the others. When Slate finally locates
them, he uses his wiles to pick them off one at a time. He
takes one of the injured gang members back to Roarke and offers to call off his activities in exchange for his motorcycle.
Roarke refuses, and the rest of the gang, who are afraid of
Slate, abandon him. Now both have a fight with chains. Slate
bests Roarke and rides away with his cycle. Lane stays behind to comfort the injured Roarke.

MADIGAN'S MILLIONS. 1969. 77 minutes. Color. *Director:*
    Stanley Prager. *Screenplay:* Jim Henaghan, José-Luis
    Bayonas, and Dan Ash. *Cinematography:* Manuel Rojas.
    Cast: Dustin Hoffman (Jason Fister); Elsa Martinelli
    (Vicky Shaw); Cesar Romero (Mike Madigan); with Gustavo
    Rojo, Franco Fabrizi, Fernando Hilbeck, Riccardo Garrone,
    Gérard Tichy, George Raft, Fernando Gilbert, José María
    Caffarel, Alfredo Mayo, Umberto Raho.

Hell's Belles

Now that Dustin Hoffman has attained a great degree of popularity, he probably does not want to be reminded of *Madigan's Millions*, a so-called crime comedy. Originally the film was paired with *Fearless Frank* (which, like this film, was made in 1967), obviously to cash in on the success Jon Voight and Hoffman had earlier in 1969 in *Midnight Cowboy*. An IRS investigator (Hoffman) goes to Rome to confiscate a million dollars hidden by a deported American gangster (Romero). Romero is killed by other mobsters who want his money. Hoffman continues his investigation, much to the dismay of the Rome police. He meets a woman (Martinelli), who poses as Romero's mistress but is actually his daughter. Romero's money is in the possession of Martinelli and her child. Before the other gangster can locate the money, the police close in and capture them. Hoffman and Martinelli have become romantically involved and decide to get married.

MAFIA. 1969. 98 minutes. Color. *Director:* Damiano Damiani. *Screenplay:* Ugo Pirro and Damiano Damiani; based on the novel *Day of the Owl*, by Leonardo Sciascia. *Cinematography:* Tonino Delli Colli. *Cast:* Claudia Cardinale (Rosa Nicolosi); Franco Nero (Captain Bellodi); Lee J. Cobb (Don Mariano Arena); Nehemiah Persoff (Pizzuco); Serge Reggiani (Parrinieddu); Rosanna Lopapero (Caterina); Gaetano Cimarosa (Zecchinetta).

Most films about the Mafia released in this country deal with only the American Mafia. In *Mafia* the action takes place in the Mafia's home territory--Sicily. Judging from the stories coming out of Sicily in the last few years, the Mafia still exerts a tremendous amount of control.
A police inspector (Nero) is investigating the murder of a man who was part of the construction business. However, no one at the murder scene is willing to talk. One woman (Cardinale), who refuses to testify, has her husband disappear on her. When it is suspected that he might have been murdered, the Mafia brands her an adultress, so as to disqualify her as a believable witness. Other witnesses are harassed and more murders are committed, until Nero finds that the foul play is part of a highway-construction scheme of the Mafia. He eventually identifies the leaders of the organization, but his supervisors, who are afraid of the Mafia (police detectives are still killed openly by the Mafia in Sicily), relieve Nero of his duties. His place is taken by a family man, and everybody knows that family men will mind their own business and tread a soft course.

MICHAEL AND HELGA. 1969. 87 minutes. Color. *Director:*
Erich F. Bender. *Screenplay:* Erich F. Bender, Dr. Roland
Cämmerer, and Klaus E.R. von Schwarze. *Cinematography:*
Fritz Baader and Erdmann Beyer. *Cast:* Ruth Gassmann
(Helga); Felix Franchy (Michael); Hildegard Linden (Doc-
tor); Elfi Rueter (Young Mother); Christian Margulies
(Christian); Christian Fredersdorf (Father, 1st Family);
Ursula Mellin (Mother, 1st Family); Jochel Piel (Father,
2nd Family); Lisa Ravel (Mother, 2nd Family); with Sonja
Lindorf, Elke Hart, Sabine Dall, Claus Hoeft, Peter Bach,
Ulla Best.

While *Helga* followed a woman's pregnancy, this sequel
deals with what happens after the birth of the child. The
couple enroll in a child-care class, where they learn about
such things as the Oedipus complex, infant sexuality, and mas-
turbation and puberty. A doctor also tells them about their
own sex life, and such things as birth control and marriage
counseling. The final part of the film details the findings
of both Kinsey and Masters and Johnson. This leads into a
discussion about foreplay, various techniques during inter-
course, and orgasm. In the end the couple experience sex supposedly without any neurotic hangups.

THE OBLONG BOX. 1969. 91 minutes. Color. *Director:* Gordon
Hessler. *Screenplay:* Lawrence Huntington, additional
dialogue by Christopher Wicking, based on the story by
Edgar Allan Poe. *Cinematography:* John Coquillon. *Cast:*
Vincent Price (Julian Markham); Christopher Lee (Dr.
Neuhartt); Alister Williamson (Sir Edward Markham); Hilary
Dwyer (Elizabeth Markham); Peter Arne (Samuel Trench);
Harry Baird (N'Galo); Carl Rigg (Mark Norton); Maxwell
Shaw (Tom Hackett); Michael Balfour (Ruddock); Godfrey
James (Weller); Rupert Davies (Joshua Kemp); Sally Geeson
(Sally Baxter); Ivor Dean (Hawthorne); with Uta Levka,
James Mellor, Danny Daniels, John Barrie, Hira Talfrey,
John Wentworth, Betty Woolfe, Martin Terry, Anne Clune,
Jackie Noble, Ann Barrass, Janet Rossini, Zeph Gladstone,
Tara Fernando, Tony Thawton, Anthony Bailey, Richard
Cornish, Colin Jeavons, Andreas Malandrinos, Hedgar
Wallace, Martin Wyldeck, The Oh! Ogunde Dancers.

Michael Reeves, the director of *Conqueror Worm*, was to
have directed *The Oblong Box*, but when he died Gordon Hessler
took over the directorial chores. In the first 15 or 20 minutes Hessler makes effective use of the subjective camera,

which was rather novel for a horror film in the 60s. Now with all the various versions of *Friday the 13th*, *Halloween*, and the other "splatter" films using the same device, it has become a horror-movie cliché.
In 19th-century England Vincent Price keeps his unbalanced brother (Williamson), who has been horribly disfigured by natives in Africa, chained in one of the rooms of their family mansion. The family lawyer (Arne) helps Williamson escape from the house by giving him a drug that simulates death. Price buries his brother, but grave robbers dig him up and take him to a local doctor (Lee). Williamson stays at Lee's house and puts on a mask, while he plans revenge against those who he feels are against him. After killing Arne and Lee, Williamson is shot by Price, but before he dies he bites his brother. Price, who had been responsible for the crime in Africa that resulted in his brother's mutilation, now takes on Williamson's appearance.

SPIRITS OF THE DEAD. 1969. 117 minutes. Color. *English-Version Narration:* Clement Biddle Wood. "Metzengerstein": *Director:* Roger Vadim. *Screenplay:* Roger Vadim and Pascal Cousin, based on the story by Edgar Allan Poe. *Cinematography:* Claude Renoir. *Cast:* Jane Fonda (Countess Frederica); Peter Fonda (Baron Wilhelm); Carla Marlier (Claude); François Prévost (Friend of the Countess); James Robertson-Justice (Countess's Adviser); Anny Duperey (1st Guest); Philippe Lemaire (Philippe); Serge Marquand (Hugues); Andreas Voutsinas (2nd Guest); Audoin de Bardot (Page); Douking (du Lissier). "William Wilson": *Director:* Louis Malle. *Screenplay:* Louis Malle; dialogue by Daniel Boulanger; based on the story by Edgar Allan Poe. *Cinematography:* Tonino Delli Colli. *Cast:* Brigitte Bardot (Giuseppina); Alain Delon (William Wilson); Katia Christina (Young Girl); Umberto D'Orsi (Hans); Daniele Vargas (Professor); Renzo Palmer (Priest). "Toby Dammit": *Director:* Federico Fellini. *Screenplay:* Federico Fellini and Bernardino Zapponi; based on the story "Never Bet Your Head," by Edgar Allan Poe. *Cinematography:* Giuseppe Rotunno. *Cast:* Terence Stamp (Toby Dammit); Salvo Randone (Priest); Fabrizio Angeli (1st Director); Ernesto Colli (2nd Director); Marina Yaru (Child); Anne Tonietti (Television Commentator); Aleardo Ward (1st Interviewer); Paul Cooper (2nd Interviewer); with Antonia Pietrosi, Rick Boyd, Polidor.

Despite the talent that was behind this trilogy of Poe tales, each one seems to be worse than the last.

In "Metzengerstein" Jane Fonda portrays a sort of 12th century French female Caligula, who becomes attracted to one of her distant cousins (Peter Fonda). When he rejects her advances, she plans vengeance on him. She orders his stables burned down, and he is killed in the blaze attempting to save his horses. She becomes strangely attracted to a horse that mysteriously appears. One day a fire starts on her property, and the newfound mystery horse rides her into the flames. The only thing of interest here is the sexual attraction developed between the real life brother and sister.

"William Wilson" deals with the theme of the doppelgänger. Wilson (Delon) confesses a murder to a priest (Palmer). From there, flashbacks relate the dissolute nature of Delon. He has a double who always hounds him. Finally the two have a duel. By murdering his double, Delon has murdered himself-- in effect killing his conscience.

The title character in "Toby Dammit" is a boozy English actor (Stamp) who has come to Italy to make a Catholic Western. He is haunted by a smiling blonde girl (Yaru). Stamp is given a new Maserati at a bizarre awards party and drives off in a state of intoxication. When he attempts to pass over a bridge, a wire strung across the road decapitates him. The young girl goes and picks up his head. This hallucinatory half-baked version of $8\frac{1}{2}$ comes across as a Fellini parody.

TWO GENTLEMEN SHARING. 1969. 105 minutes. Color. *Director:* Ted Kotcheff. *Screenplay:* Evan Jones; based on the novel by David Stuart Leslie. *Cinematography:* Billy Williams. *Cast:* Robin Phillips (Roddy); Judy Geeson (Jane); Hal Frederick (Andrew); Esther Anderson (Caroline); Norman Rossington (Phil); Hilary Dwyer (Ethne); Rachel Kempson (Mrs. Ashby-Kydd); Daisey Mae Williams (Amanda); Ram John Holder (Marcus); Earl Cameron (Charles); Shelagh Fraser (Helen); David Markham (Mr. Pater); Avice Landon (Mrs. Pater); Philip Stone (Mr. Burrows); Elspeth March (Mrs. Burrows); Thomas Baptiste (Mutt); Linbert Spencer (Jeff); Willy Payne (Bizerte); Thors Piers (Eugene Valentine); Nathan Dambuza (Chicomo); Robert Burnell (O'Reilly); Hamilton Dyce (Dickson Senior); John Humphrey (Dickson Junior); Harold Lang (Young Man); Lionel Ngakane (Bill); Tommy Ansah (Driver); George Baizley (Caretaker); Harcourt Curacao (Band Leader); Carl Adam (Negro Visitor); Anna

Wing (Neighbor); Benny Nightingale (Elevator Operator);
Charles Leno (Doorman); with Phillamore Davidson, Norman
Mitchell, John Chandos, David Edwards, John Snow, Gary
Sobers, Les Flambeaux Steel Band.

This British production was made for Paramount Pictures
but was distributed in the United States by AIP. A 1969 British entry at the Venice Film Festival, *Two Gentlemen Sharing*
presents a rather caustic view of race relations and effete
liberalism in Great Britain.

A young white executive (Phillips) places an advertise-
ment for a roommate, and a black lawyer (Frederick) responds
to the ad. They discover that they have a common bond in both
being Oxford graduates, so they become roommates. They take
their two girlfriends (Dwyer and Anderson) to a nightclub,
where Phillips finds himself attracted to a woman (Geeson)
who is being fawned over by a group of black men. Geeson and
the two roommates go to the mansion of Phillips's parents one
weekend, and his parents become upset by Frederick's presence.
When Frederick and Anderson are caught making love by his big-
oted landlady, they decide to move out. Eventually they plan
to return to their native Jamaica to avoid the racism in England. At a party for Frederick Phillips becomes drunk and
proclaims he wants to marry Geeson, but she rejects him because of his psychological weakness. A male guest (Holder)
makes advances to Phillips, but he rejects him. The police
come to break up the loud party, and Phillips is now left all
alone in his apartment.

THE YOUNG REBEL. 1969. 111 minutes. Color. *Director:*
Vincent Sherman. *Screenplay:* David Karp, Enrique Llovet,
and Enrico Bomba; adaptation by Enrique Llovet; based on
the novel *Cervantes*, by Bruno Frank. *Cinematography:*
Edmond Richard. *Cast:* Horst Buchholz (Miguel de Cervan-
tes); Gina Lollobrigida (Giulia); José Ferrer (Hassam
Bey); Louis Jourdan (Cardinal Acquava); Francisco Rabal
(Rodrigo); Fernando Rey (Phillip II); Soledad Miranda
(Nessa); with Maurice de Canonge, Antonio Casas, Angel
Del Pozo, José Jaspe, Ricardo Palacios, Claudine Dalmas,
José Nieto, Enzo Curcio, Guadenzio Di Pietro, Andres
Mejuto, Vidal Molina, Fernando Hilbeck, Concha Humbria,
Jorge Rigaud.

Miguel de Cervantes is best remembered as the author of
Don Quixote. However, his early life reads almost as interesting as an historical novel. This international co-

production follows de Cervantes's life as a young man with
relative accuracy.

Miguel de Cervantes (Buchholz) becomes a young assistant
to a Cardinal (Jourdan), while Jourdan seeks support from
Spain's Philip II (Rey) to fight against the Moors. Buchholz
later becomes friends with an Arab diplomat (Ferrer), and quits
his ecclesiastical position when he finds that Jourdan is un-
derhanded in his dealings with Ferrer. He has an affair with
a prostitute (Lollobrigida), but the church orders all prostitutes out of Rome. Buchholz now has become totally disen-
chanted with the workings of the church, as he joins his brother (Rabal) in fighting in the Battle of Lepanto. He is
wounded, and on his way back to Spain he and Rabal are captured by Arab buccaneers and taken to Algiers. After spending a good deal of time as slaves, both are released when
Ferrer gains political control in Algiers. The brothers attempt an unsuccessful revolt among the other Christian slaves.
Before they can be executed, they are ransomed and sent back
to their home in Spain.

THE SEVENTIES

ANGEL UNCHAINED. 1970. 92 minutes. Color. *Director:* Lee
Madden. *Screenplay:* Jeffrey Alladin Fiskin; based on a
story by Lee Madden and Fiskin. *Cinematography:* Irving
Lippman. *Cast:* Don Stroud (Angel); Luke Askew (Tremaine);
Larry Bishop (Pilot); Tyne Daly (Merilee); Neil Moran
(Magician); Jean Marie (Jackie); Bill McKinney (Shotgun);
Jordan Rhodes (Tom); Peter Laurence (Dave); Pedro Regas
(Injun); Linda Smith (Wendy); Nita Michaels (Matty); J.
Cosgrove Butchie (Ray); Tim Ryan (Hood); Alan Gibbs and
J.N. Roberts (Dunners); Bill Burton (Marauder); Bud
Elkins (Speed); Jerry Randall (Candy); Aldo Ray (Sheriff).

Normally hippies and bikers, with their antithetical values, would never be on the same side of any issue. In *Angel
Unchained* they are allied in combating that put-upon group--
the rural redneck.
A cycle-gang member (Stroud) decides to begin a new life
for himself by leaving his gang. Stroud sets out venturing
across the country. In the Southwest he witnesses a young
member of a hippie commune (Daly) being hassled by the local
hicks, who want the hippies out of their community. Stroud
takes her back to the commune and meets their leader (Askew),
who asks Stroud to join their group. The locals attack the
commune farm with their dune buggies. Tensions rise, and
Askew asks Stroud to have his former gang members come to protect them. Stroud agrees, even though he realizes his old
gang's negative attitude toward hippies. The gang arrives and
there is clear animosity between the two groups--that is, until the folks from town attack the commune. The hippies and
the bikers band together to force the intruders out, but Askew
is killed in the melee.

BLOODY MAMA. 1970. 90 minutes. Color. *Director:* Roger
Corman. *Screenplay:* Robert Thom; based on a story by
Thom and Donald A. Peters. *Cinematography:* John Alonzo.
Cast: Shelley Winters (Kate "Ma" Barker); Pat Hingle (Sam
Adams Pendlebury); Don Stroud (Herman Barker); Diane Varsi
(Mona Gibson); Bruce Dern (Kevin Dirkman); Clint Kimbrough
(Arthur Barker); Robert De Niro (Lloyd Barker); Robert

184

Walden (Fred Barker); Alex Nicol (George Barker); Michael
Fox (Dr. Roth); Scatman Crothers (Moses); Stacy Harris
(Agent McClellan); Pamela Dunlap (Rembrandt); Lisa Jill
(Young Kate); Steve Mitchell (Sheriff); Roy Idom (Ferry-
boat Passenger).

This orgy of blood-letting was directed by Roger Corman
to cash in on the popularity of *Bonnie and Clyde*. Made on
location in Arkansas, it shows an outlaw family so twisted
that they make the family in *The Grissom Gang* seem like your
typical suburban-shopping-mall family of four.
    Shelley Winters portrays Depression-era gang leader "Ma"
Barker, who maintains complete control over her four grown
sons (Stroud, Kimbrough, De Niro, and Walden). The five begin
a criminal career after they leave the ineffectual "Pa" Barker
(Nicol) back home in the Ozarks. This malignant backwoods
brood first rob a ferryboat. During the robbery Stroud, a
sadistic psychopath, murders one of the ferry passengers.
Later on the police capture him and Walden when attempting to
rob people at a picnic. In prison Walden gains a lover (Dern),
who becomes Winters's lover when he is released. Stroud is
also released and joins back up with the family along with
his prostitute girlfriend (Varsi). The gang kidnaps a wealthy
man (Hingle) and ask for a large ransom. The boys like Hingle,
but Winters orders him killed after the ransom has been paid.
Her sons let him go, and Stroud defies his mother and assumes
leadership of the gang. While they are hiding out in Florida,
the police detect them when they hear Dern and Stroud taking
pot shots at an alligator. Trapped in their hideout, the gang
are killed in a bloody shootout with the cops.

BORA BORA. 1970. 90 minutes. Color. *Director:* Ugo
    Liberatore. *Screenplay:* Ugo Liberatore. *Cinematography:*
    Leonida Barboni. *Cast:* Haydée Politoff (Marita Ferris);
    Corrado Pani (Roberto Ferris); Doris Kunstmann (Susanne);
    Rosine Copie (Tehina); Antoine Coco Puputauki (Mani).

Bora Bora is, in the words of *Variety*, "an essay on mental degradation, human promiscuity and incoherent evaluation
of sexual expression in sophisticated Europeans" (December 4,
1968, p. 26).
    A husband (Pani) follows his wife (Politoff) to the South
Seas after they have had an argument. He finds that she has
already left without leaving a forwarding address. After meeting a nymphomaniac (Kunstmann), Pani learns that his wife is
living on a nearby island with her native lover (Puputauki).

Pani goes to the island, but he is rejected by Politoff. He
decides to stay on the island and absorb some of the lifestyle.
The local inhabitants offer him a young teenage virgin (Copie)
as his mistress. The islanders build him a beach house, but
soon after Copie leaves him. Now Politoff moves in with her
husband. In an attempt to go native Pani decides to prove
how open and giving he is by offering his house to Politoff
and Puputauki. His jealousy eventually gets the better of
him and he picks a fight with Puputauku, in which he is easily
dispatched. Both Pano and Politoff realize that they cannot
cope with the mores of the islands, so they burn the house
down and leave the island together.

A BULLET FOR PRETTY BOY. 1970. 88 minutes. Color. *Direc-*
   tor: Larry Buchanan. *Screenplay:* Henry Rosenbaum; based
   on a story by Enrique Touceda and Larry Buchanan. *Cine-*
   matography: James R. Davidson. *Cast:* Fabian Forte
   (Charles "Pretty Boy" Floyd); Jocelyn Lane (Betty); Astrid
   Warner (Ruby); Michael Haynes (Ned Short); Adam Roarke
   ("Preacher"); Robert Glenn (Hossler); Anne MacAdams
   (Beryl); Camilla Carr (Helen); Jeff Alexander (Wallace);
   Desmond Dhooge (Harvey); Bill Thurman (Huddy); Hugh Feagin
   (Jack Dowler); Jessie Lee Fulton (Mrs. Floyd); James
   Harrell (Mr. Floyd); Gene Ross (William); Ed Lo Russo
   (Bo); Charlie Dell (Charlie); Eddie Thomas (Ben Dowler);
   Frank DeBenedett (Lester Floyd); Ethan Allen (Seth); Troy
   K. Hoskins (Sheriff Taylor); Lucky Mosley, Charles
   Redding, David Beuret, Walt Becklund, Ron Scott (Depu-
   ties).

   A Bullet for Pretty Boy is a companion piece to *Bloody*
Mama, although the cast and direction are not up to the standards of the latter film. Unlike "Ma" Barker, Floyd is presented here as a young man who did not consciously plan a career in crime but became involved in it through circumstances
not of his choosing.
   During the marriage of Charles Floyd (Forte) an argument
ensues with one of his wife's (Warner) former suitors (Feagin).
This leads to the accidental death of Feagin. Forte is con-
victed of manslaughter but escapes from prison four years
later. He hides out in a Kansas City whorehouse and later
joins a gang of bank robbers headed by Ned Short (Haynes).
He is captured again after a series of robberies. On the train
to prison Forte kills a guard and escapes to Oklahoma to visit
his wife. He picks up a local lowlife (Roarke), and the two
of them join with Haynes's gang. Eventually Roarke and Haynes

are killed by the police. After a robbery of his hometown bank Forte is trapped in a farmhouse and murdered by the authorities.

COUNT YORGA, VAMPIRE. 1970. 92 minutes. Color. *Director:* Robert Kelljan. *Screenplay:* Robert Kelljan. *Cinematography:* Arch Archambault. *Cast:* Robert Quarry (Count Yorga); Roger Perry (Dr. Hayes); Michael Murphy (Paul); Michael Macready (Michael); Donna Anders (Donna); Judy Lang (Erica); Edward Walsh (Brudah); Julie Connors (Cleo); Paul Hansen (Peter); Sybil Scotford (Judy); Marsha Jordan (Mother); Deborah Darnell (Vampire); Erica Macready (Nurse); George Macready (Narrator).

Robert Quarry makes a dashing and stylish vampire in this popular AIP film. It was the recipient of an uncommon amount of critical praise, with one periodical noting how "the understated acting and the tightly controlled increasingly staccato tempo make this the most distinctive essay in the macabre since *Night of the Living Dead*" (Kenneth Thompson, *Monthly Film Bulletin*, January 1970, p. 6).

Two couples (Macready, Anders, Murphy, and Lang) go to a seance at the mansion of the enigmatic Count Yorga (Quarry). The four are unaware that both Anders and Lang have been hypnotized by Quarry during the evening. When leaving the mansion, the van belonging to Murphy and Lang becomes stalled in mud, so they spend the night inside it. Quarry comes upon them, knocks Murphy unconscious, and bites Lang in the neck. Lang's subsequent unusual behavior (like trying to eat a cat) causes Murphy to consult a doctor (Perry). His investigation convinces him that she is the victim of a vampire. Both Anders and Lang are taken by Quarry to his mansion, while the two young men and Perry follow them there. They find the house inundated with female vampires. After both Murphy and Perry are killed, Macready drives a stake through the hearts of Quarry and Lang. He rescues Anders and takes her away, not realizing that she is already a vampire.

THE CRIMSON CULT. 1970. 87 minutes. Color. *Director:* Vernon Sewell. *Screenplay:* Mervyn Haisman and Henry Lincoln; based on a story by Jerry Sohl; suggested by the story "The Dreams in the Witch-House," by H.P. Lovecraft. *Cinematography:* John Coquillon. *Cast:* Boris Karloff (Professor Marsh); Christopher Lee (J.D. Morley); Mark Eden

Count Yorga, Vampire

(Robert Manning); Virginia Wetherell (Eve); Barbara Steele (Lavinia Morley); Rupert Davies (Vicar); Michael Gough (Elder); Rosemarie Reede (Esther); Derek Tansley (Judge); Michael Warren (Chauffeur); Ron Pember (Gas Station Attendant); Denys Peek (Peter Manning/Blacksmith); Nita Lorraine (Woman with Whip); Carole Anne and Jennie Shaw (Virgins); Vivienne Carlton (Sacrifice Victim); Roger Avon (Sergeant Tyson); Paul McNeil (Party Guest); Christine Pryor, Kerry Dean, Stephanie Marrion, and Rosalind Royale (Party Girls); Millicent Scott (Stripper at Party); Vicky Richards (Belly Dancer at Party); Tasma Brereton (Painted Girl at Party); Kevin Smith (Drunk at Party); Lita Scott (Girl with Cockerel); Terry Raven and Douglas Mitchell (Drivers in Car Chase).

The Crimson Cult is not only one of Boris Karloff's last films, but a perfectly dreadful and slow-paced film as well. Barbara Steele, the queen of 60s horror films, is totally wasted here portraying a centuries-old witch with green-tinted skin and a ram's-head headpiece with peacock or pheasant feathers coming out of it.

An antique dealer (Eden) goes to a manor house to search for his brother (Peek), who had not returned from a business trip. The mansion's owner (Lee) claims he does not know Eden's brother. His arrival has coincided with a local celebration for the "Black Witch of Greymarsh," who was one of Lee's ancestors. Eden becomes interested in Lee's niece (Wetherell) and decides to stay as Lee's guest. He begins having nightmares in which he finds himself in the presence of the long-dead witch (Steele) of the manor. A local expert on witchcraft (Karloff) tells him that his family has a witches' curse on it. Eden and Wetherell become trapped in a basement chamber of the house by Lee, who is avenging himself on the ancestors of those responsible for his ancestor's death. Karloff and the police arrive to save them, just as Lee sets fire to the mansion and dies in the flames.

CRY OF THE BANSHEE. 1970. 87 minutes. Color. *Director:* Gordon Hessler. *Screenplay:* Tim Kelly and Christopher Wicking; based on a story by Kelly. *Cinematography:* John Coquillon. *Cast:* Vincent Price (Lord Edward Whitman); Essy Persson (Lady Patricia); Elizabeth Bergner (Oona); Patrick Mower (Roderick); Hilary Dwyer (Maureen); Hugh Griffith (Mickey); Janet Rossini (Bess); Sally Geeson (Sarah); Carl Rigg (Harry Whitman); Pamela Farbrother (Margaret); Stephan Chase (Sean); Marshall Jones (Father

Tom); Quinn O'Hara (Maggie); Andrew McCulloch (Bully Boy);
Michael Elphick (Burke); Pamela Moiseiwitsch (Maid);
Godfrey James (Head Villager); Gertan Klauber (Tavern
Keeper); Peter Benson (Brander); Terry Martin (Rider);
Richard Everett (Timothy); Louis Selwyn (Apprentice);
Mickey Baker (Rider); Carol Desmond (Girl); Joyce Mandre,
Robert Hutton, Peter Forest, Guy Deghy (Party Guests);
Jane Deady (Naked Girl); with Ann Barrass, Nancy Meckler,
Hugh Portnow, Stephen Roa, Maurice Colbourne, Dinah Stabb,
Tony Sibbald, Neil Johnton, Rowan Wylie, Tim Thomas, Ron
Sahewk, Maya Roth, Philly Howell, Guy Pierce.

In its preoccupation with witches and demons, and in its
historical setting, *Cry of the Banshee* bears some resemblance
to *Conqueror Worm*. The inclusion of veteran stage and screen
actress Elizabeth Bergner, here making an ignoble comeback,
cannot disguise the penurious production values and the hap-
hazard script.

In 16th-century England a local Lord (Price) organizes
the townspeople in destroying a local Druid cult. The cult
leader (Bergner) has some of her children murdered by Price,
and she vows revenge on him and his family. She conjures up
a banshee in the form of a young man (Mower), who obtains a
job on Price's property as a stable hand. He quickly becomes
infatuated with Price's daughter (Dwyer). Meanwhile Price has
located the Druids' ceremonial area and orders Bergner and
her followers to be put to death. Price later finds Dwyer
near death, and in a struggle with Mower (now in banshee form),
Dwyer summons up enough strength to kill him and save her father. However, Mower is resurrected and ends up killing both
Price and his offspring.

DORIAN GRAY. 1970. 93 minutes. Color. *Director:* Massimo
    Dallamano. *Screenplay:* Massimo Dallamano, Marcello
    Coscia, and Günther Ebert; based on the novel *The Picture
    of Dorian Gray*, by Oscar Wilde. *Cinematography:* Otello
    Spila. *Cast:* Helmut Berger (Dorian Gray); Richard Todd
    (Basil Hallward); Herbert Lom (Henry Wotton); Marie
    Liljedahl (Sybil Vane); Margaret Lee (Gwendolyn Wotton);
    Maria Rohm (Alica); Beryl Cunningham (Adrienne); Isa
    Miranda (Mrs. Ruxton); Eleonora Rossi Drago (Esther);
    Renato Romano (Alan); Stewart Black (James Vane).

Helmut Berger's androgynous appearance in *The Damned* no
doubt led to his starring role in Wilde's classic tale. Taking
place in swinging London of the 60s, this version is vastly
inferior both in mood and in quality to the version produced

in Hollywood in 1945. Intentional or not, this is a "campy"
Dorian Gray. Berger's portrait resembles that of a young stud
standing on some street-corner "meat rack" in San Francisco.
     Dorian Gray (Berger), a student, has his portrait painted
by an artist friend (Todd). A wealthy patron (Lom) of Todd's
advises Berger to sell his soul and remain young forever, instead of having his beautiful looks suffer the ravages of age.
Berger begins to lead a life of the utmost greed and callous-
ness. He is responsible for the suicide of a woman (Liljedahl)
he jilted, and becomes a "kept" man of a wealthy older woman
(Miranda). When Berger actually exhibits some human feeling,
in this case remorse and guilt over the death of a friend
(Romano), he finds that the portrait of him is beginning to
age. In agony he rips the painting with a knife, and falls
down in pain as if suffering from a stab wound. Slowly his
corpse turns into a putrified mass.

THE DUNWICH HORROR. 1970. 90 minutes. Color. *Director:*
     Daniel Haller. *Screenplay:* Curtis Lee Hanson, Henry
     Rosenbaum, and Ronald Silkosky; based on the story by
     H.P. Lovecraft. *Cinematography:* Richard C. Glouner.
     Cast: Sandra Dee (Nancy Walker); Dean Stockwell (Wilbur
     Whateley); Ed Begley (Dr. Henry Armitage); Sam Jaffe (Old
     Whateley); Donna Baccala (Elizabeth Hamilton); Lloyd
     Bochner (Dr. Cory); Joanne Moore Jordan (Lavinia); Talia
     Coppola (Cora); Barboura Morris (Mrs. Cole); Michael Fox
     (Dr. Raskin); Jason Wingreen (Police Chief); Michael
     Haynes (Guard); with Beach Dickerson, Toby Russ, Jack
     Pierce.

     Filmed around the rugged coastline of California's Men-
docino County, this film, taken from one of Lovecraft's most
famous stories, is enhanced by some good special effects.
What saddles the film down is the perverse miscasting of people like Sandra Dee and Ed Begley.
     A college student interested in the supernatural (Dee)
meets a young man in the school library (Stockwell) who is
reading passages from a book on the occult called the
Necronomicon. She offers to drive him home, not realizing
that he is a descendant of a family that is possessed by demons. When they arrive at Stockwell's mansion, he gives her
a drug so she will stay the night. Dee is attracted to him
and agrees to stay for an entire weekend. A friend of Dee's
(Baccala) and a local authority on the occult (Begley) go looking for her when they learn that Stockwell's mother went mad
after giving birth to him and his monstrous brother (the title

character). Stockwell has the *Necronomicon* in his possession, which he plans to use during a fertility rite involving Dee. Baccala accidentally lets loose Stockwell's demon brother from the mansion, and he/it terrorizes the countryside looking for his brother. Begley finally approaches the brothers and offers a curse that destroys them both. However, unknown to Dee, she is already impregnated with a demon child.

EXPLOSION. 1970. 96 minutes. Color. *Director:* Jules
    Bricken. *Screenplay:* Jules and Alene Bricken; based on
    a story by Jules Bricken and Robert Hartford-Davis. *Cin-
    ematography:* Joseph Brun. *Cast:* Don Stroud (Richie
    Kovacs); Gordon Thomson (Alan Evans); Michele Chicoine
    (Doris Randolph); Cec Linder (Mr. Evans); Richard Conte
    (Dr. Philip Neal); Robin Ward (Peter Evans); Ted Stidder
    (Timms); Murray Matheson (Jaguar Owner); Ann Sears (Jag-
    uar Owner's Wife); Sherry Mitchell (Susan); Olga Kaya
    (Valerie); Harold Saunders (Inspector Kelso).

Filmed in British Columbia, this Canadian feature was one of the first internationally distributed films to come from the Canadian Film Development Corporation. The CFDC would play an important role throughout the 70s, but it never helped develop a truly Canadian cinema similar to the renaissance that occurred in Australia about the same time.
    A young man (Ward) is talked out of going to Canada to avoid the draft by his father (Linder) and his girlfriend (Chicoine). Ward goes into the army and is killed in Vietnam. His distraught brother (Thomson) defies his father and decides to escape induction. He meets a hippie (Stroud), and the two of them go to Canada. They steal a car, and later the in-creasingly psychotic Thomson kills two cops who get in his way. When they reach Vancouver, Stroud calls the authorities after he hears Thomson's father make an appeal for him to give himself up. Thomson forces Stroud to escape with him through the wilds of British Columbia. They are finally trapped by the police and Thomson is shot.

GAS-S-S-S. 1970. 79 minutes. Color. *Director:* Roger Corman.
    Screenplay: George Armitage. *Cinematography:* Ron Dexter.
    Cast: Robert Corff (Coel); Elaine Giftos (Cilla); Bud
    Cort (Hooper); Talia Coppola (Coralie); Ben Vereen
    (Carlos); Cindy Williams (Marissa); Alex Wilson (Jason);
    Lou Procopio (Marshall McLuhan); Phil Borneo (Quant);

Jackie Farley (Ginny); Country Joe McDonald (FM Radio); George Armitage (Billy the Kid); Pat Patterson (Demeter); Alan Braunstein (Dr. Drake); David Osterhout (Texas Ranger); Bruce Karcher (Edgar Allan Poe); Mike Castle (Hippie); Jim Etheridge and Gary Treadwell (Renegade Cowboys); Peter Fain (Policeman); Stephen Graham (Thief); Bob Easton (Fanatic Religious Leader); with Country Joe and the Fish and Juretta Taylor.

Gas-s-s-s (. . . or It May Become Necessary to Destroy the World in Order to Save It!) was the last film Roger Corman made for AIP. It is fitting that his last film for them displays many of the political and cultural touchstones of the 60s. There is no critical middle ground with this film. One either rejects it as being chaotic and overdone or feels that it creates "something of a Swiftian satire out of its odyssey through an American hinterland turned topsy-turvy but all too recognisable in its patterns of power..." (Richard Combs, *Monthly Film Bulletin*, January 1974, p. 8).

Nerve gas at a defense lab, accidentally released, will kill everyone over 25 within a very short time. Two young people (Giftos and Corff) leave Texas, which has become an armed camp between opposing factions. They head for a commune in New Mexico to start a new life. Along their journey they meet such people as a modern-day Billy the Kid (Armitage), a rock singer (McDonald), a group of fascistic football players, and Marshall McLuhan (Procopio). They finally reach the commune along with the people they have picked up along the way. When the commune is threatened by the football players, the group bands together to defend itself. At this point numerous heroes of young people appear--e.g., J.F.K., Che Guevara, Martin Luther King--to lead them into a new life. (How is that for a *deus ex machina*.)

HORROR HOUSE. 1970. 79 minutes. Color. *Director:* Michael Armstrong. *Screenplay:* Michael Armstrong; additional dialogue by Peter Marcus. *Cinematography:* Jack Atcheler. *Cast:* Frankie Avalon (Chris); Jill Haworth (Sheila); Mark Wynter (Gary); Dennis Price (Inspector Wainwright); George Sewell (Kellett); Gina Warwick (Sylvia); Richard O'Sullivan (Peter); Carol Dilworth (Dorothy); Julian Barnes (Richard); Veronica Doran (Madge); Robin Stewart (Henry); Jan Holden (Peggy); Clifford Earl (Police Sergeant); Robert Raglan (Bradley); Freddie Lees (Dave).

Frankie Avalon made it to London, and Carnaby Street and Chelsea, after shaking the sand out of his hair, for this feeble attempt at horror. The idea in *Horror House*, with a group of young people being menaced by a maniacal killer, has been used many times since, and to much greater effect.

Chris (Avalon) has a party for his fab-mod-trendy London friends. One of them (Barnes) suggests they visit an abandoned, and supposedly haunted, house where several murders have taken place. When the group enters the house, they attempt to have a séance, hoping that a ghost will materialize. This is unsuccessful, so they decide to explore the house instead. One of the group is found horribly murdered, and Avalon convinces the rest not to tell the authorities. It seems that they are already in hot water for suspected drug use. An inspector (Price) begins to question the young people anyway. Avalon decides they must play detective themselves and search the house for clues, so the police will get off their backs. During their search another youth is murdered. Avalon ends up alone with Barnes, who is the murderer. He kills Avalon just before the police arrive.

JULIUS CAESAR. 1970. 117 minutes. Color. *Director:* Stuart Burge. *Screenplay:* Robert Furnival; based on the play by William Shakespeare. *Cinematography:* Ken Higgins. *Cast:* Charlton Heston (Marc Antony); Jason Robards, Jr. (Brutus); John Gielgud (Julius Caesar); Richard Johnson (Cassius); Robert Vaughn (Casca); Richard Chamberlain (Octavius Caesar); Diana Rigg (Portia); Jill Bennett (Calpurnia); Christopher Lee (Artemidorus); Alan Browning (Marullus); Norman Bowler (Titinius); Andrew Crawford (Volumnius); David Dodimead (Lepidus); Peter Eyre (Cinna the Poet); Edwin Finn (Publius); Derek Godfrey (Decius Brutus); Michael Gough (Metellus Cimber); Paul Hardwick (Messala); Thomas Heathcote (Flavius); Ewan Hooper (Strato); Robert Keegan (Lucilius); Preston Lockwood (Trebonius); John Moffatt (Popilius Lena); André Morell (Cicero); David Neal (Cinna the Conspirator); Steven Pacey (Lucius); John Tate (Clitus); Damien Thomas (Pindarus); Laurence Harrington (Carpenter); Ron Pember (Cobbler); Ken Hutchinson (1st Plebian); Michael Keating (2nd Plebian); Derek Hardwicke (3rd Plebian); Michael Wynne (4th Plebian); David Leland (5th Plebian); Ronald McGill (Servant to Caesar); Linbert Spencer (2nd Servant to Caesar); Trevor Adams (3rd Servant to Caesar); Robin Chadwick (Servant to Octavius); Christopher Cazenove (Servant to Anthony); Roy Stewart (Slave to Lepidus); Liz Geghardt (Maid to Calpurnia).

Julius Caesar is long on star quality and production values, but somewhat lackluster in the final results. What is so timeless and universal about Shakespeare is that his plays lend themselves to so many different interpretations. This particular version cannot stand up to the 1953 version. Marlon Brando's oration in the earlier work literally stops the film whereas Charlton Heston, portraying Marc Anthony here, is mainly doing one of his pompous "schticks" from a C.B. DeMille film. Gielgud's classic Cassius from 1953 is essayed here in a monotonous drone by the usually exemplary Jason Robards. The film contains all the right visual qualities in this tale of political corruption, ambition, and intrigue. One must wonder why *Julius Caesar* was remade, when a fine version was created 17 years before.

KAMA SUTRA. 1970. 90 minutes. Color. *Director:* Kobi Jaeger. *Screenplay:* George Wilson, Kobi Jaeger, and P.D. Shenoy. *Cinematography:* Richard Reuven Rimmel. *Cast:* Bruno Dietrich (Mike); Barbara Schöne (Anke); Richard Abbott (Peter); Franziska Bronnen (Helga); Karen Kaehler (Carola); Persis Khambatta (Nanda); Faryal Karim (Asha); Jai Kumar (Dlipi); Will Quadflieg (Narrator); with Prem Nath.

This is sort of a German-made *Mondo Cane*, depicting the erotic aspects of the *Kama Sutra* in a pseudo-documentary form. It shows the various principles of the *Kama Sutra* and how they have been applied throughout history. Also shown are young European jet setters and wealthy Indians partaking in the pleasures of the *Kama Sutra*. Apparently there was a sequence added to the American prints that displays Westerners indulging in drugs, wife swapping, and body painting. All in all, *Kama Sutra* is a film that bastardizes the original intent of the Indian *Kama Sutra*.

PACIFIC VIBRATIONS. 1970. 92 minutes. Color. *Director:* John Severson. *Screenplay:* John Severson. *Cinematography:* John Severson. *Cast:* Jock Southerland, Billy Hamilton, Rolf Aurness, David Nuuhiwa, Merv Larson, Jeff Hakman, Mike Tabeling, Corky Carroll, Rick Griffin, Angie Reno, Brad McCaul, Spyder Wills, Mickey Dora, Chuck Dent, Steve Bigler, Mike Purpus.

Pacific Vibrations is a documentary ostensibly about surfing. Where Bruce Brown's film *The Endless Summer* dealt with

the search for the "perfect wave," this film has other matters
on its mind. By 1970 the ecology movement was just beginning,
and *Pacific Vibrations* reflects some of these concerns. Not
only are California and Hawaiian surfers shown riding high
waves, but the problems of the shoreline are examined. Concern
is expressed about the influx of industrial expansion and private homes on the already-overcrowded beach communities, and
the elimination of sea life. In this kind of environment the
areas for surfers become fewer and fewer. By 1970 surfing
was still practiced on the West Coast and Hawaii as much as
it had five to ten years before, but it no longer was in the
national consciousness. In the 60s the music of groups like
The Beach Boys and Jan and Dean made kids from every provincial
backwater from Paducah, Kentucky, to Ames, Iowa, an honorary
surfer.

THE SAVAGE WILD. 1970. 103 minutes. Color. *Director:* Gordon
  Eastman. *Screenplay:* Gordon Eastman. *Cinematography:*
  Gordon Eastman. *Cast:* Gordon Eastman (Gordon); Carl Spore
  (Red); Maria Eastman (Maria); Arlo Curtis (Arlo); Jim
  Timiaough (Jim); Robert Wellington Kirk (Bob); John Payne
  (John); Charles Abou (Cha-lay); Alex Dennis (Cha-lay's
  Brother); Charley Davis (Charley); Wilbur O'Brian (Heli-
  copter Pilot); with Yukon, Teton, Missy (Timber Wolves).

In *High, Wild and Free* filmmaker Gordon Eastman and his
sons explored the wildlife of British Columbia, in what
amounted to a travelogue. In *The Savage Wild* Eastman takes
his camera north, near the Arctic Circle, to film a documentary
dramatization about timber wolves. With its central theme
concerning the raising of wild animals in captivity, this film
could be called "Born Free Goes North."
  Eastman takes his family to the extreme northern edge of
Canada to study timber wolves, a rapidly diminishing species
often pursued by bounty hunters. Eastman and his group capture
three wolf cubs and decide to raise them. A bounty hunter
(Spore) who hunts from an airplane, attempts to kill one of
the cubs. His plane loses control and he is killed. When
the cubs have grown to maturity, they are set free to hunt on
their own.

SCREAM AND SCREAM AGAIN. 1970. 94 minutes. Color. *Director:*
  Gordon Hessler. *Screenplay:* Christopher Wicking; based
  on the novel *The Disoriented Man*, by Peter Saxon.

Cinematography: John Coquillon. *Cast:* Vincent Price (Dr. Browning); Christopher Lee (Fremont); Peter Cushing (Benedek); Judy Huxtable (Sylvia); Alfred Marks (Superintendent Bellaver); Anthony Newlands (Ludwig); Peter Sallis (Schweitz); David Lodge (Detective Strickland); Uta Levka (Jane); Christopher Matthews (David Sorel); Judi Bloom (Helen Bradford); Clifford Earl (Detective Jimmy Joyce); Kenneth Benda (Professor Kingsmill); Michael Gothard (Keith); Marshall Jones (Konratz); Julian Holloway (Griffin); Edgar D. Davies (Rogers); Yutte Stensgaard (Erika); Lincoln Webb (Wrestler); Nigel Lambert (Ken Sparten); Steve Preston (Fryer); Lee Hudson (Matron); Leslie Ewin (Tramp); Kay Adrian (Nurse); Rosalind Elliot (Valerie); with The Amen Corner.

Vincent Price teamed up here (unsuccessfully) with the two stars of Hammer horror films—Christopher Lee and Peter Cushing. Not only does Cushing have a negligible role, bordering on a cameo, but the entire film is marred by a confusing story and a musical score that sounds as if it were left over from television's *The Mod Squad*.

A police detective (Marks) is investigating a string of brutal murders. A doctor (Matthews) informs Marks that two of the bodies have been desanguinated. The police use a decoy (Bloom) to trap the killer, who possesses extraordinary strength. They chase him throughout the countryside to the clinic of a doctor (Price), where the murderer kills himself by jumping into a vat of acid. While all this has been going on, we have also witnessed events in an Eastern European country, where an agent (Jones) has been killing enemies of the state. Jones blackmails a British agent (Lee) to stop the police's investigation in the series of murders. All of the plot threads are tied together when Jones confronts Price and orders him to stop building his human composites. He has been the brains behind a scheme to build a race of supermen, and Price's experimental beings have been killing too many people. In a fight Jones kills Price, but Lee comes upon the scene to dispose of Jones by pushing him into an acid bath.

TIGER BY THE TAIL. 1970. 99 minutes. Color. *Director:* R.G. Springsteen. *Screenplay:* Charles A. Wallace. *Cinematography:* Alan Stensvold. *Cast:* Cristopher George (Steve Michaelis); Tippi Hedren (Rita Armstrong); Dean Jagger (Top Polk); John Dehner (Sheriff Chancey Jones); Charo (Darlita); Lloyd Bochner (Del Ware); Glenda Farrell (Sarah Harvey); Alan Hale, Jr. (Billy Jack Whitehorn);

Skip Homeier (Deputy Sheriff Laswell); R.G. Armstrong
(Ben Holmes); Dennis Patrick (Frank Michaelis); Martin
Ashe (Jimmy-San Ricketts); Frank Babich (Reporter);
Marilyn Devin (Julie Foster); Ray Martell (Garcia); Burt
Mustin (Tom Dugger); Fernando Pereira (Mendoza); Olga
Velez (Candita); Della Young and Tricia Young (Bikini
Girls); with The Mescalero Apache Horn Dancers, and
Meredith Neal and the Boot Heel Boys.

The theme of the returning war veteran having to continue
to fight when he comes home was a common theme to the *films
noirs* of the 40s. Here that theme is directed by veteran "B"
director R.G. "Bud" Springsteen in a made-to-order, predictable, television-movie fashion. As with many of these films,
the main actors are second-rate but are backed up by a strong
group of supporting character actors.
     A Vietnam veteran (George) returns to make amends with
his brother (Patrick), who runs a racetrack. He finds that
Patrick has been murdered during a robbery attempt. George
believes that the robbery is only a ruse to hide the fact that
Patrick was killed over a power play for control of the track.
He pressures one of the shareholders (Bochner) to admit complicity in the murder, but Bochner is killed before he can
divulge the names of the others involved. It turns out that
two lawmen (Homeier and Armstrong) took part in Patrick's murder. After Armstrong shoots Homeier, George has a fight with
him and kills him with his own gun. He now takes over the
operation of the racetrack.

24-HOUR LOVER. 1970. 90 minutes. Color. *Director:* Marran
     Gosov. *Screenplay:* Marran Gosov. *Cinematography:* Hubs
     Hagen and Niklas Schilling. *Cast:* Harold Leipnitz (George
     Weissborn); Sybille Maar (Irene); Herbert Bötticher
     (Alfred); Brigitte Skay (Marion); Monika Lundi (Lisa);
     Renate Roland (Peggy); Marianne Wischmann (Vera); Claudia
     Wedekind (Rosa); Sylvie Beck (Monika); Isolde Brauner
     (Mia); Werner Schwier (Doctor); Jana Novakova (Ulla);
     Doris Kiesow (Lenna); Herbert Weissbach (Grandfather);
     Inge Langen (Claudia); with Sammy Drechsel, Henry van
     Lyck, Nino Korda.

This West German sex farce sometimes goes under the title
of *Crunch*. A single middle-aged man (Leipnitz) is embarrassing
his conservative middle-class family by his promiscous behavior. His brother (Bötticher) especially wants Leipnitz to
settle down and get married, because his promotion as a school

teacher depends on it. The sexually overextended Leipnitz
has to go into the hospital. When he recuperates he brings a
nurse home and tells his family that they are going to be married. However, he continues to bring different fiancées home
to meet the family. He finally marries one of his cousins
(Maar). On the day of his marriage the joyous Leipnitz slides
down a bannister. He hurts himself doing so, which puts an
end to his sexual escapades. Presumably this is why the film
is also known as *Crunch*.

UP IN THE CELLAR. 1970. 92 minutes. Color. *Director:*
    Theodore J. Flicker. *Screenplay:* Theodore J. Flicker;
    based on the novel *The Late Boy Wonder*, by Angus Hall.
    Cinematography: Earl Rath. *Cast:* Wes Stern (Colin Slade);
    Joan Collins (Pat Camber); Larry Hagman (Maurice Camber);
    Nira Barab (Tracy Camber); Judy Pace (Harlene Jones);
    David Arkin (Hugo Cain); Joan Darling (Madame Krigo); Bill
    Svanoe (Campus Policeman); with Charles Pinney and David
    Cargo.

    The title should let you know that this is a film that
does not take itself too seriously. *Up in the Cellar* is a
satire on campus politics, ambitious right-wing politicians,
and to a lesser degree black/white relations. Like other top-
ical films from AIP, this film "is truer to the actual issues
and atmosphere of its time than many a more prestigious major
studio production..." (Tony Rayns, *Monthly Film Bulletin*, January 1974, p. 15).
    A college student (Stern) loses his scholarship when his
writing is judged unfairly by a computer. The college president (Hagman), who is running for political office, refuses
to overturn the computer's decision. A politically active
student (Arkin), who sort of represents the "militant moder-
ates," convinces Stern to take revenge on Hagman by committing
suicide at one of Hagman's political rallies. His attempt is
foiled by Hagman. Stern now decides to cause a campus scandal
by seducing Hagman's wife (Collins), daughter (Barab), and
black mistress (Pace). His plan backfires on him when it turns
out that Hagman is receiving sympathy from the embarrassing
disclosures. Hagman eventually divorces Collins and goes away
with Pace. Stern is now left free to join the mother and
daughter.

THE VAMPIRE LOVERS. 1970. 88 minutes. Color. *Director:*
Roy Ward Baker. *Screenplay:* Tudor Gates; adaptation by
Gates, Harry Fine, and Michael Style; based on the story
"Carmilla," by J. Sheridan Le Fanu. *Cinematography:* Moray
Grant. *Cast:* Ingrid Pitt (Carmilla/Mircalla/Marcilla);
Pippa Steel (Laura); Madeline Smith (Emma Morton); Peter
Cushing (General Spielsdorf); George Cole (Roger Morton);
Dawn Addams (The Countess); Kate O'Mara (Governess);
Douglas Wilmer (Baron Hartog); Jon Finch (Carl Ebhardt);
Kirsten Betts (1st Vampire); Harvey Hall (Renton); Janet
Key (Gretchin); Charles Farrell (Landlord); John Forbes-
Robertson (Man in Black); Shelagh Wilcox (Housekeeper);
Graham James and Tom Browne (Young Men); Joanna Shelley
(Woodman's Daughter); Olga James (Village Girl).

It is such films as this that have gained Ingrid Pitt a
mild cult following, but one nowhere near approaching that of
Barbara Steele. *The Vampire Lovers*, with its inclusion of
nudity and lesbianism in a vampire-story format, came out years
before *The Hunger*. This film concentrates on its gothic sur-
roundings, while *The Hunger* is imbued with a sort of decadent-
chic viewpoint.
     In order to seek revenge for the murder of his sister, a
baron (Wilmer) goes to a cemetery where he drives stakes into
the hearts of the vampire members of the Karnstein family.
However, one of the vampires (Pitt) has managed to escape his
revenge. Years later Pitt appears at the home of a General
Spielsdorf (Cushing) and quickly becomes part of his household.
Pitt, in order to gain revenge on those who condemned her family, wastes no time in seducing and killing Cushing's daughter
(Steel). She next goes after Steel's best friend (Smith) and
slowly drains her of her blood through her seductive methods.
The family butler (Hull) informs Smith's father (Cole) what
has happened, and he asks the help of Wilmer and Steel's fiancé (Finch). It is Finch who confronts the female vampire.
He corners Pitt in her crypt, where Wilmer both beheads and
impales her.

VENUS IN FURS. 1970. 86 minutes. Color. *Director:* Jess
Franco. *Screenplay:* Malvin Wald and Jess Franco; based
on the novel *Venus im Pelz*, by Leopold von Sacher-Masoch.
Cinematography: Angelo Lotti. *Cast:* James Darren (Jimmy
Logan); Barbara McNair (Rita); Maria Rohm (Wanda Reed/
Venus); Klaus Kinski (Ahmed); Dennis Price (Kapp);
Margaret Lee (Olga); Adolfo Castretti (Inspector); Paul
Müller (Nightclub Owner); with Mirella Pamphili.

The novel by von Sacher-Masoch (from whose writings the term "masochism" is derived) *Venus im Pelz* was filmed a couple of other times in the late 60s and early 70s. This particular version of *Venus in Furs* was directed by Jess Franco (he often uses aliases), a filmmaker who made several tawdry European sex films in the 60s and 70s. This piece of soft-core contains a mixture of reality and dreams, with James Darren's voiceover, to create an oneiric effect.

A young musician (Darren) finds the dead body of a beautiful woman (Rohm) on an Istanbul beach. Earlier he had witnessed her horrible death by three debauched kinky types (Kinski, Price, and Lee). He leaves for Brazil, where he falls in love with a cabaret singer (McNair). In a nightclub one night Darren notices a woman who looks very much like the dead Rohm. Like a moth attracted to a flame, he becomes instantly interested in her. Rohm seduces the three people who were her murderers, and each shortly dies thereafter. Darren is fearful of Rohm's power, so he takes McNair and returns to Istanbul. He walks back to the spot on the beach where he first found Rohm's body, and now finds his own body lying dead on the sand.

WEDDING NIGHT. 1970. 99 minutes. Color. *Director:* Piers Haggard. *Screenplay:* Robert I. Holt and Lee Dunne; additional dialogue by Piers Haggard; based on a story by Holt. *Cinematography:* Ray Sturgess. *Cast:* Dennis Waterman (Joe O'Reilly); Tessa Wyatt (Mady); Alexandra Bastedo (Gloria); Eddie Bryne (Tom); Martin Dempsey (Father Keegan); Maire O'Donnell (Kate); Patrick Laffan (Dr. Farnum); Garden Odyssey Enterprise (Rock Group); with Peter Mayock, Eileen Page, Trevor Bailey, Chris Curran, Vernon Hayden, Cecil Nash, Christian Lyons, Martin Lyons.

This film was made in Ireland and deals primarily with the Catholic church's attitude toward birth control. When *Wedding Night* first appeared at the 1979 Cork Film Festival, it caused a great deal of controversy. To make a film in Ireland critical of the Catholic church's stand on birth control is tantamount to going to Israel to produce a film about the benefits of eating pork.

Following the wedding of a young couple (Waterman and Wyatt), Wyatt's mother dies of a miscarriage after having borne many children through the years. Casting blame on her father's sexual treatment of his wife, Wyatt withholds herself from her husband. Waterman attempts to understand her feelings. He goes back to his job in London, while Wyatt stays in Ireland to help her motherless family. When the couple get back

together, their marital troubles intensify, as Waterman now
tries to force himself sexually on the unwilling Wyatt. She
returns to Ireland after Waterman begins to see an old girlfriend (Bastedo). To ease her dread of pregnancy, a local
doctor (Laffan) recommends a contraceptive for Wyatt, but her
family priest (Dempsey) advises her against it. Because of
all the pressure, Wyatt is hospitalized. She attempts suicide,
and when Waterman comes to see her they are reunited.

WUTHERING HEIGHTS. 1970. 105 minutes. Color. *Director:*
    Robert Fuest. *Screenplay:* Patrick Tilley; based on the
    novel by Emily Brontë. *Cinematography:* John Coquillon.
    Cast: Anna Calder-Marshall (Catherine Earnshaw); Timothy
    Dalton (Heathcliff); Harry Andrews (Mr. Earnshaw); Pamela
    Brown (Mrs. Linton); Judy Cornwell (Nellie); James Cossins
    (Mr. Linton); Rosalie Crutchley (Mrs. Earnshaw); Hilary
    Dwyer (Isabella Linton); Julian Glover (Hindley Earnshaw);
    Hugh Griffith (Dr. Kenneth); Morag Hood (Frances); Ian
    Ogilvy (Edgar Linton); Peter Sallis (Mr. Shielders);
    Aubrey Woods (Joseph); with Wendy Allnutt, John Comer,
    Dudley Foster, Gordon Gostelow, Lois Daine, Keith Buckley,
    James Berwick, Patricia Doyle, Mark Wilding, Sandra
    Bryant, Bruce Beeby, Jonathan Brewster, Gillian Hayes,
    Libby Granger, Gertan Klauber.

    Samuel Z. Arkoff and James H. Nicholson thought enough
of this remake to produce it themsélves. Filmed in the Yorkshire area of England, and using a cast of mostly unknowns,
this version of *Wuthering Heights* is rather predictable and
one-dimensional, much like a television film. However, it
does contain implications of Heathcliff being Catherine's il-
legitimate half-brother--a theme studiously avoided in the
1939 version.
    A young orphan named Heathcliff (Dalton) is taken by a
wealthy man (Andrews) to live with his family. Despite the
initial hostility of Andrews's children, his daughter (Calder-
Marshall) and Dalton fall in love. Things change when her
boorish brother (Glover) takes over Wuthering Heights manor,
and Calder-Marshall marries someone else. Dalton leaves for
a number of years and returns a wealthy man. He plans revenge
on those who have ostracized him by buying Wuthering Heights
from the now-drunken Glover, and marrying Calder-Marshall's
sister-in-law (Dwyer), whom he treats with contempt. After
Calder-Marshall has died in childbirth, Dalton sees her ghost
at Wuthering Heights. While there he is shot by Glover. Seriously wounded, Dalton follows Calder-Marshall's ghost out into
the Yorkshire moors, where they are reunited in death.

THE ABOMINABLE DR. PHIBES. 1971. 94 minutes. Color. *Director:* Robert Fuest. *Screenplay:* James Whiton and William Goldstein. *Cinematography:* Norman Warwick. *Cast:* Vincent Price (Dr. Anton Phibes); Joseph Cotten (Dr. Vesalius); Hugh Griffith (Rabbi); Terry-Thomas (Dr. Longstreet); Virginia North (Vulnavia); Aubrey Woods (Goldsmith); Susan Travers (Nurse Allen); Alex Scott (Dr. Hargreaves); Edward Burnham (Dr. Dunwoody); Peter Gilmore (Dr. Kitaj); Peter Jeffrey (Inspector Trout); Maurice Kaufmann (Dr. Whitcombe); Norman Jones (Sergeant Schenley); John Cater (Waverley); Derek Godfrey (Detective Crow); Sean Bury (Lem Vesalius); Walter Horsbrugh (Ross); Barbara Keough (Mrs. Frawley); Dallas Adams (1st Police Official); Alan Zipson (2nd Police Official); David Hutcheson (Dr. Hedgepath); Alister Williamson (1st Policeman); Thomas Heathcote (2nd Policeman); Ian Marter (3rd Policeman); Julian Grant (4th Policeman); Caroline Munro (Victoria Phibes); with John Laurie and Charles Farrell.

It is appropriate that Vincent Price's 100th film should be one in which he portrays one of his most famous characters-- Dr. Phibes. This horror film takes a tongue-in-cheek view of its subject, with its use of old songs, Phibes's home (an Art Deco disco), and Phibes himself, who drinks and speaks through a hole in his neck.

Price portrays a rich genius who was badly mutilated in a car crash, which took his wife's life. He is determined to gain revenge against the surgeons whom he feels are responsible for her death. The method of death on which he bases his scheme is the series of biblical plagues. After some ingenious murders, in which he uses such things as rats, bats, locusts, and bees, the police begin to suspect him. Joseph Cotten, one of the surgeons wanted by Price, has his son (Bury) kidnapped by him. He puts the boy on an operating table with a tube of acid above it, but before the tubes can explode, Cotten rescues his son. Price now joins his wife's corpse in their sealed burial tomb.

BATTLE OF NERETVA. 1971. 102 minutes. Color. *Director:* Veljko Bulajic. *Screenplay:* Ratko Djurovic, Stevo Bulajic, Veljko Bulajic, Ugo Pirro, and Alfred Weidenmann. *Cinematography:* Tomislav Pinter. *Cast:* Yul Brynner (Vlado); Sergei Bondarchuk (Martin); Curt Jergens (General Lohring); Sylva Koscina (Danica); Hardy Kruger (Colonel Kranzer); Franco Nero (Captain Riva); Orson Welles (Senator); Ljubisa Samardjic (Novak); Lojze Rozman (Commander Ivan); Milena Dravic (Nada); Oleg Vidov (Nikola); Bata

Zivojinovic (Stole); Fabijan Sovagovic (Mad Bosko); Boris
Dvornik (Stipe); Pavle Vuisic (Jordan); Anthony Dawson
(General Morelli); Howard Ross (Sergeant Mario); Charles
Millot (Djurka); with Barbara Bold, Ralph Persson, Renato
Rossini.

Battle of Neretva supposedly was the most expensive picture ever filmed in Eastern Europe (outside of the Soviet Union) and even received an Academy Award nomination for Best
Foreign Film of 1969. When it was finally released by AIP in
1971, the 175-minute film had been cut by over 70 minutes, and
received only a scattering of playdates in the United States.
    This is another story of the gallant freedom fighters of
World War II, with a musical score supplied by Bernard
Herrmann. It was not until roughly the mid-70s that films
from Eastern Europe started to deal with problems in contemporary society, instead of concentrating on the heroics of the
past. Here the location is Yugoslavia in 1943, which is under
German and Italian control. A group of partisans are escaping
the enemy by retreating to their mountain hideout. The bridge
they need to cross to get to the mountains is ordered destroyed
by none other than Marshal Tito. They quickly construct a
wooden bridge over the remnants of the damaged one and are
able to evade the Germans. The partisans confront a group of
Yugoslav Nazi sympathizers, the Chetniks. The two groups have
a ferocious and bloody battle, in which the short-handed partisans are victorious.

BLOOD AND LACE. 1971. 87 minutes. Color. *Director:* Philip
    Gilbert. *Screenplay:* Gil Laskey. *Cinematography:* Paul
    Hipp. *Cast:* Gloria Grahame (Mrs. Deere); Melody Patterson
    (Ellie Masters); Milton Selzer (Mr. Mullins); Len Lesser
    (Tom Kredge); Vic Tayback (Calvin Carruthers); Terri
    Messina (Bunch); Ronald Taft (Walter); Dennis Christopher
    (Pete); Peter Armstrong (Ernest); Maggie Corey (Jennifer);
    Mary Strawberry (Nurse); Louise Sherrill (Edna Masters).

    This is a real find--a true piece of "schlock Guignol."
Blood and Lace has all the trappings of the modern-day "slice
and dice films," such as death by a meat cleaver and by a hammer, frozen corpses, shadows, and twist endings. It also contains a rather pessimistic attack on such things as orphanages,
orphans, social workers, and even filial relations.
    A young girl (Patterson) is brought to the local orphanage
after her prostitute mother (Sherrill) has been murdered by
an unknown assailant. The orphanage is run by the sadistic

Mrs. Deere (Grahame) and her vicious henchman (Lesser). When
orphans run away from them, Lesser tracks them down, murders
them, and stores their bodies in a freezer. The bodies are
then put on display in the orphanage hospital for a head count
when the local social worker (Selzer) comes by. A detective
(Tayback) begins to snoop around the institution. After Lesser
has pole-axed Selzer with a cleaver, a mysterious masked man
appears and knocks Lesser out. It turns out to be Tayback,
who knows that Patterson murdered her mother. He agrees to
keep quiet about the murder, if she will marry him. It is
now learned that Tayback is her father.

BLOOD FROM THE MUMMY'S TOMB. 1971. 94 minutes. Color. *Di-
rectors:* Seth Holt and Michael Carreras. *Screenplay:*
Christopher Wicking; based on the novel *Jewel of the Seven
Stars*, by Bram Stoker. *Cinematography:* Arthur Grant.
Cast: Andrew Keir (Professor Julian Fuchs); Valerie Leon
(Margaret Fuchs/Queen Tera); James Villiers (Corbeck);
Hugh Burden (Dandridge); George Coulouris (Berigan); Mark
Edwards (Tod Browning); Rosalie Crutchley (Helen Dicker-
son); Aubrey Morris (Doctor Putnum); David Markham (Doctor
Burgess); Joan Young (Mrs. Caporal); James Cossins (Older
Male Nurse); Graham James (Youth in Museum); David Jackson
(Younger Male Nurse); Jonathan Burn (Saturnine Young Man);
Tamara Ustinov (Veronica); Penelope Holt and Angela
Ginders (Nurses); Tex Fuller (Patient); Madina Luis, Omar
Amoodi, Abdul Kader, Oscar Charles, Ahmed Osman, Soltan
Lalani, and Saad Ghazi (Priests).

    This was one of Hammer Films's better attempts in updating
classic horror themes. *Blood from the Mummy's Tomb* contains
such in-jokes as a character with the name of old-time horror
director Tod Browning, and uses such devices as severed hands,
sacred cats, and the obligatory mad scientist. Director Seth
Holt died shortly before the film was completed, so Michael
Carreras stepped in to complete the film. This film was remade
in 1980 as *The Awakening*, starring Charlton Heston.
    An archaeological expedition in Egypt finds the tomb of
Queen Tera and brings it back to England. Twenty-one years
later the leader (Keir) gives his daughter (Leon) Tera's ring.
The spirit of the dead queen is reincarnated as it slowly possesses Leon's body. Three members of the expedition violently
die, as Tera is out to reclaim the artifacts from the tomb.
One of the expedition members (Villiers), who believes in
Tera's power, attempts to revive her mummified body during an
ancient ceremony. He is foiled by Keir, as he destroys the

mummy, thereby bringing the house they are in down to the
ground. The only survivor is Leon, who is now in a hospital,
wrapped in bandages like a mummy.

BUNNY O'HARE. 1971. 92 minutes. Color. *Director:* Gerd
    Oswald. *Screenplay:* Stanley Z. Cherry and Coslough
    Johnson; based on a story by Cherry. *Cinematography:*
    Loyal Griggs and John Stephens. *Cast:* Bette Davis (Bunny
    O'Hare); Ernest Borgnine (Bill Gruenwald); Jack Cassidy
    (Detective Horace Greeley); Joan Delaney (R.J. Hart); Jay
    Robinson (Banker John C. Rupert); Brayden Linden (Frank);
    Robert Foulk (Commissioner Dingle); J. Rob Jordan (Police-
    man Nerdman); Reva Rose (Lulu); John Astin (Ad); Karen
    Mae Johnson (Lola); Francis R. Cody (Rhett); Darra Lyn
    Tobin (Elvira); Hank Wickham (Speed); Governor David Cargo
    (State Trooper Cargo); with Herb Marlis, Bruno Ve Sota,
    Robert Ball, Carlos José Ramirez, David Rain, Madeleine A.
    Russo, Bud Elkins, Ann Lafan, Gene Krischer, Grady Hill,
    Cordy Garcia, Sgt. Robert Mader, Carole Smith, Randi
    Proctor, Luanne Roberts, Barbara Raines, Larry Linville,
    Tony Genaro, Bob Isenberg, Buck Kartalian, Irenee Byatt,
    Roberta Reeves, Ed Call, Robert Baur.

The goings on after the production of *Bunny O'Hare* are
much more interesting than the film itself. AIP apparently
reshot and reedited the film much to Bette Davis's dismay.
Thinking she had signed up to make a film that was a social
satire, she sued AIP for its tampering with the production.
In response AIP countersued. Never have so many spent so much
time on so little. *Bunny O'Hare* is such a slapstick cartoon
mess that it was artistically irretrievable from the very beginning.
    A widow (Davis) is evicted from her home and takes to the
road with a plumber (Borgnine). She learns that he is a bank
robber who had escaped from prison years before. Together
they decide to rob branches of the New Mexico bank that issued
a foreclosure on her house. The two dress up as a pair of
aging hippies, as they are chased across New Mexico by a right-
wing cop (Cassidy) who hates hippies. Two real hippies (Linden
and Johnson), from whom Davis and Borgnine copied their outfits, decide to rob banks so they can give the money to the
farm workers. Eventually they are caught at the Mexican border, as the undetected Davis and Borgnine make their escape
into Mexico.

CARRY ON HENRY VIII. 1971. 90 minutes. Color. *Director:* Gerald Thomas. *Screenplay:* Talbot Rothwell. *Cinematography:* Alan Hume. *Cast:* Sidney James (King Henry VIII); Kenneth Williams (Sir Thomas Cromwell); Joan Sims (Marie of Normandy); Charles Hawtrey (Sir Roger de Loggerley); Terry Scott (Cardinal Wolsey); Barbara Windsor (Bettina); Kenneth Connor (Lord Hampton of Wick); Julian Holloway (Sir Thomas); Peter Gilmore (King Francis); Julian Orchard (Duc de Pincenay); Gertan Klauber (Bidet); David Davenport (Major Domo); Margaret Nolan (Lass); William Mervyn (Physician); Norman Chappell (1st Plotter); Douglas Ridley (2nd Plotter); Derek Francis (Farmer); Bill Maynard (Fawkes); Leon Greene (1st Warder); David Prowse (2nd Warder); Monica Dietrich (Katherine Howard); Marjie Lawrence (Serving Maid); Patsy Rowlands (Queen); Peter Butterworth (Earl of Bristol); Billy Cornelius (Guard); John Bluthal (Royal Tailor); Alan Curtis (Conte Di Pisa); William McGuirk (Flunkey); Anthony Sagar (Heckler); David Essex (Young Man); Peter Rigby, Trevor Roberts, and Peter Munt (Henry's Courtiers); John Clive (Dandy); Jane Cardew (Henry's 2nd Wife); Brian Wilde (Warder); Valerie Shute (Maid).

Apparently the Carry On series has its supporters in Great Britain, since so many of them were made. They never have gained much favor in the United States, but AIP distributed a handful of them anyway. *Carry on Henry VIII* reaches the summit, or the nadir, of the Carry On series, depending on one's taste. This particular film is what the British refer to as a "bawdy romp," replete with sexual situations and double entendres. Monty Python exhibits a different brand of British humor; the Carry On films are more in the vein of Benny Hill and such British stage shows as *No Sex Please, We're British.*

Carry On Henry VIII, suffice it to say, turns the life of that (in)famous monarch on its head. It contains a would-be queen who eats garlic, a host of suitors in a variety of bedchambers, a number of bosomy wenches, and a king who almost gets England in a war with France over a lady's honor.

CHRISTA. 1971. 95 minutes. Color. *Director:* Jack O'Connell. *Screenplay:* Jack O'Connell. *Cinematography:* Henning Kristiansen. *Cast:* Birthe Tove (Christa); Daniel Gélin (André); Baard Owe (Torben); Clinton Greyn (Derek); Gaston Rossilli (Umberto); Susan Hurley (Student Air Hostess);

Inger Stender and Inge Levin (Air Hostesses); with Ciro
Elias.

Before it appeared at the 1971 Cannes Film Festival
Christa was reported to have had an original running time of
four hours. Also known under the misleading title *Swedish
Fly Girls*, this U.S.-Danish co-production has some fine photography but is hampered by a weak script and a loud musical score
by Manfred Mann.
    A young airline hostess (Tove) lives in a free-and-easy
commune in Copenhagen. Her belief in free love leads her to
pick up an international assortment of men from her airplane
travels. Tove meets an Englishman (Greyn) with whom she falls
in love and wants to marry. The father (Owe) of her illegiti-
mate son learns of her marriage plans. He threatens to gain
custody of the boy by going to court to prove she is an unfit
mother. When Owe gets in serious business difficulties and
Tove refuses to let him take their son, he purposely crashes
his car and is killed.
    What one remembers from this film is not the Sirkian melo-
dramatics of the plot. Instead it is the dialogue, which is
a strange amalgam of English dubbing and subtitles.

CHROME AND HOT LEATHER. 1971. 95 minutes. Color. *Director:*
    Lee Frost. *Screenplay:* Michael Allen Haynes, David
    Neibel, and Don Tait. *Cinematography:* Lee Frost. *Cast:*
    William Smith (T.J.); Tony Young (Mitch); Michael Haynes
    (Casey); Peter Brown (Al); Marvin Gaye (Jim); Michael
    Stearns (Hank); Kathy Baumann (Susan); Wes Bishop (Sheriff
    Lewis); Herb Jeffries (Ned); Bob Pickett (Sweet Willy);
    George Carey (Lieut. Reardon); Marland Proctor (Captain
    Barnes); Cherie Moor (Kathy); Ann Marie (Helen); Robert
    Ridgely (St. Mack); Lee Parrish (NCO Club Bartender);
    Larry Bishop (Gabe).

    Even by 1971 AIP was still trying to milk the cycle films
for all they were worth. In the wonderfully titled *Chrome and
Hot Leather*, as well as *The Hard Ride*, the role of the returning Vietnam veteran comes into play. What makes this particular film unusual is that, along with its revenge motif, it
pokes some fun at the cycle genre.
    A young girl (Moor) and her friend (Ann Marie) are killed
in an auto accident caused by some rough cyclists. Her ex-
Green Beret boyfriend (Young) vows vengeance and enlists the
aid of his three army buddies (Gaye, Brown, and Stearns) in
finding the gang. All four go through a training period

learning to ride motorcycles, and then they split up to look
for the cyclists. Young encounters the gang leader (Smith)
in a bar, where Smith's girlfriend (Baumann) takes a liking
to Young. When Smith learns of the couple's romantic interlude, he takes his men and beats up Young. He is rescued by
his three friends, and they leave to prepare for their mili-
tarized assault on the gang. They trap the cyclists in a desert canyon and, through the use of tear gas and mortar rounds,
they capture them all.

THE DIRT GANG. 1971. 89 minutes. Color. *Director:* Jerry
    Jameson. *Screenplay:* William Mercer and Michael C.
    Healey. *Cinematography:* Howard A. Anderson. *Cast:* Paul
    Carr (Monk); Michael Pataki (Snake); Lee De Broux (Jesse);
    Jon Shank (Padre); Nancy Harris (Big Beth); T.J. Escott
    (Biff); Jessica Stuart (Stormy); Tom Anders (Marty); Joe
    Mosca (Willie); Michael Forest (Zino); Jo Anne Meredith
    (Dawn Christian); Nanci Beck (Mary); Charles Macauley
    (Curt); Hal England (Sidney); Ben Archibek (Jason);
    William Benedict (Station Attendant).

A renegade group of cyclists in the Southwest come upon
a movie company making a film in the desert. They charge onto
the set looking to cause havoc and wanting some food. The
movie's director (Macauley) offers to feed the gang, but one
of the stuntmen (Forest), an ex-biker, suggests that Macauley
call the police before the gang gets out of hand. The leader
(Carr) of the cyclists recognizes Forest as the one who put
out his eye in a biker duel a few years before. Carr challenges him to another duel, but Forest refuses. The gang make
themselves at home on the movie set, and begin a wild orgy.
Carr attempts to goad Forest into a duel by offering the script
girl (Beck) to one of the more repellent bikers (Pataki).
Forest agrees to the duel if Pataki stops his assault on Beck.
The next day Forest and Carr get on a couple of cycles and
have a battle with chains. Forest picks up a spear used as a
movie prop, and Carr is stabbed with it when he tries to ride
Forest down. Without a gang leader, the rest of the cyclists
meekly roar away across the desert.

DR. JEKYLL AND SISTER HYDE. 1971. 97 minutes. Color. *Direc-*
    tor: Roy Ward Baker. *Screenplay:* Brian Clemens. *Cine-*
    matography: Norman Warwick. *Cast:* Ralph Bates (Dr.
    Jekyll); Martine Beswick (Sister Hyde); Gerald Sim

(Professor Robertson); Lewis Fiander (Howard); Dorothy
Alison (Mrs. Spencer); Neil Wilson (Older Policeman);
Ivor Dean (Burke); Paul Whitsun-Jones (Sergeant Danvers);
Philip Madoc (Byker); Tony Calvin (Hare); Susan Broderick
(Susan); Dan Meaden (Town Crier); Virginia Wetherell
(Betsy); Geoffrey Kenion (1st Policeman); Irene Bradshaw
(Yvonne); Anna Brett (Julie); Jackie Poole (Margie);
Rosemary Lord (Marie); Petula Portell (Petra); Pat
Brackenbury (Helen); Liz Romanoff (Emma); Will Stampe
(Mine Host); Roy Evans (Knife Grinder); Derek Steen (1st
Sailor); John Lyons (2nd Sailor); Jeannette Wild (Jill);
Bobby Parr (Young Apprentice); Julia Wright (Street
Singer).

This Hammer film takes as its starting point characters
created by Robert Louis Stevenson and injects bisexual and
lesbian overtones into them. The two main actors, Ralph Bates
and Martine Beswick, do have a resemblance to one another,
with Beswick especially looking like Barbara Steele. As with
many of the Hammer films, the plot deficiencies in *Dr. Jekyll
and Sister Hyde* are more than made up for by an attractive
visual design on a small budget.
   Dr. Jekyll (Bates) believes that the elixir of life lies
in the hormones of dead young women. He obtains various bodies
from morgues, and through the work of a couple of grave robbers
(Dean and Calvin). The potion that Bates concocts turns him
into a beautiful young woman (Beswick). He is both attracted
and repelled by his new identity and must resort to murdering
women for their hormones when Dean and Calvin no longer are
able to supply him with bodies. Bates becomes involved in an
affair with a young girl (Broderick), just as Beswick, his
Hyde persona finds herself attracted to Broderick's brother
(Fiander). The murderous female side of Bates is gradually
consuming his own personality. An associate (Sim) of Bates
alerts the police to his behavior, and in a chase Bates falls
to his death from a rooftop.

THE HARD RIDE. 1971. 89 minutes. Color. *Director:* Burt
   Topper. *Screenplay:* Burt Topper. *Cinematography:* Robert
   Sparks. *Cast:* Robert Fuller (Phil); Sherry Bain (Sheryl);
   Tony Russell (Big Red); William Bonner (Grady); Marshall
   Reed (Father Tom); Mikel Angel (Ralls); Biff Elliot
   (Mike); Al Cole (Mooch); Phyllis Selznick (Rita); R.L.
   Armstrong (Jason); Robert Swan (Ted); Larry Eisley (Rice);
   Frank Charolla (Meyers); Herman Rudin (Little Horse);
   Alfonso Williams (Lenny); Ford Lile (Floyd); John Cestare

(A1); Del Russell (Nico); with Rachel English, John Lomma, Ron Stokes, Robert Tessier, Jo Felino, Gus Peters, Tony De Costa, Tony Haig, Doug Matheson, David Bradley.

This is a biker film that uses about a dozen songs, most of which are of the inflated self-righteous variety. *The Hard Ride* is "a thinly disguised cross between *The Wild Angels* and *Easy Rider*, whose monotony is only occasionally relieved by some nice photography of the High Sierras by Robert Sparks" (Keith Alain, *Monthly Film Bulletin*, July 1972, p. 139).

A Vietnam veteran (Fuller) brings back home the body of his black comrade (Williams). Before he died, Williams left a letter that arranged for Fuller to be the owner of his custom-built motorcycle. Fuller must also find a fellow cyclist friend of Williams (Russell) to attend his funeral. A leader of a motorcycle gang (Bonner) desires the cycle in Fuller's possession. Fuller is tricked in going to the gang's hideout, but he escapes after a brief fight. He enlists the aid of Williams's old girlfriend (Bain) to locate Russell. When they find him, he admits that he was not Williams's friend but only wanted his motorcycle. The men have a tussle for Bain's affections, which results in each one gaining respect for one another. Fuller is kidnapped by Bonner, but Russell comes to the rescue with his gang. Fuller is killed in the struggle between the rival groups. Both gangs now mend their differences and have a funeral for both Fuller and Williams.

THE HOUSE THAT SCREAMED. 1971. 94 minutes. Color. *Director:* Narcisco Ibáñez Serrador. *Screenplay:* Luis Verna Penafiel. *Cinematography:* Manuel Berenguer. *Cast:* Lilli Palmer (Mme. Fourneau); Cristina Galbo (Theresa); John Moulder Brown (Luis); Mary Maude (Irene); Candida Lasoda (Mlle. Desprez); Tomás Blanco (M. Baldie); Pauline Challoner (Catherine); Maribel Martin (Isabelle); Conchita Paredes (Suzanne); Victor Israel (Brechard); Teresa Hurtado (Andrée); Anne Marie Pol (Jacqueline); Maria Jose Valero (Helene); Maria del Carmen Duque (Julie); Gloria Blanco (Cecile); Clovis Dave (Henry); Elisa Mendez (Marie); Juana Azorin (Susie); Blanca Sendino (Marthe); Paloma Pages (Regine); Sofia Casares (Marguerite).

Made in 1969, this Spanish film is nothing more than a ripoff of the *Psycho* theme, about the perverse relationship between a mother and son. For those interested in horror films taking place in a school for girls, one should look to Dario Argento's *Suspiria* and not *The House That Screamed*.

In 19th-century France a dictatorial widow (Palmer) runs a school for girls, where her randy son (Brown) has his hands full with all his amorous affairs. A new student (Galbo) learns that various girls have disappeared. When another student is brutally murdered in the school greenhouse, Galbo attempts to escape, but she too is murdered by an unknown assailant. The leader of the school girls (Maude) finds Galbo's bloodstains, and tries to flee by going to the attic(?). Palmer follows her there and finds the dead Maude and her son. Brown has been killing the girls so he can use their body parts to create an idealized woman--just like his mother (Norman Bates, is that you?).

THE INCREDIBLE TWO-HEADED TRANSPLANT. 1971. 88 minutes. Color. *Director:* Anthony M. Lanza. *Screenplay:* James Gordon White and John Lawrence. *Cinematography:* Jack Steely, Glen Gano, and Paul Hipp. *Cast:* Bruce Dern (Roger); Pat Priest (Linda); Casey Kasem (Ken); Albert Cole (Cass); John Bloom (Danny); Berry Kroeger (Max); Larry Vincent (Andrew); Jack Lester (Sheriff); Darlene Duralia (Miss Pierce); Jerry Patterson (Deputy); Ray Thorn, Donald Brody, and Mary Ellen Clawsen (Motorcyclists); Janice P. Gelman, Mike Espe, Andrew Schneider, and Eva Sorensen (Teenagers); Bill Collins and Jack English (Highway Patrolmen); Robert Miller (Station Attendant); Laura Lanza and Carolyn Gilbert (Nurses); Leslie Cole (Danny as a Young Boy).

It would be a form of madness to praise this film too highly, but how can anyone not be drawn to a film with this subject matter that has for a theme song a romantic ditty called "Incredible." The actors in this film seem to have had a high old time while making it. Bruce Dern seems to relish the perfect bit of miscasting given to him, Albert Cole acts like the type of sexual psychopath of a woman's worst nightmares, and John Bloom's (a sort of Junior Plenty version of John Candy) portrayal of a retarded man transcends acting.

Dern is a scientist who is conducting head transplants with animals in the hopes of eventually transplanting the heads of people with irreversible brain damage. A psychopath (Cole) escapes from a mental hospital and attacks Dern's attractive wife (Priest). Dern arrives on the scene and blows Cole away with a shotgun. He decides to aid the local mentally retarded handyman (Bloom) by giving him Cole's head. Before the experiment can be fully completed, Cole takes over Bloom's body (Bloom: "My neck hurts." Cole: "Our necks hurt, dummy!").

With Cole's brain controlling Bloom's giant body, the transplant escapes and terrorizes the countryside, as it attacks
smooching teenagers and a group of bikers. Dern and his aide
(Kroeger) go out to look for the transplant before the police
can find it. They trap Cole/Bloom in an abandoned cave, where
a cave-in kills them all.

KIDNAPPED. 1971. 100 minutes. Color. *Director:* Delbert
   Mann. *Screenplay:* Jack Pulman; based on the novels *Kid-
   napped* and *David Balfour*, by Robert Louis Stevenson. *Cin-
   ematography:* Paul Beeson. *Cast:* Michael Caine (Alan
   Breck); Trevor Howard (Lord Advocate Grant); Jack Hawkins
   (Captain Hoseason); Donald Pleasence (Ebenezer Balfour);
   Lawrence Douglas (David Balfour); Vivien Heilbron
   (Catriona Stewart); Gordon Jackson (Charles Stewart);
   Freddie Jones (Cluny); Jack Watson (James Stewart); Andrew
   McCulloch (Andrew); Eric Woodburn (Doctor); Roger Booth
   (Duke of Cumberland); Russell Waters (Lord Advocate's
   Secretary); John Hughes (Simon Campbell); Claire Nielson
   (Barbara Grant); Geoffrey Whitehead (Lieutenant Dun-
   cansby); Peter Jeffrey (Riach); Terry Richards (Mungo
   Campbell).

This is at least the fourth filmed version of *Kidnapped*,
although this particular rendition also includes characters
and situations from Stevenson's *David Balfour*. It is a colorful and respectable adaptation much in the tradition of a
tasteful television historical epic. To receive any enjoyment
from the film one must look to the performances of Donald
Pleasence, as a frenzied miser, and Michael Caine, who sleep-
walks through his role much like a young Bob Mitchum.
   Kidnapped deals with the adventures of young David Balfour
(Douglas) after his uncle (Pleasence) has had him kidnapped to
be sold as a slave. He meets up with Scottish outlaw Alan
Breck (Caine), who has been fighting against English rule.
Their exploits with the various warring Scottish clans lead
them through a series of adventurous escapades. Douglas begins
a romance with a young woman (Heilbron), as Caine eventually
gives himself up to the English for a murder he committed.

MURDERS IN THE RUE MORGUE. 1971. 86 minutes. Color. *Director:* Gordon Hessler. *Screenplay:* Christopher Wicking
   and Henry Slesar; based on the story by Edgar Allan Poe.
   Cinematography: Manuel Berenguer. *Cast:* Jason Robards,

Jr. (Cesar Charron); Herbert Lom (Marot); Christine
Kauffmann (Madeleine); Adolfo Celi (Inspector Vidocq);
Michael Dunn (Pierre); Lilli Palmer (Madeleine's Mother);
Maria Perschy (Genevre); José Calvo (Hunchback); Peter
Arne (Aubert); Virginia Stach (Lucie); Dean Selmier
(Jacques); Marshall Jones (Luigi Orsini); Rosalynd Elliot
(Gabrielle); Ruth Platt and Xan Das Bolas (Orsini's As-
sistants); Maria Martin (Mme. Adolphe); Rafael Hernandez,
Pamela McInnes, and Sally Longley (Members of the Reper-
tory Company).

This lavish and colorful production of the Poe story only
uses that story's title as a starting point for a tale that
has more to do with *The Phantom of the Opera*. Using theatre
people as the main subjects, *Murders in the Rue Morgue* not only
deals with the dichotomy between theatre and life but injects
dream sequences as well.
  Jason Robards runs a theatrical troupe in turn-of-the-
century France. His actress wife (Kauffmann) has been experi-
encing a series of strange dreams having to do vaguely with
the company's production of the Poe story. When a cast member
is murdered with acid, a police detective (Celi) comes to the
theatre to investigate. Soon a series of other murders occur,
and suspicion falls on a former member (Lom) of the company,
who years before had acid accidentally thrown in his face by
Kauffmann's mother (Palmer). Lom then supposedly killed Palmer
and committed suicide. Kauffmann agrees to go to a country
home with a fan (Dunn) of hers. Here she meets Lom, who relates to her how Robards really killed her mother and disfigured him. Robards learns that the revengeful Lom is still
alive and attempts to kill him, but Lom is successful in be-
heading him. Lom next traps Kauffmann in the deserted theatre,
but she manuevers him to fall to his death. However, when
she goes to bed, she realizes that Lom's spirit is still alive.

1,000 CONVICTS AND A WOMAN. 1971. 92 minutes. Color. *Direc-
    tor:* Ray Austin. *Screenplay:* Oscar Brodney. *Cinematog-
    raphy:* Gerald Moss. *Cast:* Alexandra Hay (Angela Thorne);
    Sandor Eles (Paul Floret); Harry Baird (Carl); Neil
    Hallett (Governor Thorne); Robert Brown (Ralph); Frederick
    Abbott (Forbus); David Bauer (Gribney); Peter J. Elliott
    (Matthews); Tracy Reed (Linda); Stella Tanner (Mrs. Jack-
    son); with Peter Weston, Stanley Davies, Joe Dunne, Dinny
    Powell, Ronnie Brody, Terry Richards.

This vile little misogynistic tract has as its main character a Lolita-like young girl who goes after anyone wearing a pair of pants.

Angela Thorne (Hay) returns from school to her family's manor, which has been turned into an experimental British prison. Her father (Hallett) is the warden, but he does not know, nor wants to know, that his daughter is seducing prison inmates and guards. Hay teases a prisoner (Bauer) who happens to be a sex offender. After he has attempted to rape her, Bauer is put into a security cell. When he tries to escape, he accidentally falls to his death. Hallett is prepared now to send Hay away to school again. Before he can, two convicts (Eles and Baird) escape and take Hay as a hostage. During their escape Eles decides to return to the prison, as Baird and Hay seek shelter in a cabin. While the two are making love, Hallett comes upon them. Hay now realizes that Eles and Baird's escape was only a ruse to reveal the truth about her behavior to her father.

THE RETURN OF COUNT YORGA. 1971. 97 minutes. Color. *Director:* Bob Kelljan. *Screenplay:* Bob Kelljan and Yvonne Wilder. *Cinematography:* Bill Butler. *Cast:* Robert Quarry (Count Yorga); Mariette Hartley (Cynthia Nelson); Roger Perry (Dr. David Baldwin); Yvonne Wilder (Jennifer); Tom Toner (Reverend Thomas); Rudy De Luca (Lieutenant Madden); Philip Frame (Tommy); George Macready (Professor Rightstat); Walter Brooks (Bill Nelson); Edward Walsh (Brudah); Craig Nelson (Sergeant O'Connor); David Lampson (Jason); Karen Huston (Ellen); Helen Baron (Mrs. Nelson); Jesse Wells (Mitzi); Mike Pataki (Joe); Corrine Conley (Witch); Allen Joseph (Michael Farmer); Peg Shirley (Claret Farmer); Liz Rogers (Laurie Greggs); Paul Hansen (Jonathan Greggs).

Following the success of the previous year's *Count Yorga, Vampire*, AIP had that film's director, Bob Kelljan, make the sequel, which in some ways is better than its predecessor. The tongue-in-cheek approach to vampires becomes a bit broad as the film winds down to a climax, but one wonders, what with Quarry's penchant for female followers, whether the filmmakers had the Manson family in mind.

Count Yorga (Quarry), a vampire, has a castle near an orphanage. After he has attacked a young boy (Frame), he attends the orphange's costume party. Later that night he sends his female vampires to kill the family of one of the orphanage's administrators (Hartley). Quarry hypnotizes her and brings her to his castle. The murders continue. Hartley's psychiatrist fiancé (Perry) becomes suspicious and calls in the police. He and the two detectives (De Luca and Nelson) explore Quarry's castle, where they are attacked by his followers. In a struggle Perry throws Quarry to his death, and Hartley is rescued.

In *Count Yorga, Vampire* the young hero takes his girlfriend away from the castle, not realizing that she is a vampire. Here Hartley goes to kiss Perry when she is rescued, and finds that he has turned into a vampire.

SCHIZOID. 1971. 96 minutes. Color. *Director:* Lucio Fulci. *Screenplay:* Lucio Fulci, Roberto Gianviti, Jose Luis Martinez Molla, and Andre Tranche. *Cinematography:* Luigi Kuveiller. *Cast:* Florinda Bolkan (Carol Hammond); Stanley Baker (Inspector Corvin); Jean Sorel (Frank Hammond); Leo Genn (Edmund Brighton); Alberto De Mendoza (Brandon); Silvia Monti (Deborah); Mike Kennedy (Hubert); Georges Rigaud (Dr. Kerr); Anita Strindberg (Julia Durer); Penny Brown (Jenny); Edy Gall (Joan); Ezio Marano (Lowell); Franco Balducci (McKenna); Erszi Paal (Mr. Gordon); Jean Degrande (Director); Gaetano Imbro and Luigi Antonio Guerra (Policemen).

Known in Europe as *Lizard in a Woman's Skin*, this Italian/French/Spanish co-production uses many of the visual devices found in the Italian horror-murder films made by the likes of Mario Bava and Dario Argento. They are all here--the handheld camera, tilts, zooms, swish pans--all in the service of a story of murder and decadence in modern London.
A wealthy young woman (Bolkan) goes to see a psychoanalyst (Rigaud) after she has a terrifying dream in which she stabs a woman to death. Soon after a telephone call from an unknown woman tells Bolkan's husband (Sorel) and father (Genn) that a member of their family is hiding a secret. One of the local orgy givers (Strindberg) is found murdered under the same cirstances as found in Bolkan's dream. Bolkan is put into police custody and is placed in a sanitarium. She is released from the hospital, as Genn and her stepdaughter (Gall) attempt to clear her name. Gall is later found murdered, and a policeman (Baker) questions Bolkan. In their discussion she accidentally lets out some information that indicates she knew about the blackmail call to her family. Further questioning reveals that Bolkan had been Strindberg's lover and had murdered her when Strindberg threatened to expose their affair.

SOME OF MY BEST FRIENDS ARE. . . 1971. 109 minutes. Color.
Director: Mervyn Nelson. *Screenplay:* Mervyn Nelson. *Cin-*
ematography: Tony Mitchell. *Cast:* Alan Dellay (Peter
Thomas); Nick Denoia (Phil); Dan Drake (Lloyd); David Drew
(Howard); Jim Enzel (Gable); Tom Bade (Tanny); David Baker
(Clint); Paul Blake (Kenny); Gary Campbell (Terry Nabour);
Carleton Carpenter (Miss Untouchable); Rob Christian
(Eric); Candy Darling (Karen-Harry); Jeff David (Leo);
Tommy Fiorello (Ernie); Fannie Flagg (Helen); Joe George
(Al); Gil Gerard (Scott); Uva Harden (Michel Mireaux);
Rue McClanahan (Lita Joyce); Hector Martinez (José); Peg
Murray (Mrs. Nabour); Dick O'Neil (Tim Holland); Larry
Reed (Louis Barone); Gary Sandy (Jim Paine); Lou Steele
(Barnett Hartman); Clifton Steere (Giggling Gertie);
Sylvia Sims (Sadie); Joe Taylor (Nebraska); Ben Yaffee
(Marvin Hocker); with Rita Bennett, Bob Bonds, Mona
Crawford, Cornelius Frizell, Fritzi Goldstein, Sally
Hammer, Jack Kasabian, Mary Love, Harvey Noel, Dan Quinn,
Alisson Russo, Karolyn Russo, Cathy Stritch, Bil Tarman,
Seymour Weinstein.

  Some of My Best Friends Are. . . no doubt was inspired
by *The Boys in the Band.* This is sort of a gay *The Iceman*
Cometh, set in a New York City bar on Christmas Eve. Perhaps
it is the Christmastime setting that accounts for so much homosexual angst being displayed. I suppose that if it had been
a Halloween evening it would have lent itself to comedy instead
of the lugubrious melodramatics exhibited here.
  The story deals with the personal crises of the patrons.
Supposedly this is a typical night at the bar, with every cliché intact. This particular establishment, if we are to believe it, harbors all sorts of gays--old queens, the kid from
the "sticks," the confused married man, and the self-loathing
street hustler. The few women in the film are no less stereo-
typed with a tough as nails hostess, a "fag hag," and a mother
who comes into the bar to disown her son (on Christmas Eve no
less). With this motley group coming and going, one wonders
whether this is really a gay bar or Grand Central Station.

TAM LIN. 1971. 104 minutes. Color. *Director:* Roddy
McDowall. *Screenplay:* William Spier; based on the poem
"The Ballad of Tam Lin," by Robert Burns. *Cinematography:*
Billy Williams. *Cast:* Ava Gardner (Michaela Cazaret);
Ian McShane (Tom Lynn); Stephanie Beacham (Janet Ainsley);
Cyril Cusack (Vicar Julian Ainsley); Richard Wattis
(Elroy); David Whitman (Oliver); Madeline Smith (Sue);
Fabia Drake (Miss Gibson); Sinead Cusack (Rose); Jennie

Hanley (Caroline); Joanna Lumley (Georgia); Pamela
Farbrother (Vanna); Bruce Robinson (Alan); Rosemary Blake
(Kate); Michael Bills (Michael); Peter Henwood (Guy);
Heyward Morse (Andy); Julian Barnes (Terry); Oliver Norman
(Peter); Virginia Tingwell (Lottie).

For years Roddy McDowall wanted to make a film as a tribute to Ava Gardner. Made in England, under the auspices of
Commonwealth United, *Tam Lin (The Devil's Widow)* was purchased
by AIP along with some other films when Commonwealth United
went bankrupt.
    Ava Gardner portrays a rich and aging woman who attempts
to stay youthful by keeping a good deal of sturdy beefcake
and young trendies around her. Her current favorite boy is a
photographer (McShane). He falls in love with the daughter
(Beacham) of a local clergyman (Cusack), but is warned by one
of Gardner's hangers-on (Wattis) that he could meet with an
"accident" if he attempts to leave Gardner's home. McShane
escapes anyway but is brought back by Wattis and his clutch of
gay bully boys. During a costume party McShane is drugged and
made the victim in a "game" called "murders." He is chased
out of the house and into the nearby forest, where Beacham
saves him at the last moment. Gardner, realizing that the
"game" is over, accepts McShane's departure.
    Technically highly stylized and theatrical in its acting,
Tam Lin seems to borrow somewhat from the sort of household
that Mae West was supposed to have kept (much less malignant
of course).

WHO SLEW AUNTIE ROO? 1971. 89 minutes. Color. *Director:*
    Curtis Harrington. *Screenplay:* Robert Blees and Jimmy
    Sangster; based on a story by David Osborn. *Cinematog-*
    raphy: Desmond Dickinson. *Cast:* Shelley Winters (Rosie
    Forrest-"Auntie Roo"); Mark Lester (Christopher); Chloë
    Franks (Katy); Ralph Richardson (Mr. Benton); Lionel
    Jeffries (Inspector Willoughby); Hugh Griffith (The Pig-
    man, Mr. Harrison); Rosalie Crutchley (Miss Henley); Pat
    Heywood (Dr. Mason); Judy Cornwell (Clarine); Michael
    Gothard (Albie); Jacqueline Cowper (Angela); Richard
    Beaumont (Peter); Charlotte Sayce (Katherine); Marianne
    Stone (Miss Wilcox);

This mixture of fairy tale and horror is very loosely
based on the story of Hansel and Gretel. The emotional wreck
that Shelley Winters portrays here is made somewhat ambiguous,
since it is a child's misconception of her motives that leads

to her demise. While she is a troubled woman, she is far from
being evil.

Shelley Winters invites orphans into her mansion each year
for Christmas. Her love for children intensified after her
own daughter had been killed years before. Winters now keeps
her daughter's skeleton up in the attic, while she regularly
has seances with a fake medium (Richardson), in the hope of
communicating with her daughter. When the orphans arrive for
Christmas, Winters becomes fond of a girl (Franks) who reminds
her of her dead daughter. Franks's impressionable brother
(Lester) believes that Winters is a witch. When Franks disappears, Lester returns to the mansion to look for her. The
girl is quite content being with Winters, but when Lester witnesses her preparing a meal he thinks she is going to eat them.
He is able to lock Winters in a kitchen cupboard and sets fire
to it. As Winters burns to death, the two children flee from
the house with her jewelry.

YOG--MONSTER FROM SPACE. 1971. 84 minutes. Color. *Director:*
Inoshiro Honda. *Screenplay:* El Ogawa. *Cinematography:*
Taiiachi Kankura. *Cast:* Akira Kubo (Taro Kudo); Atsuko
Takahashi (Ayako Hoshino); Yoshio Tsuchiya (Kyoichi Miya);
Kenji Sahara (Makoto Obata); Noritake Saito (Rico);
Yukiko Kobayashi (Saki); Satoshi Nakamura (Ombo); Chotaro
Togin (Yokoyama); Wataru Omae (Sakura); Sachio Sakai (Ed-
itor); Yu Fujiki (Promotion Division Manager); Yuko
Sugihara (Stewardess).

To ascribe auteurist tendencies to Inoshiro Honda would
lead one on the road to an asylum, but his films are fun in
an innocent, childlike way. In *Yog--Monster from Space* the
monsters are not variations of prehistoric beasts as in other
Japanese films, but giant Earth animals--an octopus, a sea
turtle, a crab, etc. As in a number of other Japanese monster
films, this one casts a negative light on the Japanese entre-
preneurial spirit.

An unmanned spaceship comes back to Earth and lands on a
small Japanese island. An unseen alien force (in the form of
a blue cloud) enters the cells of animals as a first step on
the way to taking over humankind. A group of people come to
the island to research it as a possible site for a tourist
complex. They are promptly terrorized by giant creatures.
The group decides to attack the monsters with bats, since they
let out a high-pitched scream that the beasts hate. One of
the people (Sahara) has been taken over by the alien power
and attempts to sabotage their effort. Two of the animals

(the sea turtle and the crab) fight and fall into a volcano.
The contaminated Sahara now decides to save humankind by killing himself.

BARON BLOOD. 1972. 90 minutes. Color. *Director:* Mario Bava.
    Screenplay: Vincent Forte and William A. Bairn. *Cinema-
    tography:* Emilio Varriani. *Cast:* Joseph Cotten (Alfred
    Becker--The Baron); Elke Sommer (Eva Arnold); Massimo
    Girotti (Karl Hummel); Antonio Cantafora (Peter Kleist);
    Alan Collins (Fritz); Nicoletta Elmi (Gretchen); Rada
    Rassimov (Christine Hoffman); Dieter Tressler (Herr
    Dortmundt); Humi Raho (Police Inspector); Valerie Sabel
    (Martha Hummel).

Many of the horror films made by Bava and other Italian
directors are enhanced by vivid camerawork and lighting, even
when the plot is negligible. *Baron Blood* is no exception,
with a mixture of high and low angles, point-of-view shots,
an inordinate use of the zoom, and an eerie blue lighting effect. Photographing the film in a dark, gloomy castle inten-
sifies this photographic effect.
    A young man (Cantafora) and his uncle (Girotti) visit the
Austrian castle of one of his sadistic ancestors. At the castle they meet a woman (Sommer) who is planning to turn the
castle into a tourist hotel. Contafora learns that his blood-
thirsty ancestor had a curse put on him by a witch, whose incantation can bring his dreaded ancestor back to life. Sommer
and Catafora test the incantation, and the so-called Baron
Blood comes to life. The castle is put up for auction and is
bought by a wheelchair-bound stranger (Cotten). After the
nefarious Baron Blood has appeared and killed a number of people, suspicion falls on the mysterious Cotten. He in fact
turns out to be the Baron and imprisons Contafora, Sommer,
and Girotti. Before he can torture them to death, the dead
spirits of his murder victims arise and seek their revenge.
As the three escape, they are able to hear Cotten cry out from
the torture inflicted upon him by the dead spirits.

BLACULA. 1972. 92 minutes. Color. *Director:* William Crain.
    Screenplay: Joan Torres and Raymond Koenig. *Cinematog-
    raphy:* John Stevens. *Cast:* William Marshall (Mamuwalde--
    Blacula); Vonetta McGee (Tina); Denise Nicholas (Mi-
    chelle); Thalmus Rasulala (Gordon Thomas); Gordon Pinsent
    (Lieutenant Peters); Charles Macauley (Count Dracula);

Emily Yancy (Nancy); Lance Taylor, Sr. (Swenson); Ted
Harris (Bobby); Rick Metzler (Billy); Jitu Cumbuka (Skil-
let); Logan Field (Barnes); Ketty Lester (Juanita); Elisha
Cook, Jr. (Sam); Eric Brotherson (Real Estate Agent).

The panache with which William Marshall performs his role
makes *Blacula* the best of that small group of black horror
films. From about 1972 to 1976 AIP made a number of movies
that have been called blaxploitation films, films made by
whites primarily for the big city black audiences.
An 18th century African prince (Marshall) journeys to Europe in an attempt to abolish the slave trade. He ends up in
Transylvania, where he falls under the vampiric spell of Count
Dracula (Macauley). For over 150 years Marshall lies in state
in a coffin waiting for the moment to reawake and search for
human blood. Two antique dealers lend him the opportunity
when they send his body to California while cleaning out
Dracula's castle of furnishings. They become his first victims, as Marshall, now in Los Angeles, finds a young woman
(McGee) whom he believes is the reincarnation of his wife.
His smooth delivery wins McGee over. Her friends (Nicholas
and Rasulala) do not trust him ("That is one strange dude."),
especially after he does not materialize in a photograph.
Marshall turns McGee into a vampire and kills a number of people. He is finally tracked down in a factory. When McGee
has a stake put through her heart, Marshall walks out into
the daylight and turns into dust.

BOXCAR BERTHA. 1972. 88 minutes. Color. *Director:* Martin
    Scorsese. *Screenplay:* Joyce H. and John William Corring-
    ton; based on the book *Sisters of the Road*, by "Boxcar"
    Bertha Thompson. *Cinematography:* John Stephens. *Cast:*
    Barbara Hershey (Bertha); David Carradine (Big Bill
    Shelley); Barry Primus (Rake Brown); Bernie Casey (Von
    Morton); John Carradine (H. Buckram Sartoris); Victor
    Argo and David R. Osterhout (Railroad Detectives); Harry
    Northup (Harvey Posey).

Taking in some of the same sorts of characters and similar
terrain of *Bonnie and Clyde*, *Boxcar Bertha* has more of an au-
thentic feeling to it than the former film. A good part of
this is due not only to Scorsese's fervid direction, but the
plain-looking pair of Hershey and Carradine are light years
away from the star turns of Warren Beatty and Faye Dunaway in
Bonnie and Clyde.
In Arkansas during the Depression a young girl (Hershey)

is taken under the wing of two railroad workers (Carradine and Casey). They lose track of one another while hopping freight trains, and when Hershey meets Carradine again he has become a union organizer. Her exploits get her involved with a gambler (Primus), who involves her in a shooting. All four characters become train robbers, with Carradine offering his share to the union. He is kicked out of the union but continues to rob the trains. When Primus is killed, Hershey becomes involved in prostitution for a short period. She meets Casey, who tells her that Carradine is very sick and in hiding. The two are reunited, but Carradine is fatally beaten by railroad detectives.

CARRY ON CAMPING. 1972. 88 minutes. Color. *Director:* Gerald Thomas. *Screenplay:* Talbot Rothwell. *Cinematography:* Ernest Steward. *Cast:* Sidney James (Sid Boggle); Kenneth Williams (Dr. Soper); Joan Sims (Joan Fussey); Charles Hawtrey (Charlie Muggins); Bernard Bresslaw (Bernie Lugg); Terry Scott (Peter Potter); Barbara Windsor (Babs); Hattie Jacques (Miss Haggerd); Peter Butterworth (Joshua Fiddler); Julian Holloway (Jim Tanner); Betty Marsden (Harriet Potter); Dilys Laye (Anthea Meeks); Trisha Noble (Sally); Sandra Caron (Fanny).

Carry on Camping and *Carry on Doctor* were made in the 60s, but they reached the United States years later. The usual motley Carry On group is assembled here--the leering men, willing women, a battle ax (Jacques), and the busty blonde (Windsor). In its cartoon view of sexuality the Carry On Series acts as sort of a British equivalent of the Russ Meyer films.

Here the story revolves around two amorous men (James and Bresslaw), who want to warm up their "chilly" girlfriends (Sims and Laye) by taking them to a nudist camp. When they arrive, they find the camp filled with campers--fully clothed. Also at the camp are a group of young women from a finishing school called Chayste Place. James and Bresslaw soon become attracted to, and woo, two of the girls (Windsor and Caron). Their liaison is ruined when a group of hippies with amplified musical equipment show up. Both men blow up the hippie's equipment (in a victory for the middle class and the Conservative Party), but the girls leave with the longhairs. Jones and Bresslaw now return to Sims and Laye.

CARRY ON DOCTOR. 1972. 95 minutes. Color. *Director:* Gerald
    Thomas. *Screenplay:* Talbot Rothwell. *Cinematography:*
    Alan Hume. *Cast:* Frankie Howerd (Francis Bigger); Sidney
    James (Charlie Roper); Kenneth Williams (Dr. Tinklee);
    Charles Hawtrey (Mr. Barron); Jim Dale (Dr. Kilmore);
    Barbara Windsor (Sandra May); Hattie Jacques (The Matron);
    Joan Sims (Chloe Gibson); Anita Harris (Nurse Clarke);
    Bernard Bresslaw (Ken Biddle); Peter Butterworth (Mr.
    Smith); June Jago (Sister Hoggett); Dilys Laye (Mavis
    Winkle); Derek Francis (Sir Edmund Burke); Peter Gilmore
    (Henry); Dandy Nichols (Mrs. Roper); Valerie Van Ost
    (Nurse Parkin); Julian Orchard (Fred); Julian Holloway
    (Simmons); Alexandra Dane (Prenatal Instructress).

The film *Britannia Hospital* uses the British hospital as
a metaphor for a society that is steadily beginning to unravel
at the seams. *Carry On Doctor* never uses its humor to challenge the institution it is satirizing. The hospital here is
an enclosed little world of loonies, phonies, and eccentrics,
who have a priapic hospital staff as their overseers.
    The story has something to do with the rivalry between
two doctors (Dale and Williams), as well as their romantic encounters with two attractive nurses (Windsor and Harris).
Tired jokes about such things as hypodermic syringes and castor
oil are used in abundance. The preoccupation the British have
for bodily functions was exemplified in ads for the film, which
described it as a "bedpanorama of hospital life." Included
in the cast is comedian Frankie Howerd, who does exhibit a
sort of sleazy charm missing from the rest of the cast. *Carry
On Doctor* is not in the same league with that classic Three
Stooges short about doctors and hospitals, *Men in Black*.

THE DEATHMASTER. 1972. 88 minutes. Color. *Director:* Ray
    Danton. *Screenplay:* R.L. Grove. *Cinematography:* Wilmer
    C. Butler. *Cast:* Robert Quarry (Khorda); Bill Ewing
    (Pico); Brenda Dickson (Rona); John Fiedler (Pop); Betty
    Anne Rees (Esslin); William Jordan (Monk Reynolds); Le
    Sesne Hilton (Barbado); John Lasell (Detective); Freda T.
    Vanterpool (Dancer); Tari Tabakin (Mavis); Kitty Vallacher
    (Bridey); Charles Hornsby (Charles); Bob Woods (Police-
    man); Michael Cronin (Mike); Olympia Sylvers (Olympia);
    Ted Lynn (Surfer); Bob Pickett (Kirkwood).

Robert Quarry made a much more sophisticated vampire as
Count Yorga than he does here as a vampire/hippie guru. This

pathetic and tired low-budget entry in the vampire genre was
directed by actor-turned-director Ray Danton.

A surfer (Lynn) is brutally murdered on a Southern California beach by a corpse that had emerged from a coffin that
had washed ashore. A nearby hippie commune, living in an old
mansion, is visited by a strange man called Khorda (Quarry).
The impressionable group, perhaps hoping it is the second coming of Charlie Manson, accept Quarry as their guru. A member
(Jordan) of the group refuses to go along with Quarry and is
soon murdered. In no time Quarry makes a vampire out of
Jordan's girlfriend (Rees). Another doubter (Ewing) escapes
from the mansion, where Quarry and his assistant (Hilton) are
keeping the young people prisoner. He returns with a town
local (Fiedler) and the police. Everything appears to be normal at the residence, and the cops leave. Ewing and Fiedler
continue to investigate and find a black mass in progress.
Eventually there is a confrontation in the cellar, where Ewing
accidentally kills Fiedler. He manages to implant a stake in
the heart of Hilton, and Quarry stumbles and is also impaled.
Ewing now goes upstairs and finds that all his friends have
turned to ashes.

DR. PHIBES RISES AGAIN. 1972. 89 minutes. Color. *Director:*
    Robert Fuest. *Screenplay:* Robert Fuest and Robert Blees;
    based on characters created by James Whiton and William
    Goldstein. *Cinematography:* Alex Thomson. *Cast:* Vincent
    Price (Dr. Anton Phibes); Robert Quarry (Biederbeck);
    Valli Kemp (Vulnavia); Fiona Davis (Diana); Peter Cushing
    (The Captain); Beryl Reid (Mrs. Ambrose); Terry-Thomas
    (Lombardo); Hugh Griffith (Ambrose); Peter Jeffrey (In-
    spector Trout); John Cater (Waverly); Gerald Sim
    (Hackett); John Thaw (Shavers); Keith Buckley (Stuart);
    Lewis Flander (Baker); Milton Reid (Man Servant).

If anything, *Dr. Phibes Rises Again* is even more "campy"
and outrageous in its excesses than its predecessor. The off-
center characters and situations in this film are partly at-
tributable to the director, Robert Fuest, who also directed a
number of episodes of the popular television show *The Avengers.*
    Dr. Phibes (Price) wakes up from his entombment from the
last film and goes off to Egypt with his wife's body and his
assistant (Kemp). It seems he has learned of an underground
river that possesses the elixir of life. The elixir will resurrect his wife and give the two of them eternal life. Also
on the trail of the elixir is Biederbeck (Quarry) and his assistants. Price begins killing off members of Quarry's party,

as two Scotland Yard inspectors (Cater and Jeffrey) venture
on the trail of both men. Price kidnaps Quarry's lover (Davis)
in return for the key that will give him access to the magical
waters. Quarry begs to go with Price on his discovery of the
river, but Price goes off alone with his wife's coffin.
Quarry's body now begins to decay at a rapid rate, just as the
two policemen arrive on the scene.

F.T.A. 1972. 96 minutes. Color. *Director:* Francine Parker.
  Screenplay: Robin Menken, Michael Alaimo, Rita Martinson,
  Holly Near, Len Chandler, Pamala Donegan, Jane Fonda,
  Donald Sutherland, and Dalton Trumbo. *Cinematography:*
  Juliana Wang, Eric Saarinen, and Joan Weidman. *Featuring:*
  Jane Fonda, Donald Sutherland, Len Chandler, Pamala
  Donegan, Michael Alaimo, Rita Martinson, Holly Near, Paul
  Mooney, and Yale Zimmerman.

AIP shelved this film after it bombed at the box office.
F.T.A. (Free Theater Associates, otherwise known as "Fuck the
Army") is an antiwar alternative to the standard USO tours
given to servicemen overseas. In late 1971 Jane Fonda and
Donald Sutherland organized a group of performers to put on a
show for military personnel in Hawaii, Okinawa, the Philippines, and Japan. The group was not allowed to enter any military installation, so their show was performed wherever they
could find the space. The stage show revolved around comedy
skits, musical numbers, and readings, which consisted of antiwar, antiracist and antichauvinist sentiments. Part of the
film also deals with some documentary footage of Vietnam, as
well as interviews with disillusioned soldiers.
  Despite the fact that F.T.A. is preaching to the con-
verted, it is an important testament in showing the antiestab-
lishment state of mind in the early 70s. In its own way it
is as important in presenting an evocation of a particular
time as fictional AIP films like *The Trip* and *Wild in the
Streets* were in the 60s.

FROGS. 1972. 90 minutes. *Director:* George McCowan. *Screen-
  play:* Robert Hutchison and Robert Blees; based on a story
  by Robert Hutchison. *Cinematography:* Mario Tosi. *Cast:*
  Ray Milland (Jason Crockett); Sam Elliott (Pickett Smith);
  Joan Van Ark (Karen); Adam Roarke (Clint); Judy Pace
  (Bella); Lynn Borden (Jenny); Mae Mercer (Maybelle);
  David Gilliam (Michael); Nicholas Cortland (Kenneth);

George Skaff (Stuart); Lance Taylor, Sr. (Charles); Holly
Irving (Iris); Dale Willingham (Tina); Hal Hodges (Tay);
Carolyn Fitzsimmons (Lady in the Car); Robert Sanders
(Young Boy in the Car).

Frogs is an ecological disaster film and horror/monster
film wrapped up in an allegory about American economic greed.
This was the first feature directed by George McCowan, and it
certainly was auspicious. One critic even called it "the most
promising debut from an American Filmmaker within the general
area of science fiction and horror since Romero's *Night of the
Living Dead*" (David Pirie, *Monthly Film Bulletin*, July 1972,
p. 138).

Each year, in a mansion on a Southern island, the patriarch of a family (Milland) has his ne'er-do-well family members
come to celebrate his birthday and the Fourth of July. Two
family members (Van Ark and Roarke) run into an ecology photographer (Elliott) on the island and invite him to stay at the
mansion during the family celebration. Soon various family
members are killed one by one, as nature gains its revenge
from years of the family's pesticide pollution of the island.
People are killed by members of the animal kingdom like alli-
gators, snakes, leeches, turtles, spiders, and, of course,
frogs. Elliott takes the survivors and launches a boat to
the mainland, where they find nothing but deserted buildings.
Milland has adamantly refused to leave the family mansion,
and in the end he is overrun by frogs.

One of the best scenes in the film is when Milland's
Reaganite, economic-royalist daughter (Irving) complains about
how controls on pollution reduce her income. After this she
goes into the swamp, where she is attacked and killed by blood-
sucking leeches.

GODZILLA VS. THE SMOG MONSTER. 1972. 85 minutes. Color.
    Director: Yoshimitu Banno. *Screenplay:* Kaoru Mabuchi
    and Yoshimitu Banno. *Cinematography:* Yoichi Manoda.
    Cast: Akira Yamauchi (Doctor Yano); Hiroyuki Kawase (Ken
    Yaro); Toshie Kimura (Mrs. Toshie Yano); Toshio Shibaki
    (Yukio Keuchi); Keiko Mari (Miki Fujiyama).

When Godzilla ends up fighting on the side of civilization
you know that there must be an incredible menace to be overcome. Godzilla the pollution fighter here does battle with a
gigantic piece of living industrial sludge!

The inhabitants of an industrial coastal community have
polluted the skies with their factories and have made their

waterways an open sewer with industrial debris. Out of all
this waste product has evolved a smog monster, a 200-foot-tall
mass of slime called Hedorah. It has the capacity to fly and
spread an acid smog, as well as spew out poisonous mud. Needless to say, it creates a good deal of destruction and havoc.
When the young people of the city hold an anti-Hedorah rally
on top of Mount Fujiyama, Godzilla suddenly appears. With
the aid of giant electrodes Godzilla battles Hedorah and destroys the manmade monster.

LOLA. 1972. 88 minutes. Color. *Director:* Richard Donner.
Screenplay: Norman Thaddeus Vane. *Cinematography:* Walter
Lassally. *Cast:* Charles Bronson (Scott Wardman); Susan
George (Lola Londonberry); Trevor Howard (Grandfather);
Honor Blackman (Lola's Mother); Michael Craig (Lola's
Father); Orson Bean (Hal); Kay Medford (Scott's Mother);
Paul Ford (Scott's Father); Jack Hawkins (Judge Millington
-Draper); Robert Morley (Judge Roxburgh); Lionel Jeffries
(Mr. Creighton); Norman Vaughan and Jimmy Tarbuck (Come-
dians); Polly Williams (Lola's Sister); Anthony Kemp
(Lola's Brother); Cathy Jose (Felicity); Peggy Aitchison
(Mrs. Finchley); Elspeth March (Secretary); Eric Chitty
(Client); Leslie Schofield and Derek Steen (Policemen);
Gordon Waller (Marty); Reg Lever (Old Gentleman); Tony
Arpino (New York Judge); Eric Barker (Marriage Clerk);
John Rae (Hotel Receptionist); John Wright (Hotel Waiter).

When this film, under the title *Twinky*, came out in 1970,
it was said that "Richard Donner drives what one hopes will
be the final nail in the coffin of the swinging sixties"
(*Monthly Film Bulletin*, February 1970, p. 37). Even by 1970
many of the devices that *Lola* uses, such as freeze frames,
slow motion, and an innocuous musical score, had become old-
hat. For the cynical among us this film is almost totally
unwatchable, as it becomes another in the endless list of "turkeys" starring Charles Bronson.

In London a writer of softcore porn (Bronson) finds himself attracted to a 16-year-old schoolgirl (George). They
elope to Scotland to get married. Back in London, Bronson
finds himself uncomfortable around George's teenybopper friends
and his new in-laws (Blackman and Craig). The couple move to
New York City, where Bronson's parents (Medford and Ford) are
outraged by the May-December marriage. By law, George must
attend school. During a demonstration, in which George participates, Bronson attempts to take her away and ends up hit-
ting a cop. While Bronson is serving a brief jail sentence,

George has found them a new apartment. Bronson finds it difficult to continue his writing because of the stressful marriage.
After an argument George leaves for a couple of days. Bronson
finds her and offers to start all over, but George realizes
their marriage is a failure. She performs a homemade divorce
and rides away on her bicycle.

NIGHT OF THE BLOOD MONSTER. 1972. 84 minutes. Color. *Direc-
  tor:* Jess Franco. *Screenplay:* Anthony Scott Veitch; based
  on a story by Peter Welbeck. *Cinematography:* Manuel
  Merino. *Cast:* Christopher Lee (Judge Jeffries); Maria
  Schell (Mother Rosa); Leo Genn (Lord Wessex); Hans Haas
  (Harry); Maria Rohm (Mary); Margaret Lee (Alicia); Peter
  Martell (Barnaby); Howard Vernon (Jack Ketch); Milo
  Quesada (Satchel).

Night of the Blood Monster has the distinction of being
the most misleading title of any film distributed by AIP. It
apparently contained a different title in just about every
country it appeared. What sounds like a horror film is in
fact about political intrigue in 17th-century England. It
bounced around Europe for a couple of years before AIP picked
up the American distribution rights.
    The Lord High Chief Justice (C. Lee) of England is out
to find conspirators against the throne of King James. In so
doing he has no hesitation in condemning anyone suspicious of
witchcraft. Lee takes a liking to a young woman (Rohm) whose
sister (M. Lee) is executed for supposedly being a witch.
Rohm is in love with a young man (Haas), who is a supporter of
the Duke of Monmouth--a rival to King James. Lee has Rohm
brought to him after she is arrested with some rebel women.
When Haas attempts to rescue her, he is captured by Lee's men.
King James is overthrown by the insurgent forces and Lee is
now put under house arrest. But before he can be executed,
he dies in his jail cell.

PICKUP ON 101. 1972. 93 minutes. Color. *Director:* John
  Florea. *Screenplay:* Anthony Blake. *Cinematography:* Carl
  F. Marquard. *Cast:* Jack Albertson (Obediah Bradley);
  Lesley Warren (Nickie); Martin Sheen (Les Cavanaugh);
  Michael Ontkean (Chuck); Hal Baylor (Railroad Cop); George
  Chandler (Pawnship Owner); Mike Road (Desk Sergeant);
  Eddie Firestone (Auto Mechanic); William Mims (Antique
  Shop Owner); Robert Donner (Jessie--1st Farmer); Kathleen

Harper (Jesse's Wife); Harold J. Stone (2nd Farmer); Buck
Young, Peggy Stewart, Greg Young, and Cynthia Johnson
(Family in Car); Don Spruance (Highway Patrolman).

This road movie received very little critical attention,
even though it stars Jack Albertson and Martin Sheen. It is
safe to assume that AIP shelved this film soon after its release.

A college student (Warren) quits school and heads for a
commune in New Mexico. She runs into a hobo (Albertson), and
both of them are given a ride by a rock musician (Sheen) on
his way to Los Angeles. His car breaks down, and the three
of them become stranded. They are hassled by the local cops,
and Sheen and Albertson are arrested for a short period of
time. After Sheen has left the two of them in the middle of
the night, Albertson tells Warren that he is headed back to
be buried at a farm he once owned, since he feels he will die
soon. They run into Sheen again, and he and Warren argue about
taking Albertson back to the farm. Albertson decides to leave
them by hopping a train, but his heart gives out and he falls
dead near the train tracks. Warren and Sheen now take his
body to the farm. When the current owner (Stone) refuses to
let them bury him, they have him cremated and spread his ashes
from a hillside overlooking the land.

RAW MEAT. 1972. 87 minutes. Color. *Director:* Gary Sherman.
   Screenplay: Ceri Jones; based on an idea by Gary Sherman.
   Cinematography: Alex Thomson. *Cast:* Donald Pleasence
   (Inspector Colquhoun); Norman Rossington (Detective Ser-
   geant Rogers); David Ladd (Alex Campbell); Sharon Gurney
   (Patricia Wilson); Christopher Lee (Stratton-Villiers);
   Hugh Armstrong (The Man); James Cossins (James Manfred);
   June Turner (The Man's Wife); Heather Stoney (Policewoman
   Alice Marshall); Hugh Dickson (Dr. Bacon); Clive Swift
   (Inspector Richardson); Suzanne Winkler (Prostitute); Ron
   Pember (Ticket Collector); James Culliford (Barman); Jack
   Woolgar (Platform Inspector); Colin McCormick and Gary
   Winkler (Police Constables).

Also known under its more conventional title of *Death
Line*, this was a real surprise when this author saw it on the
bottom half of a double bill. Not only does it contain an
intriguing plot convention (people living for generations under
the London underground system), but director Gary Sherman has
a very sure sense of the formal elements needed for a successful horror film.

Raw Meat

Two students (Ladd and Gurney) find an unconscious man
(Cossins) in a London subway station. Returning with help,
they find that Cossins has disappeared. A police inspector
(Pleasence) questions the two of them and notes that various
people have been disappearing in the station at night. He
learns that 80 years before a cave-in during construction of
the subway trapped both men and women workers. One of the
last descendants (Armstrong) of the cave-in survivors lives
in the tunnels below the underground stations. Filthy, in
rags, and covered with sores, the cannibalistic Armstrong kidnaps people so as to feed their blood to the last surviving
woman (Turner), who is pregnant. When she dies, he apprehends
the unsuspecting Gurney, while she is standing on a station
platform. Ladd goes into the tunnels to look for her before
the plague-ridden Armstrong can attempt to replenish his race.
He saves her by killing Armstrong just before he can rape her.
Pleasence arrives and looks with amazement at the bones and
decomposing bodies of this hidden world underneath London.

SLAUGHTER. 1972. 92 minutes. Color. *Director:* Jack
  Starrett. *Screenplay:* Mark Hanna and Don Williams. *Cin-
  ematography:* Rosalio Solano. *Cast:* Jim Brown (Slaughter);
  Stella Stevens (Ann Cooper); Rip Torn (Dominick Hoffo);
  Don Gordon (Harry Bastoli); Cameron Mitchell (A.W. Price);
  Marlene Clark (Kim Walker); Robert Phillips (Morelli);
  Marion Brash (Jenny); Norman Alfe (Mario Felice); Eddie
  Lo Russo (Little Al); Buddy Garion (Eddie); Ronald C. Ross
  (1st Hood); Roger Cudney (Gio); Lance Winston (Intern);
  Juan Jose Laboriel (Uncle); Francisca Lopes de Laboriel
  (Aunt); Ricardo Adalio (2nd Hood); Geraldo Zepeda (3rd
  Hood).

Slaughter was one of the first in a long line of AIP blaxploitation crime-revenge films. Some of the later films
starred the estimable Pam Grier, but here Jim Brown shows that
the transition from carrying a football to acting does not
come all that easy. Counter to Brown, we have Rip Torn portraying a mobster with the unique relish he brings to all his
roles, be it Richard Nixon or a broken-down country-and-western
singer.
  An ex-Green Beret (Brown) sets out to find the ones who
planted the bomb that killed his mother and hoodlum father.
He surprises three hoods and kills two of them, but he learns
that he has also destroyed important evidence needed for government prosecution of a crime syndicate. He is blackmailed
by a government agent (Mitchell) to go to Mexico and find the

mob's computerized records or face a charge of murder. In
Mexico Brown starts a torrid affair with the girlfriend
(Stevens) of one of the mobsters (Torn). Torn masterminds
several attempts to eliminate Brown, but all are unsuccessful.
All along Torn has been planning to take over control from his
boss (Alfe). After he kidnaps Stevens, he is chased down by
Brown. Trapped in the wreckage of a car, Torn confesses to
the murder of Brown's parents. Brown pumps a bullet hole in
the car's gas tank, and lets Torn burn to death.

THE THING WITH TWO HEADS. 1972. 90 minutes. Color. *Direc-*
     tor: Lee Frost. *Screenplay:* Lee Frost, Wes Bishop, and
     James Gordon White; based on a story by Frost and Bishop.
     Cinematography: Jack Steely. *Cast:* Ray Milland (Dr.
     Maxwell Kirshner); Rosy Grier (Jack Moss); Don Marshall
     (Dr. Fred Williams); Roger Perry (Dr. Philip Desmond);
     Chelsea Brown (Lila); Kathy Baumann (Patricia); John
     Dullagan (Thomas); John Bliss (Donald); Bruce Kimball
     (Police Lieutenant); Jane Kellem (Miss Mullen); Lee Frost
     (Sergeant Hacker); Wes Bishop (Dr. Smith); Roger Gentry
     (Police Sergeant); Britt Nilsson (Nurse); Rick Baker (Go-
     rilla); Phil Hoover (Policeman); Rod Steele (Medical
     Salesman); Michael Viner (Prison Guard); Dick Whittington
     (Himself).

     It takes a certain audacity to make a film like *The Thing*
with Two Heads. Against my better judgment I found myself
laughing throughout this film, because, once it is all said
and done, this is not a horror/science-fiction film but a comedy about such things as mad doctors and racial prejudice.
     A brilliant surgeon (Milland), who is in the forefront
in the field of brain transplants, finds that he is dying of
cancer. Milland also happens to be a vicious bigot, which
we witness in an embarrassing scene where he confronts a black
doctor (Marshall) he hired sight unseen. In order to stay
alive he has decided to have his head removed from his cancer-
racked body and transplanted onto a healthy body. When Milland
becomes unconscious, his aides can only find the body of a
black convict (Grier) who is on death row. Since he is an
innocent man, Grier jumps at the chance of participating in
the experiment. After the operation, Milland now finds that
his head is existing on the body of the 300 pound Grier, whose
head is still attached to his own body. Seeking to prove his
innocence and to see his girlfriend (Brown), Grier escapes
from the lab, with Milland's chalky-white head bobbing on his
left shoulder. After a long chase through the Southern

California hills he makes it to Brown's house. She hardly
does a double take at Grier's new appearance. Quizzically
Brown asks him, "I was wondering. Do you have two of anything
else?" Milland knocks Grier out with his own fist and returns
to the laboratory to remove Grier's head. Marshall and Brown
rescue Grier, as Marshall separates Milland's head from his
body. The three go away in a car with Grier singing "Oh Happy
Day."

THE UNHOLY ROLLERS. 1972. 88 minutes. Color. *Director:*
Vernon Zimmerman. *Screenplay:* Howard R. Cohen; based on
a story by Vernon Zimmerman and Cohen. *Cinematography:*
Mike Shea. *Cast:* Claudia Jennings (Karen Walker); Louis
Quinn (Mr. Stern); Betty Anne Rees (Mickey); Roberta
Collins (Jennifer); Alan Vint (Greg); Candice Roman
(Donna); Jay Varela (Nick); Charlene Jones (Beverly Bray-
ton); Joe E. Tata (Marshall); Maxine Gates (Angie
Striker); Kathleen Freeman (Karen's Mother); John Harmon
(Doctor); Karl Rizzo and Mike Miller (Referees); John
Steadman (Guard); John Mitchell (Horace McKay); Roxanna
Bonilla (Consuelo); Dan Seymour (Used Car Dealer); Eve
Bruce (Woman in Bar); Alvin Hammer (Man in Bar); Vic Argo
(Vinnie); Jack Griffin (Poker Player); Dennis Redfield
(Duane); Ray Galvin (Foreman); Louis Pampino and Matt
Bennett (Workers); Hunter van Leer (Larry); Rick Hurst
and Ray O'Keefe (Movers); Terry Wolfe (Grocery Boy); Perry
Cook (Supermarket Manager); Abbi Henderson (Girl in Super-
market); Kres Mersky (Girl in Bar); Kathleen Pagel (Tina);
Cecil Reddick (Man in Phone Booth); Louis and the Rockets
(Band in the Bar).

If there is a feminine equivalent of a heel, then that
is what the late Claudia Jennings is in *The Unholy Rollers*.
The roller games (or roller derby), a pseudo-sport, has not
been the subject of many films. This film, along with *Kansas
City Bomber*, *Derby*, and, to an extent, *Rollerball*, attempts
to capture this peculiar strata of proletarian enjoyment.
An attractive young woman (Jennings) walks off her factory
job and becomes a roller-derby skater. Her problem is that
she cannot abide by the choreographed roughhousing on the
track, but fights for real. Jennings quickly becomes a star,
and in the process becomes a hated figure to the rival team,
a pain in the neck to her own team, an object of desire to
her lesbian teammate (Rees), and a mistress to the star
(Varela) of the men's team. The team owner (Quinn) hires another young skater (Jones) to replace Jennings eventually.

Shortly thereafter Jennings is beaten by a group of her teammates for injuring Rees. Both her own mates and the rival
team gang up on her on the rack, but she dishes out as much
as she receives. The still-defiant Jennings leaves the arena
at game's end and goes out into the street on her skates to
play a game of tag with speeding cars.

THE WILD PACK. 1972. 102 minutes. Color. *Director:* Hall
    Bartlett. *Screenplay:* Hall Bartlett; based on the novel
    Capitaes Da Areia, by Jorge Amado. *Cinematography:*
    Ricardo Aronovich. *Cast:* Kent Lane (Bullet); Tisha
    Sterling (Dora); John Rubinstein (Professor); Butch
    Patrick (No Legs); Mark de Vries (Dry Turn); Peter Nielsen
    (Lollypop); Alejandro Rey (Father Jose Pedro); Eliana
    Pittman (Dalvah); Ademir da Silva (Big John); Guilherme
    Lamounier ("The Cat"); Dorival Caymmi (John Adam); Chris
    Rodriguez (Police Chief); Macio (Ezequiel); Aloysio de
    Oliveira (Chancellor); Creusa Millett (Priestess); Freddie
    Gedeon (Almiro); with Jimmy Fraser, Lorrene Baker, William
    Hobson, Marusa Urban.

    Filmed in Bahia, one of the poorest areas of Brazil, this
film won the Grand Prize at the 1971 Moscow International Film
Festival. Sometimes known as *The Sandpit Generals* (the name
given to young people in Brazil who beg and scavange to survive) it covers somewhat the same ground that the later Brazilian film *Pixote* does. Where that film uses a group of Brazilian nonprofessionals, this film is peppered with young American actors portraying Brazilian waifs.
    A group of youths commit criminal acts in order to sur-
vive. They make their home in a deserted warehouse, where
they are presided over by Bullet (Lane). Into their group
comes a young girl (Sterling) and her brother (Fraser). Lane
allows Sterling to stay as long as no one touches her. She
soon becomes a combination mother and sister to the boys. The
gang learns that a rival group is going to inform on them to
the police, and in the ensuing gang fight Lane kills another
youth (Macio). During a voodoo funeral service for one of
their members (da Silva) the police arrive and arrest Lane
and Sterling. Both are sent to prison, but Lane escapes and
takes the now-fever-ridden Sterling with him. After she dies,
Lane organizes a group of the "sandpit generals" to march on
the government to be heard. The film ends with the sound of
gunfire during the demonstration.

BATTLE OF THE AMAZONS. 1973. 92 minutes. Color. *Director:*
Al Bradley (Alfonso Brescia). *Screenplay:* Mario Amendola
and Bruno Corbucci; based on a story by Fernando Izcaino
Casas. *Cinematography:* Fausto Rossi. *Cast:* Lincoln Tate
(Zeno); Lucretia Love (Eraglia); Robert Vidmark (Ilio);
Solvy Stubing (Sinade); Paolo Tedesco (Valeria); Mirta
Miller (Melanippe); Benito Stefanelli (Erno); Genie Woods
(Antiope); Giancarlo Bastianoni (Filodos); Luigi Ciavarro
(Turone); Pilar Clement (Elperia); Sonia Ciuffi (Fara);
Riccardo Pizzuti (Medonte); Marco Stefanelli (Medio);
Franco Ukmar (Artemio).

This seems very much like the type of film AIP imported
with some regularity in the early and mid-60s. The only thing
that makes *Battle of the Amazons* different from its predeces-
sors is its "R" rating, due to the heavy violence and the well-
endowed bare breasts.
    A tribe of warlike women--the Amazons--rule a large area
of Asia Minor. They use male slaves for procreation purposes
and then slay them and all the male offspring. To them "the
only good man is a dead man." A former soldier (Tate) is captured and tortured by the Amazons but escapes and ends up in
a village that has been the object of raids by the Amazons.
Tate gets his band of former soldiers to help defend the villagers and repulse the army of women. After a number of skir-
mishes there is one large battle between the two factions.
The men are barely holding their own when the women of the
village come to their rescue and rout the Amazons.

BLACK CAESAR. 1973. 92 minutes. Color. *Director:* Larry
Cohen. *Screenplay:* Larry Cohen. *Cinematography:* Fenton
Hamilton. *Cast:* Fred Williamson (Tommy Gibbs); Phillip
Roye (Joe Washington); Gloria Hendry (Helen); Julius W.
Harris (Mr. Gibbs); Val Avery (Cardoza); Minnie Gentry
(Mama Gibbs); Art Lund (John McKinney); D'Urville Martin
(Reverend Rufus); William Wellman, Jr. (Alfred Coleman);
James Dixon (Bryant); Myrna Hansen (Virginia Coleman);
Don Pedro Colley (Crawdaddy); Patrick McAllister (Cross-
field); Cecil Alonso (Motor); Allen Bailey (Sport); Omer
Jeffrey (Tommy as a Boy); Michael Jeffrey (Joe as a Boy).

This film tells about the rise and fall of a black
Godfather-type mobster. In fact, the film is known overseas
as *The Godfather of Harlem*. Its director, Larry Cohen, has

Black Caesar

made some very interesting exploitation films, such as *It's Alive*, *The Private Files of J. Edgar Hoover*, and *Q*, the first film made by Samuel Arkoff's new AIP--Arkoff International Pictures.

After shooting down a gang leader, Tommy Gibbs (Williamson), who has worked for the Mafia in Harlem for many years, tells a local Mafioso (Avery) that he wants a piece of the territory. Avery is impressed by Williamson's gall and puts him in control of two blocks. He solidifies his position by murdering the gang's bookkeeper and steals their records. Eventually he takes over from Avery, and the mob becomes increasingly upset with Williamson's newfound power. He is shot by a rogue cop (Lund), who had been his enemy for years. Seriously wounded, Williamson goes back to retrieve the mob's records once again. He confronts Lund and kills him. Williamson then struggles through the crowded streets of Manhattan to make it back to Harlam, and die.

BLACK JACK. 1973. 87 minutes. Color. *Director:* William T. Naud. *Screenplay:* William T. Naud and Dick Gautier; based on a story by Naud, Gautier, and Peter Marshall. *Cinematography:* Thomas E. Spaulding. *Cast:* Brandon De Wilde (Josh); Keenan Wynn (General Harry Gobohare); Tim O'Connor (Senator Bob Recker); Dick Gautier (Diver); James Daly (The President); Robert Lansing (Major Reason); Larry Hovis (Captain Breen); Georg Stanford Brown (Lynch); Bernie Kopell (Penrat); Joseph Turkel (Corazza); Dub Taylor (Officer Roddenberry); Phil Vandervort (Woody); with Michael Fox, Karl Lucas, Emby Mellay, Chet Stratton.

This broad and bizarre black comedy was produced under the title "God Bless the Bomb." *Black Jack* is a mixture of *Airplane* and *Dr. Strangelove*. Even if the humor here is more slapstick than trenchant, any film that displays so much disrespect for the military cannot be all bad.

On their way to prison three radicals (De Wilde, Brown, and Vandervort) escape and go to a Strategic Air Command base. They are surprised that the plane they are hiding on suddenly is taken on a flight. Up in the air Brown orders the plane's captain (Lansing) to fly to Cuba. When Lansing refuses, Brown puts him, the protesting De Wilde, and the rest of the crew under lock and key. Now Brown and a sympathetic crew member (Gautier) are in control of the plane. When a general (Wynn) orders jets to overtake the plane, Brown orders activation of the airplane's hydrogen bomb. De Wilde finally wrests control from Brown, and decides to bomb Fort Knox, so as to stop the

finances going to the Vietnam War. The President (Daly) attempts to get De Wilde to change his mind but is unsuccessful.
The ending has De Wilde approaching his destination, as he
contemplates his fate.

BLACK MAMA, WHITE MAMA. 1973. 87 minutes. Color. *Director:*
Eddie Romero. *Screenplay:* H.R. Christian; based on a
story by Joseph Viola and Jonathan Demme. *Cinematography:*
Justo Paulino. *Cast:* Pam Grier (Lee Daniels); Margaret
Markov (Karen Brent); Sid Haig (Ruben); Lynn Borden
(Densmore); Zaldy Zshornack (Ernesto); Laurie Burton
(Logan); Eddie Garcia (Captain Cruz); Alona Alegre
(Juana); Dindo Fernando (Rocco); Vic Diaz (Vic Cheng);
Wendy Green (Ronda); Lotis M. Key (Jeanette); Alfonso
Carvajal (Galindo); Bruno Punzalah (Truck Driver); Ricardo
Herrero (Luis); Jess Ramos (Alfredo); with Carpi Asturias.

The female-prison film is a genre all its own, considering
the number made in the 70s and 80s. In *Black Mama, White Mama*
the main conflict resides between two young women, one a white
middle-class revolutionary and the other a black member of the
lumpen proletariat. Both find themselves chained together
just like Tony Curtis and Sidney Poitier were in *The Defiant
Ones*. As with other films of this type, e.g., *Caged Heat* and
Terminal Island, there is just enough violence and sexual titillation to keep things moving.
    A black prostitute (Grier) and a white revolutionary
(Markov) are prisoners on an unnamed Latin American island
prison run by a lesbian (Borden). Grier and Markov get in a
fight and are chained together and transferred to another prison on the island. They escape en route and disguise themselves
as nuns. Grier wants to go after a suitcase full of her pimp's
stolen money, while Markov desires to meet her fellow revolutionaries and conspire to overthrow the island's corrupt re-
gime. The women are searched for by three people: a powerful
local gangster (Haig); Markov's guerrilla boyfriend
(Zshornack); and Grier's pimp (Diaz). Both women join up with
the revolutionaries after they have been attacked by Haig's
men. When they reach the coast, their band is attacked by
Diaz and his group. Markov is killed in the ensuing gunfight.
Everyone departs, leaving Markov's body as a souvenir for the
local police.

THE CANNIBAL GIRLS. 1973. 84 minutes. Color. *Director:* Ivan
Reitman. *Screenplay:* Robert Sandler. *Cinematography:*
Robert Saad. *Cast:* Eugene Levy (Clifford Sturges); Andrea
Martin (Gloria Wellaby); Ronald Ulrich (Reverend Alex
St. John); Randall Carpenter (Anthea); Bonnie Neilson
(Clarissa); Mira Prawluk (Leona); Bob McHeady (Sheriff);
Alan Gordon (1st Victim); Allan Price (2nd Victim); Earl
Pomerantz (3rd Victim); May Jarvis (Mrs. Wainwright);
with Gina Marrocco, Rick Maguire, Kingfish, Marion
Swadron, Ray Lawlor, Neil Lundy, Joan Fox, David Clement,
Julie Thilpot, Doug Ganton, Lyn Logan.

The Cannibal Girls was made independently on a shoestring
budget, like many other horror films. What this film and other
"quickie" horror films such as *The Evil Dead* have in common
is their debt to George Romero's *Night of the Living Dead*.
The two stars of the film, Eugene Levy and Andrea Martin, were
two of the most talented members of *SCTV*, and this particular
film, with its tongue-in-cheek attitude, could very well play
as a skit on that program. As a gimmick AIP used a buzzer on
the soundtrack to signal when a horrific moment was coming,
and then used a chime to signal when things were safe.
    A musician (Levy) and his girlfriend (Martin) are stranded
with car trouble in a small town. They hear of a local legend
about the cannibal girls, who are controlled by an evil minister to kill men and eat them on the spot. The farmhouse where
the cannibal girls were supposed to have lived is now a restaurant, so Levy and Martin go there and find that their host
is a minister (Ulrich). The three are served dinner by three
attractive young women (Carpenter, Neilson, and Prawluk). Levy
and Martin agree to stay the night. In the middle of the night
they find the cannibal girls and Ulrich in their room. Martin
escapes, and Levy catches up to her and convinces her that
she had a nightmare. Levy takes her back to the farmhouse,
where Ulrich thanks him for bringing her back. Martin realizes
she has been betrayed by Levy, so she kills him. The three
girls, Ulrich, and the at-first-reluctant Martin dine on Levy.

COFFY. 1973. 91 minutes. Color. *Director:* Jack Hill.
    Screenplay: Jack Hill. *Cinematography:* Paul Lohmann.
    Cast: Pam Grier (Coffy); Booker Bradshaw (Brunswick);
    Robert DoQui (King George); William Elliott (Carter);

Allan Arbus (Vitroni); Sid Haig (Omar); Barry Cahill
(McHenry); Morris Buchanan (Sugar-Man); Lee de Broux
(Nick); Bob Minor (Studs); John Perak (Aleva); Ruben
Moreno (Ramos); Carol Lawson (Priscilla); Linda Hayes
(Meg); Lisa Farringer (Jeri).

If there were any justice in the world, Pam Grier would
have become one of the first black female stars, instead of
Diana Ross. In the last few years she has been relegated to
small, but effective, roles in such films as *Fort Apache, the
Bronx* and such thankless roles as the long suffering wife in
Greased Lightning.
Grier is a nurse who is pretending to be a drug addict
so that she can exact revenge against those responsible for
ruining the life of her young sister, who was a junkie. After
she has killed a drug dealer (Buchanan), Grier is given some
valuable information about a top drug dealer (DoQui) by a policeman friend (Elliott). She maneuvers her way into DoQui's
employ and begins to sabotage his dealings with his drug customers by substituting sugar for heroin. Grier's councilman
boyfriend (Bradshaw), who has a working relationship with the
mob, informs on her to a local Mafia head (Arbus). She escapes
a planned execution and goes to Arbus's house and murders him.
Her last stop is Bradshaw's beach house, where, despite his
entreaties, she kills him as well.

DEEP THRUST--THE HAND OF DEATH. 1973. 88 minutes. Color.
    Director: Heang Feng. No other credits available. *Cast:*
    Angela Mao, Chang Yi, Pai Ying, June Wu, Anne Liu.

This film's title, a play on *Deep Throat*, is about as racy
as it gets. This Hong Kong-made feature with an unknown cast
is only one in a slew of martial arts films that infiltrated
the American market in the early 70s. The acting and story
values are about on a par with the film Woody Allen used in
What's Up Tiger Lily? No one in this film has the persona of
the one and only Bruce Lee. The story has something to do
with one man's war against a gambling syndicate. He is confronted by a female martial arts expert who is out to gain
revenge against him for the suicide of her sister. The confrontation between the two Tai-Chi masters is the climax of
the film.
One of the ads for *Deep Thrust--The Hand of Death* said,
"The strong bend before the clever and the quick." Full of
kicks, chops, gouges, and leaps, there is one scene here where
one fighter actually sticks his finger through an opponent's
stomach.

DILLINGER. 1973. 107 minutes. Color. *Director:* John Milius. *Screenplay:* John Milius. *Cinematography:* Jules Brenner. *Cast:* Warren Oates (John Dillinger); Ben Johnson (Melvin Purvis); Michelle Phillips (Billie Frechette); Cloris Leachman (Anna Sage-The Lady in Red); Harry Dean Stanton (Homer Van Meter); Steve Kanaly (Lester "Pretty Boy" Floyd); Richard Dreyfuss (George "Baby Face" Nelson); Geoffrey Lewis (Harry Pierpont); Frank McRae (Reed Young-blood); John Ryan (Charles Mackley); John Martino (Eddie Martin); Roy Jenson (Samuel Cowley); Read Morgan (Big Jim Wollard); Jerry Summers (Tommy Carroll); Terry Leonard (Theodore "Handsome Jack" Klutas); Bob Harris (Ed Fulton).

This was the directorial debut of John Milius, Hollywood's reigning macho man. In *Dillinger* Milius seems more concerned with the action provided by John Dillinger and his gang than with any sort of character development. As a case in point, Richard Dreyfuss's "Baby Face" Nelson is portrayed as a crazy self-destructive cartoon character. In sum, this "is the distilled essence of the AIP film: fast and florid and trashy as all hell" (Peter Schjeldahl, *The New York Times Film Reviews*, 1973-74. New York: Arno, 1975, p. 98).

Narrated by FBI man Melvin Purvis (Johnson), the film follows the exploits of John Dillinger and his gang during a period of little over a year in 1933-34. Dillinger (Oates) engineers the escape of a gangster, which results in the murder of FBI agents in Kansas City. After Oates has held up a bank, his gang split up and go out West. He is captured in Tucson and sent to prison in Indiana. It does not take him long to break out and reunite with his girlfriend (Phillips) and two new gang members--"Pretty Boy" Floyd (Kanaly) and "Baby Face" Nelson (Dreyfuss). The group is pursued to a hideout in Wisconsin by Johnson and his men. After a lengthy and bloody gun battle, all the gang are killed except Oates and Phillips. A Chicago madam (Leachman) informs Johnson of Oates' whereabouts, and while leaving the Biograph Theatre Oates is gunned down by Johnson in an ambush.

HEAVY TRAFFIC. 1973. 76 minutes. Color. *Director:* Ralph Bakshi. *Screenplay:* Ralph Bakshi. *Cinematography:* Ted C. Bemiller and Gregg Heschong. *Cast:* Joseph Kaufmann (Michael); Beverly Hope Atkinson (Carole); Frank De Kova (Angie); Terri Haven (Ida); Mary Dean Lauria (Molly); Jacqueline Mills (Rosalyn); Lillian Adams (Rosa); and the voices of Jim Bates, Jamie Farr, Robert Easton, Charles Gordone, Morton Lewis, Bill Striglos, Jay Lawrena, Lee Weaver, Phyllis Thompson, Kim Hamilton, Carol Graham,

Candy Candido, Helen Winston, William Keene, Peter Hobbs, John Bleifer.

Despite its less-than-coherent structure, Ralph Bakshi's *Heavy Traffic* might very well be the most audacious, inventive, and raunchy animated feature ever produced in the United States. Bakshi displays his general disgust for humanity by focusing on New York City as a background for such specimens of humanity as junkies, whores, Mafioso, drag queens, and corrupt cops. While much of the film is animated, some live-action (as well as paintings and photographs) are used.

The story deals with a character named Michael, a typical product of New York mixed marriage (Jewish and Italian). He wants to be a cartoonist but also desires to lose his virginity. As we explore Michael's environment, we witness his accidentally pushing a woman off a roof during a gang bang; his involvement with Carole, a black barmaid; his rejectioning of an old whore his Mafioso father bought him as a present; and his beating to death of one of Carole's pickups. Michael's journey eventually ends when a legless admirer of Carole's accidentally shoots a bullet into Michael's head.

Heavy Traffic was given an "X" rating, mainly for its language, and it contains enough scathing portraits of various ethnic and social groups to get anyone angry. However, the response to the film was nowhere near as hostile as that received by Bakshi's next film, *Coonskin*.

THE ITALIAN CONNECTION. 1973. 92 minutes. Color. *Director:* Fernando Di Leo. *Screenplay:* Augusto Finocchi, Ingo Hermess, and Fernando Di Leo. *Cinematography:* Franco Villa. *Cast:* Henry Silva (Dave); Woody Strode (Frank); Mario Adorf (Luca Canali); Adolfo Celi (Don Vito Tressoldi); Luciana Paluzzi (Eva); Sylva Koscina (Lucia); Cyril Cusack (Corso); Franco Fabrizi (Enrico); Femi Benussi (Nana); Gianni Macchia (Nicolo); Francesca Romana Coluzzi (Triney).

This is another Mafioso film, with a good deal of action of the one-shot—fall-over, bloodless variety. In its theme of a small-time crook being hunted by the syndicate, this film is reminiscent of that fine *film noir*, *Night and the City*.

A large shipment of drugs sent to an Italian underworld mob disappears in Milan. The boss of the New York mob (Cusack) hires two professional hit men (Silva and Strode) to go to Italy to kill the person responsible for stealing the drugs. When the two arrive, suspicion falls on a Milanese pimp

(Adorf). The local crime boss (Celi) promises to help Silva and Strode locate Adorf. The shrewd Adorf is able to elude Celi's men, until he is trapped and decides to fight back. After he has killed Celi's security men, he confronts Celi, who admits he is the one who double-crossed his own organization. He offers to split the drug money with Adorf, but Adorf pulls the trigger on him anyway. The climax comes with Adorf being chased by Silva and Strode through an auto junkyard, where the three have it out with guns, resulting in multiple deaths.

LITTLE CIGARS. 1973. 92 minutes. Color. *Director:* Chris
    Christenberry. *Screenplay:* Louis Garfinkle and Frank Ray
    Perilli. *Cinematography:* John M. Stephens. *Cast:* Angel
    Tompkins (Cleo); Billy Curtis (Slick Bender); Jerry Maren
    (Cadillac); Frank Delfino (Monty); Felix Silla (Frankie);
    Emory Souza (Hugo); Joe De Santis (Travers); Phil
    Kenneally (Ganz); Jon Cedar (Faust); Rayford Barnes (Gus);
    Walter Brakel (Lieutenant Garrett); Nick Benedict (1st
    Cop); Joe Billings (Gambler); Frank Bonner (Bellman);
    Simmy Bow (1st Yokel); Leon Charles (2nd Yokel); Roger
    Creed (Peters); Jojo D'Amore (Unemployed Actor); Jack
    Denton (Lieutenant Dixon); Buddy Douglas (Art Barnes);
    Jack English (2nd Cop); Lindy Heidt (Archie); Sam Javis
    (Gas Pump Jockey); Merryl Jay (Theater Cashier); Mort
    Lewis (Clancy); Sally Marr (Buxom Lady); Gordon McGill
    (Security Man); Paul Micale (Unemployed Man); Ralph
    Montgomery (1st Hick); J.D. Nichols (Truck Driver); Angelo
    Rossitto (Angelo); Glen Stensel (Bartender); Bunny Summers
    (Matron); Todd Susman (Buzz); Bud Walls (1st Beer Drink-
    er); Alan Warnick (Unemployed Man).

Little Cigars is sort of a modern day permutation of Snow White and the Seven Dwarfs. Since up to this time AIP had exploited everything else, why not Midgets? One of the stars of the film is Billy Curtis, who starred in the 1938 all-midget western, *The Terror of Tiny Town*.
    The girlfriend (Tompkins) of a mobster (De Santis) takes off across country with a huge amount of his money. She hides out as a waitress in some provincial backwater and is befriended by two midgets (Maren and Delfino), who are attracted to the large, shapely blond. They are part of a five-man outfit that puts on shows for the local rubes. The group are actually crooks, who steal from people's cars while the others are performing. De Santis's goons (Cedar and Kenneally) show up, but Tompkins escapes from them and joins up with the midget troupe as their sexy attraction. She soon has an affair with

the group's leader (Curtis) and suggests they go into big-time
robbery. They begin by robbing such places as grocery stores,
where the men can hide in broccoli crates, and graduate to
robbing an unemployment office. After a job Tompkins and
Curtis take the money and leave the others behind. She also
plans to skip out on Curtis, but when she sees the other midgets beat him up for their share of the loot, she has a change
of heart and the two go away together.

MANSON. 1973. 83 minutes. Color. *Director:* Laurence
    Merrick. *Screenplay:* Joan Huntington. *Cinematography:*
    Leo Rivers. *Featuring:* Charles Manson, Vincent Bugliosi,
    Patricia Krenwinkle, Leslie Van Houten, Tex Watson, Robert
    Beausoliel, Steve Grogan, Bruce Davis, and Mary Bruner.

    This award-winning documentary depicts the events sur-
rounding the orgy of murder committed by Charles Manson and
his "family" in Los Angeles in the late 60s. Particular emphasis is given to Manson's early life, as well as the backgrounds of his followers. Needless to say, most of them came
from typical All-American families, as so many mass killers
have. The prosecuting attorney in the Tate-LaBianca murders,
Vincent Bugliosi, narrates part of the film, and most of the
rest is mainly told in the first person by others who were
involved in the events prior to, and after the murders. There
have been rumors for years in California that Manson followers
can still be found in the state and are just waiting for the
word from Manson to go out and kill again. *Manson* sheds quite
a bit of light on the dark, malignant side of the 60s, especially in view of subsequent personality cults, such as Jim
Jones and Reverend Moon.

SAVAGE SISTERS. 1973. 89 minutes. Color. *Director:* Eddie
    Romero. *Screenplay:* H. Franco Moon and Harry Corner.
    Cinematography: Justo Paulino. *Cast:* Gloria Hendry (Lynn
    Jackson); Cheri Caffaro (Jo Turner); Rosanna Ortiz (Mei
    Ling); John Ashley (W.P. Billingsley); Sid Haig (Mala-
    vasi); Eddie Garcia (Captain Morales); Rita Gomez (Matron
    Ortega); Leopoldo Salcedo (General Balthazar); Vic Diaz
    (One-Eye).

    This film was probably made around the same time as *Black
Mama, White Mama,* for the films have a similar plot, the same
director, and the same producer (John Ashley), and both were

filmed in the Philippines. In *Hollywood Boulevard*, a satire
on the AIP and New World type of exploitation film, there is
a part that pokes fun at these tough-babe-guerrillas-in-a-
banana-republic type of film.

In a tropical country a local hustler (Ashley, who, with
his flower-print shirts and mustache is sort of a poor man's
Tom Selleck) uses three women--a former hooker (Hendry) now
working for the police, and two revolutionaries (Caffaro and
Ortiz)--to help him find $1,000,000 in U.S. currency. They
are opposed by the local military leaders (Garcia and Salcedo)
and a scruffy bandito (Haig). There are the standard number
of attacks, ambushes, low-cut blouses, and thighs, until Ashley
and the women come upon the money. Ortiz claims that the money
belongs to the women and gives Ashley a couple of kung-fu moves
to convince him. They give Ashley $1,000; Hendry keeps her
share, while Ortiz and Caffaro decide to use the rest of the
money to aid the revolution.

SCREAM BLACULA SCREAM. 1973. 96 minutes. Color. *Director:*
    Bob Kelljan. *Screenplay:* Joan Torres, Raymond Koenig,
    and Maurice Jules; based on a story by Torres and Koenig.
    Cinematography: Isidore Mankofsky. *Cast:* William Marshall
    (Mamuwalde-Blacula); Pam Grier (Lisa); Don Mitchell
    (Justin); Michael Conrad (Sheriff Dunlop); Richard Lawson
    (Willis); Lynne Moody (Denny); Beverly Gill (Maggie);
    Bernie Hamilton (Ragman); Barbara Rhoades (Elaine); Janee
    Michelle (Gloria); Don Blackman (Doll Man); Van Kirksey
    (Prof. Walston); Bob Minor (1st Pimp); Al Jones (2nd
    Pimp); Arnold Williams (Louis); Eric Mason (Milt); Sybil
    Scotford (Librarian); Judith Elliotte (Prostitute); Dan
    Roth (Cop); Nicholas Worth (Dennis); Kenneth O'Brien
    (Joe); Craig Nelson (Sarge); James Payne (Attendant);
    Richard Washington (1st Cop); Bob Hoy (2nd Cop); James
    Kingsley (Sergeant Williams); Arnita Bell (Woman).

When we left William Marshall in *Blacula*, he was nothing
more than dust and bones. Resurrected here by director Bob
Killjan, of Count Yorga fame, the Shakespearean-trained
Marshall seeks to have his soul restored to peace through voodoo. The screenplay is something of a travesty, being a "combination of ghetto argot, California psycho-babble and the
Transylvanian idiom developed by the late Bela Lugosi" (Harry
and Michael Medved, *The Golden Turkey Awards*. New York: Perigee, 1980, p. 106). Marshall's victims in this film are a
bit out of the ordinary, since they look and dress as if they
are going out for a night on Hollywood Boulevard.

A renegade voodoo priest (Lawson) finds a bag of bones, which are the remains of Blacula. A voodoo spell brings Marshall back to life, and he makes Lawson his first victim. Marshall comes upon a party where he meets another, and much more attractive, member (Grier) of a voodoo sect, whom he asks for help in restoring his soul. Meanwhile he continues to turn people into vampires, so as to continue to live. A sheriff (Conrad) and Grier's policeman fiancé (Mitchell) investigate the source of the vampire attacks. Marshall has Grier prepare a voodoo ceremony in his house, but when the police arrive, a melee occurs. Marshall threatens to turn Grier into a vampire, but she drives a stake through the heart of a voodoo-doll replica of Marshall, and he dies once more.

THE SCREAMING TIGER. 1973. 101 minutes. Color. *Director:* Chien Lung. *Screenplay:* Wang Pi Jen. *Cinematography:* No credit given. *Cast:* Wang Yu, Chang Ching Ching, Ma Chi, Lei Ming, Tzu Lan, and Chin Lien.

With this film martial-arts expert Wang Yu was supposed to have taken over the mantle of karate champion from the late Bruce Lee. Here he portrays a young man out to gain revenge against the man responsible for killing his father and sister. The villain happens to be Japanese. After a series of martial-arts battles Wang Yu finally comes upon the villain, who is the head of a karate school and a band of pickpockets. The men have a lengthy fight, which starts in the hills and progresses to the top of a speeding train and finally to the edge of a waterfall, before Wang Yu emerges victorious.

SISTERS. 1973. 92 minutes. Color. *Director:* Brian De Palma *Screenplay:* Brian De Palma and Louisa Rose; based on a story by De Palma. *Cinematography:* Gregory Sandor. *Cast* Margot Kidder (Danielle Breton); Jennifer Salt (Grace Collier); Charles Durning (Joseph Larch); Bill Finley (Dr. Emil Breton); Lisle Wilson (Philip Woode); Barnard Hughes (Mr. McLennen); Mary Davenport (Mrs. Collier); Dolph Sweet (Detective Kelly).

This stylish and humorous homage to Alfred Hitchcock is probably Brian De Palma's best film. Freely borrowing plot devices from such Hitchcock films as *Psycho*, *Vertigo*, *Rear Window*, and *Rope*, *Sisters* can easily stand on its own as an effective piece of horror. It is aided considerably by Bernar Herrmann's eerie score.

A young French-Canadian model (Kidder) meets a young actor
(Wilson) on a television game show and after dinner takes him
to her apartment on Staten Island. They are followed there
and watched by Kidder's estranged husband (Finley). The next
morning Wilson wakes Kidder up, and she suddenly, in a frenzy,
stabs him to death. A newspaper reporter (Salt) witnesses
the murder from her apartment across the way and calls the
police. Finley comes into the apartment and has Kidder hide
the body in a rollaway sofa. The police refuse to believe
Salt's story, so she hires a private detective (Durning) to
search the apartment and follow the sofa when it is moved.
Doing some research, Salt learns that Kidder is the surviving
half of siamese twins separated by Finley, who now feels protective toward the murderously schizophrenic Kidder. Salt
follows the pair to a private clinic, where she is drugged by
Finley. Kidder assumes her dead sister's personality whenever
men approach her, and when Finley kisses her she stabs him.
Just then the police arrive, but the drug administered to Salt
has made her unconscious of the first murder.

SLAUGHTER'S BIG RIP-OFF. 1973. 94 minutes. Color. *Director:*
    Gordon Douglas. *Screenplay:* Charles Johnson; based on a
    character created by Don Williams. *Cinematography:*
    Charles Wheeler. *Cast:* Jim Brown (Slaughter); Ed McMahon
    (Duncan); Brock Peters (Reynolds); Don Stroud (Kirk);
    Gloria Hendry (Marcia); Richard Williams (Joe Creole);
    Art Metrano (Burtoli); Judy Brown (Norja); Russ Marin
    (Crowder); Eddie Lo Russo (Arnie); Jackie Giroux (Mrs.
    Duncan); Tony Brubaker (Ed Pratt); Gene LeBell (Leo);
    Fuji (Chin); Russ McGinn (Harvey); with Hoke Howell, Chuck
    Hicks, Nick Benedict, Scatman Crothers, J. Jay Saunders,
    George Gaynes, Leu Camacho, Piper Alvez, Lisa Farringer,
    Lillian Gray, Junero Jennings, Marianna Case, Lisa Moore,
    Frank Tallman, Bill Cameron, Pamela Miller, Valda Hanson,
    Shannon Lane, Gayle Lynn Davis, Sable Sperling, Nick
    Ferrari, Chuck G. Niles, Reg Parton.

This came out on the heels of the successful *Slaughter*
and, if anything, is worse than the original. Even veteran
director Gordon Douglas cannot overcome the clichés in a film
where the main character seems to have taken lessons in moral-
ity and willpower from G. Gordon Liddy.
    Jim Brown once again is Slaughter, the avenger of crime
syndicates, who finds that the mob is still on his trail even
after the tail-whipping he gave them in *Slaughter*. He hunts
the killer of a friend who had been murdered by gangsters while
attending a posh garden party. Brown refuses to work with the

police, preferring instead the role of the lone wolf. With
the aid of a flashy pimp (Williams) and various other members
of Los Angeles's night community, he finds the killer--dead.
The police persuade Brown to procure the list of syndicate
members, which he does through the help of Williams. Both a
crooked cop (Marin) and a crime boss (McMahon) put assassins
on Brown's trail, but he eludes them. By now he has been
forced to return the list, because his girlfriend (Hendry) has
been threatened by the mob. Brown carries out an assault on
McMahon's house, where he dispatches his men and obtains the
crime list from the frightened McMahon.

ABBY. 1974. 91 minutes. Color. *Director:* William Girdler.
  Screenplay: G. Cornell Layne; based on a story by William
  Girdler and Layne. *Cinematography:* William Asman. *Cast:*
  William Marshall (Bishop Garnet Williams); Carol Speed
  (Abby Williams); Terry Carter (Reverend Emmett Williams);
  Austin Stoker (Cass Potter); Juanita Moore (Mamma Potter);
  Charles Kissinger (Dr. Hennings); Elliott Moffitt
  (Russell); Nathan Cook (Taft Hassan); Bob Holt (Voice of
  the Demon); Nancy Lee Owens (Mrs. Wiggins); with Joann
  Holcomb, Bill Wilson, Don Henderson, John Miller, Joan
  Ray, Robin James, Casey Brown, Billy Bradford.

     Directed and co-written by the late William Girdler, who
made the strange and ludicrous *The Manitou*, *Abby* is nothing
more than a blaxploitation version of *The Exorcist*. This paltry production remains as a fine example of a movie that is
"enjoyable on the level of a *Mad* magazine film parody" (*Variety*, January 1, 1975, p. 14).
     A black clergyman/archaeologist (Marshall) goes to Nige-
ria, where he unearths a carved wooden box that contains the
spirit of a god of evil and carnality. Back in Louisville
the wife (Speed) of Marshall's minister son (Carter) begins
acting strangely. This results in Speed having a seizure during a church service. She becomes more violent in her behavior and begins the lifestyle of a swearing, promiscuous "bar
fly" of a woman. She is hospitalized, and Carter asks his
father to return from Africa. Speed has already forced her
way out of the hospital when Marshall arrives on the scene.
He becomes convinced that she is possessed by the spirit of
the artifact he found in Africa. Carter and Speed's brother
(Stoker) finally track her down in a closed nightclub, where
Marshall performs a successful exorcism on her.

ACT OF VENGEANCE. 1974. 90 minutes. *Director:* Robert
Kelljchian (Kelljan). *Screenplay:* Betty Conklin and H.R.
Christian. *Cinematography:* Brick Marquard. *Cast:* Jo Ann
Harris (Linda); Peter Brown (Jack); Jennifer Lee (Nancy);
Lisa Moore (Karen); Connie Strickland (Teresa); Patricia
Estrin (Angie); Ross Elliot (Sergeant Long); Steve Kanaly
(Tom); Tony Young (Bud); Lada Edmund, Jr. (Tiny); John
Pickard (Dr. Schelman); Ninette Bravo (Joyce); Stanley
Adams (Bernie); Joan McCall (Gloria); Anneka De Lorenzo
(Chris); Jay Fletcher (Pimping Percy); Marie O. Henry
(Kathleen); Ginger Mason (Diane); Holly Harris (Woman at
Ranch); Cheryl Waters (Tamara); Alyscia Maxwell (Rigina);
Hank Rolike (Vendor); Esther Sutherland (Woman at Laundro-
mat); James Kingsley (Athlete); Dennis Cross (Larry);
Clint Young (Dave); Troy Melton (Bartender); Marc Seaton
(Buddy); Guy Hemric (1st Suspect); Fred Lerner (2nd Sus-
pect).

Act of Vengeance has a novel premise as well as a ballsy,
tough-talking script. This film preceded by a few years the
more highly promoted *Lipstick*, with which it shares a number
of aspects.
   A young woman (Harris) is upset by the callous treatment
the police give her when she reported she was raped. She meets
four other women (Moore, Estrin, Lee, and Strickland), who
have also been victims of the masked rapist known as "Jingle
Bells" (he makes the women sing that song when he is raping
them). The five setup a "rape squad" and begin passing out
leaflets and taking self-defense courses. They become a vigilante force by trapping men who abuse women, and in one instance they even dye a man's scrotum. All the while "Jingle
Bells" is watching their activities and becoming "turned on."
One girl (Mason), who has been used as bait, is killed before
the women can rescue her. "Jingle Bells" then teases them to
meet him at the zoo at night. He kills one of them (Moore),
and one by one he finds the rest, tying them up and putting
them in cages. Finally Harris is the only one left. She rid-
icules his sexual performance, which forces him into the open.
When he tries to attack her, she stabs him to death.

BAMBOO GODS AND IRON MEN. 1974. 96 minutes. Color. *Direc-
tor:* Cesar Gallardo. *Screenplay:* Kenneth Metcalfe and
Joseph Zucchero. *Cinematography:* Felipe J. Sacdalan.
Cast: James Inglehart (Calvin Jefferson); Shirley

Washington (Arlene Jefferson); Chiquito (Charley); Marissa
Delgado (Pandora); Eddie Garcia (Ambrose); Ken Metcalfe
(Leonardo King); Joe Zucchero (Ivan Soroka); Michael Boyet
(Gunman).

A film is in trouble any time the people behind the camera
find it necessary to appear in their own production. In the
case of *Bamboo Gods and Iron Men* both screenwriters make the
unfortunate decision of portraying villains. Not only are
the martial-arts sequences second-rate but the film is also
hampered by the pathetic comedy routines of someone called
Chiquito.
    A Manila businessman (Metcalfe) has the centuries-old
diary of a Chinese scientist, who claimed to have discovered
a material that would control the world. One of his emissaries
(Zucchero) locates the tomb where the material is hidden inside a pouch. In Hong Kong he hides the pouch in the luggage
of an American boxer (Inglehart), who is on his way to Manila
as part of his honeymoon. Metcalfe has Zucchero killed by
one of his gunmen (Garcia). Meanwhile Inglehart has rescued
a young Chinese man (Chiquito) from drowning. Chiquito feels
so beholden to him that he refuses to leave his side, as he
accompanies Inglehart and his wife (Washington) to Manila.
In Manila Inglehart avoids various traps set for him by
Metcalfe and Garcia. In desperation Metcalfe has Washington
kidnapped and offers the pouch as ransom. Inglehart and
Chiquito go to Metcalfe's home after Chiquito has found the
pouch in a box containing a Buddha. The police arrive and
join in the battle with Inglehart. When the pouch is opened,
it turns out to be only gunpowder.

THE BAT PEOPLE. 1974. 94 minutes. Color. *Director:* Jerry
    Jameson. *Screenplay:* Lou Shaw. *Cinematography:* Matthew
    Leonetti. *Cast:* Stewart Moss (Dr. John Beck); Marianne
    McAndrew (Cathy Beck); Michael Pataki (Sergeant Ward);
    Paul Carr (Dr. Kipling); Arthur Space (Tramp); Robert
    Berk (Motel Owner); Pat Delaney (Nurse in Laboratory);
    George Paulsin (Young Man in Car); Bonnie Van Dyck (Young
    Girl in Car); Jeni Kulik (Murdered Nurse); Laurie Brooks
    Jefferson (Nurse Who Describes the Murder).

A doctor of immunology (Moss) stops to study a bat cave
with his wife (McAndrew) on the way to their honeymoon vacation. He is bitten by a bat and later begins to have a glazed
look and shudders in his body. When Moss later has a convul-
sion, he witnesses McAndrew being chased by a swarm of bats

and is unaware that she has also been bitten. He is taken to a hospital to undergo a rabies test, and while there his hand turns into a bat claw and he kills a nurse (Kulik). A series of similar killings occur as Moss eludes a police detective (Pataki). McAndrew is reunited with Moss one night, and while they are making love he turns into a large batlike creature. When she screams, Moss flees back to the bat cave. While McAndrew and Pataki drive out to the cave, she exhibits the same shudders her husband did after he had first been bitten. A large group of bats fly out of the cave (urged on by a particularly ugly one) and attack their car. Pataki is eaten alive, as McAndrew follows a call emanating from the cave, where she is reunited with her husband.

DERANGED. 1974. 82 minutes. Color. *Directors:* Jeff Gillen
and Alan Ormsby. *Screenplay:* Alan Ormsby. *Cinematog-
raphy:* Jack McGowan. *Cast:* Roberts Blossom (Ezra Cobb);
Cosette Lee (Ma Cobb); Leslie Carlson (Narrator); Robert
Warner (Harlan Koontz); Marcia Diamond (Jenny Koontz);
Brian Sneagle (Brad Koontz); Arlene Gillen (Miss Johnson);
Robert McHeady (Sheriff); Marion Waldman (Maureen Selby);
Jack Mather (Drunk); Micki Moore (Mary); Pat Orr (Sally).

Back in the late 50s law authorities searched the Wisconsin farmhouse of Ed Gein. Their grisly find made notoriety
as one of the most notorious crimes in American criminal history. Strewn around Gein's house were the remains of women's
bodies--beheaded, eviscerated, and skinned. *Deranged* follows
the Gein case almost to the letter, whereas *Psycho* (loosely
based on the case) studiously avoids many of the gory details.
Aided by a good script, and a terrifyingly believable performance by Roberts Blossom, "*Deranged* has a compulsive conviction
that knocks the altogether slicker *The Texas Chainsaw Massacre*
for six" (Tom Milne, *Monthly Film Bulletin*, March 1976, p. 51).
    A middle-aged farmer (Blossom) cares for his beloved moth-
er (Lee), who has always warned him about the dangers of con-
sorting with women. Lee dies, and after months alone Blossom
goes out to the cemetery to dig up her body and bring it back
home. To restore her he studies taxidermy and embalming.
Blossom digs up more bodies to keep him and his mother company,
but they fall short of being witty conversationalists. He
ends up killing three women from town, as he makes clumsy attempts at looking for a wife. A girlfriend (Orr) of a neighbor's son (Sneagle) disappears, so the boy and his father
(Warner) and the sheriff (McHeady) go to Blossom's house to
investigate. There they find body parts everywhere, and the

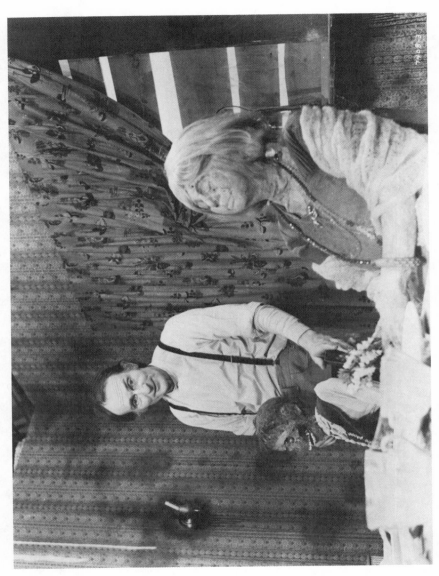

Deranged

blood-covered Blossom in a state of incoherence.

Contrary to rumors, Ed Gein is not running a barbecue joint in Green Bay. In 1976 he was again judged too mentally ill to be released.

THE DESTRUCTORS. 1974. 89 minutes. Color. *Director:* Robert Parrish. *Screenplay:* Judd Bernard. *Cinematography:* Douglas Slocombe. *Cast:* Michael Caine (John Deray); Anthony Quinn (Steve Ventura); James Mason (Jacques Brizard); Maureen Kerwin (Lucianne Brizard); Marcel Bozzuffi (Calmet); Catherine Rouvel (Brizard's Mistress); Maurice Ronet (Briac); Andre Oumansky (Marsac); Alexandra Stewart (Mrs. Matthews); Patrick Floersheim (Jo Kovakian); Georges Beller (Minierini); Jean-Louis Fortuit (Fortuit); Jerry Brouer (Kurt); Georges Lycan (Henri); Pierre Koulak (Wilson); Hella Petri (Countess); Vernon Dobtcheff (Lazar); Barbara Sommers (Sally); Martine Kelly (Janet); Danik Zurakowski (The Girl); Pierre Salinger (Williams); Bill Kearns, Alan Rosset, James Jones, Gene Moskowitz and Sam White (Card Players); Jean Bouchard (Rouget); Bob Lerick (1st Man at Airfield); Jacques Chevalier (2nd Man at Airfield); Jack Jourdain (3rd Man at Airfield); Robert Rondo (Matthews); John Rico (Informer); Charles Millot (Butler); Charles Morosi (Coroner); Brooks Poole (Kevin Matthews); Dominique Gilles (Helicopter Pilot); Georges Pelligrin (Pelligrin); Ed Marcus (Fargas).

A big name cast is used to negligible results in this tired *policier* patterned somewhat after *The French Connection.* Also known as *The Marseilles Contract*, this is one of those international co-productions in which the market value of the star names is supposed to overshadow the incongruities of the plot, e.g., Quinn escapes from killers by running to a vacant field instead of staying with a crowd of people.

The head of an American antidrug unit in Paris (Quinn) is out to end the operation of a big-time Marseilles drug smuggler (Mason). After one of his agents is murdered, Quinn asks the help of a French detective (Ronet) to find him a hired assassin to kill Mason. An old friend of Quinn's (Caine) turns out to be the hit man. Caine swiftly joins Mason's organization after becoming acquainted with Mason's daughter (Kerwin). Caine's cover is eventually exposed when one of Mason's men (Bozzuffi) tells him about Caine's background. Quinn comes to Marseilles, where he and Caine have planned to stop one of Mason's drug shipments. The plan is betrayed by the crooked Ronet, and in a shootout Caine, Ronet, and Bozzuffi are killed.

Quinn now goes to Mason's mansion during a grand party and uses a silencer to kill him amidst the group of revelers.

DIRTY O'NEIL. 1974. 89 minutes. Color. *Directors:* Howard
    Freen and Lewis Teague. *Screenplay:* Howard Freen. *Cin-
    ematography:* Stephen V. Kate. *Cast:* Morgan Paull (Jimmy
    O'Neil); Art Metrano (Lassiter); Pat Anderson (Lisa);
    Jean Manson (Ruby); Katie Saylor (Vera); Raymond O'Keefe
    (Lou); Tom Huff (Bennie); Bob Potter (Al); Sam Laws
    (Clyde); Liv Lindeland (Mrs. Crawford); with Susan McIver,
    June Fairchild, John Steadman, Amtra Ford.

This story of sex and small-town cops was paired on double
bills with *They Call Her One Eye* and mainly played the big-
city grindhouses and suburban drive-ins. As a matter of fact,
since *Dirty O'Neil* deals with the amorous exploits of a cop
in a town overflowing with attractive women, it seems the perfect film for people to watch at drive-ins, as they sit in
their deck chairs and nurse their six-pack.
    A young cop in a California town (Paull) spends much of
his time away from his desultory police work wooing the local
beauties. As is usually the case, a nurse (Anderson), whom
he cares for the most, will not have anything to do with him.
Paull's idyllic existence is rudely interrupted one day when
three Hell's Angels come to town. They rape the waitress
(Manson) at the local diner and rob it as well. Paull catches
two of them in the middle of the robbery, and chases the third,
until he catches and kills him with a bulldozer. Slightly
injured, Paull, while in the hospital, now finds that Anderson
has now changed her attitude towards him.

FOXY BROWN. 1974. 94 minutes. Color. *Director:* Jack Hill.
    Screenplay: Jack Hill. *Cinematography:* Brick Marquard.
    Cast: Pam Grier (Foxy Brown); Antonio Fargas (Link Brown);
    Peter Brown (Steve Elias); Terry Carter (Michael Ander-
    son); Kathryn Loder (Katherine Wall); Harry Holcombe
    (Judge Fenton); Sid Haig (Hays); Juanita Brown (Claudia);
    Sally Ann Stroud (Deb); Bob Minor (Oscar); with H.B.
    Haggerty, Boyd Red Morgan, Judy Cassmore, Tony Giorgio,
    Fred Lerner, and Jack Bernardi.

Foxy Brown is very much like the previous year's *Coffy*,
also starring Pam Grier as the eponymous *noir* heroine, and
directed by Jack Hill. While *Coffy* had a tone of all-pervasive

corruption, this film just seems to revel in its slashings, burnings, and castrations. The only thing that *Foxy Brown* has going for it is Pam Grier, who, for most of us, is more than enough.

Grier's narc boyfriend (Carter) is murdered by members of a drug and vice ring, after being "fingered" by Grier's brother (Fargas). She swears revenge, and forces from Fargas the names of the syndicate's leaders (Loder and Brown). Grier obtains a job with Loder's protection and blackmail racket and slowly begins to subvert the organization. After being raped and tortured, Grier escapes before Loder's men can inject her with drugs. She joins forces with the head of a black neighborhood group (Minor) to prevent a shipment of heroin from coming into the neighborhood. With Minor and his group Grier goes to Mexico to foil the drug shipment plans of Loder and Brown. Brown is castrated by Minor, and Grier brings his private parts in a jar to Loder.

GOLDEN NEEDLES. 1974. 96 minutes. Color. *Director:* Robert Clouse. *Screenplay:* S. Lee Pogostin and Sylvia Schneble. *Cinematography:* Gilbert Hubbs. *Cast:* Joe Don Baker (Dan Mason); Elizabeth Ashley (Felicity); Ann Sothern (Finzie); Burgess Meredith (Winters); Jim Kelly (Jeff); Roy Chiao (Lin Toa); Frances Fong (Sulin); Tony Lee (Kwan); Alice Fong (Lotus); Clarence Barnes (Claude); Pat Johnson (Winters' Man); Edgar Justice (Bobby).

Golden Needles is a retrograde example of the mindless escapist school of filmmaking that reached its peak with *Raiders of the Lost Ark*. Instead of searching for the Lost Ark of the Covenant, the protagonists here are looking for a gold statue. The figurine contains acupuncture needles, which if applied properly will yield the power of virility. Despite the exotic Hong Kong locations, *Golden Needles* "carries all the earmarks of a reject episode of *Hawaii Five-O*" (Verina Glaessner, *Monthly Film Bulletin*, November 1974, p. 251).

A woman (Ashley) is employed by a rich collector (Meredith) to find a valuable gold statue from the Sung Dynasty. The statue is stolen from her, and through a friend (Lee) she meets a fortune hunter (Baker), who agrees to help her for at least ten percent of the take. A female martial-arts expert (F. Fong) is also after the statue for the Hong Kong government. Baker and company locate what they think is the real statue and ship it to Meredith in Los Angeles. It turns out to be a fake, so back they go to Hong Kong, where Baker finds the real statue in Lee's houseboat. He flees from a Chinese gang by running through teeming crowds of Hong Kong shoppers. The police arrive to save Baker, and he and Ashley agree to give the statue to the Hong Kong government.

HELL UP IN HARLEM. 1974. 96 minutes. Color. *Director:* Larry
　　Cohen. *Screenplay:* Larry Cohen. *Cinematography:* Fenton
　　Hamilton. *Cast:* Fred Williamson (Tommy Gibbs); Julius W.
　　Harris (Papa Gibbs); Gloria Hendry (Helen Bradley);
　　Margaret Avery (Sister Jennifer); D'Urville Martin (Rev-
　　erend Rufus); Tony King (Zacharia); Gerald Gordon (Mr.
　　DiAngelo); James Dixon (Irish); Charles MacGuire (Hap);
　　Bobby Ramsen (Frankfurter); Esther Sutherland and Annie
　　Horten (The Maids).

Before he began appearing in films, Fred Williamson had been a defensive back in the National Football League, where he was known as "The Hammer," for his aggressive style of play. His career as an actor brought out his natural muscular bent in films that seemed tailor-made for him. *Hell Up in Harlem* is so much like *Black Caesar*, the previous Larry Cohen film starring Williamson, that this could easily be called *Black Caesar II*.

Williamson here is a Harlem criminal determined to be the overlord of Harlem. He has in his possession incriminating evidence against white city officials who are involved in graft and corruption. He uses this knowledge, along with the aid of his father (Harris) and a sidekick (King), to build a criminal empire. It does not take long for King to become resentful of the power wielded by Williamson and Harris. The district attorney (Gordon) uses King's jealousy to help overthrow Williamson. When the heat gets to be too much for him, Williamson goes to the West Coast but returns to New York after an attempt is made on his life. He finds that his father is dead and King has gained control of much of his territory. In a final struggle Williamson kills King and, later, Gordon as well. The ending of the film leaves open the possibility for a sequel.

HOUSE OF WHIPCORD. 1974. 101 minutes. Color. *Director:*
　　Pete Walker. *Screenplay:* David McGillivray; based on a
　　story by Peter Walker. *Cinematography:* Peter Jessop.
　　Cast: Barbara Markham (Mrs. Wakehurst); Patrick Barr (Jus-
　　tice Bailey); Ray Brooks (Tony); Anne Michelle (Julia);
　　Penny Irving (Ann-Marie de Vernay); Sheila Keith (Walker);

Dorothy Gordon (Bates); Robert Tayman (Mark Dessart);
Ivor Salter (Jack); Judy Robinson (Claire); Karen David
(Karen); Jane Hayward (Estelle); Celia Quicke (Denise);
Celia Imrie (Barbara); Ron Smerczak (Ted); David
McGillivray (Cavan); Barry Martin (Al); Tony Sympson
(Henry); Rose Hill (Henry's Wife); David Butler (Ticket
Collector); Denis Tinsley (Police Sergeant); Pete Walker
(Cyclist).

The director of *House of Whipcord*, Pete Walker, is known
for a string of British sex films. While this film has certain
titillating aspects, it nonetheless casts a critical eye on
Puritanical sexual repression. The "official" British persona
exemplifying proper behavior through a regimen of diffidence
and decorum is shattered when confronted with such films as
House of Whipcord, or the rumps and bosoms of the tabloid
press.

A model (Irving) is approached by a man (Tayman) after
she has appeared in court for an embarrassing nude encounter.
He invites her to a country house, where Irving soon finds
herself a prisoner of a former judge (Barr) and an ex-warden
(Markham), who have set up the country home as a prison for
young women of "loose" morals. Irving and the other female
prisoners experience a series of beatings, solitary confine-
ment, and threats of execution. Eventually Irving's roommate
(Michelle) finds out about Irving's imprisonment. Michelle
goes there and is able to inform her boyfriend (Brooks) of
the prison just before Markham shows her Irving's corpse.
Brooks comes to the rescue with the police, and the prisoners
are freed from the clutches of the sadists and closet lesbians.

MACON COUNTY LINE. 1974. 89 minutes. Color. *Director:*
Richard Compton. *Screenplay:* Max Baer and Richard
Compton; based on a story by Baer. *Cinematography:* Daniel
Lacambre. *Cast:* Alan Vint (Chris Dixon); Cheryl Waters
(Jenny); Geoffrey Lewis (Hamp); Joan Blackman (Carol
Morgan); Jessie Vint (Wayne Dixon); Max Baer (Deputy Reed
Morgan); Sam Gilman (Deputy Bill); Timothy Scott (Lon);
James Gammon (Elisha); Leif Garrett (Luke Morgan); Emile
Meyer (Gurney); Doodles Weaver (Augie); Avil Williams
(Public Defender); Jay Adler (Impound Yard Man); Roger
Camras (Man in Car); David Orange (1st Highway Patrolman);
Roger Pancake (2nd Highway Patrolman); Carolyn Judd (Wait-
ress); John DeMattio (Pimp); Kate Monahan (Ida); Linda
Atnip (Police Despatcher); Edward Cross (Ed); Von Deming
(Policeman); Ross Hildebrand (Man in Truck); Annie
Compton (Policewoman); Jan Green (Whore).

Macon County Line combines the revenge theme of *Death Wish* and hayseed exploitation found in such television shows as *The Dukes of Hazzard*. This is supposedly based on a true story, which is easy to believe, considering that the red-neck behavior and the preoccupation with guns exhibited here is in keeping with the reputation that the rural South has.

In the Deep South in 1954 a young man (Alan Vint) goes out with his brother (Jesse Vint) "bombing" down country roads and having a high old time before he is to go into the Army. They pick up a girl (Waters) and become stranded in a town when their car breaks down. The local sheriff (Baer) asks them to leave town, and the three decide to spend the night parked along the side of the road. Baer picks up his young son (Garrett) from a military school and takes the unwilling youngster on a hunting trip to make a "man" out of him. They return home to find Baer's wife (Blackman) raped and murdered. Baer goes out looking for the Vints, thinking they are responsible. While he is on their trail, the real murderers (Gammon and Scott) have been caught. Baer's deputy (Gilman) goes to stop Baer before anyone can be hurt. Baer has trapped the three in a houseboat, and in a shootout all but Alan Vint are killed. Baer's psychologically shattered son is now put in a mental institution.

Macon County Line attempts a criticism of the macho mystique and lowlife behavior in general, but like so many American films it seems to enjoy what it is supposedly condemning.

MADHOUSE. 1974. 89 minutes. Color. *Director:* Jim Clark. *Screenplay:* Greg Morrison and Ken Levison; based on the novel *Devilday*, by Angus Hall. *Cinematography:* Ray Parslow. *Cast:* Vincent Price (Paul Toombes); Peter Cushing (Herbert Flay); Robert Quarry (Oliver Quayle); Adrienne Corri (Faye); Natasha Pyne (Julia); Michael Parkinson (Himself); Linda Hayden (Elizabeth Peters); Barry Dennen (Blount); Ellis Dayle (Alfred Peters); Catherine Willmer (Louise Peters); John Garrie (Harper); Ian Thompson (Bradshaw); Jenny Lee Wright (Carol); Julie Crosthwaite (Ellen); Peter Halliday (Psychiatrist).

No doubt AIP's advertising angle for *Madhouse* stressed the teaming up of their own reigning horror star (Price) with that of Hammer Films (Cushing), as well as Count Yorga (Quarry). *Madhouse* includes a number of clips from some of Vincent Price's AIP horror films and borrows a plot device that has been used in other films, such as *Straight Jacket*.

Price is a once-famous horror star, whose career ended

when his fiancée was found decapitated. After spending 12
years as a recluse, he is asked by an actor/writer friend
(Cushing) to come to England to star in a television show, in
which he would portray his most famous role--Doctor Death.
Price stays in Cushing's home and finds a strange discovery
in the basement--a former lover (Corri), now married to
Cushing, who lives in the basement, disfigured and lording
it over a colony of spiders. Soon a number of women are found
murdered by the same modus operandi used by Price's Doctor
Death character. The police naturally suspect him. The publicity girl (Pyne) at the television studio, who has befriended
Price, tells him she has found evidence about the murders.
He goes to the studio and finds Pyne dead and is attacked by
someone wearing the Doctor Death costume. The near-mad Price
locks himself in the studio and starts a fire that apparently
kills him. Cushing takes over the Doctor Death role, and when
he comes home one night he encounters the still-alive Price.
Cushing admits to the other killings, and in a struggle Price
kills him. Price now dons the Doctor Death makeup in front
of the laughing and insane Corri.

THE NINE LIVES OF FRITZ THE CAT. 1974. 76 minutes. Color.
Director: Robert Taylor. *Screenplay:* Robert Taylor, Fred
Halliday, and Eric Monte; based on characters created by
Robert Crumb. *Cinematography:* Ted C. Bemiller and Greg
Heschong. *Character Voices:* Skip Hinnant, Reva Rose,
Bob Holt, Dick Whittington, Robert Ridgley, Fred Smoot,
Luke Walker, Peter Leeds, Louisa Moritz, Larry Moss,
Stanley Adams, Joan Gerber, Pat Harrington, Jr., Jim
Johnson, Carol Androsky, Jay Lawrence, Lynn Toman, Ralph
James, Eric Monte, Glynn Turman, Ron Knight, Gloria Jones,
Renny Roker, Peter Hobbs, Buddy Aret, John Hancock, Chris
Graham, Felton Perry, Anthony Mason, and Serena Grant.

Ralph Bakshi directed the original version of *Fritz the
Cat*, based on the character created in Robert Crumb's underground comics. This film does not contain quite the vigor of
the previous version, but it still contains enough negative
references to women and ethnic groups to get many people very
upset. Using the world of underground comics as a starting
point for an animated feature seems to offer fresh ground for
filmmakers. Although it is doubtful whether the mass audience
is ready for the more scatological creations to be found in
such comics as *Amputee Love* and *Insect Fear*.
Fritz the Cat is being nagged by his wife, so in a drugged
fantasy he thinks about lives he could have led. After

seducing his sister, he becomes an assistant to Adolf Hitler. Adhering to no conventional sense of time, the film jumps to the point where Fritz takes a space ride with a black woman, and they go forward in time to a point where Henry Kissinger is President (evidently Seymour Hersh's book has had a reverse effect). Most immigrants in the United States have gone back to their native lands, except the blacks, who all live in New Jersey. A black general declares war on America and is victorious. Fritz hides in a sewer and meets an effeminate Satan. He wakes up from his fantasy, and his wife throws him out of the house.

SEIZURE. 1974. 93 minutes. Color. *Director:* Oliver Stone. *Screenplay:* Edward Mann and Oliver Stone; based on a story by Stone. *Cinematography:* Roger Racine. *Cast:* Jonathan Frid (Edmund Blackstone); Martine Beswick (Queen of Evil); Joe Sirola (Charlie); Christina Pickles (Nicole Blackstone); Herve Villechaize (The Spider); Ann Meacham (Eunice); Roger De Koven (Serge); Troy Donahue (Mark); Mary Woronov (Mikki); Henry Baker (Jackal); Lucy Bingham (Betsy the Maid); Alexis Kirk (Arris); Mike Meola (Gas Station Attendant); Timothy Rouse (Milkman); Richard Cox (Gerald); Timothy Ousey (Jason).

A writer of supernatural novels (Frid) invites some friends to spend the weekend with him and his family at his country home in Quebec. Not long after the guests arrive, he finds his dog killed and a strange face peering at him through a window. He relates to one of his guests (De Koven) that he has dreamed that they are going to be visited by three characters from his latest novel--the Queen of Evil (Beswick), a giant (Baker), and a sinister dwarf (Villechaize). Each of the three appear and begin to kill off the guests, as they prey on the emotional weaknesses of their victims. Realizing that they will try to kill him next, Frid offers his son (Ousey) to them. He runs out of the house and kills Baker. Villechaize catches up with Frid and begins to strangle him. At this point he wakes up from what had been a nightmare but finds that Beswick, and not his wife (Pickles), is in bed with him. Frid is found the next morning by Pickles--dead from fright.
Obviously director Oliver Stone was well versed in the horror genre, since he borrows so freely from other films, such as *The Cabinet of Dr. Caligari* and *Dead of Night*. What adds to the pleasure of the proceedings is the inclusion of Jonathan Frid, who gained quite a bit of popularity portraying

a vampire in the television show *Dark Shadows*.

SUGAR HILL. 1974. 97 minutes. Color. *Director:* Paul
Maslansky. *Screenplay:* Tim Kelly, Alvin Kazar, and
Maurice Jules. *Cinematography:* Bob Jessup. *Cast:* Marki
Bey (Diana "Sugar" Hill); Robert Quarry (Morgan); Don
Pedro Colley (Baron Samedi); Richard Lawson (Valentine);
Betty Anne Rees (Celeste); Zara Culley (Mama Maitresse);
Larry D. Johnson (Langston); Charles Robinson (Fabulous);
Rick Hagood (Tank Watson); Ed Geldhart (O'Brien); Thomas
C. Carroll (Baker); Albert J. Baker (George); Raymond E.
Simpson (King); Charles Krohn (Captain Merrill); J.
Randall Bell (Parkhurst); Peter Harrell III (Police Pho-
tographer); Big Walter Price (Preacher); Judy Hanson (Mas-
seuse); Tony Brubaker (Head Zombie); Gary W. Chason (Lab
Technician); Roy L. Downey (Stevedore); Garrett Scales
(Crew Chief); John E. Scarborough (Uniformed Cop).

Sugar Hill openly copies the voodoo found in *Scream Blacula Scream* and the beauteous female avenger in *Coffy* and *Foxy
Brown*. Nevertheless, it can stand on its own terms as an effective excursion in the black horror genre. The idea of black
slaves coming back from the dead to kill their white oppressors
must have hit a strong note with black audiences. *Sugar Hill*
is usually shown on television under the title *The Zombies of
Sugar Hill*, with about eight minutes cut from the original
version.
    A black owner of a nightclub (Johnson) is killed by the
underlings of a white mobster (Quarry), because he would not
sell his club. Johnson's girlfriend (Bey) swears vengeance
upon his murderers and goes to ask the help of an old voodoo
priestess (Culley). Culley conjures up the leader of the zombies (Colley) to lead his soulmates in acts of revenge against
Quarry and his gang. Members of Quarry's group are killed off
one by one by the zombies, who are centuries-old slaves. A
detective (Lawson) and a local historian (Bell) begin to investigate the murders. Finally Bey tricks Quarry and his girlfriend (Rees) into visiting Culley's ramshackle mansion.
Quarry is shown all his murdered gang members and in a panic
flees through the swamps, where he falls in quicksand. Colley
now takes Rees for himself, as he goes back into the world of
the dead.

SUPER STOOGES VS. THE WONDER WOMEN. 1974. 90 minutes. Color.
    Director: Al Bradley (Alfonso Brescia); *Screenplay:* Aldo
    Crudo and Alfonso Brescia. *Cinematography:* Fausto Rossi.
    Cast: Nick Jordon (Aro); Marc Hannibal (Togo); Yueh Hua
    (Chang); Malisa Longo (Pentesillea); Karen Yeh (May May
    Wong); Genie Woods (Akela); Riccardo Pizzuti (Philodos);
    Kirsten Gilles (High Priestess).

No, this film does not star Curly, Larry, and Moe, but
Aro, Togo, and Chang. This farce produced by the Shaw Brothers
of Hong Kong is a mixture of the Italian gladiator movie and
the Chinese sword films made popular by Run Run Shaw and company. This is like those films one sees ads for in *Variety*,
when they have those large issues during the Cannes Film Festival and MIFED. These films rarely come to one's neighborhood
theatre, but instead are displayed to the supposedly less dis-
criminating audiences in places like Bangkok.
    The plot line is very similar to that of *Battle of the
Amazons*. Long ago in a land far, far away lived a band of
wonder women, who terrorized the villagers of the nearby communities. The peasants are protected by the magical powers
of the old wise Dharma. When he is slain by a bandit leader
(Pizzuti), a younger and stronger man (Jordon) takes his place.
He is aided by two warriors, one from China (Hua) and the other
from Africa (Hannibal). Jordon's fertile imagination, and the
power passed on to him from the Dharma, enables him to invent
early prototypes of a catapult, parachute, and a Sherman tank.
Using these inventions, the three warriors are able to defeat
the wonder women.

THEY CALL HER ONE EYE. 1974. 89 minutes. Color. *Director:*
    Alex Fridolinski. *Screenplay:* Bo A. Vibenius. *Cinema-
    tography:* Andreas Bellis. *Cast:* Christina Lindberg
    (Frigga); Heinz Hopf (Tony); Despina Tomazani (Lesbian).

They Call Her One Eye is a sleazy blend of sex and sadism,
made in Sweden. AIP probably picked this film up for distribution because it was another of those female-revenge stories,
which had proved so successful with the black market.
    A young woman (Lindberg), who has been mute since a trau-
matic childhood rape, accepts a ride into the local town from
a handsome stranger (Hopf). She accepts his invitation to
come to his apartment, where he drugs her with a series of
heroin injections. Once Hopf has enslaved her, he uses Lindberg as a prostitute for his kinky clientele. When she attacks
her first client, Hopf blinds one of her eyes. He forges a

They Call Her One Eye

letter to her parents telling of her lifestyle, and in shame
they commit suicide. Now Lindberg plans her revenge against
Hopf and her customers by learning hand-to-hand combat and
how to use firearms. Using different colored eye patches to
coordinate with her clothes, Lindberg one by one slays the
customers who have degraded her. After she takes care of two
gunmen hired by Hopf to stop her, she challenges him to a duel.
She outwits Hopf and shoots him in the leg. Then, taking a
page from Asian torture practices, Lindberg buries Hopf up to
his neck and puts a rope around his head, which is attached
to a horse. When the horse goes to reach for a bucket of grain
it pulls Hopf's head off.

TRUCK STOP WOMEN. 1974. 88 minutes. Color. *Director:* Mark
    L. Lester. *Screenplay:* Mark L. Lester and Paul Deason;
    based on a story by Deason. *Cinematography:* John A.
    Morrill. *Cast:* Claudia Jennings (Rose); Lieux Dressler
    (Anna); Gene Drew (Mac); Dolores Dorn (Trish); Dennis
    Fimple (Curly); Jennifer Burton (Tina); Paul Carr (Seago);
    John Martino (Smith); Eric Nord (Sheriff); with Len
    Lesser, Speed Sterns, Jo Ann Atkinson.

Truck Stop Women is the quintessential exploitation film.
Sex, violence, and car chases combined with some good dialogue
and characterizations make this a very interesting film. One
critic even went so far as to call it "the most consistently
funny American comedy in a very long time" (Tony Rayns, *Monthly
Film Bulletin*, March 1975, p. 65).
    In New Mexico a truck stop owned by a woman (Dressler)
offers more than a cup of java and a sinker to the truckers.
She presides over girls who offer themselves to the drivers.
This prostitution racket is a ruse for what is an extensive
hijacking scheme orchestrated by Dressler and her two mechanics
(Drew and Fimple). An Eastern gang syndicate decides to muscle
in on Dressler's profits. One of the mobsters (Martino) even
seduces Dressler's daughter (Jennings) into working against
her mother. Martino arranges accidents so as to disrupt
Dressler's business, so she decides to play "hard ball" as
well. She has a showdown with Martino and his hoods by arrang-
ing a theft of a cattle truck, which contains stolen money.
After some lively action Martino's men take the truck, but
Dressler stops them on the road. In the climax, in a ghost
town, mother and daughter confront one another with guns.
    Truck Stop Women features one trend found in American
films of the mid-70s--the aggressive (both sexual and otherwise), take-charge woman. This is not only a great drive-in

movie but a must for any repertory theatre that wants to screen
a fine example of the 70s road movie.

TRUCK TURNER. 1974. 91 minutes. Color. *Director:* Jonathan
Kaplan. *Screenplay:* Oscar Williams, Leigh Chapman, and
Michael Allin; based on a story by Jerry Wilkes. *Cine-
matography:* Charles F. Wheeler. *Cast:* Isaac Hayes (Matt
"Truck" Turner); Yaphet Kotto (Harvard Blue); Alan Weeks
(Jerry); Annazette Chase (Annie); Nichelle Nichols
(Dorinda); Sam Laws (Nate); Paul Harris (Gator); Scatman
Crothers (Duke); Dick Miller (Fogarty); Don Megowan
(Garrity); Henry Kingi (Candy Man); Rhavan Briggs
(Felice); Earl Maynard (Panama); Stan Shaw (Fontana); Mel
Novak (Doctor); John Dennis (Desmond's Guard); John Evans
(Police Lieutenant); Clarence Lockett (Preacher); Johnny
Ray McGhee (Hired Killer); Stymie Beard (Jail Guard);
Annik Borel (Stalingrad); Randy Gray (Kid in Hospital);
Donnie Williams (Highway Dept. Man); Sharon Madigan
(Nurse); Bob Harris (Snow); Charles Cyphers (Drunk); John
Kramer (Desmond); Cheryl Sampson (Taffy); Edna Richardson
(Frenchie); Bernadette Gladden (Raquel); Tara Strohmeier
(Turnpike); Lisa Farringer (Annette); Ruth Warshawski
(Saleslady); Richard Blackwell (Wins); Douglas Anderson
(Charlie); Jon Jacobs (Dave); Jim Millhollin (Judge Advo-
cate); Larry Gabriel (Travis); Esther Sutherland (Black
Mamma); Eddie Smith (Druggist); Don Watters (Val);
Clarence Barnes (Toro); Wendell Tucker (Wendell); Jac
Emeil (Reno).

After composing the music for some of the blaxploitation
shoot-em-ups, Isaac Hayes was picked to portray another in a
string of black macho superheroes. These films were made to
display plenty of action and bloodletting, and in that context
Truck Turner is something of a success.
   Hayes and his partner (Weeks) act as skip tracers, who
go out and capture bail jumpers. A disreputable white lawyer
(Miller) hires them to pick up a criminal known as Gator
(Harris). Hayes and Weeks corner Harris and kill him. When
Harris's brothel-owner girlfriend (Nichols) finds out about
the murder, she offers a group of criminals her girls if they
kill Hayes and Weeks. After a number of unsuccessful attempts
on their lives a big-time mobster (Kotto) moves in to finish
the job. After Weeks is ambushed and killed, Hayes goes on
a personal rampage to Nichols's establishment. Afterwards he
has a gun battle with Kotto, in, of all places, a hospital
ward. Emerging victorious, Hayes now tries to bring some nor-
malcy back to his life.

WAR GODDESS. 1974. 89 minutes. Color. *Director:* Terence
Young. *Screenplay:* Dino Maiuri, Massimo De Rita, and
Serge De La Roche; based on a story by Richard Aubrey
and Richard Graves. *Cinematography:* Aldo Tonti. *Cast:*
Alena Johnston (Antiope); Sabine Sun (Oreitheia); Rosanna
Yanni (Penthesilea); Helga Line (High Priestess); Godela
H. Meyer (Molpadia); Rebecca Potok (Melanippe); Malisa
Longo (Leuthera); Lucy Tiller (Alana); Almut Berg
(Cynara); Virginia Rhodes (Aste); Veronique Floret
(Marpessa); Anna Petocchi (Melia); Ulrike Pesch (Lauris);
Luciana Paluzzi (Phaedra); Angelo Infanti (Theseus);
Fausto Tozzi (General); Angel Del Pozzo (Captain); Franco
Borelli (Perithous); Benito Stefanelli (Commander).

Yet another film about Amazons, but this one contains
more bare breasts and women loving women than some of the others. The director, Terence Young, who is known more for some
of the James Bond films he has directed, here actually has
his name above the title in some advertisements. You would
think he would try to keep it quiet, since this is the typical
AIP film, one "that encourages any spectator to feel more intelligent than what he's watching and laugh at the sheer sil-
liness of it all" (Jonathan Rosenbaum, *Monthly Film Bulletin*,
December 1974, pp. 275-76).
The queen of the Amazons (Johnston) decides, against her
warlike half-sister's (Sun) objections, to seek a rapprochement
with Greek soldiers, so they may use them for breeding purposes. The Greek king (Infanti) is attracted to Johnston and
forces himself upon her. Afterward Johnston and her female
warriors are set upon by the Scythians and are rescued by
Infanti and his army. Sun is plotting against Johnston because
she is pregnant with Infanti's child. She gives birth to a
boy, but Amazon law requires that only females be allowed to
survive, so the child is taken away from her. When Sun attempts to kill Johnston in her sleep, a tussle ensues that
evolves into a love-making session between the two women. Now
that they are united in sisterhood, they march on with the
rest of the Amazons to the yearly mating ritual with the
Greeks.

BUCKTOWN. 1975. 94 minutes. Color. *Director:* Arthur Marks.
Screenplay: Bob Ellison and Arthur Marks. *Cinematography:*
Robert Birchall. *Cast:* Fred Williamson (Duke Johnson);
Pam Grier (Aretha); Thalmus Rasulala (Roy); Tony King
(T.J.); Bernie Hamilton (Harley); Art Lund (Chief Patter-
son); Tierre Turner (Steve); Morgan Upton (Sam); Carl

Weathers (Hambone); Jim Bohan (Clete); Robert Burton
(Merle); Gene Simms (Josh); Bruce Watson (Bagman).

Bucktown is a socially reactionary blaxploitation film,
which would never be in the running for a brotherhood award.
Fred Williamson has claimed that he is not interested in socially uplifting films, and *Bucktown* is a prime example of
his philosophy. Since the film deals with the cleaning up of
a vice-ridden Southern town, it tackles the same subject area
as *The Phenix City Story*, but it never achieves that film's
surge of robust vigilante emotion.

A tough ghetto dude (Williamson) comes to the crime-filled
Southern town of Buchanan (known as "Bucktown") to bury his
murdered bar-owner brother. Buchanan is an almost-all-black
town controlled by a corrupt, white five-man police force.
Williamson takes over the ownership of his brother's saloon
and takes up with his brother's girlfriend (Grier). Determined
to clean up the town's corruption, he summons the help of some
of his tough big-city friends. With their aid Williamson is
able to get rid of the police force, but the town's crime profits are now taken over by Williamson's friend (Rasulala) and
his companions. Williamson, realizing the truth of the old
adage, "The more things change, the more they stay the same,"
commandeers a tank from a nearby military base in an effort to
rest control from Rasulala and his hoods. All of Rasulala's
men are killed, as Williamson challenges him to a fist fight,
with the loser leaving town. Naturally, Williamson is victorious after a bloody bout.

COOLEY HIGH. 1975. 107 minutes. Color. *Director:* Michael
    Schultz. *Screenplay:* Eric Monte. *Cinematography:* Paul
    vom Brack. *Cast:* Glynn Turman (Robert "Preach" Morris);
    Lawrence-Hilton Jacobs (Larry "Cochise" Jackson); Garrett
    Morris (Mr. Mason); Cynthis Davis (Brenda); Corin Rogers
    (Pooter); Maurice Leon Havis (Willie); Joseph Carter
    Wilson (Tyrone); Sherman Smith (Stone); Norman Gibson
    (Robert); Maurice Marshall (Damon); Steven Williams
    (Jimmy Lee); Jackie Taylor (Johnny Mae); Christine Jones
    (Sandra); Lynn Caridine (Dorothy); Mary Larkins (Preach's
    Mother); Cherene Snow (Tooty); Alicia Williams (Dee);
    Lily Schine (Cochise's Mother); Mukai Richardson (Bev-
    erly); Juanita McConnell (Martha); Sharon Murff (Loretta);
    Jimmy Whig (Trick); Nathaniel Reed and Frank Beetson (De-
    tectives); Marlene Howton (Girl in Toilet); Colostine
    Boatwright and Keita L. Keita (Prostitutes); James
    Kingsley and James George (Police at Pier); Mary Jane

Schaefer (School Teacher); Brandon Schultz (Tommy).

When *Cooley High* first came out, it was called by some a black *American Graffiti*. The only similarity, it seems to me, is that both films deal with teenagers. Where *American Graffiti* dealt with the ennui of small-town white-bread WASPS, *Cooley High* concentrates on the big-city vitality of young ghetto blacks, who for the most part live for the moment. Written by Eric Monte (who also created the television show *Good Times*), and directed by black filmmaker Michael Schultz, *Cooley High* seems to be partly autobiographical in its depiction of a black Chicago high school circa 1964. Ironically, the real Cooley Vocational High School is only a stone's throw away from Chicago's fashionable Gold Coast.

The story revolves around three high school students (Turman, Jacobs, and Rogers). Where Turman has just received a scholarship and eventually wants to be a Hollywood writer, most of his friends concern themselves with having a good time. The group is shown cutting school, joy-riding, fighting, drinking wine, and "makin' out." Turman and Jacobs are picked up for car theft just before a big exam. A sympathetic teacher (Morris) convinces the police to let them go. Two others (Smith and Gibson) who were arrested think that Jacobs informed on them. When they are set free, they find him and beat him to death. Turman reads a poem over his grave and decides to leave Chicago.

CORNBREAD, EARL AND ME. 1975. 94 minutes. Color. *Director:* Joe Manduke. *Screenplay:* Leonard Lamensdorf; based on the novel *Hog Butcher*, by Ronald Fair. *Cinematography:* Jules Brenner. *Cast:* Moses Gunn (Benjamin Blackwell); Rosalind Cash (Sarah Robinson); Bernie Casey (Atkins); Larry Fishburne III (Wilford); Madge Sinclair (Leona Hamilton); Keith Wilkes (Nathaniel "Cornbread" Hamilton); Tierre Turner (Earl Carter); Antonio Fargas ("One Eye"); Vincent Martorano (Golich); Charles Lampkin (Fred Jenkins); Stack Pierce (Sam Hamilton); Logan Ramsey (Deputy Coroner); Thalmus Rasulala (Charlie); Bill Henderson (Watkins); Sarina C. Grant (Mrs. Parsons); Stefan Gierasch (Sergeant Danaher).

AIP released this atypical film for the predominately black market. The type of maudlin sentimentality conveyed in *Cornbread, Earl and Me* is more in keeping with those softheaded made-for-television films. What this film has in its favor is a fairly accurate picture of life in a black ghetto.

A young high school basketball star (Wilkes) plans to
leave the ghetto by receiving an athletic scholarship to college. He has been able to keep "clean" while living in a rough
neighborhood and is idolized by two younger boys (Fishburne
and Turner). Wilkes leaves a soda shop one rainy night with
a bottle of pop in one hand and his basketball in the other.
While he is walking home, two cops (Casey and Martorano) who
are chasing a sexual psychopath mistake Wilkes for the suspect.
They see the pop bottle in his hand, and think it is a gun and
shoot him dead. His parents (Pierce and Sinclair) hire a lawyer (Gunn) to sue the city. Now the common coverup ensues,
as the police realize that witnesses can be intimidated.

FRIDAY FOSTER. 1975. 90 minutes. Color. *Director:* Arthur
    Marks. *Screenplay:* Orville Hampton. *Cinematography:*
    Harry May. *Cast:* Pam Grier (Friday Foster); Yaphet Kotto
    (Colt Hawkins); Godfrey Cambridge (Ford Malotte); Thalmus
    Rasulala (Blake Tarr); Eartha Kitt (Madame Rena); Ted
    Lange (Fancy Dexter); Jim Backus (Enos Griffith); Scatman
    Crothers (Reverend Noble Franklin); Tierre Turner (Cleve);
    Paul Benjamin (Senator David Lee Hart); Jason Bernard
    (Charles Foley); Edmund Cambridge (Lieutenant Jake Wayne);
    Julius Harris (Monk Riley); Rosalind Miles (Cloris
    Boston); Carl Weathers (Yarbro); Tony Brubaker (Chet
    Freed); Stan Stratton (Shawn North); John Anthony Bailey
    (1st Cop); James Cousar (2nd Chauffeur); William Gill
    (Minister); Almeria Quinn (Dresser); Alice Jubert (Sena-
    tor Hart's Secretary); William Sims (1st Chauffeur); Candy
    All (Prostitute); Samuel Daris (Dooley); Frenchia Guizon
    (2nd Cop); Bebe Drake Hooks (Neighbor); Harold Jones
    (Buzzy); Charles Stroud (Drunk); Mel Carter (Gate Guard).

Friday Foster is somewhat of a black version of *The Parallax View*--an intricately plotted political conspiracy thrill-
er. Instead of portraying a revengeful woman, Pam Grier here
plays an innocent bystander who becomes involved in circumstances beyond her control.
    A model-turned-photographer (Grier) is covering the ar-
rival of a black multimillionaire (Rasulala) when she witnesses
an assassination attempt on his life. The next day at a fashion show Grier sees one of the men (Weathers) involved in the
unsuccessful assassination. Soon a fashion-model friend of
Grier's (Miles) is murdered, and the police tell her that Miles
was involved with various Washington politicos. With the help
of a private detective (Kotto) Grier goes to Washington to
investigate the connection between Miles's death and the

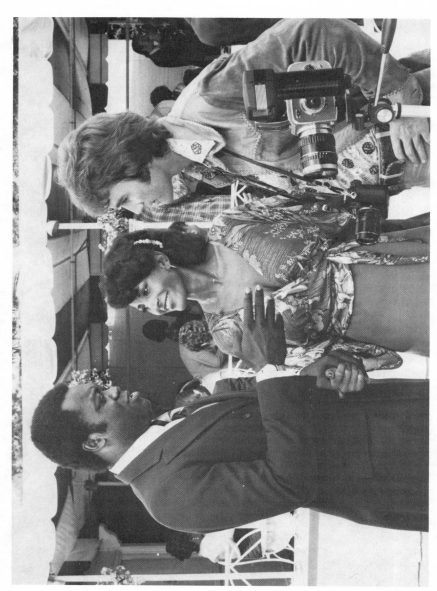

Friday Foster

previous assassination attempt. She meets Rasulala in Washington and learns that he is trying to find out about the code phrase "Black Widow," which Miles whispered to Grier just before she died. Grier learns that a political group headed by Rasulala, a Senator (Benjamin), and a clergyman (Crothers) is going to be attacked by a white supremicist (Backus), who is behind operation "Black Widow." She and Kotto go to Benjamin's country home, where the attack is to take place, and thwart the conspirators' plans.

HENNESSY. 1975. 103 minutes. Color. *Director:* Don Sharp. *Screenplay:* John Gay; based on a story by Richard Johnson. *Cinematography:* Ernest Steward. *Cast:* Rod Steiger (Niall Hennessy); Lee Remick (Kate Brook); Richard Johnson (Inspector Hollis); Trevor Howard (Commander Rice); Peter Egan (Williams); Eric Porter (IRA Leader Tobin); Ian Hogg (Gerry); Stanley Lebor (Hawk); John Hallam (Boyle); Patrick Stewart (Tilney); David Collings (Covey); John Shrapnel (Tipaldi); Hugh Moxey (Burgess, the MP); Peter Copley (Home Secretary); Isolde Cazelet (Mrs. Hanagan); Diana Fairfax (Maureen Hennessy); Patsy Kensitt (Angie Hennessy); Margery Mason (Housekeeper); Elizabeth Romilly (Shop Assistant); Alan Barry (Sergeant Duggan); Paul Brennan (Maguire); Oliver Maguire (Mick); Graham Ashley (Police Commissioner); Charles Kay (Parliamentary Guide); Christopher Blake (Young Soldier); Paul Blake (Rally Leader); Paul Gregory (Lieutenant).

Hennessy is similar to *The Day of the Jackal*, in that we already know that the assassination attempt will be foiled at the last minute, so that some of the suspense is averted. Apparently the subject matter of this film, as well as the inclusion of stock footage of Queen Elizabeth, upset EMI, AIP's British distributor, so an explanatory prologue was added.

In Belfast in 1972 a former IRA explosives expert (Steiger), who is now leading a quiet family life, sees British soldiers accidentally shoot and kill his wife (Fairfax) and daughter (Kensitt) during a street battle with Catholic youths. The emotionally distraught Steiger decides to pose as a Member of Parliament and blow up the Parliament building when Queen Elizabeth presides over the state opening of the Houses of Parliament. The IRA members fear that Steiger's suicidal act will cast blame on them, so they decide to have him shot before he can complete his plan. On the other side is a Special Branch officer (Johnson) sent to London to stop Steiger. Steiger hides out at the home of a friend from his old IRA

days (Remick). On the day of the bombing he disguises himself
and straps explosives to his body. Johnson locates him in
Parliament just before the Queen is to speak. He takes Steige
outside, but he breaks free. Johnson then shoots him, and
the explosives go off.

KILLER FORCE. 1975. 100 minutes. Color. *Director:* Val
  Guest. *Screenplay:* Michael Winder, Val Guest, and Gerald
  Sanford. *Cinematography:* David Millin. *Cast:* Telly
  Savalas (Harry Webb); Peter Fonda (Mike Bradley); O.J.
  Simpson ("Bopper" Alexander); Maud Adams (Clare Chambers)
  Hugh O'Brian (Lewis); Christopher Lee (Chilton); Ian Yule
  (Legrand Woods); Michael Mayer (Adams); Victor Melleney
  Sr. (Ian Nelson); Richard Loring (Roberts); Stuart Brown
  (George Chambers); Marina Christelis (Danielle); Dale
  Cutts (Plotter); Don McCorkindale (Radio Operator); Frank
  Douglas (Barman); Frank Shelley (Keller); Peter Van
  Dissell (Rick); Ian Hamilton (Doctor); Erica Rogers (Lady
  Doctor); Kevin Basel (Guardhouse Sergeant); David Anderso
  (2nd Gate Guard); Anthony Fridjhon (Pilot-SM4); Clive
  Scott (Pilot-Webb); Giles Ridley (Young Security Guard);
  Cocky Thlothlalemaje (Franklyn); Marigold Russell (Sales-
  girl).

    Made in South Africa, *Killer Force* would be totally dis-
missible if it were not for the note of moral ambiguity in
the characters portrayed by Peter Fonda and Telly Savalas.
Savalas, who is on the side of the law, has a villainous demeanor, while Fonda makes a sympathetic aging hippie thief.
    In a South African diamond mine the head of security
(Savalas) is ordered to investigate the disappearance of some
diamonds. Another member of the security force (Fonda) is the
leader of a group of mercenaries who are planning a large
theft. He organizes the heist by leading the group into the
security compound, using his knowledge of the alarm system to
escape detection. After they have stolen a good many diamonds
they have a shootout with the security guards. Fonda picks
up his girlfriend (Adams), who is the daughter of a company
executive, and takes his two remaining cohorts (Simpson and
O'Brian) into the desert. Both men are killed, as Fonda and
Adams make their way to an unused helicopter and escape with
the loot. The ending has Savalas vowing to capture them.

THE LAND THAT TIME FORGOT. 1975. 91 minutes. Color. *Director:* Kevin Connor. *Screenplay:* James Cawthorne and Michael Moorcock; based on the novel by Edgar Rice Burroughs. *Cinematography:* Alan Hume. *Cast:* Doug McClure (Bowen Tyler); John McEnery (Captain von Schoenvorts); Susan Penhaligon (Lisa Clayton); Keith Barron (Bradley); Anthony Ainley (Dietz); Godfrey James (Borg); Bobby Farr (Ahm); Declan Mulholland (Olson); Colin Farrell (Whiteley); Ben Howard (Benson); Roy Holder (Pleaser); Andrew McCulloch (Sinclair); Ron Pember (Jones); Grahame Mallard (Deusett); Andrew Lodge (Reuther); Brian Hall (Schwartz); Stanley McGeagh (Hiller); Peter Sproule (Hindle); Steve James (1st Sto-Lu).

The Land That Time Forgot is sort of a throwback to those films from the 50s and early 60s that dealt with a group of people stumbling across a prehistoric world. Many of these were made for kiddie matinees, since it usually took an eight-year-old's vivid imagination and lack of discrimination to make these films palatable. While the special effects here render some fine color sequences, the spastic movements of the prehistoric beasts remain risible.

During World War I a British transport ship is sunk by a German submarine, and some of the survivors are taken aboard. The sub loses its way and lands in a remote bay in Antarctica, in the legendary land of Caprona. Caprona is a prehistoric world that has been left with a moderate climate, thanks to the heat from nearby volcanoes. Inhabiting this land are prehistoric monsters, strange plants, and an early form of prehistoric man known as the Sto-Lu. The group, which consists of McClure, McEnery, Penhaligon, et al., come across an ape man (Farr), as well as large deposits of oil. The group set up a camp, as the Germans begin oil drilling. Penhaligon is captured by the Sto-Lu but is rescued by McClure. When a volcano erupts, the two of them take the opportunity to escape from the Germans. The submarine is destroyed by lava, so McClure and Penhaligon continue their journey northward on foot.

LIVE A LITTLE, STEAL A LOT. 1975. 101 minutes. Color. *Director:* Marvin Chomsky. *Screenplay:* E. Arthur Kean; based on a story by Allan Dale Kuhn. *Cinematography:* Michael

Hugo. *Cast:* Robert Conrad (Allan); Don Stroud (Jack
Murphy); Donna Mills (Ginny Eaton); Robyn Millan (Sharon
Kagel); Luther Adler (Max "The Eye"); Paul Stewart
(Avery); Morgan Paull (Arnie Holcomb); Ben Frank (Hopper
McGee); Burt Young (Sgt. Bernasconi); Pepper Martin (Sgt.
Terwilliger); Don Matheson (Hauser); Lindsay Crosby (S.A.
Thomas); Mimi Saffian (Sally); Nancy Conrad (Edna); Buffy
Dee (Bucks); Jess Barker and Al Bordighi (Museum Guards);
with Lloyd McLinn, Mel Stevens, Harvey Levine, Harriet
Haindl, Kip King, Caruth C. Byrd, Joe Mell, Oak R. Gentry
Herb Vigran.

This film documents the robbery of the Star of India sap-
phire and other gems from the American Museum of National History in October 1964. One of the two robbers, Allan Kuhn,
acted as a technical adviser on the film and wrote the origina
story. *Live a Little, Steal a Lot* contains one of those priv-
ileged moments one finds in an otherwise ordinary film. In
an article on "B" films Wallace Markfield mentions a scene in
which Don Stroud totally ignores a woman's substantial cleavag
in order to devour an onion role ("Remembrance of 'B' Movies
Past," *The New York Times Film Reviews*, 1975-76. New York,
Arno, 1977, p. 69).

The film begins with the two thieves (Conrad and Stroud)
stealing the gems and then proceeds in flashback to show how
these two dissimilar personalities met. The cool, calm, and
fastidious Conrad and the brutish and boisterous Stroud set
out on a series of robberies in Miami mansions and a Bahaman
hotel. Along with their girlfriends (Millan and Mills) they
move to Manhattan. After they have stolen the jewels, the
police quickly learn their identities, and their "fence" refuses to handle the merchandise for them. They go back to
Miami, where the money from the previous robberies is quickly
used up. Backed into a corner, Conrad finally convinces Strou
to accept a plea-bargaining agreement with the authorities,
as long as they give up the jewelry.

THE MCCULLOCHS. 1975. 93 minutes. Color. *Director:* Max
Baer. *Screenplay:* Max Baer. *Cinematography:* Fred
Koenekamp. *Cast:* Forrest Tucker (J.J. McCulloch); Max
Baer (Culver Robinson); Julie Adams (Hannah McCulloch);
Janice Heiden (Ali McCulloch); Dennis Redfield (Steven
McCulloch); Don Grady (R.J. McCulloch); William Demarest
(Father Gurkin); Harold J. Stone (George Garner); Vito
Scotti (Tony Stathos); Sandy Kevin (Rad Jackson); Chip
Hand (Gary McCulloch); Lillian Randolph (Missy); Doodles

Weaver (Pop Holson); James Gammon (Detective No. 1);
Candice Smith (Marsha Kearney); Mike Mazurki (Cliff
Randall).

The McCullochs is reminiscent of those western family
melodramas of the 50s, in which a hard-nosed family patriarch
alienated almost everybody. One notices a similarity between
the father in this film and the one in *Macon County Line*. Both
films were written by Max Baer and display a slightly jaundiced
view of the so-called "man's man."
  The time and place is the Midwest in the early 50s.
Forrest Tucker has become the successful head of a trucking
company by being meaner and smarter than anyone else. He
prides himself on being the toughest man in town and runs his
family accordingly. His sons find it increasingly difficult
to measure up to their father's expectations. One of his more
sensitive sons (Redfield) kills a man in a drunken rage.
Tucker's favorite son (Grady), the football hero, dies in Ko-
rea. The other one (Hand) becomes fed up with Tucker's bully-
ing and leaves home. An employee (Baer) of Tucker's wants to
marry his daughter (Heiden), but Tucker feels he is not good
enough for her. The entire town knows that the only way Baer
will gain approval from Tucker is to best him in a fight. They
start a brawl in a bar, which ends out in the street. Baer
is winning, but concedes to Tucker. Now that he has a newfound
respect for Baer, Tucker allows him in as a member of the family.

OLD DRACULA. 1975. 89 minutes. Color. *Director:* Clive
  Donner. *Screenplay:* Jeremy Lloyd. *Cinematography:* Tony
  Richmond. *Cast:* David Niven (Count Dracula); Teresa
  Graves (Countess Vampira); Peter Bayliss (Maltravers);
  Jennie Linden (Angela); Nicky Henson (Marc); Linda Hayden
  (Helga); Bernard Bresslaw (Pottinger); Cathie Shirriff
  (Nancy); Andrea Allan (Eve); Veronica Carlson (Ritva);
  Minah Bird (Rose); Christopher Sandford (Milton); Freddie
  Jones (Gilmore); Frank Thornton (Mr. King); Aimi MacDonald
  and Patrick Newell (Couple in Hotel Room); Kenneth Cranham
  (Paddy the Delinquent); Carol Cleveland (Jane, His Vic-
  tim); Luan Peters (Pottinger's Secretary); Marcia Fox
  (Air Hostess); David Rowlands (Drunk); Ben Aris (Police-
  man); Nadim Sawacha (Airline Representative); Holma
  MacDonald, Nicola Austine, and Penny Irving (Playboy Bun-
  nies).

Old Dracula is a pathetic camp version of Dracula, using
the atmosphere of swinging London and Playboy bunnies to give
it a contemporary feeling. This film even goes so far as to
leave in the viewer's mind that there is something wrong about
being black.

David Niven portrays Dracula as an urbane aristocrat who
rents out his British castle as a hotel for tourists. A group
of Playboy bunnies come there for a photographic session, and
Niven and his servant (Bayliss) check to see if any of them
have the same blood type as Niven's dead wife (Graves). In
order to bring her back to life they take blood samples from
the girls, but the samples are accidentally mixed up. The
new blood turns Graves from a Caucasian to a black. Niven
becomes upset with this turn of events and seeks out new blood
to correct the error. He exerts mind control over a writer
(Henson) who is friends with the bunnies. Niven takes blood
samples from the girls once again, and their chaperone (Linden
becomes suspicious. He takes her prisoner in his castle, but
Henson rescues her. During the operation on Graves, Niven is
bitten by her and he turns black as well. The two of them
and Bayliss quickly leave the country before Henson can convince the police of his story.

PART 2, WALKING TALL. 1975. 109 minutes. Color. *Director:*
Earl Bellamy. *Screenplay:* Howard B. Kreitsek. *Cinema-
tography:* Keith Smith. *Cast:* Bo Svenson (Buford Pusser);
Luke Askew (Pinky Dobson); Noah Beery (Carl Pusser); John
Chandler (Ray Henry); Robert DoQui (Obra Eaker); Bruce
Glover (Grady Coker); Richard Jaeckel (Stud Pardee);
Brooke Mills (Ruby Ann); Logan Ramsey (John Witter); Ange
Tompkins (Marganne Stilson); Lurene Tuttle (Grandma
Pusser); Leif Garrett (Mike Pusser); Dawn Lyn (Dawna
Pusser); William Bryant and Lloyd Tatum (FBI Men); Levi
Frazier, Jr. (Runaway Moonshiner); Red West (Sheriff
Tanner); Jon R. Wilson (Lumber-Truck Driver); Ken Zimmer-
man (Water-Truck Driver); Archie Grinalds (AC Hand); Alle
Mullikin (Floyd Tate); Libby Boone (Joan Lashley); Jimmy
Moore (Miles); Frank McRae (Steamer Riley); Gary M.
Darling (Rudy).

Buford Pusser, the sheriff of McNairy County, Tennessee,
gained national attention when CBS News did a story about his
one-man effort to rid his county of crime, which led to the
successful film *Walking Tall*. This sequel is not really as
violent as the original and was to have featured the actual
Buford Pusser before he died on August 20, 1974.

Pusser (Svenson), after recovering from injuries suffered
in an assassination attempt, is welcomed back by county authorities. A local crime lord (Ramsey) orders two men (Askew and
Chandler) to murder Svenson before he can be reelected.
Svenson survives various attempts on his life, one of which
takes the life of his black assistant (DoQui). He engages in
a motorboat chase to catch Askew, who crashes and ends up in
the hospital. He escapes from there, but Svenson catches him
and gets him to tell where Chandler is hiding. In a shootout
he kills Chandler but is wounded in the process.

If this film, and its predecessor, are at all reasonably
accurate, it seems that Pusser spent much of his time going
after the "small fry," instead of those who really wielded
local power. If Pusser is not quite the hero the media made
him out to be, perhaps we should remember one of the lessons
from *The Man Who Shot Liberty Valance*--in time the legend sometimes becomes more important than the man.

THE REINCARNATION OF PETER PROUD. 1975. 104 minutes. Color.
  Director: J. Lee Thompson. *Screenplay:* Max Ehrlich. *Cin-
  ematography:* Victor J. Kemper. *Cast:* Michael Sarrazin
  (Peter Proud); Jennifer O'Neill (Ann Curtis); Margot
  Kidder (Marcia Curtis); Cornelia Sharpe (Nora Hayes);
  Paul Hecht (Dr. Samuel Goodman); Tony Stephano (Jeff
  Curtis); Normann Burton (Dr. Frederick Spear); Anne Ivers
  (Ellen Curtis); Debralee Scott (Suzy); Jon Richards (News-
  paper Custodian); Steve Franken (Dr. Charles Crennis);
  Fred Stuthman (Pop Johnson); Lester Fletcher (Car Sales-
  man); Paul Nevens (Room Clerk); Breanna Benjamin (Miss
  Hagerson); Addison Powell (Reeves); Phillip Clark (Number
  Five); Gene Boland (Charlie); Albert Henderson (Police
  Sergeant); Connie Garrison (Ellie); Sam Laws (Satan's
  Disciple); Mary Margaret Amato (Nurse); Terry Green (Col-
  lege Student); Jacqueline Manning (Lab Assistant); Henry
  Cosimini (Square Dance Caller); Douglas Rutherford (Club
  Steward); Marjorie Morely Eaton (Astrologer); Shelley
  St. Clair (Bookstore Clerk).

The Reincarnation of Peter Proud ventures upon subject
matter that is better left in the pages of the *National Enquirer*. Directed in a heavy-handed manner by J. Lee Thompson,
one of the film's saving graces is a good performance by Margot
Kidder, as a middle-aged, love-starved alcoholic.

A young California college professor (Sarrazin) has been
bothered by recurring dreams, especially one in which he is
being drowned by a woman. A parapsychologist (Hecht) informs

him that the dreams are some form of psychic disturbance. Sarrazin believes he is the reincarnation of the murdered man in his dream, so, using clues from his dreams, he deduces that the man lived in New England in the 1940s. He goes to New England to investigate and meets the woman murderer (Kidder), who was the man's wife, and her daughter (O'Neill). Sarrazin and O'Neill soon develop a sort of reincarnated incest, as they make plans to marry. He does not realize that Kidder sees him as a reborn version of the philandering husband she murdered in 1946. When he attempts to recreate the dream in order to drive it from his psyche, Kidder attacks and drowns him for his incestuous ways.

RETURN TO MACON COUNTY. 1975. 90 minutes. Color. *Director:* Richard Compton. *Screenplay:* Richard Compton. *Cinematography:* Jacques Marquette. *Cast:* Nick Nolte (Bo Hollinger); Don Johnson (Harley McKay); Robin Mattson (Junelle); Robert Viharo (Sergeant Whittaker); Eugene Daniels (Tom); Matt Greene (Pete); Devon Ericson (Betty); Ron Prather (Steve); Phillip Crews (Larry); Laura Sayer (Libby); Walt Guthrie (Big Man in the Coffee Shop); Mary Ann Hearn (Pat); Sam Kilman (Cook); Bill Moses (Sheriff Jackson); Pat O'Connor (Officer Harris); Kim Graham (Girl in Car); Don Higdon (Boy in Car); James M. George (Police Officer); Jeannie Detwiler (Hitchhiker).

This is not really a sequel to the successful *Macon County Line*, since most of the characters in that film had been killed off. What we have here is a mixture of *Easy Rider*, *American Graffiti*, and *Two-Lane Blacktop*, along with a soundtrack full of music from people like Fats Domino, Chuck Berry, and Eddie Cochran.

In 1958 two young hick hot rodders (Nolte and Johnson) are driving their customized Chevy to California for a big race. Along the way they pick up a very "spacey" gun-toting waitress (Mattson). Johnson enters their car in a local drag race and wins. The losers beat him up, but he is saved when Mattson comes brandishing a gun. Meanwhile Nolte gets into an altercation with a cop (Viharo). Now both the youths who lost the race and Viharo chase after the three. A casual sexual interlude between Nolte and Mattson puts a strain on Nolte's friendship with Johnson. Viharo has disobeyed orders and has pursued the three across state lines to an abandoned farm. One of the youths (Daniels) who is after them, appears and steals the Chevy, but Viharo mistakes him for Nolte, or Johnson, and shoots him dead. The deranged Viharo is taken

away by other law officers. Mattson decides to separate from
Nolte and Johnson, so the two, now without a car, make it on
foot to California.

SHEBA BABY. 1975. 90 minutes. Color. *Director:* William
    Girdler. *Screenplay:* William Girdler; based on a story
    by Girdler and David Sheldon. *Cinematography:* William
    Asman. *Cast:* Pam Grier (Sheba Shayne); Austin Stoker
    (Brick Williams); D'Urville Martin (Pilot); Rudy
    Challenger (Andy); Dick Merrifield (Shark); Christopher
    Joy (Walker); Charles Kissinger (Lieut. Phil Jackson);
    Charles Broaddus (Hammerhead); Maurice Downes (Killer);
    Ernest Cooley (Whale); Edward Reece, Jr. (Racker); William
    Foster, Jr. (Waldo); Bobby Cooley (Tank); Paul Grayber
    (Fin); Sylvia Jacobson (Tail); Leroy Clark, Jr. (Custom-
    er); Mike Clifford (2nd Policeman); Rose Ann Deel (Police-
    woman); Clayton Rose (Bum); Frank Sgroi (1st Hood); Bobby
    Evans (2nd Hood); Bobby Stewart (3rd Hood); James Durston
    (4th Hood); Melvin Jones (1st R.R. Man); Herman Thompson
    (2nd R.R. Man); Bill Wilson (3rd R.R. Man); Robert Drane
    (1st Officer); Mary Minor (1st Pilot's Girl); Henriette
    Brands (2nd Pilot's Girl); Joyce Jones (3rd Pilot's Girl);
    Bobby Davis (Hit Man); Walter Evans (2nd Customer);
    Charles Norton, Bill Embry, Dennis Williams, and Mike
    Abrams (Boat Guards); Phil Kelley and Lloyd Poore (Dock
    Guards); Mary Perries and Jackie Patterson (Shayne
    Clerks); Richard Taylor (Bartender); Joan Ray (Nurse);
    Toni Gorman, Tara Lang, and Jeanie Care (Party Girls).

    Like *Abby*, another AIP film directed by William Girdler,
Sheba Baby was filmed in the seldom-used location of Louisville, Kentucky. This is very much like the previous AIP films
starring Pam Grier, but fortunately for her this one fulfilled
her contract to AIP.
    A Chicago private detective (Grier) goes to Louisville
when she learns that local mobsters are attempting to muscle
in on her father's (Challenger) money-lending business. She
is almost killed by a bomb meant for her father. When
Challenger is shot and killed, Grier ignores warnings by a
local cop (Kissinger) and sets out to find her father's killers. She is aided in her search by her father's partner
(Stoker), with whom she has developed a relationship. Grier
learns that the head of the local mob is a successful businessman (Merrifield). She barges aboard his yacht but is recognized by one of his gang and is taken prisoner. Stoker comes
with the cops, and a gun battle ensues. Merrifield escapes

on a speedboat as Grier chases after him and kills him with a
spear gun. Despite Stoker's pleas, she returns to Chicago
but promises to visit often.

SIX PACK ANNIE. 1975. 88 minutes. Color. *Director:* Graydon
    F. David. *Screenplay:* Norman Winski, David Kidd, and
    Wil David. *Cinematography:* Daniel Lacambre. *Cast:*
    Lindsay Bloom ("Six Pack" Annie Bodine); Jana Bellan (Mary
    Lou); Joe Higgins (Sheriff Waters); Larry Mahan (Bustis);
    Stubby Kaye (Mr. Bates); Raymond Danton (Mr. O'Meyer);
    Richard Kennedy (Jack Whittlestone); Danna Hansen (Aunt
    Tess); Pedro Gonzales-Gonzales (Carmello); Bruce
    Boxleitner (Bobby Joe); Sid Melton (Angelo); Louisa Moritz
    (Flora); Vince Barnett (Bartender); Steve Randall (Long
    John); Doodles Weaver (Hank); Ronald Marriott (Luke);
    Donald Elson (Mr. Piker); Oscar Cartier (Louis Danton);
    Montana Smoyer (Edna Whittlestone); Ralph James (Ace);
    Terry Mace (John); Danny Michael Mann (Tony).

Six Pack Annie was premiered without any advertising
buildup or trade screenings. With its Daisy Mae-like cartoon
characterizations and dress styles from Frederick's of Hollywood, perhaps even AIP was embarrassed to give this film much
public exposure.
    Big and blond Annie Bodine (Bloom) is courted by just
about every male in rural Titwillow, Georgia. Bloom works in
a small diner owned by her aunt (Hansen), which is about to
be foreclosed by the local banker (Elson). Along with a friend
(Bellan), Bloom goes to Miami to receive money to stop the
foreclosure from her supposedly well-off sister (Moritz).
Moritz turns out to be a cheap prostitute living in a seedy
part of town, so Bloom decides to look for a "sugar daddy"
among all the wealthy men of Miami. She has various unsuccessful encounters, until she meets a rich Texan (Kennedy) in a
Cuban bar. He gives her a lucky stone on a necklace and
$6,000. When she takes the drunken Kennedy back to the hotel,
his wife (Smoyer) appears and takes Kennedy and the $6,000
away. The disheartened Bloom returns to Titwillow and the
diner. A traveling salesman (Kaye) enters the restaurant,
sees the stone around Bloom's neck, and offers her $7,000.
The diner is now saved from foreclosure.

THE WILD PARTY. 1975. 100 minutes. Color. *Director:* James
    Ivory. *Screenplay:* Walter Marks; based on the narrative

poem by James Moncure March. *Cinematography:* Walter
Lassally. *Cast:* James Coco (Jolly Grimm); Raquel Welch
(Queenie); Perry King (Dale Sword); Tiffany Bolling
(Kate); Royal Dano (Tex); David Dukes (James Morrison);
Dena Dietrich (Mrs. Murchison); Regis J. Cordic (Mr.
Murchison); Jennifer Lee (Madeline True); Marya Small
(Bertha); Bobo Lewis (Wilma); Annette Ferra (Nadine);
Eddie Laurence (Kreutzer); Tony Paxton (Sergeant); Waldo
K. Berns (Policeman); Nina Faso (Lady in Black); Baruch
Lumet (Tailor); Martin Kove (Editor); Ralph Manza (Fruit
Dealer); Lark Geib (Rosa); Fredric Franklyn (Sam); J.S.
Johnson (Morris); Michael Grant Hall (Oscar D'Armano);
Skipper (Phil D'Armano); Don De Natale (Jackie the Danc-
er); Tom Reese (Eddy); Geraldine Baron (Grace); Jill
Giraldi (Crippled Girl); Barbara Quinn (Mildren); Gloria
Gadhoke (Redhead); Clea Ariell, Susan Arnold, Joe
Arrowsmith, Jonathan Becker, Bob Buckingham, Jennifer
Chessman, Chuck Comisky, Bill Dance, Rick Dano, Kathleen
Dimmick, Mark David Jacobson, Rick Kanter, Kevin Matthews,
Luke Matthiessen, Gordon Maus, Bill Merickel, Tommie
Merickel, Anthony Pecorano, Jack Sachs, Carmen Saveiros,
Mark Swope, Ayesha Taft, and Whitney Tower (Party Guests).

The Wild Party was severely reedited by AIP in order to
give greater emphasis to the scandalous nature of its subject
matter. This look at Hollywood of the 1920s was filmed at the
historic Mission Inn in Riverside, California, and portrays
certain qualities of the movie industry that still exist: "the
shallowness of stardom, the venality (sexual and professional)
of heartless executives, the fragility of fame, the rarity of
friendship and loyalty" (John Pym, *Monthly Film Bulletin*, August 1982, p. 162).
A silent-film actor (Coco) throws a party at his mansion
to screen a film of his, which he hopes will lead to a comeback. He invites a number of guests, including the two studio
executives (Cordic and Laurence) whom he wishes to influence.
The film is shown to a very negative response, which causes
Coco desperately to suggest revisions in the film. Soon he
becomes drunk and insults his mistress (Welch), as she begins
to gain the attention of a young actor (King). The party rapidly degenerates, as guests begin leaving for another party.
The ones who stay have gone upstairs for some bedroom recreation. One of the guests (Bolling) tells Coco he is too old
for Welch, and when Welch and King are called downstairs from
the bedroom, Coco shoots both of them.

AT THE EARTH'S CORE. 1976. 90 minutes. Color. *Director:*
Kevin Connor. *Screenplay:* Milton Subotsky; based on the
novel by Edgar Rice Burroughs. *Cinematography:* Alan Hume.
Cast: Doug McClure (David Innes); Peter Cushing (Dr. Abner
Perry); Caroline Munro (Dia); Cy Grant (Ra); Godfrey James
(Ghak); Sean Lynch (Hoojah); Keith Barron (Dowsett); Helen
Gill (Maisie); Anthony Verner (Gadsby); Robert Gillespie
(Photographer); Michael Crane (Jubal); Bobby Parr (Sagoth
Chief); Andee Cromarty (Slave Girl); Laurie Davis (Riot
Rouser).

This sequel to *The Land That Time Forgot* includes the
usual stilted prehistoric creations and some unconvincing rear
projection. Some of the fanciful characters in the film sound
as if they came from a George Lucas film--Hooja, Ghak, Jubal,
et al.

In the 19th century two men, a scientist (Cushing) and
his financial backer (McClure), are testing a piece of excava-
tion equipment they have dubbed the "iron mole." The machine
goes out of control and burrows a hole through the earth.
Cushing and McClure enter the hole and end up in a prehistoric
land called Pellucidar. They are captured by some apelike
men and taken to a city controlled by female birdlike creatures. McClure becomes a slave to these beings which are
called Mahars. Meanwhile Cushing has found evidence that the
Mahars emerge from only one incubation chamber. McClure escapes from his enslavement and takes a beautiful young princess
(Munro) with him. He gains the trust of her people after he
has defended her from a dinosaur, and a primitive (Crane) who
wants her. McClure and one of Munro's people (Grant) lead an
attack on the Mahar incubation chamber. Grant is killed in
the effort, but the chamber as well as the Mahars are done
away with. McClure and Cushing board their mechanical con-
traption to return to the surface, while Munro stays behind
with her people.

BOBBIE JO AND THE OUTLAW. 1976. 89 minutes. Color. *Direc-
tor:* Mark W. Lester. *Screenplay:* Vernon Zimmerman. *Cin-
ematography:* Stanley Wright. *Cast:* Marjoe Gortner (Lyle
Wheeler); Lynda Carter (Bobbie Jo James); Jesse Vint
(Slick Callahan); Merrie Lynn Ross (Pearl James); Belinda
Balaski (Essie Beaumont); Gene Drew (Sheriff Hicks);
Peggie Stewart (Hattie James); Gerrit Graham (Magic Ray);
John Durren (Deputy Gance); Virgil Frye (Joe Grant); James
Gammon (Big Turner); Howard Kirk (Mr. Potts); Aly Yoder
(Mrs. Potts); Joe Kurtzo, Jr. (Flattop); Chuck Russell

(Deputy); Richard Breeding (Deputy Leroy); Jesse Price
(Buford the Grocer); Kip Allen (Hotel Manager); Jose
Toledo (Indian); Robert Fleming (Ten Gallon Hat).

It is appropriate that Marjoe Gortner, who conned people
as a child evangelist, should portray a character here in the
Charlie Manson mold. Despite the somewhat frivolous title of
Bobbie Jo and the Outlaw, this film revels in the exploits of
a gang on a crime spree.
A young quick-draw expert (Gortner) escapes from the police in New Mexico after stealing a car. He meets a waitress
(Carter), who tags along with him. An old Indian (Toledo)
administers a hallocinogenic mushroom to Gortner, which makes
him think he is Billy the Kid. Later on he and Carter pick
up her sister (Ross) and her punk boyfriend (Vint). Together
the group robs a store, and Gortner murders a man. A young
girl (Balaski) whom they had picked up informs the sheriff
(Drew) where the gang is hiding. The group survives a couple
of police ambushes and eventually meets up with sort of a cowboy flower-child cult leader (Graham). Finally, in Abilene,
Texas, the law corners the gang, and all are killed, except
Carter.

CRIME AND PASSION. 1976. 92 minutes. Color. *Director:* Ivan
    Passer. *Screenplay:* Jesse Lasky, Jr., and Pat Silver;
    based on the novel *An Ace Up Your Sleeve*, by James Hadley
    Chase. *Cinematography:* Denis C. Lewiston. *Cast:* Omar
    Sharif (Andre Ferrin); Karen Black (Susan); Joseph Bottoms
    (Larry); Bernhard Wicki (Herman Rolf); Heinz Ehrenfreund
    (Henkel); Elma Karlowa (Masseuse); Volker Prechtel (Inn-
    keeper); Erich Padalewski (Car Salesman); Robert Abrams
    (Mr. Blatt); Franz Muxeneder (Priest); Margarete Soper
    (Sylvia).

This is a strange mixture of international financial dou-
ble-dealings and slapstick, which AIP apparently tampered with
after they picked up the rights for domestic distribution.
Crime and Passion has the dubious distinction of probably being
the weakest film from Czech emigré director director Ivan
Passer.
A financial adviser (Sharif) finds himself in deep financial trouble. Every time that he feels anxious, Sharif must
immediately satisfy his sexual urges. After he has done so
with his chief aide (Black), she gives him an idea to gain
some new financial rewards. She will marry a wealthy German
(Wicki) and then divorce him for a large cash amount that she

and Sharif will share. Black marries Wicki, and Sharif does
not hear from her for almost a year. By this time he has been
called before an international financial commission to explain
his business dealings, especially in relation to Wicki's money.
In order to pay the misappropriated money, Sharif goes in
search of Black. He ends up finding her at a ski resort with
a young American skier (Bottoms). Black attempts to give
Sharif the cold shoulder and tells him she has not divorced
Wicki, because his previous wives have died mysteriously.
Sharif leaves Black after various attempts are made on his
life. In Wicki's absence Black and Bottoms now have the run
of his castle to themselves.

THE DEVIL WITHIN HER. 1976. 90 minutes. Color. *Director:*
Peter Sasdy. *Screenplay:* Stanley Price; based on a story
by Nato de Angeles. *Cinematography:* Kenneth Talbot.
Cast: Joan Collins (Lucy Carlesi); Eileen Atkins (Sister
Albana); Donald Pleasence (Dr. Finch); Ralph Bates (Gino
Carlesi); Caroline Munro (Mandy); Hilary Mason (Mrs.
Hyde); John Steiner (Tommy); Janet Key (Jill); George
Clayton (Hercules); Judy Buxton (Sheila); Derek Benfield
(Police Inspector); Stanley Lebor (Police Sergeant); John
Moore (Priest); Phyllis McMahon (Nun); Andrew Secombe
(Delivery Boy); Susan Richards (Old Lady); Floella
Benjamin and Penny Darch (Nurses); Lopez and Suzie
Lightning (Strippers); Janet Brett and Val Hoadley (Danc-
ers).

The Devil Within Her is a blatant composite of *The Exorcist*, *Rosemary's Baby*, and *It's Alive*; but in a way it is very
watchable trash. Though in almost all respects irredeemable,
the film is enjoyable for those who have an affection for midnight movies and Joan Collins. When you eliminate its imitative qualities, you are left with the marvelous description
by Vincent Canby: "The moral of the movie: don't mess around
with amorous dwarfs" (*The New York Times Film Reviews*, 1975-76.
New York: Arno, 1977, p. 234).
A former stripper (Collins) gives birth to a large and
unusually strong baby boy. She tells a former co-worker
(Munro) that she believes the baby is possessed by a curse
put on her by a dwarf (Clayton), who works at the strip club
and had been rejected by her. Soon after the baby's nurse
(Key) is found drowned. Collins's sister-in-law (Atkins),
who is a nun, comes to visit and also thinks that the baby is
possessed. Collins and her husband (Bates) plan to go away
on a trip, while the child goes through a series of medical

tests. Before they leave, Bates is killed one night in their
garden. A doctor (Pleasence) comes to aid the now-half-mad
Collins, and he is clubbed to death. Atkins decides to perform
an exorcism on the child, but just before she can Collins is
knifed to death. While Atkins prays over the baby, we see
Clayton slowly dying while performing his nightclub act. The
exorcism has been a success.

DRAGONFLY. 1976. 95 minutes. Color. *Director:* Gilbert
Cates. *Screenplay:* N. Richard Nash. *Cinematography:*
Gerald Hirschfeld. *Cast:* Beau Bridges (Jesse Arlington);
Susan Sarandon (Chloe); Mildred Dunnock (Mrs. Barrow);
Michael B. Miller (Gabriel Arlington); Linda Miller (Willa
Arlington); Martin Burke (Lonnie Arlington); James Otis
(Clifford); James Noble (Dr. Leo Cooper); Ann Wedgeworth
(Pearlie Craigle); Frederick Coffin (Walter Craigle);
Harriet Rogers (Mrs. Patterson).

This story of a released mental patient was an attempt
by AIP to change its image by producing an uplifting picture.
There is an in-joke in *Dragonfly*: Beau Bridges, after being
institutionalized for years, goes to see a film; it happens
to be AIP's *Dillinger*, and the violence in it makes Bridges
physically ill.
A young man (Bridges) has just been released from a mental
hospital, where he had been confined since the age of 13. Even
though he is fearful of the outside world, he ventures back
to the Connecticut town where he hopes to find his family,
who had abandoned him. In a movie theatre he meets a young
woman (Sarandon), who befriends him and takes him home with
her. His innocence appeals to her, and in a short time
Bridges, with newfound confidence, gets a job. While looking
for his family, he learns of the farm where his brother
(Miller) lives. A happy reunion turns acrimonious, as Miller
tells Bridges where their mother (Dunnock) lives. Bridges
finally confronts her (she is the truly disturbed one in the
family) and is able to sort out his tormented past (if only
things were that easy). He now looks to a happy future with
Sarandon.

THE FOOD OF THE GODS. 1976. 89 minutes. Color. *Director:*
Bert I. Gordon. *Screenplay:* Bert I. Gordon; based on a
portion of the novel by H.G. Wells. *Cinematography:*
Reginald Morris. *Cast:* Marjoe Gortner (Morgan); Pamela

Franklin (Lorna Scott); Ralph Meeker (Jack Bensington);
Ida Lupino (Mrs. Skinner); Jon Cypher (Brian Oster);
Belinda Balaski (Rita); Tom Stovall (Thomas); John McLiam
(Mr. Skinner); Chuck Courtney (Davis); Reg Tunnicliffe
(Ferry Attendant).

Bert I. Gordon had been making films about giant mutations
20 years before *The Food of the Gods.* I suppose that he continued to make these films until he finally got it right. Except for some remarks that display an awareness of environmental pollution, this picture is similar to other Gordon films.
One wonders how he convinced such capable people as Ida Lupino
and Ralph Meeker to appear in such a project.

Two football players (Gortner and Courtney) are vacationing on an island in the Pacific Northwest, where Courtney is
stung to death by giant wasps. After Gortner has repelled an
attack from a giant chicken, he meets a middle-aged couple
(Lupino and McLiam) who live on the island. The couple keep
in jars, labeled FOTG, a mushy white substance that emanates
from the ground, which Lupino thinks comes from the gods. Animals that eat this substance grow to an enormous size. A
greedy businessman (Meeker) comes to the island with his assistant (Franklin) to buy FOTG for industrial purposes. Another couple (Balaski and Stovall) appear, and soon all the
inhabitants are being menaced by giant rats, chickens, wasps,
etc. The group is killed off one by one, until only Gortner,
Franklin, Balaski, and Stovall are left. The two men dynamite
a dam, which drowns the rats that are attacking them, and the
four leave the island. Two jars of the FOTG are left; they
eventually are given in the form of milk, to some schoolchil-
dren.

FUTUREWORLD. 1976. 107 minutes. Color. *Director:* Richard T.
Heffron. *Screenplay:* Mayo Simon and George Schenck. *Cin-
ematography:* Howard Schwartz. *Cast:* Peter Fonda (Chuck
Browning); Blythe Danner (Tracy Ballard); Arthur Hill
(Duffy); Yul Brynner (Gunslinger); John Ryan (Schneider);
Stuart Margolin (Harry); Jim Antonio (Ron); Allen Ludden
(Game Show Host); Robert Cornthwaite (Mr. Reed); Angela
Greene (Mrs. Reed); Darrell Larson (Eric); Nancy Bell
(Erica); John Fujioka (Mr. Takaguchi); Dana Lee (Mr.
Takaguchi's Aide); Burt Conroy (General Karnovski);
Dorothy Konrad (Mrs. Karnovski); Alex Rodine (KGB Man);
Joanna Hall (Maiden Fair); Judson Pratt (Bartender);
Andrew Masset (Male Robot); James Connor (Robot Clark);
Ray Holland (Chief Technician); Mike Scott (Steven); Ed

Geldhart (Frenchy); David Perkins (Fantasy Technician);
Charles Krohn (Holcombe); Hirsch Scholl (Arab); Barry
Gilmore (Guard); Catherine McClenny (Secretary); Barry
Gremillion (Page); Jim Everhart (Shorty); Jan Cobbler
(Hostess); Howard Finch (Reporter).

This sequel to *Westworld* was filmed at the NASA Center
in Houston. In the previous film malfunctioning robots caused
chaos, and in *Futureworld* it seems that the robots have taken
over and are programming themselves.

In 1985 a news reporter (Fonda) and a television reporter
(Danner) go to report on the reopening of Delos--a sort of
adult Disney World, where adults may go to act out their fan-
tasies. Delos's head scientist (Ryan, as a Henry Kissinger
lookalike) has placed robots in control of the amusement complex. Fonda and Danner are drugged, and when they awake they
are told by a sympathetic technician (Margolin) that their
doubles, as well as those of important world leaders, exist
in Delos. Ryan and the center's director (Hill) plan to control the world by replacing important leaders with replicants
that will do their bidding. Fonda, wanting to break the news
story, is confronted by Hill, who turns out to be a robot.
Fonda and Danner do away with their doubles and escape from
Delos.

THE GREAT SCOUT AND CATHOUSE THURSDAY. 1976. 102 minutes.
   Color. *Director:* Don Taylor. *Screenplay:* Richard
   Shapiro. *Cinematography:* Alex Phillips, Jr. *Cast:* Lee
   Marvin (Sam Longwood); Oliver Reed (Joe Knox); Robert
   Culp (Jack Colby); Elizabeth Ashley (Nancy Sue); Kay Lenz
   (Cathouse Thursday); Strother Martin (Billy); Sylvia Miles
   (Mike); Howard Platt (Vishniat); Jac Zacha (Trainer);
   Erika Carlson (Monday); C.C. Charity (Tuesday); Ana
   Verdugo (Wednesday); Phaedra (Friday); Leticia Robles
   (Saturday); Luz Maria Pena (Holidays).

This low-brow *Cat Ballou* takes place in the first decade
of the 20th century, like *The Wild Bunch* and *Ride the High
Country*. Where the two latter films are elegies to the Old
West, this film seems more intent on displaying bathroom wall
humor.

A former scout (Marvin) and his half-breed sidekick (Reed)
steal a wagon full of jailbound prostitutes. They set off for
the town of an ex-partner (Culp), who had cheated them out of
some money years before. In the ensuing years Culp has become
a wealthy and powerful man. Reed frees the prostitutes, but

one of them (Lenz) takes a liking to Marvin and joins up with
them. Reed and Marvin attempt to extract the money from Culp
by kidnapping his boisterous foul-mouthed wife (Ashley), whom
Culp is anxious to get rid of anyway. They finally are able
to steal Culp's box of cash, while he is staging a boxing
match. Culp chases after them and agrees to fight Marvin for
the money. He defeats Marvin, but as Reed, Marvin, and Lenz
leave, Culp finds his cashbox full of scalps.

J.D.'S REVENGE. 1976. 95 minutes. Color. *Director:* Arthur
Marks. *Screenplay:* Jaison Starkes. *Cinematography:* Harry
May. *Cast:* Glynn Turman (Ike); Lou Gossett (Reverend
Elija Bliss); Joan Pringle (Christella); Carl Crudup
(Tony); James Louis Watkins (Carl); Fred Pinkard (Theotis
Bliss); Jo Anne Meredith (Sara Divine); Alice Jubért
(Roberta Bliss/Betty Jo); David McKnight (J.D. Walker);
Stephanie Faulkner (Phyllis); Fuddle Bagley (Enoch Land);
Earl Billings (Captain Turner); Paul Galloway (Garage
Man); Barbara Tasker (Sheryl); Tom Alden (Higgins); Melvin
Bijou, Jr. (Football Player); Blue Lu Barker (Bar Keep);
James Borders IV (Atwood); Joseph Collins (Proprietor);
Daniel Dunn (Detective); Fred Ford (Doctor); Theodore
Gilliam (Professor Summit); Chauncey Leon Gilbert (Foot-
ball Player); Ruth Kempf (Woman Passenger); Bob Minor
(Husband); Tony Owens (Leader); Samuel "Catfish" Routh
(Barker); Hazel Roberts (1942 Woman); Timothy Roseborough
(Madman); Carol Sutton (Waitress); Rhonda Shear (1942
Girl); Sylvia Williams (Matron).

This is another blaxploitation horror item that bears a
resemblance to *The Reincarnation of Peter Proud*. Most critics,
while damning the film, were unanimous in their praise of Glynn
Turman, as he changes from a straight, hard-working young law
student to a flamboyant, jive-talking street hustler.
    A law student in New Orleans (Turman) goes to a nightclub
with his wife (Pringle) and two friends (Crudup and Faulkner).
Volunteering for an experiment in hypnosis, Turman has a dream
of being someone else. He soon experiences blackouts and eventually a total change of personality as he begins to carry a
knife, straighten his hair, wear orange suits, and become a
habitué of skid row dives. Nonetheless, he finds himself drawn
to an evangelist (Gossett), who happens to be a link to his
past. It turns out that Turman is the reincarnation of J.D.
Walker (McKnight), a hoodlum murdered in a meat-packing plant
in 1942. J.D. was wrongfully accused of killing his sister,
who had been married to Gossett. As J.D., Turman finds himself

attracted to Gossett's daughter (Jubért), or J.D.'s niece.
He finally finds his way to the abandoned plant, with Gossett,
Jubért, Pringle, and Gossett's brother (Pinkard) following
him. Here the solution to the decades-old murder is found.

A MATTER OF TIME. 1976. 97 minutes. Color. *Director:*
Vincente Minnelli. *Screenplay:* John Gay; based on the
novel *The Film of Memory*, by Maurice Druon. *Cinematog-
raphy:* Geoffrey Unsworth. *Cast:* Liza Minnelli (Nina);
Ingrid Bergman (The Contessa); Charles Boyer (Count
Sanziani); Spiros Andros (Mario Morello); Tina Aumont
(Valentina); Anna Proclemer (Jeanne Blasto); Gabriele
Ferzetti (Antonio Vicaria); Arnolda Foa (Pavelli); Orso
Maria Guerrini (Gabriele d'Orazio); Fernando Rey (Charles
Van Maar); Isabella Rossellini (Sister Pia); Geoffrey
Coppleston (Hotel Manager); Dominot (Hotel Porter); Jean
Mas (Kaiser Wilhelm); Amedeo Nazzari (Tewfik); Virgilio
Volpe (Restaurant Owner); Philippe Hersent (Cook); Jacques
Stany (Reporter); Marino Masé (Hotel Forum Porter);
Richard Oneto (Hotel Forum Manager); Gianpiero Albertini
(Mr. De Perma); Andrea Esterhazy (Jeweler); Loris
Bazzocchi (Cab Driver); Vlado Stergar (Bank Clerk); Rick
Battaglia (Nina's Father).

Excoriated by the critics when it appeared, *A Matter of
Time* was even disowned by its director, Vincente Minnelli.
This big, expensive, glossy piece of nostalgic kitsch was severely hampered by sluggish pacing and poor dubbing. For this
writer any film with Liza Minnelli in it is enough to cause
an allergic reaction.
Liza Minnelli is a famous movie star, who relates a story
about her arrival in Rome from an Italian village in 1949.
She obtains a job as a chambermaid at a run-down hotel, where
there lives an elderly Contessa (Bergman), whom she befriends.
The old woman shares with Minnelli her stories of being an
elegant young woman in Europe at the turn of the century.
Minnelli is enchanted by Bergman's reminiscences and envisions
herself in a series of fantasy sequences living out Bergman's
earlier life. Likewise, Bergman seems to be reliving her life
through the impetuous youthfulness of Minnelli. Bergman is
visited by her former husband (Boyer), who finds that all the
years away from her make it difficult for him to take care of
her. A young screenwriter (Andros) convinces Minnelli to do
a screen test, which turns out to be very successful. As she
seeks her fame and fortune, Minnelli remembers the trite statement told to her by Bergman: "Be an original."

THE MONKEY HUSTLE. 1976. 90 minutes. Color. *Director:*
Arthur Marks. *Screenplay:* Charles Johnson; based on a
story by Odie Hawkins. *Cinematography:* Jack L. Richards.
Cast: Yaphet Kotto (Daddy Foxx); Kirk Calloway (Baby D);
Thomas Carter (Player); Donn Harper (Tiny); Lynn Caridine
(Jan-Jan); Patricia McCaskill (Shirl); Lynn Harris (Sweet
Potatoe); Rudy Ray Moore (Goldie); Rosalind Cash (Mama);
Randy Brooks (Win); Debbi Morgan (Vi); Fuddle Bagley (Mr.
Molet); Frank Rice (The Black Knight); Carl Crudup (Joe);
Duchyll Smith (Beatrice); Steve Williams (The Manager);
Frank Barrett (Leon); Ralph Johnson (Cobra); Dewellie
Colbert (Moe); Robin Morgan (Tanya); Altyrone Brown
(Bugger); Nate Reed (Cook); Charles Smith (1st Guard);
George Roby (2nd Guard); Robert Townsend (Musician); Recoe
Walker (Musician); Jeffrey Hazle (The Queen); Reginald
Parker (Doorman); Nate Mallet (City Man); Clifford Thomas
(Alderman); Roberta Williams (Prostitute); Alvin Henry
(Rubbish Man).

The Monkey Hustle came out during the tail end of AIP's
blaxploitation cycle. This is the sort of film, along with
Superfly, that usually elicited protests from black leaders
for glorifying the lowest elements of the black community.
Set in Chicago, *The Monkey Hustle* does not contain as many
scenes of action and sex as your typical blaxploitation film,
but it does offer a number of polished, letter-perfect performances from people like Yaphet Kotto, Rosalind Cash, and a
cast of virtual unknowns.
    The plot is told in the form of vignettes, as it follows
the denizens of a Chicago ghetto in their attempt to stop a
proposed freeway from ruining their neighborhood. Yaphet Kotto
is a street hustler who has a number of young boys at his call
for various forms of thievery. The petty hustlers and thieves
spend much of their time ripping each other off, as they exchange words in an impenetrable (as least to white viewers)
ghetto slang.
    The Monkey Hustle was made with few allowances for white
audiences. Despite the criticism leveled at films like this
for role models they portray, it contains more raw energy and
enthusiasm than such tame, and well-meaning, films as *Sounder*.

SCORCHY. 1976. 99 minutes. Color. *Director:* Hikmet Avedis.
Screenplay: Hikmet Avedis. *Cinematography:* Laszlo Pal.
Cast: Connie Stevens (Sergeant Jackie Parker); Cesare
Danova (Phillip Bianco); Marlene Schmidt (Claudia Bianco);
William Smith (Carl Henrich); Normann Burton (Chief Frank

O'Brien); John Davis Chandler (Nicky); Joyce Jameson
(Mary Davis); Greg Evigan (Alan); Nick Dimitri (Steve);
Nate Long (Charlie); Ingrid Cedergren (Suzi); Ellen
Thurston (Maria); Ray Sebastian (Counterman); Mike Easy
(Dimitri); Gene White (Big Boy).

Scorchy is not much more than an extended version of television's *Police Woman*, with Connie Stevens standing in for
Angie Dickinson. The film did poor business on its initial
run in Seattle, where it was filmed, and went downhill from
there. This is not too surprising, since Connie Stevens is
no Pam Grier and is considerably over her head in *Scorchy* (she
is better doing the Ace Hardware commercials).
An undercover narc (Stevens) has been out to trap a drug
dealer (Danova) for over two years. She poses as a tourist
aboard a plane from Rome bound for Seattle, where she is keeping her eye on a shipment of heroin hidden in a statue.
Stevens has ingratiated herself with Danova and his operatives
over the course of two years to the point of gaining their
trust. The statue is sold to an art collector unaware of its
contents. In order to retrieve it, Danova asks Stevens to
take part in the theft. After the heroin has changed hands
several times, Danova obtains it and escapes to an island in
Puget Sound, where he is to give the drugs to his contact.
Stevens and other law-enforcement authorities arrive for the
bust, but Danova escapes with the money made from the drug
shipment. Stevens chases after him in a helicopter and bests
him in a final confrontation.

SHOUT AT THE DEVIL. 1976. 147 minutes. Color. *Director:*
Peter Hunt. *Screenplay:* Wilbur Smith, Alistair Reid,
and Stanley Price; based on a novel by Smith. *Cinematog-
raphy:* Michael Reed. *Cast:* Lee Marvin (Flynn O'Flynn);
Roger Moore (Sebastian Oldsmith); Barbara Parkins (Rosa
O'Flynn); Rene Kolldehoff (Fleischer); Ian Holm (Moham-
med); Karl Michael Vogler (Von Kleine); Horst Janson
(Kyller); Gernot Endemann (Braun); Maurice Denham (Mr.
Smythe); Jean Kent (Mrs. Smythe); Heather Wright (Cyn-
thia); Bernard Horstall (Captain Joyce); Robert Lang (Cap-
tain Henry); Peter Copley (Admiral Howe); Murray Melvin
(Lieutenant Phipps); Geoff Davidson (MacKintosh); Gerard
Paquis (French Pilot); George Coulouris (El Keb); Renu
Setna (Mr. Raji); Simon Sabela (1st Village Chief);
Shalimar Undi (Nanny); Joe Matela (Sergeant Dumu); Paul
Matela (Native Runner); Solomon Dungane (Luti); Ray
Msengana (Ahmed); Nicholas Kourtis (Arab).

This overly long, mediocre all-star epic takes place during the same time and in roughly same geographic location as *The African Queen.* Saddled with a long-winded story, the makers of this film filled the screen with scenes of combat, shipwrecks, hostile natives, time bombs, crocodile attacks, and just about anything else they could think of.

In 1913 in East Africa a gin-soaked poacher (Marvin) gets an expatriate Englishman (Moore) to become his partner. They spend their time raiding territory controlled by German authorities. After the two have a close escape with the local German commissioner (Kolldehoff), Moore meets Marvin's daughter (Parkins), and they fall in love and marry. With the outbreak of World War I Kolldehoff sends a raiding party that burns down Marvin's home and kills the daughter of Moore and Parkins. The three wage war on Kolldehoff and his men, as they agree to blow up a German cruiser for the British Navy. Marvin and Moore sneak aboard the ship with a time bomb and escape. Meanwhile Kolldehoff has taken Parkins prisoner, and Marvin decides to sacrifice himself for his daughter so Moore may rescue her. The ship blows up with Marvin on board, but Kolldehoff escapes, only to be shot by Moore.

A SMALL TOWN IN TEXAS. 1976. 95 minutes. Color. *Director:* Jack Starrett. *Screenplay:* William Norton. *Cinematography:* Bob Jessup. *Cast:* Timothy Bottoms (Poke Jackson); Susan George (Mary Lee); Bo Hopkins (Duke); Art Hindle (Boogie); John Karlen (Lenny); Morgan Woodward (C.J. Crane); Hank Rolike (Cleotus); Buck Fowler (Bull Parker); Clay Tanner (Junior); Patrice Rohmer (Trudy); Mark Silva (Kevin); Santos Reyes (Jesus Mendez); Dodi Bieberly (Mrs. Carter); Claude Ennis Starrett, Jr. (Buford Tyler); James N. Harrell (Old Codger); Ron McPherson (PR Man); Leotis Duffie (Butler); Kathryn Lacy (Mrs. Crane); Starrett Berry (Cooter); L.A. Steele (Cowboy); Joe Michel (Band Leader); Fay Armstrong (Woman at Mansion); James Brewer III (Potsy Singer); Amy Andrewartha (Lucy).

A Small Town in Texas takes a swipe or two at Texas, political conspiracies, assassinations, and reactionary politics, but ruins much of its desired effect by indulging in endless car chases. For some nonsensical reason there are still people (hopefully not too many over the age of 18) who receive some orgasmic thrill watching people in cars chase one another and crash right and left.

A young man (Bottoms) returns to his hometown in Texas after spending five years in prison for possession of marijuana. He finds that his girlfriend and mother of his child

(George) is sleeping with the local sheriff (Hopkins), who
had put Bottoms in jail. A local politician (Reyes) is assas-
sinated during a public gathering, and Bottoms witnesses
Hopkins killing the assassin, stealing an envelope from the
dead body, and hiding it. Hopkins is only a part of a conspiracy orchestrated by the town's wealthiest man (Woodward).
Bottoms steals the envelope which contains $25,000, and Hopkins
goes on his trail. During a chase two policemen are killed,
and Hopkins issues a warrant on Bottoms for murder. Bottoms
breaks through a police barricade to pick up George and his
son and escapes. Woodward decides to let Hopkins kind of "hang
slowly in the wind," by allowing him to go it alone in captur-
ing Bottoms. He and Bottoms have a lengthy car chase, and
Hopkins crashes and is killed. Bottoms returns to town in
hopes of exposing the conspiracy.

SPECIAL DELIVERY. 1976. 99 minutes. Color. *Director:* Paul
   Wendkos. *Screenplay:* Don Gazzaniga. *Cinematography:*
   Harry Stradling, Jr. *Cast:* Bo Svenson (Jack Murdock);
   Cybill Shepherd (Mary Jane); Tom Atkins (Zabelski);
   Sorrell Booke (Hubert Zane); Gerrit Graham (Swivot);
   Michael C. Gwynne (Carl Graff); Jeff Goldblum (Snake);
   Robert Ito (Mr. Chu); Lynette Mettey (Marj); Richard Drout
   Miller (Artie); John Quade (Barney); Vic Tayback (Wyatt);
   Edward Winter (Lorenzo Pierce); Kim Richards (Juliette);
   Marla Adams (Mrs. Zane); Phillip R. Allen (Browne);
   Timothy Blake (Mother); Alex Colon (Lopez); Lawrie
   Driscoll (Policeman); Ed Peck (Man in Booth); Joe de Reda
   (Torgan); Mel Scott (Anderson).

Special Delivery contains some of the photographic effects
and milieu commonly associated with *film noir*, along with a
broad comedic streak. Produced by Bing Crosby Productions,
it reflects Crosby's conservative tastes in its castigation
of such easy targets as porno theatres and people with long
hair.
   Four Vietnam veterans plan a daring daylight bank robbery,
but two of the group are caught and one is accidentally killed
in a getaway attempt. Bo Svenson is the only one that escapes,
as he stashes part of the holdup money in a mailbox. Two people, a neighborhood junkie (Gwynne) and young woman (Shepherd),
witness Svenson hiding the loot. Gwynne mentions to a drug
dealer (Ito) the whereabouts of the money, so Ito decides to
go after Svenson and the money himself. Shepherd finagles
her way into Svenson's good graces. They soon become lovers
and begin to think of ways to retrieve the money. The two of
them are able to outwit and outfight anyone who challenges

them for the money, until they steal a van and take the entire
mailbox with them. Svenson and Shepherd use part of the money
to go on a world cruise. On the cruise Svenson is spotted and
recognized by the wife (Adams) of the president (Booke) of the
bank from where the money was stolen. Things are left pur-
posefully up in the air as to whether she turns them in or not

SQUIRM. 1976. 92 minutes. Color. *Director:* Jeff Lieberman.
Screenplay: Jeff Lieberman. *Cinematography:* Joseph
Mangine. *Cast:* Don Scardino (Mick); Patricia Pearcy (Ger
Sanders); R.A. Dow (Roger Grimes); Jean Sullivan (Naomi
Sanders); Peter MacLean (Sheriff Jim Reston); Fran Higgin
(Alma Sanders); William Newman (Quigley); Barbara Quinn
(Sheriff's Girl); Carl Dagenhart (Willie Grimes); Angel
Sande (Millie); Carol Jean Owens (Bonnie); Kim Iocouvozzi
(Hank); Walter Dimmick (Danny); Julia Klopp (Mrs. Klopp);
Ralph Flanders (1st Man at Lunch Counter); Albert Smith
(2nd Man at Lunch Counter); Jim Shirah (3rd Man at Lunch
Counter); Harold Mumm (Bus Driver); W.A. Lindblatt (Power
Line Repairman); with Leslie Thorsen.

Squirm is supposedly based on an incident that occurred
in Georgia in 1975. This effective horror item includes some
good special effects using foot-long sandworms and is liberall
spiced with touches of black humor. Its writer/director, Jeff
Lieberman, went on to direct one of the best cult films of
the 70s--*Blue Sunshine*.

A storm in a small Georgia town has knocked the power
lines to the ground. The next day a local simpleton (Dow)
attacks a young woman (Pearcy), while she is fishing. Dow
falls in the boat and is attacked by some hungry worms being
used for bait. Pearcy and a friend from the North (Scardino)
tell the disbelieving sheriff (MacLean) their story, and soon
after the worm-riddled body of Dow's father (Dagenhart) is
found. The electricity from the power lines had entered the
ground and electrified the worms into man-eaters. Scardino
leaves Pearcy at her mother's house, as he goes into the woods
to look for material to barricade the house against a worm
attack. He is attacked and knocked unconscious by the crazed
Dow. When Scardino comes to, he finds the house Pearcy is in
covered with worms. Inside the house the worm-ravaged Dow
has made Pearcy a prisoner in the attic. Scardino rescues
her by throwing Dow into a horde of worms, as he and Pearcy
hide in a wooden chest for the night. When daylight appears,
the nocturnal worms have disappeared and the two come safely
out of their hidingplace.

STREET PEOPLE. 1976. 92 minutes. Color. *Director:* Maurizio
Lucidi. *Screenplay:* Ernest Tidyman, Randall Kleiser,
Gianfranco Bucceri, Niccola Badalucco, Roberto Leoni, and
Maurizio Lucidi; based on a story by Bucceri and Leoni.
Cinematography: Aiace Parolin. *Cast:* Roger Moore
(Ulysses); Stacy Keach (Charlie); Ivo Garrani (Salvatore
Francesco); Ettore Manni (Bishop Lopetri); Ennio Balbo
(Continenza); Fausto Tozzi (Nicoletta); Pietro Martellanz
(Pano); Romano Puppo (Fortunate); with Rosemarie Lindt,
Loretta Persichetti, Luigi Casellato, Aldo Rendine,
Salvatore Torrisi, Emilio Vale, Franco Fantasia.

This attempt to profit from the escapades of the Mafia
was literally written by a committee of six. At times it seems
that *Street People* is so chaotic that each writer was not aware
of what the others were doing. Most of the exteriors of this
Italian-made film were shot in San Francisco; and the film
includes a *Bullitt*-inspired car chase.
A Mafioso (Garrani) is tricked when three men steal heroin, hide it in a crucifix, and ship it to San Francisco.
Garrani asks a local Mafia don (Balbo) for revenge against the
three, so Balbo hires Garrani's lawyer nephew (Moore) to find
out who they are. In San Francisco a hit man and a partner
of Moore's (Keach) has found the whereabouts of the three men,
who have not yet sold the heroin and are in debt. After Balbo
is murdered, Moore (who is as confused as the rest of us about
what is happening) learns that Garrani was the man who killed
his father when he was a boy. Realizing that Garrani has created a ruse to sell the heroin, Moore and Keach go out to look
for Garrani's three confederates. When all the requisite people are done away with, Moore confronts Garrani and kills him.
Keach now decides to sell the heroin, but Moore gets rid of
it instead.

THE BLACK PIRATE. 1977. 121 minutes. Color. *Directors:*
Sergio Sollima and Alberto Silvestri. *Screenplay:* Un-
available. *Cinematography:* Alberto Spagnoli. *Cast:* Kabir
Bedi (The Black Pirate); Carole Andre (Honorata); Mel
Ferrer (Van Gould); Angelo Infante (Morgan); Tony Renis
(Jose); Dagmar Lassander (Marqesa); Sonja Jeanine (Yara).

This overly long and high-budgeted Italian adventure film
was made in 1974 but did not reach the United States market
until 1977. *The Black Pirate* was inspired by the successful
Italian television show about Sandokan, a dashing swordsman.
This is a mixture of ESP and camp fantasy in which a

Spanish pirate (Bedi) is out to overthrow a Dutch ruler
(Ferrer) in the southern Caribbean region around Colombia and
Venezuela. There is plenty of action and some colorful locations, but the spare storyline becomes repetitive over a perio
of two hours. It seems that *The Black Pirate* was without a
strong producer to exert a guiding influence. As it is, this
film does not seem to offer anything different from a similar
film, *Guns of the Black Witch*, made many years before.

BREAKER! BREAKER! 1977. 86 minutes. Color. *Director:* Don
    Hulette. *Screenplay:* Terry Chambers. *Cinematography:*
    Mario Di Leo. *Cast:* Chuck Norris (J.D. Daves); George
    Murdock (Judge Trimmings); Terry O'Connor (Arlene
    Trimmings); Don Gentry (Sergeant Strode); John Di Fusco
    (Arney); Ron Cedillos (Deputy Boles); Michael Augenstein
    (Billy Daves); Dan Vandegriff (Wilfred); Douglas Stevenso
    (Drake).

   Breaker! Breaker! exploits the popularity of the truck
driver's lifestyle and citizen-band radios, which were quite
the rage a number of years ago. This film could easily have
been called "The Revenge of the Zen Trucker," as this is one
of the first films for karate champion and martial-arts expert
Chuck Norris, who has gone on to make a slew of highly profitable films.
   A trucker (Norris) returns to his hometown in California
after having worked on the Alaskan pipeline. Norris wants to
settle down for a while and lets his younger brother (Augenstein) drive his large 18-wheel truck for him. Augenstein is
arrested one day by two corrupt cops (Cedillos and Gentry),
who take him to a town presided over by an equally corrupt
judge (Murdock). The town makes a living exploiting truckers
and motorists by assessing unreasonable traffic fines.
Augenstein has a set of false charges read to him by Murdock,
and has a large fine imposed on him. When Augenstein attempts
to escape, he is beaten and put in prison. Norris goes to
look for his missing brother and involves himself in a bar
brawl, in which one of the locals is killed. Murdock puts
Norris in jail and gives him a death sentence. A woman whom
Norris has befriended (O'Connor) uses a CB to alert the truckers of Norris's plight. A convoy of trucks comes to rescue
him and Augenstein and, in the process, level the town.

CHATTER BOX. 1977. 73 minutes. Color. *Director:* Tom De
    Simone. *Screenplay:* Mark Rosin and Norman Yonemoto; based
    on a story by Tom De Simone. *Cinematography:* Tak
    Fujimoto. *Cast:* Candice Rialson (Penelope); Larry Gelman
    (Dr. Pearl); Jane Kean (Eleanor Pittman); Perry Bullington
    (Ted); Arlene Martell (Marlene); Michael Taylor (Dick);
    Cynthia Hoppenfield (Linda Ann); Robert Lipton (Jon
    David); Rip Taylor (Mr. Jo); Professor Irwin Corey (Him-
    self); Sandra Gould (Mrs. Bugatowski); Trent Dolan (Frank
    Rio).

This short feature has all the subtlety of *The Gong Show.*
Chatter Box is not readily available nowadays, especially on
television, since the film deals with a woman who, as the ads
say, "has a unique way of expressing herself."
A young woman (Rialson) discovers that she has a second
voice box in her vagina, called Virginia. Not only can Virginia speak, she can sing as well. Her fiancé (Bullington)
leaves her when Virginia comments negatively about his performance in bed. Rialson consults a psychiatrist (Gelman)
with show-business connections, and after he introduces her
to an AMA convention she becomes an overnight sensation on
television talk shows. She (or should I say Virginia) becomes
a recording star, with thousands of adoring fans. Rialson's
star-struck mother (Kean) eventually comes to accept her daughter's stardom and sees Virginia as a separate personality.
The strain of all this attention is too much for Rialson, as
she yearns to free herself from the situation. How she finally
straightens out her career and her sex life is left to the
viewer to find out. This was a Lips Production.

CRACKING UP. 1977. 74 minutes. Color. *Directors:* Rowby
    Goren and Chuck Staley. *Screenplay:* The Ace Trucking
    Company, The Credibility Gap, Proctor and Bergman, The
    Graduates, Neil Israel, and "Kansas City" Bob McClurg.
    Cinematography: Bob Collins. *Cast:* Phil Proctor (Walter
    Concrete); Peter Bergman (Barbara Halters); with Michael
    Mislore, Fred Willard, Paul Zegler, Steve Bluestein, The
    Credibility Gap, Harry Shearer, Michael McCane, David
    Landers, The Graduates, Jim Fisher, Jim Staahl, Gino
    Insana, "Kansas City" Bob McClurg, Leslie Ackerman, Rowby
    Goren, Neil Israel, Rick Murray, C.D. Taylor, Edie

McClurg, Mary McCusker, Cris Pray, Ron Prince, Lynn Marie
Stuart, Steven Stucker, Kurt Taylor, Paul Willson, Fee
Waybill.

Various alumni from such improvisational groups as The
Ace Trucking Company and Firesign Theatre here attempted a
parody of television news and sitcoms revolving around a news-
cast about a California earthquake. Like a number of other
films made for college-age audiences, *Cracking Up* was test-
marketed in Champaign, Illinois. Even in this large college
town the film was able to manage only about seven people per
screening. To parody television sitcoms, as well as such people as Billy Graham and Kathryn Kuhlman, seems to be redundant
The improvisational bits wear thin very quickly, especially
the drug jokes. Use is made of video in this production, and
the only bright spot in the film is the musical track by The
Tubes, who perform such songs as "Proud to Be an American"
and "White Punks on Dope." It seems that about the only comedic films made for adults nowadays are the Richard Pryor concert films, and some of the ones made by Woody Allen.

THE DAY THAT SHOOK THE WORLD. 1977. 111 minutes. Color.
   Director: Veljko Bulajic. *Screenplay:* Paul Jarrico; base
   on a story by Stefan Bulajic and Vladimir Bor. *Cinema-
   tography:* Jan Curik. *Cast:* Christopher Plummer (Archduke
   Franz Ferdinand); Florinda Bolkan (Duchess Sophie);
   Maximilian Schell (Djuro Sarac); Ifran Mensur (Gavrilo
   Princip); Rado Bajic (Nedeljko Cabrinovil); with Jan
   Hrusinsky, Branko Duric, Libuse Safrankova, Iana Jvandova
   Otomar Korbelar, Henjo Haase.

   As in any film dealing with a historical assassination--
e.g., *The Day of the Jackal* or *Nine Hours to Rama*--the suspens
here is vitiated by a pedestrian conclusion. Filmed on location, *The Day That Shook the World* deals with the event that
precipitated World War I, one that, as far as anyone knows,
was never recorded by newsreel cameras.
   Hoping to forestall a war between Bosnia and Serbia, Arch
duke Franz Ferdinand of the Austro-Hungarian Empire (Plummer)
ventures to Sarajevo in 1914 to witness war maneuvers. When
a revolutionary (Schell) learns of the visit of Plummer and
his wife (Bolkan), he organizes a group of three assassins to
murder Plummer. This would set off political events that
Schell believes will give Bosnia independence. The authoritie
are keeping an eye on the conspirators, as Bolkan had voiced
her doubts about the political climate when she and Plummer

arrived in Sarajevo. Schell is captured by the police when
they hear a rumor about the assassination attempt. Schell is
convinced by the authorities that an assassination would cause
Austria to declare war on the Balkans. He unsuccessfully attempts to talk one of the conspirators (Mensur) out of committing the act and later is captured and tortured by the secret police. The next day a bomb attempt on Plummer, while
riding in his car, is foiled. Later in the same motorcade
Mensur appears out of a crowd and shoots and kills the royal
couple. Soon after Austria declares war on Serbia. Russia
enters the war on the side of Serbia, and this leads to an
all-out European war.

EMPIRE OF THE ANTS. 1977. 91 minutes. Color. *Director:*
    Bert I. Gordon. *Screenplay:* Jack Turley; based on a story
    by H.G. Wells; adaptation by Bert I. Gordon. *Cinematog-
    raphy:* Reginald Morris. *Cast:* Joan Collins (Marilyn
    Fryser); Robert Lansing (Dan Stokely); Edward Power
    (Charlie Pearson); John David Carson (Joe Morrison);
    Jacqueline Scott (Margaret Ellis); Albert Salmi (Sheriff
    Art Kincade); Pamela Shoop (Coreen Bradford); Robert Pine
    (Larry Graham); Brooke Palance (Christine Graham); Harry
    Holcombe (Harry Thompson); Irene Tedrow (Velma Thompson);
    Tom Fadden (Sam Russell); Jack Kosslyn (Thomas Lawson);
    Ilse Earl (Mary Lawson); Janie Gavin (Ginny); Norman
    Franklin (Anson Parker); Florence McGee (Phoebe Russell);
    with Jim Wheelus, Mike Armstrong, Tom Ford, Charles Red,
    Hank Hooker, Hugh M. Hooker.

    Bert I. Gordon's preoccupation with giant mutations is a
worthy subject for a psychiatrist's couch. This film is no
different from *The Food of the Gods*, with paltry special effects and a clumsy script. When this writer first saw *Empire
of the Ants* in a downtown San Francisco grindhouse, the street-
wise mid-week audience were laughing at things that Gordon
did not intend to be amusing.
    A businesswoman (Collins) escorts a group of potential
land buyers to look at some undeveloped land near the Florida
Everglades. One couple, separated from the tour, are killed
by giant ants, who have grown by ingesting radioactive waste.
When the rest of the group discover the presence of the ants,
they are led by a boat captain (Lansing) through the forest
with hopes of reaching a town. After some of the party have
been killed, the survivors get in a rowboat and arrive at a
nearby town. All of the people of the community are under
the control of the ant empire, with a queen ant controlling

the workers at the town's sugar refinery. A couple of the group are taken prisoner, but Lansing burns the queen ant with a flame thrower. Another group member (Carson) burns down the refinery and kills all the ants. The four survivors now escap in a boat.

FINAL CHAPTER--WALKING TALL. 1977. 112 minutes. Color. *Director:* Jack Starrett. *Screenplay:* Howard B. Kreitsek; based on a story by Kreitsek. *Cinematography:* Robert B. Hauser. *Cast:* Bo Svenson (Buford Pusser); Margaret Blye (Luan Patton); Forrest Tucker (Carl Pusser); Morgan Woodward (The Boss); Libby Boone (Joan); Leif Garrett (Mike Pusser); Bruce Glover (Grady Coker); Taylor Lacher (Martin French); Dawn Lyn (Dwana Pusser); Sandy McPeak (Lloyd Tatum); Robert Phillips (Johnny); Logan Ramsey (John Witter); Clay Tanner (O.Q. Teal); Lurene Tuttle (Grandma); David Adams (Robbie); Vance Davis (Aaron); H.B. Haggerty (Bulo); John Malloy (Mel Bascomb).

With this final installment the life and legend of Buford Pusser has been milked dry. The makers of this film were so desperate for a storyline that they even included Pusser selling his story to Hollywood. In the best docudrama tradition, *Final Chapter--Walking Tall* carries the usual mixture of sentimentality and self-righteous vigilante violence.

The film begins by showing that there is virtually no crime in the county where Buford Pusser (Svenson) is sheriff. A civil-liberties lawyer (Lacher) is on hand to question Svenson's method of law enforcement. Before long a new group of criminals move into an "open" territory between Svenson's jurisdiction and a neighboring county. Svenson runs for re-election, and is defeated when Lacher convinces the voters that his methods are outdated. Finding it difficult to get any work except odd jobs, Svenson decides to sell his story to Hollywood. The film is a success, as he is tabbed to portray himself in the sequel. His success has made him once again a folk hero to the populace. The local crime boss (Ramsey) realizes that Svenson's popularity will probably get him reelected sheriff, thus closing down his criminal operation. While driving his new car to Memphis, Svenson loses control of the vehicle, crashes, and is killed. Without any substantial proof, the filmmakers intimate that his car had been sabotaged.

GRAYEAGLE. 1977. 104 minutes. Color. *Director:* Charles B.
Pierce. *Screenplay:* Charles B. Pierce. *Cinematography:*
Jim Roberson. *Cast:* Ben Johnson (John Colter); Iron Eyes
Cody (Standing Bear); Lana Wood (Beth Colter); Jack Elam
(Trapper Willis); Paul Fix (Running Wolf); Alex Cord
(Grayeagle); Jacob Daniels (Scar); Jimmy Clem (Abe
Stroud); Cindy Butler (Ida Colter); Charles B. Pierce
(Bugler); Blackie Wetzell (Medicine Man); Cheyenne Rivera
and Wayne Wells (Shoshone Braves); Bill Lafromboise and
Don Wright (Indians at Fort); Jim Hirst (Young Running
Wolf); John Welsh (Lum Stroud).

Filmed on location in Montana on a small budget, *Grayeagle*
touches upon some of the same themes found in *The Searchers*.
A number of the Indian characters here are portrayed with some
nobility, but the film falls short of portraying the West from
an Indian's viewpoint. It is unfortunate that the film, which
attempts to give the Indian their due, is hampered by the Uncle
Tom Tom character that Western film veteran Iron Eyes Cody
portrays.
A young Cheyenne warrior (Cord) kidnaps the daughter
(Wood) of a trapper (Johnson). He and his retainer (Cody)
form a posse to look for her but run into an outlaw band headed
by a real nut case (Pierce). While the posse is taking care
of Pierce and his gang, Cord has had to fight a Shoshone
(Daniels), whom Wood shoots. Cord takes her to an old chief
(Fix) who is on his death bed. Fix is Wood's real father,
thanks to a liaison he had had with her mother years before.
He just wants to see his daughter before he dies, and afterward Cord promises Wood to take her back home. Near Johnson's
cabin Cord and Wood are attacked by Shoshones. Wood is now
under Johnson's protection, and just as they think that Cord
has been killed, he rides toward them to be reunited with her.

THE HOUSE BY THE LAKE. 1977. 89 minutes. Color. *Director:*
William Fruet. *Screenplay:* William Fruet. *Cinematog-
raphy:* Robert T. Saad. *Cast:* Brenda Vaccaro (Diane);
Don Stroud (Lep); Chuck Shamata (Harry Blatt); Richard
Ayres (Runt); Kyle Edwards (Frankie); Don Granbery
(Stanley); Ed McNamara (Spragg); Michael Kirby (Ralph);
Richard Donat (Policeman); Denver Mattson (Smokey); Al
Bernardo (Mr. Doobie); Roselle Stone (Mrs. Doobie); Elaine
Yarish (Campground Girl).

The House by the Lake

This grand prize winner at the Sitges International Terror Film Festival is another revenge film in the mold of *Straw Dogs*. The beautiful scenery of rural Ontario is counterpointed with the violence being perpetrated on a couple by four drunken punks.

A wealthy young dentist (Shamata) takes a model (Vaccaro) to his country home for the weekend in the hopes of seducing her. Along the way Shamata lets Vacarro drive his "souped up" Corvette. They encounter another car containing four hoodlums (Stroud, Ayres, Granbery, and Edwards), who refuse to let them pass. A race ensues, and the car that Stroud is driving ends up in a ditch. The four follow Shamata and Vaccaro to the country home, where they break in and cause havoc. Stroud murders Shamata, and all four rape Vacarro. In the process of being raped by Ayres, Vacarro gets a piece of glass and cuts his throat. She then lures the two others (Granbery and Edwards) to their deaths--one in a boathouse set on fire and the other in some quicksand. Vacarro, who is near total collapse, tries to escape from Stroud by driving away in a jeep. Stroud shoots at the jeep with a volley of shotgun fire and then attempts to assault it himself. Vacarro keeps on driving and runs him over, continuing on her way to the nearest highway.

THE ISLAND OF DR. MOREAU. 1977. 104 minutes. Color. *Director:* Don Taylor. *Screenplay:* John Herman Shaner and Al Mamrus; based on the novel by H.G. Wells. *Cinematography:* Gerry Fisher. *Cast:* Burt Lancaster (Dr. Moreau); Michael York (Andrew Braddock); Nigel Davenport (Montgomery); Barbara Carrera (Marla); Richard Basehart (Saver of the Law); Nick Cravat (M'Ling); The Great John "L" (Boarman); Bob Ozman (Bullman); Fumio Demura (Hyenaman); Gary Baxley (Lionman); John Gillespie (Tigerman); David Cass (Bearman).

This is a remake of *Island of Lost Souls*, first made in the early 30s and starring Charles Laughton as Dr. Moreau. That black-and-white film had a claustrophobic quality that this version lacks, and Burt Lancaster portrays Moreau as a sort of misguided humanist, whereas Laughton was truly demented.

A young seaman and survivor of a shipwreck (York) lands on a remote Pacific island. While exploring the island, he is knocked unconscious, and when he wakes up he finds himself in the presence of the island's owner (Lancaster) and his aide (Davenport). He also meets a young woman (Carrera) who is a

permanent guest of Lancaster's. York soon learns that
Lancaster is conducting experiments in eugenics, whereby he
attempts to change animals into humans, teaching them non-
violent human traits. The jungle is filled with Lancaster's
experiments, beings who are half-men and half-bear, lion, tiger, boar, etc. When one of them (Ozman) breaks the Law that
Lancaster has formulated, he is hunted down. York shoots Ozma
to save him from future experiments. Lancaster decides to
make York his next experiment, as York gradually takes on animal features. Davenport tries to stop Lancaster's experiments
on York, so Lancaster shoots him. When the animal men see
that Lancaster has broken the Law, they kill him and set fire
to his home and laboratory. Carrera frees York, and they get
a boat and head out to sea. Just before they are picked up
by a passing ship, York's features change back to human form.

JOYRIDE. 1977. 92 minutes. Color. *Director:* Joseph Ruben.
    Screenplay: Joseph Ruben and Peter Rainer. *Cinematog-
    raphy:* Stephen M. Katz. *Cast:* Desi Arnaz, Jr. (Scott);
    Robert Carradine (John); Melanie Griffith (Susie); Anne
    Lockhart (Cindy); Tom Ligon (Sanders); Cliff Lenz
    (Henderson); Robert Loper (Simon Williams); Diana Grayf
    (Rhonda); Diane O'Mack (Debbie); Susan Ludlow (Personnel
    Lady); Ted D'Arms (Site Manager); Gail Rosella (Cashier);
    Richard Mazzola (Car Salesman); Michael O'Neill (Hender-
    son's Assistant); Duncan MacLean (Diner Owner); Richard
    Riehle (Bartender); Richard Tietjen (Sam); Paul Fleming
    (Big Ed).

    Three young people (Arnaz, Carradine, Griffith) quit thei
humdrum jobs in the San Fernando Valley and journey to Alaska
to search for adventure and better paying jobs. Arnaz and
Carradine apply for jobs on the Alaskan pipeline, but they
must join a union. When Griffith ignores the advances of a
union official (Ligon), he sees to it that the two young men
will not work on the pipeline. The three have their posses-
sions stolen from their van, and soon after both Arnaz and
Carradine are able to secure jobs on the pipeline after all.
They are fired for blowing the whistle on the corrupt Ligon.
With nothing more to lose the disillusioned trio decide to
hold up the pipeline payroll office. In so doing they kidnap
an employee (Lockhart) and ask for a $300,000 ransom. The
ransom is paid, and they escape after a shootout and car chase
Jealousy causes friction between them, as Carradine finds Arna
making love with Griffith. Uncertain now of their own loyal-
ties, the three drive into the Canadian woods to avoid the

police. Arnaz steals another car as they elude the authorities. Now with most of the ransom money they drive off to an
uncertain future.

THE LITTLE GIRL WHO LIVES DOWN THE LANE. 1977. 94 minutes.
Color. *Director:* Nicolas Gessner. *Screenplay:* Laird
Koenig; based on the novel by Koenig. *Cinematography:*
Rene Verzier. *Cast:* Jodie Foster (Rynn Jacobs); Martin
Sheen (Frank Hallet); Alexis Smith (Mrs. Hallet); Mort
Shuman (Miglioriti); Scott Jacoby (Mario Podesta); Dorothy
Davis (Town Hall Clerk); Clesson Goodhue (Bank Manager);
Hubert Noel and Jacques Famery (Bank Clerks); Mary Morter
and Judie Wildman (Tellers).

This is a cold, detached, and clinical film about a young
murderess, who gains our complete sympathy.
A 13 year old girl (Foster) has leased a house with her
father in a small New England town. No one knows that Foster's
father had committed suicide when he learned he was terminally
ill. Before he died, he rented the house for her and told
her to live on her own as if nothing had happened. The local
child molester (Sheen) occasionally comes by the house, obviously intrigued by Foster. Sheen's nosy mother (Smith), the
real-estate agent who had leased the house, calls to see
Foster's father. Smith goes into the house's cellar for some
household items. She screams when she finds a body, hits her
head, and is killed. The body in the cellar is that of
Foster's mother, whom she had poisoned when she attempted to
take Foster away with her. A local boy (Jacoby) befriends
Foster, and they soon become lovers. She confides to him about
the bodies in the cellar, so he helps her bury them. Jacoby
contracts pneumonia and is sent to the hospital. Now alone,
Foster is visited by Sheen, who has become suspicious about
his mother's disappearance. He attempts to blackmail Foster,
but she gives him a cup of tea with the same poison she used
on her mother.

THE PEOPLE THAT TIME FORGOT. 1977. 90 minutes. Color. *Di-
rector:* Kevin Connor. *Screenplay:* Patrick Tilley; based
on the novel by Edgar Rice Burroughs. *Cinematography:*
Alan Hume. *Cast:* Patrick Wayne (Ben McBride); Doug
McClure (Bowen Tyler); Dana Gillespie (Ajor); Sarah
Douglas (Charly); Thorley Walters (Dr. Edward Norfolk);
Shane Rimmer (Hogan); Tony Britton (Captain Lawton); John

306 *American International Pictures*

Hallam (Chang-Sha); Dave Prowse (Executioner); Milton
Reid (Sabbala); Kiran Shah (Bolum); Richard Parmentier
(Lieutenant Whitby); Jimmy Ray (Lieutenant Graham); Tony
McHale (Telegraphist).

Filmed in Spain, this paltry sequel to *The Land That Time
Forgot* is filled with the same cavemen and papier-mâché prehistoric monsters. It seems to have been a vehicle to exploit
the scantily clad body of Dana Gillespie.
An expedition takes off in 1918 to search for a lost explorer (McClure, who had disappeared in the land of Caprona
in the prior film). The plane carrying the expedition members
crashes on an icy island in Antarctica. Three members of the
party (Wayne, Walters, Douglas) explore the area and end up
rescuing a cavegirl (Gillespie) from a dinosaur attack. She
takes them to look for McClure, who has lived with her for
the last couple of years. All of them are eventually captured
by a murderous race of warriors, who are holding McClure prisoner. The tribe plans to sacrifice Gillespie and Douglas by
throwing them into a volcano. Wayne organizes the rest of
the group in a rescue attempt to free the two women. While
fighting the hostile primitives, McClure is killed, but the
rest of the group make it back past lava flows to their now-
repaired aircraft.

RECORD CITY. 1977. 96 minutes. Color. *Director:* Dennis
Steinmetz. *Screenplay:* Ron Friedman. *Cinematography:*
William M. Klages. *Cast:* Michael Callan (Eddie); Jack
Carter (Manny); Ruth Buzzi (Olga); Frank Gorshin (Chame-
leon); Sorrell Booke (Coznowski); Ted Lange (Wiz); Ed
Begley, Jr. (Pokey); Rick Dees (Gordon); Kinky Friedman
(Himself); Alice Ghostley (Worried Wife); Leonard Barr
(Sickly Man); Joe Higgins (Doyle); Susan Tolsky (Goldie);
Larry Storch (Blind Man); Stuart Getz (Rupert); Maria
Grimm (Rita); Dennis Bowen (Danny); Alan Oppenheimer
(Blind Man); Isaac Ruiz (Macho); Harold Sakata (Gucci);
Wendy Schall (Lorraine); Elliott Street (Hitch); Timothy
Thomerson (Marty); Deborah White (Vivian).

This plotless AIP comedy is a series of episodic events
revolving around a large record store. Produced for what appears to have been saturation distribution, *Record City* is
similar to *Car Wash* in its use of vignettes instead of an established plot. Many familiar faces are used: Jack Carter as
the store owner; Michael Callan as the store manager; Ruth
Buzzi as the store cleaning lady; Frank Gorshin as a potential

robber. Much of the action is very predictable, with Joe
Higgins, the good-old-boy cop portraying--you guessed it--a
good-old-boy cop. For film buffs there is a scene with a blind
man knocking over record racks that is copied directly from
W.C. Fields film *It's a Gift*. Anyone who has ever been in a
large record store knows that the impersonal nature of these
establishments does not lend itself to comedy very readily.

ROLLING THUNDER. 1977. 99 minutes. Color. *Director:* John
Flynn. *Screenplay:* Paul Schrader and Heywood Gould; based
on a story by Schrader. *Cinematography:* Jordan Cronen-
weth. *Cast:* William Devane (Major Charles Rane); Tommy
Lee Jones (Johnny Vohden); Linda Haynes (Linda Forchet);
Lisa Richards (Janet); Dabney Coleman (Maxwell); James
Best (Texan); Cassie Yates (Candy); Luke Askew (Automatic
Slim); Lawrason Driscoll (Cliff); Jordan Gerler (Mark);
James Victor (Lopez); Jane Abbott (Sister); Jerry Brown
(1st Patrolman); Jacque Burandt (Bebe); Anthony Castillo
(Street Urchin); Charles Escamilla (T. Bird); Robert K.
Guthrie (3rd Reporter); Ray Gutierrez (Tex-Mex); James
N. Harrell (Grandpa); Randy Herman (Sanchez); Michael
Nakamura (Torturer); Pete Ortega (Emilio); Paul A. Partian
(Brother-in-Law); James Connor Pribble (2nd Patrolman);
Cheyenne Rivera (Gato); Carol Sowa (Betty Ann); Robert
Raymond Reves (2nd Reporter); Arturo R. Tamez, Jr. (Bar-
tender); Bob Tisdale (Mr. Williams); Autry Ward (2nd Tex-
an); Wert Ward (Card Player); William Vance Witte (Bob);
Michael R. Witte (1st Reporter); Alan Wong (Bila).

The main character in *Rolling Thunder* is very much like
the protagonist of *Taxi Driver* (also written by Paul Schrader),
in that both men are walking time bombs, who could resort to
violence at any moment. This film was bounced around from
studio to studio and apparently had some scenes taken out when
preview audiences complained about the excessive violence.
An emotionally drained POW (Devane) returns to his home
in San Antonio after spending many years in a North Vietnamese
prison camp. Upon his arrival he finds that his wife
(Richards) is in love with a friend of his (Driscoll). Devane
is given a typical hometown welcome, which includes a silver
dollar for every day in captivity. One day four men enter
Devane's home looking for the money. When he refuses to tell
them where it is they grind his hand in a kitchen disposal
and murder his wife and son. Now with a razor-sharp prosthetic
hook replacing his hand, Devane methodically sets out to find
the four men and kill them. He takes on his journey a young

woman (Haynes), who had worn his POW bracelet while he was a prisoner. The trail takes them into rough Mexican border towns. With Haynes acting as his confederate, Devane is able to extract information on the men's whereabouts, which leads to a local whorehouse. Along with an Army buddy (Jones), he leads a military-style attack on the four men and their associates.

STRANGE SHADOWS IN AN EMPTY ROOM. 1977. 99 minutes. Color. *Director:* Martin Herbert (Alberto De Martino). *Screenplay:* Vincent Mann and Frank Clark. *Cinematography:* Andrew Ford. *Cast:* Stuart Whitman (Captain Tony Saitta); John Saxon (Sergeant Matthews); Martin Landau (The Doctor); Tisa Farrow (Julie); Carole Laure (Louise Saitta); Gayle Hunnicutt (Margie Cohn); with Jean Leclerc, Jean Marchand, Anthony Forest, Andree St. Laurent, Peter MacNeil, Julie Wildman, James Tapp, Jerome Thibergen, Terence Ross, Dave Nichols, Jene Chandler.

This film's American title makes it sound like a spooky mystery or horror film, but its European title, *Blazing Magnum*, is much more indicative of the subject matter. Filmed in Montreal, this is a standard *policier* with plenty of fast car chases and red herrings.

A police detective (Whitman) learns that his younger sister (Laure) has been murdered. He searches in the high and low spots of Montreal using hardnosed techniques: he would rather rough someone up before asking any questions. Through his garnering of evidence Whitman uncovers his sister's shady lifestyle. One by one his suspects are killed by Laure's murderer. When Whitman goes to the hospital to visit Laure's roommate (Farrow), he finds Laure's former boyfriend ready to kill her. In a chase Whitman shoots the murderer down when he attempts to escape in a helicopter.

TENTACLES. 1977. 102 minutes. Color. *Director:* Oliver Hellman (Ovidio Assonitis). *Screenplay:* Jerome Max, Tito Carpi, Steve Carabatsos, and Sonia Molteni. *Cinematography:* Roberto D'Ettore Piazzoli. *Cast:* John Huston (Ned Turner); Shelley Winters (Tillie Turner); Bo Hopkins (Will Gleason); Henry Fonda (Mr. Whitehead); Cesare Danova (John Corey); Alan Boyd (Mike); Claude Akins (Captain Robards); Delia Boccardo (Vicki Gleason); Sherry Buchanan (Judy); Franco Diogene (Chuck); Marc Fiorini (Don); Helena Makela

(Jane's Mother); with Allesandro Poggi, Roberto Poggi,
Giancarlo Nacinelli, Consolato Marciano, Phillip Dallas,
Leonard C. Lightfoot, John White, William Van Raaphorst,
Joanne Van Raaphorst, Patrick Mulvihill, Janet Myers,
Krisha M. Brekke, Janet Raycraft, Kenneth Lunden, Rita
Real, Alan Scharf, Ross Gordon, Ronald Shapiro, Joseph
Johnson.

One wonders whether John Huston, Shelley Winters, and
Henry Fonda were just hard up for the money: what other reason
would there be for performers of their stature to appear in
this pathetic Italian-made ripoff of *Jaws*? Instead of a shark,
we have a giant octopus who strips and sucks it victims dry
along the Southern California coast. *Tentacles* might well
have one of the worst musical soundtracks of all time.
A couple of skeletons appear in the water off a California
seaport town. A local reporter (Huston) suggests that the
nearby construction of an underwater tunnel plays a part in
the deaths. The head of the construction firm (Fonda) threatens to sue Huston, even though one of his own executives
(Danova) used illegal high-frequency waves in the project.
The waves have disturbed a giant octopus residing in the area.
Soon people are being attacked and killed by the monster. An
oceanographer (Hopkins) decides to use two of his trained killer whales against the octopus. The whales and the octopus
have a savage battle and the monster is killed.

THE TOWN THAT DREADED SUNDOWN. 1977. 90 minutes. Color.
    Director: Charles B. Pierce. *Screenplay:* Earl E. Smith.
    Cinematography: Jim Roberson. *Cast:* Ben Johnson (Captain
    J.D. Morales); Andrew Prine (Deputy Norman Ramsey); Dawn
    Wells (Helen Reed); Jimmy Clem (Sergeant Mal Griffin);
    Charles B. Pierce (Patrolman A.C. Benson); Cindy Butler
    (Peggy Loomis); Earle E. Smith (Dr. Kress); Christine
    Ellsworth (Linda Mae Jenkins); Mick Hackworth (Sammy
    Fuller); Jim Citty (Police Chief Sullivan); Robert Aquino
    (Sheriff Otis Barker); Misty West (Emma Lou Cook); Rick
    Hildreth (Buddy Turner); Steve Lyons (Roy Allen); Bud
    Davis (Phantom Killer); Vern Stiersen (Narrator); Joe
    Catalanatto (Eddie Le Doux); Roy Lee Brown (Rainbow
    Johnson); Jason Darnell (Captain Gus Wells); Mike Downs,
    Bill Deitz, and Carolyn Moreland (Reporters); Michael
    Brown (Police Officer); Woody Woodman (FBI Agent); James
    B. McAdams (Sheriff's Deputy); John Stroud (Dr. Preston
    Hickson); Mason Andres (Reverend Harden); Richard Green
    (High School Principal); Dorothy Darlene Orr (Dispatcher);
    Don Adkins (Suspect).

For a few months in 1946, in the Texarkana area near the Texas and Arkansas border, a hooded psychopath killed five people and injured three others. This film traces the police work done in the case, graphically showing the series of killings as well. Curiously, the panic in the local community, where people booby-trapped their houses and kept shotguns within arm's reach, is hardly delved into.

A young couple (Ellsworth and Hackworth) are brutally murdered in a secluded lovers' lane. A few weeks later a lawman (Prine) finds another murdered couple, so a Texas Ranger (Johnson) is called into the case. The police pose as decoys to lure the killer, but this cannot prevent him from striking again. A psychological profile is compiled on the murderer. A woman (Wells) is shot and wounded by the assailant, but when the police arrive he has disappeared. The murders suddenly stop, and the person responsible was never found.

Everything here reeks of low-budget, but this film packed them in on the Southern drive-in circuit. The paltriness of the production extends not only to the actors supporting Johnson and Prine but also to the stilted semidocumentary quality of the narration.

THE CHOSEN. 1978. 105 minutes. Color. *Director:* Alberto De Martino. *Screenplay:* Sergio Donati, Alberto De Martino, and Michael Robson; based on a story by Donati and De Martino. *Cinematography:* Erico Menczer. *Cast:* Kirk Douglas (Robert Caine); Simon Ward (Angel Caine); Agostina Belli (Sarah Golan); Anthony Quayle (Professor Griffith); Virginia McKenna (Eva Caine); Alexander Knox (Meyer); Ivo Garrani (Prime Minister); Spiro Focas (Harbin); Massimo Foschi (Arab Assassin); Adolfo Celi (Dr. Kerouac); Romolo Valli (Monsignor Charrier); Geoffrey Keen (Gynecologist); John Carlin (Robertson); Gerald Hely (Clarke); Peter Cellier (Sheckley); Penelope Horner (Caine's Secretary); Joanne Dainton (Gynecologist's Nurse); Caroline Langrisch (Angel's Girlfriend); Alan Hendricks (Demonstrator).

Definitely influenced by the foolish mumbo jumbo of *The Omen*, *The Chosen* (also known as *Holocaust 2000*) combines the themes of the Antichrist and ecological disaster through nuclear power.

The executive of a company that is building a nuclear plant in the Middle East (Douglas) is told a strange story by a journalist (Belli). A biblical prophesy envisions a seven-headed monster that will destroy the world under the influence

of the Antichrist. Soon after Douglas's wife (McKenna) is
killed, and opposition develops to the building of the power
plant. Douglas asks for a safety endorsement from his son's
(Ward) mathematics instructor (Knox). Later he learns that
his company's computer has conjured up the prophesy, and that
the plant's design resembles a seven-headed monster. Before
he dies, a computer expert (Quayle) tells Douglas he has created a monster. Douglas finds that Ward's brain and heart
are nonhuman (why was this not found when he was an infant?).
The diabolical Ward puts his father in an asylum and takes
over the nuclear project. Douglas escapes just as Ward announces the completion of the plant on his birthday in the
year 2000.

FORCE 10 FROM NAVARONE. 1978. 118 minutes. Color. *Director:*
Guy Hamilton. *Screenplay:* Robin Chapman; story by Carl
Foreman; based on the novel by Alistair Maclean. *Cine-
matography:* Christopher Challis. *Cast:* Robert Shaw (Major
Mallory); Harrison Ford (Lieutenant-Colonel Mike Barnsby);
Barbara Bach (Maritza Petrovitch); Edward Fox (Sergeant
Miller); Franco Nero (Captain Radicek [Nicolai Lescovar]);
Carl Weathers (Sergeant Walter Weaver); Richard Kiel(Cap-
tain Drazak); Alan Badel (Major Petrovitch); Angus
MacInnes (Lieutenant Doug Reynolds); Michael Byrne (Major
Schroeder); Philip Latham (Commander Jensen); Petar Buntic
(Lieutenant Marko); Michael Sheard (Sergeant Bauer);
Leslie Schofield, Antony Langdon, and Richard Hampton
(Interrogation Officers); Paul Humpoletz (Sergeant
Bismark); Dicken Ashworth (Nolan); Christopher Malcolm
(Rogers); Nick Ellsworth (Salvone); Jonathan Blake
(Oberstein); Roger Owen (Blake); Frances Mughan, Mike
Sirett, Graham Crowther, and Jim Dowdall (Force 10 Team);
Michael Osborne (Naval Lieutenant); Edward Peel (MP Driv-
er); Michael Josephs (German Storeman); Jürgen Anderson
and David Gretton (Engineers); Paul Jerrico (Lieutenant);
Edward Kalinski (Young German Soldier); Robert Gillespie
(Sergeant); Wolf Kahler (German Soldier); Hans Kahler
(Pilot); Ramiz Pasic (Mallory's Boy).

Rarely has a war film with so much action been pulled
off with such a pedestrian lack of imagination. Whereas *The
Guns of Navarone* began slowly and built up interest, this film
begins with action and then rapidly becomes bogged down.
Two British survivors (Shaw and Fox) of the Navarone mission are assigned to an American unit led by Harrison Ford.
Shaw and Fox's assignment is to identify and kill a German

spy, who is impersonating a leader of the Yugoslavian partisans. Meanwhile Ford and his group have orders to blow up a
vital German bridge in Yugoslavia. A plane carrying the group
is shot down, and the survivors are captured by Chetniks (Yu-
goslavs loyal to the Germans) and given over to German authorities. A partisan (Bach) aids them in escaping from the Germans. They decide to blow up the bridge by dynamiting a dam,
so they make an assault on a German supply yard to gain access
to explosives. During the raid the German spy (Nero) is uncovered and killed by Ford. Now Fox and Shaw blow up the dam,
with the ensuing flood destroying the bridge. With the mission
a success the members of the unit now find themselves caught
behind German lines.

HERE COME THE TIGERS. 1978. 90 minutes. Color. *Director:*
Sean S. Cunningham. *Screenplay:* Arch McCoy. *Cinematog-*
raphy: Barry Abrams. *Cast:* Richard Lincoln (Eddie Burke);
James Zvanut (Burt Honneger); Samantha Grey (Bette Burke);
Manny Lieberman (Felix the Umpire); William Caldwell
(Kreegen); Fred Lincoln (Aesop); Xavier Rodrigo (Buster
Rivers); Kathy Bell (Patty O'Malley); Noel John Cunningham
(Noel "Peanuts" Cady); Sean P. Griffin (Art Bullfinch);
Max McClellan (Mike "The Bod" Karpel); Kevin Moore ("Eagle
Scout" Terwillinger); with Ted Oyama, Philip Scuderi,
Nancy Willis.

This egregious imitation of *The Bad News Bears* was directed by Sean S. Cunningham, the man who brought us *Friday*
the 13th. Filmed on a small budget in Westport, Connecticut,
this film is geared more toward the suburban-shopping-mall
audience than those in large cities.
A young policeman (Lincoln) takes over a little-league
baseball team made up of youngsters who are a racially mixed
group of misfits and delinquents. The team--filled with such
characters as a flirtatious blonde, a deaf pitcher, a certified
juvenile delinquent, and a cleanup batter who wields a bat
like a Samurai sword--gradually is molded into a winning unit.
Just before the big championship game they become embroiled
in a pool-hall fight. Their Samurai swinging cleanup hitter
straightens things out with a few judicious karate chops. During the melee the team's pitcher injures his shoulder, and a
top flight surgeon is brought in to correct the boy's problem.
Needless to say, the team wins the championship game.

HIGH-BALLIN. 1978. 100 minutes. Color. *Director:* Peter
Carter. *Screenplay:* Paul Edwards; based on a story by
Richard Robinson and Stephen Schneck. *Cinematography:*
René Verzier. *Cast:* Peter Fonda (Rane); Jerry Reed
(Duke); Helen Shaver (Pickup); Chris Wiggins (King
Caroll); David Ferry (Harvey); Christopher Langevin
(Tanker); Myrna Lorrie (Country Singer); Mary Pirie
(Vonetta); Wendy Thatcher (Hijacker); Harvey Atkin (Buzz);
Les Carlson (Bud); Arnie Achtman (Cue); Ardon Bess (Po-
liceman); George Buza (Warehouseman); Alan Crofoot
(Bushes); Len Doncheff (Decal); John Friesen (Pictures);
Michael Hogan (Reggie); Eric House (Slater); Kay Hawtrey
(Ma); Michael Ironside (Butch); Cec Linder (Policeman);
Chris Lumiere (Freddie); Brian Nasimok (Warehouseman);
Patrick Patterson (Gatesman); Linda Rennhofer (Waitress);
Prairie Oyster (Country Band).

Plenty of CBs, 18-wheelers, and auto crashes make *High-
Ballin* the sort of film that appeals to the good-old-boy rural
audience. Peter Fonda looks so out of place here that it appears he just stepped off the set of *Easy Rider.*
A motorcycle racer (Fonda) visits a friend (Reed) who is
an independent truck driver. Reed and other indies are being
constantly threatened by a group of hijackers in the employ
of a trucking company owner (Wiggins), who wants the truckers
to sign up with his outfit. When Reed loses his truck, Fonda
offers to help him. The two of them deliver a truckload of
bootleg alcohol on a truck bought by Reed after mortgaging
his house. Wiggins has his men stop them from the delivery
by ambushing them at night in a motel. Reed is shot and injured, and Fonda goes after Wiggins and his chief henchman
(Ferry) when they kidnap his girlfriend (Shaver). By this
time all of the independent truckers come to the rescue to
fight Wiggins's group of hijackers. Fonda now contemplates
going into business with Reed.

THE INCREDIBLE MELTING MAN. 1978. 86 minutes. Color. *Director:* William Sachs. *Screenplay:* William Sachs. *Cinematography:* Willy Curtis. *Cast:* Alex Rebar (Colonel Steve
West); Burr DeBenning (Dr. Ted Nelson); Myron Healey (General Perry); Michael Aldredge (Sheriff Blake); Ann Sweeny
(Judy Nelson); Lisle Wilson (Dr. Loring); Rainbeaux Smith
(Model); Julie Drazen (Carol); Stuart Edmond Rodgers and

Chris Whitney (Little Boys); Edwin Max (Harold); Dorothy
Love (Helen); Janus Blythe (Nell); Jonathan Demme (Matt);
Mickey Lolich (1st Security Guard); Westbrook Claridge
(2nd Security Guard); De Forest Covan (Janitor); Sam
Gelfman (Fisherman); Bonnie Inch (Nurse); Keith Michl
(Maintenance Man); Leigh Mitchell (Carol's Mother); Don
Walters (Photographer); Voices--Nowell Alexander (Steve
West); Rosemary Lovell (Nora); Dave Hull (Houston Con-
trol); Jennifer Mulaire (Newscaster).

This film is a throwback to those grade-"Z" science-
fiction films of the 50s like *The Hideous Sun Demon*. In directing his first film, William Sachs includes some unintentionally ludicrous moments, but the film also betrays at times
an off-the-wall sense of humor. Alex Rebar is very believable
as the title character, even if he does resemble a combination
of a candle and a chocolate sundae left out in the sun.
The sole survivor of a space flight to Saturn (Rebar) is
taken to a hospital with serious burns and a mysterious skin
infection. As the infection increases, Rebar escapes from
the hospital. His condition, which is causing his skin to
melt, requires him to eat human flesh in order to slow down
the melting process. Military authorities attempt to keep
his condition a secret, since there is going to be another
Saturn flight. A doctor friend of Rebar's (DeBenning) goes
out to look for him. Rebar goes on a killing spree that includes a number of gruesome murders. DeBenning finally comes
upon him in a power plant, where Rebar saves him from a near-
fatal fall. When two security guards appear, they accidentally
shoot DeBenning. Rebar kills both men and soon after melts
down into an unrecognizable puddle.

ISLAND OF THE DAMNED. 1978. 110 minutes. Color. *Director:*
    Narciso Ibáñez Serrador. *Screenplay:* Luis Peñafiel and
    Narciso Ibáñez Serrador; based on the novel by Juan José
    Plans. *Cinematography:* José Luis Alcaine. *Cast:* Lewis
    Fiander (Tom); Prunella Ransome (Evelyn); Maria Druille,
    Lourdes de la Cámara, Roberto Nauta, José Luis Romero,
    Javier de la Cámara, Marian Salgado, Cristina Torres,
    Luis Mateos, Adela Blanco, Juan Carlos Romero, Julio
    Jesús Parra, Carlos Parra, Juan Antonio Balandin, and
    Pedro Balandin (The Children); with Antonio Iranzo, Miguel
    Narros, Maria Luisa Arias, Marisa Porcel, Juan Cazalilla,
    Luis Ciges, Antonio Canal, Aparacio Rivero, Fabián Conde,
    Andrés Goinez.

AIP picked up the American rights to this 1976 Spanish film, but apparently it never received the wide release it deserved. Serrador brings a stylistic flourish to the horror genre much like some of the Italian directors, such as Bava and Argento. The most frightening aspect of this film is not that the children are murderers but that they kill with a bright-eyed, laughing sangfroid.

An English couple (Fiander and Ransome) are vacationing on a small island in the Mediterranean near the Balearics. Fiander finds that the local town seems to be deserted except for children, as almost all of the adults have hastily departed. From the hotel they witness a young girl beat a man to death. Then a group of children hang him, while they cut at him with a scythe. Most of the adults in the area have been killed, since they did not protect themselves, lest they kill a child. It seems that the children are gaining revenge on adults for the suffering of children through centuries of war and starvation. When Fiander and Ransome attempt to leave the island, they become trapped in a police station. During the night the pregnant Ransome is attacked and killed from inside her body by the unborn child. Fiander runs to the harbor with a machine gun in hand. He is fighting off the children when the police arrive and kill him, thinking that he has gone berserk. The children then kill the police and set out to continue their mayhem on the mainland.

JENNIFER. 1978. 90 minutes. Color. *Director:* Brice Mack. *Screenplay:* Kay Cousins Johnson; based on a story by Steve Krantz. *Cinematography:* Irv Goodnoff. *Cast:* Lisa Pelikan (Jennifer Baylor); Bert Convy (Jeff Reed); Nina Foch (Mrs. Calley); Amy Johnston (Sandra Tremayne); John Gavin (Senator Tremayne); Jeff Corey (Luke Baylor); Louise Hoven (Jane Delano); Ray Underwood (Dayton Powell); Wesley Eure (Pit Lassiter); Florida Friebus (Miss Tooker); Georganne La Piere (DeeDee Martin); Sally Pansing (Brenda); Leslie E. King (Tammy); Ruth Cox (Nancy); Lillian Randolph (Martha); Randy T. Williams (Bill); Domingo Ambrizi (Jose); Kimberly Eilbacher (Jennifer as a Child).

Jennifer has all the trappings of a low budget *Carrie*, the only difference being that Jennifer gains revenge on her classmates by using snakes. Character actor Jeff Corey, who late in his career made a speciality of portraying spooky, semidemented characters, here portrays Jennifer's religious-fanatic father.

A young girl from Appalachia (Pelikan) is one of the few
scholarship students at an exclusive private girls' school.
She and her father (Corey) live in the back of a small pet
store that they run. Corey is a follower of a fundamentalist
snake-handling cult. As a young girl Pelikan was known for
her strange telekinetic powers, especially her control over
the snakes that the cult worshiped. At school she is harassed
by the local blonde bitch (Johnston), who is attempting to
drive Pelikan out of school. All of Johnston's plans are unsuccessful, until she and her boyfriend (Underwood) kill a
cat bought from the pet store and blame Pelikan for the death.
The money-grubbing headmistress of the school (Foch) plans to
expel Pelikan, but before this can happen Pelikan exacts her
revenge on her tormentors. One night Johnston and her friends
kidnap Pelikan. When they anger her to the breaking point,
she conjures up giant snakes, which kill some (including
Johnston) and injure others.

THE LAST SURVIVOR. 1978. 88 minutes. Color. *Director:*
    Ruggero Deodato. *Screenplay:* Tito Cardi, Giafranco
    Clerici, and Renzo Genta. *Cinematography:* Marcello
    Masciocchi. *Cast:* Massimo Foschi (Robert Harper); Me Me
    Lay (Jungle Girl); Ivan Rassimov (Rolf); with Sheik Razak
    Shikur, Judy Rosly, Suleiman, Shamsi.

The makers of this film claimed that it is based on the
real-life discovery of an unknown Stone Age tribe in the Philippines some years ago. *The Last Survivor* seems more intent
on exploiting the seldom-filmed subject of a cannibal civilization than on displaying anthropological concerns.
    Two men (Foschi and Rassimov) set out to look for two
oil company employees in the Philippine jungle. After they
find evidence of foul play, a woman who has come with them
(Rosly) is kidnapped. While looking for her, Foschi and
Rassimov find a cannibal tribe eating their remains. They use
a raft to return to their plane, but Rassimov falls in the
river and is presumably drowned. Foschi collapses in the jungle and is captured and taken prisoner by another group of
cannibals. A sympathetic native woman (Lay) helps him escape
through the jungle. While hiding in a cave, they come across
the injured Rassimov. Before they can make it to their plane,
they are victims of a cannibal attack, as Lay is killed and
eaten. The cannibals seem to gain some sort of respectful
curiosity toward Foschi when he kills one of them and devours
his intestines. They allow the two men to take off in the
plane, but while they are in the plane the injured Rassimov
dies.

MATILDA. 1978. 105 minutes. Color. *Director:* Daniel Mann.
Screenplay: Albert S. Ruddy and Timothy Galfas; based on
the novel by Paul Gallico. *Cinematography:* Jack Woolf.
Cast: Elliott Gould (Bernie Bonnelli); Robert Mitchum
(Duke Parkhurst); Harry Guardino (Uncle Nono); Clive
Revill (Billy Baker); Karen Carlson (Kathleen Smith);
Lionel Stander (Pinky Schwab); Art Metrano (Gordon Baum);
Roy Clark (Wild Bill Wildman); Larry Pennell (Lee
Dockerty); Roberta Collins (Tanya Six); Lenny Montana
(Mercanti); Frank Avianca (Renato); Doe De Fish, Pat
Henry, Matty Jordan, and Shep Saunders (Hoods); Don Dunphy
(Ringside Announcer); Mike Willesee (Australian Announc-
er); George Latka (Referee); Fred Carney (Clay); Charlie
Brill (Barker); David Clarke (Sheriff); John Cunningham
(Dave Holter); Rex Everhart (1st ASPCA Attendant); Bob
Hodges (2nd ASPCA Attendant); Ted Hartley (Payne Smith);
Harry Holcombe (Mr. Hardy); Elizabeth Kerr (Mrs. Hardy);
James Jeter (3rd ASPCA Attendant); Jimmy Lennon (Ring
Announcer); Ed Max (Matson); John Thomas (3rd Referee);
Bill Quinn (Donoghue); Rita Karin (Spectator); Gary Morgan
(Matilda the Kangaroo).

Matilda is sort of a marsupial *Rocky* (the only difference
being that the boxing kangaroo is smarter), which was a box-
office disaster. The expensive promotional campaign, which
had ties with a tennis-ball company and McDonald's, could not
help this film's prospects. It is reported that, on the first
day of its run in San Francisco, absolutely no one came to
see it; it played only to the theatre employees. Only Robert
Mitchum was able to escape this fiasco with any semblance of
dignity.
A former boxer (Revill) convinces a New York theatrical
promoter (Gould) to hire Matilda, Revill's boxing kangaroo.
Gould persuades a sportswriter (Mitchum) to watch Matilda in
an exhibition bout with a hungover fighter (Pennell), who is
managed by a mobster (Guardino). Much to everyone's surprise,
Matilda knocks Pennell out. Gould begins the kangaroo on a
boxing career that will take the animal to the championship.
Along the way Gould is hampered in his efforts by a woman from
an animal-protection society (Carlson) and by Guardino's hoods,
who attempt to kidnap the kangaroo. Though Matilda can box,
he (despite the name, he is a male) cannot take a punch and
loses the championship fight.

MEAN DOG BLUES. 1978. 100 minutes. Color. *Director:* Mel
Stuart. *Screenplay:* George Lefferts. *Cinematography:*
Robert B. Hauser. *Cast:* Gregg Henry (Paul Ramsey); Kay

Lenz (Linda Ramsey); George Kennedy (Captain Omar
Kinsman); Scatman Crothers (Mudcat); Tina Louise (Donna
Lacey); Felton Perry (Jake Turner); Gregory Sierra (Jesus
Gonzales); James Wainwright (Sergeant Hubbell Walker);
William Windom (Victor Lacey); John Daniels (Yakima
Jones); Marc Alaimo (Transfer Guard); Edith Atwater
(Linda's Mother); James Boyd (Sonny); Edward Call (Road
Gang Guard); Christina Hart (Gloria Kinsman); Chris
Hubbell (Elroy Smith); Stephen Johnson ("Mary" Emerson);
Logan Ramsey (Edmund Oberlin); Geno Silva (Tonto); Lee
Weacer (Cheatem); Ian Wolfe (Judge); David Lewis (Dr.
Caleb Odum); Billy Beck (Deadman); Herb Armstrong (Bai-
liff); James Bacon (Court Clerk); Hunter van Leer (Guard
at Conjugal Barracks); Kimberly Allan (Max); Andy Albin
(Truck Driver); Georgie Paul (Masseuse); John Dennis
(Deputy Sheriff); Bill Catching (Mr. Vogel).

Mean Dog Blues is an amalgam of the powerful 1933 Warner
Brothers film *I Am a Fugitive from a Chain Gang* and the prison
movies made more successfully by New World Pictures. This
film is so imitative that even George Kennedy portrays a character that is very similar to the one that won him an Academy
Award in *Cool Hand Luke*.
A young musician hitching a ride to Nashville (Henry) is
picked up by a wealthy drunk (Windom) and his wife (Louise).
Windom kills a pedestrian but puts the blame on Henry, who is
railroaded into a prison sentence on a work farm run by a couple of brutal overseers (Wainwright and Kennedy). Henry, dis-
liked by the other prisoners after he interferes with a homosexual rape, soon after becomes "bait" for Kennedy's training
of his vicious guard dog. Henry's wife (Lenz) is attempting
to get him out of prison, and when she visits the farm
Wainwright tries to rape her. Louise decides to help Lenz by
persuading her influential husband to have the governor set
Henry free. A pardon is sent to the prison, just as Kennedy
catches Henry with his daughter (Hart). He forces Henry to
partake in a death race with his savage guard dog, which Henry
kills. He is now finally set free and has a reunion with Lenz.

THE NORSEMAN. 1978. 90 minutes. Color. *Director:* Charles
    B. Pierce. *Screenplay:* Charles B. Pierce. *Cinematog-
    raphy:* Robert Bethard. *Cast:* Lee Majors (Thorvald Helge);
    Cornel Wilde (Ragnar); Mel Ferrer (King Eurich); Jack
    Elam (Death Dreamer); Chris Connelly (Rolf); Kathleen
    Freeman (Indian Woman); Danny Miller (Rauric); Seaman
    Glass (Gunnar); Jimmy Clem (Olaf); Susie Coelho (Winetta);

Jacob Jerry Daniels (Kiwonga); Deacon Jones (Thraul); Charles Pierce, Jr. (Young Eric); Bill Lawler (Bjorn); Fred Biletnikoff, Steve Denny, William Lower, Mike Kaminsky, Frank Anderson, Glen Hollis, Curtis Jordon, David Kent, John Welsh, Cicil Kent, Anthony Vitale, Kevin Myhre, Sandy Sanders, and Eric Carandall (Norsemen); Ron Britt (Indian Boy).

This unintentionally humorous film would appeal only to audiences in neighborhood theatres in Greenland. Co-produced by Lee Majors and Farrah Fawcett, *The Norseman* is filled with outlandish qualities: Majors as a Viking in a blow-dry hairdo, Vikings who look more Mediterranean than Nordic, and action scenes shot in slow motion. If you look closely, you can see an oil tanker near one of the Norsemen's ships.

A Viking warrior (Majors) takes his hardy band of men on an expedition to Vineland (North America). He is looking for his father (Ferrer), the Norse king, who along with his men has been a prisoner of an Indian tribe for more than a year. The Vikings survive a number of attacks by the Indians after they arrive. A friendly Indian girl (Coelho) leads Majors and his men to an underground chamber where Ferrer and his men are being held. They lead the prisoners away, as the Indians attack them. In a pitched battle near their boats the Vikings beat off the Indians and set off for home.

OUR WINNING SEASON. 1978. 92 minutes. Color. *Director:* Joseph Ruben. *Screenplay:* Nick Niciphor (some sources list Joseph Ruben). *Cinematography:* Stephen Katz. *Cast:* Scott Jacoby (David Wakefield); Deborah Benson (Alice Barker); Dennis Quaid (Paul Morelli); Randy Herman (Jerry McDuffy); Joe Penny (Dean Berger); Jan Smithers (Cathy Wakefield); P.J. Soles (Cindy Hawkins); Robert Wahler (Burton Fleishaur); Wendy Rastatter (Susie Wilson); Damon Douglas (Miller); Joanna Cassidy (Sheila); Jeff Soracco (Eddie Rice); J. Don Ferguson (Coach Michael Murphy); Ted Henning (Mr. Weizle); Chris Shelt (1st Pledge); George Griffin (2nd Pledge); Joe Dorsey (Officer McNally); Carl Mariani (Priest); Pete Robinson (Sergeant); Doug McCroskey (Assistant Manager); Earleen Carey (Waitress at Snack Bar); Fred Waugh (1st Cop); Roy Tatum (2nd Cop).

Set back in 1967, this film does what AIP began doing more and more in the 70s--that is exploit other successful films. *Our Winning Season* seems to combine the hijinks of *American Graffiti* with the coming-of-age of *The Last Picture*

Show and the triumph of the underdog from *Rocky*.

A high school track star (Jacoby) hopes to receive an athletic scholarship, but he must win the state-championship mile race against an old rival (Wahler), whom he has never beaten. Both Jacoby and Wahler go to the same school, where they belong to different social groups that spend time harassing one another. Jacoby meets his former track idol (Penny), who has dropped out of college and is soon to leave for Vietnam. Penny helps Jacoby train for the race, all the while urging him to go to college so he will not be drafted. After Penny has been killed in Vietnam, Jacoby steps up his training, using Penny as an inspiration. Naturally Jacoby wins the big race and his track scholarship.

THE PRIVATE FILES OF J. EDGAR HOOVER. 1978. 112 minutes.
   Color. *Director:* Larry Cohen. *Screenplay:* Larry Cohen.
   Cinematography: Paul Glickman. *Cast:* Broderick Crawford
   (J. Edgar Hoover); Jose Ferrer (Lionel McCoy); Michael
   Parks (Robert F. Kennedy); Ronee Blakley (Carrie DeWitt);
   Rip Torn (Dwight Webb, Jr.); Celeste Holm (Florence
   Hollister); Michael Sacks (Melvin Purvis); Dan Dailey
   (Clyde Tolson); Raymond St. Jacques (Martin Luther King,
   Jr.); Andrew Duggan (Lyndon B. Johnson); John Marley (Dave
   Hindley); Howard Da Silva (Franklin D. Roosevelt); June
   Havoc (Hoover's Mother); James Wainwright (Young Hoover);
   Lloyd Nolan (Attorney General Stone); Ellen Barber (Miss
   Harper); Lloyd Gough (Walter Winchell); Brad Dexter
   (Alvin Karpis); Jennifer Lee (Ethel Brunette); George
   Plimpton (Quenton Reynolds); Jack Cassidy (Damon Runyon);
   William Jordan (John F. Kennedy); Henderson Forsythe
   (Harry Suydam); George D. Wallace (Senator Joseph
   McCarthy); Fred J. Scollay (Putnam); William Wellman, Jr.
   (Dwight Webb, Sr.); Art Lund (Benchley); Mary Alice Moore
   (Miss Bryant); Jim Antonio (Senator McKellar); Gregg Abels
   (President's Aide); Dan Resin (President's Adviser); James
   Dixon (Reilly); Penny Du Pont (Newscaster); Alvin Miles
   (Valet); John Bay (Heywood Broun); Brooks Morton (Earl
   Warren); Richard Dixon (President Nixon); James Dukas
   (Frank the Waiter); Ron Faber (Hijacker); Ed Masy, Hans
   Mannship, Dana Rowe, Colin Bremmen, Jack Drummond, Joe
   Norton, Ken Harvey, Paul Thomas, and Sam Crew (FBI
   Agents); Margo Lynn Curtis and Tanya Roberts (Steward-
   esses); Larry Pine (Kelly); John Stefano (Harry); Wyman
   Kane (Senator); Gordon Zimmerman (Lepke); Marty Lee (Media
   Man); Reno Garrel (Officer); Frank Kohnbach, Marshall
   Gordon and Joe Mayo (White House Aides); Joe Arrowsmith

(Newspaperman); with Gwynn Gillis and Bruce Weitz.

Larry Cohen chooses to portray in this film what many
people suspected of J. Edgar Hoover but were often too afraid
to say. He presents Hoover as a man obsessed with sex, a puritanical prude with a mother fixation, and perhaps a closet
homosexual. Many of the American critics excoriated this film,
comparing it to a visual *National Enquirer*, and even nit-
picking about the poor color used in some sequences. It took
the British and European critics to see the film's merits:
one called it "arguably the most radical Hollywood genre film
in years" (Paul Taylor, *Monthly Film Bulletin*, February 1977,
p. 31).

The 50-year career of FBI director J. Edgar Hoover
(Crawford) is followed from Dillinger to Watergate. Along
the way the film traces various events in Hoover's private,
but mostly public, life, as narrated by a former FBI agent
(Torn). Shown are: Hoover's theft of headlines in the
Dillinger killing, his aiding Joe McCarthy (Wallace) in his
witch hunts, his relationship with the Kennedys (Parks and
Jordan), the wiretapping of Martin Luther King, Jr. (St.
Jacques), and the role that he and the FBI might have played
in the Watergate scandal.

All along Larry Cohen makes the connection between how
public policy is often influenced by private behavior.

YOUNGBLOOD. 1978. 90 minutes. Color. *Director:* Noel
    Nosseck. *Screenplay:* Paul Carter Harrison. *Cinematog-
    raphy:* Robbie Greenberg. *Cast:* Lawrence-Hilton Jacobs
    (Rommel); Bryan O'Dell (Youngblood); Ren Woods (Sybil);
    Tony Allen (Hustler); Vince Cannon (Corelli); Art Evans
    (Junkie); Jeff Hollis (Basketball Pusher); Dave Pendleton
    (Reggie); Ron Trice (Bummie); Sheila Wills (Joan); Ralph
    Farquhar (Geronimo); Herbert Rice (Durango); Lionel Smith
    (Chaka); Maurice Sneed (Skeeter-Jeeter); Ann Weldon (Mrs.
    Gordon); Isabel Cooley (School Principal); Bernie Weissman
    (Bodyguard); Earl Billings (Bowling Alley Manager); T.K.
    Carter (Bubba Cossell); Frank E. Ford (2nd Dalton Boy);
    Provot Gupta (Basketball Player in Dream); Ron Neal (Gym
    Teacher); Michael Pagan (Youth in Knife Fight); Hank Ross
    (Dalton War Councillor).

Youngblood was surely one of the last attempts by AIP to
capture the black urban audience, with which it had much success. Incidentally, while one of the main characters is nick-
named "Youngblood," this ghetto term really means a tough,
aggressive young man.

A teenage boy living in a black ghetto in Los Angeles
(O'Dell) seeks acceptance from his peers. One of his friends
(Trice) urges him to join a local gang called The Kingsmen,
whose leader is an older Vietnam veteran (Jacobs). After a
confrontation with another gang O'Dell is fully accepted as a
member of The Kingsmen. His brother (Pendleton) buys his family a house, but O'Dell instead moves in with Jacobs and his
wife (Wills). When several members of the gang succumb to
drug addiction, the other gang members decide to drive the
pushers out of the neighborhood. O'Dell finds that his new
girlfriend (Woods) has become a junkie, and compounding his
agony is the fact that Pendleton is part of the mob supplying
the drugs. He and Jacobs steal a large amount of drug money
from the gang, and Jacobs is injured in the process. The denouement comes when the two young men find themselves trapped
by Pendleton and other mob members.

THE AMITYVILLE HORROR. 1979. 117 minutes. Color. *Director:*
Stuart Rosenberg. *Screenplay:* Sandor Stern; based on
the book by Jay Anson. *Cinematography:* Fred J. Koenekamp.
Cast: James Brolin (George Lutz); Margot Kidder (Kathleen
Lutz); Rod Steiger (Father Delaney); Don Stroud (Father
Bolen); Murray Hamilton (Father Ryan); John Larch (Father
Nuncio); Natasha Ryan (Amy); K.C. Martel (Greg); Meeno
Peluce (Matt); Michael Sacks (Jeff); Helen Shaver
(Carolyn); Amy Wright (Jackie); Val Avery (Sergeant
Gianfriddo); Irene Dailey (Aunt Helena); Marc Vahanian
(Jimmy); Elsa Raven (Mrs. Townsend); Ellen Saland (Bride);
Eddie Barth (Agucci); Hank Garrett (Bartender); James
Tolkan (Coroner); Carmine Foresta (1st Cop at the House);
Peter Maloney (Newspaper Clerk); Charlie Welch (Carpen-
ter); J.R. Miller (Boy); Patty Burtt (Girl); Michael
Hawkins (1st New York State Trooper); Richard Hughes (2nd
New York State Trooper); Jim Dukas (Neighbor); Baxter
Harris (2nd Cop at the House); Michael Stearns (Police-
man); Jack Krupnick (Dead Father).

The Amityville Horror is supposedly based on fact, but
then supermarket tabloids claim to be factual as well. This
film panders to those who actually believe that there is a
hell, and that absolute evil does exist. The worse sin a horror film can commit is not to be scary, and *The Amityville
Horror* is not. It does contain a performance by Rod Steiger
that is a tour-de-force of overacting, complete with rolling
his eyeballs and weeping.
A pair of newlyweds (Brolin and Kidder) and Kidder's three

children move into a house, in which, a year before, a young
man had murdered his family. They soon experience inexplicable
occurrences--drafts, black goo coming out of walls and toilets,
and a room full of flies. A local priest (Steiger) visits
the house and suddenly becomes ill. Meanwhile Brolin has become more and more withdrawn and sullen and begins to neglect
his work. A friend (Sacks) informs him that the old house was
once occupied by a satanist. Soon after Steiger is struck
blind while praying for the family's safety. Brolin is slowly
being taken over by the house's evil spirit, as Kidder learns
that the house's previous killer looked like Brolin. She and
her children leave when the house begins to bend and shake.
Brolin enters the basement to rescue their dog and finds that
the entrance to hell lies in a basement opening. He escapes
just before the forces of hell can engulf him.

CALIFORNIA DREAMING. 1979. 92 minutes. Color. *Director:*
      John Hancock. *Screenplay:* Ned Wynn. *Cinematography:*
      Bobby Byrne. *Cast:* Glynnis O'Connor (Corky); Seymour
      Cassel (Duke); Dorothy Tristan (Fay); Dennis Christopher
      (T.T.); John Calvin (Rick); Tanya Roberts (Melanie); Jimmy
      Van Patten (Mike); Todd Susman (Jordy); Alice Playten
      (Corrine); Ned Wynn (Earl); John Fain (Tenner); Marshall
      Efron (Ruben).

California Dreaming is a feeble last gasp of a company
in trouble, as AIP vainly attempts here to rejuvenate the
beach-party films of the 60s. Some of the 40ish denizens of
the beach community in this film look as if they have been
living there since the beach-party days.
      A callow young man (Christopher) from the Midwest comes
to the West Coast to immerse himself in the Southern California
beach lifestyle. He falls in love with a girl (O'Connor),
who is tired of the beach lifestyle and wants to settle down,
but not with him. Christopher is unsuccessful in becoming
part of the local surfer clique, so O'Connor's father (Cassel)
teaches him some of the finer arts of life: volleyball, surfing, and, of course, getting along with girls. Before we know
it, Christopher is one of the crowd. For the rest of the film
he seems to spend his time interfering in other people's private lives. In the end Christopher has wised up a bit and
realizes that the California Dream is an illusion--yes, it is
time to grow up.

C.H.O.M.P.S. 1979. 89 minutes. Color. *Director:* Don
Chaffey. *Screenplay:* Dick Robbins, Duane Poole, and
Joseph Barbera; based on a story by Barbera. *Cinematog-
raphy:* Charles F. Wheeler. *Cast:* Wesley Eure (Brian
Foster); Valerie Bertinelli (Casey Norton); Conrad Bain
(Ralph Norton); Chuck McCann (Brooks); Red Buttons
(Braken); Larry Bishop (Ken Sharp); Hermoine Baddeley
(Mrs. Fowler); Jim Backus (Mr. Gibbs); Robert Q. Lewis
(Merkle); Austin Willis (Head Engineer); William Flatley
(1st Engineer); Dinah Anne Rogers (2nd Engineer); James
Reynolds (Reporter); Joe E. Baker (Moving and Storage
Foreman); Phil Adams (1st Hood); Paul Nuckles (2nd Hood);
Baynes Barron (1st Policeman); Steve Mitchell (2nd Police
man); Peter Griffin (3rd Policeman); Larry Easley (Secur-
ity Guard); Michael Rougas (T.V. Newsman); Joe Hornok
(Dog Catcher); Sheldon Konblett (Shelter Officer); Joe
Ross (Man at Wall); Regis Toomey (Chief Patterson).

C.H.O.M.P.S., one of the few AIP films that was released
with a "G" rating, can be easily confused with a product from
the Disney Studio. As AIP was slowly being incorporated by
Filmways, it put out some quite dreadful films, *C.H.O.M.P.S.*
and *California Dreaming* being prime examples.
A small town is being hit with a rash of burglaries. A
young engineer with a security company (Eure) is attempting
to come up with an alarm system that will stymie the burglars.
Eure builds a device he calls C.H.O.M.P.S.--Canine Home Protection System, a mechanical dog made in the image of his own
mutt. The electronic computerized dog has X-ray vision, teeth
that can bite through metal, and paws that perform karate
chops. The owner of a rival security company (Backus) seeks
to steal Eure's invention. He hires two incompetent Laurel-
and-Hardy-type thieves (McCann and Buttons) to steal the plans
for the electronic dog. Eure's boss (Bain) sets up a demonstration experiment, but he confuses Eure's real dog with the
mechanical one. Not much more need be said.

THE EVICTORS. 1979. 92 minutes. Color. *Director:* Charles
B. Pierce. *Screenplay:* Charles B. Pierce. *Cinematog-
raphy:* Chuck Bryant. *Cast:* Michael Parks (Ben Watkins);
Jessica Harper (Ruth Watkins); Vic Morrow (Jake Rudd);
Sue Ann Langdon (Olie Gibson); Dennis Fimple (Bumford);
Bill Thurman (Preacher Higgins); Jimmy Clem (Buckner);
Harry Thomasson (Wheeler); Twyla Taylor (Mrs. Bumford);
Mary Branch (Mrs. Mullins); John Meyer (Mr. Mullins);
John Milam (Mr. Rhinehart); Roxanne Harter (Mrs.

The Evictors

Rhinehart); Foster Litton (Sheriff); Owen Guthrie, Ron
White, and Thomas Ham (G-Men); Donald Hodge, Raymond
Meyers, Ervin Reed, William Rexon, Robert Sibley, and
Stanley Taylor (Deputies); Lucius Farris (Lee); Jesse
Cagle (Banker); Marilyn Gorsylowsky (Lady at Party); Glen
Roberts (Dwayne Monroe); S.F. Vaughan (Man at Store);
John Fertitta (Doctor).

The director of *The Evictors*, Charles B. Pierce, with
his string of low-budget films, might very well be the Roger
Corman of the 70s and 80s. This particular film seems to have
been almost totally ignored when it came out. It was subse-
quently sold to some of the cable movie channels, where it
turns up occasionally as a pleasant surprise.

In Louisiana in 1942 a local real-estate agent (Morrow)
sells a house to a young couple (Parks and Harper). In a series of flashbacks we witness the house's violent history.
The original owners died in a shootout with authorities when
they refused to be evicted. A neighbor (Langdon) relates to
Harper how a number of people living in the house during the
30s were murdered. Harper periodically notices a strange man
on the property. One day the man (Roberts) kills a local ped-
dler (Farris) working for Harper and then goes after her.
While alone in the house she is able to fend him off. When
Parks comes home at night, she mistakes him for Roberts and
shoots him dead. She decides to leave the area and goes to
say goodbye to Langdon. While there Harper finds that Langdon
and Roberts are husband and wife. They are the original owner
of her house and have been killing the other owners of the
house ever since. The deranged Roberts kills Langdon, but
before he can kill Harper, Morrow appears and shoots him.
Morrow is Roberts's brother and also one of the house's original owners. We next see Morrow and Harper five years later,
and now married. He sells the house to an elderly couple,
who, we learn at the end, were killed a year later.

JAGUAR LIVES! 1979. 90 minutes. Color. *Director:* Ernest
    Pintoff. *Screenplay:* Yabo Yablonsky. *Cinematography:*
    John Cabrera. *Cast:* Joe Lewis (Jonathan Cross-"Jaguar");
    Christopher Lee (Adam Caine); Donald Pleasence (General
    Villanova); Barbara Bach (Anna); Capucine (Zina Vanacore)
    Joseph Wiseman (Ben Ashir); Woody Strode (Sensei); John
    Huston (Ralph R. Richards); Gabriel Melgar (Ahmed);
    Anthony De Longis (Brett); Sally Faulkner (Terry); Gail
    Grainger (Consuela); Anthony Heaton (Coblintz); Luis
    Prendes (Habish); Simon Andreu (Petrie); James Smilie

(Reardon); Oscar James (Collins); Ray Jewers (Jessup);
Ralph Brown (Logan).

This martial-arts film amounts to nothing more than a
world travelogue and came at least five or six years after the
height of the martial-arts rage. The hero, Joe Lewis, is sort
of a poor man's Chuck Norris (and neither man is in the same
league with Bruce Lee).

A secret agent (Lewis) is resting on a farm owned by his
martial-arts teacher (Strode). Another agent (Bach) comes to
him with orders to destroy the criminal organization responsible for the death of one of his agent friends (De Longis).
Lewis learns that the gang he is after are international drug
traffickers. His search takes him from a Central American
banana republic to Madrid, Brazil, Hong Kong, Macao, and Tokyo.
By now the audience is suffering from jet lag. The intrepid
Lewis finds himself betrayed in Macao. He is sent from there,
unconscious, to Tokyo. He overhears a conversation between
an English drug dealer (Lee) and the mysterious head of the
drug organization, who is only known as "Esteban." Lee wants
Lewis to join him, but he refuses, so Lee lets him go. Lewis
is next attacked by a group of martial arts flunkies hired by
"Esteban," but he defeats them all. When he confronts
"Esteban," he finds it is his old secret-agent partner, De
Longis, who was thought dead. The two men engage in a furious
martial arts battle with Lewis emerging victorious.

LOVE AT FIRST BITE. 1979. 96 minutes. Color. *Director:* Stan
    Dragoti. *Screenplay:* Robert Kaufman; based on a story
    by Kaufman and Mark Gindes. *Cinematography:* Edward
    Rosson. *Cast:* George Hamilton (Count Vladimir Dracula);
    Susan Saint James (Cindy Sondheim); Richard Benjamin (Dr.
    Jeff Rosenberg); Dick Shawn (Lieutenant Ferguson); Arte
    Johnson (Renfield); Sherman Hemsley (Reverend Mike);
    Isabel Sanford (Judge); Barry Gordon (Flashlight Vendor);
    Ronnie Schell (Gay in Elevator); Bob Basso (TV Repairman);
    Bryan O'Byrne (Priest); Michael Pataki (Mobster); Hazel
    Shermet (Lady in Elevator); Basil Hoffman (Desk Clerk);
    Stanley Brock (Cab Driver); Danny Dayton (Billy); Robert
    Ellenstein (VW Man); David Ketchum (Customs Inspector);
    Lidia Kristen (Female Commissar); Eric Laneuville
    (Russell); Susan Tolsky (Model Agent); Robin Dee Adler
    (Woman in Nightgown); John Anthony Bailey and Shelly
    Garrett (New York Thugs); Paul Barselow (Bloodbank Guard);
    Laurie Beach (Little Girl); Jacque Lynn Colton (Lady with
    Cat); Charlie Dell (Busboy); John Dennis (Motorcycle Cop);

Ding Dingle (TWA Agent); Alan Haufrect (Photographer);
Michael Heit (2nd Bellboy); David Landsberg (Morty); Ralp
Manza (Limo Driver); Tiger Joe Marsh (Citizen Outside
Castle); Ed Marshall (News Reporter); Joe Medalis (In-
tern); Rose Michtom (Elderly Lady); Deborah Kim Moore
(Nurse); Robert Nadder (Bellevue Doctor); Dino Natali
(Man Outside Castle); Jerold Pearson (Hippy in Customs);
Judy Penrod (Stewardess); Hal Ralston (Police Sergeant);
Lavelle Roby (Mourner); Merrie Lynn Ross (Lady in Apart-
ment); Whitney Rydbeck (Male Commissar); Rolfe Sedan (Maî
tre d'); Cicely Walper (Grandmother).

Geoge Hamilton displays a flair for comedy in this spoof
of the Dracula legend, which was one of AIP's last successful
films. While the comedic elements become a bit excessive,
there are moments of inspiration. Hamilton's vampire is one
who uses a Bela Lugosi accent, gets drunk from the blood of a
wino, and finds that in modern-day New York City he cannot
scare anyone.

Count Dracula (Hamilton) goes to New York with his assistant (Johnson) when the Rumanian government expropriates
his castle for a training site for gymnasts. In New York his
incarnation as a bat does not impress people, and he and
Johnson must "obtain blood from blood banks to keep him alive.
While he is "getting down" in a disco, Hamilton meets a fashion model (Saint James). She falls in love with this kinky
foreigner after he bites her in the neck while making love.
Her psychiatrist boyfriend of nine years (Benjamin) recognizes
the marks on her neck as vampire bites. He makes an unsuccess
ful attempt to kill Hamilton with some silver bullets (which
are for werewolves, not vampires). Hamilton plans to take
Saint James with him back to Europe, but Benjamin kidnaps her.
Hamilton rescues her and confesses his love. He bites her on
the neck one more time, and they turn into bats and fly away
together.

METEOR. 1979. 103 minutes. Color. *Director:* Ronald Neame.
Screenplay: Stanley Mann and Edmund H. North; based on
the story by North. *Cinematography:* Paul Lohmann. *Cast:*
Sean Connery (Dr. Paul Bradley); Natalie Wood (Tatiana
Donskaya); Karl Malden (Harry Sherwood); Brian Keith (Dr.
Dubov); Martin Landau (General Adlon); Trevor Howard (Sir
Michael Hughes); Richard Dysart (Secretary of Defense);
Henry Fonda (The President); Joseph Campanella (General
Easton); Bo Brundin (Rolf Manheim); Katherine De Hetre
(Jan Watkins); James G. Richardson (Alan Marshall); Roger

Robinson (Bill Hunter); Michael Zaslow (Sam Mason); John
McKinney (Peter Watson); John Findlater (Astronaut Tom
Easton); Paul Tulley (Astronaut Bill Frager); Allen
Williams (Astronaut Michael McKendrick); Bibi Besch (Helen
Bradley); Gregory Gay (Russian Premier); Zitto Kazann
(Hawk-Faced Party Member); Clyde Kusatsu (Yamashiro);
Burke Byrnes (Coast Guard Officer); Joe Medalis (Bar-
tender); Charles Bartlett and Raymond O'Keefe (Guards);
Henry Olek (Army Translator); Peter Bourne (U.N. Presi-
dent); Stanley Mann (Canadian Representative); Ronald
Neame (British Representative); Philip Sterling (Russian
Representative); Arthur Adams (Ghanaian Representative);
Fred Carney (U.S. Representative); Sybil Danning (Girl
Skier); Meschino Paterlini (Boy Skier); Jon Yune (Siberian
Man); Eileen Saki (Siberian Woman); Chris Baur, Paul
Camen, Dorothy Catching, Bill Couch, William Darr, Joan
Foley, Paul Laurence, Johnny Moio, Read Morgan, Conrad
Palmisano, Tony Rocco, and Jesse Wayne (Communications
Center Technicians); Carole Hemingway (Sherwood's Secre-
tary); Clete Roberts (Network Newscaster); Stu Nahan
(Football Announcer); Osman Ragheb (Swiss TV Newscaster);
Yu Wing (Chinese Fisherman); Yau Tsui Ling (Chinese Fish-
erman's Wife); Rick Slaven (Canteen Worker); James Bacon
and Yani Begakis (News Reporters); Selma Archerd (Woman
in Subway); Domingo Ambrizi (Boy with Radio).

As with most disaster films, depth of character becomes
secondary to the disaster itself. Names like Sean Connery
and Natalie Wood are used solely for their drawing power, and
any incipient relationship between the two of them is
squelched. *Meteor* took a number of years to complete, since
it had a consortium of international financial backers.
    A five-mile-long meteor dubbed "Orpheus" is on a collision
course with Earth. Both Russian and American scientists band
together to avert a world disaster. The two superpowers agree
to position their nuclear missiles away from one another and
aim them toward the hurtling meteor. Pieces of the meteor
begin falling to Earth, which gives the special effects people
a chance to concoct an earthquake in Siberia, a tidal wave in
Hong Kong, and a huge avalanche in the Alps. An American scientist (Connery) is put in charge of orchestrating a missile
attack and is aided by a Russian scientist (Keith) and his
assistant (Wood). The group coordinate their activities from
an underground center in New York City. A piece of the meteor
severely damages part of New York, including the command center. Connery, Keith, and Wood, among others, escape into the
subway system, which is overflowing with fetid mud. While
they are attempting to stay afloat, so to speak, they learn

that the Russian and American missiles have destroyed the meteor.

SEVEN. 1979. 100 minutes. Color. *Director:* Andy Sidaris.
Screenplay: William Driskill and Robert Baird; based on
a story by Andy Sidaris. *Cinematography:* Quito. *Cast:*
William Smith (Drew Sevano); Barbara Leigh (Alexa); Guich
Koock ("Cowboy"); Art Metrano (Kinsella); Martin Kove
(Skip); Richard Le Pore ("The Professor"); Christopher
Joy (T.K.); Susan Kiger (Jennie); Robert Relyea (Harris);
Little Egypt (Maile); Lenny Montana ("The Kahuna"); Reggi
Nalder ("The Hermit"); Ed Parker (Ed Parker); Tadashi
Yamashita (Swordsman); Terry Kiser (Senator); Seth Sakai
(Keoki McDowell); Tino Tuiolosega (Mr. Lee); Henry Ayau
("Butterfly"); Russ Howell ("Skater"); Peter Knecht (Kimo
Maderos); Kwan Hilim (Mr. Chin); Sandra Bernadou (Rhonda)
Charles Picerni (The Kahuna's Driver); Nick Georgiade
(Niko); John Alderman (Paul); Terry Jastrow (Angela);
Lionel Tarape (Keoki's Bodyguard); Titus Napoleon (Tommy)
Les Marshall (Agent at Tunnel); John Allen (Man with Yellow Lei); Jeff Suarez (2nd Agent); Bertha Smilow (Lady
at Race Track); Jay C. Hill (Man at Counter); Yukon King
(Fat Cat at Aquarium).

Television sports director Andy Sidaris wrote and directed
this crime film, which is little more than an *Hawaii Five-O*
episode, only more violent. AIP did not even have trade
screenings for *Seven*, as it was relegated to regional saturation bookings, where you take the money and run. One of the
main actors, William Smith, is perhaps best remembered as being
Nick Nolte's repulsive nemesis in *Rich Man, Poor Man*.
An agent for a federal agency hires a shady middleman
(Smith) to find professional assassins to kill the seven members of a Hawaiian crime syndicate, who have been responsible
for the deaths of three federal agents and a United States
Senator. Smith locates six hired killers to do the job, and
he plans to take care of the criminal mastermind (Montana)
himself. The film follows the assassins as they track down
the mobsters one by one and shows how they dispose of them in
different ways. Perhaps the most ingenious execution is the
one that involves one of those inflatable sex dolls. After
all of them have killed their respective targets, they set
their sites on a hula dancer (Little Egypt), who had been the
informer responsible for the deaths of the federal agents.

SOMETHING SHORT OF PARADISE. 1979. 91 minutes. Color. *Director:* David Helpern, Jr. *Screenplay:* Fred Barron. *Cinematography:* Walter Lassally. *Cast:* Susan Sarandon (Madeleine Ross); David Steinberg (Harris Sloane); Jean-Pierre Aumont (Jean-Fidel Mileau); Marilyn Sokol (Ruthie Miller); Joe Grifasi (Barney Collins); Robert Hitt (Edgar Kent); David Rasche (David Ritchie); Bob Kaliban (George Pendleton); Ted Pugh (Frank Barnett); Ann Robey (Gail Barnett); William Francis (Hotel Manager); Adrienne Jalbert (Fru-Fru); Terrence O'Hara (Donny Conrad); Fred Nassif (Desk Clerk); Sonya Jennings (Beth); Ellen March (Lisa); Loretta Tupper (Alice Quine); Martha Sherrill (Mrs. Peel).

Something Short of Paradise is the sort of film made by those survivors of the 60s who have moved from political commitment to dealing with "personal relationships," and "true feelings," and other forms of California-style psycho-babble. Here we are supposed to be charmed by a couple and their relationship while they pursue their respective careers. The white pseudo-hip/intellectual middle class is limned much better by Woody Allen in *Annie Hall* than it is here.
     A magazine writer in New York City (Sarandon) meets a movie-theater owner (Steinberg) at a party given by Sarandon's best friend (Sokol). Their relationship blossoms in the beginning, and shortly thereafter it turns into an on-again/off-again affair, as Steinberg shows himself to be leery of making an emotional commitment. He eventually proposes, but the thought of marriage frightens Sarandon, as she would like to keep things as they are. A French film star (Aumont) arrives in New York and Sarandon covers his press conference. Aumont's publicist (Hitt) "fixes" her up with Aumont as a media event for the French star, and Sarandon accepts the offer. When Steinberg hears of this, he runs off to the airport thinking that the two of them are going to Paris. He and Sarandon are now once again confronted with the nature of their relationship.

SUNNYSIDE. 1979. 100 minutes. Color. *Director:* Timothy Galfas. *Screenplay:* Timothy Galfas and Jeff King; based on a story by King and Robert L. Schaffel. *Cinematography:* Gary Graver. *Cast:* Joey Travolta (Nick Martin); John Lansing (Denny Martin); Stacey Pickren (Donna Rosario); Andrew Rubin (Eddie Reaper); Michael Tucci

(Harry Cimoli); Talia Balsam (Ann Rosario); Chris Mulkey
(Reggie Flynn); Joan Darling (Mrs. Martin); Richard
Beauchamp (Hector); Heshimu Cumbuka (Ice); Jonathan Gries
(Wild Child); E. Lamont Johnson (Rage); Peter Kwong
(Alvin); Eric Laneuville (Gearbox); Randy Martin (Randy);
John Megna (B.B.); Thomas Rosales, Jr. (Tommy); Frank
Sivero (Dezi); Marion Waters (Watty); Michael T.
Williamson (Hot Dog); John Alderson (Jack Flynn); Brenda
Alexis (Rita); Herbert Braha (Rudy); Grand Bush (Teddy);
David Byrd (Roy Reaper).

It is quite evident that *Sunnyside* was primarily made to
exploit Joey Travolta's resemblance to his more famous brother
With its two brothers, one a tough street kid and the other
an aspiring artist, this film reminds one of that classic 1940
film *City for Conquest*, with Jimmy Cagney and Arthur Kennedy.
A young member (Travolta) of a street gang seeks to move
away from a tough area of Queens known as Sunnyside. Travolta
is part do-gooder and part street tough, as he hesitates leaving until he helps the community rid itself of a rival street
gang called The Warlocks. In order to clean the area up,
Travolta agrees to an alliance with The Warlocks' leader
(Rubin) in shutting down a crooked carnival. He and the gang
split the money taken from the carnival, as he uses his share
to move himself and his mother into a nice section of Manhattan. Before Travolta can move, The Warlocks challenge his
old gang, and he feels a responsibility to go back and help
them. In the ensuing gang fight both Travolta and Rubin are
killed.

DEFIANCE. 1980. 103 minutes. Color. *Director:* John Flynn.
   Screenplay: Thomas Michael Donnelly; based on a story by
   Donnelly and Mark Tulin. *Cinematography:* Ric Waite.
   Cast: Jan Michael Vincent (Tommy Gamble); Theresa Saldana
   (Marsha Bernstein); Fernando Lopez ("Kid"); Danny Aiello
   (Carmine); Santos Morales (Paolo); Don Blakely (Abbie
   Jackson); Frank Pesce (Herbie); Rudy Ramos (Angel Cruz);
   Lee Fraser (Bandana); Randy Herman (Tito); Alberto Vasquez
   (Slagg); Church Ortiz (Luis); Art Carney (Abe); East Carlo
   (El Bravo); Lenny Montana ("Whacko"); James Victor (Father
   Rivera); Tom Reese (1st Cop); Ernie Orsatti (2nd Cop);
   Marvin Katzoff (Sol); G. Anthony Sirico (Davey); Joe
   Campanella (Karenski); Brian Dean (Rondini); Pamela Gatell
   (Angel's Lady); Margarita Garcia (Cashier); Phil Levy
   (Earnie); Chino "Fats" Williams (Local); David Cadiente
   (Elroy); Wendy Oates (Carmine's Wife); Barbara Smith

Defiance

(Herbie's Wife); Dawn Adams (Priest's Assistant); James
Oscar Lee (Police Officer); Victor Mendez (Window Singer)

Defiance is an urban vigilante film a cut above the repellent and racist *Fighting Back* and *Boardwalk*. AIP held up
release of the film until the furor arising from other urban-
gang films, such as *The Warriors* and *Boulevard Nights*, died
down. What sets this film apart is the melding of some interesting characters and the growing involvement of Jan Michael
Vincent with the community's problems.
A merchant seaman (Vincent) is temporarily suspended from
his union. While waiting for the suspension to be lifted, he
takes an apartment in the Lower East Side of New York, which
is undergoing the familiar change of ethnic groups. A gang
called The Souls, led by the vicious Angel Cruz (Ramos), terrorizes the mainly Jewish and Italian residents of the neighborhood. Vincent remains a loner who is just waiting for the
moment he can get on another ship. He begins to have an affair
with a young woman (Saldana) who lives in his building. An
altercation on the street with one of the Souls puts him on
their enemies list. Vincent slowly integrates himself into
the community, as he befriends an orphan (Lopez), a punch-
drunk ex-boxer (Montana), and a middle-aged, layabout, ex-gang
member (Aiello--you know this is a tough area when Danny Aiello
is one of the more civilized elements). Vincent decides to
leave when a ship assignment comes about, but on his way he
finds that The Souls have murdered Montana. He now confronts
the rest of the gang, as his once-timid neighbors stand behind
him and help rid themselves of the gang.

GORP. 1980. 91 minutes. Color. *Director:* Joseph Ruben.
Screenplay: Jeffrey Konvitz. *Cinematography:* Michel Hugo
Cast: Michael Lembeck (Jay Kavell); Philip Casnoff (Mark
Bergman); Dennis Quaid ("Mad" Grossman); Fran Drescher
(Evie); David Huddleston ("Walrus" Wallman); Mark Deming
("Lobster" Newberg); James Greenleaf ("Fat" Solowitz);
Peter Marc (Steinberg); Vincent Bufano (De Neckio); Bill
Kirchenbauer (Wino Willie); Curt Ayers (Duffo Weiss);
Steve Bonino ("Batshit"); Richard Beauchamp (Ramirez);
Glen Super ("Dracula" Kesselman); Lou Wagner (Federman);
Robert Trebor (Rabbi Blowitz); Dale Robinette (Irvington)
John Reilly (Don Sharpe); Julius Harris (Fred the Chef);
DeWayne Jessie (Sweet Moe); Douglas Dirkson (Bible Looie)
Rudy Diaz (Indian Joe); Rosanna Arquette (Judy); Lisa
Shure (Vicki); Judith Drake (Big Bertha); Janet Sarno
(Mrs. Kramer); Robert Elston (Mr. Kramer); Four Scott

(Kramer's Son); Shirley Gunther (Wallman's Wife); Fred
Hinds (Seven-Year-Old Boy); Pete Robinson (Man in Bar);
Debi Richter (Barbara); Mickey Gilbert, Stan Barrett,
Joe Finnegan, and Stacie Elias (Stunt Players).

Gorp is a kosher version of the Canadian film *Meatballs*,
in that it deals with the antics of teenagers at a summer camp.
The success of *Animal House* spawned a number of imitations,
like the aforementioned films and *Porky's*, which accomplished
the almost-impossible task of making *Animal House* look good
in comparison.
    A Jewish summer camp in the Catskill Mountains is the
scene of mischief for a group of young people. Two second-
year waiters at the camp lodge (Lembeck and Casnoff) are the
chief instigators of the local hijinks. Along with a group
of new waiters they cause havoc for the camp owner
(Huddleston), as well as lust after some of the new female
counselors (that clean mountain air will do it every time).
The waiters make night-time raids on the girls' compound, engage in wild food fights, and substitute stag films for nature
films on a day when parents come to visit. With the subsequent
success of *Porky's* there apparently is a vast under-21 audience
for fare such as this.

TITLE INDEX

Abby, 248, 279
Abominable Dr. Phibes, The,
 203
"Ace Up Your Sleeve, An",
 283
Act of Vengeance, 249
*Adventures of Marco Polo,
 The*, 80
African Queen, The, 292
Airplane, 237
Alakazam the Great, 63
Alien, 36
Aloma of the South Seas, 38
Altered States, 93
Amazing Colossal Man, The,
 12-13, 28, 38, 41
Amazing Transparent Man, The,
 55-56
American Bandstand, 160
American Graffiti, 268, 278,
 319
Amityville Horror, The, 322
Amputee Love, 259
Angel, Angel, Down We Go,
 169
Angel Unchained, 184
Angels from Hell, 155
Angry Red Planet, The, 55-56
Animal House, 335
Annie Hall, 331
Apache Woman, 3
*Around the World in Eighty
 Days*, 153
Assignment--Outer Space, 63-
 64
Astounding She-Monster, The,
 27
At the Earth's Core, 282
Atragon, 100
Attack of the Giant Leeches,
 43

Attack of the Puppet People,
 28
Avengers, The, 224
Awakening, The, 205

Bad News Bears, The, 312
"Ballad of Tam Lin, The", 217
Bamboo Gods and Iron Men, 249-
 250
Bang, Bang, You're Dead, 130
Baron Blood, 220
Bat People, The, 250
Battle Beyond the Sun, 86, 90,
 140
Battle of Algiers, The, 104
Battle of the Amazons, 235,
 262
Battle of Neretva, 203-204
Beach Blanket Bingo, 117, 121
Beach Party, 87, 96
Beast With Five Fingers, The,
 89
*Beast with a 1,000,000 Eyes,
 The*, 4, 37
Becket, 108
Beware of Children, 64
"Beyond the Mountains", 158
Beyond the Time Barrier, 55-
 56, 57
Bicycle Thief, The, 176
Big T.N.T. Show, The, 131
Bikini Beach, 101
Billy Jack, 146
Bird of Paradise, 37
Black Caesar, 235-236, 256
"Black Cat, The", 84
Black Fox, 51
Black Jack, 237
Black Mama, White Mama, 238,
 244
Black Pirate, The, 295-296

Black Sabbath, 103
Black Sunday, 65-67, 106, 122
Blacula, 220-221, 245
Blazing Magnum, 308
Blood and Lace, 204
Blood Bath, 131-132
Blood From the Mummy's Tomb, 205
Blood of Dracula, 13-14
Bloody Mama, 184, 186
Blue Sunshine, 294
Boardwalk, 334
Bobbie Jo and the Outlaw, 282-283
Bonnie and Clyde, 30, 160, 185, 221
Bonnie Parker Story, The, 29-30, 35
Bora Bora, 185
Born Losers, 145-146
Born Wild, 168
Boulevard Nights, 334
Boxcar Bertha, 221
Boys in the Band, 217
Brain Eaters, The, 29
Brain That Wouldn't Die, The, 77-78
Breaker! Breaker!, 296
Breaker Morant, 138
Breaking Away, 98
Britannia Hospital, 223
Brute and the Beast, The, 156
Bucket of Blood, A, 21, 26, 44-45
Bucktown, 266-267
Bullet for Pretty Boy, A, 186
Bullitt, 98, 120, 295
Bunny O'Hare, 206
Burn, Witch, Burn, 77, 79

Cabinet of Dr. Caligari, The, 260
Caged, 8
Caged Heat, 238
California, 87-88

California Dreaming, 323-325
Cannibal Girls, The, 239
"Capitaes Da Areia", 234
"Captive City, The", 117
Car Wash, 306
"Carmilla", 200
Carrie, 315
Carry on Camping, 222
Carry on Doctor, 222-223
Carry on Henry the VIII, 207
"Case of Charles Dexter Ward, The", 92
"Cask of Amontillado, The", 84
Cat Ballou, 287
Cat Girl, 14
Cat People, 14
"Cervantes", 182
Chastity, 170
Chatter Box, 297
C.H.O.M.P.S., 324
Chosen, The, 310
Christa, 207-208
Chrome and Hot Leather, 208
Circus of Fear, 150
Circus of Horrors, 58-59
City for Conquest, 332
Cobra, The, 146
Coffy, 239, 254, 261
"Colour Out of Space, The", 118
Comedy of Terrors, The, 88
Commando, 103-104
"Conjure Wife", 77
Conquered City, 117-118
Conqueror Worm, The, 156-158, 179, 190
Cool and the Crazy, The, 30, 31
Cool Hand Luke, 318
Cooley High, 267-268
Coonskin, 242
Cornbread, Earl and Me, 268
"Cosmic Frame, The", 18
Count Yorga, Vampire, 187-188, 215-216
Cracking Up, 297-298
Crawling Hand, The, 89

Creature From Galaxy 27, *The*, 36
Creature From the Black Lagoon, *The*, 12
Crime and Passion, 283
Crimson Cult, *The*, 187, 189
Crunch, 198-199
Cry of the Banshee, 189-190
Curse of the Demon, 79
Cycle Savages, *The*, 170-171
Cyclops, *The*, 41

Daddy-O, 46
Damned, *The*, 190
Dark Shadows, 261
"David Balfour", 213
"Day It All Happened, Baby, The", 166
Day of the Jackal, *The*, 271, 298
"Day of the Owl", 178
Day That Shook the World, *The*, 298
Day the Earth Froze, *The*, 104
Day the Hot Line Got Hot, *The*, 171
Day the World Ended, *The*, 6, 28
Dead of Night, 260
Death Line, 229
Death Wish, 137, 147, 258
Death Wish II, 137
Deathmaster, *The*, 223
Deep, *The*, 98
Deep Throat, 240
Deep Thrust--The Hand of Death, 240
Defiance, 332-334
Defiant Ones, *The*, 238
Dementia 13, 89
Deranged, 251-252
Derby, 233
De Sade, 172
"Descent into the Maelstrom, A", 127-128
Desperate Ones, *The*, 158
Destroy All Monsters, 173

Destructors, *The*, 253
Devil Doll, *The*, 28
Devil Within Her, *The*, 284
"Devilday", 258
Devil's Angels, 147
Devil's 8, *The*, 173
Devil's Widow, *The*, 218
Diary of a Bachelor, 105
Diary of a High School Bride, 46-47
Die, Monster, Die!, 118
Dillinger, 241, 285
Dirt Gang, *The*, 209
Dirty Dozen, *The*, 173
Dirty Game, *The*, 133
Dirty O'Neil, 254
"Disoriented Man, The", 196
Dr. Goldfoot and the Bikini Machine, 119, 134
Dr. Goldfoot and the Girl Bombs, 134
Dr. Jekyll and Sister Hyde, 209-210
Dr. Phibes Rises Again, 224
Dr. Strangelove, 237
"Don Quixote", 182
Don't Knock the Rock, 25
"Doomed City, The", 127
Door-to-Door Maniac, 67
Dorian Gray, 190-191
Dragonfly, 285
Dragstrip Girl, 15-16, 19
Dragstrip Riot, 31
"Dreams in the Witch-House, The", 187
"Drop of Water, The", 103
Dukes of Hazzard, *The*, 258
Dunwich Horror, *The*, 191

Easy Rider, 211, 278, 313
8½, 181
Empire of the Ants, 28, 299
End as a Man, 25
Endless Summer, *The*, 195
Erik the Conqueror, 90
Europe in the Raw, 152
Evictors, *The*, 324-326
Evil Dead, *The*, 239

Evil Eye, 105-106
Exorcist, The, 248, 284
Explosion, 192
Eye Creatures, The, 19

"Facts in the Case of M.
  Valdemar, The", 84
"Fall of the House of Usher,
  The", 60
"Farewell My Lovely", 125
Fast and the Furious, The,
  3
Fearless Frank, 174, 178
Female Jungle, 7-8
Fighting Back, 334
"Film of Memory, The", 289
Final Chapter--Walking Tall,
  300
Fireball 500, 134-136
  153
Five Guns West, 4-5
Five Minutes to Live, 67
Flesh and the Spur, 16-17
Flight of the Lost Balloon,
  67
Food of the Gods, The, 285-
  286, 299
Force 10 From Navarone, 311
Fort Apache, The Bronx, 240
Foxy Brown, 254-255, 261
*Frankenstein Conquers the
  World*, 135
Free, White and 21, 91, 115
French Connection, The, 253
Friday Foster, 269-270
Friday the 13th, 180, 312
Fritz the Cat, 259
Frogs, 225-226
F.T.A., 225
Fury of the Vikings, 90
Futureworld, 286-287

Gaslight, 37
Gas-s-s-s, 192-193
*Ghost in the Invisible
  Bikini, The*, 136
Ghost of Dragstrip Hollow,
  47

Girl Getters, The, 137
Girls in Prison, 8-9
Glass Sphinx, The, 159
Glory Stompers, The, 147-148
Go Go Mania, 120
God Forgives, I Don't, 174
Godfather of Harlem, The, 235
Godzilla Vs. the Smog Monster,
  226
Godzilla Vs. the Thing, 106
Golden Ivory, 43
Golden Needles, 255
Goldfinger, 149
Goliath and the Barbarians, 48
Goliath and the Dragon, 58, 60
*Goliath and the Sins of
  Babylon*, 91
Goliath and the Vampires, 107,
  111
Gong Show, The, 297
Good Times, 268
Gorp, 334-335
Grayeagle, 301
Greased Lightning, 240
*Great Scout and Cathouse
  Thursday, The*, 287
Great Spy Chase, The, 137
Grissom Gang, The, 185
Guns of Navarone, The, 311
Guns of the Black Witch, 68,
  296
Gunslinger, 9

Halloween, 180
"Hamp", 138
Hand, The (1960), 69
Hand, The (1981), 89
Hard Ride, The, 208, 210-211
Haunted Palace, The, 92
Hawaii Five-O, 255, 330
Headless Ghost, The, 48-49
Heavy Traffic, 241-242
Helga, 159-160, 179
Hell Squad, 31, 39
Hell Up in Harlem, 256
Hell's Angels 69, 175
Hell's Belles, 176-177
Hennessy, 271

Here Come the Tigers, 312
Hideous Sun Demon, The, 12,
  314
High-Ballin, 313
High School Hellcats, 32
High, Wild and Free, 160, 196
Hills Have Eyes, The, 162
"Hog Butcher", 268
Hollywood Boulevard, 245
Hollywood's World of Flesh,
  152
Holocaust 2000, 310
"Hop-Frog", 108
Horror House, 193-194
Horrors of the Black Museum,
  49-50, 58
Hot Rod Gang, 33
Hot Rod Girl, 9-10
House By the Lake, The, 301-
  302
House of Fright, 69
House of a Thousand Dolls,
  148
House of Usher, 60, 74, 81
House of Whipcord, 256-257
House That Screamed, The, 211
How to Make a Monster, 33-34
How to Stuff a Wild Bikini,
  120-121
Hunger, The, 200

I Am a Fugitive from a Chain
  Gang, 318
"I Am Legend", 107
I, the Jury, 11
I Want to Live, 63
I Was a Teenage Frankenstein,
  14, 17, 34
I Was a Teenage Gorilla, 71
I Was a Teenage Werewolf, 13,
  17-18
Iceman Cometh, The, 217
Ikarie XB1, 116
Incredible Melting Man, The,
  313
Incredible Shrinking Man,
  The, 28
Incredible Two-Headed
  Transplant, The, 212

Insect Fear, 259
Intruder, The, 4
Invaders From Mars, 19
Invasion of the Body
  Snatchers, 10, 116, 174
Invasion of the Saucer Men,
  18-19
Invasion of the Star
  Creatures, 79-80
Island of Dr. Moreau, The, 303
Island of Lost Souls, 303
Island of the Damned, 314
It Conquered the World, 10,
  29
Italian Connection, The, 242
It's a Gift, 307
It's Alive, 237, 284

J.D.'s Revenge, 288
Jaguar Lives!, 326
Jailbreakers, The, 61
Jaws, 309
Jennifer, 315
Jet Attack, 34
"Jewel of the Seven Stars",
  205
Journey to the Lost City, 61-
  62
Journey to the Seventh Planet,
  70, 83
Joyride, 304
Julius Caesar, 194-195

Kagi No Kagi, 144
"Kalevala", 104
Kama Sutra, 195
Kansas City Bomber, 233
Kidnapped, 213
Killer Force, 272
Killers Three, 160
King and Country, 138
King Dinosaur, 13
Konga, 70-71

Land That Time Forgot, The,
  273, 282, 306
Last Man on Earth, The, 107-
  108

Last Picture Show, The, 319-320
Last Survivor, The, 316
"Late Boy Wonder, The", 199
Leave It to Beaver, 169
"Ligeia", 127
Lipstick, 249
Little Cigars, 243
Little Girl Who Lives Down the Lane, The, 305
Little Shop of Horrors, The, 26-44
Live a Little, Steal a Lot, 273-274
Lizard in a Woman's Skin, 216
Lola, 227
Lost Battalion, 71
Lost Weekend, The, 91
Lost World of Sinbad, The, 123
Lost Women, 27
Love at First Bite, 327
Loves of Hercules, The, 53

McCullochs, The, 274-275
Machine Gun Kelly, 35
Macon County Line, 257-258, 275, 278
Mad Max, 164
Madhouse, 258
Madigan's Millions, 176, 178
Mafia, 178
Man From Cocody, The, 139
Man From U.N.C.L.E., The, 40, 131
"Man in the Iron Mask, The", 82
Man Who Shot Liberty Valance, The, 277
Manitou, The, 248
Manson, 244
Marco Polo, 80, 83
Marseilles Contract, The, 253
Maryjane, 161
Masque of the Red Death, The, 108
Master of the World, 72

Matilda, 317
Matter of Time, A, 289
Mean Dog Blues, 317-318
Meatballs, 335
Men in Black, 223
Meteor, 328
"Metzengerstein", 180-181
Michael and Helga, 179
Midnight Cowboy, 178
Million Eyes of Su-Muru, The, 149
Mind Benders, The, 93
Mini-Skirt Mob, The, 162
Mod Squad, The, 197
Mondo Cane, 126, 166, 195
Mondo Topless, 152
Monkey Hustle, The, 290
"Monsters from Nicholson Mesa", 79
"Morella", 84
Most Dangerous Game, The, 110
Mothra, 106
Motorcycle Gang, 19, 31
Murders in the Rue Morgue, 213-214
Muscle Beach Party, 109

Naked Africa, 35-36, 43
Naked Eye, The, 51
Naked Paradise, The, 20, 37
Naked Prey, The, 110
Nashville Rebel, The, 139
Navajo Run, 110
Nebo Zovyot, 86
"Never Bet Your Head", 180
Night and the City, 242
Night of the Blood Beast, 36-37
Night of the Blood Monster, 228
Night of the Living Dead, 187, 226, 239
Night Tide, 94-95
Nine Hours to Rama, 298
Nine Lives of Fritz the Cat, The, 259
99 River Street, 11
No Kidding, 64

"No Sex Please, We're
  British", 207
Norseman, The, 318-319
North by Northwest, 131
Nutty Professor, The, 124

Oblong Box, The, 179
Oklahoma Woman, The, 11
Old Dracula, 275-276
Omen, The, 310
"One Night of 21 Hours", 122
1,000 Convicts and a Woman,
  214
Operation Bikini, 94, 96
Operation Camel, 72
Operation Dames, 51, 53
Operation Malaya, 5
Operation Snafu, 121
Our Gang, 20
Our Winning Season, 319
Outlaw Treasure, 5-6

Pacific Vibrations, 195-196
Pajama Party, 110-111
Panic in the Year Zero, 80-81
Parallax View, The, 269
Paratroop Command, 51, 53
Part 2, Walking Tall, 276
Paths of Glory, 138
"Paxton Quigley Had the
  Course", 165
Peeping Tom, 58
People That Time Forgot, The,
  305
Peyton Place, 29
Phantom from 10,000 Leagues,
  The, 6, 11-12
Phantom of the Opera, The,
  214
Phantom Planet, The, 73
Phenix City Story, The, 267
Pickup on 101, 228
"Picture of Dorian Gray,
  The", 190
Pit and the Pendulum, The,
  74, 81
Pixote, 234
Plan 9 from Outer Space, 27

Planet of Blood, 140
Planet of the Vampires, 122
Police Woman, 291
Porky's, 335
Portrait of a Sinner, 74-75
Prehistoric World, 39
Premature Burial, The, 81
Prisoner of the Iron Mask, 82
*Private Files of J. Edgar
  Hoover, The,* 237, 320
Psycho, 211, 246, 251
Psycho-Circus, 150
Psych-Out, 163
Pyro, 111

Q, 237
Queen of Blood, 140

Raiders of the Lost Ark, 255
Rancho Notorious, 16
Range Rider, The, 88
Raven, The, 84, 88, 96, 98
Raw Meat, 229-230
Rear Window, 246
Rebecca, 37
Rebel, The, 135
"Rebel Against the Light", 141
Rebel Without a Cause, 18
Record City, 306
Reform School Girl, 20
*Reincarnation of Peter Proud,
  The,* 277, 288
Reptilicus, 82-83
Return of Count Yorga, The,
  215
Return to Macon County, 278
"Return to the Wood", 138
Rich Man, Poor Man, 330
Ride the High Country, 287
Riot on Sunset Strip, 150-151
Road Hustlers, The, 163-164
Road Racers, 52, 100
Road Warrior, 164
Roaring Twenties, The, 29
Robot Monster, 27
"Robur, the Conquerer", 72
Rock All Night, 21
Rock Around the World, 14,
  22, 120

Rocky, 317, 320
Rollerball, 233
Rolling Thunder, 307
Rope, 246
Rosemary's Baby, 284
"Rough and the Smooth, The",
  74-75
Runaway Daughters, 22

Sampo, 104
Sampson and the Seven
  Miracles of the World, 83
Sampson and the Slave Queen,
  97
Samurai Pirate, 123
Sandpit Generals, The, 234
Sands of Beersheba, 141
Saturday Night Live, 144
Savage Seven, The, 164
Savage Sisters, 71, 244
Savage Wild, The, 196
Schizoid, 216
Scorchy, 290-291
Scream and Scream Again, 196
Scream Blacula Scream, 245,
  261
Screaming Skull, The, 36-37
Screaming Tiger, The, 246
SCTV, 239
Searchers, The, 176, 301
Secret Agent Fireball, 141
Seizure, 260
Sergeant Deadhead, 123-124
Seven, 330
Seven Samurai, 92
Sexy Magico, 152
Shake, Rattle and Rock!,
  23-25
She Creature, The, 12, 47, 94
She Gods of Shark Reef, 20,
  37-38
Sheba Baby, 279
Shout at the Devil, 291
Sign of the Gladiator, 48,
  52-53
Sisters, 246
"Sisters of the Road", 221
Six Pack Annie, 280

$64,000 Question, The, 40
Ski Party, 124-125
Slaughter, 231, 247
Slaughter's Big Rip-Off, 247
Small Town in Texas, A, 292
Some of My Best Friends
  Are..., 217
Some People, 112
Something Short of Paradise,
  331
Sorority Girl, 25
Sounder, 290
South of Pago Pago, 38
Space Men, 64
Special Delivery, 293
Spider, The, 38
Spirits of the Dead, 180
Spy in Your Eye, 142
Squirm, 294
Star Trek, 29
"Stop at a Winner", 121
Straight Jacket, 258
"Strange Case of Dr. Jekyll
  and Mr. Hyde, The", 69
Strange One, The, 25
Strange Shadows in an Empty
  Room, 308
Straw Dogs, 303
Street People, 295
Student Nurses, The, 131
Stunt Man, The, 163
Submarine Seahawk, 53
Sugar Hill, 261
Suicide Battalion, 38-39
Summer Holiday, 97-98
Sunnyside, 331-332
Super Stooges Vs. the Wonder
  Women, 262
Superfly, 290
Superman, 9
Suspiria, 169, 211
Swedish Fly Girls, 208
Swinger's Paradise, 125

Taboos of the World, 126
Tabu, 37
Tales of Terror, 84, 88
Tam Lin, 217-218

T.A.M.I. Show, The, 113, 131
Tank Battalion, 39
Tank Commandos, 53, 85
*Tarzan and the Valley of
  Gold,* 143
Taxi Driver, 307
Teenage Caveman, 39
"Telephone, The", 103
Tentacles, 308-309
Terminal Island, 131, 238
Terror, The, 98
Terror from the Year 5000, 40
Terror of Tiny Town, The, 243
Texas Chainsaw Massacre, The,
  251
That Man From Rio, 139
They Call Her One Eye, 254,
  262-263
Thing With Two Heads, The,
  232
39 Steps, The, 131
Those Fantastic Flying Fools,
  152-153
*Those Magnificent Men in
  Their Flying Machines,* 153
3 in the Attic, 165
Thunder Alley, 153
Thunder over Hawaii, 20
Thunder Road, 164
Tiger By the Tail, 197
Time Machine, The, 114
Time Travelers, The, 113-114
"Toby Dammit", 180-181
Tokyo Olympiad, 126-127
Tomb of Ligeia, The, 127
Torpedo Bay, 114
*Town That Dreaded Sundown,
  The,* 309
Trip, The, 154, 166, 225
Truck Stop Women, 264
Truck Turner, 265
Trunk to Cairo, 143
24-Hour Lover, 198
Twinky, 227
Twist All Night, 75-77
Two Gentlemen Sharing, 181-
  182
Two-Lane Blacktop, 278

2001: A Space Odyssey, 55

Undead, The, 25-26
Under Age, 115
Unearthly Stranger, The, 115-
  116
Unholy Rollers, The, 233
Up in the Cellar, 199

Vampire Lovers, The, 200
Velvet Vampire, The, 131
Venus in Furs ("Venus im
  Pelz"), 200, 206
Vertigo, 246
"Vie du Marquis de Sade", 172
"Vij, The", 65
*Viking Women and the Sea
  Serpent, The,* 26
Voodoo Woman, 27
*Voyage to the End of the
  Universe,* 116

Walk in the Sun, 51
Walking Tall, 276
War Goddess, 266
War Gods of the Deep, 127-128
War Italian Style, 154
War of the Colossal Beast,
  13, 34, 41-42
War of the Zombies, The, 128-
  129
Warriors, The, 168, 334
Warriors 5, 85
Wedding Night, 201
Westworld, 287
What's Up Tiger Lily?, 144,
  240
White Dawn, The, 174
White Slave Ship, 85
White Huntress, 36, 41, 43
Who Slew Auntie Roo?, 218
Why Must I Die?, 62-63
Wild Angels, The, 145, 147,
  166, 211
Wild Bunch, The, 287
Wild Eye, The, 165-166
Wild in the Streets, 165-166,
  225

Wild One, The, 19, 36
Wild Pack, The, 234
Wild Party, The, 280-281
Wild Racers, The, 167
"William Wilson", 180-181
"Witchfinder General", 156
"Wurdalak, The", 103
Wuthering Heights, 202

*X--The Man With the X-Ray
    Eyes*, 99

Yancy Derringer, 88
Yog--Monster from Space, 219
Yojimbo, 92
Young Animals, The, 167
*Young, the Evil and the
    Savage, The*, 168
Young Racers, The, 99-100
Young Rebel, The, 182
Youngblood, 321

Zombies of Sugar Hill, 261

NAME INDEX

Abbott, Bud, 155
Abbott, Frederick, 214
Abbott, Jane, 307
Abbott, Richard, 195
Abels, Gregg, 320
Abou, Charles, 196
Abrams, Barry, 312
Abrams, Mike, 279
Abrams, Robert, 283
Ace Trucking Company, The,
    297-298
Achtman, Arnie, 313
Ackerman, Forrest J., 113,
    140
Ackerman, Leslie, 297
Ackles, David, 131
Acone, Tony, 148
Acosta, Rosi, 71
Adalio, Ricardo, 231
Adam, Carl, 181
Adam, Ronald, 127
Adami, Alfredo, 155
Adams, Arthur, 329
Adams, Beverly, 120-121, 147
Adams, Dallas, 203
Adams, David, 300
Adams, Dawn, 334
Adams, Dawn (Addams), 69-70,
    200
Adams, Dennis, 55
Adams, Joseph, 116
Adams, Julie, 274
Adams, Lillian, 241
Adams, Marla, 293-294
Adams, Mary, 13
Adams, Maud, 272
Adams, Nick, 118-119, 135
Adams, Phil, 324
Adams, Stanley, 153, 249, 259
Adams, Trevor, 194
Addis, Cecil, 31

Addis, David, 53
Adelman, Joe, 30
Adkins, Don, 309
Adler, Jay, 22, 257
Adler, Judy, 115
Adler, Luther, 274
Adler, Robin Dee, 327
Adorf, Mario, 133, 242
Adrian, Iris, 3
Adrian, Kay, 197
Agar, John, 16, 28, 34, 70
Ahearne, Tom, 165
Ai, Kyoko, 173
Aidman, Charles, 169
Aiello, Danny, 332, 334
Aikens, Van, 107
Aimé, Monique, 148
Ainley, Anthony, 273
Aitchison, Peggy, 227
Akins, Claude, 308
Alaimo, Marc, 318
Alaimo, Michael, 225
Alan, Clark, 46
Alaniz, Rico, 41
Albano, Pietro, 82
Alberti, Anna, 68
Albertini, Adalberto, 48, 159
Albertini, Gianpiero, 289
Albertson, Jack, 228-229
Albin, Andy, 318
Alcaide, Chris, 9, 21
Alcaine, José-Luis, 314
Alcott, Robert, 115,
Alden, Honey, 165
Alden, Norman, 145, 160
Alden, Tom, 288
Alderman, John, 330
Alderson, John, 332
Alderton, John, 137
Aldham, Gillian, 158
Aldredge, Michael, 313

Alegre, Alona, 238
Aleong, Aki, 19, 94
Alesia, Frank, 111, 136
Alessandri, Roberto, 175
Alexander, George, 41
Alexander, Jeff, 186
Alexander, Jim, 105
Alexander, Nowell, 314
Alexander, Richard, 16
Alexander, Terence, 93
Alexis, Brenda, 332
Alfe, Norman, 231-232
Alfonsi, Lidia, 103
Algren, Nelson, 174
Alison, Dorothy, 210
All, Candy, 269
Allan, Andrea, 275
Allan, Kimberly, 318
Allen, Ethan, 186
Allen, Jack, 48
Allen, John, 330
Allen, Kip, 283
Allen, Phillip R., 293
Allen, Ron, 169
Allen, Tony, 321
Allen, Woody, 144, 240, 298, 331
Allin, Michael, 265
Allison, Bart, 128
Allnutt, Wendy, 202
Allyn, Alice, 51
Almagor, Gila, 143
Almanzar, James, 79
Almars, Marvin, 47
Almendros, Nestor, 167
Alonso, Arsenio, 71
Alonso, Cecil, 235
Alonso, Chelo, 48, 52
Alonso, Pablito, 104
Alonzo, John, 184
Alspaugh, William, 160
Altamura, Tullio, 68
Altariba, Beatrice, 100
Altgens, James, 56, 91
Alvez, Piper, 247
Alvieri, Tommaso, 155
Amadio, Silvio, 82, 85
Amado, Jorge, 234

Amato, Mary Margaret, 271
Ambrizi, Domingo, 315, 329
Amen Corner, The, 197
Amendola, Mario, 235
Ament, Duane, 87, 94, 109
American Revolution, The, 168
Ames, Allyson, 73
Ames, Heather, 13, 32, 34
Ames, Lionel, 62
Amigo, César, 71
Amoodi, Omar, 205
Amsterdam, Morey, 35, 87, 109
Anchóriz, Leo, 104
Andar, David, 60
Anders, Donna, 181
Anders, Luana, 20, 74, 89-90, 94-95, 99, 154
Anders, Merry, 113
Anders, Richard, 147, 164
Anders, Tom, 209
Andersen, Asbjorn, 82, 83
Andersen, Susy, 103, 128-130
Anderson, Christian, 164
Anderson, David, 272
Anderson, Douglas, 265
Anderson, Esther, 181-182
Anderson, Frank, 319
Anderson, Gerald, 49
Anderson, Howard A., 290
Anderson, Jürgen, 311
Anderson, Nancy, 47
Anderson, Nina, 104
Anderson, Pat, 254
Anderson, Robert, 32
Anderson, Verily, 64
Andre, Carole, 295
André, Gaby, 60
Andreas, Elena, 136
Andreas, Herb, 136
Andrei, Franco, 122
Andres, Mason, 309
Andreu, Simon, 326
Andrewartha, Amy, 292
Andrews, Andy, 89
Andrews, Dana, 142, 146
Andrews, David, 112
Andrews, Harry, 137, 202
Andrews, Mark, 9-10

Andros, Spiros, 289
Androsky, Carol, 259
Angel, Heather, 81-82
Angel, Mikel, 210
Angeli, Fabrizio, 180
Angeli, Pier, 85-86, 142
Angelillo (Angiolillo),
    Luciana, 142, 166
Angelini, Nando, 68
Angst, Richard, 61, 133, 172
Animals, The, 120
Ankrum, Morris, 34
Ann Marie, 208
Anne, Carole, 189
Annicelli, Corrado, 68
Annis, Francesca, 64
Ansah, Tommy, 181
Anson, Jay, 322
Anthony, Joseph, 117
Antinori, Lamberto, 118
Antonelli, Ennio, 155
Antonelli, Laura, 134
Antonini, Gabriele, 83
Antonio, Jim, 286, 320
Appleby, John, 117
Aquino, Robert, 309
Aranda, Angel, 122-123
Arbessier, Louis, 133
Arbus, Allan, 240
Archambault, Arch, 187
Archambeault, George, 35
Archdale, Alexander, 48
Archerd, Army, 166
Archerd, Selma, 329
Archibek, Ben, 209
Arden, Arianne, 56
Arden, Eve, 124
Ardisson, Giorgio, 90-91
Arel, Fabienne, 167
Arena, Maurizio, 103
Arent, Eddie, 150
Aret, Buddy, 259
Argento, Dario, 122, 169,
    211, 216, 315
Argo, Victor (Vic), 221, 233
Arias, Maria Luisa, 314
Arie, Bruno, 174
Ariell, Clea, 281

Aris, Ben, 275
Arishima, Ichiro, 123
Arkin, David, 199
Arkoff, Samuel Z., 4, 202
Arlen, Richard, 89
Arlen, Roxanne, 9
Arling, Arthur E., 124
Armitage, George, 192-193
Armstrong, Fay, 292
Armstrong, Herb, 318
Armstrong, Hugh, 229, 231
Armstrong, Michael (Mike),
    193, 299
Armstrong, Peter, 204
Armstrong, R.G., 198
Armstrong, Richard, 170
Armstrong, R.L., 210
Armstrong, Tex, 134
Arnal, Issa, 119
Arnaz, Desi, Jr., 304-305
Arne, Peter, 179-180, 214
Arnold, Grace, 71
Arnold, Susan, 281
Aronovich, Ricardo, 234
Arpino, Tony, 227
Arquette, Rosanna, 334
Arrowsmith, Joe, 281, 320
Arthur, Louise, 46
Arthur, Maureen, 33, 153, 160
Arthure, Richard, 138
Ash, Dan, 176
Ashcroft, Ronnie, 27
Ashe, Martin, 198
Asher, Jack, 69
Asher, Jane, 108-109
Asher, William, 87, 101, 109,
    117, 120, 134
Ashley, Elizabeth, 255-256,
    287-288
Ashley, Graham, 271
Ashley, John, 16, 19, 33-34,
    38-39, 87, 101, 109, 117,
    120, 124, 244-245
Ashworth, Dicken, 311
Askew, Luke, 184, 276-277,
    307
Askins, Monroe, 13, 25-26,
    153

Aslan, Grégoire, 130
Asman, William, 248, 279
Astin, John, 206
Asturias, Carpi, 238
Atcheler, Jack, 193
Atkin, Harvey, 313
Atkins, Eileen, 284-285
Atkins, Tom, 293
Atkinson, Beverly Hope, 241
Atkinson, Frank, 14
Atkinson, Jo Ann, 264
Atkinson, Ray, 111, 121
Atnip, Linda, 257
Atterbury, Malcolm, 13, 18, 33
Atwater, Edith, 318
Aubrey, Jean, 121
Aubrey, Richard, 266
Aubry, Danielle, 101, 169
Audiard, Michel, 137
Audran, Stephane, 170
Augenstein, Michael, 296
Aumont, Jean-Pierre, 331
Aumont, Tina, 289
Aureli, Andrea, 97
Aurness, Rolf, 195
Austin, Ray, 214
Austine, Nicola, 275
Autumn, 170
Avalon, Frankie, 63, 80-81, 87, 94, 96, 101-102, 109-110, 117, 119-121, 123-125, 134-135, 149, 193-194
Avedis, Hikmet, 290
Avery, Margaret, 256
Avery, Val, 235-237, 322
Avianca, Frank, 317
Avon, Roger, 189
Ayau, Henry, 330
Ayer, Harold, 161
Ayers, Curt, 334
Ayres, Maray, 170-171
Ayres, Robert, 14, 301, 303
Azorin, Juana, 211

Baader, Fritz, 160, 179
Babich, Frank, 198
Baccala, Donna, 191-192

Bach, Barbara, 311-312, 326-327
Bach, Peter, 179
Backus, Jim, 94, 269, 271, 324
Bacon, James, 318, 329
Bacon, Roger, 87, 111
Badalucco, Niccola, 295
Baddeley, Hermoine, 324
Bade, Tom, 217
Badel, Alan, 311
Baer, John, 36
Baer, Max, 257-258, 274-275
Baers, Marlo, 87
Baez, Joan, 131
Baghino, Giovanni, 68
Bagley, Fuddle, 288, 290
Bagolini, Silvio, 82
Bail, Chuck, 164
Bailey, Allen, 235
Bailey, John (Anthony), 179, 269, 327
Bailey, Trevor, 201
Bain, Conrad, 324
Bain, Sherry, 210-211
Baird, Harry, 179, 214-215
Baird, Robert, 330
Bairn, William A., 220
Baizley, George, 181
Bajic, Rado, 298
Bakalyan, Richard, 29-30, 51, 80, 94
Baker, Albert J., 261
Baker, Art, 145
Baker, Bruce, 120
Baker, Bryden, 11
Baker, David, 217
Baker, Diane, 141
Baker, Everett, 4
Baker, Fay, 25
Baker, Henry, 260
Baker, Joe Don, 255-256
Baker, Joe E., 324
Baker, John, 14
Baker, Lorrene, 234
Baker, Mickey, 190
Baker, Rick, 232
Baker, Roy Ward, 200, 209
Baker, Stanley, 216

Baker, Tom, 156
Bakshi, Ralph, 241-242, 259
Balandin, Juan Antonio, 314
Balandin, Pedro, 314
Balaski, Belinda, 282-283, 286
Balbo, Ennio, 295
Baldassarre, Raffaele, 90
Baldini, Renato, 142
Balducci, Franco, 85, 216
Baldwin, Bill, Sr., 150
Balfour, Michael, 179
Ball, Robert, 29, 79, 206
Baloh, Miha, 85
Balsam, Martin, 117
Balsam, Talia, 332
Baltimor, Franco, 142
Balutin, Jacques, 137
Bambert, Judy, 16, 44
Banas, Bob, 46
Band Without a Name, 153
Banghart, Kenneth, 166
Banks, Doug, 29
Banks, Linda, 171
Banno, Yoshimitu, 226
Baptiste, Thomas, 181
Bar Boo, Luis, 175
Barab, Nira, 199
Baracco, Adriano, 142
Barbarians, The, 113
Barber, Ellen, 320
Barbera, Joseph, 324
Barboni, Leonida, 117, 185
Barclay, Mary M., 48
Bardot, Brigitte, 180
Barger, Douglas, 160
Barger, Sonny, 175
Barker, Blue Lu, 288
Barker, Eric, 121, 227
Barker, Jess, 274
Barnes, Clarence, 255, 265
Barnes, Gordon, 38
Barnes, Julian, 193-194, 218
Barnes, Rayford, 243
Barnett, Ken, 105
Barnett, Trevor, 48
Barnett, Vince, 119, 280
Baron, Emma, 82, 107

Baron, Geraldine, 281
Baron, Helen, 215
Barr, Leonard, 306
Barr, Patrick, 256-257
Barrass, Ann, 179, 190
Barrett, Frank, 290
Barrett, John, 128
Barrett, Linda, 86
Barrett, Stan, 335
Barrie, John, 179
Barron, Baynes, 134, 153, 161, 173, 324
Barron, Fred, 331
Barron, Keith, 273, 282
Barron, Robert, 53, 163
Barrow, Baynes, 39
Barrows, George, 136
Barry, Alan, 271
Barry, Hilda, 49
Barry, Julian (Sergio Martino) 141
Barry, Wendy, 97
Barrymore, John Drew, 128-130
Barselow, Paul, 88, 327
Barth, Eddie, 322
Bartlett, Charles, 329
Bartlett, Hall, 234
Barton, Kirk, 86
Barton, Michele, 121
Barty, Billy, 25
Barzell, Wolfe, 141
Basehart, Richard, 303
Basel, Kevin, 272
Basil, Toni, 111
Baskin, William, 96, 119
Bassett, Ronald, 156
Basso, Bob, 327
Bastedo, Alexandra, 201-202
Bastianoni, Giancarlo, 175, 235
Bates, Jim, 241
Bates, Ralph, 209-210, 284-285
Battaglia, Rick, 289
Battaglia, Rudy, 169
Battin, Brent, 87
Bauer, David, 214-215

Baumann, Kathy, 208-209, 232
Baur, Chris, 329
Baur, Robert, 206
Bava, Mario, 65, 67, 90, 103,
  105-106, 122, 134, 216,
  220, 315
Baxley, Gary, 303
Baxt, George, 58, 77
Baxter, Bruce, 71
Bay, John, 320
Bayldon, Geoffrey, 75
Bayliss, Peter, 275-276
Baylor, Hal, 6, 228
Bayonas, José-Luis, 176
Bazzocchi, Loris, 289
Beach, Ann, 121
Beach Boys, The, 113, 196
Beach, John, 87
Beach, Laurie, 327
Beacham, Stephanie, 217-218
Bean, Orson, 227
Beard, Stymie, 265
Beatles, The, 22, 120
Beaton, Timothy, 93
Beatty, Warren, 221
Beauchamp, Richard, 218,
  332-334
Beaumont, Charles, 77, 81,
  92, 108
Beaumont, Richard, 218
Beaumont, Stephanie, 137
Beausoliel, Robert, 244
Beck, Billy, 134, 318
Beck, Jim, 29, 51
Beck, John, 165
Beck, Nanci, 209
Beck, Sylvie, 198
Becker, Jonathan, 281
Becklund, Walt, 186
Beckwith, Reginald, 79
Beckwar, George, 41
Bedi, Kabir, 295-296
Beeby, Bruce, 202
Beery, Noah, 276
Beeson, Paul, 118, 213
Beetson, Frank, 267
Begakis, Yani, 329
Begley, Ed, 166, 191-192

Begley, Ed, Jr., 306
Behm, Marc, 143
Behrens, Marla, 82
Beint, Michael, 156
Beirute, Jorge, 143
Bekassy, Stephen, 56
Belinda, 152
Bell, Arnita, 245
Bell, J. Randall, 261
Bell, Kathy, 312
Bell, Michael, 153
Bell, Nancy, 286
Bell, Rodney, 11
Bell, Tom, 141
Bellamy, Ann, 145
Bellamy, Earl, 276
Bellan, Jana, 280
Beller, George, 253
Bellero, Carlo, 68
Belli, Agostina, 310
Belli, Melvin, 166
Belli, Pino, 114
Bellis, Andreas, 262
Belove, Leonard, 30
Bemiller, Ted C., 241, 259
Benda, Kenneth, 197
Bender, Russ, 10, 12, 16, 18-
  19, 27, 33, 38-39, 41, 47,
  80, 147, 161, 168
Bender, Erich F., 159, 179
Bendix, William, 74-75
Benedict, Nick, 243, 247
Benedict, William, 209
Benfield, Derek, 284
Bengell, Norma, 122-123
Benjamin, Breanna, 277
Benjamin, Floella, 284
Benjamin, Paul, 269, 271
Benjamin, Richard, 327-328
Bennet, Spencer, 53
Bennett, Brian, 125
Bennett, Charles, 127
Bennett, Frances, 69
Bennett, Jill, 194
Bennett, Julie, 144
Bennett, Matt, 233
Bennett, Nicholas, 71
Bennett, Rita, 217

Benson, Deborah, 319
Benson, Linda, 109, 111
Benson, Peter, 190
Benson, Tony, 150
Bent, Linda, 121, 134
Bentley, John, 43, 53
Benussi, Femi, 242
Ben-Yosef, Avraham, 141
Bercovici, Eric, 103, 117
Bercovitch, Reuben, 135
Berenguer, Manuel, 111, 171, 211, 213
Berg, Almut, 266
Berg, Peter, 172
Berger, Helmut, 190-191
Berger, Mel, 164-165
Berger, Senta, 130, 172
Bergman, Ingrid, 289
Bergman, Peter, 297
Bergner, Elizabeth, 189-190
Berk, Robert, 250
Berlinger, Warren, 153-154
Berlinski, Zeev, 143
Bernadou, Sandra, 330
Bernard, Carl, 48
Bernard, Jason, 269
Bernard, Judd, 253
Bernardi, Jack, 254
Bernardo, Al, 301
Bernay, Lynn, 26, 74
Bernds, Edward, 20, 32
Berns, Waldo K., 281
Bernsen, Caren, 154
Bernstein, Richard, 39, 62
Berry, Chuck, 113, 278
Berry, Kerry, 120
Berry, Starrett, 292
Bert, Flo, 12
Bertinelli, Valerie, 324
Bertone, Guido, 85
Bertoya, Paul, 155
Berwick, James, 202
Beryl, Tania, 142
Besbas, Peter, 72
Besch, Bibi, 329
Bess, Ardon, 313
Best, James, 307
Best, Ulla, 179

Beswick, Martine, 209-210, 260
Bethard, Robert, 318
Bethmann, Sabine, 62
Bettoja, Franca, 107-108
Betts, Kirsten, 200
Beuret, David, 186
Bevilacqua, Alberto, 103, 122
Bey, Marki, 261
Beyer, Erdmann, 179
Bianchi, Eleanora, 91
Bianchi, Tino, 65, 142
Biancoli, Oreste, 80, 83, 90
Bierberly, Dodi, 292
Bigelow, Ben, 32
Bijou, Melvin, Jr., 288
Bikel, Theodore, 158-159
Bigler, Steve, 195
Biletnikoff, Fred, 319
Billings, Earl, 288, 321
Billings, Joe, 243
Bills, Michael, 218
Binder, Steve, 113
Bindi, Clara, 65
Bingham, Lucy, 260
Biondi, Lidia, 146, 159
Birch, Harry, 230
Birch, Paul, 3-6
Birchall, Robert, 266
Bird, Minah, 275
Bird, Norman, 79, 93
Biro, Barney, 46
Biroc, Joe, 12
Birriel, Felippe, 67
Bishop, Larry, 164, 166, 173, 184, 208, 324
Bishop, Wes, 208, 232
Bissell, Whit, 17-18
Bissett, Donald, 48
Black, Eva, 152
Black, Karen, 283-284
Black, Stewart, 190
Blackman, Don, 245
Blackman, Honor, 227
Blackman, Joan, 257-258
Blackwell, Richard, 265
Blaine, Jerry, 13
Blair, Janet, 79
Blair, Nicky, 22, 34-35

Blaisdell, Paul, 6, 10, 12, 19, 27, 47
Blake, Angela, 17
Blake, Anthony, 228
Blake, Christopher, 271
Blake, Dennis, 128
Blake, Jonathan, 311
Blake, Josephine, 48
Blake, Paul, 217, 271
Blake, Rosemary, 218
Blake, Timothy, 293
Blakely, Dennis, 150
Blakely, Don, 332
Blakley, Ronee, 320
Blaksted, Jorgen, 82
Blanche, Francis, 137
Blanchot, Jacky, 133
Blanco, Adela, 314
Blanco, Gloria, 211
Blanco, Tomás, 211
Blees, Robert, 218, 224-225
Bleifer, John, 242
Blier, Bernard, 137
Bliss, John, 232
Bloch, Lars, 166
Block, Irving, 26
Blockbusters, The, 21
Bloom, John, 212-213
Bloom, Judi, 197
Bloom, Lindsay, 280
Blossom, Roberts, 251-253
Bluestein, Steve, 297
Blume, Jochen, 62
Bluthal, John, 207
Blye, Margaret, 300
Blythe, Janus, 314
Boatman, Robert, 131
Boatwright, Colostine, 267
Boccardo, Delia, 166, 308
Bochner, Lloyd, 191, 197-198
Body, Martin, 14
Bogarde, Dirk, 93, 138-139
Bogart, Hal, 19, 28, 34
Bogdanovich, Peter, 145, 154
Bohan, Jim, 267
Boido, Rico, 122
Boland, Gene, 277
Bolas, Xan Das, 214

Bold, Barbara, 204
Bolkan, Florinda, 216, 298
Bolke, Bradley, 105
Bollante, Letitia, 85
Bolling, Tiffany, 281
Bolzoni, Adriano, 142, 146, 159
Bomba, Enrico, 182
Bonar, Ivan, 161
Bond, Derek, 69, 125-126
Bond, Diane, 111, 148
Bond, Lenore, 79
Bondarchuk, Sergei, 203
Bonds, Bob, 217
Bonet, Nai, 105, 147
Bongioanni, Gianni, 166
Bonilla, Roxanna, 233
Bonino, Steve, 334
Bonner, Frank, 243
Bonner, William, 210-211
Bono, Sonny, 170
Booke, Sorrell, 293-294, 306
Boon, Kurt, 167
Boon, Robert, 140
Boone, Libby, 276, 300
Boone, Pat, 148
Booth, Calvin, 18
Booth, Nesdon, 20
Booth, Roger, 213
Bor, Vladimir, 298
Borden, Lynn, 225, 238
Borders, James, 288
Bordighi, Al, 274
Borel, Annik, 265
Borelli, Franco, 266
Borgnine, Ernest, 206
Borik, Alcide, 141
Borneo, Phil, 192
Borromel, Charles, 85
Borzage, Bill, 60
Boschero, Dominique, 141-142
Bosetti, Giulio, 117
Bosic, Andrea, 82
Bottar, Frank (Franco Bottari), 168
Bötticher, Herbert, 198
Bottoms, Joseph, 283-284
Bottoms, Timothy, 292-293

Bouchard, Jean, 253
Bouchey, Willis, 80
Boulanger, Daniel, 180
Bourne, Peter, 329
Bourvil, 133
Bouvard, Philippe, 133
Bow, Simmy, 33, 243
Bowen, Dennis, 306
Bowler, Clive Colin, 137
Bowler, Norman, 194
Bowman, Tom, 150
Boxer, John, 22
Boxleitner, Bruce, 280
Boyce, George, 120
Boyd, Alan, 308
Boyd, James, 318
Boyd, Rick, 180
Boyer, Charles, 171, 289
Boyer, John, 124
Boyet, Michael, 250
Bozan, Aghul Rain, 142
Bozzuffi, Marcel, 253
Brace, Peter, 150
Brackenbury, Pat, 210
Brackett, Sarah, 108
Bradbury, Basil, 79
Bradbury, Jeanette, 64
Braddock, Martin, 32, 47
Bradford, Billy, 248
Bradford, Marshall, 3, 17, 39
Bradford, Raymond, 115
Bradley, Al (Alfonso
  Brescia), 235, 262
Bradley, David, 31, 211
Bradley, Leslie, 20, 39
Bradshaw, Booker, 239-240
Bradshaw, Irene, 210
Brady, Scott, 94, 96, 163-
  164, 171
Braha, Herbert, 332
Brakel, Walter, 243
Brambell, Wilfred, 156
Brame, Bill, 170
Branch, Mary, 324
Brandel, Marc, 117
Brando, Marlon, 195
Brands, Henriette, 279
Brandstetter, Frank, 143

Brandt, Mogens, 72, 82
Brash, Marion, 231
Brauner, Isolde, 198
Braunstein, Alan, 193
Bravo, Ninette, 249
Breakston, George, 41
Breck, Peter, 89
Bredell, Elwood, 8
Breeding, Richard, 283
Brekke, Krisha M. 309
Bremmen, Colin, 326
Brendel, El, 12
Brennan, Paul, 271
Brenner, Jules, 241, 268
Brent, Doris, 77
Brereton, Tasma, 158, 189
Bresslaw, Bernard, 222-223,
  275
Brett, Anna, 201
Brett, Janet, 284
Brewer, James, 292
Brewster, Jonathan, 202
Brice, Pierre, 97
Bricken, Alene, 192
Bricken, Jules, 192
Bridges, Beau, 285
Bridges, Jim, 18
Bridges, Lloyd, 3-4
Briggs, Rhavan, 265
Brighton, Bruce, 77
Brignone, Guido, 52
Briley, Anne, 98
Brill, Charlie, 317
Brill, Marty, 169
Brinegar, Paul, 33
Brinkley, John, 44
Britt, Ron, 319
Britton, Tony, 74-75, 305
Broaddus, Charles, 279
Brock, Stanley, 327
Brockmann, Jochen, 62
Brodie, Steve, 171
Brodney, Oscar, 214
Brodrick, Susan, 210
Brody, Donald, 212
Brody, Raymond, 138
Brody, Ronnie, 214
Brolin, James, 322-323

Bromley, Sydney, 118
Bronne, Franziska, 195
Bronson, Charles, 35, 72
227-228
Brontë, Emily, 202
Brooke, Steven, 128
Brooks, Jan, 53
Brooks, Randy, 290
Brooks, Ray, 112, 256-257
Brooks, Walter, 215
Brotherson, Eric, 221
Brouer, Jerry, 253
Brown, Altyrone, 290
Brown, Bruce, 195
Brown, Caroll (Bruno
Carotenuto), 141
Brown, Casey, 248
Brown, Chelsea, 232-233
Brown, Eleonora, 168-169
Brown, Ewing, 27
Brown, Gaye, 108
Brown, Georg Stanford, 237
Brown, James, and the Flames,
113, 125
Brown, Jerry, 307
Brown, Jim, 231-232, 247-248
Brown, Joe E., 88
Brown, John Moulder, 211-212
Brown, Juanita, 254
Brown, Judy, 247
Brown, Michael, 309
Brown, Pamela, 202
Brown, Penny, 216
Brown, Peter, 208, 249, 254-
255
Brown, Ralph, 327
Brown, Robert, 108, 214
Brown, Roy Lee, 309
Brown, Scotty, 84
Brown, Stuart, 272
Browne, Tom, 200
Browning, Alan, 194
Browning, Tod, 205
Brubaker, Tony, 247, 261, 269
Bruce, Barbara, 128
Bruce, Dorothy, 16
Bruce, Eve, 233
Bruce, Paul, 145

Brun, Joseph, 192
Brudin, Bo, 328
Bruner, Mary, 244
Brutsche, Jerry, 87, 111, 117,
120, 124, 136, 176
Bryant, Chuck, 324
Bryant, Gerald, 22
Bryant, Michael, 93
Bryant, Sandra, 202
Bryant, William, 276
Bryar, Claudia, 17
Bryne, Eddie, 201
Brynner, Yul, 203, 286
Buccella, Maria Grazia, 133,
139
Bucceri, Gianfranco, 295
Buchanan, Larry, 91, 115, 186
Buchanan, Morris, 240
Buchanan, Robert, 106
Buchanan, Sherry, 308
Buchholz, Horst, 182-183
Buchman, Harold, 121
Buckingham, Bob, 281
Buckley, Keith, 138, 202, 224
Bufano, Vincent, 334
Buffington, Sam, 18
Bugliosi, Vincent, 244
Bulajic, Stevo (Stefan), 203,
298
Bulajic, Veljko, 203, 298
Bullington, Perry, 297
Bulloch, Jeremy, 97-98
Bullock, Dick, 176
Buntic, Petar, 311
Burandt, Jacque, 307
Burden, Hugh, 205
Burge, Stuart, 194
Burgess, Madeleine, 69
Burke, Martin, 285
Burn, Jonathan, 205
Burnell, Robert, 181
Burnet, Susan, 137
Burnham, Edward, 203
Burnham, Jeremy, 114, 137
Burns, Mark, 137
Burns, Robert, 217
Burr, Raymond, 11
Burroughs, Edgar Rice, 143,
273, 282, 305

Burton, Bill, 184
Burton, Jennifer, 264
Burton, Jhean (Jeanne), 44,
    62
Burton, Julian, 44, 108
Burton, Laurie, 238
Burton, Normann, 277, 290
Burton, Robert, 17, 267
Burtt, Patty, 322
Bury, Sean, 203
Bush, Grand, 332
Bushman, Francis X., 73,
    136
Bushman, Susan, 163
Butchie, J. Cosgrove, 184
Butera, Sam, and the
    Witnesses, 75-77
Butler, Bill, 174, 215
Butler, Cindy, 301, 309
Butler, David, 257
Butler, Wilmer C., 223
Butterworth, Peter, 207,
    222-223
Buttons, Red, 324
Buttram, Pat, 124
Butula, Tony, 31
Buxton, Frank, 144
Buxton, Judy, 284
Buza, George, 313
Buzzi, Ruth, 306
Byatt, Irenee, 206
Byrd, Caruth C., 274
Byrd, David, 332
Byrds, The, 131
Byrne, Bobby, 323
Byrne, Michael, 311
Byrnes, Burke, 329
Byrnes, Edward, 20-21
Byron, Kathleen, 79
Bysol, Jim, 30

Caba, Irene G., 148
Cabot, Bruce, 48
Cabot, Susan, 25-26, 35
Cabrera, John, 326
Cadiente, David, 332
Caffarel, José Maria, 176
Caffaro, Cheri, 244-245

Cagle, Jesse, 326
Cagney, Jimmy, 332
Cahill, Barry, 240
Cahn, Julie, 145
Cahn, L. Edward, 8, 12, 16,
    18-19, 22-23, 27, 34, 38
Caine, Michael, 213, 253
Calder-Marshall, Anna, 202
Caldwell, William, 312
Caleita, Maria, 172
Calhoun, Joan, 169
Calhoun, Rory, 80
Calker, Darrell, 56
Call, Ed (Edward), 206, 318
Callan, Michael, 306
Callard, Kay, 14
Calloway, Kirk, 290
Calnan, Matilda, 128
Calo, Carla, 48, 60
Calvin, John, 323
Calvin, Tony, 210
Calvo, José, 214
Calvo, Rafael Luis, 104
Camacho, Leu, 247
Cambridge, Edmund, 269
Cambridge, Godfrey, 269
Camel, Joe, 82
Camen, Paul, 329
Cameron, 94
Cameron, Bill, 247
Cameron, Earl, 64, 181
Cämmerer, Dr. Roland, 179
Campanella, Joseph, 328, 332
Campbell, Archie, 139
Campbell, Bob, 4-5
Campbell, Choker, 23
Campbell, Gary, 217
Campbell, Margaret, 9, 25
Campbell, R. Wright, 4, 35,
    39, 99, 108
Campbell, Robert, 99-100
Campbell, William, 89, 99-100,
    131-133
Campo, Wally, 31-32, 35, 53,
    72, 84, 147
Campogalliani, Carlo, 48
Campoy, Rafael Sánchez, 159
Camras, Roger, 257

Canal, Antonio, 314
Canale, Gianna Maria, 107
Canalejas, José, 174
Canby, Vincent, 284
Candelli, Stelio, 122
Candido, Candy, 242
Candy, John, 212
Cannon, Esma, 64
Cannon, Vince, 321
Cantafora, Antonio, 220
Capitani, Remo, 174
Capucci, Fabrizio, 48
Capucci, Franco, 85
Capucine, 326
Carabatsos, Steve, 308
Carandall, Eric, 319
Carbone, Anthony, 44, 74
Carbonell, Carmen, 158
Carby, Fanny, 112
Cardew, Jane, 207
Cardi, Tito, 316
Cardinale, Claudia, 178
Cardos, John, 160, 163-164
Care, Jeanie, 279
Carey, Earleen, 319
Carey, George E., 150, 208
Carey, Joyce, 74
Carey, Philip, 113-114
Carey, Timothy, 101, 117
Cargo, David, 199, 206
Caridine, Lyn (Lynn), 267, 290
Carlan, Richard, 21
Carleton, Claire, 20
Carlin, John, 310
Carlisle, Bruce, 3, 8
Carlo, East, 332
Carlson, Erika, 287
Carlson, Karen, 317
Carlson, Leslie (Les), 251, 313
Carlson, Veronica, 275
Carlton, Rex, 77, 115
Carlton, Vivienne, 189
Carmel, Eddie, 77
Carmona, Guillermo, 104
Carney, Art, 332
Carney, Fred, 317, 329

Caron, Sandra, 222
Carpenter, Carleton, 217
Carpenter, Frank, 6
Carpenter, John, 5
Carpenter, Randall, 239
Carpi, Fabio, 165
Carpi, Tito, 308
Carr, Camilla, 186
Carr, Larry, 17
Carr, Paul, 209, 250, 264
Carradine, David, 221-222
Carradine, John, 8, 221
Carradine, Robert, 304
Carras, Anthony, 94
Carrera, Barbara, 303-304
Carreras, Michael, 205
Carricart, Robert, 34
Carroll, Brandon, 31-32
Carroll, Corky, 195
Carroll, Marilyn, 31
Carroll, Thomas C., 261
Carroll, Victoria, 121, 163
Carruthers, Ben, 174
Carson, Jack, 58
Carson, John David, 299-300
Carter, Allan, 31
Carter, Georgianna, 36
Carter, Jack, 306
Carter, Lynda, 282-283
Carter, Marya, 73
Carter, Mel, 269
Carter, Peter, 313
Carter, T.K., 321
Carter, Terry, 248, 254-255
Carter, Thomas, 290
Cartier, Oscar, 280
Cartwright, Percy, 69
Carvajal, Alfonso, 238
Casares, Sofia, 211
Casas, Antonio, 182
Casas, Fernando Izcaino, 235
Cascales, Jose Antonio, 159
Case, Marianna, 247
Casellato, Luigi, 295
Casetti, Tiziana, 82
Casey, Bernie, 221-222, 268-269
Cash, Johnny, 67

Cash, Rosalind, 268, 290
Casnoff, Philip, 334-335
Cass, David, 303
Cass, Henry, 69
Cass, Ronald, 97, 125
Cassaday, Bill, 13
Cassavetes, John, 147
Cassel, Seymour, 323
Cassidy, Jack, 206, 320
Cassidy, Joanna, 319
Cassidy, Maureen, 22
Cassidy, Regina, 115
Cassmore, Judy, 254
Castellano, Franco, 134, 154
Castelnuovo, Nino, 156
Casten, Peter, 103
Castillo, Anthony, 307
Castillo, Gloria, 18, 20-23
Castle, Mary, 61
Castle, Mike, 193
Castle, Peggie, 11
Castretti, Adolfo, 200
Castro, Luis, 158
Catalanatto, Joe, 309
Catching, Bill, 318
Catching, Dorothy, 329
Cater, John, 203, 224-225
Cates, Gilbert, 285
Cavara, Paolo, 165
Cavell, Marc, 94, 145, 147
Cawthorne, James, 273
Caymmi, Dorival, 234
Cazalilla, Juan, 314
Cazelet, Isolde, 271
Cazenove, Christopher, 194
Ca'Zorzi, Alberto, 114
Cebrian, Fernando, 148
Cedar, Jon, 243
Cedergren, Ingrid, 291
Cedillos, Ron, 296
Celano, Guido, 62, 107
Celi, Adolfo, 214, 242, 310
Cellier, Peter, 310
Cembrowska, Susan, 73
Cervi, Gino, 52
Cesarvilla, Carlos, 103-104, 111
Cestare, John, 210

Cevenini, Alberto, 122
Cezon, Connie, 8
Chabot, Amedee, 109
Chace, Haile, 52
Chadwick, Robin, 194
Chaffey, Don, 324
Chakiris, George, 171
Challenger, Rudy, 279
Challis, Christopher, 311
Challoner, Carla, 58
Challoner, Pauline, 211
Chamberlain, Cyril, 22, 64
Chamberlain, Richard, 194
Chambers, Don, 31
Chambers, Terry, 296
Chandler, George, 228
Chandler, Jene, 308
Chandler, Joan, 31
Chandler, John, 276-277
Chandler, John Davis, 291
Chandler, Lee, 170
Chandler, Len, 225
Chandler, Patti, 111, 117, 119-120, 124, 134, 136, 149
Chandler, Raymond, 125
Chandos, John, 182
Chanel, Hélène, 83
Chaney, Lon, Jr., 92
Chang, Paul, 149
Chang'e, 146
Chapman, Edward, 75
Chapman, Leigh, 265
Chapman, Marguerite, 55
Chapman, Robin, 311
Chappell, Norman, 207
Charity, C.C., 287
Charles, Arlene, 119
Charles, Leon, 243
Charles, Oscar, 205
Charles, Ray, and his Orchestra, 131
Charles, Tommy, 23
Charo, 197
Charolla, Frank, 210
Chase, Annazette, 265
Chase, James Hadley, 283
Chase, Stephen, 189
Chason, Gary W., 261

Chatlak, Mariela, 158
Chau-Luong-Ham, 83
Chavez, Carlos, 61
Checchi, Andrea, 48, 65, 90-91, 114
Chekov, Anton, 103
Cheng, Mary, 149
Cher, 170
Cherry, Joretta, 115
Cherry, Stanley Z., 206
Chertok, Barry, 86
Chessman, Jennifer, 281
Cheung, Margaret, 149
Chevalier, Jacques, 253
Chevron, John, 91
Chi, Ma, 246
Chiao, Roy, 255
Chicoine, Michele, 192
Ching, Chang Ching, 246
Chiquito, 250
Chit-Chu-La, 83
Chitty, Eric, 227
Chiurco, Isabella, 85
Chocolate Watch Band, The, 150
Chomsky, Marvin, 273
Chow, Michael, 80
Christelis, Marina, 272
Christenberry, Chris, 243
Christian, Chris, 58
Christian, H.R., 238, 249
Christian-Jaque, 133, 139
Christian, Rob, 217
Christian, Roger, 87, 109
Christina, Katia, 180
Christophe, Françoise, 90
Christopher, Dennis, 204, 323
Christopher, Jordan, 169-170
Church, Frank, 131
Cianci, Antonio, 83
Ciavarro, Luigi, 235
Ciges, Luis, 314
Cimarosa, Gaetano, 178
Ciral, Karen, 170-171
Cisar, George, 34
Citty, Jim, 309
Ciuffi, Sonia, 235
Clair, Jany, 82

Claridge, Westbrook, 314
Clark, Dick, 23, 160-161, 166
Clark, Frank, 308
Clark, Fred, 119, 123, 155
Clark, Jim, 258
Clark, Ken, 43
Clark, Leroy, Jr., 279
Clark, Marlene, 231
Clark, Petula, 131
Clark, Phillip, 277
Clark, Roy, 317
Clarke, David, 317
Clarke, Gary, 31, 33-34
Clarke, Jason, 170
Clarke, Robert, 27-28, 56
Claussen, Joy, 105
Clawsen, Mary Ellen, 212
Clay, Jim (Aldo Cecconi), 141
Clay, Philippe, 139
Clayton, George, 284-285
Cleaves, Robert, 145
Clem, Jimmy, 301, 309, 318, 324
Clemens, Brian, 209
Clement, David, 239
Clement, Pilar, 235
Clements, John, 93
Clerici, Giafranco, 316
Cleveland, Carol, 275
Cliff, John, 17
Clifford, Mike, 279
Clitheroe, Jimmy, 152-153
Clive, John, 207
Clouse, Robert, 255
Clune, Anne, 179
Coates, Phyllis, 8-9
Cobb, Edmund, 13, 16, 19, 22, 84
Cobb, Lee J., 178
Cobbler, Jan, 287
Coburn, Norman, 122
Cochran, Eddie, 278
Cockrell, Gary, 122
Coco, James, 281
Coco, Sasha, 58
Cody, Francis R., 206
Cody, Iron Eyes, 301
Coelho, Susie, 318-319

Coffin, Frederick, 285
Coffin, Tris, 89
Cohen, Herman, 14, 17, 33, 48-49, 70
Cohen, Howard R., 233
Cohen, Larry, 235, 256, 320-321
Cohn, Gordon, 109
Colbert, Dewellie, 290
Colbert, Nicholas, 86
Colbert, Pam, 87
Colbourne, Maurice, 190
Colchart, Thomas, 86
Cole, Al (Albert), 210, 212-213
Cole, Donna, 4
Cole, George, 200
Cole, Leslie, 212
Cole, Phyllis, 19
Cole, Selette, 62
Coleman, Ben, 170
Coleman, Bryan, 22, 69
Coleman, Dabney, 307
Colin, Joel, 29
Colizzi, Giuseppe, 174
Coll, Julio, 111
Colley, Don Pedro, 235, 261
Colli, Ernesto, 180
Collier, Marian, 52
Collings, David, 271
Collins, Alan (Luciano Pigozzi), 141, 168, 220
Collins, Bill, 212
Collins, Bob, 297
Collins, Jo, 120, 124, 134
Collins, Joan, 199, 284-285, 299
Collins, Joseph, 288
Collins, Roberta, 233, 317
Colman, Booth, 161
Colon, Alex, 293
Colton, Jacque Lynn, 327
Coluzzi, Francesca Romana, 242
Comer, John, 202
Comisky, Chuck, 281
Compton, Annie, 257
Compton, Richard, 257, 278

Conde, Fabián, 314
Conklin, Betty, 249
Conklin, Chester, 3-4
Conley, Corrine, 215
Connell, Maureen, 43
Connell, W. Merle, 61
Connelly, Chris, 318
Connery, Sean, 121-122, 328-329
Connor, James, 286
Connor, Kenneth, 207
Connor, Kevin, 273, 282, 305
Connor, Patrick, 48
Connors, Chuck, 9-10
Connors, Joan, 46, 53
Connors, Julie, 187
Connors, Touch (Mike), 4-6, 11, 16, 23-24, 27, 38-39
Conrad, Jess, 71
Conrad, Michael, 245-246
Conrad, Nancy, 274
Conrad, Robert, 274
Conroy, Burt, 286
Contardi, Livia, 90, 128
Conte, Richard, 192
Conti, Audrey, 18
Continenza, Sandro, 85
Contini, Alfio, 174
Contino, Dick, 46
Contner, J. Burgi, 160, 165
Contreras, Roberto, 88
Convy, Burt (Bert), 44, 315
Conway, Gary, 17, 26, 33-34
Conway, Karla, 134
Conway, Russ, 37
Conway, Tom, 12, 27
Cook, David, 138
Cook, Ed (Edwin), 145, 148
Cook, Elisha, 92, 221
Cook, Myron, 13
Cook, Nathan, 248
Cook, Perry, 161, 233
Cooley, Bobby, 279
Cooley, Ernest, 279
Cooley, Isabel, 38-39, 321
Coon, Caroline, 148
Cooney, Ray, 69
Coop, Denys, 93, 138

Cooper, Gary, 80
Cooper, Jeff, 145
Cooper, Linda, 161
Cooper, Paul, 180
Copie, Rosine, 185-186
Copley, Peter, 138, 271, 291
Coppleston, Geoffrey, 289
Coppola, Francis Ford, 86,
  89-90, 98, 167
Coppola, Talia, 167, 191-192
Coquillon, John, 156, 179,
  189, 197, 202
Corbett, Harry H., 112
Corbucci, Bruno, 235
Corbucci, Enzio, 105
Corbucci, Sergio, 107
Cord, Alex, 301
Cord, Bill, 37
Cordic, Regis J., 281
Corevi, Antonio, 108, 128
Corey, Jeff, 315-316
Corey, Maggie, 204
Corey, Professor Irwin, 297
Corff, Robert, 192-193
Corman, Roger, 3-6, 9-11, 20-
  21, 25-26, 35, 37, 39, 44,
  60, 74, 81, 84, 86, 90, 92,
  96, 98-99, 108, 120, 127,
  145, 154, 172, 184-185,
  192-193, 326
Corn, Danielle, 175
Cornelius, Billy, 207
Corner, Harry, 244
Cornet, Francisco, 104
Cornish, Richard, 179
Cornthwaite, Robert, 286
Cornwall, Dan, 138
Cornwell, Judy, 153, 167,
  202, 218
Corona, Elvira, 46
Corra, Dora, 68
Corri, Adrienne, 74, 258-259
Corrington, John William, 221
Corrington, Joyce H., 221
Cort, Bud, 192
Cortese, Valentina, 105-106
Cortez, Stanley, 55, 136
Cortland, Nicholas, 225

Cory, Steve, 161
Coscia, Marcello, 65, 85, 190
Cosimini, Henry, 277
Cossins, James, 202, 205,
  229, 231
Costello, Carol, 169
Costello, Lou, 155
Costello, Ward, 40
Cosulich, Callisto, 122
Cottafavi, Vittorio, 58, 60
Cotten, Joseph, 220
Coubert, Chana, 106
Couch, Bill, 203, 329
Couglin, Kevin, 161-162, 166
Coulouris, George, 205, 291
Counsell, Elizabeth, 93
Court, Hazel, 81, 96, 108-109
Courtenay, Tom, 138-139
Courtland, Christi, 108
Courtney, Chuck, 286
Cousar, James, 269
Cousin, Jody, 139
Cousin, Pascal, 180
Covan, De Forest, 314
Cowan, Ashley, 89
Cowper, Jacqueline, 218
Cox, Richard, 260
Cox, Ruth, 315
Crabtree, Arthur, 49
Craig, Ed, 51
Craig, John, 147
Craig, Michael, 117-118, 227
Craig, Wendy, 93
Craig, Yvonne, 124
Crain, William, 220
Crane, Barbara, 25
Crane, Dagne, 105
Crane, Michael, 282
Cranham, Kenneth, 275
Cranshaw, Joseph (Patrick),
  55, 115
Cranston, Joseph, 89
Cravat, Nick, 303
Crawford, Andrew, 194
Crawford, Broderick, 60, 320-
  321
Crawford, Kelton, 80
Crawford, Mona, 217

Crisa, Erno, 91-92
Creed, Roger, 243
Crehan, Donna, 18
Crehan, Dorothy, 20
Crenshaw, Hugh, 91
Cressoy, Pierre, 80
Crew, Sam, 320
Crews, Phillip, 278
Crisa, Erno, 91-92
Crisman, Nino, 133
Crockett, Jan, 105
Crofoot, Alan, 313
Cromarty, Andee, 282
Cronenweth, Jordan, 307
Cronin, Michael, 223
Crosby, Bing, 293
Crosby, Floyd, 3-4, 20-21,
    33, 35-39, 60, 74, 81, 84,
    88, 96, 99, 101, 110, 117,
    120, 123, 134
Crosby, Gary, 94
Crosby, Lindsay, 148, 274
Crosby, Warren, 39
Cross, Dennis, 33, 249
Cross, Edward, 257
Cross, Jimmy, 13
Crosthwaite, Julie, 258
Crothers, Scatman, 185, 247,
    265, 269, 271, 318
Crowley, Kathleen, 8
Crowther, Graham, 311
Croydon, John, 5
Crudo, Aldo, 262
Crudup, Carl, 288, 290
Crumb, Robert, 259
Crutchley, Rosalie, 202,
    205, 218
Cuby, Joseph, 125
Cudney, Roger, 231
Culbert, Patricia, 167
Culley, Zara, 261
Culliford, James, 229
Culp, Robert, 287-288
Cumbuka, Heshimu, 332
Cumbuka, Jitu, 221
Cummings, Bob, 87
Cunningham, Beryl, 190
Cunningham, John, 317

Cunningham, June, 49
Cunningham, Noel John, 312
Cunningham, Sean S., 312
Curacao, Harcourt, 181
Curb, Mike, 148
Curcio, Enzo, 182
Curik, Jan, 298
Curnow, Graham, 49-50
Curran, Chris, 201
Curtis, Alan, 207
Curtis, Arlo, 196
Curtis, Billy, 243-244
Curtis, Howard, 111
Curtis, Margo Lynn, 320
Curtis, Mel, 73
Curtis, Tony, 238
Curtis, Willy, 313
Cusack, Cyril, 217-218, 242
Cusack, Sinead, 217
Cushing, Peter, 197, 200, 224,
    258-259, 282
Cuthbertson, Allan, 153
Cutting, Richard, 21
Cutts, Dale, 272
Cypher, Jon, 286
Cyphers, Charles, 265

Daarstad, Eric, 31
Dade, Stephen, 128
Dagenhart, Carl, 294
Dailey, Allen, 79
Dailey, Dan, 320
Dailey, Irene, 322
Daine, Lois, 202
Dainton, Joanne, 310
Daisies, Anthony (Antonio
    Margheriti), 63
Dalban, Robert, 137, 139
Dale, Dick, and the Del Tones,
    87, 109
Dale, Jim, 223
Dall, Sabine, 179
Dallamano, Massimo, 190
Dallas, Jean, 69
Dallas, Philip, 309
Dalmas, Claudine, 182
Dalton, Abby, 21, 26
Dalton, Timothy, 202

Daly, James, 237-238
Daly, Mark, 22
Daly, Tom, 55, 171
Daly, Tyne, 184
Dalzell, Arch R., 154, 162
Dambuza, Nathan, 181
Damiani, Damiano, 178
Damon, Mark, 60-61, 99-100, 103, 168
D'Amore, Jojo, 243
Dance, Bill, 281
Dane, Alexandra, 223
Dane, Peter, 146
Daniel, Carmel, 55
Daniel, Leslie, 77-78
Danieli, Emma, 68, 107
Daniels, Danny, 179
Daniels, Eugene, 278
Daniels, Jacob (Jerry), 301, 319
Daniels, Jody, 94
Daniels, John, 318
Daniely, Lisa, 22
Danner, Blythe, 286-287
Danning, Sybil, 329
Dano, Rick, 281
Dano, Royal, 281
Danova, Cesare, 290, 308-309
Dante, Michael, 94
Danton, Ray (Raymond), 223-224, 280
A'Antonio, Carmen, 53
D'Arc, Giselle, 27
Darc, Mireille, 137-138
Darch, Penny, 284
Darden, Severn, 174
Daris, Samuel, 269
Darling, Candy, 217
Darling, Gary M., 276
Darling, Joan, 174, 199, 332
Darmour, Roy, 18
D'Arms, Ted, 304
Darnell, Deborah, 187
Darnell, Jason, 309
Darr, William, 329
Darren, James, 200-201
Darrin, Diana, 8, 13, 20
Darrow, Susannah, 164

Darwell, Jane, 8
Daryl, Jacqueline, 97-98
da Silva, Ademir, 234
Da Silva, Howard, 320
D'Astrea, Irene, 171
Dave, Clovis, 211
Davenport, David, 207
Davenport, Mary, 246
Davenport, Nigel, 303-304
David, Graydon F., 280
David, Jeff, 217
David, Karen, 257
David, Richard, 112
David, Ronnie, 111
David, Wil, 280
Davidson, Geoff, 291
Davidson, James R., 186
Davidson, John Porter, 137
Davidson, Phillamore, 182
Davies, David, 108
Davies, Edgar D., 197
Davies, Rupert, 156, 158, 179, 189
Davies, Stanley, 214
Davis, Bette, 206
Davis, Billy, 120
Davis, Bobby, 279
Davis, Bruce, 244
Davis, Bud, 309
Davis, Charley, 196
Davis, Cynthia, 267
Davis, Dorothy, 305
Davis, Fiona, 224-225
Davis, Gayle Lynn, 247
Davis, Jean, 27
Davis, Jim, 163-164
Davis, Karl, 29
Davis, Laurie, 292
Davis, Monica, 164
Davis, Robert, 7-8
Davis, Spencer, Group, 120
Davis, Vance, 300
Davison, Davey, 169
Davreux, Denise, 149
Dawkins, Paul, 156
Dawn, Doreen, 108
Dawson, Anthony (Antonio Margheriti), 168, 204

Day, Robert, 143
Dayle, Ellis, 258
Dayne, Marjorie, 171, 173
Dayton, Danny, 327
Dayton, Ronnie, 111, 119, 121, 124, 147, 161, 176
Deady, Jane, 190
Dean, Brian, 332
Dean, Ivor, 179, 210
Dean, James, 18
Dean, Jeanne, 13
Dean, Kerry, 189
Dean, Madgal, 163
Dean, Susan, 105
de Angeles, Nato, 284
De Angelis, Remó, 159
Deardon, Basil, 93
Deason, Paul, 264
de Bardot, Audoin, 180
DeBenedett, Frank, 186
DeBenning, Burr, 313-314
De Brea, Astrid, 124
De Broux, Lee, 209, 240
de Canonge, Maurice, 182
De Carellis, Aldo, 168
De Carmine, Renato, 114
de Cervantes, Miguel, 182
De Concini, Ennio, 65, 80, 105, 133
De Costa, Tony, 211
Dee, Buffy, 274
Dee, Sandra, 191-192
Deel, Rose Ann, 279
Deems, Mickey, 105
Dees, Rick, 306
De Felice, Lionello, 91
De Feo, Francesco, 52, 82
De Filippo, Pasquale, 68
De Fish, Doe, 317
De Francesco, Aldo, 142
Deghy, Guy, 190
Degrande, Jean, 216
De Hetre, Katherine, 328
Dehner, John, 197
Deitz, Bill, 309
De Kova, Frank, 35, 39, 241
De Koven, Roger, 260
de la Cámara, Javier, 314

de la Cámara, Lourdes, 314
Delancey, Shirley, 13
Delaney, Joan, 206
Delaney, Pat, 250
De La Roche, Serge, 266
Delbo, Jean-Jacques, 90
del Carmen Duque, Maria, 211
Delderfield, Ronald Frederick, 121
De Leo, Rosy, 97
De Leone, Francesco, 68, 82
Delfino, Frank, 243
Del Fra, Lino, 85
Delgado, Marissa, 250
Delgado, Roger, 93
Dell, Charlie, 186, 327
Della Giovanna, Ettore, 126
Dellay, Alan, 217
Delli Colli, Franco, 107
Delli Colli, Tonino, 178, 180
Delon, Alain, 180-181
De Longis, Anthony, 326-327
De Lorenzo, Anneka, 249
de los Arcos, Luis, 111
Del Piano, Mike, 79
Del Pozo (Pozzo), Angel, 159, 182, 266
Del Ruth, Roy, 62
Deltgen, René, 62
De Luca, Lorella, 52
De Luca, Rudy, 215-216
De Luise, Dom, 105
Delutri, Gabe, 31, 61
De Marchi, L., 126
De Marco, Diane, 119
Demarest, William, 274
De Marney, Terence, 118
De Martino, Alberto, 310
De Martino, Ferruccio, 128
DeMattio, John, 257
Demby, William, 103
de Mendoza, Alberto, 158-159, 216
DeMille, C.B., 164, 195
Deming, Mark, 334
Deming, Von, 257
Demme, Jonathan, 238, 314
Dempsey, Martin, 201-202

Demura, Fumio, 303
De Nardo, Gustavo, 103
De Natale, Don, 281
Denham, Maurice, 291
De Niro, Robert, 184-185
Dennen, Barry, 258
Denning, Richard, 6, 8, 11, 20
Dennis, Alex, 196
Dennis, Joe, 71
Dennis, John, 265, 318, 327
Denny, Steve, 319
Denoia, Nick, 217
Dent, Chuck, 195
Denton, Coby, 145
Denton, Jack, 243
Deodato, Ruggero, 316
de Oliveira, Aloysio, 234
De Palma, Brian, 246
De Paola, Alessio, 170
de Pedro, Jaime, 104
de Reda, Joe, 293
De Rita, Massimo, 128, 266
Dern, Bruce, 145, 154, 163, 170-171, 184-185, 212-213
DeRosa, Franco, 168-169
De Rouen, Reed, 69
Derr, Richard, 165
De Sabata, Eliana, 80, 105
de Sade, Marquis, 172
De Santis, Joe, 243
De Santis, Gino, 85
De Sica, Vittorio, 176
De Simone, Tom, 297
Desmond, Carol, 190
Desny, Ivan, 85-86
De Souza, Edward, 153
Detwiler, Jeannie, 278
Devane, William, 307-308
Devello, Ashik, 93
Devereau, Audrey, 77
Devin, Marilyn, 198
Devine, Andy, 164
Devlin, Don, 13, 39, 51
Devlin, Joe, 23-24
Devon, Richard, 13, 25-26, 35
de Vries, Mark, 234
Dewar, Ian, 93

De Wilde, Brandon, 237-238
De Witt, Alan, 84, 88
De Witt, Jack, 21
De Wolff, Francis, 69
Dexter, Anthony, 73
Dexter, Brad, 320
Dexter, Maury, 161-162, 167, 176
Dexter, Ron, 192
Dhooge, Desmond, 186
Dial, Rudolph, 116
Dialina, Rika, 103
Diamond, Jack, 40
Diamond, Marcia, 251
Dias, Selma Vaz, 14
Diaz, Rudy, 334
Diaz, Vic, 238, 244
Di Benedetto, Gianni, 106, 168
Dickerson, Beech (Beach), 21, 39, 160, 164, 191
Dickinson, Angie, 291
Dickinson, Desmond, 49, 70, 218
Dickson, Brenda, 223
Dickson, Hugh, 229
Diddley, Bo, 131
Dierkes, John, 81, 92, 99
Diestel, George, 28
Dietrich, Bruno, 195
Dietrich, Dena, 281
Dietrich, Monica, 207
Diffenderfer, Mike, 109
Diffring, Anton, 58-59
Di Fraia, Adelmo, 118
Di Fusco, John, 296
Dijon, Alan, 64
Di Leo, Fernando, 156, 242
Di Leo, Mario, 296
Dillon, Brendan, 81
Dillon, Robert, 99, 101, 109
Dillon, Tom, 94
Dilworth, Carol, 193
Dimitri, Nick, 291
Dimmick, Kathleen, 281
Dimmick, Walter, 294
Dinehart, Alan, Jr., 52
Dingle, Ding, 328

Diogene, Franco, 308
Dionisio, Sylvia, 168
Di Paolo, Dante, 83, 105
Di Pietro, Guadenzio, 182
Dirkson, Douglas, 334
Disney, Walt, 63
Dix, Robert, 163-164
Dixon, James, 235, 256, 320
Dixon, Ole, 72
Dixon, Richard, 320
Djurovic, Ratko, 203
Dobson, James, 34
Dobtcheff, Vernon, 253
Dockstader, George, 16, 47
Dodimead, David, 194
Dolan, Lindsay, 97
Dolan, Trent, 297
Doleman, Guy, 137
Dolen, Jim, 106
Domerel, Myrtle, 44
Domerque, Faith, 88
Dominici, Arturo, 48, 65-66
Dominici, Germana, 65
Domino, Fats, 23, 278
Dominot, 389
Donahue, Troy, 152-153, 260
Donan, Martin (Mario Donen),
    141
Donat, Richard, 301
Donati, Sergio, 310
Doncheff, Len, 313
Donegan, Pamala, 225
Donlevy, Brian, 120
Donnelly, Thomas Michael, 332
Donner, Clive, 112, 275
Donner, Richard, 227
Donner, Robert, 228
Donno, Eddie, 164
Donoro, Jackie, 67
Donovan, 131
Donte, Joseph, 46
DoQui, Robert, 173, 239-240,
    276-277
Dora, Mickey, 87, 109, 120,
    124, 195
Doran, Veronica, 193
Doria, Enzo, 90
Dorn, Dolores, 264

Dornan, Sallie, 124
Doro, Mino, 128, 130
Doro, Virginia, 106
Dorr, Lester, 33
Dorsey, Joe, 319
D'Orsi, Umberto, 180
Dottesio, Attilio, 97
Douglas, Angela, 112
Douglas, Buddy, 243
Douglas, Damon, 319
Douglas, Frank, 272
Douglas, Gordon, 247
Douglas, Kirk, 310-311
Douglas, Lawrence, 213
Douglas, Sally, 158
Douglas, Sarah, 305-306
Douking, 180
Dow, R.A., 294
Dowdall, Jim, 311
Dowling, Barbara, 90
Downes, Maurice, 279
Downey, Roy L. 261
Downs, Cathy, 11-12
Downs, Frederick, 40
Downs, Mike, 309
Doyle, Patricia, 202
Drache, Heinz, 150
Dragoti, Stan, 327
Drake, Dan, 217
Drake, Fabia, 217
Drake, Judith, 334
Drake, Oliver, 5
Drane, Robert, 279
Draper, Peter, 137
Dravic, Milena, 203
Drazen, Julie, 313
Drechsel, Sammy, 198
Dreifuss, Arthur, 150
Drescher, Fran, 334
Dressler, Lieux, 264
Drew, David, 217
Drew, Gene, 264, 282-283
Drexel, Steve, 33
Dreyfuss, Richard, 241
Driscoll, Lawrason, 307
Driscoll, Lawrie, 293
Driskill, William, 330
Druille, Maria, 314

Drummond, Jack, 320
Druon, Maurice, 289
Dubois, Marie, 171-172
Dubov, Paul, 3, 6, 12, 23, 27
Dubray, Claire, 33
Ducharme, Connie, 111
Duffie, Leotis, 292
DuFour, Val, 25
Dugan, Michael, 153
Duggan, Andrew, 320
Dugue, Antonio, 158
Dukas, James (Jim), 320, 322
Dukes, David, 281
Dullaghan, John, 232
Dullea, Keir, 172
Dumas, Alexandre, 82
Dumbrille, Douglas, 23
Dumont, Margaret, 23-24
Dunaway, Faye, 30, 221
Duncan, Kenne, 16-17, 27
Duncan, Pamela, 25-26
Dungane, Solomon, 291
Dunlap, Pamela, 185
Dunlop, Jack, 91
Dunn, Daniel, 288
Dunn, Michael, 214
Dunne, Eithne, 90
Dunne, Joe, 214
Dunne, Lee, 201
Dunning, Jessica, 79
Dunnock, Mildred, 285
Dunphy, Don, 317
Dunton, Roger, 120
Duperey, Anny, 180
Dupont, Elaine, 47
Du Pont, Penny, 320
Dupuis, Joan, 18
Duralia, Darlene, 212
Durant, Don, 37
Duric, Branko, 298
Durning, Charles, 246-247
Durren, John, 282
Durston, James, 279
Dusina, Nancy, 96
Dvornik, Boris, 204
Dwain, Hal, 91
Dwyer, Hilary, 156, 158, 179, 181-182, 202

Dwyer, Leslie, 118, 189-190
Dyce, Hamilton, 181
Dymon, Frankie, Jr., 112
Dyrector, Marcus, 31
Dysart, Richard, 328

Earl, Clifford, 193, 197
Earl, Ilse, 299
Easley, Larry, 324
Eason, Myles, 75
Eastman, Gordon, 160, 196
Eastman, Maria, 196
Easton, Robert (Bob), 193, 241
Easy, Mike, 291
Eaton, Marjorie Morely, 94, 277
Eaton, Shirley, 149
Ebert, Günther, 190
Echols, Jill, 148
Eddy, Duane, 164
Eden, Elana, 143
Eden, Mark, 187, 189
Eden, Rolf, 172
Edgley, George, 91, 115
Edmond, Terence, 93
Edmund, Lada, Jr., 173, 249
Edwards, David, 182
Edwards, Gordon, 32
Edwards, Kyle, 301, 303
Edwards, Mark, 205
Edwards, Paul, 313
Efron, Marshall, 323
Egan, Peter, 271
Ehrenfreund, Heinz, 283
Ehrlich, Max, 277
Eilbacher, Kimberly, 315
Einer, Bob, 18
Einstein, Albert, 170
Eisinger, Jo, 133
Eisley, Larry, 210
Eitner, Don, 140
Ekberg, Anita, 52, 146-147, 159
Elam, Jack, 301, 318
Eldridge, John, 112
Eles, Sandor, 214-215
Elhardt, Ingrid, 104-105

Elhardt, Kaye, 119
Elias, Ciro, 208
Elias, Louis, 119
Elias, Stacie, 335
Elkins, Bud, 175, 184, 206
Ellenstein, Robert, 327
Ellerbe, Harry, 60, 92
Elliot, Biff, 210
Elliot, Jeff, 131
Elliot, Rosalynd, 197, 214
Elliott, Peter J., 214
Elliott (Elliot), Ross, 89, 249
Elliott, Sam, 225-226
Elliott, William, 239-240
Elliotte, Judith, 245
Ellis, Christopher, 93
Ellis, Mirko, 85
Ellison, Bob, 266
Ellsworth, Christine, 309-310
Ellsworth, Nick, 311
Elmes, Nick, 117
Elmi, Nicoletta, 220
Elphick, Michael, 190
Elsenbach, John, 139
Elson, Donald, 280
Elston, Robert, 334
Embry, Bill, 279
Emeil, Jac, 265
Emmanuel, Jacques, 139
Emmet, Michael, 36, 43
Endemann, Gernot, 291
Endfield, Cy, 172
Enemies, The, 150
Engl, Sigi, 124
England, Hal, 209
English, Jack, 212, 243
English, Marla, 12, 16, 22-23, 27
English, Rachel, 211
Englund, Jan, 18, 20, 38-39
Enlow, Darlene, 105
Enzel, Jim, 217
Erickson, Del, 9
Erickson, Judy, 73
Ericson, Devon, 278
Erwin, Edward, 55
Escamilla, Charles, 307

Escott, T.J., 209
Espe, Mike, 212
Esperanza, Rosetta, 152
Essakali, Hassan, 130
Essex, David, 207
Essler, Fred, 9
Esterhazy, Andrea, 289
Estridge, Robin, 64
Estrin, Patricia, 249
Etheridge, Jim, 193
Eure, Wesley, 315, 324
Evans, Alan, 82
Evans, Art, 322
Evans, Bobby, 279
Evans, Charles, 23
Evans, Frank, 29
Evans, Haydn, 64
Evans, Jeanne, 12
Evans, John, 268
Evans, Linda, 117
Evans, Michael, 150
Evans, Roy, 210
Evans, Walter, 279
Everett, Elaine, 176
Everett, Richard, 190
Everhart, Jim, 287
Everhart, Rex, 317
Evers, Herb, 77-78
Evigan, Greg, 291
Ewen, Gwenda, 69
Ewin, Leslie, 197
Ewing, Bill, 223-224
Exciters Band, The, 101
Eyre, Peter, 194
Eytle's Tommy, Calypso Band, 22

Faber, Ron, 320
Fabian, 134-135, 153-154, 161-162, 167, 173-174
Fabre, Dominique, 171
Fabrizi, Franco, 176, 242
Fabrizi, Valeria, 114
Fabrizio, Arnaldo, 91
Fadden, Tom, 299
Fahey, Myrna, 60-61
Fain, John, 87, 109, 111, 120, 323

Fain, Peter, 171, 193
Fair, Jody, 29, 33, 43, 47
Fair, Ronald, 268
Fairchild, June, 254
Fairfax, Diana, 271
Fairman, Paul W., 18
Faith, Dolores, 73
Faithful, Geoffrey, 5
Falls, Shirley, 19, 35
Famery, Jacques, 305
Fantasia, Andrea, 82
Fantasia, Frank (Franco), 64, 295
Farbrother, Pamela, 189, 218
Fargas, Antonio, 254-255, 268
Farinon, Gabriella, 63-64
Farley, Frederick, 86
Farley, Jackie, 193
Farley, Richard, 97
Farmer, Mimsy, 147, 150, 152, 267
Farmer, Suzan, 118-119
Farnese, Alberto, 52
Farquhar, Ralph, 321
Farr, Bobby, 273
Farr, Jamie, 241
Farrell, Charles, 200, 203
Farrell, Colin, 273
Farrell, Glenda, 197
Farrell, Paul, 118
Farretta, Donato, 53-54
Farringer, Lisa, 240, 247, 265
Farris, Lucius, 326
Farrow, Tisa, 308
Faso, Nina, 281
Faulkner, Edward, 124
Faulkner, Sally, 326
Faulkner, Stephanie, 288
Fawcett, Farrah, 319
Faye, Joey, 105
Feagin, Hugh, 186
Fedden, Leander, 98
Fegte, Ernst, 56
Feindel, Jock, 6
Feliciani, Mario, 107
Felino, Jo, 211
Felleghi, Tom, 156

Fellini, Federico, 180
Fellows, Maurice, 137
Fenemore, Hilda, 22
Feng, Heang, 240
Ferguson, J. Don, 319
Fernando, Dindo, 238
Fernando, Tara, 179
Ferra, Annette, 281
Ferrara, Al, 150
Ferrara, Romano, 142
Ferrari, Nick, 247
Ferrer, Jose, 182-183, 320
Ferrer, Mel, 295-296, 318-219
Ferrero, Fiorella, 85
Ferris, Barbara, 137
Ferris, Fred, 112
Ferris, Mark, 79
Ferris, Paul, 158
Ferry, David, 313
Ferry, Jean, 139
Fertitta, John, 326
Ferzetti, Gabriele, 114, 289
Fiander, Lewis, 210, 314-315
Fiedler, John, 223-224
Field, Logan, 221
Field, Shirley Ann, 49
Field, Susi, 158
Fields, Verna, 167
Fields, W.C., 307
Fife, Alan, 111, 117, 120, 136
Filer, Tom, 4
Filippini, Rino, 126
Fimple, Dennis, 264, 324
Finch, Howard, 287
Finch, Jon, 200
Findlater, John, 329
Fine, Harry, 200
Finley, Bill, 246-247
Finn, Edwin, 194
Finn, Mickey, 38
Finnegan, Joe, 94, 335
Finnerman, Perry, 46
Finocchi, Augusto, 242
Fiorello, Tommy, 217
Fiorini, Marc, 308
Fiorino, Giovanna, 23
Firesign Theatre, 298

Firestone, Eddie, 228
Fishburne, Larry, 268-269
Fisher, Audrey, 141
Fisher, David, 174
Fisher, George, 150
Fisher, Gerry, 303
Fisher, Jim, 297
Fisher, Michael, 160, 164
Fisher, Terence, 69
Fiskin, Jeffrey Alladin, 184
Fitzgerald, Edward, 88
Fitzsimmons, Carolyn, 226
Fix, Paul, 301
Flagg, Fannie, 217
Flambeaux Steel Band, Les, 182
Flanagan, Kellie, 166
Flander, Lewis, 224
Flanders, Ralph, 294
Flanders, Tommy, 163
Flatley, William, 324
Fleming, Paul, 304
Fleming, Robert, 283
Fletcher, Jay, 249
Fletcher, Lester, 277
Fletcher, Neil, 56
Flicker, Theodore J., 199
Floersheim, Patrick, 253
Florea, John, 228
Floret, Veronique, 266
Florman, Arthur, 40
Flournoy, Don, 56
Flynn, John, 307, 332
Foa, Arnolda, 289
Focas, Spiro, 310
Foch, Nina, 315-316
Foley, Joan, 329
Fonda, Henry, 133, 308-309, 328
Fonda, Jane, 180-181, 225
Fonda, Peter, 145, 154, 180-181, 272, 286-287, 313
Fong, Alice, 255
Fong, Frances, 255
Fong, Jon, 149
Fontages, Françoise, 148
Forbes, John, 6
Forbes-Robertson, John, 200

Ford, Amtra, 254
Ford, Andrew, 308
Ford, Frank E., 321
Ford, Fred, 288
Ford, Harrison, 311-312
Ford, Paul, 227
Ford, Ross, 20
Ford, Tom, 299
Foreman, Carl, 311
Forest, Anthony, 308
Forest, Mark, 60, 91-92
Forest, Michael, 209
Forest, Peter, 190
Foresta, Carmine, 322
Forester, Cay, 67
Forrest, Mike, 26
Forster, Jaime, 28
Forsythe, Henderson, 320
Forte, Fabian, 186-187
Forte, Vincent, 220
Fortuit, Jean-Louis, 253
Foschi, Massimo, 310, 316
Foster, Barry, 138
Foster, Carey, 111
Foster, Dudley, 202
Foster, Jodie, 305
Foster, Julia, 137
Foster, Preston, 113
Foster, Ronald, 46-47
Foster, Susan, 145
Foster, William, Jr., 279
Foulk, Robert, 206
Four Pennies, The, 120
Fourmost, The, 120
Fowler, Buck, 292
Fowler, Gene, Jr., 17
Fox, Edward, 93, 311-312
Fox, Joan, 239
Fox, Marcia, 275
Fox, Mike (Michael), 35, 185, 191, 237
Foy, Madeline, 29, 34
Frame, Philip, 215
Francen, Victor, 62
Franchel, Emile, 49
Franchetti, Rina, 156
Franchi, Franco, 134, 155
Franchy, Felix, 179

Francioli, Germana, 85
Francis, Derek, 127, 153,
 207, 223
Francis, William, 331
Francisco, Sanchez, 130
Franco, Jess, 200-201, 228
Frank, Ben, 274
Frank, Bruno, 182
Frank, Joanna, 164-165, 168
Frank, T.C. (Tom Laughlin),
 145
Frankel, Cyril, 121
Franken, Steve, 113, 277
Frankham, David, 72, 84
Franklin, Gretchen, 118
Franklin, Norman, 299
Franklin, Pamela, 286
Franklyn, Fredric, 281
Franks, Chloë, 218-219
Frann, Mary, 139-140
Fraser, Jimmy, 234
Fraser, Lee, 332
Fraser, Sally, 10, 38, 41, 52
Fraser, Shelagh, 181
Frassineti, Augusto, 114
Frattari, Benito, 152
Frazier, Levi, Jr., 276
Fred, Franklyn, 141
Freda, Riccardo, 83
Frederick, Hal, 181-182
Fredericks, Dean, 73
Fredersdorf, Christian, 179
Freed, Bert, 62, 166
Freeman, Dave, 152
Freeman, Joan, 80-81
Freeman, Kathleen, 233, 318
Freen, Howard, 254
Frees, Paul, 166
Fregonese, Hugo, 80
Frei, Sally, 119
Frend, Charles, 114
Fresno, Maruchi, 158
Frid, Jonathan, 260
Fridjhon, Anthony, 272
Fridolinski, Alex, 262
Friebus, Florida, 315
Friedman, Kinky, 306
Friedman, Ron, 306

Friesen, John, 313
Frizell, Cornelius, 217
Frobe, Gert, 152-153
Frohlich, Alan, 120
Frome, Milton, 119
Frost, Alan, 8, 29
Frost, Lee, 208, 232
Frost, Warren, 41
Fruet, William, 301
Fry, Gil, 75
Frye, Virgil, 140, 282
Fuento, Arturo, 175
Fuest, Robert, 202-203, 224
Fujiki, Yu, 100-101, 106, 219
Fujimoto, Tak, 297
Fujioka, John, 286
Fujita, Susume, 106
Fujiyama, Yoko, 100-101
Fulci, Lucio, 156, 216
Fuller, Bobby, Four, 136
Fuller, Lance, 3-4, 8-9, 12,
 22, 27
Fuller, Robert, 210-211
Fuller, Tex, 205
Fulton, Jessie Lee, 186
Funato, Jun, 123
Funicello, Annette, 87, 101-
 102, 109-111, 117, 119-121,
 125, 134, 153-154
Furdeaux, Beatrice, 40
Furie, Sidney J., 125
Furnival, Robert, 194
Fux, Herbert, 148

Gaba, Marianne, 119-120
Gabriel, Larry, 265
Gadhoke, Gloria, 281
Gage, Leona, 84
Gaines, Mel, 16
Galbo, Cristina, 211
Galfas, Timothy, 317, 331
Gall, Edy, 216
Gallardo, Cesar, 249
Galli, Ida, 128, 130
Gallico, Paul, 317
Galloway, Paul, 288
Galvin, Ray, 233
Gammon, James, 257-258, 275,
 282

Ganley, Gail, 13
Gano, Glen, 212
Gans, Ron, 167
Ganton, Doug, 239
Garcia, Cordy, 206
Garcia, Eddie, 238, 244-245, 250
Garcia, Margarita, 332
Garcia, Tito, 174
Garde, Annie Birgit, 70, 72
Garden Odyssey Enterprise, 201
Gardiner, Reginald, 124
Gardner, Ava, 217-218
Garfinkle, Louis, 243
Gargiullo, Giorgio, 166
Garion, Buddy, 231
Garland, Beverly, 9-10, 20
Garland, Richard, 25-26, 80
Garner, Ed, 87, 109, 111, 120, 134, 136
Garnet, Bob, 41
Garr, Terry (Teri), 161
Garrani, Ivo, 65, 103, 118, 295, 310
Garrel, Reno, 320
Garrett, Hank, 322
Garrett, John, 46
Garrett, Leif, 257-258, 276, 300
Garrett, Sharon, 87
Garrett, Shelly, 327
Garrie, John, 258
Garrison, Connie, 277
Garrone, Riccardo, 103, 176
Garth, Michael, 11
Garwood, John, 164
Garwood, Judith, 155
Gassman, Vittorio, 133
Gassmann, Ruth, 160, 179
Gatell, Pamela, 332
Gately, Frederick, 39
Gates, Maxine, 233
Gates, Tudor, 200
Gautier, Richard (Dick), 161, 237
Gavin, Janie, 299
Gavin, John, 315

Gavlin, Fred, 31, 53
Gay, Gregory, 329
Gay, John, 271, 289
Gaye, Lisa, 23
Gaye, Marvin, 113, 208
Gayle, Saundra, 147, 155
Gaynes, George, 247
Gazarra, Ben, 25, 117-118
Gazzaniga, Don, 293
Gebel, Eva-Marie, 172
Gebhardt, Fred, 73
Gedeon, Freddie, 234
Geeson, Judy, 181
Geeson, Sally, 179, 181-182, 189
Geghardt, Liz, 194
Geib, Lark, 281
Gein, Ed, 251, 253
Geldhart, Ed, 261, 287
Gelfman, Sam, 314
Gélin, Daniel, 207
Gelman, Janice P., 212
Gelman, Larry, 297
Gemma, Giuliano, 91
Genaro, Tony, 206
Genn, Leo, 150, 216, 228
Genta, Renzo, 316
Gentile, Fedele, 60
Gentilomo, Giacomo, 107
Gentry, Don, 296
Gentry, Minnie, 235
Gentry, Oak R. 274
Gentry, Roger, 232
George, Christopher, 173-174, 197-198
George, M. James, 267, 278
George, Joe, 217
George, Susan, 227-228, 292-293
Georgiade, Nick, 330
Gerard, Gil, 217
Gerber, Joan, 259
Gering, Richard, 46
Gerler, Jordan, 307
Germani, Gaia, 114
Gerrity, William, 163
Gerry and the Pacemakers, 113
Gerson, Jeanne, 37

Gerstle, Frank, 53, 145
Gertzman (Gertsman), Maury, 33
Gessner, Nicolas, 305
Getz, Stuart, 306
Ghaffouri, Daniel, 170
Ghazi, Saad, 205
Ghostley, Alice, 306
Giacchetti, Fosco, 48
Giacobini, Franco, 90
Gianviti, Roberto, 91, 216
Gibbs, Alan, 164, 184
Gibson, Michael, 52
Gibson, Norman, 267
Gielgud, John, 194-195
Gierasch, Stefan, 268
Gifford, Alan, 64
Giftos, Elaine, 192-193
Gil, Jaime Camas, 159
Gilbert, Carolyn, 212
Gilbert, Chauncey Leon, 288
Gilbert, Denise, 171
Gilbert, Fernando, 176
Gilbert, Helen, 8
Gilbert, Lou, 174
Gilbert, Mickey, 335
Gilbert, Philip, 204
Gilbert, Terry, 97
Gilbreath, Bob, 34
Gilchrist, Connie, 35
Giles, Sandra, 46
Gill, Beverly, 245
Gill, Helen, 282
Gill, William, 269
Gillen, Arlene, 251
Gillen, Jeff, 251
Gilles, Dominque, 253
Gilles, Kirsten, 262
Gillespie, Dana, 305-306
Gillespie, John, 303
Gillespie, Robert, 282, 311
Gillette, Robert, 67
Gilliam, David, 225
Gilliam, Theodore, 288
Gillis, Gwynn, 321
Gilman, Sam, 257-258
Gilmore, Art, 38
Gilmore, Barry, 287

Gilmore, Denis, 127
Gilmore, Peter, 203, 207, 223
Ginders, Angela, 205
Gindes, Mark, 327
Ging, Jack, 47
Gingold, Hermione, 152
Giordani, Aldo, 85
Giorgelli, Gabriella, 133
Giorgio, Bill, 28, 38, 41
Giorgio, Tony, 254
Giovannini, Giorgio, 67
Giraldi, Jill, 281
Girard, Cindy, 51
Girardon, Michele, 85
Girardot, Annie, 133
Girdler, William, 248, 279
Girotti, Mario, 175
Girotti, Massimo, 220
Giroux, Jackie, 247
Gizzi, Loris, 97
Gladden, Bernadette, 265
Gladstone, Zeph, 179
Glass, Seaman, 318
Glazier, Menashe, 143
Gleason, Regina, 39
Glenn, Robert, 186
Glickman, Paul, 320
Glori, Vittorio Musy, 52
Glouner, Richard C., 191
Glover, Bruce, 276, 300
Glover, Julian, 202
Gobet, Sandrine, 169
Gobin, Gabriel, 133
Godfrey, Derek, 194, 203
Godsell, Vanda, 71
Godwin, Ron, 170
Gogol, Nikolai, 65
Goinez, Andrés, 314
Golan, Menahem, 143-144
Goldblatt, Harold, 93
Goldblum, Jeff, 293
Goldman, Louis, 26
Goldstein, Fritzi, 217
Goldstein, William, 203, 224
Goldwyn, Sam, 23
Golonka, Arlene, 105
Gomez, Rita, 244
Gonzales-Gonzales, Pedro, 280

Goode, Frederic, 120
Goodhue, Clesson, 305
Goodnoff, Irv, 315
Goodwin, Harold, 118, 122
Gordon, Alan, 239
Gordon, Barry, 327
Gordon, Bert I., 12-13, 28,
    38, 41, 285-286, 299
Gordon, Claire, 71
Gordon, Colin, 79
Gordon, Don, 231-232
Gordon, Dorothy, 257
Gordon, Gale, 123
Gordon, Gerald, 256
Gordon, Kelly, 46
Gordon, Larry, 173
Gordon, Leo, 43, 92, 98, 147
Gordon, Marianne, 121
Gordon, Marshall, 320
Gordon, Nora, 49
Gordon, Ross, 309
Gordon, Roy, 41
Gordon, Susan, 28
Gordone, Charles, 241
Gore, Lesley, 113, 125
Goren, Rowby, 297
Gorman, Toni, 279
Gorog, Laszlo, 38
Gorshin, Frank J., 9, 15-16,
    18-19, 22, 39, 306
Gorsylowsky, Marilyn, 326
Gortner, Marjoe, 282-283,
    285-286
Gosov, Marran, 198
Goss, Helen, 69
Gossett, Lou, 288-289
Gostelow, Gordon, 202
Gotell, Walter, 58
Gothard, Michael, 197, 218
Gottlieb, Carl, 161
Gough, Lloyd, 320
Gough, Michael, 49-50, 70-71,
    189, 194
Gould, Berni, 75
Gould, Elliott, 317
Gould, Heywood, 307
Gould, Sandra, 297
Gowdy, Michael, 64

Grabowski, Norman, 124
Gracia, Sancho, 148
Graduates, The, 297
Grady, Don, 274-275
Graham, Arthur, 5
Graham, Bill, 109
Graham, Billy, 298
Graham, Carol, 241
Graham, Chris, 259
Graham, Gerrit, 282-283, 293
Graham, Kim, 278
Graham, Stephen, 193
Grahame, Gloria, 204-205
Grainger, Gail, 326
Granbery, Don, 301, 303
Granger, Libby, 202
Granger, Stewart, 103-104
Grant, Arthur, 127, 205
Grant, Cy, 282
Grant, Gloria, 33
Grant, Julian, 203
Grant, Moray, 200
Grant, Sarina (Serena) C.,
    259, 268
Grasshoff, Alexander, 61
Grau, Marta, 171
Graver, Gary, 331
Graves, Peter, 10
Graves, Richard, 266
Graves, Teresa, 275-276
Gray, Coleen, 73
Gray, Dorian, 103
Gray, Lillian, 247
Gray, Lisa, 149
Gray, Randy, 265
Grayber, Paul, 279
Grayf, Diana, 304
Great John "L", The, 303
Greci, José, 91-92
Green, Garard, 69
Green, Jan, 257
Green, Joseph, 77
Green, Nigel, 108-109
Green, Richard, 309
Green, Teddy, 97-98
Green, Terry, 277
Green, Wendy, 238
Greenberg, Robbie, 321

Greene, Angela, 36, 286
Greene, Howard, 49
Greene, Leon, 207
Greene, Matt, 278
Greene, Otis, 27
Greenlaw, Verina, 108
Greenleaf, James, 334
Greer, Dabbs, 9
Gregg, Christina, 100
Gregory, Fabian, 164
Gregory, Iain, 137
Gregory, Patricia, 23
Gregory, Paul, 271
Gremillion, Barry, 287
Gretton, David, 311
Grey, Samantha, 312
Greyn, Clinton, 207-208
Gribble, Donna Jo, 20
Grier, Pam, 231, 238-240,
    245-246, 254-255, 266-267,
    269-271, 279-280, 291
Grier, Rosey, 232-233
Gries, Jonathan, 332
Grifasi, Joe, 331
Griffin, George, 319
Griffin, Jack, 233
Griffin, Peter, 324
Griffin, Rick, 195
Griffin, Robert (Bob), 18, 35
Griffin, Sean P., 312
Griffith, Charles B., 9-10,
    16, 20-21, 25, 44, 145, 147
Griffith, D.W., 17
Griffith, Hugh, 189, 202-203,
    218, 224
Griffith, James, 55
Griffith, Kenneth, 58
Griffith, Melanie, 304
Griggs, Loyal, 206
Grimm, Maria, 306
Grimstrup, Borge Moller, 82
Grinalds, Archie, 276
Grizzi, Loris, 68
Grogan, Steve, 244
Gross, Ortrud, 172
Grove, R.L., 223
Guardino, Harry, 317
Guerra, Luigi Antonio, 216

Guerra, Tonio, 165
Guerra, Ugo, 68, 103, 126
Guerrini, Mino, 103, 105
Guerrini, Orso Maria, 289
Guest, Val, 272
Guevara, Che, 193
Guglielmi, Marco, 142
Guida, Wandisa, 82, 141
Guizon, Frenchia, 269
Gunn, Moses, 268-269
Gunther, Shirley, 335
Gupta, Provot, 321
Gurney, Robert J., Jr., 18,
    40
Gurney, Sharon, 229, 231
Guth, Raymond, 29, 94
Guthrie, Carl, 52
Guthrie, Owen, 326
Guthrie, Robert K., 307
Guthrie, Walt, 278
Gutierrez, Ray, 307
Gwillim, Jack, 58
Gwynn (Gwynne), Michael C.,
    112, 293

Haas, Hans, 228
Haase, Henjo, 298
Hackett, Buddy, 109-110
Hackett, John, 84
Hackworth, Mick, 309-310
Hadden, Robert, 30
Hagen, Hubs, 198
Hagen, Jean, 80
Hagen, Paul, 72
Hagen, Ross, 162, 173
Haggard, Merle, 160-161
Haggard, Piers, 201
Haggerty, Don, 109
Haggerty, Fred, 58
Haggerty, H.B., 254, 300
Hagood, Rick, 261
Hagman, Larry, 199
Hahn, Jess, 137
Hahn, Paul, 13, 55
Haig, Sid, 131, 238, 240, 244-
    245, 254
Haig, Tony, 211
Haigh, Peter, 156

Haindl, Harriet, 274
Haisman, Mervyn, 187
Hajnal, Stephen, 77
Hakman, Jeff, 195
Hale, Alan, Jr., 89, 197
Haley, Bill, and the Comets, 25
Hall, Angus, 199, 258
Hall, Bobby, 175
Hall, Brian, 273
Hall, Frank, 27
Hall, Harvey, 108, 200
Hall, Joanna, 286
Hall, Michael (Grant), 13, 281
Hall, Zooey, 168
Hallam, John, 271, 306
Haller, Daniel, 118, 147, 167, 191
Haller, Ernest, 62
Hallest, Knud, 82
Hallett, Neil, 214-215
Halliday, Clive L., 81
Halliday, Fred, 259
Halliday, Peter, 258
Halloran, John, 29
Halsey, Bret (Brett), 32, 53, 142
Ham, Thomas, 326
Hama, Mie, 123, 144
Hamdy, Emad, 159
Hamilton, Bernie, 245, 266
Hamilton, Billy, 195
Hamilton, Fenton, 235, 256
Hamilton, George, 327-328
Hamilton, Guy, 311
Hamilton, Ian, 272
Hamilton, Jill, 149
Hamilton, Jim, 32
Hamilton, Joe (Joseph), 34-35, 39
Hamilton, Kim, 145, 241
Hamilton, Murray, 322
Hamilton, Sue, 119, 124, 134, 136
Hammer, Alvin, 233
Hammer, Len, 105
Hammer, Sally, 217

Hampshire, Susan, 125-126
Hampton, Orville H., 34, 150, 269
Hampton, Richard, 311
Hancock, Hunter, 22
Hancock, John, 259, 323
Hand, Chip, 274-275
Handl, Irene, 64-65
Hanley, Jennie, 218
Hanna, Mark, 9, 12, 16, 20, 25, 34, 231
Hannahan, John, 30
Hannawalt, Charles, 89
Hannibal, Marc, 262
Hansen, Danna, 280
Hansen, Myrna, 235
Hansen, Paul, 187, 215
Hanson, Curtis Lee, 191
Hanson, Judy, 261
Hanson, Valda, 247
Harari, Clément, 141
Harden, Uva, 217
Hardenberg, Sarah, 98
Hardwick, Paul, 194
Hardwicke, Derek, 194
Harins, Bob, 175
Harmon, David P., 21
Harmon, John, 233
Harper, Donn, 290
Harper, Gerald, 125
Harper, Jessica, 324, 326
Harper, Kathleen, 229
Harper, Toni, 121
Harrell, James (N.), 186, 292, 307
Harrell, Peter, 261
Harrington, Curtis, 94, 140, 218
Harrington, Laurence, 194
Harrington, Pat, Jr., 259
Harris, Anita, 223
Harris, Baxter, 322
Harris, Bob, 119, 155, 241, 265
Harris, Holly, 62, 249
Harris, Jo Ann, 161, 249
Harris, Julius W., 235, 256, 269, 334

Harris, Lynn, 290
Harris, Michael, 13, 16
Harris, Nancy, 209
Harris, Owen, 53
Harris, Paul, 265
Harris, Robert H., 33-34
Harris, Stacy, 185
Harris, Ted, 221
Harris, Viola, 32
Harrison, Kathleen, 121
Harrison, Paul Carter, 321
Harrison, Richard, 72, 141-142
Harrison, Sandra, 13-14
Hart, Christina, 318
Hart, Elke, 179
Hart, John, 150
Hart, Kathryn, 99
Hart, Pamela, 97-98
Hart, Richard, 122
Hart, Susan, 110, 119, 128, 136
Harter, Roxanne, 324
Hartford, James, 119, 134
Hartford-Davis, Robert, 192
Hartley, Mariette, 215-216
Hartley, Ted, 317
Harvey, Bob, 87, 111, 117, 120, 124, 136
Harvey, James, 69
Harvey, Ken, 320
Harvey, Marilyn, 27-28
Harvey, Phil, 62-63
Hasley, Charles, 109
Hattie, Hilo, 38
Hatton, Raymond, 6, 8, 16, 18-19, 23
Haufrect, Alan, 167, 328
Hauser, Robert B., 300, 317
Havard, Dafydd, 106
Haven, Terri, 241
Havis, Maurice Leon, 267
Havoc, June, 320
Hawdon, Robin, 93
Hawkins, Jack, 213, 227
Hawkins, Michael, 322
Hawkins, Odie, 290
Hawkins, Virginia, 171

Hawkwood, John, 168
Haworth, Jill, 193
Hawtrey, Charles, 207, 222-223
Hawtrey, Kay, 313
Hay, Alexandra, 214-215
Hayashida, Shigeo, 126
Hayden, Linda, 258, 275
Hayden, Nora, 55-56, 72-73
Hayden, Schuyler, 150, 152
Hayden, Vernon, 201
Hayers, Sidney, 58, 77
Hayes, Allison, 9, 25-26, 32, 89
Hayes, Gillian, 202
Hayes, Isaac, 265
Hayes, Linda, 240
Hayes, Melvyn, 97-98, 125
Haynes, Dick, 73
Haynes, Linda, 307-308
Haynes, Michael, 186, 191, 208
Hayward, Jane, 257
Hayward, Susan, 63
Haze, Jonathan, 3-6, 9-11, 20-21, 26, 39, 44, 79-80, 98-99, 131
Hazle, Jeffrey, 290
Healey, Michael C., 209
Healey, Myron, 313
Hearn, Mary Ann, 278
Hearne, Jon, 32
Hearne, Reginald, 69
Heathcote, Thomas, 121, 194, 203
Heaton, Anthony, 326
Hecht, Paul, 277
Hedren, Tippi, 197
Heffley, Wayne, 53, 161
Heffron, Richard T., 286
Heiden, Janice, 274-275
Heidt, Lindy, 243
Heilbron, Vivien, 213
Heims, Jo, 110
Heinrich, Mimi, 70, 82
Heit, Michael, 328
Hellen, Marjorie, 39
Heller, Otto, 74

Hellman, Otto, 74
Hellman, Monte, 98
Hellman, Oliver (Ovidio
    Assonitis), 308
Hell's Angels, 145
Helpern, David, Jr., 331
Helton, Percy, 23
Hely, Gerald, 310
Hemingway, Carole, 329
Hemmings, David, 112, 137
Hemric, Guy, 109, 111, 120,
    249
Hemsley, Sherman, 327
Henaghan, Jim, 176
Henderson, Abbi, 233
Henderson, Albert, 277
Henderson, Bill, 268
Henderson, Chuck, 51
Henderson, Don, 248
Henderson, Douglas, 18, 134
Hendricks, Alan, 310
Hendry, Gloria, 235, 244-245,
    247, 256
Hennessy, Peter, 14, 22
Henning, Ted, 319
Henry, Alvin, 290
Henry, Gregg, 317-318
Henry, Marie O., 249
Henry, Mike, 143
Henry, Pat, 317
Henry, Ric, 175
Henry, Thomas B., 13-14
Henson, Nicky, 156, 275
Henwood, Peter, 218
Herbert, 128
Herbert, Martin (Alberto De
    Martino), 308
Herbert, Percy, 118
Herbst, Itzhak, 143
Herlin, Jacques, 91
Herman, Jack, 56
Herman, Randy, 307, 319, 332
Herman's Hermits, 120
Hermess, Ingo, 242
Hernandez, Rafael, 214
Hernandez, Robert, 41
Herrero, Ricardo, 238
Herrick, Fred, 40-41

Herrin, John, 73
Herrmann, Bernard, 204, 246
Hersent, Philippe, 60, 68,
    128, 289
Hersh, Seymour, 260
Hershey, Barbara, 221-222
Herzog, Werner, 130
Heschong, Greg(g), 241, 259
Hessler, Gordon, 172, 179,
    189, 196, 213
Heston, Charlton, 194-195,
    205
Hewitt, David L., 113
Hewlett, Arthur, 128
Hewlett, Brian, 108
Heyland, Michael, 128
Heyward, Lewis M., 110, 122-
    123, 127, 134, 136, 156,
    159
Heywood, Pat, 218
Hice, Eddie, 176
Hickman, Dwayne, 119-121, 124-
    125
Hicks, Chuck, 247
Hicks, John, 91, 115
Hicks, Pat, 69
Hickson, Joan, 64-65
Higdon, Don, 278
Higgins, Fran, 294
Higgins, Joe, 280, 306-307
Higgins, Ken, 125, 194
Hilbeck, Fernando, 111, 158,
    176, 182
Hildebrand, Helmut, 62
Hildebrand, Ross, 257
Hildreth, Rick, 309
Hilim, Kwan, 330
Hill, Arthur, 286-287
Hill, Benny, 207
Hill, Grady, 206
Hill, Jack, 8, 29, 98, 131,
    239, 254
Hill, Jay C., 330
Hill, Robert, 37
Hill, Rose, 257
Hill, Terence, 174-175
Hill, Toby, 61
Hills, Beverly, 88

Hilton, George, 156
Hilton, Le Sesne, 223–224
Hilton, Tony, 69
Hinckley, John
Hindle, Art, 292
Hinds, Fred, 335
Hingle, Pat, 184–185
Hinnant, Skip, 259
Hintermann, Carlo, 118
Hipp, Paul, 204, 212
Hirata, Akihiko, 100
Hirschfeld, Gerald, 285
Hirst, Jim, 301
Histman, George, 146
Hitchcock, Alfred, 130, 246
Hitler, Adolf, 260
Hitt, Robert, 331
Hix, Don, 46
Hoadley, Val, 284
Hoag, Mitzi, 147, 154
Hoban, Gordon, 145
Hobbs, Peter, 242, 259
Hobson, William, 234
Hodge, Donald, 326
Hodges, Bob, 317
Hodges, Hal, 226
Hodgins, George, 31
Hodson, James Lansdale, 138
Hoeft, Claus, 179
Hoffman, Basil, 327
Hoffman, Dustin, 176, 178
Hoffman, Harold, 115
Hogan, Jack, 29–30, 51
Hogan, Michael, 313
Hogg, Ian, 271
Holbrook, Hal, 166–167
Holcomb, Joann, 248
Holcombe, Harry, 254, 299, 317
Holden, Jan, 193
Holden, Joyce, 40
Holder, Ram John, 181
Holder, Roy, 273
Holdren, Judd, 13
Hole, William, Jr., 47, 75
Holen, Lee, 160
Holland, Anthony, 174
Holland, Ray, 286

Hollis, Glen, 319
Hollis, Jeff, 321
Holloway, Joan, 105
Holloway, Julian, 197, 207, 222–223
Holloway, Nancy, 139
Holloway, Stanley, 121
Holloway, Sterling, 23–25, 63
Holloway, Susan, 155
Holm, Celeste, 320
Holm, Claus, 61–62
Holm, Ian, 61–62, 291
Holman, Rex, 80
Holmes, Joi, 111
Holmes, Luree, 109–110, 119–120, 124, 136
Holsen, Ivy, 85
Holt, Penelope, 205
Holt, Robert (Bob) I., 201, 248, 259
Holt, Seth, 205
Homeier, Skip, 198
Honda, Inoshiro, 100, 106, 135, 173, 219
Hondells, The, 117, 125
Honeycomb, The, 120
Hood, Morag, 202
Hood, Nöel, 64
Hooker, Hank, 299
Hooker, Hugh M., 299
Hooker, Joe, 175
Hooks, Bebe Drake, 269
Hooper, Ewan, 194
Hoover, J. Edgar, 321
Hoover, Phil, 232
Hope, Teri, 111
Hopf, Heinz, 262, 264
Hopkins, Bo, 292–293, 308–309
Hoppenfield, Cynthia, 297
Hopper, Dennis, 94–95, 140, 147–148, 154
Horner, Penelope, 310
Hornok, Joe, 324
Hornsby, Charles, 223
Horsbrugh, Walter, 203
Horstall, Bernard, 291
Horten, Annie, 256

Horvath, Charles, 88
Hoshi, Yuriko, 106
Hoskins, Troy K., 186
Hossein, Robert, 133
House, Derina, 98
House, Eric, 313
House, Max, 167
Houston, Glyn, 58
Hoven, Louise, 315
Hovis, Larry, 237
Howard, Ben, 273
Howard, Judy, 47
Howard, Ronny, 67
Howard, Sandy, 105
Howard, Trevor, 213, 227, 271, 328
Howell, Hoke, 247
Howell, Jean, 3
Howell, Peter, 64
Howell, Philly, 190
Howell, Russ, 330
Howerd, Frankie, 223
Howes, Reed, 22
Howton, Marlene, 267
Hoy, Bob, 245
Hoyos, Rudolpho, 88
Hoyt, Clegg, 21
Hoyt, John, 28, 99, 113
Hrusinsky, Jan, 298
Hsiao, Susanne, 172
Hua, Yueh, 262
Huang, Essie, 149
Hubbell, Chris, 318
Hubbs, Gilbert, 255
Hubeňáková, Svatava, 116
Hubschmid, Paul, 61-62
Huddleston, David, 334-335
Hudis, Norman, 22, 64
Hudson, Bill (William), 12
Hudson, John, 37
Hudson, Larry, 53
Hudson, Lee, 197
Hudson, Vanda, 58
Huerta, Chris, 158
Huff, Tom, 254
Huffaker, Clair, 143
Hughes, Andrew, 173
Hughes, Barnard, 246

Hughes, Carolyn, 29, 51
Hughes, David, 29
Hughes, Derek, 164
Hughes, Glenn, 46
Hughes, John, 213
Hughes, Mary, 109, 111, 119-120, 124, 134, 136
Hughes, Richard, 322
Hughes, William, 13
Hugo, Michael (Michel), 274, 334
Hulette, Don, 296
Hull, Dave, 314
Hull, Henry, 72
Humbria, Concha, 182
Hume, Alan, 207, 223, 273, 282, 305
Hummel, Asgard, 160
Hummer, Jackie, 176
Humphrey, John, 5, 181
Humpoletz, Paul, 311
Hundar, Robert, 80
Hunnicutt, Gayle, 145, 308
Hunt, Dolly, 170
Hunt, Peter, 291
Hunter, Bernard, 22
Hunter, Bruce, 86
Hunter, Henry, 161
Hunter, James, 138
Hunter, Tab, 94, 96, 128
Huntington, Joan, 244
Huntington, Lawrence, 179
Huong-Thien, 80
Hurley, Susan, 207
Hurndell, Williams, 128
Hurst, Rick, 233
Hurt, John, 36, 46
Hurtado, Teresa, 211
Huston, John, 172, 308-309, 326
Huston, Karen, 215
Huston, Patti (Patricia), 29, 51
Hutcheson, David, 203
Hutchinson, Ken, 194
Hutchison, Robert, 225
Hutton, Robert, 61, 190
Huxtable, Judy, 197

Huyck, William, 173
Hyde-White, Wilfrid, 121, 130, 149
Hyer, Martha, 101, 111-112, 148-149, 155
Hylton, Jane, 58

Ichikawa, Kon, 126
Idelson, William, 89
Idom, Roy, 185
Ihnat, Steve, 31
Imbro, Gaetano, 216
Imrie, Celia, 257
Inch, Bonnie, 314
Incontrera, Annabella, 107
Inescort, Frieda, 12
Infanti (Infante), Angelo, 266, 295
Inglehart, James, 249-250
Inglés, Rufino, 175
Ingraham, Jack, 4-5
Ingram, Jean, 124
Ingrassia, Ciccio, 134, 155
Inkijinoff, Valery, 62, 83
Innes, Edward, 55
Insana, Gino, 297
Iocouvozzi, Kim, 294
Iranzo, Antonio, 314
Ireland, John, 3, 9
Ireland, O. Dale, 31
Irey, Carol, 99
Ironside, Michael, 313
Irving, Holly, 226
Irving, Penny, 256-257, 275
Irwin, Joe, 116
Isaac, Alberto, 168
Isenberg, Bob, 206
Ishihara, May, 166
Ishikawa, Komei, 63
Israel, Neil, 297
Israel, Victor, 211
Ito, Emi, 106-107
Ito, Hisaya, 173
Ito, Robert, 293
Ito, Yumi, 106-107
Ivers, Anne, 277
Ives, Burl, 152-153
Ivo, Tommy, 16, 47

Ivory, James, 280
Iwamoto, Hiroshi, 106

Jackson, Brad, 26
Jackson, David, 205
Jackson, Freda, 118-119
Jackson, Gordon, 213
Jackson, Larry E., 163
Jackson, Sherry, 162
Jacobbi, Ruggero, 82, 85
Jacobs, Jon, 265
Jacobs, Lawrence-Hilton, 267-268, 321-322
Jacobson, Mark David, 281
Jacobson, Sylvia, 279
Jacoby, Scott, 305, 319-320
Jacques, Hattie, 222-223
Jaeckel, Richard, 276
Jaeger, Kobi, 195
Jaffe, Sam, 191
Jagger, Dean, 197
Jaglom, Henry, 163
Jago, June, 64, 223
Jalbert, Adrienne, 331
James, Elizabeth, 145-146
James, Godfrey, 156, 179, 190, 273, 282
James, Graham, 200, 205
James, Lawrence, 150
James, Olga, 200
James, Oscar, 327
James, Ralph, 259, 280
James, Robin, 248
James, Sidney, 207, 222-223
James, Sonny, 139
James, Steve, 273
Jameson, Jerry, 209, 250
Jameson, Joyce, 84, 88-89, 201
Jamison, Mikki, 124
Jan and Dean, 113, 196
Janis, Ursula, 148
Janiss, Vivi, 11
Janson, Horst, 291
Jar, Morris, 156
Jarrico, Paul, 171, 298, 311
Jarvis, Al, 73
Jarvis, May, 239

Jaspe, José, 148, 182
Jastrow, Terry, 330
Javis, Sam, 243
Jay, Merryl, 243
Jeanine, Sonja, 295
Jeavons, Colin, 179
Jefferson, I.J., 163
Jefferson, Laurie Brooks, 250
Jeffrey, Michael, 235
Jeffrey, Omer, 235
Jeffrey, Peter, 203, 213, 224-225
Jeffries, Herb, 208
Jeffries, Lionel, 152-153, 218, 227
Jen, Wang Pi, 246
Jenks, Frank, 12-13, 23
Jennings, Claudia, 233-234, 264
Jennings, Junero, 247
Jennings, Sonya, 331
Jennings, Waylon, 139-140
Jens, Salome, 40-41
Jensen, Hardy, 82
Jenson, Roy, 241
Jergens, Adele, 6, 8-9, 22-23
Jergens, Curt, 203
Jergens, Diane, 71
Jessel, Patricia, 64
Jessie, DeWayne, 334
Jessop, Peter, 256
Jessup, Bob, 261, 292
Jeter, James, 317
Jewers, Ray, 327
Jill, Lisa, 185
Jim Jr., 96
Jocelyn, June, 13, 28, 38-39, 41
Johansen, Svend, 72, 82
Johns, Margo, 71
Johns, Stratford, 152
Johnson, Arte, 327-328
Johnson, Ben, 241, 301, 309-310
Johnson, Candy, 87, 101, 109-110
Johnson, Charles, 247, 290

Johnson, Coslough, 206
Johnson, Cynthia, 229
Johnson, Don, 278-279
Johnson, E. Lamont, 332
Johnson, J.S., 281
Johnson, Jason, 18
Johnson, Jim, 259
Johnson, Joseph, 309
Johnson, Karen Mae, 206
Johnson, Kay Cousins, 315
Johnson, Larry D., 261
Johnson, Margaret, 79
Johnson, Pat, 255
Johnson, Ralph K., 91, 290
Johnson, Richard, 194, 271-272
Johnson, Russell, 21
Johnson, Stephen, 318
Johnson, Toni, 37
Johnson, Virginia, 179
Johnston, Alena, 266
Johnston, Amy, 315-316
Johnston, Oliver, 127
Johnston, Rosemary, 47
Johnton, Neil, 190
Joint, Alf, 156
Jolley, Stanford I., 92
Jones, Al, 245
Jones, Bonnie, 105
Jones, Ceri, 229
Jones, Charlene, 233
Jones, Christine, 267
Jones, Christopher, 165-167
Jones, Deacon, 319
Jones, Dick, 30, 120
Jones, Evan, 138, 181
Jones, Freddie, 213, 275
Jones, G. Stanley, 89
Jones, Gloria, 259
Jones, Harold, 269
Jones, James, 253
Jones, Jennifer, 169
Jones, Jim, 244
Jones, Joyce, 279
Jones, Marshall, 189, 197, 214
Jones, Melvin, 279
Jones, Michael, 176

Jones, Norman, 203
Jones, Morgan, 3
Jones, Tommy Lee, 307-308
Jones-Moreland, Betsy, 26
Jordan, J. Rob, 206
Jordan, Joanne Moore, 191
Jordan, Marsha, 187
Jordan, Matty, 317
Jordan, William, 223-224, 320
Jordon, Curtis, 319
Jordon, Mike, 60
Jordon, Nick, 262
Jose, Cathy, 227
Joseph, Allen, 215
Joseph, Robert L., 67
Joseph, Jackie, 38
Josephs, Michael, 311
Jourdain, Jack, 253
Jourdan, Louis, 182-183
Joy, Christopher, 274, 330
Jubért, Alice, 269, 288-289
Judd, Carolyn, 257
Judge, Arline, 89
Juhl, Bente, 70
Juhlin, Benny, 82
Jules, Maurice, 245, 261
Julian, Arthur, 120
Julien, Max, 163-164
Juráček, Pavel, 116
Juran, Nathan, 67
Jussef, Raggah, 72
Justice, Barry, 138
Justice, Edgar, 255
Jvandova, Jana, 298

Kaas, Preben, 72
Kader, Abdul, 205
Kadler, Karen, 10
Kaehler, Karen, 195
Kafafian, Eddie, 16, 19, 23
Kahler, Hans, 311
Kahler, Wolf, 311
Kahn, Lilly, 14
Kaiser, Burt, 8
Kaliban, Bob, 331
Kalinski, Edward, 311
Kalis, Jan, 116
Kallis, Stanley, 51-52

Kaminsky, Mike, 319
Kamis, Ahmed, 159
Kamoi, Kip, 43
Kanaly, Steve, 241, 249
Kandel, Aben, 14, 17, 33, 48-
    49, 70
Kane, Sid, 79
Kane, Wyman, 320
Kankura, Taiichi, 173, 219
Kannon, Jackie, 105
Kannon, Mary, 86
Kanter, Marianne, 147
Kanter, Rick, 281
Kaplan, Jonathan, 265
Karcher, Bruce, 193
Karim, Faryal, 195
Karin, 143
Karin, Rita, 317
Karlen, John, 292
Karlin, Miriam, 121
Karloff, Boris, 88-89, 96, 98-
    99, 101, 103, 118-119, 136,
    187, 189
Karlowa, Elma, 283
Karn, Bill, 67
Karnes, Thomas, 131
Karp, David, 182
Kartalian, Buck, 147, 206
Kasabian, Jack, 217
Kasem, Casey, 148, 171, 212
Kate, Stephen V., 254
Katz, Stephen (M.), 304, 319
Katzoff, Marvin, 332
Kauffmann, Christine, 214
Kaufman, Philip, 174
Kaufman, Robert, 119, 124,
    134, 327
Kaufmann, Joseph, 241
Kaufmann, Maurice, 150, 203
Kavanagh, Kevin, 149
Kawada, Clifford, 38
Kawaji, Kenchiro, 135
Kawase, Hiroyuki, 226
Kay, Bernard, 156
Kay, Charles, 271
Kaya, Olga, 192
Kaye, Ian, 97
Kaye, Mary Ellen, 22-23, 27

Kaye, Stubby, 280
Kazann, Zitto, 329
Kazar, Alvin, 261
Keach, Stacy, 295
Kean, E. Arthur, 273
Kean, Jane, 297
Keane, Charles, 9
Kearney, Carolyn, 9
Kearns, Bill, 253
Keast, Paul, 17
Keating, Michael, 194
Keaton, Buster, 110-111, 117, 120-121, 124, 154-155
Keats, Viola, 121
Keegan, Robert, 194
Keen, Geoffrey, 49, 93, 114, 310
Keene, William, 242
Keir, Andrew, 114, 205
Keita, Keita L., 267
Keith, Brian, 328-329
Keith, Sheila, 256
Kellem, Jane, 232
Kellerman, Sally, 20-21
Kelley, Phil, 279
(Kelljchian) Kelljan, Robert, 163, 187, 215, 245, 249
Kelly, David Blake, 69
Kelly, Don, 39
Kelly, Jim, 255
Kelly, John, 143
Kelly, Kevin, 55
Kelly, Martine, 253
Kelly, Patsy, 136
Kelly, Tim, 189, 261
Kemmer, Ed, 38
Kemmerling, Warren, 110
Kemp, Anthony, 227
Kemp, Valli, 224
Kemper, Victor J., 277
Kempf, Ruth, 288
Kempson, Rachel, 181
Kendall, Suzy, 150
Kendall, William, 69
Kendrick, Henry, 147, 176
Kenion, Geoffrey, 210
Kennaway, James, 93
Kenneally, Phil, 243

Kennedy, Arthur, 332
Kennedy, Douglas, 29, 55, 67-68
Kennedy, Frank, 176
Kennedy, George, 318
Kennedy, Mary Jo, 167
Kennedy, Mike, 216
Kennedy, Richard, 280
Kenney, June, 25-26, 28, 38
Kensitt, Patsy, 271
Kent, Cicil, 319
Kent, David, 319
Kent, Gary, 163-164
Kent, Jean, 291
Keough, Barbara, 203
Kermer, Norberto, 53
Kerns, Ira, 139
Kerr, Bruce, 77
Kerr, Elizabeth, 317
Kerr, John, 74
Kerr, Millicent, 64
Kerwin, Maureen, 253
Kessler, Alice, 90
Kessler, Bruce, 155, 160
Kessler, Ellen, 90
Kessler, Kathy, 109
Ketchum, David, 327
Kevin, Sandy, 274
Key, Janet, 200, 284
Key, Lotis M., 238
Khambatta, Persis, 195
Kiamos, Eleni, 105
Kidd, David, 280
Kidd, John, 156
Kidder, Margot, 246-247, 277-278, 322-323
Kiebach, Max, 172
Kiel, Richard, 73, 311
Kieling, Wolfgang, 148
Kiesow, Doris, 198
Kiger, Susan, 330
Kildany, Marion, 111
Kilgas, Nancy, 23, 32
Kilgore, Jim, 113
Kilman, Sam, 278
Kilpatrick, Shirley, 27
Kimball, Bruce, 232
Kimberley, Maggie, 156

Kimbrough, Clint, 184-185
Kimura, Takeshi, 123
Kimura, Toshie, 226
Kincaid, Aron, 119, 124-125, 136
King, Alan, 121-122
King, Duane, 109
King, Jeff, 331
King, Kip, 153, 274
King, Leslie E., 315
King, Martin Luther, 193, 321
King, Perry, 281
King, Tony, 256, 266
King, Yukon, 330
Kingfish, 239
Kingi, Henry, 265
Kingsley, James, 245, 249, 267
Kingsley, Martin, 9, 11
Kingsmen, The 120
Kinsey, Alfred, 179
Kinski, Klaus, 130, 149-150, 153, 200-201
Kirby, Michael, 301
Kirchenbauer, Bill, 334
Kirino, Nadao, 173
Kirk, Alexis, 260
Kirk, Howard, 282
Kirk, Robert Wellington, 196
Kirk, Tommy, 110-111, 136
Kirksey, Van, 245
Kirkwood, Gene, 150
Kiser, Terry, 330
Kissinger, Charles, 248, 279
Kissinger, Henry, 260, 287
Kita, Akemi, 100
Kitt, Eartha, 269
Klages, William M., 306
Klauber, Gertan, 190, 202, 207
Kleiser, Randall, 295
Klingler, Werner, 133
Klopp, Julia, 294
Knecht, Peter, 330
Kneubuhl, John, 36
Knight, Ron, 259
Knight, Sandra, 98-99, 131
Knox, Alexander, 310-311

Knox, Herman, 155
Knox, Ken, 56
Kobayashi, Tetsuko, 100
Kobayashi, Yukiko, 173, 219
Koch, Marianne, 143-144
Kodl, James, 8
Koenekamp, Fred (J.), 274, 322
Koenig, Laird, 305
Koenig, Raymond, 220, 245
Kohnbach, Frank, 320
Koizumi, Hajime, 100, 106, 135
Koizumi, Hiroshi, 100, 106
Kokojan, Henry, 115
Kolb, Clarence, 23
Kolldehoff, Rene, 291-292
Kolmar, Kerry, 111
Komai, Tetsu, 39
Konblett, Sheldon, 324
Konrad, Dorothy, 286
Konvitz, Jeffrey, 334
Konzal, Jack, 170
Koock, Guich, 330
Kopell, Bernie, 237
Korbelar, Otomar, 298
Korda, Nino, 198
Koscina, Sylva, 203, 242
Kosslyn, Jack, 13, 28, 38, 41, 299
Kossoff, David, 69, 97
Kosugi, Yoshio, 106
Kotcheff, Ted, 181
Kotler, Oded, 141
Kotto, Yaphet, 265, 269-271, 290
Kotze, John, 149
Koulak, Pierre, 253
Kourtis, Nicholas, 291
Kova, Irene, 116
Kovack, Nancy, 143
Kovacs, Laszlo, 163-164
Kove, Martin, 281, 330
Kowalski, Bernard L., 36, 43
Kramarsky, David, 4
Kramer, Billy J., and the Dakotas, 113, 120
Kramer, Jack N., 32

Kramer, John, 265
Krantz, Steve, 315
Kreitsek, Howard B., 276, 300
Krenwinkle, Patricia, 244
Kresel, Lee, 63, 68, 82
Krims, Milton, 103
Krischer, Gene, 206
Krish, John, 115
Kristen, Lidia, 327
Kristen, Marta, 117
Kristiansen, Henning, 207
Kroeger, Berry, 212-213
Krohn, Charles, 261, 287
Krone, Fred, 176
Krüger, Christiane Laura, 172
Kruger, Hardy, 203
Krupnick, Jack, 322
Kruschen, Jack, 20-21, 55-56
Kubo, Akira, 173, 219
Kuhlman, Kathryn, 298
Kuhn, Allan Dale, 273-274
Kulchitskiy, Nikolay, 86
Kulik, Jeni, 250-251
Kumar, Jai, 195
Kunstmann, Doris, 185
Kurobe, Susumu, 144, 173
Kurt, Lisbet, 72
Kurtzo, Joe, Jr., 282
Kusabue, Mitsuko, 123
Kusakawa, Naoya, 173
Kusatsu, Clyde, 329
Kuveiller, Luigi, 216
Kwong, Peter, 332
Kwouk, Burt, 130

Laborie, Jacques, 133
Laboriel, Francisca Lopes de, 231
Laboriel, Juan Jose, 231
Lacambre, Daniel, 167, 257, 280
Lacey, Keith, 64
Lacher, Taylor, 300
Lachman, Stanley, 13
Lack, Otto, 116
Lack, Simon, 121
Lackteen, Frank, 16-17

Lacy, Kathryn, 292
Ladd, David, 229, 231
Ladd, Diane, 145
Ladue, Lyzanne, 124
Lafan, Ann, 206
Laffan, Patrick, 201-202
Lafromboise, Bill, 301
Lain, Jewell, 38-39
Lakso, Ed, 51-52
Lalani, Soltan, 205
Lamb, Charles, 22
Lamb, John, 128
Lambert, Jack, 35, 121
Lambert, Nigel, 197
Lamensdorf, Leonard, 268
Lamont, Adele, 77
Lamonte, Franco, 68
Lamounier, Guilherme, 234
Lamour, Dorothy, 110-111
Lampkin, Charles, 268
Lampson, David, 215
Lan, Tzu, 246
Lancaster, Burt, 303-304
Lancaster, Stuart, 145
Lanchester, Elsa, 110-111
Lancia, Cesare, 68
Landau, Martin, 308, 328
Landers, David, 167, 297
Landers, Lew, 33
Landfield, David, 87, 94
Landi, Aldo Bufi, 97
Landis, Monty, 122, 152
Landon, Avice, 181
Landon, Michael, 17-18
Landsberg, David, 328
Lane, Andrea, 80
Lane, Jocelyn, 176-177, 186
Lane, Kent, 234
Lane, Larry H., 176
Lane, Shannon, 247
Laneuville, Eric, 327, 332
Lang, Fritz, 61-62
Lang, Harold, 181
Lang, Judy, 154, 187-188
Lang, Robert, 291
Lang, Tara, 279
Langan, Glenn, 6, 12-13
Langberg, Ebbe, 72

Langdon, Antony, 311
Langdon, Sue Ann, 324, 326
Lange, Ted, 269, 306
Langen, Inge, 198
Langevin, Christopher, 313
Langrisch, Caroline, 310
Langtry, Kenneth (Aben
  Kandel), 17, 33, 48
Lanphier, James, 67-68
Lansing, John, 331
Lansing, Robert, 237, 299
Lanza, Anthony M., 147, 212
Lanza, Laura, 212
Lapenieks, Vilis, 94, 140
La Piere, Georganne, 315
Larch, John, 322
Larkins, Mary, 267
Larson, Darrell, 286
Larson, Merv, 195
Lasater, Carolyn, 105
Lascelles, Andrea, 148
Lasell, John, 223
La Shelle, Joseph, 17
Laskey, Gil, 204
Lasky, Jesse, Jr., 283
Lasoda, Candida, 211
Lassally, Walter, 227, 281,
  331
Lassander, Dagmar, 295
Lasser, Louise, 144
Lassick, Sid, 29
Laszlo, Ernest, 28
Latham, Jack, 166
Latham, Philip, 311
Latka, George, 317
Lauenstein, Tilly, 172
Lauffen, Richard, 62
Laughlin, Tom, 145-146
Laughton, Charles, 303
Launer, John, 18
Laure, Carole, 308
Lauren, Rod, 89
Laurence, Eddie, 281
Laurence, Paul, 329
Laurence, Peter, 184
Lauria, Mary Dean, 241
Laurie, Al, 46
Laurie, John, 203

Lautner, Georges, 137
Lavi, Daliah, 152
Lawler, Bill, 319
Lawler, Patti, 18
Lawlor, Ray, 239
Lawrena, Jay, 241
Lawrence, Jay, 259
Lawrence, Joel, 52
Lawrence, John, 41, 147, 212
Lawrence, Maggie, 53
Lawrence, Marjie, 207
Lawrence, Sid, 164
Laws, Sam, 254, 265, 277
Lawson, Carol, 240
Lawson, Christine, 97
Lawson, Linda, 94
Lawson, Richard, 245-246, 261
Lay, Me Me, 316
Laye, Dilys, 222-223
Layne, Bill, 8
Layne, G. Cornell, 248
Leachman, Cloris, 241
Lear, Jerry, 53
Leavitt, Sam, 9, 119
LeBell, Gene, 247
Lebor, Stanley, 271, 284
Leclerc, Jean, 308
Ledford, Jonathan, 55, 91,
  115
Lee, Bruce, 240, 246, 327
Lee, China, 119, 144
Lee, Christopher, 69-70, 150,
  179-180, 187, 189, 194, 197,
  228-229, 272, 326-327
Lee, Chosette, 251
Lee, Dana, 286
Lee, James Oscar, 334
Lee, Jennifer, 249, 281, 320
Lee, Joanna, 29
Lee, John, 14
Lee, Louise, 149
Lee, Margaret, 130, 150, 190,
  200-201, 228
Lee, Marty, 320
Lee, Penelope, 127
Lee, Randee, 171
Lee, Sharon, 20
Lee, Teri, 140

Lee, Tony, 255
Lee, Vicki, 99
Lee, Waveney, 71
Lee, Woody, 16
Leeds, Peter, 259
Lees, Freddie, 193
Le Faber, Eleanor, 60
Le Fanu, J. Sheridan, 200
LeFebvre, Jim, 150
Lefferts, George, 317
Lehmann, Beatrix, 122
Lehmann, Ted, 164
Leicester, William, 107
Leiber, Fritz, 77
Leigh, Barbara, 330
Leigh-Hunt, Ronald, 69
Leipnitz, Harald, 198-199
Leith, Virginia, 77-78
Leland, David, 194
Lely, Gilbert, 172
Lemaire, Philippe, 180
Lembeck, Harvey, 87, 101,
    110-111, 117, 119-121, 124,
    134-136
Lembeck, Michael, 334-335
Le Mesurier, John, 121, 128,
    130
Lemoine, Michel, 82
Lemont, John, 70
Lennon, Jimmy, 317
Lennon, Toby, 156
Leno, Charles, 182
Lenti, Lara, 148
Lenz, Cliff, 304
Lenz, Kay, 287-288, 318
Lenzi, Giovanna, 174
Lenzi, Umberto, 97
Leon, Valerie, 205-206
Leonard, Terry, 241
Leone, Sergio, 52
Leonetti, Matthew, 250
Leoni, Roberto, 295
LePore, Richard, 62, 330
Lerick, Bob, 253
Lerner, Fred, 249, 254
Leroy, Philippe, 166
Leslie, David Stuart, 181
Leslie, Dudley, 74

Leslie, Gloria, 113
Leslie, Mari Ann, 119
Lesser, Len, 120, 134, 204-
    205, 264
Lessy, Ben, 110-111
Lester, Jack, 164, 212
Lester, Ketty, 221
Lester, Mark, 218-219,
    264, 282
Lever, Reg, 227
Levin, Inge, 208
Levine, Harvey, 274
Levinson, Janice, 120, 124
Levison, Ken, 258
Levka, Uta, 172, 179, 197
Levstik, Vida, 85
Levy, Eugene, 239
Levy, Phil, 332
Levy, Weaver, 34
Lewis, Bobo, 281
Lewis, David, 318
Lewis, Forrest, 150
Lewis, Geoffrey, 241, 257
Lewis, Jack, 55
Lewis, Jean, 8
Lewis, Jerry, 18, 44, 124
Lewis, Joe, 326-327
Lewis, Judy, 96
Lewis, Louise, 13-14, 18
Lewis, Morton (Mort), 241,
    243
Lewis, Robert Q., 124, 324
Lewiston, Denis C., 283
Lewiston, Peter, 22
Li, Alicia, 96
Libertore, Ugo, 185
Licudi, Gabriella, 115-116
Lido, Pini, 106
Liddy, G. Gordon, 247
Lieberman, Jeff, 294
Lieberman, Leo, 25
Lieberman, Manny, 312
Lien, Chin, 246
Light, Joe, 170
Lightfoot, Leonard C., 309
Lightning, Suzie, 284
Ligon, Tom, 304
Lile, Ford, 210

Liljedahl, Marie, 190-191
Lilli, Virgilio, 126
Lime, Yvonne, 18, 31-32
Lincoln, Fred, 312
Lincoln, Henry, 187
Lincoln, Richard, 312
Lindberg, Christina, 262-264
Lindblatt, W.A., 294
Lindeland, Liv, 254
Linden, Brayden, 206
Linden, Hildegard, 179
Linden, Jennie, 275
Linder, Cec, 192, 313
Lindop, Audrey Ersking, 74
Lindorf, Sonja, 179
Lindsay, Carol, 20, 37
Lindt, Rosemarie, 295
Line, Helge, 266
Ling, Yau Tsui, 329
Linville, Larry, 206
Lippman, Irving, 143, 184
Lipton, Robert, 161, 297
Litel, John, 22
Lithgow, Tom, 43
Little Egypt, 330
Little Richard, 25
Littlejohn, Gary, 164, 170
Littleton, Thomas, 86
Littlewood, Tom, 22
Litton, Foster, 326
Liu, Anne, 240
Livingston, Stanley, 29
Lizzani, Carlo, 133
Llovet, Enrique, 182
Lloyd, E. James (Tom
  Laughlin), 145
Lloyd, Jeremy, 275
Loben, Lawrence, 86
Locher, Felix, 88
Locke, Harry, 121
Lockett, Clarence, 265
Lockhart, Anne, 304
Lockhart, Marshall, 164
Lockwood, Julia, 64
Lockwood, Preston, 194
Loder, Kathryn, 254-255
Lodge, Andrew, 273
Lodge, David, 197

Lodge, Jean, 108
Loffredi, Franco, 60
Loftin, Carey, 119
Logan, Lyn, 239
Logan, Vincent, 97
Lohmann (Loman), Paul, 175,
  239, 328
Lok, Christine, 149
Lolich, Mickey, 314
Lollobrigida, Gina, 182-183
Lom, Herbert, 130, 190-191,
  214
Lomax, Louis, 166
Lombard, Carole, Singers, 134
Lomma, John, 211
London, Barbara, 163, 170
Long, Nate, 291
Longdon, Terence, 121
Longhairs, The, 150
Longhurst, Henry, 150
Longley, Sally, 214
Longo, Germano, 68
Longo, Malisa, 168, 262, 266
Lönnrot, Elias, 104
Lonvang, Ib, 72
Lopapero, Rosanna, 178
Loper, Robert, 304
Lopez, 284
Lopez, Fernando, 332, 334
Lor, Denise, 105
Lord, Rosemary, 210
Loren, Donna, 101, 109-110,
  117, 124
Lorenzon, Livio, 48, 68, 91
Loring, Richard, 272
Lorraine, Nita, 189
Lorre, Peter, 84, 88-89, 96-
  97, 109
Lorrie, Myrna, 313
Lo Russo, Eddie (Ed), 186,
  231, 247
Losey, Joseph, 138
Lotti, Angelo, 200
Loughney, John, 56
Louis and the Rockets, 233
Louise, Tina, 318
Love, Dorothy, 314
Love, Lucretia, 235

Love, Mary, 217
Lovecraft, H.P., 92, 118, 187, 191
Lovegrove, Arthur, 69
Lovell, Rosemary, 314
Lovett, Dorothy, 62
Lovin' Spoonful, The, 131, 144
Lowell, Jan, 32, 46
Lowell, Mark, 28, 32, 46
Lower, William, 319
Loy, Barbara, 155
Loy, Mino, 152
Lozer, Curtis, 32
Lucas, George, 282
Lucas, Karl, 237
Lucas, Rodney, 116
Luccoli, Fausto, 142
Lucero, Enrique, 143
Lucht, Darlene, 92, 109
Lucidi, Maurizio, 295
Lucisano, Fulvio, 154
Luckham, Cyril, 112
Lucking, William, 176
Lüddecke, Werner Jörg, 61
Ludden, Allen, 286
Ludlow, Susan, 304
Lugosi, Bela, 245
Luis, Madina, 205
Lukather, Dorys, 11
Lukschy, Wolfgang, 133
Lulli, Folco, 52, 85, 90
Lulli, Piero, 91
Lumet, Baruch, 281
Lumiere, Chris, 313
Lumley, Joanna, 218
Luna, Barbara, 39
Lund, Annalena, 91
Lund, Art, 235, 237, 266, 320
Lund, Deanna, 119
Lund, Jana, 32
Lund, John, 4-5
Lunden, Kenneth, 309
Lundi, Monika, 198
Lundy, Neil, 239
Lung, Chien, 246
Lunsford, Beverly, 89
Lupino, Ida, 286

Lupo, Alberto, 114
Lupo, Michele, 91
Lupus, Peter, Jr., 109-110
Lvova, Ludmilla, 168
Lycan, Georges, 253
Lyden, Pierce, 11
Lyell, David, 156
Lyn, Dawn, 276, 300
Lynch, Alfred, 121-122
Lynch, Ken, 29, 51
Lynch, Sean, 282
Lynde, Paul, 117
Lynn, Ann, 137
Lynn, George, 17
Lynn, Jack, 156
Lynn, Laura, 87
Lynn, Loretta, 139
Lynn, Stella, 34
Lynn, Ted, 223-224
Lyon, Richard, 48
Lyons, Christian, 201
Lyons, John, 210
Lyons, Lori, 73
Lyons, Martin, 201
Lyons, Steve, 309
Lytken, Ole, 72
Lyttelton's Humphrey, Band, 22

Maar, Sybille, 198-199
Mabuchi, Kaoru, 135, 173, 226
MacAdams, Anne, 115, 186
McAdams, James B., 309
McAllister, Patrick, 235
McAndrew, Marianne, 250-251
MaCaul, Brad, 195
Macauley, Charles, 209, 220-221
McBain, Diane, 153-154, 161-162
McBane, Maria, 134
McCall, Joan, 249
McCall, Mitzi, 35
McCallum, David, 131
McCane, Michael, 297
McCann, Chuck, 324
McCann, Henry, 33, 47, 53
McCarthy, Joe, 321

McCaskill, Patricia, 290
Macchi, Valentino, 168
Macchia, Gianni (John), 87,
    117, 120, 124, 136, 242
McClanahan, Rue, 217
McClellan, Max, 312
McClenny, Catherine, 287
McClure, Doug, 273, 282, 305-
    306
McClure, Jack, 46
McClurg, Edie, 298
McClurg, "Kansas City" Bob,
    297
McConnell, Juanita, 267
McCorkindale, Don, 272
MacCormack, Joanne, 105
McCormick, Colin, 229
McCormick, Patty, 161-162,
    167-168
McCowan, George, 225-226
McCoy, Arch, 312
McCrea, Jody, 87, 94, 96,
    101, 109-111, 117, 120,
    147-148
McCroskey, Doug, 319
McCulloch, Andrew, 190, 213,
    273
McCusker, Mary, 298
McDaniel, Earl, 33, 73
McDermott, Mickey, 94
McDevitt, Chas., Skiffle
    Group, 22
MacDonald, Aimi, 275
McDonald, Country Joe, and
    the Fish, 193
MacDonald, David, 5
MacDonald, Holma, 275
MacDonald, John, 98
MacDonald, Kenneth, 12
MacDouglas, John, 156
McDowall, Roddy, 169, 217-
    218
MacDowell, Bill, 164
Mace, Terry, 280
McEndree, Maurice, 147
McEnery, John, 273
McEwan, Geraldine, 64-65
McGeagh, Stanley, 273

McGee, Bill, 91
McGee, Florence, 299
McGee, Vonetta, 220-221
McGhee, Johnny Ray, 265
McGill, Gordon, 243
McGill, Ronald, 194
McGillivray, David, 256-257
McGinn, Russ, 247
McGowan, Jack, 251
McGreevey, John, 9
MacGuire, Charles, 256
McGuirk, William, 207
McHale, Tony, 306
McHeady, Bob (Robert), 239,
    251
MacInnes, Angus, 311
McInnes, Pamela, 214
McIntyre, Paddy, 98
Macio, 234
McIver, Susan, 254
Mack, Brice, 315
McKenna, Virginia, 310-311
McKern, Leo, 138
McKinley, J. Edward, 55
McKinney, Bill, 164, 184
McKinney, John, 329
Macklin, David, 168
McKnight, David, 288
McLaren, Bruce, 100
Maclean, Alistair, 311
MacLean, Duncan, 304
McLean, Glen, 160
MacLean, Peter, 294
McLiam, John, 286
McLinn, Lloyd, 274
McMahon, Ed, 247-248
McMahon, Phyllis, 284
McManus, Joe, 171
McMullen, Robert, 176
McNair, Barbara, 200-201
McNamara, Ed, 301
McNamara, John, 38, 41
McNeil, Paul, 189
MacNeil, Peter, 308
McNeil, Ron, 46
McPeak, Sandy, 300
McPherson, Ron, 292
McRae, Frank, 241, 276

MacRae, Meredith, 87, 101
Macready, Erica, 187
Macready, George, 187, 215
Macready, Michael, 187
McShane, Ian, 217-218
Maculani, Giulio, 128
McVeagh, Eve, 165
McVey, Tyler, 36, 43
Mader, Sgt. Robert, 206
Madden, Lee, 175, 184
Maddern, Victor, 121, 150
Madigan, Sharon, 265
Madoc, Philip, 210
Madsen, Peter, 161
Magee, Patrick, 90, 99, 108, 118
Maguire, Oliver, 271
Maguire, Rick, 239
Mahan, Larry, 280
Mahony, Jock, 88, 147-148
Maiuri, Dino, 266
Majors, Lee, 318-319
Makela, Helena, 308
Malandrinos, Andreas, 179
Malatesta, Guido, 97
Malcolm, Christopher, 311
Malden, Karl, 328
Malicz, Mark, 158
Mallard, Grahame, 273
Malle, Louis, 180
Mallet, Nate, 290
Malloy, John, 300
Malone, Dorothy, 3-5, 87
Maloney, Peter, 322
Mamrus, Al, 303
Mancori, Alvaro, 107
Mancori, Guglielmo, 91
Mandre, Joyce, 190
Manduke, Joe, 268
Mangine, Joseph, 294
Mangini, Gino, 48
Mangione, Giuseppe, 52, 103
Mankofsky, Isidore, 245
Mankowitz, Wolf, 69
Mann, Daniel, 317
Mann, Danny Michael, 280
Mann, Delbert, 213
Mann, Edward, 260

Mann, Hank, 46
Mann, Manfred, 208
Mann, Stanley, 328-329
Mann, Vincent, 308
Manni, Ettore, 128, 130, 295
Manning, Jacqueline, 277
Mannship, Hans, 320
Manoda, Yoichi, 226
Mansfield, Jayne, 8
Manson, Charlie (Charles), 224, 244, 283
Manson, Jean, 254
Manza, Ralph, 281, 328
Mao, Angela, 240
Marais, Jean, 139
Maran, David, 64
Marandi, Evi, 122
Marano, Ezio, 216
Marc, Peter, 334
Marceau, Michèle, 137
Marceau, Violette, 133
Marcellini, Romolo, 126
March, Ellen, 331
March, Elspeth, 181, 227
March, James Moncure, 281
March, Myron, 116
Marchal, George (Georges), 52, 133
Marchand, Jean, 308
Marciano, Consolato, 309
Marcus, Ed, 253
Marcus, Peter, 193
Marcuse, Theodore, 141
Marcuzzo, Lucio, 142
Maren, Jerry, 243
Mares, John, 116
Maretti, Sandro, 60
Margolin, Stuart, 286-287
Margotta, Michael, 161-162, 166
Margulies, Christian, 179
Mari, Keiko, 226
Mariani, Carl, 319
Marie, Jean, 184
Marin, Luciano, 48
Marin, Russ, 247, 248
Marini, Tullio, 166
Marisenka, 111

Marisol, 148
Mark, Michael, 28
Marker, Russell, 56
Markfield, Wallace, 274
Markham, Barbara, 256-257
Markham, David, 181, 205
Markland, Ted, 155
Markov, Margaret, 238
Marks, Alfred, 197
Marks, Arthur, 266, 269, 288, 290
Marks, Walter, 280
Marks, Wes, 160
Marla, Norma, 69
Marlene, 152
Marley, John, 320
Marlier, Carla, 180
Marlis, Herb, 206
Marlowe, Gene, 3
Marlowe, Scott, 30-31
Marly, Florence, 140
Marquand, Serge, 180
Marquard, Brick, 249, 254
Marquard, Carl F., 228
Marquette, Jack (Jacques), 44, 67, 278
Marr, Eddie, 18
Marr, Sally, 243
Marrion, Stephanie, 189
Marriott, Ronald, 280
Marrocco, Gina, 239
Mars, Bruce, 161
Marsden, Betty, 222
Marsh, Anthony, 100
Marsh, Jean, 115-116
Marsh, Mae, 8
Marsh, Tiger Joe, 328
Marshall, Arthur, 32
Marshall, Darrah, 39
Marshall, Don, 232-233
Marshall, Ed, 238
Marshall, Garry, 161, 163
Marshall, Gloria, 52
Marshall, Les, 330
Marshall, Maurice, 267
Marshall, Michael, 73
Marshall, Penny, 164
Marshall, Peter L., 161, 237

Marshall, Shary, 80
Marshall, Tony, 18
Marshall, William, 73, 220-221, 245-246, 248
Marta, Jack, 29, 38, 41
Martel, Arlene, 155
Martel, K.C., 322
Martell, Arlene, 297
Martell, Peter, 146-147, 228
Martell, Ray, 198
Martellanz, Pietro, 295
Marter, Ian, 203
Martha and the Vandellas, 33
Martin, Al, 18
Martin, Andrea, 239
Martin, Barry, 257
Martin, Claudia, 136
Martin, D'Urville, 235, 256, 279
Martin, Edward R., 51
Martín, José Manuel, 174
Martin, Joseph, 46, 79
Martin, Marcella, 116
Martin, Maria, 214
Martin, Maribel, 211
Martin, Nan, 165
Martin, Pepper, 155, 274
Martin, Randy, 332
Martin, Skip, 108, 150
Martin, Strother, 287
Martin, Terry, 190
Martinelli, Elsa, 176, 178
Martinez, Adolph, 168
Martinez, Hector, 217
Martínez, Felix Mirón, 159
Martino, John, 241, 264
Martino, Luciano, 68
Martinson, Leslie, 9
Martinson, Rita, 225
Martorano, Vincent, 268-269
Marvin, Hank B., 125
Marvin, Lee, 287-288, 291-292
Mas, Jean, 289
Masciocchi, Marcello, 63, 166, 316
Masciocchi, Raffaele, 82, 166
Masé, Marino, 289
Maser, Gerhard, 163

Masing, Esther, 168
Masino, Steve, 72
Maslansky, Paul, 261
Maslow, Walter, 38-39
Mason, Anthony, 259
Mason, Buddy, 18, 88
Mason, Eric, 245
Mason, Ginger, 249
Mason, Hilary, 284
Mason, James, 114, 253-254
Mason, Lola, 77
Mason, Margery, 271
Mason, Pamela, 67, 166
Massari, Lea, 117
Masset, Andrew, 286
Massey, Anna, 172
Massie, Paul, 69-70
Masters, William, 179
Masy, Ed, 320
Matalon, Vivian, 138
Matania, Clelia, 117
Matela, Joe, 291
Matela, Paul, 291
Mateos, Luis, 314
Materassi, Giovanni, 82
Mather, Jack, 251
Mather, Marian, 64
Mathes, Marissa, 73, 131
Matheson, Don, 274
Matheson, Doug, 211
Matheson, Murray, 192
Matheson, Richard, 60, 72,
   74, 77, 84, 88, 96, 107-
   108, 172
Metras, Christian, 158
Matthews, Christopher, 197
Matthews, Kevin, 281
Matthiessen, Luke, 281
Mattson, Denver, 301
Mattson, Robin, 278-279
Maude, Mary, 211-212
Maugham, Robin, 74
Maughan, Susan, 120
Maurice, Paula, 77
Maus, Gordon, 281
Max, Edwin (Ed), 314, 317
Max, Jerome, 308
Maxwell, Alyscia, 249

Maxwell, Bill, 156
Maxwell, Frank, 92, 145
Maxwell, Len, 144
Maxwell, Paul, 13, 53
Maxwell, Stacey, 111
May, Harry, 269, 288
May, Jack, 14
May, Joe, 62
Mayer, Michael, 272
Mayers, Addison, 72
Maynard, Bill, 207
Maynard, Earl, 265
Maynard, Ken, 17
Maynard, Kermit, 16-17
Mayo, Alfredo, 104, 176
Mayo, Joe, 320
Mayock, Peter, 201
Mazurki, Mike, 275
Mazzola, Richard, 304
Meacham, Anne, 260
Meaden, Dan, 210
Meadows, Joyce, 16
Mecale, Giulio, 142
Meckler, Nancy, 190
Medalis, Joe, 328-329
Medford, Kay, 227
Meeker, Ralph, 173-174, 286
Megna, John, 332
Megowan, Don, 68, 143, 265
Mehas, Mick, 170
Mehling, Margo, 111
Mejding, Bent, 82
Mejuto, Andres, 182
Melchior, Ib, 55, 70, 82, 113,
   122
Melecco, Marta, 106
Melgar, Gabriel, 326
Mell, Joseph (Joe), 18, 274
Mellay, Emby, 237
Melleney, Victor, Snr., 272
Mellin, Ursula, 179
Mellor, James, 179
Melton, Sid, 280
Melton, Troy, 249
Melvin, Murray, 291
Menczer, Enrico, 133, 310
Mendez, Elisa, 211
Mendez, Victor, 334

Meniconi, Furio, 48
Menken, Robin, 225
Mensur, Ifran, 298-299
Menzies, Mary, 74
Meo, David, 161
Meola, Mike, 260
Mercer, Mae, 225
Mercer, William, 209
Merchant, Cathy, 92
Mercier, Michèle, 103
Meredith, Burgess, 255
Meredith, Dana, 116
Meredith, Jo Anne, 209, 288
Meredith, Judi, 140
Merey, Carla, 16
Merickel, Bill, 281
Merickel, Tommie, 281
Merino, Manuel, 148, 228
Merivale, John, 58
Merjanian, Steve, 109
Merrick, Laurence, 244
Merrifield, Dick, 279
Merrow, Jane, 137
Mersky, Kres, 233
Mervyn, William, 58, 207
Mescalero Apache Horn
  Dancers, The, 198
Mesic, Ajsa, 85
Messina, Terri, 204
Messinger, David, 46
Mestral, Armand, 85-86
Metcalf, Kenneth, 249-250
Methling, Sven, Jr., 72
Metrano, Art, 247, 254, 317,
  330
Mettey, Lynette, 293
Metzler, Rick, 221
Meyer, Emile, 257
Meyer, Eve, 51
Meyer, Godela H., 266
Meyer, John, 324
Meyer, Russ, 51, 165, 222
Meyers, Peter, 125
Meyers, Raymond, 326
Micale, Paul, 243
Michael, Gertrude, 75
Michaelian, Michael, 175
Michaels, Kay, 119

Michaels, Nita, 184
Michel, Joe, 292
Michelle, Anne, 256-257
Michelle, Donna, 117
Michelle, Janee, 245
Michl, Keith, 314
Michtom, Rose, 328
Middough, Miles, 91
Miehe-Renard, Louis, 70, 72
Mifune, Toshiro, 92, 123
Mihashi, Tatsuya, 144
Mikler, Michael T., 153
Milam, John, 324
Milan, George, 41
Milano, Nino, 60
Mileham, Mark, 64
Miles, Alvin, 320
Miles, Rosalind, 269, 271
Miles, Sylvia, 287
Milius, John, 173, 241
Millan, Robyn, 274
Milland, Ray, 80-83, 99, 225-
  226, 232-233
Miller, Bodil, 82
Miller, Chris, 9
Miller, Danny, 318
Miller, David, 131
Miller, Dick (Richard), 3, 9-
  11, 20-21, 23, 25, 44-45,
  81, 98-99, 125, 154, 167,
  265
Miller, George, 164
Miller, J.R., 322
Miller, Janice, 145
Miller, John, 248
Miller, Ken, 18, 28
Miller, Linda, 285
Miller, Magda, 69
Miller, Martin, 75
Miller, Marvin, 104
Miller, Mike (Michael B.),
  233, 285
Miller, Mirta, 235
Miller, Pamela, 247
Miller, Pat, 17
Miller, Peggy, 46
Miller, Richard (Drout), 293
Miller, Robert, 212

Miller, Roger, 131
Millett, Creusa, 234
Millhollin, Jim, 265
Millin, David, 272
Millot, Charles, 137, 204, 253
Mills, Brooke, 276
Mills, Donna, 274
Mills, Jacqueline, 241
Milne, Eithne, 98
Milner, Dan, 11
Milton, Beaufoy, 156
Milton, Billy, 118
Milton, Ernest, 14
Milton, Troy, 119
Mimieux, Yvette, 165
Mims, William, 228
Ming, Lei, 246
Minnelli, Liza, 289
Minnelli, Vincente, 289
Minor, Bob, 240, 245, 254, 255, 288
Minor, Mary, 279
Miranda, Isa, 190-191
Miranda, Soledad, 111, 182
Mislore, Michael, 297
Mitchell, Bill, 79
Mitchell, Cameron, 90-91, 231
Mitchell, Carlyle, 13
Mitchell, Carolyn, 31
Mitchell, Don, 245-246
Mitchell, Douglas, 189
Mitchell, John, 233
Mitchell, Laurie, 8, 28
Mitchell, Leigh, 314
Mitchell, Mary, 80-81, 90
Mitchell, Norman, 182
Mitchell, Sherry, 192
Mitchell, Steve, 53, 94, 185, 324
Mitchell, Ted, 91
Mitchell, Tony, 217
Mitchell, Warren, 115
Mitchum, Bob (Robert), 213, 317
Miyagawa, Kazuo, 126
Mizrahi, Anna, 150
Mizuno, Kumi, 123, 135, 144

Mock, Laurie, 150
Modern Folk Quartet, The, 131
Modugno, Lucia, 106
Moe, Marilyn, 47
Moffatt, John, 194
Moffitt, Elliott, 248
Mohler, Orv, 18
Mohr, Gerald, 55-56
Moio, Johnny, 329
Moiseiwitsch, Pamela, 190
Molina, Vidal, 182
Moll, Allan J., 166
Molla, Jose Luis Martinez, 216
Mollo, Gumersindo, 146, 174
Molteni, Sonia, 308
Monahan, Kate, 257
Monay, Maria, 16, 53
Monch, Peter, 70
Mondry, Eberhard, 160
Monlaur, Yvonne, 58
Monreal, Andres, 158
Montana, Lenny, 317, 330, 332, 334
Monte, Eric, 259, 267-268
Monteil, Beatriz, 163
Monteiro, Johnny, 71-72
Montell, Lisa, 20, 37
Montemuri, Davide, 114
Montés, Elisa, 146
Montgomery, Ralph, 243
Monti, Milly, 103
Monti, Silvia, 216
Montiforte, Frank, 111
Montresor, Dave, 63
Montuori, Marco, 60
Moody, Lynne, 245
Moody, Ron, 97
Moon, George, 118
Moon, Georgina, 93
Moon, H. Franco, 244
Moon, Reverend, 244
Mooney, Paul, 225
Moor, Cherie, 208
Moorcock, Michael, 272
Moore, Deborah Kim, 328
Moore, Jimmy, 276
Moore, John, 284

Moore, Juanita, 248
Moore, Kevin, 312
Moore, Lisa, 247, 249
Moore, Mary Alice, 320
Moore, Michael, 69
Moore, Micki, 251
Moore, Richard, 145, 147, 161, 166
Moore, Roger, 291-292, 295
Moore, Rudy Ray, 290
Moore, Terry, 62-63
Moorhead, Jean, 13, 19, 28
Mor, Tikva, 143
Morales, Mario, 122
Morales, Santos, 332
Moran, Francisco, 111
Moran, Neil, 184
Moravia, Alberto, 165
More, Kenneth, 112
Morel, Jacques, 139
Moreland, Carolyn, 309
Moreland, Gloria, 73
Moreland, Sherry, 111
Morell, André, 194
Moreno, Ruben, 240
Moretti, Renato, 118
Morey, Jack, 164
Morgan, Debbi, 290
Morgan, Gary, 317
Morgan, Priscilla, 122
Morgan, Read, 241, 329
Morgan, Red (Boyd), 55-56, 254
Morgan, Robin, 290
Morgan, Stacy, 55
Morgan, Stanley, 71
Morici, Franco, 156
Morick, David, 163
Morigi, Franco, 106
Moritz, Louisa, 259, 280
Moritz, Ulla, 70
Morley, Robert, 227
Morosi, Charles, 253
Morrill, A. John, 31, 264
Morris, Aubrey, 205
Morris, Barbara, 92
Morris, Barboura, 21, 25, 35, 44-45, 154, 191

Morris, Chester, 12
Morris, Edna, 121
Morris, Garrett, 267-268
Morris, Jan, 116
Morris, Jeff (Jeffrey), 29, 51
Morris, Reginald, 285, 299
Morrison, Greg, 258
Morrison, Hollis, 120
Morrow, Byron, 51, 80, 161
Morrow, Vic, 324, 326
Morse, Heyward, 218
Morse, Robin, 3, 21
Morter, Mary, 305
Morton, Brooks, 320
Morton, John, 80
Mosca, Joe, 209
Moschin, Gaston, 142
Moses, Bill, 278
Moskowitz, Gene, 253
Mosley, Lucky, 186
Moss, Gerald, 214
Moss, Larry, 259
Moss, Stewart, 250-251
Moxey, Hugh, 271
Moxey, John, 150
Mower, Patrick, 189-190
Msengana, Ray, 291
Mughan, Frances, 311
Muir, Gavin, 94
Mulaire, Jennifer, 314
Mulder, Ed, 175
Mulè, Francesco, 134
Mulholland, Declan, 273
Mulkey, Chris, 332
Mullaney, Jack, 119
Müller, Paul, 52, 91, 114, 200
Mullikin, Allen, 276
Mulvihill, Patrick, 308
Mumm, Harold, 294
Munoz, Loli, 148
Munro, Andrew, 51
Munro, Caroline, 203, 282, 284
Munro, Matt, 120
Munro, Pauline, 137
Munt, Peter, 207

Munzar, Ludek, 116
Murco, Vera, 85
Murdock, George, 296
Murff, Sharon, 267
Murgia, Tiberio, 106
Murnau, F.W., 37
Murphy, Audie, 143-144
Murphy, Jimmy (James), 51,
    88, 155
Murphy, Michael, 187
Murray, Jan, 153
Murray, Peg, 217
Murray, Rick, 297
Murray, Zon, 19
Murton, Lionel, 97-98
Mustin, Burt, 198
Mutrux, Floyd, 161
Muxeneder, Franz, 283
Myer, Paul, 147
Myers, Janet, 309
Myers, Peter, 97
Myhre, Kevin, 319

Nacinelli, Giancarlo, 309
Nadajan, 60
Nadder, Robert, 328
Nader, George, 148-149
Nader, Mike, 87, 109, 111,
    117, 120, 124, 134-135
Nader, Stephanie, 120, 124
Nagano, Juichi, 126
Nahan, Stu, 329
Nakajima, Haruo, 106
Nakamaru, Tadao, 123, 144
Nakamura, Kinji, 126
Nakamura, Michael, 307
Nakamura, Satoshi, 219
Nakayama, Yutaka, 106
Nalder, Reggie, 330
Nale, Spartaco, 60
Napier, Alan, 81
Napoleon, Titus, 330
Nardini, Tom, 167-168, 173
Narros, Miguel, 314
Narsico, Gracia, 16
Nash, Cecil, 201
Nash, N. Richard, 285
Nashville Teens, The, 120

Nasimok, Brian, 313
Nassif, Fred, 331
Natale, Paolo, 168
Natali, Dino, 328
Nath, Prem, 195
Nathan, Peggy, 106
Naud, William T., 237
Nauta, Roberto, 314
Navarro, George, 41
Navarro, Larry, 105
Nazzari, Amedeo, 289
Neal, David, 194
Neal, Meredith, and the Boot
    Heel Boys, 198
Neal, Ron, 321
Neame, Ronald, 328-329
Near, Holly, 169, 225
Neel, Joan, 111
Neibel, David, 208
Neilson, Bonnie, 239
Nell, Christa, 149
Nelson, Alberta, 87, 109, 111,
    117, 119-120, 124, 136
Nelson, Bert, 21
Nelson, Craig, 215-216, 245
Nelson, Dick, 13
Nelson, Ed, 18, 21, 29, 36,
    44
Nelson, Lori, 6, 9
Nelson, Mervyn, 217
Nephew, Neil, 80
Nero, Franco, 156, 178, 203,
    311-312
Néstor, José, 64
Netranga, Leo V., 53
Neuman, Dorothy, 25, 33, 47,
    98
Nevdal, Ellen, 105
Nevens, Paul, 277
Neville, John, 115-116
Newark, Derek, 128, 137
Newell, Patrick, 115, 275
Newlands, Anthony, 150, 197
Newman, James, 30
Newman, William, 294
Newton, Rick, 111
Ney, Richard, 81-82
Neyland, Anne, 19

Ngakane, Lionel, 181
Nicholas, Denise, 220-221
Nicholaus, John, Jr., 36, 43,
    53, 98
Nicholls, Anthony, 79
Nichols, Dandy, 223
Nichols, Dave, 308
Nichols, J.D., 243
Nichols, Jeff, 131
Nichols, Nichelle, 265
Nicholson, Elwood J., 73
Nicholson, Jack, 96, 98-99,
    154, 163
Nicholson, James H., 4, 202
Nicholson, Laura, 46, 109,
    111, 119
Nicholson, Loretta, 41, 46
Nicholson, Luree, 46, 87-88
Nicholson, Meredith M., 55-56
Niciphor, Nick, 319
Nicol, Alex, 36-37, 185
Nielsen, Peter, 234
Nielson, Claire, 213
Nieto, José, 182
Nightingale, Benny, 182
Nightingale, Timothy, 112
Niles, Chuck G., 247
Nilsson, Britt, 232
Nimmo, Derek, 137
Nimoy, Leonard, 29
Niven, David, 117-118, 275-
    276
Nixon, Richard, 231
Nizzari, Joyce, 111
Noble, Jackie, 179
Noble, James, 285
Noble, Trisha, 222
Noel, Chris, 105, 147-148
Noel, Harvey, 217
Noel, Hubert, 305
Nolan, Lloyd, 320
Nolan, Margaret, 158, 207
Nolan, Tom, 161, 170
Noland, Valora, 87, 109
Nolte, Nick, 278-279, 330
Nord, Eric, 264
Nordine, Ken, 174
Noriega, Eduardo, 143

Norman, John, 69
Norman, Oliver, 218
Norris, Chuck, 296, 327
North, Edmund H., 328
North, Virginia, 203
Northup, Harry, 221
Norton, Charles, 279
Norton, Joe, 320
Norton, Kay, 87
Norton, William, 292
Nosseck, Noel, 321
Nova, Renza, 116
Novak, Mel, 265
Novakova, Jana, 198
Noyman, Yoel, 143
Nuckles, Paul, 324
Nuuhiwa, David, 195

Oakland Hell's Angels, The,
    175
Oas-Heim, Gordon, 139-140
Oates, Warren, 241
Oates, Wendy, 332
O'Brian, Hugh, 272
O'Brian, Wilbur, 196
O'Brien, Kenneth, 245
O'Brien's Chris, Caribbeans,
    22
O'Byrne, Bryan, 327
O'Connell, Jack, 207
O'Connell, Michael, 61
O'Conner, Glynnis, 323
O'Connor, Pat, 278
O'Connor, Terry, 296
O'Connor, Tim, 237
O'Dell, Bryan, 321-322
Odlum, Jerome, 3
O'Donnell, Maire, 201
O'Donovan, Derry, 90
O'Flynn, Damian, 62
Ogawa, El, 219
Ogilvy, Ian, 156, 158, 202
O'Hara, Quinn, 136, 190
O'Hara, Terrence, 331
Oh! Ogunde Dancers, The, 179
O'Keefe, Ray (Raymond), 233,
    254, 329
Oklander, Ruth, 60

Olaguibel, Juan, 148, 174
Olek, Henry, 329
Oliver, Stephen, 155
Oliveras, Frank, 171
Olivieri, Enrico, 65
Olvera, Oswald, 143
O'Mack, Diane, 304
Omae, Wataru, 219
O'Mara, Kate, 200
Omura, Wataru, 173
O'Neal, Anne, 22
O'Neal, Frederick, 91
O'Neil, Dick, 217
O'Neill, Jennifer, 277-278
O'Neill, Michael, 304
O'Neill, Sheila, 98
Oneto, Richard, 289
Onorato, Glauco, 103
Ontkean, Michael, 228
Opatoshu, David, 141, 143
Opie, Linda, 109, 111
Oppenheimer, Alan, 306
Orange, David, 257
Orchard, Julian, 207, 223
O'Reilly, Patricia, 111
Orfei, Moira, 97
Ormsby, Alan, 251
Orr, Dorothy Darlene, 309
Orr, Pat, 251
Orsatti, Ernie, 332
Ortega, Pete, 307
Ortiz, Church, 332
Ortiz, Rosanna, 244-245
Osborn, David, 218
Osborn, Lynn, 12, 18
Osborne, Bud, 16
Osborne, Michael, 311
Osborne, Rupert, 71
Oscar, Henry, 128
Osman, Ahmed, 205
Osmond, Cliff, 173
Osterhout, R. David, 193, 221
Ostos, George, 169
O'Sullivan, Richard, 125, 193
Oswald, Gerd, 206
Otis, James, 285
Otsuka, Harusato, 63
Otsuka, Seigo, 63

Ott, Warrene, 73
Ottosen, Carl, 70, 82-83
Oulton, Brian, 64
Oumansky, Andre, 253
Ousey, Timothy, 260
Owe, Baard, 207-208
Owen, Bill, 121
Owen, Roger, 311
Owen, Tudor, 11
Owens, Bonnie, 160
Owens, Carol Jean, 294
Owens, James, 176
Owens, Nancy Lee, 248
Owens, Tony, 288
Owensby, Earl, 164
Oyama, Ted, 312
Ozenne, Jean, 141
Ozman, Bob, 303-304

Paal, Erszi, 216
Pace, Judy, 165, 199, 225
Pace, Roger, 41
Pacey, Steven, 194
Padalewski, Erich, 283
Padget, Bob, 39
Padilla, Manuel, Jr., 143
Pagan, Michael, 321
Page, Eileen, 201
Page, Keva, 111
Pagel, Kathleen, 233
Pages, Paloma, 211
Paget, Debra, 61-63, 84-85, 92
Pagh, Klaus, 72
Paiva, Nestor, 88
Pal, Laszlo, 290
Palacios, Ricardo, 158, 182
Palance, Brooke, 299
Palance, Jack, 85
Palella, Oreste, 133
Palethorpe, Joan, 98
Pallottini, Riccardo, 80, 83, 156
Palmara, Mimo (Mimmo), 52, 91
Palmer, Edward, 93, 156
Palmer, Edwin, 86
Palmer, Lilli, 114, 172, 211-212, 214

Palmer, Renzo, 180-181
Palmer, Robert, 158
Palmer, Terry, 93, 138
Palmer, Toni, 122
Palmisano, Conrad, 329
Paluzzi, Luciana, 62, 242, 266
Pampanini, Silvana, 68, 109-110
Pamphili, Mirella, 200
Pampino, Louis, 233
Pancake, Roger, 257
Pane, Bob, 111
Pani, Corrado, 185-186
Paniagua, Cecilio, 103
Pansing, Sally, 315
Pantera, Malou, 49
Paolella, Domenico, 68
Papadopoulos, Panos, 62
Papas, Irene, 158-159
Papiri, Umberto, 168
Paquis, Gerard, 291
Paredes, Conchita, 211
Parker, Bill, 87
Parker, Cecil, 121, 150
Parker, Ed, 330
Parker, Francine, 225
Parker, Kathleen, 168
Parker, Reginald, 290
Parker, Ross, 137
Parkin, Dean, 41-42
Parkins, Barbara, 291-292
Parkinson, Michael, 258
Parks, Michael, 320-321, 324, 326
Parmentier, Richard, 306
Parolin, Aiace, 295
Parr, Bobby, 210, 282
Parra, Carlos, 314
Parra, Julio Jesús, 314
Parrish, Julie, 134
Parrish, Lee, 208
Parrish, Leslie, 134, 173
Parrish, Robert, 253
Parry, Harvey, 119
Parry, Natasha, 74-75
Parslow, Ray, 258
Parsons, Milton, 92

Partian, Paul A., 307
Parton, Reg, 247
Partridge, Derek, 138
Pasic, Ramiz, 311
Passante, Mario, 65
Passer, Dirk, 82
Passer, Ivan, 283
Pastell, George, 71
Pastore, Piero, 82
Pastore, Pietro, 60
Pataki, Michael, 215, 250-251, 327
Pate, Michael, 88, 209
Paterlini, Meschino, 329
Patrick, Butch, 234
Patrick, Dennis, 113, 198
Patrick, Roy, 128
Patterson, Hank, 13, 28, 38
Patterson, Jackie, 279
Patterson, Jerry, 212
Patterson, Melody, 170-171, 204-205
Patterson, Pat (Patrick), 193, 313
Patterson, Troy, 28, 38-39
Patton, Bart, 89-90
Paul, George (Georgie), 60, 318
Paulette, Geraldine, 60
Paulino, Justo, 238, 244
Paull, Morgan, 254, 274
Paulsin, George, 250
Pauly, Ursule, 167
Pawley, Anthony, 30
Paxton, Tony, 281
Payne, Bobby, 87
Payne, James, 245
Payne, John, 160, 196
Payne, Willy, 181
Paz, Shlomo, 143
Peach, Kenneth, 167, 176
Peacock, Keith, 130, 150
Pearcy, Patricia, 294
Pearson, Jerold, 328
Peck, Ed, 293
Peck, William, 115
Pecorano, Anthony, 281
Peek, Denys, 189

Peel, Edward, 311
Peerce, Larry, 131
Pehlke, Heinz, 172
Pelikan, Lisa, 315-316
Pelkey, Sanita, 47
Pellevant, Antoinette, 80
Pellicer, Oscar, 171
Pelligrin, Georges, 253
Peluce, Meeno, 322
Pember, Ron, 189, 194, 229, 273
Pena, Luz Maria, 287
Penafiel, Luis (Verna), 211, 314
Pendleton, Dave, 321-322
Penhaligon, Susan, 273
Penn, Arthur, 30
Pennell, Larry, 317
Penny, Joe, 319-320
Penrod, Judy, 328
Perak, John, 240
Percival, Lance, 122
Pereira, Fernando, 198
Perier, Etienne, 171
Perilli, Frank Ray, 243
Perkins, David, 287
Perkins, Millie, 166
Perreau, Gigi, 30
Perries, Mary, 279
Perry, Edd, 86
Perry, Felton, 259, 318
Perry, Roger, 187, 215-216, 232
Perry, Ron, 90
Perry, Ty, 75
Perschy, Maria, 158, 214
Persichetti, Loretta, 295
Persoff, Nehemiah, 178
Persson, Essy, 189
Persson, Gene, 38
Persson, Ralph, 204
Pesce, Frank, 332
Pesch, Ulrike, 266
Pestriniero, Renato, 122
Peter and Gordon, 120
Peters, Brock, 247
Peters, Donald A., 184
Peters, Gus, 211

Peters, Lauri, 97-98
Peters, Lee, 156
Peters, Luan, 275
Peters, Scott, 13, 18-19, 28, 33, 38-39, 80
Petersen, Kjeld, 82
Peterson, Arthur, 168
Petit, Pierre, 133
Petocchi, Anna, 266
Petra, Hortense, 150
Petrelli, Sandra, 148
Petri, Hella, 253
Petrie, Gordon, 150
Petrini, Paolo, 85
Petroff, Hamil, 87
Petrov, Vassily, 63
Petrucci, Giovanni, 146
Petty, Jerry, 160
Pettyjohn, Angelique, 176
Phaedra, 287
Pharo, Richard G., 52
Phillips, Alex, Jr., 287
Phillips, Barney, 18
Phillips, Conrad, 58
Phillips, Greigh, 29
Phillips, Leslie, 64-65
Phillips, Michelle, 241
Phillips, Robert, 231, 300
Phillips, Robin, 181-182
Phipps, Nicholas, 97
Phoenix, Ray, 35
Pia Luzi, Maria, 85
Piazzoli, Roberto D'Ettore, 308
Piccolo, Marco, 58
Picerni, Charles, 330
Pickard, John, 249
Pickett, Bob, 208, 223
Pickford, Jimmy, 18, 23
Pickles, Christina, 260
Pickren, Stacy, 331
Piel, Jochel, 179
Pierce, Arthur G., 56
Pierce, Charles B., 301, 309, 318, 324, 326
Pierce, Charles, Jr., 319
Pierce, Guy, 190
Pierce, Jack, 191

Pierce, Maggie, 84
Pierce, Norman, 75
Pierce, Stack, 268-269
Pierfederici, Antonio, 65
Pierotti, Piero, 80, 90, 128
Pierreux, Jacqueline, 103
Piers, Thors, 181
Pietrosi, Antonia, 180
Pigozzi, Luciano, 142
Pilotto, Camillo, 80
Pilou, Nana, 152
Pimentel, Hugo, 111
Pine, Larry, 320
Pine, Philip, 11
Pine, Robert, 299
Ping, Poing, 80
Pini, Aldo, 64, 114
Pink, Sidney, 55, 70, 82, 111
Pinkard, Fred, 288-289
Pinney, Charles, 199
Pinsent, Gordon, 220
Pinter, Tomislav, 203
Pintoff, Ernest, 326
Pipolo, 134, 154
Pirie, David, 58
Pirie, Mary, 313
Pirro, Ugo, 85, 165, 178, 203
Pitt, Ingrid, 200
Pittman, Eliana, 234
Pizzuti, Riccardo, 235, 262
Place, Lou, 3, 46
Plans, Juan José, 314
Platt, Howard, 287
Platt, Ruth, 214
Platters, The, 21
Playten, Alice, 323
Pleasence, Donald, 58, 213,
    229, 231, 284-285, 326
Plimpton, George, 320
Ploski, Joe, 119
Plumb, Kenneth, 30
Plummer, Christopher, 298-299
Poe, Edgar Allan, 60, 74, 81,
    84, 92, 96, 108, 118, 120,
    127-128, 179-181, 213-214
Pogany, Gabor, 114, 128
Poggi, Allesandro, 309
Poggi, Roberto, 309

Pogostin, S. Lee, 255
Pohlmann, Eric, 64
Poitier, Sidney, 238
Pol, Anne Marie, 211
Pol, Talitha, 137
Poli, Mimmo, 82, 114
Polidor, 180
Polito, Gene, 75
Politoff, Haydée, 185-186
Pollack, Jack (Jindřich
    Polák), 116
Pollard, Michael J., 145
Pollini, Joe, 64
Pollini, Leo, 22
Pomerantz, Earl, 239
Pomerantz, Leon, 98
Pons, Beatrice, 105
Poole, Brooks, 253
Poole, Duane, 324
Poole, Jackie, 210
Poore, Lloyd, 279
Pope, Cliff, 91
Porcel, Marisa, 314
Portell, Petula, 210
Porter, Eric, 271
Porter, J. Robert, 140
Portnow, Hugh, 190
Portulari, Angela, 62
Potok, Rebecca, 266
Potter, Bob, 254
Poulsen, Majour, 72
Powell, Addison, 277
Powell, Arla, 86
Powell, Dinny, 214
Powell, Fred, 150
Powell, Lillian, 20
Power, Edward, 299
Power, Paul, 34
Powers, Jon, 104
Powers, Mala, 67-68
Prager, Stanley, 176
Prairie Oyster, 313
Prather, Ron, 278
Pratt, Judson, 286
Prawluk, Mira, 239
Pray, Cris, 298
Prechtel, Volker, 283
Prendes, Luis, 111, 326

Prescod, Pearl, 64
Prescott, Guy, 34
Prescott, Russ, 53
Preston, Steve, 197
Prévost, Francoise, 180
Pribble, James Connor, 307
Price, Allan, 239
Price, Big Walter, 261
Price, Dennis, 22, 152, 193-
    194, 200-201
Price, Jesse, 283
Price, Stanley, 284, 291
Price, Vincent, 60-61, 72,
    74, 84-85, 87-89, 92-93,
    96-97, 107-109, 119-120,
    126-128, 134, 148-149, 156-
    158, 179-180, 189-190, 197,
    203, 224-225, 258-259
Priest, Pat, 212
Prima, Louis, 75-77
Primus, Barry, 221-222
Prince, Ron, 298
Prine, Andrew, 309-310
Pringle, Joan, 288-289
Priver, Eytan, 143
Proclemer, Anna, 289
Procopio, Lou, 145, 192-193
Proctor, Marland, 208
Proctor, Phil, 297
Proctor, Randi, 206
Prohaska, Janos, 101
Prokop, Paul, 145, 148
Prosperi, Franco, 105
Provine, Dorothy, 29-30
Prowse, David (Dave), 207,
    306
Pryor, Christine, 189
Pryor, Richard, 166, 298
Ptushko, Aleksandr, 104
Puente, Jesus, 146-147
Pugh, Ted, 331
Pulman, Jack, 213
Pulver, Liselotte, 139
Punzalah, Bruno, 238
Pupa, Piccola, 136
Puppo, Romano, 295
Puputauki, Antoine Coco, 185-
    186

Purcell, Noel, 64
Purdom, Edmund, 85-86
Purpus, Mike, 195
Pusser, Buford, 276-277, 300
Putnam, Jock, 89
Pyne, Natasha, 258-259
Pyramids, The, 101

Quade, John, 293
Quadflieg, Will, 195
Quaid, Dennis, 319, 334
Quarry, Robert, 187-188, 215-
    216, 223-225, 258, 261
Quayle, Anthony, 310-311
Quesada, Milo, 100, 106, 143,
    228
Quick, Al, 148
Quick, Jim, 164
Quicke, Celia, 257
Quickly, Tommy, and the Reno
    Four, 120
Quine, Tom, 120
Quinn, Almeria, 269
Quinn, Anthony, 253-254
Quinn, Barbara, 281, 294
Quinn, Bill, 317
Quinn, Dan, 217
Quinn, Dermot, 41
Quinn, Louis, 233
Quito, 330

Rabal, Francisco, 182-183
Racca, Claudio, 85, 146
Racine, Roger, 260
Rae, John, 227
Rae, Mabel, 53
Rafferty, Chips, 5
Raft, George, 176
Ragheb, Osman, 329
Raglan, Robert, 193
Ragona, Ubaldo, 107
Raho, Umberto (Humi), 176,
    220
Raimond, Larry, 29
Rain, David, 206
Rainer, Peter, 304
Raines, Barbara, 206
Rake, Dodie, 46

Ralli, Giovanna, 85
Ralston, Hal, 328
Ramati, Alexander, 141, 143, 158
Ramati, Didi, 141
Ramirez, Carlos José, 206
Ramos, Jess, 238
Ramos, Rudy, 332, 334
Ramsen, Bobby, 256
Ramsey, Clark, 5
Ramsey, Logan, 268, 276-277, 300, 318
Ramsey, Ward, 161
Ramsing, Bob, 72
Ranchi, Federica, 60
Randall, Greta, 105
Randall, Jerry, 175-176, 184
Randall, Steve, 280
Randall, Tony, 130-131
Randall, Walter, 69
Randell, Ron, 12
Randi, Don, Trio Plus One, The, 134
Randolph, Henry, 29
Randolph, Lillian, 274, 315
Randone, Salvo, 180
Rane, Patricia, 109
Raney, Sue, 164
Rank, Claude, 139
Rank, Ursula, 149
Ransome, Prunella, 314-315
Rapp, Paulette, 87
Rasche, David, 331
Rassimov, Ivan, 122, 316
Rassimov, Rada, 220
Rastatter, Wendy, 319
Rasulala, Thalmus, 220-221, 266-269, 271
Rath, Earl, 199
Rathbone, Basil, 84-85, 88-89, 136, 140
Ratoni, Suzanna, 143
Rau, Umberto, 107
Ravel, Lisa, 179
Raven, Elsa, 322
Raven, Terry, 189
Ravick, Tom, 56
Rawlinson, Brian, 64

Rawls, Lou, 169
Ray, Aldo, 150, 152, 184
Ray, Andrew, 137
Ray, Annita, 23
Ray, Frankie, 79
Ray, Jimmy, 306
Ray, Joan, 248, 279
Ray, Philip, 93
Raybould, Harry, 13
Raycraft, Janet, 309
Raymond, Cyril, 64
Raynor, Sheila, 118
Re, Gustavo, 171
Read, Peter, 90
Reader, Jim, 147
Reading, Donna, 158
Real, Rita, 309
Rebar, Alex, 313-314
Red, Charles, 299
Reddick, Cecil, 233
Redding, Charles, 186
Redfield, Dennis, 233, 274-275
Reding, Juli, 62
Redman, Lee, 53
Redman, Louise, 64
Reece, Edward, Jr., 279
Reed, Charles, 120
Reed, Dolores, 79
Reed, Ervin, 326
Reed, Jerry, 313
Reed, Larry, 217
Reed, Marshall, 210
Reed, Michael, 130, 291
Reed, Nathaniel (Nate), 267, 290
Reed, Oliver, 137, 287-288
Reed, Ralph, 20
Reed, Sandy, 134, 153
Reed, Tracy, 214
Reed, Walter, 34
Reede, Rosemarie, 189
Rees, Betty Anne, 223-224, 233-234, 261
Reese, Tom, 281, 332
Reeves, Michael, 156, 158
Reeves, Roberta, 206
Reeves, Steve, 48

Regas, Pedro, 184
Reggiani, Serge, 85, 178
Rego, Fernando, 152
Reid, Alistair, 291
Reid, Beryl, 224
Reid, Milton, 224, 306
Reid, Susan, 69
Reider, Ed, 9
Reilly, John, 334
Reisser, Dora, 137
Reitman, Ivan, 239
Relyea, Robert, 330
Remberg, Erika, 58
Remick, Lee, 271-272
Remy, Jacques, 133
Renard, Ray, 175
Rendine, Aldo, 295
Renella, Pat, 150
Renis, Tony, 295
Rennhofer, Linda, 313
Rennie, Michael, 168-169
Reno, Angie, 195
Renoir, Claude, 180
Renson, Barbara, 154
Resin, Dan, 320
Ressel, Franco, 83, 90, 155
Reves, Robert Raymond, 307
Revill, Clive, 48-49, 317
Rexon, William, 326
Rey, Alejandro, 234
Rey, Fernando, 158-159, 182-183, 289
Reyer, Walter, 61-62
Reyes, Santos, 292-293
Reynolds, James, 324
Reynolds, Quentin, 35
Rheims, V.J., 31
Rhind, Burke, 170
Rhoades, Barbara, 245
Rhodes, Jordan, 184
Rhodes, Virginia, 266
"Rhubarb," the cat, 88
Rialson, Candice, 297
Riano, Renie, 101, 111, 134
Ribotta, Ettore, 108
Rice, Frank, 290
Rice, Herbert, 321
Rich, Anthony, 53

Richard, Cliff, 97-98, 125-126
Richard, Dawn, 18
Richard, Edmond, 182
Richards, Diane, 8
Richards, George, 128
Richards, Jack L., 290
Richards, Jon, 277
Richards, Kim, 293
Richards, Lisa, 307
Richards, Susan, 284
Richards, Terry, 213-214
Richards, Vicky, 189
Richardson, Edna, 265
Richardson, James G., 328
Richardson, John, 65
Richardson, Mukai, 267
Richardson, Ralph, 218-219
Richmond, Felice, 19
Richmond, Tony, 275
Richter, Debi, 335
Rickett, Nooney, Four, The, 111
Rickles, Don, 99, 101, 109, 117
Rico, John, 253
Riddle, Hal, 119
Ridgley, Robert, 208, 259
Ridley, Douglas, 207
Ridley, Giles, 272
Riehle, Richard, 304
Rifkin, Alan, 124
Rifkin, Ron, 173-174
Rigaud, Jorge (Georges), 182, 216
Rigby, Peter, 207
Rigg, Carl, 179, 189
Rigg, Diana, 194
Righi, Massimo, 103, 118, 122, 142
Rimmel, Richard Reuven, 195
Rimmer, Shane, 305
Rinaldi, Antonio, 122
Riquerio, Francisco, 143
Risk, Linda Sue, 161
Risso, Roberto, 118
Ritter, Tex, 139-140
Rivas, Carlos, 143

Rivera, Cheyenne, 301, 307
Rivera, Linda, 20
Rivera, Luis, 148
Rivero, Aparacio, 314
Rivers, Leo, 244
Rizzo, Karl, 233
Roa, Stephen, 190
Road, Mike, 228
Roarke, Adam, 163-165, 176-177, 186, 225-226
Robards, Jason, Jr., 194-195, 213-214
Robbins, Cindy, 18
Robbins, Dick, 324
Roberson, Jim, 301, 309
Roberto, Freddy, 53
Roberts, Clete, 329
Roberts, Glen, 325-326
Roberts, Hazel, 288
Roberts, J.N., 184
Roberts, Luanne, 206
Roberts, Tanya, 320, 323
Roberts, Trevor, 207
Robertson-Justice, James, 180
Robey, Ann, 331
Robinette, Dale, 334
Robinson, Bruce, 218
Robinson, Charles, 261
Robinson, Chris, 46-47, 170-171
Robinson, Edward G., 39
Robinson, Jay, 206
Robinson, Joe, 69, 90
Robinson, Judy, 257
Robinson, Pete, 319, 335
Robinson, Richard, 313
Robinson, Roger, 329
Robinson, Smokey, and the Miracles, 113
Robles, Leticia, 287
Robles, Renato, 71
Robles, Walter, 164, 170
Robsahn, Margaret, 100
Robson, Michael, 310
Roby, George, 290
Roby, Lavelle, 328
Rocca, Daniela, 117
Rocco, Tony, 329

Rockin' Berries, The, 120
Rodgers, Pamela, 119
Rodgers, Steve, 155
Rodgers, Stuart Edmond, 313
Rodine, Alex, 286
Rodrigo, Xavier, 312
Rodriquez, Chris, 234
Roeg, Nicolas, 108, 137
Rogers, Corin, 267-268
Rogers, Dinah Anne, 324
Rogers, Erica, 272
Rogers, Harriet, 285
Rogers, Linda, 87-88, 110
Rogers, Liz, 215
Rogers, Steve, 124
Rohm, Maria, 148-149, 190, 200-201, 228
Rohmer, Patrice, 292
Rohmer, Sax, 149
Rojas, Manuel, 176
Rojo, Gustavo, 176
Roker, Renny, 259
Roland, Renate, 198
Rolike, Hank, 249, 292
Rolling Stones, The, 113
Romain, Yvonne, 58
Román, Antonio, 122
Roman, Candice, 233
Roman, Carmen M., 148
Roman, Leticia, 105-106
Romano, Andy, 87, 110, 117, 120, 124, 136
Romano, Renato, 190-191
Romanoff, Liz, 210
Romero, Blanquita, 67
Romero, Cesar, 123, 176, 178
Romero, Eddie, 71, 238, 244
Romero, George, 226, 239
Romero, José Luis, 314
Romero, Juan Carlos, 314
Romilly, Elizabeth, 271
Rondell, Ronnie, 111, 119, 162
Rondo, Robert, 253
Ronet, Maurice, 253
Ronettes, The, 131
Rooney, Mickey, 121, 170
Rooney, Tim, 150

Roosevelt, Buddy, 16
Roquevert, Noël, 137
Rosales, Thomas, Jr., 332
Rose, Clayton, 279
Rose, David, 48
Rose, John, 116
Rose, Louisa, 246
Rose, Mickey, 144
Rose, Reva, 165, 206, 259
Rose, Sherman A., 39
Roseborough, Timothy, 288
Rosella, Gail, 304
Roseman, Ben, 94
Rosen, Marvin J., 30
Rosenbaum, Henry, 186, 191
Rosenberg, Stuart, 322
Rosin, Mark, 297
Rosly, Judy, 316
Ross, Diana, 240
Ross, Gene, 186
Ross, Hank, 321
Ross, Joe, 324
Ross, Joe E., 161
Ross, Merrie Lynn, 282-283, 328
Ross, Myrna, 117, 120, 136
Ross, Ronald C., 231
Ross, Rosalind, 164
Ross, Terence, 308
Rossellini, Isabella, 289
Rosset, Alan, 253
Rossi, Fausto, 235, 262
Rossi Drago, Eleonora, 190
Rossi Stuart, Giocomo, 107
Rossilli, Gaston, 207
Rossington, Norman, 181, 229
Rossini, Janet, 179, 189
Rossini, Renato, 204
Rossitto, Angelo, 243
Rosson, Edward, 327
Rosson, Lili, 46
Rostill, John, 125
Roth, Dan, 245
Roth, Gene, 38, 43
Roth, Maya, 190
Rothman, Stephanie, 131
Rothwell, Talbot, 207, 222-223

Rotunno, Giuseppe, 180
Roubicek, George, 79
Rougas, Michael, 18, 324
Rouse, Timothy, 260
Routh, Samuel "Catfish", 288
Rouvel, Catherine, 253
Rovere, Gina, 174
Rowe, Dana, 320
Rowlands, David, 275
Rowlands, Patsy, 122, 207
Royale, Rosalind, 189
Royce, Riza, 8
Roye, Phillip, 235
Royter, Roland, 115
Rozman, Lojze, 203
Ruben, Joseph, 304, 319, 334
Rubicon, Jessica, 152
Rubin, Andrew, 331-332
Rubin, Benny, 136
Rubini, Giulia, 48
Rubinstein, John, 234
Ruddy, Albert S., 317
Rudin, Herman, 210
Rueter, Elfi, 179
Ruffo, Leonora, 60, 107
Ruiz, Isaac, 306
Runachagua, Aysanoa, 156
Rush, Billy, 164
Rush, Richard, 153, 163-164
Rusoff, Lou, 3, 6, 8, 10-12, 14, 16, 19, 22-23, 33, 38, 47, 53, 63, 87
Russ, Toby, 191
Russell, Bing, 38-39
Russell, Chuck, 282
Russell, Del, 211
Russell, Donna, 87
Russell, George, 91, 115
Russell, Hilda Campbell, 128
Russell, Jane, 145
Russell, Ken, 93
Russell, Marigold, 272
Russell, Ray, 81, 99
Russell, Robert, 156-158
Russell, Tommie, 115
Russell, Tony, 210-211
Russo, Alisson, 217
Russo, Karolyn, 217

Russo, Madeleine A., 206
Rutherford, Douglas, 277
Ruttencutter, Frank, 170
Ryan, John, 241, 286-287
Ryan, Madge, 97-98
Ryan, Marla, 31
Ryan, Natasha, 322
Ryan, Robert, 133
Ryan, Tim, 184
Rydbeck, Whitney, 328

Saad, Robert (T.), 239, 301
Saarinen, Eric, 225
Sabel, Valerie, 220
Sabela, Simon, 291
Sacdalan, J. Felipe, 71, 249
Sachs, Jack, 281
Sachs, Leonard, 71
Sachs, William, 313-314
Sachse, Salli, 109, 119, 121,
    124, 134, 136, 147, 149,
    154, 166
Sacks, Michael, 320, 322-323
Sada, Yutaka, 106, 173
Sadek, Eshane, 146
Saffian, Mimi, 274
Safrankova, Libuse, 298
Sagar, Anthony, 207
Sahara, Kenji, 106, 219-220
Sahewk, Ron, 190
St. Clair, Shelley, 277
St. Jacques, Raymond, 320-321
Saint James, Susan, 327-328
St. John, Bill, 47
St. Laurent, Andree, 308
Saito, Noritake, 219
Saito, Takao, 123
Sakai, Sachio, 219
Sakai, Seth, 330
Sakata, Harold, 306
Saki, Eileen, 329
Sala, Vittorio, 142
Saland, Ellen, 322
Salcedo, Leopoldo, 71, 244-
    245
Saldana, Theresa, 332, 334
Salgado, Marian, 314
Salinger, Pierre, 253

Salkow, Sidney, 107
Salkowitz, Sy, 153
Sallis, Peter, 197, 202
Salmi, Albert, 299
Salt, Jennifer, 246-247
Salter, Ivor, 257
Salvi, Emmimo, 48
Salvia, Raphael J., 122
Sam and the Ape Men, 119
Samardjic, Ljubisa, 203
Samarina, Yelena, 148-149
Sampson, Bill, 124
Sampson, Cheryl, 265
Sampson, Edwards, 3
Sande, Angel, 294
Sanders, George, 23, 143-144
Sanders, Hugh, 80
Sanders, Robert, 226
Sanders, Sandy, 319
Sandford, Christopher, 275
Sandler, Robert, 239
Sandor, Gregory, 110, 145,
    246
Sandor, Steve, 175
Sands, Anita, 46-47
Sandy, Gary, 217
Sanford, Gerald, 272
Sanford, Isabel, 327
Sangiovanni, Vincente, 158
Sangster, Jimmy, 218
Sanguineti, Helen, 130
Sanguineti, William, 130
Santone, Penny, 88
Sanz, Paco, 174
Sarafian, Richard C., 30
Sarandon, Susan, 285, 331
Sargent, Dick, 4
Sarne, Michael, 64, 122
Sarno, Janet, 334
Sarrazin, Michael, 277-278
Sartarelli, Marcello, 128
Sasdy, Peter, 284
Sasso, Ugo, 48, 60
Sato, Makoto, 123
Saunders, Harold, 192
Saunders, J. Jay, 247
Saunders, Linda (Lori), 131,
    133

Saunders, Shep, 317
Saunders, Stuart, 29, 122
Sauro, Sergio, 52
Savage, Archie, 64
Savalas, Telly, 272
Saveiros, Carmen, 281
Saville, Jimmy, 120
Savona, Leopoldo, 85
Sawacha, Nadim, 275
Sawamura, Ikio, 106, 173
Sawara, Kenji, 100, 173
Saxon, Aaron, 9, 25, 96
Saxon, John, 105-106, 140, 308
Saxon, Peter, 196
Sayce, Charlotte, 218
Sayer, Jay, 26, 35
Sayer, Laura, 278
Saylor, Katie, 254
Saylor, Syd, 89
Sbragia, Gian Carlo, 60
Sbrenna, Mario, 91
Scaife, Edward, 121
Scala, Gaetano, 97
Scales, Garrett, 261
Scammel, Roy, 150
Scarborough, John E., 261
Scardamaglia, Francesco, 91
Scardino, Don, 294
Scattini, Luigi, 152, 154, 159
Schaefer, Mary Jane, 268
Schaffel, Robert L., 331
Schall, Wendy, 306
Schallert, William, 9
Schanzer, Karl, 90, 131
Scharf, Alan, 309
Schell, Maria, 228
Schell, Maximilian, 158-159, 298-299
Schell, Ronnie, 327
Schenck, George, 286
Schilling, Niklas, 198
Schine, Lily, 267
Schmidt, Marlene, 290
Schneble, Sylvia, 255
Schneck, Stephen, 313
Schneider, Andrew, 212

Schofield, Leslie, 227
Scholl, Hirsch, 287
Schöne, Barbara, 195
Schönfelder, Friedrich, 172
Schönherr, Dietmar, 104
Schrader, Paul, 307
Schrier, Leon, 31
Schultz, Brandon, 268
Schultz, Michael, 267-268
Schwartz, Howard, 286
Schwier, Werner, 198
Sciascia, Leonard, 178
Scipioni, Bruno, 85
Scollay, Fred J., 320
Scorsese, Martin, 221
Scotford, Sybil, 187, 245
Scott, Alex, 203
Scott, Beverly, 47
Scott, Clive, 272
Scott, Debralee, 277
Scott, Four, 334
Scott, Gordon, 83, 107
Scott, Harold, 69
Scott, Hedy, 134
Scott, Jacqueline, 299
Scott, Ken, 163
Scott, Larry, 109
Scott, Linda Gaye, 163
Scott, Lita, 189
Scott, Mel, 293
Scott, Mike, 286
Scott, Millicent, 189
Scott, Peter Graham, 48
Scott, Ron, 186
Scott, Terry, 207, 222
Scott, Timothy, 257-258
Scott, Tony, 94
Scott, Vernon, 94
Scotti, Andrea, 97
Scotti, Gino, 48
Scotti, Vito, 72, 274
Scuderi, Philip, 312
Scully, Vin, 134
Seaforth, Susan, 88
Seager, Sandy, 158
Sears, Ann, 192
Seaton, Marc, 249
Seay, James, 12

Sebastian, Ray, 291
Sebelious, Gregg, 104
Secombe, Andrew, 284
Sedan, Rolfe, 328
Seeds, The, 163
Seel, Charles, 17
Segal, Michael, 156
Sekizawa, Shinichi, 100, 106, 123
Selby, Tony, 128, 156
Selden, Margaret, 113
Selleck, Tom, 245
Selmier, Dean, 214
Selwyn, Louis, 190
Selzer, Milton, 204-205
Selznick, Phyllis, 210
Sendino, Blanca, 211
Sen Yung, Victor, 34
Sequi, Mario, 146
Serandrei, Mario, 65
Serato, Massimo, 97
Sernas, Jacques, 52, 107, 133
Serra, Gianna, 159
Serrador, Narcisco Ibáñez, 211, 314-315
Setan, Rene, 93
Setna, Renu, 291
Seven, Bob, 109
Seven, Johnny, 110
Severini, Leonardo, 83
Severson, John, 195
Sewell, George, 193
Sewell, Vernon, 187
Seymour, Dan, 233
Seymour, Jonah, 138
Sgroi, Frank, 279
Shacove, Gene, 166
Shadows, The, 97
Shah, Kiran, 306
Shakespeare, William, 194-195
Shamata, Chuck, 301, 303
Shamsi, 316
Shaner, John Herman, 44, 303
Shank, Jon, 209
Shapard, William, 56
Shapiro, Ronald, 309

Shari, Bonnie, 77
Sharif, Omar, 283-284
Sharp, Don, 130, 152, 271
Sharpe, Cornelia, 277
Shaughnessy, Alfred, 14
Shaver, Helen, 313, 322
Shaw, Barnett, 115
Shaw, Bobbi, 110, 117, 120, 124-125, 136
Shaw, Jennie, 189
Shaw, Larry, 109
Shaw, Lou, 250
Shaw, Maxwell, 179
Shaw, Robert, 311-312
Shaw, Run Run, 262
Shaw, Stan, 265
Shawlee, Joan, 145
Shawn, Dick, 327
Shay, John, 52
Shayer, David, 119
Shayne, Lyn, 156
Shayne, Robert, 39, 62
Shea, Mike, 233
Shear, Barry, 166
Shear, Rhonda, 288
Sheard, Michael, 311
Shearer, Harry, 297
Sheeler, Mark, 39, 62
Sheen, Martin, 228-229, 305
Sheldon, David, 279
Shell, Anna, 143
Shelley, Barbara, 14
Shelley, Frank, 272
Shelley, Joanna, 200
Shelt, Chris, 319
Shelton, Abbagail, 62
Shelton, Don, 16, 18, 32
Shelton, Joy, 64
Shenoy, P.D., 195
Shepard, Jan, 43
Shepherd, Cybill, 293-294
Shepherd, Elizabeth, 69, 127
Shepherd, Pauline, 69
Sheridan, Jay, 139
Sherman, Fred, 62, 75
Sherman, Gary, 229
Sherman, Orville, 29
Sherman, Vincent, 182

Shermet, Hazel, 327
Sherrill, Louise, 204
Sherrill, Martha, 331
Shibaki, Toshio, 226
Shikur, Sheik Razak, 316
Shimura, Takashi, 123, 135
Shirah, Jim, 294
Shirakawa, Daisaku, 63
Shirasaka, Yoshio, 126
Shirley, Peg, 215
Shirriff, Cathie, 275
Shonteff, Lindsay, 149
Shoop, Pamela, 299
Shore, Sammy, 153
Shpetner, Stanley, 29, 51
Shrapnel, John, 271
Shuey, Gene, 109
Shuman, Mort, 305
Shure, Lisa, 334
Shute, Valerie, 207
Shuttleworth, Larry, 31, 46, 53
Sibbald, Tony, 190
Sibley, Robert, 326
Sickner, William, 25
Sidaris, Andy, 330
Sidney, Susanne (Sydney, Suzanne), 155
Sierra, Gregory, 318
Signorelli, Tom, 154
Sila, Valeria, 85
Silberstein, Mona, 143
Silk, Geoff, 150
Silkosky, Ronald, 191
Silla, Felix, 243
Silva, Geno, 318
Silva, Henry, 242
Silva, Mark, 292
Silver, Joe, 105
Silver, Pat, 283
Silvestri, Alberto, 295
Sim, Gerald, 209-210, 224
Simms, Gene, 267
Simms, Jay, 80
Simon, Mayo, 286
Simonelli, John (Giovanni Simonelli), 168
Simonin, Albert, 137

Simpson, O.J., 272
Simpson, Peggy, 64
Simpson, Raymond E., 261
Sims, George, 147
Sims, Joan, 207, 222-223
Sims, Sylvia, 217
Sims, Warwick, 167
Sims, William, 269
Sinatra, Nancy, 136, 145
Sinclair, Elaine, 20
Sinclair, Madge, 268-269
Sinclair, Peter, 121
Singleton, Anthony, 93
Singuineau, Frank, 79
Siodmak, Robert, 74-75
Sirett, Mike, 311
Sirico, G. Anthony, 332
Sirk, Douglas, 169
Sirola, Joe, 260
Sison, Joe, 71
Sivero, Frank, 332
Six, Eva, 87, 94, 96
Skaff, George, 226
Skarreso, Karin, 148
Skay, Brigitte, 198
Skipper, 281
Skyler, Barbara, 51
Slate, Jeremy, 145-146, 162, 175-177
Slater, Bud, 80
Slater, John, 5
Slaven, Rick, 329
Slavin, Slick, 79
Slesar, Henry, 213
Slezak, Walter, 125-126
Slocombe, Douglas, 58, 253
Slosky, Bill, 87
Small, Marya, 281
Smerczak, Ron, 257
Smethurst, Jack, 122
Smilie, James, 326
Smilow, Bertha, 330
Smith, Albert, 294
Smith, Alexis, 305
Smith, Barbara, 332
Smith, Candice, 275
Smith, Carole, 206
Smith, Charles, 290

Smith, Cyril, 75, 121
Smith, Duchyll, 290
Smith, Earl E., 309
Smith, Eddie, 265
Smith, Emmett E., 27
Smith, Frankie, 154
Smith, John, 9, 10
Smith, Keith, 189, 276
Smith, Kevin, 189
Smith, Kirby, 47
Smith, Linda, 184
Smith, Lionel, 321
Smith, Madeline, 200, 217
Smith, Norman, 55
Smith, Paul, 101
Smith, Rainbeaux, 313
Smith, Sally, 168
Smith, Sherman, 267-268
Smith, Wilbur, 291
Smith, William, 208-209,
  290, 330
Smithers, Jan, 319
Smolen, Francis, 116
Smoot, Fred, 259
Smoyer, Montana, 280
Smyrner, Ann, 70, 82, 148-149
Sneagle, Brian, 251
Sneed, Maurice, 321
Snow, Cherene, 267
Snow, John, 182
Snyder, F.G., 103
Sobers, Gary, 182
Soble, Ron, 110
Sohl, Jerry, 118, 135, 187
Sohl, Leila, 152
Sokol, Marilyn, 331
Sokoloff, Vladimir, 18, 56
Solano, Rosalio, 231
Soles, P.J., 319
Sollima, Sergio, 295
Sommer, Elke, 220
Sommers, Barbara, 253
Soper, Margarete, 283
Soracco, Jeff, 319
Sorel, Jean, 216
Sorensen, Eva, 212
Sorenson, Peter, 104
Sothern, Ann, 255

Sottane, Liliane, 48
Sounds Incorporated, 120
Southerland, Jock, 195
Soutter, Morea, 43
Souza, Emory, 243
Sovagovic, Fabijan, 204
Sowa, Carol, 307
Sowards, Jack, 32, 53
Space, Arthur, 250
Spadaro, Odoardo, 118
Spagnoli, Alberto, 295
Spain, Fay, 15-16
Spalla, Erminio, 82
Sparks, Robert, 210-211
Sparrow, Walter, 128
Spaulding, Thomas E., 237
Spearman, Jim, 128
Speed, Carol, 248
Spencer, Bud, 174-175
Spencer, Linbert, 181, 194
Spenser, Jeremy, 138
Sperli, Alessandro, 142, 155
Sperling, Sable, 247
Speziali, Renato, 85
Spier, William, 217
Spila, Otello, 190
Spillane, Mickey, 8
Spina, Maria Grazia, 97
Spitzner, Heinz, 172
Spore, Carl, 196
Spradlin, G.D., 175
Spring, Helen, 33
Springsteen, R.G., 197-198
Sprogoe, Ove, 70
Sproule, Peter, 273
Spruance, Don, 229
Staahl, Jim, 297
Stabb, Dinah, 190
Staccioli, Ivano, 128
Stach, Virginia, 214
Stacy, John, 48, 106
Stader, Paul, 119
Staehr, Per, 72
Staley, Chuck, 297
Stamp, Terence, 180-181
Stampe, Will, 210
Standells, The, 150, 152
Stander, Lionel, 317

Stander, Martin, 82
Stang, Arnold, 63
Stanton, Harry Dean 162, 241
Stanton, Helene, 11
Stany, Jacques, 289
Stanyk, Barbara, 172
Stapleton, Vivian, 168
Stapp, Marjorie, 38-39
Stark, Graham, 121, 153
Starkes, Jaison, 288
Starrett, Claude Ennis, Jr.,
   292
Starrett, Jack, 145, 155,
   231, 292, 300
Stassino, Paul, 141
Staten, Max, 158
Steadman, John, 233, 254
Stearns, Michael, 208, 322
Steel, Alan, 97
Steel, Pippa, 200
Steele, Barbara, 65, 74, 189,
   200, 210
Steele, L.A., 292
Steele, Lou, 217
Steele, Rod, 232
Steele, Tommy, 22
Steely, Jack, 212, 232
Steen, Derek, 210, 227
Steere, Clifton, 217
Stefanelli, Benito, 235, 266
Stefanelli, Marco, 235
Stefano, John, 320
Steffen, Sirry, 89
Steiger, Rod, 271-272, 322-
   323
Stein, Ronald, 30
Steinberg, David, 174, 331
Steiner, John, 284
Steinmetz, Dennis, 306
Stemmler, Emile, 130
Sten, Anna, 22-23
Stender, Inger, 208
Stensel, Glen, 243
Stensgaard, Yutte, 197
Stensvold, Alan, 197
Stephano, Tony, 277
Stephans, Dennis, 116
Stephen, Susan, 43

Stephens, John, 206, 221, 243
Stephens, Martin, 64
Stephenson, Sheila, 121
Stergar, Vlado, 289
Sterling, Philip, 329
Sterling, Tisha, 234
Stern, Sandor, 322
Stern, Tom, 155, 175-176
Stern, Wes, 199
Sterndale-Bennett, Joan, 153
Sterns, Speed, 264
Steusloff, Helen, 161
Stevens, Connie, 31, 290-291
Stevens, Dodie, 63
Stevens, Dorinda, 49
Stevens, Geoffrey, 163
Stevens, John, 220
Stevens, Mel, 274
Stevens, Stella, 231-232
Stevens, William, 29
Stevenson, Ben, 98
Stevenson, Douglas, 296
Stevenson, Robert Louis, 69,
   210, 213
Steward, Ernest, 150, 222,
   271
Stewart, Alexandra, 253
Stewart, Andy, 86
Stewart, Bobby, 279
Stewart, Charles, 41
Stewart, Patrick, 271
Stewart, Paul, 274
Stewart, Paula, 105
Stewart, Peggy (Peggie), 229,
   282
Stewart, Robin, 193
Stewart, Roy, 194
Stidder, Ted, 192
Stiersen, Vern, 309
Stockwell, Dean, 163, 191-192
Stoker, Austin, 248, 279-280
Stoker, Bram, 205
Stokes, Ron, 211
Stokke, Tor, 72
Stoloff, Victor, 37
Stone, Danny, 158
Stone, Harold J., 99, 229,
   274

Stone, James, 4-5
Stone, Marianne, 218
Stone, Oliver, 260
Stone, Philip, 115-116, 181
Stone, Roselle, 301
Stone, Uta, 120
Stoner, Joy, 17
Stoney, Heather, 229
Storch, Larry, 306
Storck, Jackie, 30
Storck, Shelby, 30
Stott, Judith, 79
Stoumen, Louis Clyde, 51
Stovall, Tom, 286
Stradling, Harry, Jr., 293
Strahl, Franca Parisi, 85
Strangers, The, 160
Strasberg, Susan, 154, 163
Stratton, Chet, 237
Stratton, John, 40-41
Stratton, Stan, 269
Strawberry Alarm Clock, The, 163
Strawberry, Mary, 204
Street, Elliott, 306
Stresa, Nino, 48
Stricker, Vera, 72
Strickland, Connie, 249
Striglos, Bill, 241
Strindberg, Anita, 216
Stringer, Clint, 160
Stritch, Cathy, 217
Strock, Herbert L., 13, 17, 33, 89
Strode, Woody, 242, 326-327
Strohmeier, Tara, 265
Stromsoe, Fred, 119
Strong, Leonard, 34
Stroud, Charles, 269
Stroud, Don, 184-185, 192, 247, 274, 301-303, 322
Stroud, John, 309
Stroud, Sally Ann, 254
Strudwick, Peter, 113
Stuart, Alan, 22
Stuart, Greg, 31
Stuart, Jack, 159
Stuart, Jessica, 209

Stuart, Lynn Marie, 298
Stuart, Mel, 317
Stubbs, Una, 97-98, 125
Stubing, Solvy, 235
Stucker, Steven, 298
Sturgeon, Jennings, 71
Sturgess, Ray, 201
Sturlin, Ross, 36
Stuthman, Fred, 277
Style, Michael, 200
Suarez, Jeff, 330
Suberi, Cesar, 143
Subotsky, Milton, 282
Sugano, Anna, 170
Sugihara, Yuko, 219
Sugiyama, Kenji, 63
Suhr, Alex, 82
Suleiman, 316
Sullivan, Barry, 111-112, 122-123
Sullivan, Jean, 294
Summerfield, Eleanor, 121
Summers, Bunny, 243
Summers, Jeremy, 148
Summers, Jerry, 119, 241
Summers, Leslie, 119
Summers, Lorie, 87, 99, 109
Sun, Sabine, 266
Super, Glen, 334
Supremes, The, 113
Suschitzky, Wolfgang, 141
Susman, Todd, 243, 323
Sutherland, Donald, 225
Sutherland, Esther, 249, 256, 265
Sutton, Carol, 288
Sutton, Kay, 111
Suzuki, Kazuo, 173
Svanoe, Bill, 199
Svenson, Bo, 276-277, 293-294, 300
Swadron, Marion, 239
Swan, Kitty, 148
Swan, Robert, 210
Swanson, Logan, 107
Swanwick, Peter, 58
Sweeny, Ann, 313
Sweet, Dolph, 246

Sweeten, Cheryl, 110
Swerdloff, Arthur, 52
Swift, Clive, 229
Switzer, Carl, 19-20
Swope, Mark, 281
Sydney, Suzanne (Susanne
    Sidney), 19, 32
Sykes, Fairy, 160
Sylvano, Sam, 71
Sylvers, Olympia, 223
Sylvestre, Phil, 60
Sympson, Tony, 257

Tabakin, Tari, 223
Tabeling, Mike, 195
Tadake, Kenzo, 106
Taffarel, Giuseppe, 48
Tafler, Jennifer, 137
Tafler, Sydney, 64
Taft, Ayesha, 281
Taft, Ronald, 204
Tahi, Moana, 134
Tait, Don, 175, 208
Tajima, Yoshifumi, 106, 173
Takahashi, Atsuko, 219
Takarada, Akira, 106
Takashima, Tadao, 100, 135
Talbot, Kenneth, 284
Talfrey, Hira, 156, 179
Tallman, Frank, 247
Talltree, Laura, 155
Tamberlani, Nando, 82
Tamez, Arturo R., Jr., 307
Tanaka, Tadashi, 126
Tani, Akemi, 73
Tani, Yoko, 80, 83
Taniguchi, Senkichi, 123, 144
Tanikawa, Shuntaro, 126
Tanner, Clay, 292, 300
Tanner, Stella, 214
Tansley, Derek, 189
Tapias, Josefina, 171
Tapin, Martin, 116
Tapp, James, 308
Tarape, Lionel, 330
Tarbuck, Jimmy, 227
Tarlton, Alan, 43
Tarman, Bil, 217

Tarver, Leonard, 4, 37
Tasker, Barbara, 288
Tata, Joe E., 233
Tate, John, 194
Tate, Lincoln, 235
Tatum, Jean (Jeanne), 27, 47
Tatum, Lloyd, 276
Tatum, Roy, 319
Taurog, Norman, 119, 123
Tayback, Victor (Vic), 67,
    204-205, 293
Taylor, Alfred, 131
Taylor, Buck, 147
Taylor, C.D., 297
Taylor, Don, 287, 303
Taylor, Dub, 33, 237
Taylor, Fred, 40
Taylor, Jackie, 267
Taylor, Jerry, 171
Taylor, Joan, 3-4, 8-9
Taylor, Joe, 217
Taylor, Juretta, 193
Taylor, Keith, 168
Taylor, Kent, 11-12, 89
Taylor, Kurt, 298
Taylor, Lance, Sr., 221, 226
Taylor, Larry, 138
Taylor, Michael, 297
Taylor, Richard, 279
Taylor, Rip, 297
Taylor, Robert, 159, 171, 259
Taylor, Stanley, 326
Taylor, Twyla, 324
Taylor, Wayne, 19-20
Taylor, Wilda, 26
Tayman, Robert, 257
Tazaki, Jun, 100, 106, 123,
    173
Tchang, Giacomo, 83
Teague, Lewis, 254
Tedesco, Paola, 235
Tedrow, Irene, 299
Teege, Joachim, 153
Tejada, Luis, 158
Tekneci, Saliha, 105
Tensi, Francesco, 118
Terra, Renato, 60, 65, 107,
    133

Terrell, Ken, 72
Terrell, Steve, 16, 18-19, 22
Terry, Martin, 156, 179
Terry The Tramp, 175
Terry-Thomas, 130, 153, 203, 224
Terzano, Ubaldo, 65, 90, 103
Tessari, Duccio, 80, 107
Tessier, Robert, 145, 147, 211
Tetrick, Bob, 38
Tex, 145
Tezuka, Osamu, 63
Thatcher, Leora, 105
Thatcher, Wendy, 313
Thaw, John, 224
Thawnton, Tony, 179
Thayer, Lorna, 4
Thellung, Antonio, 52
Thibergen, Jerome, 308
Thiel, Roy, 147
Thierry, Richard (Riccardo Pallottini), 141
Thilpot, Julie, 239
Thlothlalemaje, Cocky, 272
Thom, Robert, 166, 169, 184
Thomas, Clifford, 290
Thomas, Damien, 194
Thomas, Eddie, 186
Thomas, Gerald, 64, 207, 222-223
Thomas, Gretchen, 17
Thomas, John, 317
Thomas, Paul, 320
Thomas, Peter, 156
Thomas, Tim, 190
Thomas, Winford Vaughn, 5
Thomasson, Harry, 324
Thomerson, Timothy, 306
Thompson, Bill, 176
Thompson, "Boxcar" Bertha, 221
Thompson, Charles P., 39
Thompson, Herman, 279
Thompson, Hilarie, 161
Thompson, Ian, 258
Thompson, J. Lee, 277
Thompson, Marc, 31

Thompson, Marion, 73
Thompson, Mark, 79
Thompson, Marshall, 67-68
Thompson, Palmer, 67
Thompson, Phyllis, 241
Thompson, William C., 27
Thomsen, Poul, 82
Thomson, Alex, 224, 229
Thomson, Gordon, 192
Thor, Larry, 3-4, 12, 35
Thordsen, Kelly, 18
Thorn, Ray, 212
Thorne, Dennis, 156
Thornton, Frank, 127, 275
Thornton, Ralph (pseudonym for Herman Cohen and Aben Kandel), 13-14, 17
Thorp, Ted, 35
Thorsen, Leslie, 294
Thorsen, Rex, 8
Thorsen, Russ, 9
Three Stooges, The, 223
Thrett, Maggie, 165
Thurman, Bill, 186, 324
Thurston, Ellen, 291
Thyssen, Greta, 70
Tichy, Gérard, 171, 176
Tidyman, Ernest, 295
Tierney, Lawrence, 7-8
Tietjen, Richard, 304
Tiezzi, Augusto, 97
Tiller, Lucy, 266
Tiller, Nadja, 76-75
Tilley, Patrick, 202, 305
Timiaough, Jim, 196
Tingwell, Virginia, 218
Tinsley, Denis, 257
Tinti, Gabriele, 48, 114, 166
Tipping, Brian, 138
Tirard, Ann, 156
Tisdale, Bob, 307
Tito, Marshal, 204
Tobin, Darra Lyn, 206
Todd, Richard, 190-191
Todd, Sally, 26
Todesco, Anita, 64
Tofanelli, Arturo, 103
Togami, Seuko, 135

Togin, Chotaro, 219
Toksvig, Claus, 82
Toledo, Jose, 283
Tolkan, James, 322
Tolsky, Susan, 306, 327
Tolstoy, Leo, 103
Tomaino, Titti, 106
Toman, Lynn, 259
Tomazani, Despina, 262
Tomerlin, John, 94
Tomlinson, David, 128
Tompkins, Angel, 243-244, 276
Tompkins, Darlene, 56
Toner, Tom, 215
Tong, Sammy, 38
Tonietti, Anne, 180
Tonner, Gene, 86
Tonti, Aldo, 266
Toomey, Regis, 324
Topper, Burt, 31, 46, 53,
    173, 210
Toran, Enrique, 146
Torey, Hal, 38, 75
Torgeson, Sonia, 46
Torn, Rip, 231-232, 320-321
Torres, Cristina, 314
Torres, Joan, 220, 245
Torrisi, Salvatore, 295
Tosi, Mario, 147, 225
Totter, Audrey, 34-35
Touceda, Enrique, 186
Tourneur, Jacques, 79, 88,
    127-128
Tove, Birthe, 207-208
Tower, Whitney, 281
Towers, Harry Alan, 148-150,
    152
Towne, Robert, 127
Townsend, Julian, 105
Townsend, Leo, 101, 117, 120,
    134
Townsend, Robert, 290
Tozzi, Fausto, 103, 266, 295
Tracy, Kim, 71
Tranche, Andre, 216
Trasatti, Luciano, 52
Travers, Susan, 203
Travis, Deborah, 150

Travis, Merle, 67
Travolta, Joey, 331-332
Traylor, William, 105
Treadwell, Gary, 193
Trebor, Robert, 334
Tremayne, Les, 55-56
Trenaman, John, 156
Trenker, Floriano, 152
Tressler, Dieter, 220
Trevor, Austin, 49, 71
Trice, Ron, 321-322
Triesault, Ivan, 55
Trigonis, John, 39
Trikonis, Gus, 111
Tristan, Dorothy, 323
Truchado, José, 159
Trueblood, Guerdon, 171
Truex, Barry, 31
Trumbo, Dalton, 225
Tsekaviy, G., 104
Tsu, Irene, 120
Tsuchiya, Yoshio, 135, 173,
    219
Tsukamoto, Raynum K., 96
Tsutsumi, Yasuhisa, 106
Tubes, The, 298
Tucci, Michael, 331
Tucker, Forrest, 274-275, 300
Tucker, Wendell, 265
Tuiolosega, Tino, 330
Tulin, Mark, 332
Tulley, Paul, 329
Tulli, Marco, 82
Tullis, Jerry, 116
Tunnicliffe, Reg, 286
Tupper, Loretta, 331
Turgeon, Peter, 109
Turkel, Joseph, 29-30, 173,
    237
Turley, Jack, 299
Turman, Glynn, 259, 267-268,
    288
Turnbull, Bob, 31
Turner, Ike, 131
Turner, Joe, 23
Turner, June, 229, 231
Turner, Larry, 74
Turner, Tierre, 266, 268-269

Turner, Tina, 28, 131
Tuttle, Lam Nam, 96
Tuttle, Lurene, 276, 300
Tyler, Leon, 16, 23, 47
Tyrrell, Geoffrey, 14

Uehara, Ken, 100
Uekusa, Keinosuke, 63
Ukmar, Franco, 235
Ulius, Betty, 163
Ullman, Elwood, 119, 136
Ulmer, Edgar G., 55-56
Ulrich, Ronald, 239
Underwood, Ray, 315-316
Undi, Shalimar, 291
Unger, Freddy, 141
Uno, Koji, 106
Unsworth, Geoffrey, 120, 289
Upton, Morgan, 266
Urban, Marusa, 234
Ure, Mary, 93
Urquhart, Gordon, 8, 29
Urquhart, Robert, 41, 43
Usher, Gary, 87, 109
Ustinov, Tamara, 205

Vaccaro, Brenda, 301-303
Vadim, Roger, 180
Vahanian, Marc, 322
Vailati, Bruno, 114
Valdemarin, Mario, 142
Vale, Emilio, 295
Valentine, A.J., 67
Valentine, Elmer, 170
Valero, Maria Jose, 211
Vallacher, Kitty, 223
Valli, Romolo, 310
Vallone, Raf, 158-159
Valturri, Pat, 168-169
Van Ark, Joan, 225-226
Van Artsdalen, Butch, 109
Van Buren, Kristin, 176
Van Cleef, Lee, 10
Vandegriff, Dan, 296
Van Der Veer, Willard, 89
Van Der Vlis, Diana, 99
Vandervort, Phil, 161, 237
Van Deter, Tonia, 121

Van Dissell, Peter, 272
van Dreelen, John, 56
Van Dyck, Bonnie, 250
Van Dyke, Conny, 175-176
Vane, Norman Thaddeus, 227
Van Eyck, Peter, 133
Van Haren, Chuck, 51
Van Hoorn, Teresa, 93
Van Houten, Leslie, 244
van Leer, Hunter, 233, 318
van Lyck, Henry, 198
Van Ost, Valerie, 223
Van Patten, Jimmy, 323
Van Raaphorst, Joanne, 309
Van Raaphorst, William, 309
Van Stralen, Anton, 61, 79
Vantell (Van Tell), Terry,
    156, 159
Vanterpool, Freda T., 223
Van Vooren, Monique, 174
Varden, Norma, 67
Varela, Jay, 233
Varelli, Alfredo, 52
Vargas, Daniele, 114, 180
Vari, Giuseppe, 128
Varley, Beatrice, 49, 75
Varno, Martin, 36
Varriani, Emilio, 220
Varsi, Diane, 160-161, 166-
    167, 184-185
Vasayova, Emilie, 116
Vasquez, Alberto, 332
Vaughan, Norman, 227
Vaughan, S.F., 326
Vaughn, Robert, 39-40, 194
Vaughn, Sammy, 168
Veitch, Anthony Scott, 228
Vejlby, Bent, 82
Velasco, Maria, 72
Velez, Olga, 198
Venantini, Venantino, 85, 118
Ventura, Lino, 137-138
Verdugo, Ana, 287
Vereen, Ben, 192
Verne, Jules, 72, 153
Verner, Anthony, 282
Vernon, Howard, 228
Vernon, Richard, 127

Versini, Marie, 100
Verzier, René, 305, 313
Ve Sota, Bruno, 3, 8-9, 11, 21, 25, 29, 43, 46, 79, 92, 206
Vessel, Edy, 107
Vibenius, Bo A., 262
Vichinsky, Shlomo, 143
Vickers, Yvette, 20, 43-44, 87
Vico, Antonio, 158
Victor, Charles, 74
Victor, Gloria, 46, 79
Victor, James, 307, 332
Vidmark, Robert, 235
Vidor, King, 37
Vidov, Oleg, 203
Vigran, Herb, 274
Viharo, Robert, 278
Villa, Franco, 242
Villechaize, Herve, 260
Villena, Fernando, 122-123
Villiers, James, 138, 205
Vincent, Gene, 33
Vincent, Jan Michael, 332, 334
Vincent, Larry, 212
Vincent, Romo, 124, 169
Vincent, Virginia, 110
Vincenzi, Luciana, 146
Viner, Michael, 232
Vint, Alan, 233, 257-258
Vint, Jessie, 257-258, 282-283
Viola, Joseph, 238
Visconti, Luigi, 114
Vitale, Anthony, 319
Vitkovich, Viktor, 104
Vitolazzi, Rocco, 107
Vogel, Paul C., 150
Vogler, Karl Michael, 291
Voight, Jon, 174, 178
Volpe, Virgilio, 289
vom Brack, Paul, 267
von Almassy, Susanne, 172
von Borsody, Hans, 103, 143
von Hagen, Ruth, 85
von Harbou, Thea, 61

von Holt, Renate, 153
von Mayrhauser, Caroline, 30
von Nutter, Rick, 63-64
von Sacher-Masoch, Leopold, 200-201
von Schwarze, Klaus E.R., 179
Voskovec, George, 158
Voss, V.I., 27
Voutsinas, Andreas, 180
Vuisic, Pavle, 204
Vuolo, Tito, 16

Wada, Natto, 126
Waddilove, Philip, 158
Wagner, Lou, 334
Wagoner, Porter, 139
Wahler, Robert, 319-320
Wainer, Lee, 147
Wainwright, James, 318, 320
Waite, Ric, 332
Wakabayashi, Akiko, 123, 144
Walcott, Gregory, 34-35
Wald, Malvin, 200
Walden, Robert, 185
Waldman, Marion, 251
Walker, Luke, 259
Walker, Michael, 176
Walker, Pete, 256-257
Walker, Recoe, 290
Walker, Robert, Jr., 160-161, 164-165
Wallace, Charles A., 197
Wallace, Connie, 96
Wallace, Edgar, 69
Wallace, George D., 320-321
Wallace, Hedgar, 179
Wallace, Helen, 20
Wallace, Jack, 64
Waller, Gordon, 227
Walley, Deborah, 117, 119, 123-124, 136
Walls, Bud, 243
Walper, Cicely, 328
Walsh, Dick, 32
Walsh, Edward, 185, 215
Walsh, Katherine, 154
Walters, Don, 314
Walters, Luana, 8

Walters, Susan, 154–155
Walters, Thorley, 305–306
Wang, George, 142
Wang, Juliana, 225
Ward, Aleardo, 180
Ward, Autry, 307
Ward, Michael, 75
Ward, Peggy, 124
Ward, Robin, 192
Ward, Simon, 310–311
Ward, Skip, 52
Ward, Wert, 307
Ware, Derek, 158
Ware, Howard, 115
Ware, Midge, 67
Warner, Astrid, 147, 176, 186
Warner, Robert, 251
Warnick, Alan, 243
Warren, Dodie, 161
Warren, John F., 169
Warren, Kenneth, 58, 122
Warren, Lesley, 228–229
Warren, Michael, 189
Warren, Val, 101
Warrenton, Gil, 31, 46–47,
   51, 53, 72, 80, 94
Warshawski, Ruth, 265
Warwick, Gina, 193
Warwick, John, 49
Warwick, Norman, 203, 209
Washington, Richard, 245
Washington, Shirley, 250
Watanabe, Hiroko, 169
Waterman, Dennis, 201–202
Waters, Cheryl, 249, 257–258
Waters, Ed, 25
Waters, George W., 39, 62
Waters, Marion, 332
Waters, Russell, 213
Watkin, Pierre, 23
Watkins, James Louis, 288
Watson, Bruce, 267
Watson, Jack, 71, 213
Watson, Jan, 119
Watson, John, 14
Watson, Malcolm, 58
Watson, Tex, 244
Watters, Don, 265

Wattis, Richard, 217–218
Watts, Gwendolwn, 137
Waugh, Fred, 319
Waybill, Fee, 298
Wayne, Jesse, 329
Wayne, Patrick, 305–306
Weacer, Lee, 318
Weathers, Carl, 267, 269, 311
Weaver, Doodles, 33, 257, 275,
   280
Weaver, Lee, 241
Webb, David, 156
Webb, Dean, 112
Webb, Lincoln, 197
Webber, Peggy, 37
Weber, André, 137
Weber, Richard, 73
Webster, Joy, 69
Webster, Mary, 72
Webster, Paddy, 14
Wedderspoon, Ted, 31
Wedekind, Claudia, 198
Wedgeworth, Ann, 285
Weeks, Alan, 265
Weidenmann, Alfred, 203
Weidman, Joan, 225
Weighell, Alan, 22
Weinrib, Lennie, 84
Weinstein, Seymour, 217
Weis, Don, 110, 136
Weissbach, Herbert, 172, 198
Weissman, Bernie, 321
Weitz, Bruce, 321
Welbeck, Peter, 130, 148–150,
   152, 228
Welch, Charlie, 322
Welch, Raquel, 281
Welch, Bruce, 125
Weldon, Ann, 321
Weldon, Jimmy, 73
Welles, Mel, 21, 25
Welles, Orson, 203
Wellman, Harold, 109
Wellman, William, Jr., 145,
   235, 320
Wells, Dawn, 309–310
Wells, Dolores, 87, 101, 109,
   113

Wells, H.G., 285, 299, 303
Wells, Jesse, 215
Wells, Wayne, 301
Welsh, Bill, 16
Welsh, John, 71, 74, 301, 309
Wendkos, Paul, 293
Wenner, Leslie, 111
Wentworth, John, 179
Wermer, Ed, 89
Werner, Klaus, 160
Weske, Brian, 121
West, Frederick E., 8-12, 16, 18, 22-23, 27, 34
West, H.E., 94
West, James, 87
West, Mae, 218
West, Misty, 309
West, Red, 276
Westbrook, John, 108-109, 127
Westerfield, James, 101
Weston, Click, 139
Weston, David, 108-109
Weston, Jerry Bob, 31
Weston, Peter, 214
Westwood, Patrick, 22, 74
Wetherell, Virginia, 189, 210
Wetzell, Blackie, 301
Whalen, Michael, 6, 11-12
Wheeler, Charles (F.), 247, 265, 324
Wheeler, Kay, 33
Wheelus, Jim, 299
Whig, Jimmy, 267
Whiskey, Nancy, 22
Whitaker, David, 127
White, Deborah, 306
White, Gene, 291
White, James Gordon, 147, 162, 167, 173, 176, 212, 232
White, Jeannine, 120
White, Jesse, 110-111, 136
White, John, 309
White, Ron, 326
White, Sam, 253

Whitehead, Geoffrey, 213
Whitehead, O.Z., 80
Whiteman, Russ, 17
Whiteside, Robert, 33
Whitman, David, 217
Whitman, Kip, 147
Whitman, Stuart, 308
Whitney, Cece, 139
Whitney, Chris, 314
Whiton, James, 203, 224
Whitsun-Jones, Paul, 108, 210
Whittaker, Ian, 121
Whittaker, Stephen, 170
Whittington, Dick, 232, 259
Whorf, David, 75
Wickham, Hank, 206
Wicki, Bernhard, 283-284
Wicking, Christopher, 179, 189, 196, 205, 213
Wiggins, Chris, 313
Wilburn Brothers, The, 139
Wilcox, John, 97, 112
Wilcox, Shelagh, 200
Wild, Jeannette, 210
Wildaker, Poul, 82
Wilde, Brian, 207
Wilde, Colette, 58
Wilde, Cornel, 318
Wilde, Oscar, 190
Wilde, Wendy, 46
Wilder, Yvonne, 215
Wilding, Mark, 202
Wildman, Julie, 305, 308
Wildt, Helmut, 133
Wiles, John, 48
Wilke, Birthe, 82
Wilken, Alfred, 82
Wilkerson, Guy, 92
Wilkes, Jerry, 265
Wilkes, Keith, 268-269
Wilkins, Martin, 27
Wilkinson, June, 75, 77
Willard, Fred, 297
Willesee, Mike, 317
Willett, E. Hunter, 163
Williams, Alfonso, 210-211
Williams, Alicia, 267
Williams, Allen, 329

Williams, Arnold, 245
Williams, Avil, 257
Williams, Billy, 181, 217
Williams, Bob, 32
Williams, Chino "Fats", 332
Williams, Cindy, 192
Williams, Daisey Mae, 181
Williams, Dennis, 279
Williams, Don, 231, 247
Williams, Donnie, 265
Williams, Doug, 88
Williams, Guy, 18
Williams, Kenneth, 207, 222-223
Williams, Oscar, 265
Williams, Polly, 227
Williams, Randy T., 315
Williams, Rhoda, 32
Williams, Richard, 247-248
Williams, Roberta, 290
Williams, Rosemary, 121
Williams, Steven (Steve), 267, 290
Williams, Sue, 121
Williams, Sumner, 52
Williams, Sylvia, 288
Williams, Vince, 29
Williamson, Alister, 179-180, 203
Williamson, Fred, 235-237, 256, 266-267
Williamson, Michael T., 332
Willingham, Calder, 25
Willingham, Dale, 226
Willis, Austin, 324
Willis, Marlene, 28
Willis, Nancy, 312
Willis, Norman, 27
Willmer, Catherine, 258
Wills, Annika, 112
Wills, Chill, 134
Wills, Sheila, 321-322
Wills, Spyder, 195
Willson, Paul, 298
Wilmer, Douglas, 200
Wilson, Alex, 192
Wilson, Bill, 248, 279
Wilson, Brian, 87, 120

Wilson, Bryna, 144
Wilson, Earl, 117
Wilson, George, 195
Wilson, John, 138
Wilson, Jon R., 276
Wilson, Joseph Carter, 267
Wilson, Lisle, 246-247, 313
Wilson, Neil, 210
Wilson, Richard, 165
Wilson, Ronald, 69
Wiltrup, Age (Aage), 70, 72, 82
Winchell, Walter, 166
Winder, Michael, 272
Winding, Victor, 137
Windom, William, 318
Windsor, Barbara, 121, 207, 222-223
Windsor, Marie, 9
Windsor, Tod, 124
Windust, Irene, 52
Wing, Anna, 182
Wing, Yu, 329
Wingreen, Jason, 191
Winkler, Gary, 229
Winkler, Suzanne, 229
Winner, Michael, 137
Winski, Norman, 280
Winslow, Dick, 150
Winston, Helen, 242
Winston, Lance, 231
Winter, Edward, 293
Winter, Pauline, 93
Winters, Jonathan, 63
Winters, Shelley, 166, 184-185, 218-219, 308-309
Winton, Wayne, 94
Wisbar, Frank, 103
Wisborg, Ole, 82
Wischmann, Marianne, 198
Wiseman, Joseph, 326
Wish, Jerome, 155
Witney, William, 29-30, 51, 72
Witte, Michael R., 307
Witte, William Vance, 307
Witty, Christopher, 64
Wolfe, Ian, 318

Wolfe, Terry, 233
Wolff, Frank, 174-175
Wolfit, Donald, 74
Won, Barbara, 152
Wonder, Little Stevie, 101, 109
Wong, Alan, 307
Wood, Clement Biddle, 180
Wood, Gary, 148
Wood, Howarth, 43
Wood, Jeane, 25
Wood, Lana, 301
Wood, Michael, 168
Wood, Natalie, 328-329
Woodburn, Eric, 213
Woodbury, Joan, 113
Woodman, Woody, 309
Woods, Aubrey, 202-203
Woods, Bob, 223
Woods, Donald, 67
Woods, Genie, 235, 262
Woods, Ren, 321, 322
Woodward, Morgan, 292-293, 300
Wooland, Norman, 74
Woolf, Gary, 79
Woolf, Jack, 317
Woolfe, Betty, 179
Woolgar, Jack, 229
Woronov, Mary, 260
Worth, Lothrop, 17
Worth, Nicholas, 245
Wray, Fay, 31
Wright, Amy, 322
Wright, Don, 301
Wright, Heather, 291
Wright, Howard, 29, 38, 41, 67
Wright, Jenny Lee, 258
Wright, John, 227
Wright, Julia, 210
Wright, Stanley, 282
Wright, Tony, 74-75
Wu, June, 240
Wyatt, Tessa, 201-202
Wyer, Reg(inald), 77, 115, 152
Wyldeck, Martin, 179

Wylie, Rowan, 190
Wymark, Patrick, 156
Wyndham, Don, 166
Wyngarde, Peter, 79
Wynn, Keenan, 101, 237
Wynn, Ned, 111, 120, 323
Wynne, Michael, 194
Wynter, Mark, 193

Yablonsky, Yabo, 326
Yabushita, Teiji, 63
Yadin, Joseph, 143
Yafa, Stephen H., 165
Yaffee, Ben, 217
Yagdfeld, Grigoriy, 104
Yakushev, V., 104
Yamada, Kazuo, 144
Yamamoto, Ren, 106
Yamashita, Tadashi, 330
Yamauchi, Akira, 226
Yancy, Emily, 221
Yanni, Rosanna, 266
Yardley, Susan, 87
Yarish, Elaine, 301
Yarnell, Bruce, 163-164
Yaru, Marina, 180-181
Yates, Cassie, 307
Yates, George Worthing, 28, 38, 41
Yates, Peter, 97-98
Yeh, Ely, 83
Yeh, Karen, 262
Yeldham, Peter, 130
Yi, Chang, 240
Ying, Pai, 240
Yoder, Aly, 282
Yonemoto, Norman, 297
York, Jay, 155
York, Michael, 303-304
York, Tony, 160-161
Yorton, Chester, 109
Young, Buck, 229
Young, Burt, 274
Young, Clint, 249
Young, Della, 198
Young, Eliezer, 143
Young, Faron, 139
Young, Greg, 229

Young, Joan, 205
Young, Robert, 89
Young, Skip, 38
Young, Terence, 133, 266
Young, Tony, 208-209, 249
Young, Tricia, 198
Youngman, Henny, 139
Yu, Tchang, 156
Yu, Wang, 246
Yule, Ian, 272
Yune, Jon, 329

Zacha, Jac, 287
Zalman, 143
Zamperla, Nazzareno, 97
Zapien, Danny, 170
Zapponi, Bernardino, 180
Zaslow, Michael, 329
Zegler, Paul, 297
Zepeda, Geraldo, 231
Zichel, Rosy, 128
Zielstorff, Ilse, 160
Ziemann, Sonja, 172
Zimbalist, Efrem, Jr., 146
Zimeas, John, 60
Zimmerman, Gordon, 320
Zimmerman, Ken, 276
Zimmerman, Vernon, 233, 282
Zimmerman, Yale, 225
Zipson, Alan, 203
Zivojinovic, Bata, 204
Zoulfikar, Omar, 146
Zounds, Archibald, Jr., 60
Zshornack, Zaldy, 238
Zsigmond, William (Vilmos),
  113
Zucchero, Joseph, 249-250
Zuccoli, Fausto (Frank), 154,
  168
Zur, Bomba, 143
Zurakowski, Danik, 253
Zvanut, James, 312